THE RESEARCH EXPERIENCE

EDITED BY
M. PATRICIA GOLDEN

NORTHEASTERN UNIVERSITY, BOSTON

F. E. PEACOCK PUBLISHERS, INC. ITASCA, ILLINOIS

FOR MY FAMILY AND MY STUDENTS

and dedicated to
the memory of my friend
Norman Kaplan

Contents

hard to follow?

stats hard

Preface

Students come into a social research methods course with many misconceptions, not only about social research but also about sociology and what the sociologist does. Many of them also come with an inordinate fear of the material and a lack of confidence in their ability to cope with it. Research methods texts tend to compound the difficulties by presenting the research process as an orderly and patterned progression, from problem selection through data collection, data analysis, and presentation of findings in the form of a research report. Initially, at least, it seems so simple and logical, so "scientific." On the surface, sociology seems capable of perfection.

Neat outlines of the research process, however, overlook much of what is actually involved in doing research. Methods texts touch on only some of the problems one encounters. Research reports do not record the many choices, decisions, and refinements made along the way. Therefore, students can get a very distorted picture of the research process and of the research experience. Biased or limited treatments may not be acknowledged as such. Methodological preferences, whether personal or routed in theoretical orientations, may not be made clear to the student. To their own misunderstandings, students may add the prejudices of a particular textbook or teacher. It may be some time before they learn that there are alternative ways to do research.

Further, to the beginning student, social research often seems abstract and intellectual. Problems and difficulties are usually discussed in terms of theoretical and methodological principles. Rightly so, but sometimes even these principles are lost in the detail of technique. The implications of personal and pragmatic considerations and constraints, which may influence one's choices and restrict one's possibilities, are often ignored. The urgencies and limitations imposed by inadequate resources of time, money, and personnel are not reported. The idiosyncratic interests that influenced the selection of a problem or the choice of an integrating principle remain the private domain of the researcher. The many compromises and modifications that are made as a result of circumstances are left out of the final product. That the ideal and the actual experiences of social research may differ in significant ways is a reality seldom communicated to the novice researcher.

This book makes two basic assumptions: (1) that students should be exposed to a wide range of research possibilities, and they should have the privilege of making their own choices and developing their own biases, and (2) that students should be introduced to the experiential as well as the conceptual aspects of research, that is, not only to the basic principles that influence the nature of the research process, but also to the compelling personal and pragmatic considerations and constraints which sometimes alter, modify, and impede that process. Accordingly, the content of the book is organized in terms of these two goals. Further details of this organization can be found under the heading "Plan of the Book" at the end of Chapter 1.

The book is intended to complement the material covered in a basic research methods text. The articles included were chosen primarily for their methodological approach rather than their substantive content. Students should thus be advised to look for methodological points rather than substantive findings. The object is to provide material which is stimulating for students and provokes their interest in sociology and, at the same time, exposes them to significant research strategies and important procedures.

ACKNOWLEDGMENTS

My students and I, building on the work of others—especially Phillip E. Hammond, *Sociologists at Work* (New York: Basic Books, 1964)—conceived and developed the idea of this book together, and it would not have been possible without their help. The basic premise grew out of discussions with students in my first few years of teaching. From the point when I decided to act on their expressed needs and suggestions, students have been involved in every stage of the process of editing this book. They helped in sifting, sorting, and finally selecting articles that would be interesting and informative for students just beginning to explore social research.

Though the ultimate decisions were mine, their inputs were invaluable in determining who would be approached to participate. At later stages students read draft manuscripts and provided reviews, and sometimes detailed comments, which were shared with contributors. Though most of my undergraduate students these last few years have to some extent been involved in this project as readers and critics, I cannot, of course, thank them all individually. Because of their special involvement in and commitment to this project, however, I would like to express a particular debt of gratitude to the following students: Marsha Baron, Nancy Bennotti, Neal Beroz, Diane Bolling, Ming Chiu, Bruce Colby, Sally Dalton, Michele Diamond, Alexandra Eadie, Robert Feinberg, Sheila Friend, Jan Gamer, Judith Gillis, Patricia Gittens, David Hankard, Carole Hardy, Sharan Harlan, Donald Holl, Florence Kayes, Bruce Kirchner, Robin Lewis, Marie Mann, Janet Minton, Sheryl Nese, Pauline Scanlon, Linda Smith, Gloria Taylor, Loren Thompson, Darby Van Buskirk, Linda Weinrich, Nancy Weisberg, Laura Wool.

Though my students have been instrumental to the development and successful completion of this project, only the contributors have made it possible. Their participation is, of course, indispensable; the worth of the book derives from the quality of their contributions. From discussions with others who have been involved in similar editorial undertakings, I am aware that I have been very fortunate to have had, throughout, unusual cooperation and commitment from all of the contributors. I am most grateful for their participation and for their interest and support.

Besides my students and the contributors, there are others, colleagues and friends, to whom I am indebted. Were it not for the encouragement of my colleagues, especially Jack Levin, Blanche Geer, and Norman Kaplan, I probably would not have embarked on this project at all. They convinced me that it was a worthwhile idea and prodded me to develop a proposal. While I was preparing the proposal, a number of people also took the time to discuss the concept of the book with me and to offer their comments. Robert Rosenthal, Joseph Lengermann, Roberta Rovner-Pieczenik, Al Schwartzbaum, and Zick Rubin must be singled out in this regard. Their assistance and favorable comments at a crucial point were very important and much appreciated. In the early stages, Earl Rubington helped by suggesting numerous articles for my students and me to consider. Stan Kaszanek provided thoughtful criticisms of a number of contributions. And Jack Levin, Alex Rysman, Carol Owen, and Earl Rubington read and commented on earlier versions of the first chapter. The final product has benefited by their many helpful suggestions.

Because I, too, once was a student, I would like to acknowledge the influence of my professors, Wayne Thompson, Ned Rosen, and Robin Williams, who gave me broad exposure to the social science disciplines and who encouraged me, early in my career, to consider the possibilities rather than develop preferences.

Very special thanks are due Valerie Cahoone for her invaluable assistance with various administrative activities related to assembling this book, especially obtaining permissions and keeping in touch with contributors. She gave much time and attention to improving the organization of the book and shared many of the painful moments. Her very significant contribution is acknowledged with affection and respect.

Tom LaMarre of F. E. Peacock Publishers has been patient and supportive beyond expectation. His confidence, from the beginning, in the basic concept of the book has been gratifying, and his advice and counsel in developing and executing that concept have been especially helpful. The care and attention provided by the editors at Peacock, especially Joyce Usher, Marjorie Evensen, and Gloria Reardon, have in both small details and important ways improved the presentation and enhanced the quality of the book. Their assistance is much appreciated and gratefully acknowledged.

Finally, I want to thank my family—my mother, and all my aunts, uncles, and cousins—for a lifetime of support and encouragement, and, especially, for their understanding and patience throughout this endeavor.

Boston, Massachusetts   M. PATRICIA GOLDEN

CHOICES AND CONSTRAINTS IN SOCIAL RESEARCH

CHAPTER 1

CHAPTER 1

CHOICES AND CONSTRAINTS IN SOCIAL RESEARCH

Though many do not admit it, and some are unaware of it, most social scientists have their favorite approaches when it comes to theory or research. The first course in social research, however, seems an inappropriate point at which to make choices about and commitments to lifelong theoretical or research orientations. Before making such choices, students should consider all the possibilities, regarding the appropriateness not only of a particular research strategy for a specific problem but also of general orientations to sociology and social research.

Consequently, this book advocates no particular research approach to the exclusion of others. Because the type of material presented here is intended to complement the many excellent textbooks already available, the specific procedures and precautions associated with using various methods are not reiterated. Once the choices have been made, there are many sources, including many of the contributions to this book, for obtaining such "how to" and "how not to" formulas.

For students, what is more often lacking is a coherent discussion of the considerations and constraints that influence the researcher's choices in the first place. The comparative advantages and limitations of various methods must be weighed and a decision taken. When to use a particular method or how to choose between two alternatives remains for many students a confusing and ambiguous exercise, often encumbered by ill-conceived and unclear stereotypes about research. Assuming that questionnaires are only used in surveys or that exploratory research always involves fieldwork, for example, student researchers can sometimes get inaccurate impressions and make unwise decisions about the way things are "usually" done. Preferences (often those picked up from a particular textbook or teacher or course), rather than possibilities, may dictate choices. If students lack sufficient experience and information, they may make choices for themselves and judgments of others based on fragmented and incomplete knowledge.

Still another element which is often missing in a student's first encounter with social research methods is exposure to the experiential aspects of the research process. For the student who has had very limited first-hand experience with research, it is often difficult to imagine how the abstract principles in the textbook translate into actual research activities. And it is sometimes easy to overlook the fact that considerations and constraints other than those cited in the textbook can also influence one's choices.

This chapter outlines some of the factors that must be dealt with and the dilemmas that must be faced in making choices at different points in the research process. It also provides some guidelines in terms of which the choices made by the contributors to this book and the constraints that were imposed on them can be considered. An effort also has been made to clarify the sometimes confusing and conflicting ways in which certain terminology is

TABLE I
Summary: Choices and Constraints in Social Research

Research Strategies	Type of "Unit in setting"	Purpose	Criteria Maximized	Primary Goal
Field study	Real groups in natural (Field) setting	Exploratory/Descriptive	Naturalness (and insight)	To understand system character of *context*
Experiment Laboratory	Treatment groups in contrived (Lab) setting	Causal	Control	To establish relationships between *variables* (internal validity)
Field	Treatment groups in natural (Field) setting	Causal	Some control/Some naturalness	To establish relationships between *variables in context* (internal validity)
Simulation	Treatment groups in simulated/contrived (Lab) setting	Causal/Descriptive/Exploratory	Some control	To establish relationships between *variables in context* (internal validity)
Survey	Sample in variable setting (Behavior is not dependent on setting)	Descriptive/Causal/Exploratory	Representativeness	Generalizability to other *units* and their attributes (external validity)
Available data	Sample in variable setting	Descriptive/Causal/Exploratory	Representativeness/Naturalness	Generalizability to other *units* (external validity)

Evaluation (Babbie Ch. 10)

used by researchers with slightly different research orientations. The material covered is summarized in Table 1.

The Starting Point: Selecting a Topic

The first choice a researcher must make generally involves the selection of a research topic. The range of possibilities is broad, practically synonymous with human experience. The concern here, however, is not to chronicle the possible topics but to outline some of the factors that might influence one's choices among that wide range of topics. Choosing a research topic is usually treated as if it were simply an intellectual exercise. In this context, the relative validity of *theory, previous research,* and *personal experience* as possible sources for research topics may be debated. While personal hunches and guesses based on one's experience are not ruled out as potential sources for research topics, many authors, especially those concerned with the cumulative aspects of sociological knowledge, stress the superiority of research questions rooted in theory. Others argue that such considerations must not deter one from the creative avenues opened up by personal insights and practical experience.

Alternatively, choosing an area for research is sometimes treated as an issue of personal or social *values.* Many textbooks make the distinction between *pure* or *basic* research, supposedly based on the desire to know in order to know, and *applied* or *practical* research, which has as its goal a particular behavioral outcome. While some researchers would argue that the two goals are not mutually exclusive, the basic value decision is nevertheless reduced to choosing between one orientation and the other. No doubt choosing a topic—whether related to race relations, social mobility, or criminal justice—because one "wants to change society" involves values. Likewise, choosing to do research, perhaps in these same areas, because of a desire to explore and expand knowledge in a particular field is seldom a value-free decision.

Questions of the relationship between values and research are important; they permeate the research process. Certainly the vital roles of both theory and experience as starting points for formulating a research problem cannot be ignored. For one who may have limited resources and expertise, however, such considerations might be regarded as a luxury. For the novice researcher (and maybe even for one more experienced), the reasons for choosing a particular topic are seldom so high-minded. Very often the choice of a research topic is influenced and constrained by far more pressing and mundane personal and pragmatic considerations. At least for beginners, the starting point is most likely to be *personal interest.* It is easier to get started on and to stay involved in something that interests one. No doubt, as they read this book, students will like certain selections and certain sections better than others. Such individual preferences are to be expected.

The researcher's personal interest could be theoretical in nature. For his research reported in Chapter 4, for example, Joseph Lengermann had a theoretical interest in a particular *problem*—the relationship between organizational structure and professionalism. His starting point did not require study of a particular group or setting. For others, however, the starting point may be precisely an interest in a particular *group* (an order of Catholic nuns) or a particular kind of group (the working class—see Herbert Gans, Chapter 2); a particular *setting* (Metrocourt—see Roberta Rovner-Pieczenik, Chapter 5) or a particular kind of setting (prisons—see Craig Haney, W. Curtis Banks, and Philip G. Zimbardo, Chapter 3). It could even be a *method.* Joy Browne (Chapter 2), for example, admits to looking for a group and a setting in which she could do participant observation, and the starting point for Anthony Doob and Alan Gross (Chapter 6) was their desire to use "unobtrusive methods" in a field setting. In certain situations, the interest may be vague and unfocused. For some, like Gans or Browne, their research "interest" does not become clearly specified or articulated until they are well underway and have spent much time.

Professional preferences also play a part. Important social issues may precipitate research interest within a discipline, or the availability of research funds can become a compelling factor in choice of a topic. Even the specific orientations of journals or journal editors (see Doob and Gross) can become a factor in choosing research topics. One might choose not to undertake research whose publication cannot be anticipated.

Pragmatic constraints such as the need to support one's family or the desire to stay in school can also affect the choice of a research topic. One's employer or one's professor may provide a research topic, ready-made and unalterable. Ultimately, every researcher must choose a topic which is manageable, within the limits of his or her available resources. Insufficient money or time or expertise can be powerful inhibiting forces when considering not only the range of possible research topics but also the range, and scale, of possible research approaches.

Problems, Units, and Settings: Specifying the Who, What, and Where of Social Research

In any research project there are a number of elements that can vary—things about the person or case, things about the setting, or things related to the behavior under study. Each of these sources of variation must be taken into account and specified. Not only must the researcher select particular variables (behaviors) to be studied, but also the particular social units (persons or cases) that will be performing those behaviors, and in what circumstances (setting), must also be determined. Behaviors differ not only between individual units but also within such units, as at different times or in different settings. Two women, one married and one divorced, might have different

THE RESEARCH EXPERIENCE

feelings about divorce, but one of them might also have different feelings under different circumstances, such as before and after divorce. Variations in the data which can be attributed to each of these sources, as well as to any interactions between them (e.g., the combination of being female and being divorced), must be taken into account, either at the point of data collection or, alternatively, at the point of data analysis.

The Research Problem

Whatever the origin—theoretical, practical, personal—the researcher ultimately must settle on some aspect of human behavior (the what) as the focus of his or her study. Formulating a research problem involves more than deciding on a research topic. Within a particular area of research, a great number of specific questions might be investigated. General concerns about the real world must eventually be translated into a clearly defined, rather specific, researchable "problem." This is sometimes referred to as "narrowing the topic."

Statement of the research problem focuses attention and directs effort toward examining some specific aspects of human behavior. It is usually phrased (preferably in clear and unambiguous terms) as a question about the relationship between two or more variables. Not every research topic, however, can be translated into a feasible, testable research problem. The nature of the research problem and its degree of specificity and refinement, consequently, influence one's approach to the research process.

Hypotheses More "scientific" approaches to research, those more concerned with causality and explanations, may require not only a well-formulated problem but also a specific, precise, testable hypothesis. Hypotheses are suggested explanations, usually in the form of a statement or proposition about the relationship between two variables. The *independent variable* is the assumed "cause," or determining factor. The *dependent variable* (sometimes called the criterion variable) is the assumed effect, or outcome. While hypotheses are sometimes based on "hunches" or previous research, those derived from theory are considered preferable. Research can begin with well-formulated hypotheses, or hypotheses can be formulated as the end product of the research (see Gans, Chapter 2). Starting with specific hypotheses is of particular concern to researchers with a scientific orientation, those who demand a more systematic and empirical approach to research investigations.

The Research Unit

Human behavior requires human actors (the who), social entities of some size and form (a dating couple, a football team, a college, a country). The nature of the social units about which the researcher wishes to become more informed must be specified. Most of the terms used to refer to the units of a study imply that these units are human or made up of human elements: actors, subjects, respondents, groups. Writers who use more general terms— like cases, elements, or units of analysis—attempt to take into account the fact that the units of the study can also be such nonhuman entities as cities, prisons, floor tiles, or even the words on a printed page. Babbie (1975) distinguishes four types of social units: individual human beings (such as workers, students, parents), groups (such as families, friendship groups, street gangs), organizations (such as churches, schools, insurance companies), and social artifacts (such as books, songs, automobiles, buildings).

The type of units studied, whether individuals, families, cities, or horn honks, is usually determined by the nature of the problem. The characteristics of the social unit under study, however, can themselves influence the conduct of the research. It should be obvious that if one's starting point is interest in a particular group or a particular type of social entity, this interest will have relevance for one's approach to the investigation.

Whatever the nature of the social units under study, it is possible to distinguish at least three different ways in which they can be grouped by the researcher: (1) real groups, (2) treatment groups, and (3) samples.

Real Groups The first type, a "real" group, is one that exists and has an ongoing life of its own, independent of the research or the researcher. Such a group (the car salesmen at a particular dealership—see Browne, Chapter 2; or the leadership of a particular country—see Charles Moskos, Jr., Chapter 2) has boundaries, and its members are aware of each other and involved in behavior which is dependent on a particular natural setting. Such a group could not be contrived by the researcher, nor could the group be studied in any other context. Likewise, individual elements could not be studied in isolation. This type of group is of particular interest to fieldworkers.

Treatment Groups The second type of group is a treatment group (those given a particular type of article to read, female author or male author—see Philip Goldberg, Chapter 3; or those assigned to a particular experimental condition, hurry or no-hurry—see John Darley and C. Daniel Batson, Chapter 3). This type of group is contrived or constructed, the individual elements or subjects being brought together by the researcher (usually an experimenter) so that their behavior can be studied in a setting created by the researcher and under conditions which allow the researcher to manipulate the independent variable. The units of such a group (whether individuals or rats or machines) need have no relationship to one another outside the context of the research situation, at least no relationship which is of interest to the researcher.

Samples In the third type of group, usually called a sample, the elements need not be aware of or in communication with one another and are not necessarily ever together in one place. The behavior under study, such as

THE RESEARCH EXPERIENCE

which political candidate one planned to vote for, may not be setting dependent.

This type of social entity has some of the characteristics of each of the other two. The activities of its members are not interfered with or manipulated in any contrived way. Behaviors are taken as they are, and variables are studied as they occur naturally, in interaction with other factors. Nevertheless, the group is created or constructed by the researcher. The responses of or data about the elements can be obtained in a variety of settings or locales and brought together for analysis. The elements themselves, though they may have things in common (being female, living in Texas, being an "intact" family, being a large city) or may sometimes even be aware of each other, need never meet. Because they are taken as "representatives" of a larger population of elements whose responses or characteristics can be inferred from those of the sample, there is great emphasis on the way the elements are selected. Principles of probability and techniques of random sampling are the tools commonly used by investigators (usually survey researchers) who use samples.

The Research Setting

Human behavior also takes place within a particular setting or context (the where). Other quite commonly used words for this which might be considered synonyms include: situation (stresses the aspect of meaning to the subject), occasion (stresses the temporal aspect), environment (stresses physical place), milieu, surroundings, embedding system (Runkel & McGrath, 1972: 22).

In social research, the words context and setting can refer to a specific, concrete setting (the West End—see Gans, Chapter 2), or to a kind of setting (prisons—see Haney, Banks, and Zimbardo, Chapter 3). The most common usage, however, simply dichotomizes settings as *field* or *laboratory*, according to whether the behavior takes place in a natural or a contrived setting. It should also be recognized that some behaviors do not depend on a particular setting. In any case, settings, too, must be taken into account in choosing a research strategy.

The Research Purpose: Focusing on the Why of Social Research

Once the research problem has been formulated and the cases and setting specified, the researcher must work out an appropriate research strategy. The choice of a particular research strategy is influenced not only by the nature of the research problem and the type of "unit in setting" but also by the particular purpose or emphasis of the investigator. How much does one want to know? How much does one already know? How far can one go? Consideration of these questions helps in making certain crucial decisions about research strategies. Given the same research problem one might make different choices, depending on one's purpose.

Classification of Purposes

Research purposes can be classified into several broad categories: (1) to explore, (2) to describe and classify, (3) to establish relationships, and (4) to show causality.

To Explore   When the researcher wants to become familiar with a problem, a group, or a setting, an exploratory approach to the research is most appropriate. In this case gaining insight and acquiring understanding in greater depth are probably more important than obtaining full, accurate, and detailed information. Hypotheses are more likely to be the result of rather than the impetus for such research. It would certainly be necessary to adopt strategies which would allow for openness and flexibility, and discovery and consideration of as many factors as possible would be the paramount concern.

To Describe and Classify.   Description focuses on what is, emphasizing accuracy, validity, and completeness. Whether the description is in narrative form or presented as statistical summaries, the relevant characteristics must be specified and classified in some detail.

To Establish Relationships   Taking description one step further, the investigator may attempt to show that two or more phenomena are related or correlated in a specified way. When we say that two variables are related, we mean that they "go together"; either they occur at the same time, or they vary together (changes in one phenomenon are accompanied by changes in the other) in some specified way. Showing that such a relationship exists, however, does not establish that one variable leads to, or "causes," the other.

To Show Causality   The researcher who wants to go beyond description and do more than establish that certain phenomena are related must be concerned with causality. The concern is not only to show what is but also to determine why, that is, to explain. Once something has been explained, it should then be possible to predict its occurrence. Explaining a phenomenon (the dependent variable: the effect or outcome) involves demonstrating that its occurrence or variation in it is the result of certain other specific determining factors (the independent variable or variables: the assumed cause). Demonstrating such a relationship is facilitated when the independent variable(s) can be manipulated. To establish cause, however, the researcher must be able to show not only that two phenomena are related but also that they occur in a particular sequence (i.e., time order) and that the outcome is not the result of other possible "causal" factors. Before-after procedures are useful for accomplishing the former, while the way units are selected is important in ensuring the latter.

Some authors use these terms—exploratory, descriptive, causal—as labels for types of research design. In a way, purpose and design become synonyms. But like many others, we prefer the more commonly used labels—experiments, surveys, field studies—for classifying research strategies. While certain strategies may be more suitable and more frequently used for certain purposes (such as field studies for exploratory research), purpose does not necessarily dictate design. Howard Schuman's survey (see Chapter 4), for example, uses survey research to explore the sources of antiwar sentiment in America. The prison simulation of Haney, Banks, and Zimbardo (Chapter 3), while experimental in design, was intended to explore the effects of situational variables on interpersonal dynamics.

Research Goals: Deciding How to Do the Study

. As in choosing a research topic, a number of crucial considerations and constraints influence the researcher's decision about an appropriate research strategy.

A Strategy to Fit the Problem

Once the research problem has been specified, the next step involves choosing a method for studying it. This is one point about which there seems to be some degree of consensus in the social sciences. The rule is that the method should fit the problem and the purpose. The assumption is that, given the specific problem, the researcher will consider all the possible alternative strategies before choosing the most (though not necessarily the only) appropriate one. But there is no one right way to approach a particular problem. Neither is there one particular research strategy that is right for every problem. Further, this position overlooks the many constraints imposed by personal and pragmatic considerations. Doing fieldwork, for example, involves a great investment of time and energy. Large-scale survey research can be expensive. A novice researcher especially, with limited resources, may very well have to settle for the best of several equally unsatisfactory strategies.

Personal, Professional, and Pragmatic Constraints

Probably the most imposing constraint is the availability of important resources: time, money, personnel, energy. Finding enough time to use the appropriate method correctly can be difficult if a project has to be done within the length of a course, or if, as in the case of many graduate students, one's grant or tenure is for a limited period. Fast-breaking events (see H. Edward Ransford, Chapter 4) may leave little time for planning and polish.

Except for the independently wealthy or the well connected, financing a research project can be prohibitive. Because they lack either experience or contacts, few students have access to substantial research funds. Preparing applications can be time-consuming (see Lengermann, Chapter 4) and often fruitless, and relying on personal finances is limiting, to say the least. Most student projects are of necessity modest, and compromises and modifications are commonplace.

Competent personnel can facilitate the research process. But, if one cannot find or afford reliable interviewers, coders, keypunchers, or computer programmers when one needs them (see Ransford, Chapter 4, and Stella Jones, Chapter 4), the research experience can indeed be frustrating.

To see one's research through to the end, mostly one needs to survive. If one gets tired or begins to run out of time, it can be difficult to keep going and maintain interest. Without interest, perseverance may be impossible. It should be obvious that if one has enough money, one probably can buy sufficient time and competent personnel—and maybe even a much-needed vacation.

The importance of personal interests and inclinations cannot be ignored. As pointed out earlier, social researchers sometimes choose the problem to suit the method. One who enjoys doing fieldwork is quite likely to reject topics or job opportunities which necessitate dealing with large amounts of quantitative data. One who likes fiddling with numbers or who (despite the inherent frustrations) enjoys using the computer is likely to be more open to research ideas and career possibilities that utilize these skills and inclinations.

The general and specific preferences within the discipline may also play a part. Historically, for example, the work of psychologists has tended to be experimental in nature and largely carried out within the confines of the laboratory. It should not be surprising then that sociologists with a social-psychological orientation would tend to use experimental methods. Likewise, sociologists in the symbolic interaction, or Chicago, tradition would probably be more comfortable in the field. Just as topics can be "in" or "out," so too can methods. During certain periods, or in certain regions or departments, different methodologies have predominated within the discipline. For some researchers, using those methods that are in vogue can become a compelling constraint.

The personal and pragmatic constraints outlined above do not exhaust the issues which must be considered in choosing a method. Assuming the motivation for doing research is more professional than personal, there are still other important considerations which pertain to the strengths and limitations of particular research strategies (or designs, the terminology preferred in the context of experimental research) for meeting particular research goals. Given a particular research problem, the researcher must determine the purpose of his or her research; consider the relative importance of various research goals in the light of that purpose; compare the relative effectiveness of different research strategies for accomplishing these goals; and, choose a particular research strategy from among those available.

Criteria for Comparing Alternative Research Strategies

Designing, or planning, the research involves choosing the actors (who), the behaviors (what), and the setting (where) in which they will be studied, and doing so within the context of the research purpose. Given a specific problem and a specific purpose, certain research goals become more important than others. Certain research strategies, in turn, are more fruitful than others for accomplishing these goals. The criteria for judging the adequacy of a particular strategy include (1) control, (2) representativeness, and (3) naturalness.

Control When the researcher's goal is *to establish relationships between independent and dependent variables,* control is the most crucial criterion for judging the adequacy of the research strategy. This means control not only of independent variables, those central to the research study, but also of those extraneous, perhaps unknown or unobserved, variables that may also affect the dependent variable. The idea is to minimize the number of elements, both within the subjects and within the environment, that can vary in the research situation, so that the important relationship between the independent and dependent variables can be highlighted and established without ambiguity.

In experimental research, *manipulation of the independent variable* is one way of accomplishing such an unambiguous situation. This can be done by either (1) imposing an experimental condition, or treatment, on the subjects, or (2) creating an experimental variable by classifying the subjects on some trait already existent in them, such as sex, age, or amount of education. When, for practical or ethical reasons, control cannot be introduced at the point of data collection (as in experiments), after-the-fact statistical controls introduced at the point of data analysis on such already existent traits can sometimes be useful.

When variables—such as characteristics of the subjects, or the setting, or the particular phenomena under study—cannot or should not be incorporated as independent variables (perhaps because one does not know what they are or because there are too many variables), there are two other ways to accomplish control. One is *holding variables constant,* as by "matching" characteristics of the subjects or creating an environment which can be regulated by the researcher. The other is *randomizing variables,* in relation to the way subjects are assigned to groups, the way task variables are presented, or the time of day the study takes place. Randomization[1] which involves giving

---

1. Random procedures involve giving each element of a population or universe the same chance as every other—in *random sampling,* of being selected from the population or universe; in *randomization,* of being assigned to a particular treatment condition, experimental or control.

all elements the same chance of being chosen for a particular assignment, is the only alternative available when the researcher does not know what variables may be affecting the dependent variable. Usually, the researcher tries to achieve control by *manipulating* task (or behavioral) variables, *holding constant* environmental variables, and *randomizing* (sometimes in combination with matching) subject variables.

Control is actually a way of accomplishing *internal validity.* Internal validity involves minimizing the amount of error (both constant and random)[2] due to extraneous variables, so that it is possible to conclude with confidence that differences in the dependent variable are attributable to differences in the independent variable. This requires *precise measurement of behavior.* The central concern is to establish, and to explain, relationships between variables.

Representativeness The second criterion for comparing research strategies involves weighing the relative advantages of obtaining detailed data about particular cases as opposed to securing less complex information, usually about a broader selection of cases, which might be more universally applicable. Examining complex patterns and the details of individual cases leaves less time and money for examining issues in a more general context. For given purposes, however, different emphases are important. A psychiatrist, for example, appropriately attempts to determine, with as much detail as possible, the unique patterns of an individual case. A social anthropologist may spend long periods studying particular cultures in depth. But information such as this cannot be assumed to be applicable to other cases or other settings.

Is it sufficient to establish that two variables are related in the group and in the circumstances studied or does the researcher want to apply the results to other persons and other situations? Given the latter requirements, representativeness of the units and the setting(s) becomes a primary concern. Achieving representativeness may involve large-scale probability sampling. By random sampling—that is, by selecting cases so that each element within the population has the same chance of being selected as every other element—the results can be assumed to apply to all cases in the universe, or population (of individuals, groups, things, settings, times) from which they have been drawn. Though studies having such concerns are often more limited in terms of the amount and type of information which can be sought about individual cases, there is the advantage of wider applicability.

Discussions regarding representativeness are usually phrased in such "contrast" terms as universal vs. particular; extensive vs. intensive; scope (breadth) vs. depth; complex vs. general. The question of representativeness

---

2. Constant or biasing error is introduced into the research process by some factor that systematically affects the characteristic being measured. Random error is due to transient aspects of the variables, actors, or setting that are likely to vary from one measurement to the next (Selltiz et al., 1959).

THE RESEARCH EXPERIENCE

is related to the question of *generalizability*. Representativeness is important because it allows one to *generalize to other actors or units or settings,* and their *attributes,* or characteristics. Is the researcher satisfied with describing or explaining something about the group or setting he has studied, or does he want to "go beyond" the specific findings, that is, to generalize or extrapolate the findings to some broader "population" (of units or settings) which the units and settings are presumed to "represent." Findings that can be generalized to other units or other settings have *external validity.* In applied research, especially, such a priority is essential.

Naturalness As pointed out above, one of the chief ways in which an experimenter can achieve control is by manipulating the independent, or treatment, variable. It is often argued, however, that by doing this the researcher has interfered with the natural process of events and has created an "artificial" situation. If the research is carried out in a controlled environment as well (as, for example, in a laboratory experiment), the charge of artificiality is magnified.

Further, if the focus of the research is on establishing a relationship between independent and dependent variables (i.e., on internal validity), often the researcher shows little concern for how subjects are selected. Unrelated individuals or social elements are brought together in artificially constructed "treatment" groups solely for the purposes of the researcher. Manipulated behaviors in contrived settings by researcher-created "treatment" groups may maximize rigor and control but can hardly be expected to reflect the natural behaviors of real persons in concrete natural settings.

When a primary concern is understanding *the system character of the context* (Runkel & McGrath, 1972) of a particular phenomenon or event (the interaction at a Billy Graham rally—see Weldon Johnson, Chapter 3; or the traffic patterns on a street corner—see Doob and Gross, Chapter 6), the naturalness of the behavior and the setting becomes the most important criterion for judging the adequacy of the research strategy. The focus is on the complex, ongoing patterns of interaction brought about by "real" social entities performing their normal activities in a natural setting (the Italians in the West End—see Gans, Chapter 2; or, the legal actors in Metrocourt—see Rovner-Pieczenik, Chapter 5).

Research Strategies: Comparing the Alternatives

To determine which research strategy is the most useful and appropriate for a particular purpose, the relative advantages and limitations of different strategies for accomplishing specific research goals must be compared. Though they do not exhaust the possibilities (or the names attached to those possibilities), the next four chapters of this book cover the major research strategies available to the investigator: (1) field studies, (2) experiments, (3) surveys, and (4) using available data. Within each chapter, studies are included which were done for different purposes and which use different data collection techniques and measurement procedures. Because there are particular problems related to the operationalization of variables, two research projects which were specifically conceived and designed to deal with the problems of operationalization are included in a separate chapter on measurement (Chapter 6).

Field Studies

Of the alternative research strategies available, field studies come closest to approximating real life. There is maximum concern with understanding the patterns of interaction in a *particular context*. Because their objective is to study, in all its complexity, the behavior of real actors in actual settings, such approaches are strong on realism and meaningfulness. The researcher tries to interfere as little as possible with the ongoing behavior and to understand as fully as possible the interaction of the many variables in the particular setting.

While such approaches may make it difficult to focus on or to isolate specific elements of the research situation, they do lend themselves to openness, flexibility, and discovery. Consequently, it should not be surprising that field studies are often the preferred research strategy where the purpose is to explore or to describe. An anthropological fieldworker interested in a particular tribe or a sociologist interested in a particular community would be quite likely to use a field study approach. Their emphasis would be on finding out as much as possible about the particular group or phenomenon. Because control is difficult to achieve in field studies, they are seldom used where explanation is the researcher's purpose.

In summary: field studies use *real groups* in *natural settings;* they focus on a *particular context,* are strong on *naturalness,* weak on control and representativeness, and are most likely to be used in *exploratory* or *descriptive* research.

Experiments

When one is testing a hypothesis, control is of paramount importance. For maximizing control in one's research, an experimental strategy in which one manipulates the independent variable is desirable. Several strategies are available to the experimental researcher: (1) laboratory experiments, (2) field experiments, and (3) experimental simulations.

Laboratory Experiments By manipulating the independent variables central to the investigation, and by holding constant other extraneous environmental and personal variables, laboratory experiments can provide the most complete control. The experimenter deliberately creates, for the specific purpose of the research, a contrived setting which lends itself to research procedures that, because they can be manipulated or controlled, are usually more precise, more accurate, more detailed, more definite, and more easily quantifiable. Achieving such control permits a focus on the behaviors under study, on the relationships between variables. It is certainly the preferred strategy among those who favor a more "scientific" and "behavioral" approach to research, psychologists and social psychologists in particular.

The very precision and control which can be accomplished in laboratory experiments, however, also provides the basis for the strongest criticisms of this research strategy. Some consider laboratory experiments "artificial" and therefore meaningless. The difficulty is that, while experiments are high on internal validity, they are weak on external validity. The findings cannot be generalized to other individuals or other settings. But, if one's purpose is to explain the relationship between variables and if one is not concerned with generalizing, it may not matter that the units and the setting are not representative of real life.

In summary: laboratory experiments use *treatment groups* in *contrived settings;* they focus on *relationships between variables* (i.e., on behaviors), are strong on *control,* weak on naturalness and representativeness, and are most likely to be used in *causal* research.

Field Experiments Field experiments are an attempt to wed some of the advantages of both field studies and experiments. Consequently, they also present some of the difficulties of both. By introducing experimental manipulation into real situations, the researcher tries to gain maximum control of behavior without sacrificing the reality of the situation. Therefore field experiments are more artificial than field studies and have less control than lab experiments. It must be recognized that, because control of the environment is minimal, extraneous environmental variables can still influence the outcome. Johnson (see Chapter 3), for example, assigned subjects to active and passive participation at a Billy Graham meeting, but he did not anticipate that such large crowds would arrive so early, making it impossible for some students to take up their assigned positions inside the stadium.

In summary: field experiments use *treatment groups* in *natural settings;* they focus primarily on *relationships between variables* (i.e., on behaviors), while giving attention to the *particular context;* they achieve *some control* and *some* degree of *naturalness,* and are most likely to be used for *causal* research.

Experimental Simulations An experimental simulation is a research strategy which has some things in common with laboratory experiments but is different in several important ways. Like laboratory experiments, experimental simulations create a setting for the specific purposes of the research. The difference lies in the fact that in the latter, the setting is created to be like (that is, to "represent") some particular class or kind of naturally-occurring real-life situation (prison—see Haney, Banks, and Zimbardo,

Chapter 3). Further, while some degree of control is built into the study by manipulation of the independent variable and by selection and assignment of the subjects, still other variables are left free to vary.

In summary: experimental simulations use *treatment groups* in a *"representative" contrived setting;* they focus on *relationships between variables* (i.e., behaviors) in the *particular "simulated" context,* in order to be able to make *"generalizations"* about interaction in that particular type of setting. They attempt to *control* certain elements of the experiment, and, at the same time, to create a situation which is "close to life." There is a difficulty here in that "representativeness" and "generalizations" are not used in precisely the same way that these terms are used elsewhere in this chapter. Probability (i.e., random sampling) procedures are not involved in the way these "contrived" settings are determined. "Representativeness" is more likely to be based on the *researcher's* idea of what is "typical." With proper planning, experimental simulations can be used for various purposes.

Survey Research

Survey research is used when the researcher wants to obtain information —usually a large amount of it—which can be generalized to a whole class of units, or actors. Accomplishing this generalizability requires using samples that represent these larger populations. The phenomenon being studied (attitudes toward the Vietnam War—see Schuman, Chapter 4) is usually independent of particular settings. Comprehensiveness, or coverage of a great many topic areas, is sometimes emphasized at the expense of depth, and accuracy is usually considered important. Variables are supposed to be studied as they are in reality. While some would argue that the naturally occurring interaction of factors is not altered, others (see, e.g., Derek Phillips, 1971) would counter that the introduction of the survey instrument is reactive in itself and creates a totally unnatural situation. No manipulation of the independent variable means, of course, less control. To compensate, however, for the absence of control at the point of data collection, one can usually introduce statistical controls (e.g., by holding variables constant) at the point of data analysis.

Since opinion polls are the type of survey research with which most people are familiar, there is a tendency to associate surveys with description. They are certainly the preferred procedure among political scientists and social policymakers. Surveys can, however, be used as well in exploratory (see Schuman, Chapter 4) or causal research (see Lengermann, Chapter 4; or Ransford, Chapter 4). It depends on one's purpose. To engage in causal survey research, the type of statistical controls mentioned above is used.

In summary, surveys use *samples* which are *"independent of" settings;* they focus on *generalizations about classes of units, or actors,* are especially strong on *representativeness,* though control and naturalness need not be sacrificed entirely. While surveys are used most often in *descriptive* and *causal* research, *exploratory* purposes should not be ruled out.

Using Available Data

Variations on the basic research strategies—field studies, experiments, surveys—have been developed to deal with available data, some of the varieties of which are discussed later in this chapter (see p. 21). Using what is available can provide many opportunities for the researcher to be creative and imaginative. It should be recognized, however, that the researcher has little control over the original form of the data. These data must be taken as they are. Content analysis and secondary analysis are research strategies which attempt to use such data to advantage.

Content Analysis A strategy which has been developed to facilitate systematic study of public and private documents is content analysis, which has been used rather widely in the study of mass media (see Levin and Spates, Chapter 5). While quantification of content has often been a preoccupation of content analysts, the basic principles underlying this strategy are not much different from those that must be considered in other contexts. Concern for the representativeness of the sample of content chosen for analysis, for example, differs from survey analysis largely in that the units of the study are nonhuman—usually artifacts such as words on a page, in a book, or a song, or segments on radio or television.

Secondary Analysis The strategy of secondary analysis uses social science data that have been collected, usually by another researcher or organization, for other purposes, or at least not for the researcher's particular current purpose. Using census data to do research for which the data were not originally intended (see Kasarda, Chapter 5) is an example, as is using any other survey data already collected. Given the tremendous cost of collecting data, being able to use what is available is an advantage which should not be easily dismissed. Once the source is decided on, the principles of design and analysis are little different from those for survey analysis.

The Time Dimension

The time it takes to do research is, of course, one of the constraints with which the researcher must contend. There are, however, several other important ways in which the time dimension can affect the planning and execution of one's research. Two points in particular should be mentioned, each primarily related to a particular type of research strategy.

Before-After Testing To establish causality, as noted above, it is necessary not only to show that the independent and dependent variables are related but also to show that the dependent variable did not occur before the independent variable in time. In an experimental design, information on the time order of the variables can be obtained by measuring the dependent variable (Y), both prior to and subsequent to the manipulation of the independent, or treatment, variable (X). In the classic experimental model, "before-after with experimental and control group," the before and after measures are made for both the experimental group (which was exposed to the treatment variable) and the control group (which was not). Comparing the differences between the before and after tests for the two groups provides a basis for inferring that the independent variable "caused" or was responsible for the change in the dependent variable.

Cross-sectional and Longitudinal Studies   Time is also of concern to survey researchers and to those who use available data. They must determine whether or not to collect the data and take the measurements at one point in time or at several points in time. Again, the problem is related to the question of causality. Cross-sectional studies base their conclusions on data obtained at only one point in time and hence have limitations which make it difficult to establish causality. Longitudinal studies, on the other hand, obtain data at several points or for several periods in time and are more useful when establishing causality is of concern to the researcher.

A Word on Terminology

The names for the types of research strategies which have been chosen as the organizing headings for chapters of this book reflect general usage in the discipline, but they are not universally favored. There is not even unanimity about what these names represent. Try to distinguish, for example, between a design, an approach, a format, or a strategy. It is probably true that the latter three terms have evolved to encompass those ways of doing research that are not causal and do not involve setting up a "design" (the terminology usually preferred by those who do experimental studies). Indeed, for some research specialists the dichotomy between experimental and nonexperimental research is the only important one.

Part of the ambiguity of the terminology probably arises out of our reluctance to attach the word "design" to research that favors more open and flexible "approaches." Still another factor contributing to the use of multiple terms may be our uncertainty about where the boundaries lie between designing the research and collecting the data. One confusing problem for the beginning student is that some writers include as a research design or strategy what other authors would regard as a technique of data collection. The use of participant observation comes to mind. In some instances it is used almost as a synonym for field study and treated as a special type of research strategy; in others it is discussed as a particular variation of the use of observation to obtain data.

Discussions of certain other attributes of research—reactive vs. nonreactive, quantitative vs. qualitative—are also confusing in this regard. Are

THE RESEARCH EXPERIENCE

these characteristics of research strategies, data collection techniques, or measurement procedures? Actually these terms have been used variously by different authors, in all three contexts. Indeed, the latter terms have even been used by some to characterize "kinds" of sociology. At bottom, reactivity and quantitativeness are probably routed in measurement procedures, but the ambiguity is acknowledged here by discussing them "in between."

Reactivity Techniques for obtaining and measuring data can be said to vary in the degree of intervention or intrusion they make on the research process. Though obtrusiveness or reactivity was cited by Aaron Cicourel in a 1964 text, particular concern with and widespread use of these and related terms seem to date from the publication of _Unobtrusive Measures_ by Webb et al. in 1966.

Reactiveness involves the extent to which the research activities intrude on the situation or behavior under study—the degree to which the investigation affects the research process. In a sense, all research is to some extent intrusive; differences in intervention are really a matter of degree. Field studies and surveys, for example, are intrusive only in that they require some procedure of data collection. Depending on the nature of the procedure and the _precision of the measurement,_ data collection can be more or less intrusive. Unstructured observations or interviews which can remain a part of the ongoing behavior of participants are probably less intrusive than standardized questionnaires.

Because experimental strategies also involve _manipulation of the independent variable,_ and usually more precise and standardized measures, they are generally more intrusive than other research strategies, although some field experiments (see Doob and Gross, Chapter 6) can be less so. The _control of the physical environment_ which is common in laboratory experiments and experimental simulations and the precise measures used to ensure rigor and control combine to make experimental strategies intrusive as a rule. Precise measures need not be obtrusive, however; Webb et al. outline a number of procedures—physical traces, archival data, participant and/or hidden observation—for minimizing reactivity. Nevertheless, it can be argued that control and precision of measurement often mean more intrusive research operations.

Reactivity is a rather encompassing term affected by aspects of design, data collection, _and_ measurement. Experiments and surveys are considered more intrusive than field studies, and asking questions more intrusive than using simple (participant) observation, archival data, or physical traces. The many-faceted idea seems to be affected by the degree of control of the research design; the degree of structure, participation, and directness in the data gathering; and the degree of precision and quantification in the measurement process.

Quantitativeness Some social scientists (e.g., Bernard Phillips, 1966) also place research on a qualitative-quantitative continuum. While this attribute would also seem to be primarily related to the precision and refinement of the measurement procedures used, it is often translated into a broader characterization of particular research strategies, presumably based on the assumption that certain research strategies are more likely than others to use quantitative measures. Fieldworkers, in this view, are presumed to rely more heavily on participant observation, document analysis, and detailed case study approaches. Their research thus is characterized as "qualitative." Because of the need for control and standardization and precision in experiments, experimental researchers, in contrast, are cited as being more "quantitative." Even disciplines can be so characterized—psychology as more quantitative, anthropology as more qualitative.

Other social scientists object to having their research or their discipline placed on such an axis. The fieldworker who might be classified as "qualitative" because he or she employs participant observation could argue that this is a false distinction, for if the situation demanded he or she would also conduct surveys and quantify data. Others do not object to classifying research as more or less quantitative. Though the word may be unsatisfactory for the purpose, it conveys a meaning for which no other seems more adequate. Certainly, some fieldworkers (Wax, 1971) do not include among their repertoire of preferred techniques standardized instruments such as structured interviews or questionnaires, which seem to lend themselves more easily to quantification and precision.

Data Collection, Measurement, and Analysis: Executing the Strategy

Selltiz et al. (1959) describe a research design as "the arrangement of conditions for collection and analysis of data in a manner that aims to combine relevance to the research purpose with economy in procedure."

Getting the Data

Whatever research strategy is chosen, there are only a few basic ways to obtain the data. The most widely used techniques involve *observing behavior* and *asking questions*. Questions can be asked face to face (or by someone other than the respondent, as over the phone), in which case the procedure is called an *interview.* It does not matter whether the researcher or someone else asks the questions. Nor does it matter whether the questions being asked refer to the interviewee (who is then called a respondent) or to someone else (in which case the interviewee is referred to as an informant). If written questions are used and the form is completed by the respondent, it is called a *questionnaire,* whether the form is sent through the mail or administered directly. A third alternative involves using *secondary and archival sources,* information already available in various public and private sources.

Archival (or available) data include both personal and public documents. Letters, diaries, autobiographies, and speeches are examples of the former. The latter encompass several types of materials: public records, including those of such agencies as police, courts (Rovner-Pieczenik, Chapter 5), or schools; census data (John Kasarda, Chapter 5); news sources and other printed matter, including radio, TV, newspapers, magazines (Jack Levin and James Spates, Chapter 5) and books (James Banks, Chapter 5). Data obtained (perhaps by observing or asking questions) for one research purpose and subsequently stored and made available for other "secondary" analyses can also be described in this way.

An effort was made to choose for this book studies using various data collection techniques in the context of differing research strategies. But it would probably be impossible to find studies that used each data collection technique in the context of each research strategy, probably because certain strategy-technique combinations are more common than others. There is no denying that fieldworkers are more likely to use participant observation, unstructured interviews, and archival data, while survey researchers prefer questionnaires and interviews. In fact, it would probably be absurd for the latter even to consider observation. Experimenters may rely most heavily on structured observation and questionnaires, but they might also use interviews or participant observation (as does Johnson—see Chapter 3).

There are a number of dimensions of comparisons which are helpful in choosing among data collection procedures, as well as in determining the preferred version of a particular procedure. We are not reviewing here the specific advantages and limitations of observing behavior or asking questions or using available data. Rather, we are considering those dimensions that can be used to characterize *all* data collection techniques. Observations can be made, questions can be asked, and available information can be obtained in more or less structured form, directly or indirectly, with more or less objectivity on the part of the researcher or the respondent. The degree to which the researcher becomes involved in or participates in the data collection process also can vary.

Structure This dimension involves the extent to which the content under study has been specified and standardized in advance. More structured techniques usually have designated characteristics or categories in terms of which observations are made or question responses elicited. Less structured techniques tend to remain open, flexible, and unspecified in terms of both content and categorization. Structured techniques restrict the alternatives or categories to those provided by the researcher. "Are you satisfied with your job?" can be an open-ended question if no categories of response are provided and if no restrictions are placed on the length or type of response. If the researcher restricts choices to given alternatives (e.g., "yes" and "no"; or "very satisfied," "somewhat satisfied," etc.), the question becomes more structured. Likewise an observer who has been instructed to record particular behaviors in a specific, standardized format is doing more structured research than one who goes into the field with few preconceived notions or expectations.

Objectivity Still another dimension in terms of which the strengths and weakness of different data collection techniques and measurement procedures are debated is the degree of objectivity that can be achieved. This involves the extent to which the data are free of the researcher's or the respondent's biases or interpretation. Objective procedures are supposed to make it possible for anyone following the prescribed rules to interpret behavior and assign values in the same way.[3] One point of debate concerns whether or not any subjectivity involved is that of the researcher or of the unit or person being studied.

Though researcher biases cannot be eliminated, they can be recognized, dealt with and, it is hoped, minimized. As for the respondent, "the dilemma concerns whether or not attention is focused on factors which must be viewed as the actor views them—that is, which need the interpretation or perspective of the case under study rather than that of the researcher" (Leik, 1972). Certain kinds of information (someone's age or sex, or the population of a city) may remain relatively, though not entirely, free of a subjective element. Other variables (marital happiness, job satisfaction, educational aspiration) are less objective and may require a response from a subjective perspective. Sometimes it is desirable, even necessary, to understand the whole research situation from the point of view—or the perspective—of the respondent. Then, data collection procedures which allow for subjectivity, or interpretation from the perspective of the respondent, are crucial.

Subjectivity need not mean that standardization must be sacrificed. Projective tests and attitude scaling techniques, for example, have been developed to make it possible to elicit subjective responses in a standardized form. The important distinction is whether or not the data require or are free of interpretation by the subject or respondent.

Degree of Participation The degree to which the researcher becomes involved in the data collection process also must be considered in choosing a data collection technique. Some procedures require or give priority to frequent and intense contact with the research subjects. The data gathering is carried out as a part of the ongoing interaction, and the researcher becomes a part of it. While this aspect of data collection is most often discussed with regard to "participant" observation, the idea can be considered in any data gathering effort. Any data collection procedure can remain rather impersonal and detached, or it can become more participative and interactive. In more participative situations, the researcher can rely primarily on observa-

---

3. Babbie (1975) comments that all scientists are "subjective" to some extent—influenced by their personal motivations. He uses the term "intersubjectivity," to mean that two researchers "with different subjective orientations would arrive at the same conclusion if each conducted the same experiment."

THE RESEARCH EXPERIENCE

tion (Browne, Chapter 2; Laud Humphreys, Chapter 2; and Johnson, Chapter 3) or interviews (Moskos, Chapter 2). Such techniques are usually associated with fieldwork and long periods in the field. But participation does not necessarily mean duration. Johnson, for example, used participant observers at a Billy Graham rally. Involvement in the ongoing activity is the key consideration in participative research.

Directness The straightforwardness with which the researcher approaches data gathering is another of its dimensions. The term can perhaps be understood in two ways. The first meaning is related to _why_ one wants the data. Is a behavior observed or a response elicited for its obvious or manifest content, or for some other meaning assumed to be reflected in it? The second way in which the term can be understood has more to do with _how_ one gets the data. Does one go directly to the situation or the source for the information, or is some alternative data collection procedure utilized?

In the first meaning, for example, the researcher might look for physical traces or indirect evidence of some behavior. Observing the selective wear or rate of replacement of floor tiles in a museum (Webb et al., 1966) might be an indirect indicator of the popularity of one exhibit as compared to another. Rate of accumulation of refuse might be an indirect measure of food consumption or economic affluence. The information of interest, in each case, is obtained indirectly.

Projective techniques also elicit data about individuals indirectly, by getting them to talk about or respond to stimulus objects other than themselves. Their reactions to these ambiguous stimuli (inkblots, pictures, dolls) are taken as an indicator of their attitudes or feelings. When direct questions might be threatening, or when individuals may be unaware of or unable to recognize or express their thoughts or feelings, such techniques can be useful. Sometimes, however, indirect techniques are used to obtain information that the individual or group might not be open about or actually might not want to share. Asking a "factual" question (e.g., What percentage of the population of Metrocity is on welfare?) for which only incorrect alternative responses are supplied and then using that "incorrect" response as an indication of an individual's attitude toward the "fact," is an indirect technique. Observing one aspect of an individual's behavior in a situation not clearly related to that behavior (e.g., observing some aspect of interracial behavior in the waiting room of a doctor's office) is also indirect. In each instance, the subjects think they are doing something other than what is actually the case. Herein lies the danger with and the limitation of indirect techniques.

The difficulty with such techniques comes in the area of disclosure. Does the subject or respondent know that the information is sought for other than the manifest or stated purpose? While a subject may realize that a projective technique is seeking latent information, this is not always the case. Indirect techniques can lend themselves to disguise and deception, and care must be taken to limit abuse.

The second meaning of directness probably is more useful in distinguishing among data collection techniques than in describing variations in a particular technique. From this perspective, some data collection techniques are more indirect than others. If one wants to know something about an individual, one can ask. That's direct. In contrast, using archival data would be more indirect. And less reactive. Certainly, with historical events, there is no other alternative. Questionnaires and interviews can also be an indirect data source. Using survey data for a purpose other than that for which they were collected can be considered an indirect procedure (see, e.g., Schwartzbaum, Rothman, and McGrath, Chapter 5). Data banks containing social science information obtained (perhaps using questionnaires or interviews) for other research purposes can be a fertile, indirect source of data. Since archival data and physical traces are usually suggested as "unobtrusive" methods, use of indirect data sources can also be said to be related to the desire to mitigate reactivity.

Measurement

Variables must be defined in both conceptual and operational terms. The measurement procedures constitute the "operational definitions" of the variables of the study (horn honks as a measure of aggression—Doob and Gross, Chapter 6—or mutual gazing as a measure of romantic love—Zick Rubin, Chapter 6). Measurement involves arranging the data in such a way so as to be able, where necessary, to distinguish degree or quantity, as well as quality. Measurement consists of identifying the values or categories that may be assumed by some variable and representing those values by numbers or codes which are systematically and consistently assigned according to a set of rules. The rules for accomplishing the measurement can affect both the techniques of data collection and the procedures of analysis. If one wants to perform certain measurement procedures on a set of data, it is necessary that the data be collected in a form which makes such procedures possible. If one needs information on which distinctions of degree can be based, it is more efficient to obtain the data in such a form than to transform it later. Likewise, different types of data analysis require, or are most appropriately used with, different levels of measurement (nominal, ordinal, interval, or ratio). If data are not available at the appropriate level of measurement, certain types of analyses are impossible.

Most textbooks discuss measurement devices in terms of their (1) validity and (2) reliability. Both ideas are related to the errors involved in the way a concept is measured.

Validity Validity describes the degree to which the measure does what it purports to do, or how accurately it reflects variations in the concept it is intended to measure. The *internal validation* of a measure, sometimes called an item analysis, involves determining the extent to which there is agreement of results among the parts or components of a complex measure (e.g., among the items of an attitude scale or the parts of an aptitude test) and between the parts and the composite, or total, measure. *External* (or construct) *validation* involves determining the extent to which there is agreement of results among diverse ways of measuring the concept (e.g., with driving ability, the written test and the road test). One researcher's way of measuring a concept must give results compatible with those of other researchers using other known ways of operationalizing the same concept.

Reliability The degree to which the measure gives consistent or reproducible results is called its reliability. The same measure should give consistent results from one time to the next (*stability reliability*) or under different sets of circumstances—two different interviewers or observers using the same instrument, or two different versions of the same test (*equivalence reliability*).

Data Analysis

Though method of analysis was not a central concern in choosing the contributions to this book, the material covered does give sufficient exposure to different kinds of data analysis. These range from the sometimes complex and cumbersome categorizing and indexing procedures needed to present findings in narrative form (Browne, Chapter 2) to the more quantitative, and perhaps threatening (though they need not be) statistical procedures used in experiments and surveys—such as analysis of variance (Jeffrey Goldstein and Robert Arms, Chapter 3), multiple regression (Darley and Batson, Chapter 3), or path analysis (Kasarda, Chapter 5).

It must be recognized that analysis cannot be an afterthought in research. In order to have data appropriate for a particular procedure of data analysis, the data must be collected in proper form. The use to which the data will ultimately be put should be taken into account at an early stage in the research.

Ethical Considerations: Determining Whether It Should Be Done

Ethical considerations present still another set of variables which can impose constraints on research. The recent development by the federal government of guidelines for the "protection of human subjects" in any federally funded research project gives added weight to these dimensions. Those who resent or resist such policing of social research might argue that the integrity of knowledge is jeopardized when such limitations are placed on scientific inquiry. Indeed, such restrictions may rule out "ideal" research procedures, but social research must be ethically as well as scientifically sound.

Ethical concerns can enter at every stage of the research process, from the selection of a research problem to the use of research results. Some ethical dilemmas are present in all research. *Sponsorship* is crucial: What does the sponsor expect in return for the money? Who decides what to study? Who owns the data? Who decides how it may be used? Further, all research has *consequences*. What does the researcher owe to those from whom or about whom the data is obtained (see Rubin, Chapter 6)? Who determines whether or how the results will be used, especially where they might be unflattering or potentially harmful to certain individuals or groups (see Humphreys, Chapter 2)?

Other questions vary with the topic or the research strategy or the data collection technique. Whether or not to reveal the identity of the researcher is especially troublesome in field studies. There is much controversy in the literature about the appropriateness of disguised or secret observation (see Humphreys) and whether or not it constitutes an invasion of privacy or a violation of individual or group rights. Because experiments usually involve the manipulation of a crucial variable, they inevitably pose questions about the treatment of human subjects. Physical or psychological harm must be avoided, and subjects rights must not be usurped. "Informed consent" must be obtained. Experiments can also pose questions regarding deception: should the subjects be told what the study is actually about? Proponents of disguised observation and experimental deception argue that knowledge of the research on the part of the subjects would distort their behavior and make the research impossible.

In surveys, the anonymity and confidentiality of data are crucial. Steps must be taken to protect the identity of the respondents and to safeguard the data from unauthorized persons. Recruitment, or the circumstances under which an individual agrees to participate, is important in all research. Consent must be not only "informed" but also "free." The use of "lower participants" or captive populations (subjects or respondents are more likely to be students than teachers, prisoners than guards, patients than doctors) because it is expedient must be discouraged.

Beyond the specific constraints laid out by the federal government and various professional societies in recent guidelines, resolving ethical dilemmas ultimately involves one's personal ideology and judgment. To most people, using secret observation to determine an individual's response to "high status" and "low status" cars (Doob and Gross, Chapter 6) seems less offensive, certainly less controversial, than not revealing one's identity when observing "impersonal sex" (Humphreys). Likewise, deceiving subjects about the nature of the treatment variable seems more acceptable in some cases than in others. Few students, for example, seem alarmed that seminarians were not told that the phenomenon being studied was helping behavior, not religious education, in Darley and Batson's study reprinted in Chapter 3.

In the end, it is up to the individual researcher whether or not to accept compromising sponsorship, study lower participants, use disguised observation or engage in experimental deception, protect the identity of respondents, guarantee the confidentiality of data, or attempt to establish "reciprocity" with informants. Students should approach such decisions with an awareness of the very crucial issues involved.

Plan of the Book: Putting It All Together

This book has two basic purposes: to expose students to a wide range of research possibilities, and to introduce them to the experiential as well as the conceptual aspects of social research. To accomplish these purposes, the book is organized in two ways: research strategies and individual contributions.

Research Strategies

In line with the first purpose, the basic alternative research strategies—field studies, experiments, surveys, using available data—serve as the headings for Chapters 2 through 5 of the book. Within each of these chapters, an effort is made to include studies that were done for different purposes and that used various data collection techniques. To ensure that students are exposed to some of the particular problems related to the operationalization of variables, a separate chapter on measurement is also included (Chapter 6).

In selecting the topics or approaches to be covered and choosing the articles to be included in the book, the objectives were as follows:

1. To provide adequate *coverage* of the various strategies (field studies, surveys, experiments, using available data) and techniques (observation, interview, questionnaire) of social research.
2. To include articles on a *variety* of topics to help students become aware of the diversity of subject matter and settings which can provide a focus for research.
3. To select articles written from a *sociological* (or social-psychological) *perspective.*

The goals are to provide a broad, balanced overview of the research process and to encourage students to consider possibilities before they develop preferences.

Individual Contributions

In line with these goals, each contribution includes a personal journal to supplement the research report example. These journals demonstrate that social research is circumstantial and unexpected, as well as logical and systematic. They focus on the "context of discovery" rather than the "context of justification" (Hammond, 1964; Reichenbach, 1938). The context of justification refers to the process whereby researchers attempt to justify and defend their findings by logical means. The context of discovery refers to the evolution of ideas and events involved in developing and executing the research. It includes both the conceptual and the experiential aspects of the endeavor.

Because the personal journals must be read in conjunction with the associated research reports, the book brings together material related to both contexts—justification and discovery. The material for each study is presented in two parts:

A. Research Report: a presentation of the findings (context of justification).
B. Personal Journal: a chronicle of the research experience (context of discovery).

The first article by each contributor is a research report of the type that normally appears in the professional journals of the field. Most have been previously published, although some appear here for the first time. An effort has been made to choose research which is as close as possible in time and scope to the kind of experience students might have themselves. Student reviews at each stage of the selection process helped to ensure that the reports are as clear and comprehensible as possible to those who have not yet had any research experience.

The personal journals, most of which were written expressly for this volume, take into account the unplanned as well as the planned aspects of discovery. These first-person accounts are intended to provide a broader perspective of the research experience than is usually found in the professional literature of the field. The contributors review some of the considerations and constraints—theoretical, practical, and personal—which influenced their decisions at crucial choice points in the research experience. The individual accounts focus on different points in the research process and emphasize various aspects of the research experience. Sometimes they are very personal statements.

These articles chronicle the feeling, thinking component—the human side—of research. They confront the disorderly, the overlooked, the unpredictable, and even the boring and routine aspects of research. The idea is for students to learn not only about research but also about how the researcher works. Exposure to this type of material should help them to understand the methodology of social research and to appreciate both the difficulties and the joys involved in the process of discovery. The research experience should then be viewed not only as more difficult, but also as more possible.

Science tells us what ought to be done. When students see that even professionals face problems and have confusing and dissatisfying moments, and that social science does not fall into neat and predictable patterns on cue, they should develop a new respect for those who attempt to do research and a better perspective from which to view their own work. They should be more patient with themselves and more confident of their ability to participate in such activities. Research should become something they *could* do, even though not easily, as well as something they might want to do. Easy criticism should be replaced by thoughtful examination of the problems and the pitfalls. Actually doing research should become at once easier (for them), and harder (for anybody). It is hoped that students will see that both confidence *and* humility are prerequisites for a satisfactory research experience.

REFERENCES

Babbie, Earl R. *The practice of social research.* Belmont, Calif.: Wadsworth Publishing, 1975.

Cicourel, Aaron V. *Method and measurement in sociology.* New York: Free Press, 1964.

Denzin, Norman K. *The research act.* Chicago: Aldine, 1970.

Hammond, Phillip E. (ed.). *Sociologists at work.* New York: Basic Books, 1964.

Kerlinger, Fred N. *Foundations of behavioral research.* 2nd ed. New York: Holt, Rinehart & Winston, 1973.

Leik, Robert K. *Methods, logic and research of sociology.* Indianapolis: Bobbs-Merrill, 1972.

Phillips, Bernard S. *Social research: Strategy and tactics.* New York: Macmillan, 1966.

Phillips, Derek L. *Knowledge from what?* Chicago: Rand-McNally, 1971.

Reichenbach, Hans. *Experience and prediction.* Chicago: University of Chicago Press, 1938.

Runkel, Philip J., & Joseph E. McGrath. *Research on human behavior.* New York: Holt, Rinehart & Winston, 1972.

Selltiz, Claire; Jahoda, Marie; Deutsch, Morton; & Cook, Stuart W. *Research methods in social relations.* New York: Holt, Rinehart & Winston, 1959.

Wax, Rosalie H. *Doing fieldwork.* Chicago: University of Chicago Press, 1971.

Webb, Eugene J.; Campbell, Donald T.; Schwartz, Richard D.; & Sechrest, Lee. *Unobtrusive measures.* Chicago: Rand McNally, 1966.

FIELD STUDIES

A. RESEARCH BY
Herbert Gans
Joy Browne
Laud Humphreys
Charles C. Moskos, Jr.

B. PERSONAL JOURNALS BY
Herbert Gans
Joy Browne
Laud Humphreys
Charles C. Moskos, Jr.

CHAPTER 2

CHAPTER 2

FIELD STUDIES

Field studies are most likely to be used by researchers who are interested in studying naturally-occurring interaction in a particular context. The selections included in this chapter have such a goal in common—they all seek to get close to the realities of a particular situation. The contexts in which this goal are pursued, however, are quite different. Herbert Gans reports on fieldwork in a working-class Italian community in Boston; Joy Browne relates her experiences doing research on used-car salesmen; Laud Humphreys recounts his research in "tearooms," those public restrooms frequented by men who are interested in "impersonal" sex; and Charles Moskos, Jr., discusses some of the problems encountered in his research in the West Indies.

All of these fieldworkers studied a "real" group in which the activities and the interactions of the participants were carried out within a particular context, and these activities had a meaning independent of the research. Such groups could not be contrived by the researcher and had to be studied on their own turf. Though they shared this characteristic, the groups differed in size, make-up, and degree and kind of interaction. Gans, for example, was attempting to study a community of close to 3,000 persons although in the course of his research he met and spoke with no more than 100 to 150 people and had intense contact with only about 20 West Enders. For Browne, the situation and the group were more circumscribed, and the number of actors who had to be "taken in" was more limited. Humphreys at any one time was involved with only a limited number of actors, but the makeup of the group in which he was interested was fluid; it was altered as individuals penetrated the membrane of the "tearoom" and then withdrew. Moskos's respondents were scattered throughout six islands of the West Indies, no more than 13 to 20 in each island.

To protect the privacy of the people they studied, Gans, Browne, and Humphreys all endeavored to guard the names of group members and to conceal other identifying facts and information about them. In contrast, Moskos departed from "customary practice" and published the actual names and rankings of the West Indian leaders included in his study. He maintained that "Such a public listing of societal leaders allows for an informed evaluation of the identification procedure."

Participant observation was the primary means of data collection in three of these studies—Gans, Browne, and Humphreys. Gans actually lived in the West End, and, though most of his involvement there was as a researcher-participant, to a certain extent and for a period of time, at least, he was also a real participant. Gans embarked on this study because he wanted "to understand neighborhoods known as slums" and "to learn firsthand what differentiates working- and lower-class people from middle-class ones." In his personal journal, Gans discusses some of the problems he faced as a "middle-class outsider." Initially he found he had difficulty penetrating the

West End society; a welcoming gesture from a neighbor provided the first contact.

The friendly nature of Gans's involvement in the group he was studying presented further complications. Emotional involvement with the people may mean an opportunity to see the world from their perspective, but it can also blind the researcher to behavior patterns and distort the study. Gans maintains, however, that such identification decreases in intensity as the research proceeds; he feels that the "dangers of overidentification are also reduced by the many differences between the researcher and the people he is studying." The researcher ultimately "realizes that he cannot be like them, or that he should not even try to be."

Though Browne never became a used car salesperson, she did become a regular on the lot. But first she had to gain admittance, or entree, which she describes as a power game. To do so she chose to contact the sales manager, whom she determined to be "an effectively rather than a nominally powerful person." She counsels the researcher to "go as high as possible, so that the compromise will only have to be made once."

Browne discusses the fear that haunts fieldworkers: How much is the data being influenced by one's presence? Being aware that one might affect the nature of the interaction is probably the best way, perhaps the only legitimate way, of guarding against doing just that. Given enough time, the fieldworker should become a familiar and less relevant presence in the situation. Browne found that eventually her presence and her observation became accepted as part of the action, and she felt comfortable being there. She does note, however, that there were times when the fact that she was a young woman created a methodological problem. She had "to develop a method of convincing a sometimes overeager informant that I did not want to be *that* kind of participant." Leaving the field for awhile proved an effective way of allowing things to "cool off naturally." She thus avoided a showdown and loss of an informant.

As field techniques, Browne cautions against using tape recorders or taking notes. Listen and learn to remember, she suggests. She also provides some helpful tips on how to keep field notes. At first the researcher should record only observations; later, interpretations "may be interspersed with what actually happens." She mentions some practical ways in which the researcher can keep observations and interpretations "together but separate" in the field notes.

Once the fieldwork is complete, the researcher usually finds that there is more data than she or he can ever hope to analyze. Then begin the long, solitary months of analyzing and writing up the data. Students sometimes lose sight of this less glamorous task in the excitement of data gathering. Browne reveals some of the "agonies" involved in this phase of her work.

To study impersonal sex in public places, Humphreys decided to "pass as deviant" in order to prevent distortion of the interaction. Without revealing himself as a researcher, he took the role of a nonsexual participant, the watchqueen, in the tearoom activities. His concern in the study was with the description of a specific style of deviant behavior and the population who engage in that activity.

Humphreys maintains that "the real methodological breakthrough" of his research was the discovery of an essential strategy which involved "mobilization of the social organization being observed." Because of the fear and suspicion prevalent in the restrooms, a lookout is necessary. Humphreys feels that his assuming the role of voyeur, "the only lookout role that is not overtly sexual," was crucial to his ability to gather data on the behavior patterns in the tearoom. To observe these activities across a representative range of times and places, he observed, within a year's time, some 120 sexual acts in 19 different men's rooms in five parks of one city.

Both Gans and Humphreys supplemented their participant observation with other procedures. Such a multimethod approach is common in field-work. While participant observation may be the most frequent choice of fieldworkers, these researchers do not rule out using other data collection techniques when necessary or appropriate. For Gans, the interviewing, though helpful, was somewhat peripheral to the central participant observation phase of his study. The second stage of Humphreys's research was, however, as central to his investigation as the first. Because he wanted to obtain "a representative sample of covert deviants," he used physical traces (license plate numbers) and public records (the city directory) to identify some of the tearoom participants. Without their knowledge or consent, he drew a random sample from among this group so that he could interview them in their homes. He did this by including them in a larger survey unrelated to homosexuality and incorporating his questions on homosexuality into the broader "social health" interview which was used in that study.

Moskos's fieldwork is different from that of the others in several significant ways. First, his interest in leadership and political independence took him to a Third World context in the islands of the West Indies. Second, he relied primarily on interviews rather than participant observation. In his personal journal, Moskos reports that these interviews were usually obtained in an informal "leisurely" atmosphere, and he discusses some of the difficulties involved in structuring and specifying the data obtained in such interviews. Moskos also comments on the practical aspects of arranging and carrying out interviews with influential people, citing the inadequacy and misrepresentation of sociological training which assumes or suggests that all research should be done on lower participants and that "downward interviewing" should be the norm in social research.

Each of these fieldworkers in some way specifically addresses the question of ethics in social research. Gans wonders about the legitimacy and necessity of having withheld his identity as a researcher. Because he feared it might affect the behavior of the West Enders, he never made explicit to them his role as a researcher-participant. Later, he began to feel that he might be exploiting his friendly relationships with his neighbors. Given the benefit of hindsight, Gans reports that he feels that he could have been more open about the purpose of his being in the neighborhood. Browne acknowledges that there are problems and compromises involved in making a "bargain" with the subjects of research, but she urges honesty. One should reveal one's presence, she maintains, and as much as one can of one's purpose.

Humphreys's position on this point is more equivocal. He deals with the problems of misrepresentation, confidentiality, and consequentiality largely in response to the criticisms of others. He feared that acknowledging his presence and his purpose would have distorted, if not halted, the action in the tearooms. Though some have characterized his research as spying or "snooping" and as a threat to the individual's basic right to privacy, Humphreys argues that he faithfully fulfilled his role of watchqueen and took every possible precaution to protect the identities of his respondents. He maintains that social scientists should not avoid studying socially sensitive areas and that "the ethics of social science are situation ethics." There is a genuine concern and a difference of opinion in the social sciences with regard to secret observation. Humphreys's position is not without its critics.

Moskos considers some of the issues that must be dealt with by American social scientists working in underdeveloped countries. Such researchers, he points out, cannot be "detached from the consequences" of their work. They have a special responsibility to be aware of their obligations to the people with whom they are dealing and to consider the implications of their presence and their findings. Moskos proposes, for Third World studies, a "participatory sociology" in which "the subjects themselves help define what are proper and needed avenues of investigation." It might be a good idea for much of the rest of sociological study as well.

One final point: While most of the research articles in this collection have been previously published, only three of the personal journals have appeared elsewhere. It is no accident that all three of these previously published personal statements are in this section and that they are written by fieldworkers. This reflects a reality in the discipline of sociology: historically, fieldworkers have been far more concerned with the context of discovery than have those social scientists who use other research strategies. This reality is in all likelihood not unrelated to the theoretical perspectives of the sociologists involved. Herbert Gans reports that he was trained at the University of Chicago; Joy Browne acknowledges her commitment to "the theoretical implications of symbolic interaction"; and Laud Humphreys notes that his choice of methods was influenced by a particular "school" of sociology. For all of them, their choice of method—participant observation—was a consequence of their theoretical orientation. They share the view that hypotheses and explanations should emerge from the data and "develop *out of* such ethnographic work, rather than provide restrictions and distortions from its

THE RESEARCH EXPERIENCE

inception" (Humphreys). Discovery is important.

The *process* of discovery is important as well. Traditionally, field-workers have attempted to communicate to others how they obtained their information. They outline the procedures used and report the problems and pitfalls encountered. Their personal journals, then, become very helpful field manuals for future researchers. The absence of such materials written by those who have different theoretical perspectives, and who, consequently, choose different research strategies, is, of course, what prompted the publication of this collection.

Herbert Gans

A. THE WEST END: AN URBAN VILLAGE

OVERVIEW

To the average Bostonian, the West End was one of the three slum areas that surrounded the city's central business district, little different in appearance and name from the North or the South End. He rarely entered the West End and usually glimpsed it only from the highways or elevated train lines that enveloped it. From there he saw a series of narrow winding streets flanked on both sides by columns of three- and five-story apartment buildings, constructed in an era when such buildings were still called tenements. Furthermore, he saw many poorly maintained structures, some of them unoccupied or partially vacant, some facing on alleys covered with more than an average amount of garbage; many vacant stores; and enough of the kinds of people who are thought to inhabit a slum area.

To the superficial observer, armed with conventional images and a little imagination about the mysteries thought to lie behind the tenement entrances, the West End certainly had all the earmarks of a slum. Whether or not it actually was a slum is a question that involves a number of technical housing and planning considerations and some value judgments. For the moment, the West End can be described simply as an old, somewhat deteriorated, low-rent neighborhood that housed a variety of people, most of them poor.

In most American cities there are areas where European immigrants—and more recently Negro and Puerto Rican ones—try to adapt their nonurban institutions and cultures to the urban milieu. Thus they may be called *urban villages*. The West End was an urban village.

In this particular urban village, the population's socio-economic level was low. Indeed, the sample's median income was just under $70 a week. About a quarter earned less than $50 per week; a half between $50 and $99; and the top category, slightly less than a fifth, between $100 and $175. Most of the household heads were unskilled or semiskilled manual workers (24 and

Source: Abridged from Herbert Gans, *Urban Villagers* (New York: Free Press, 1962), pp. 3-18, 36-40, 80-89.

THE RESEARCH EXPERIENCE

37 per cent, respectively).[1] Skilled manual workers, semiskilled white-collar workers, and skilled white-collar workers (including small businessmen) each accounted for about 10 per cent of the sample.

LIFE IN THE WEST END

Until the coming of redevelopment,[2] only outsiders were likely to think of the West End as a single neighborhood. After redevelopment was announced, the residents were drawn together by the common danger, but, even so, the West End never became a cohesive neighborhood.

My first visit to the West End left me with the impression that I was in Europe. Its high buildings set on narrow, irregularly curving streets, its Italian and Jewish restaurants and food stores, and the variety of people who crowded the streets when the weather was good—all gave the area a foreign and exotic flavor. At the same time, I also noticed the many vacant shops, the vacant and therefore dilapidated tenements, the cellars and alleys strewn with garbage and the desolation on a few streets that were all but deserted.

After a few weeks of living in the West End, my observations—and my perception of the area—changed drastically. The search for an apartment quickly indicated that the individual units were usually in much better condition than the outside or the hallways of the buildings. Subsequently, in wandering through the West End, and in using it as a resident, I developed a kind of selective perception, in which my eye focused only on those parts of the area that were actually being used by people. Vacant buildings and boarded-up stores were no longer so visible, and the totally deserted alleys or streets were outside of the set of paths normally traversed, either by myself or by the West Enders. The dirt and spilled-over garbage remained, but, since they were concentrated in street gutters and empty lots, they were not really harmful to anyone and thus were not as noticeable as during my initial observations.

THE ITALIANS OF THE WEST END

This study concerns second-generation Italians[3]—the American born children of parents who came from Italy—some from the Southern Italian

1. These figures report the occupation of the past or present household head. In 18 per cent of the cases, the woman's occupation is reported, either because there was never a male household head, the husband was not in the labor force because of illness, or because his occupation was unavailable.
2. The West End had been slated for slum clearance since the early 1950s and was torn down shortly after my fieldwork ended in 1958. It was rebuilt with luxury high-rise housing, and all of the West Enders had to move elsewhere; none could afford the rents in the new development. The West Enders' reaction to the destruction of their neighborhood is described in detail in Chapters 13 and 14 of *Urban Villagers*.
3. The Center for Community Studies survey indicates that they made up 42 per cent of the West End population. They comprised 55 per cent of all second-generation residents.

provinces, others from Sicily. They now are adults, mainly in their late thirties and forties, who are raising their own children. The term "West Enders" will be used to refer to the second-generation Italian-Americans who lived in the West End.

THE STRUCTURE OF WEST END SOCIETY: AN INTRODUCTION TO THE PEER GROUP SOCIETY

The life of the West Ender takes place within three interrelated sectors: the primary group, the secondary group, and the outgroup. The primary group refers to that combination of family and peer relationships which I shall call the *peer group society*. The secondary group refers to the small array of Italian institutions, voluntary organizations, and other social bodies which function to support the workings of the peer group society. This I shall call the *community*. I use this term because *it*, rather than the West End or Boston, is the West Ender's community. The outgroup, which I shall describe as the *outside world*, covers a variety of non-Italian institutions in the West End, in Boston, and in America that impinge on his life—often unhappily, to the West Ender's way of thinking.

Although social and economic systems in the outside world are significant in shaping the life of the West Ender, the most important part of that life is lived within the primary group. National and local economic, social, and political institutions may determine the West Ender's opportunities for income, work, and standard of living, but it is the primary group that refracts these outside events and thus shapes his personality and culture. Because the peer group society dominates his entire life, and structures his relationship with the community and the outside world, I shall sometimes use the term to describe not only the primary relationships, but the West Enders' entire social structure as well.

The primary group is a peer group society because most of the West Enders' relationships are with peers, that is, among people of the same sex, age, and life-cycle status. While this society includes the friendships, cliques, informal clubs, and gangs usually associated with peer groups, it also takes in family life. In fact, during adulthood, the family is its most important component. Adult West Enders spend almost as much time with siblings, in-laws, and cousins—that is, with relatives of the same sex and age—as with their spouses, and more time than with parents, aunts, and uncles. The peer group society thus continues long past adolescence, and, indeed, dominates the life of the West Ender from birth to death. For this reason I have coined the term "peer group society."

In order to best describe the dominance of the peer group principle in the life of the West Ender, it is necessary to examine it over a typical life cycle. The child is born into a nuclear family; at an early age, however, he or she—although girls are slower to do this than boys—transfers increasing amounts of his time and allegiance to the peers he meets in the street and in school. This transfer may even begin long before the child enters school. Thus, one West Ender told me that when he wanted his two-year-old son to attend an activity at a local settlement house, bribery and threats were useless, but that the promise that he could go with two other young children on the block produced immediate assent.

From this time on, then, the West Ender spends the rest of his life in one or another peer group. Before or soon after they start going to school, boys and girls form cliques or gangs. In these cliques, which are sexually segregated, they play together and learn the lore of childhood. The sexually segregated clique maintains its hold on the individual until late adolescence or early adulthood.

Dating, the heterosexual relationship between two individuals that the middle-class child enters into after puberty—or even earlier—is much rarer among West Enders. Boys and girls may come together in peer groups to a settlement house dance or a clubroom. Even so, they dance with each other only infrequently. Indeed, at the teenage dances I observed, the girls danced mostly with each other and boys stood in the corner—a peer group pattern that may continue even among young adults.

The hold of the peer group is broken briefly at marriage. During courtship, the man commutes between it and his girl. Female peer groups—always less cohesive than male—break up even more easily then, because the girl who wants to get married must compete with her peers for male friends and must be at their beck and call. At marriage, the couple leaves its peer groups, but after a short time, often following the arrival of the first child, they both re-enter peer group life.

Most often a new peer group is formed, consisting of family members and a few friends of each spouse. This group meets after working hours for long evenings of sociability. Although the members of the group are of both sexes, the normal tendency is for the men and women to split up, the men in one room and the women in another. In addition, husband and wife also may belong to other peer groups: work colleagues or childhood friends among the men, informal clubs of old friends that meet regularly among the women. In the West End, friendship ties seem to be formed mainly in childhood and adolescence, and many of them last throughout life.

But the mainstay of the adult peer group society is the *family circle*.[4] The circle is made up of collateral kin: in-laws, siblings, and cousins predominantly. Not all family members are eligible for the peer group, but the rules of selection—which are informal and unstated—are based less on closeness of kinship ties than on compatibility. Family members come

---

4. I have borrowed this term from Michael Young and Peter Willmott, *Family and Kinship in East London,* London: Routledge and Kegan Paul, 1957.

together if they are roughly of the same age, socio-economic level, and cultural background. How closely or distantly they are related is much less important than the possession of common interests and values. Even among brothers and sisters only those who are compatible are likely to see each other regularly. This combination of family members and friends seems to continue to function as a peer group for the rest of the life cycle.

The West End, in effect, may be viewed as a large network of these peer groups, which are connected by the fact that some people may belong to more than one group. In addition, a few individuals function as communicators between the groups, and thus keep them informed of events and attitudes important to them all.

The hold of the peer group on the individual is very strong. Achievement and social mobility, for example, are group phenomena. In the current generation, in which the Italian is still effectively limited to blue-collar work, atypical educational and occupational mobility by the individual is frowned upon. Children who do well in school are called "sissies," and they cannot excel there and expect to remain in their peer group. Since allegiance to any one group is slight at this stage, however, the good student can drift into other peer groups until he finds one with compatible members. Should such peers be lacking, he may have to choose between isolation or a group that does not share his standards. Often, he chooses the latter.

Life in a peer group society has a variety of far-reaching social and psychological consequences. Pressure on man and wife affects the family structure, as does the willingness—or resignation—of the parents in relinquishing their children to their own peer group at an early age. The fact that individuals are accustomed to being with—and are more at ease with—members of their own sex means that their activities are cued primarily to reference groups of that sex. This may help to explain the narcissistic vanity among West End men, that is, their concern with clothes, and displays of muscular strength or virility. It also may help to explain the chaperoning of unmarried women, in fear that they will otherwise indulge in sexual intercourse. Not only does the separation of the sexes substitute for the development of internal controls that discourage the man from taking advantage of the woman, but they replace, as well, those controls that allow the woman to protect herself.

The peer group principle has even more important consequences for personality organization. Indeed, the role of the group in the life of the individual is such that he exists primarily in the group. School officials, for example, pointed out that teenagers were rough and active when they were with their peers, but quiet and remarkably mild and passive when alone. Their mildness is due to the fact that they exist only partially when they are outside the group. In effect, the individual personality functions best and most completely among his or her peers—a fact that has some implications for independence and dependence, conformity and individualism among the West Enders.

THE RESEARCH EXPERIENCE

MALE?

THE INDIVIDUAL AND THE GROUP

West Enders live within the group; they do not like to be alone. Indeed, for most of them, people trained from childhood to function solely within the group, being alone brings discomfort and ultimately fear. The discomfort was expressed by housewives who got their housework done quickly so as to be able "to visit." It was expressed more strongly by people who feared that the destruction of the West End would tear them away from their group and leave them isolated. It was expressed perhaps most vividly by a corner boy who explained to his friends that a prison sentence was bad "because it separates you from friends and family."

Yet the peer group is important not only because it provides this much desired companionship and the feeling of belongingness, but because it also allows its members to be individuals, and to express that individuality. In fact, it is only within the peer group that people can do so. In the middle class, people can exist as individuals outside a group, and enter a group to accomplish personal as well as shared ends. Among the West Enders, however, people grow up within a group and use it to be individuals, with the result that this group cannot work together. This is the basic paradox of the peer group society.

Although the peer group is the most important entity in the West Ender's life, he is not merely a robot whose actions are determined by the group or the cultural tradition. In fact, peer group life in many ways is just the opposite of the cohesive and tightly-knit group that has served as a model for descriptions of primary relations in other societies. It is a spirited competition of individuals "jockeying" for respect, power, and status. Indeed, to the outside observer, West Enders appear to be involved in a never ending dialectic: individual actions take them out of the group momentarily and are followed by restraints that bring them back, only to be succeeded by more individuating talk or behavior.

This is most visible among the teenage and young adult action-seekers. Within the group their behavior is a series of competitive encounters intended to assert the superiority and skillfulness of one individual over the other, which take the form of card games, short physical scuffles, and endless verbal duels. Through bragging, teasing, wisecracking, and insulting, individuals express their own verbal strength and skill, while denigrating the characteristics and achievements of others. Only when there is a common opponent does the group coalesce, but even then this is not always likely to happen. For example, among the young adults whom I observed at a tavern where they hung out nightly, a basketball team broke up because the better players did not want to play on a team with the poorer ones, who would deny them the opportunity to display their individual talents.

While there is no physical competition among the adult groups, and even card games are rare, similar competition does exist, although in considerably muted form. Most of the competitive play takes place in conversation, through an exchange of anecdotes that display the story teller's exploits, and of jokes and wisecracks that entertain the group while making one person stand out. The exchange is not vicious, nor is it used by self-centered people to call attention to themselves, or to make others look bad. In fact, any attempt by an insecure person to build himself up in the group at others' expense is considered out of place. It is politely ignored in his presence, and harshly criticized when he is out of earshot.

Group members—be they adult or adolescent—display themselves to the group, to show their peers that they are as good if not slightly better than the rest, but then they yield the floor to the next person and allow him to do likewise. The purpose of this is to create mild envy among the rest of the group.

Two other expressions of West End individualism are the rejection of formal dependence on the group, and the emphasis on the mutual nature of obligations. Despite the fact that West Enders live so much within a group, they feel that they cannot and do not want to depend on it for help. People say that "in the last analysis, you have to depend on yourself." They are loath to ask for favors from others, even within the family circle, and much more so from organized charity. The emphasis on independence is based partly on a realistic appraisal that others can extend only a limited amount of help, and that it would be unrealistic to depend on them. When economic deprivations strike one member of a low-income population, they are likely to hit others as well. Moreover, if other troubles arise, such as illness, they are apt to be serious ones. Although West Enders will offer and accept help, they do not cherish being dependent on others. They want to remain independent, for accepting aid is thought to reflect on the strength of the individual, and is thus a reflection on self-respect which places the dependent person in an inferior position.

Moreover, giving and receiving—of help or gifts—involves the individual in a spiral of reciprocatory obligations. The obligation may be latent, in which case people feel a desire to give and receive, and enjoy the resulting reciprocity. Or it may be manifest, thus becoming a duty. In this case reciprocity can turn into a burden, and people try to escape involvement. This happens most often with representatives from the outside world, like welfare agencies and settlement houses, who want to give aid in exchange for deference or loyalty to institutions.

Among close friends and relatives, goods and services are exchanged freely and obligations remain latent, unless one or the other person falls seriously behind in reciprocating, or unless the exchange becomes competitive. Should someone reciprocate with a more expensive gift than he originally received, he may be suspected of showing off, or of trying to make the other person look bad. If it continues, this can lead to an eventual alienation from the group.

THE RESEARCH EXPERIENCE

When relationships are not close, obligations are manifest. For example, after a man had done some electrical work for his sister, she invited him to dinner several times as a payment for the work—which he had done for nothing. Although she was not formally required to reciprocate, since he was her brother, she wanted to do so because she felt it to be the proper thing. This brother had married an upwardly mobile woman, and was not part of the immediate family circle.

When obligations concern authority figures and hierarchical relationships, the rejection of dependence becomes stronger, and often evolves into fear of domination. Thus, whereas West Enders will subordinate themselves to someone whom they recognize as a leader, they will bitterly reject the individual who is imposed as a leader from the outside—or who tries to impose himself.

Although the peer group is a theater for individual expression, it is also characterized by strict control of deviant behavior. The major mechanisms of social control are criticism, the expectation of criticism, and the not always successful attempts by individuals to maintain self-control.

Since everyone knows everyone else, life is an open book, and deviant acts are hard to hide. This means that such acts are committed either outside the reaches of the group—as in the case of adolescents who do their misbehaving outside the West End—or that they are not committed at all. Jokes and wisecracks, a polite way of questioning deviant behavior, usually suffice to bring the individual back into line. Similarly, the individual is expected to keep up with the activities of the group, and the pattern of individual display. The person who is too noisy or dominating is suspect, but so is the one who is too quiet. The hostess who sets too lavish a table is criticized, but even more so is the person who is unwilling to entertain or feed the group in the style to which it is accustomed.

But as so much of life is based on routine, there is little incentive for nonconforming behavior. Thus most conformity is quite voluntary. But West Enders also regulate their conduct by involuntary conformity of the type expressed in the phrase "what will the neighbors think." Indeed, the expectations of what other people will think are extremely harsh; they assume the blackest thoughts and deeds possible. For example, a neighbor who had recently had a baby carried the baby carriage up several flights, rather than leaving it in an empty store that served as storage room for several adjacent apartment buildings. She justified her behavior by explaining that, since the storage room was not in her own building, people might think she was going in there to steal something. While the exaggerated expectations do constitute a potent control against deviant behavior, they create, at the same time, an unspoken atmosphere of mutual recrimination, in which everyone is likely to expect the worst from everyone else. It must be noted, however, that such expectations are usually not held about peer group members, but only about people who are less close—neighbors, for example.

It is clear that the ascription of evil motives and deeds stems not from observations of the neighbors' behavior or inferences from their conversations, but from the individual himself. He projects on the neighbors his underlying fear that he himself might do evil things or harbor evil motives. For although West Enders believe that fate regulates actions over which they have no say, their own behavior is thought to be self-determined.

The West Ender therefore is frequently concerned over his ability to control himself. Among the adolescents and the action-seeking adults, the main concern is to stay out of "trouble"—which means not only to avoid getting caught by the police or by other agents of social control, but also not going out of control in episodic behavior, for this might detach the individual from the group. Among routine-seeking people, uncontrolled behavior is less of a problem. Their concern is to avoid getting into situations that could be misinterpreted. In short, the individual must control himself so that he cannot be suspected of negatively evaluated behavior, either by the group or by himself.

The definition of deviant behavior comes initially from the group itself and the group encourages individuals to shame each other into conformity through overt criticism. In view of the severity of social control, it would be easy to caricature peer group life as a prison for its members. To the outsider, the concern with social control and self-control might indeed seem oppressive. But he must also take into account that there is little desire for voluntary nonconformity, and, consequently, little need to require involuntary conformity. Nor do people seem to be troubled by fears about the breakdown of self-control, or about the possibility that they may be suspected of misdeeds. Although these potentialities do lurk under the surface, they do not usually disturb the positive tenor of group relations. Such fears, of course, may be private preoccupations, less visible to the sociologist than they would be to the clinical psychologist. Moreover, the people who are seriously troubled by these fears shun the kind of group I have discussed.

Tensions and problems exist in the peer group, as in every other group, but they are overshadowed by the gratifications that it provides for the individual. Perhaps the best illustration of this was given by a young man who was suffering from an ulcer, and was faced with a choice between his health and his group. As he explained it: "I can't stop drinking when I'm with my friends; I eat and drink like they do and when I'm alone I take care of my ulcer. But I don't care if it kills me; if it does, that's it."

In summary, social relationships within the peer group follow a narrow path between individualistic display and strictly enforced social control. The group is set up to provide its members with an opportunity for displaying, expressing, and acting out their individuality, as long as this does not become too extreme.

As a result, the peer group is unable to work together to achieve a common goal unless it is shared by all members of the group. Since the main function of the group is to provide an area for individual display, the members are less interested in activities that require working together than in impressing each other. Moreover, if group tasks, especially those of a novel nature, are suggested, people become fearful that they will be used as pawns by an individual who will gain the most from this activity. Consequently, the inability to participate in joint activities does inhibit community organization, even when it concerns the very survival of the group, as it did in the clearance of the West End. This, perhaps, is the peer group society's most serious weakness: that the group is used by its members to express and display individualistic strivings and that these strivings prevent the group from acting in concert.

Personal Journal ——————————————————————————

B. ON THE METHODS
USED IN THIS STUDY

THE PURPOSES AND METHODS OF THE STUDY

The findings of any study are intrinsically related to the methods used to develop them. Although this study may be described generally as based on participant-observation, a more detailed description of the methods is necessary to indicate the over-all perspective of the research, and some shortcomings of the findings.

Findings are also affected by research purposes. I had two major reasons for making this study: a desire to understand neighborhoods known as slums, and the people who live in them; and a desire to learn firsthand what differentiates working- and lower-class people from middle-class ones. These questions were based partly on my concern about middle-class bias in the planning and caretaking professions.

Having been trained in sociology at the University of Chicago during the era when Everett C. Hughes and the late Louis Wirth—to name only two—were dominant influences in the Department of Sociology, I believed strongly in the value of participant-observation as a method of social

———————
Source: Abridged from Herbert Gans, *Urban Villagers* (New York: Free Press, 1962), pp. 336-350.

research. As a result, I felt that I could best achieve my study purposes by living in a slum myself.

Although I had wanted to do the study for several years, other projects had prevented my searching for a suitable area. Consequently, I was very pleased when I was offered the opportunity of making a study in the West End—a particularly suitable neighborhood. Not only was it known as a slum, but it also was a white area, and thus somewhat easier for a white participant-observer to enter. For while the method is difficult enough to use when it requires a trip across class barriers, it is much more so when racial barriers also exist. Much as I would have liked to do the study in a Negro slum, I doubted at the time whether many Negroes would have accepted a white participant-observer in their midst. The West End was also attractive because it was adjacent to the North End, the district described in William F. Whyte's classic *Street Corner Society*. Not only were my purposes based on some of the same values that guided his study, but my belief in the desirability and feasibility of the project had also been much encouraged by his book, as well as by the detailed description of the way in which he went about his study.[1]

My actual field work employed six major approaches:

1. *Use of the West End's facilities.* I lived in the area, and used its stores, services, institutions, and other facilities, as much as possible. This enabled me to observe my own and other people's behavior as residents of the area.

2. *Attendance at meetings, gatherings, and public places.* I attended as many public meetings and gatherings as I could find, mostly as an observant spectator. I also visited area shops and taverns in this role.

3. *Informal visiting with neighbors and friends.* My wife and I became friendly with our neighbors and other West Enders, spending much time with them in social activities and conversations that provided valuable data.

4. *Formal and informal interviewing of community functionaries.* I interviewed at least one person in all of the area's agencies and institutions—talking with directors, staff members, officers, and active people in settlement houses, church groups, and other voluntary organizations. I also talked with principals, ministers, social workers, political leaders, government officials—especially those concerned with redevelopment—and store owners.

5. *Use of informants.* Some of the people I interviewed became informants, who kept me up to date on those phases of West End life with which they were familiar.[2]

6. *Observation.* I kept my eyes and ears open at all times, trying to learn something about as many phases of West End life as possible, and also

---

1. "On the Evolution of Street Corner Society," in William F. Whyte Jr., *Street Corner Society*. Chicago: University of Chicago Press, 2nd ed., 1955, pp. 279-358.

2. Anthropologists use informants to get basic information about the culture they are studying; I used them mainly to get data about specific institutions in which they were functioning, and to check observations or impressions gathered in my field work.

THE RESEARCH EXPERIENCE

looking for unexpected leads and ideas on subjects in which I was especially interested.

The data which evolved from the use of these methods were written down in field notes, and placed in a diary. They were subsequently analyzed for this report.

THE TYPES AND PROBLEMS OF PARTICIPANT-OBSERVATION

The first three of the methods I used are usually described under the rubric of participant-observation—a generic and not entirely accurate term for a variety of observational methods in which the researcher develops more than a purely research relationship with the people he is studying. The actual types of participant-observation which I used, and the problems which I encountered, therefore deserve more detailed consideration.

Variations in the participant-observation method can be described in different ways. One principle of classification is the extent to which the researcher's participation is known to the people he is studying: that is, whether it is kept secret, revealed partially, or revealed totally.[3] I have found it more useful to classify the approaches in terms of differences in the actual behavior of the researcher. This produces three types:

1. *Researcher acts as observer.* In this approach, the researcher is physically present at the event which he observes, but does not really participate in it. Indeed, his main function is to observe, and to abstain from participation so as not to affect the phenomenon being studied—or at least, to affect it no more than is absolutely unavoidable. Much of my participation was of this type, when I was using the area's facilities, attending meetings, or watching the goings-on at area stores and taverns.

2. *Researcher participates, but as researcher.* In this case, the researcher does become an actual participant in an event or gathering, but his participation is determined by his research interests, rather than by the roles required in the situation he is studying.[4] For example, in social gatherings, the researcher may try to steer the conversation to topics in which he is especially interested. In such instances, he might be described as a "research-participant."

3. *Researcher participates.*[5] In this approach, the researcher temporarily abdicates his study role and becomes a "real" participant. After the event,

---

3. This principle has been used by Raymond L. Gold, "Roles in Sociological Field Observations," *Social Forces,* vol. 36 (1958), pp. 217-223; and by Buford H. Junker, *Field Work,* Chicago: University of Chicago Press, 1960, Chap. 3.

4. He must, of course, follow the rules that guide participation in the event, or he will be ejected. For example, he cannot tell people to stop talking about a topic that does not interest him.

5. These three types cut across what Morris and Charlotte Schwartz have described as passive and active participation. See their "Problems in Participant-Observation," *American Journal of Sociology,* vol. 60 (1955), pp. 343-353, at pp. 348-350.

his role reverts back to that of an observer—and in this case, an analyst of his own actions while being a real participant. For example, he may go to a social gathering as an invited guest and participate fully and freely in the conversation without trying to direct it to his own research interests. Afterwards, however, he must take notes on all that has happened, his own activities included. Needless to say, even during the most spontaneously real participation he can never shed the observer role entirely, if only because he knows he will write it all down later.

In attending meetings and other public gatherings, I acted as observer. In using the West End's facilities, I was usually a real participant, sometimes a research-participant or observer. The informal visiting with friends and neighbors employed a mixture of real and research participation. Given the short time I had for field work, the research participation role turned out to be most productive. The real participation was most enjoyable, but it turned out to be a time-consuming approach. Also, while it is most useful when the object of study is a single group or institution, it is less so in a general community study. Although being a real participant allows the researcher to understand the functioning of a group like no other method can, it also cuts him off from other parts of the society which are closed to its members. For example, it would be impossible for a participant studying one political party to study the opposition party as well.

In using these three types of participant-observation, I encountered several problems which deserve some consideration: the difficulty of entry into the community; the identification with the people being studied; and doubts as to the ethics of the approach.

The problem of entry into West End society was particularly vexing. As the West Enders were a low-income group, they had neither been interviewed by market researchers nor been exposed to the popular sociology of the slick magazines. Consequently, they were unfamiliar with the methods and goals of sociology. Also, they were suspicious of middle-class outsiders, especially so because of the redevelopment threat. As a result, I was somewhat fearful at the beginning whether I would be able to function as a participant-observer once I had told people that I was a researcher.

The Center for Community Studies on whose staff I served had already made contact with one of the settlement houses, and the workers, being middle-class, were willing to be interviewed and to help out in the study. They also referred me to some of their loyal clients, but these, I soon found out, were in several ways unlike the large majority of West Enders. Nor did any of them resemble "Doc," the man whom William F. Whyte had met at the start of his study and who had offered to guide Whyte into the society of the North End.[6] Although the early weeks of the study were indeed anxious ones, I did not waste them, using the time to interview the staff members of

6. Whyte, *op. cit.*, p. 291.

West End institutions and the officers of its organizations. Eventually, however, the problem almost resolved itself, this time by the same sort of lucky accident that had befallen Whyte. My wife and I were welcomed by one of our neighbors and became friends with them. As a result, they invited us to many of their evening gatherings and introduced us to other neighbors, relatives, and friends. These contacts provided not only pleasant companionship, but a considerable amount of data about the workings of the peer group society.

As time went on, I became friendly in much the same way with other West Enders whom I had encountered at meetings or during informal interviews. They too introduced me to relatives and friends, although most of the social gatherings at which I participated were those of our first contact, and their circle.

After I had been in the area for about three months, I became a familiar face, and was able to carry on longer conversations with storeowners and other West Enders. Finally, the entry problem disappeared entirely. Indeed, I was now faced with a new one: having more data than I could ever hope to analyze.

Even my most notable failure in gaining entry produced useful information. Feeling that I should not limit myself entirely to being with people who spent their evenings at home, I decided to do some research in the area taverns. After making the rounds of the West End bars and finding most of them a haven for older men and Polish or Irish West Enders, I finally chanced on one which served as a hangout for a group of young Italian adults of the type that Whyte called "corner boys." From then on, I visited there only. But as much as I tried to participate in the conversation, I could not do so. The bar, though open to the general public, was actually almost a private club: the same dozen or so men came there every night, and—since some of them were unemployed or not working during daylight hours—during the day as well. Moreover, I suspect that some of them were engaged in shady enterprises. In any case, they were extremely loath to talk to strangers, especially one like myself who came unintroduced, alone, and then only irregularly about once a week. Also, much as I tried, I could not really talk about the subjects they covered or use the same abundance of four-letter profanity. After several unsuccessful attempts, I gave up trying to intrude and sat quietly by, from then on, as an observer. As it turned out, however, I learned a lot from listening to their conversations and to their comments about the television programs that they watched intermittently.

One of the factors that complicated the entry problem was my initial desire to be only an observer and a real participant, that is, to gather data simply by living in the West End and to learn from the contacts and conversations that came my way just by being there. I soon found that this was impossible. There were simply too many questions that I could not ask in my role as an ordinary—and newly arrived—resident. Given the short time I had in which to do the research, I could not wait for these questions to come up spontaneously in the conversation. Consequently, I told people that I was doing a study of the neighborhood, especially of its institutions and organizations. I also sensed quickly that they were familiar with historical "studies," and thereafter described my research as being a recent history of the area. The revelation of my research role ended a few relationships, but on the whole, it helped my study and made it easier for me to approach people with unusual questions.

In addition, I wanted initially to refrain from interviewing as much as possible, except among people such as agency staff members and organizational leaders who were used to it. I made this decision partly on epistemological grounds—doubting whether I would get trustworthy data—and partly because I was not sure that I could be both interviewer and participant-observer in the same neighborhood. When I found that I was not gathering enough data, I changed my mind and, subsequently, I did interview a number of West Enders. But this was always done quite informally and without a questionnaire, except one lodged firmly in my memory. I did no door-to-door interviewing, however, partly because I did not like to do it, and because I found it difficult to assume the detached role of the interviewer who comes as a stranger, never to be seen again. Although I never considered myself to be a West Ender, I did think myself to be enough of a participant in the life of the area to feel uncomfortable about also being an interviewer.[7]

A second problem of participant-observation is that of identification with the people one studies. Every participant-observer becomes emotionally involved not only in his study, but also with the people, since it is through their willingness to talk that he is able to do his research. And this involvement does have some advantages: it allows the observer to understand the people with whom he is living, and to look at the world through their eyes. At the same time, it can also blind him to some of their behavior patterns, and thus distort the study.[8]

The identification is probably more intense if the people being studied are suffering from deprivation, and if they are a low-status group whose point of view is not being taken notice of in the world outside. In such a situation, the researcher feels a need to do something about the deprivation, and to correct false stereotypes about the people. This reaction also befell me. I quickly became convinced that the redevelopment of the area was unjustified, and that the planning was being poorly handled. This identification can be socially useful—at least from the liberal perspective—for the sociologist then becomes an informal spokesman for groups who themselves lack the power to voice their demands in the larger society.

---

7. I did, however, help to pretest the interview schedule being used by the larger study, and interviewed, without discomfort, an ex-West Ender who had left the area some years earlier.

8. Morris and Charlotte Schwartz call this affective participation, and indicate how it can be dealt with. *Op. cit.*, pp. 350-352.

THE RESEARCH EXPERIENCE

Although identification can detract from the objectivity of the research, it need not do so—especially if the researcher knows what is happening to him. Moreover, the identification, likely to be strong at the beginning, decreases in intensity as the research proceeds. It is reduced even further in the time which elapses between the end of field work, the data analysis, and the writing of the report. Instances of overidentification in the field work can therefore be dealt with in later stages of the research. In my case, the dangers of identification were somewhat reduced by their being channeled largely into the redevelopment issue, a topic peripheral to the main purposes of my study. Thus, I expressed my identification with the West Enders through my critique of the redevelopment process, and was able to remain more detached about the social structure and culture of the West Enders.

The dangers of overidentification are also reduced by the many differences between the researcher and the people he is studying. Since the researcher is an observer more often than he is a real participant, he is always conscious of value clashes when they occur during the field work. Thus, while the participant-observer cannot argue with his informants and respondents as fully as he would like—because it might endanger his rapport—he is continually made aware of his own points of view on the subjects that come up in conversation. This not only produces insights useful to his research, but also keeps him detached from the people he is studying. He realizes that he cannot be like them, or that he should not even try to be.[9] At the same time, he becomes ever more sensitive to the fact that values arise out of the social position of those who hold them. Thus, when the researcher becomes a spokesman for the people he is studying, he is really arguing with those who fail to see this basic sociological fact. This accounts for the intensity of my reaction about the narrow-mindedness of the world at large and my dismay at the middle-class professional who expects people to share his own values even though they lack the opportunities and cultural background that have shaped his own views.

The third problem of the participant-observation approach concerns its ethical validity. Although I did tell people that I was in the West End to make a study, I described my research mainly as a survey of organizations, institutions, and the redevelopment process. I mentioned but did not stress my interest in studying the everyday life of West Enders, and did not mention at all that I attended social gatherings in the dual role of guest and observer. At the time I felt sure that this admission would either have ended the relationships, or have made life so uncomfortable for them and for me that I

9. I did not wear the middle-class uniform of suit, white shirt, and tie, however, in order to minimize my connection with the hospital that was sponsoring the research in which I was involved. Its support of the redevelopment program had antagonized many West Enders. I did not try to look like a West Ender but one day, while wandering through the area, some college students who were taking pictures there treated me—literally—as if I were a native. Their tone of well-meaning condescension made me see more clearly than ever why West Enders harbor uncomplimentary feelings toward the middle class.

could not have been either guest or observer. With some hindsight and additional participant-observation experience in another community, I feel now that I could have been more open about my role. Most people are too busy living to take much notice of a participant-observer once he has proven to them that he means no harm.

The fact that I was using friendly relationships for the collection of data, coupled with my feeling that I was thus exploiting these relationships, did create some guilt. My feelings of anxiety were somewhat alleviated, however, by the fact that my study was based neither on harmful or malicious ends. Needless to say, I had intended from the start to maintain the privacy of my informants. Thus, I have used no names in the report, and have frequently distorted facts that would make it possible for West Enders to recognize their erstwhile neighbors. In attributing quotes, I have freely used the term "neighbor" as a synonym for West Ender, and some of the people I have quoted were not really neighbors at all.

Although these explanations and safeguards do not solve the ethical problem of whether the ends of the study justified the means used in making it, I can see no easy solution to this problem The social scientist attempts to describe the world as it is, and he must therefore observe people in their normal, everyday ways. Should he hide his purpose, either by not telling them of his participant-observation role, or by asking interview questions which get at more than they seem to on the surface, he does so because he has no other alternative. If he bares all his research purposes, he may be denied access to the very society he wants to study. If he forswears participant-observation and gathers his data solely by interviewing, he can get only reports of behavior, but not behavior itself. If he is completely open about his participant-observation or interview questions, his respondents are likely to hide information from him—not necessarily by intention—by giving him access not to behavior but to appearances; not to what people do, but how they would like their doings to appear publicly.

If research methods do involve some evasion, the social scientist is saddled with a great responsibility to the people he has studied. The researcher must try to prevent any harm from coming to the people he has studied, either from his research or its publication. There is one exception: if the people studied are participants in what appears to the researcher as a gross miscarriage of justice, he has the right to publish his conclusion, even if the correction of the injustice might hurt them. Because these requirements force the researcher to set himself up as a judge over other human beings, he must take personal responsibility for these decisions and for the hurts his study could cause. Beyond that, he must be as objective as is humanly possible, not by renouncing value judgments, but by refraining from hasty and oversimplified ones, and by showing why people behave as they do, especially when this behavior violates prevalent norms.

All these precautions, of course, cannot do away with the fact that research, like all other human activities, is political; that it supports one point of view and vested interest at the expense of others.[10] The researcher must therefore take a political stand on some issues, and he should make it clear where his sympathies lie. This I have tried to do.

THE ANALYSIS OF THE DATA AND SOME OF THEIR LIMITATIONS

The actual analysis of the data was quite simple. I recorded my observations and interviews as soon as possible after they had been completed, together with the generalizations they stimulated, and placed them in a field diary. When I came to write the study, I read and reread my diary several times, and then put the generalizations and some supporting observations on index cards. Eventually, I had more than 2000 of these. I then sorted and classified them by a variety of subject headings. The classification was determined in part by my initial research purposes, in part by topics in which I had become interested during the field work, and in part by the observations made spontaneously while in the field. The content of the cards was then further digested into pages of notes listing the major generalizations and other ideas. An initial report was written from these notes in 1959.[11] Before I wrote this present version, I reread the diary and took further notes on it.

The study is based on quite simple—if not primitive—research methods, and its findings are hypotheses. Moreover, what evidence I have offered for them is illustrative rather than documentary. This is not accidental; from the start I had decided to give lower priority to methodological sophistication than to the search for hypotheses. I tried, of course, to be a careful observer, and a careful analyst of what I had observed, but I did not attempt to seek evidence for my hypotheses on a systematized basis. As a result, the findings have several limitations.

Many of the generalizations of the study fall into the category of what Merton has called "post factum sociological interpretation" in that they have been developed after the observation. Concerning this, Merton has warned:

> A disarming characteristic of the procedure is that the explanations are indeed consistent with the given set of observations. This is scarcely surprising, inasmuch as only those post factum hypotheses are selected which do accord with these observations. . . . Post factum explanations remain at the level of plausibility [low evidential value] rather than leading to "compelling evidence" [a high

---

10. For a clear statement of this fact, see John R. Seeley, "We Hidden Persuaders: Social Thought and Politics," an address to the National Federation of Canadian University Students, McMaster University, 1961, mimeographed. My conclusions about the ethics of participant-observation have benefited from discussions with him and with Fred Davis.
11. "The Urban Villagers: A Study of the Second Generation Italians in the West End of Boston," Boston: Center for Community Studies, November, 1959, mimeographed.

degree of confirmation]. Plausibility . . . is found when an interpretation is consistent with one set of data. . . . It also implies that alternative interpretations equally consistent with these data have not been systematically explored, and that inferences drawn from the interpretation have not been tested by new observations.[12]

Merton's criticism can be applied to my own findings. I did try, however, to guard against overly facile interpretation by analyzing my data immediately after collecting them, and by putting both data and analysis into the field notes. Thus, I developed interpretations at once, rather than at the end of the study. This gave me an opportunity to test these notions in subsequent data collection, and to develop alternative ones if they did not fit later observations. Since I did not begin the study with a set of explicit notions that I wanted to prove at all costs, it was not difficult to surrender poor interpretations for better ones. Most of the generalizations reported were thus developed during the field work.

Participant-observation also has another major drawback—the size and quality of the sample on which observations are based. Although my study sought to report on a population of close to 3000, I probably met and talked with no more than 100 to 150 West Enders.[13] Moreover, my most intensive contact was with about twenty West Enders, and most of my hypotheses about the peer group society are based on my observations of their ways. Because of the size of my sample, I did not attempt any statistical analysis. Nevertheless, I have used freely such quasi-statistical terms as "many," "most," "some," or "the majority of." Obviously, my use of these concepts is based on impressionistic evidence.[14]

Also, I could not determine to what extent any reported behavior pattern or attitude was distributed throughout the population, nor could I inquire into subgroupings and subcultures among the West Enders, other than the most obvious ones of class and age. Even then, I did not apply the distinction between action-seeking and routine-seeking West Enders as fully as I might have. Thus, while the report may state that the West Enders act in a certain way, or hold a given attitude, only more extensive research will be

---

12. Robert K. Merton, *Social Theory and Social Structure*, New York: The Free Press of Glencoe, 2nd ed., 1957, pp. 93-94.
13. I include in this number neither the middle-class caretakers, nor other people working in West End or with West Enders; they were not West Enders.
14. Howard S. Becker and Blanche Geer have developed new methods of participant-observation and data analysis which remove some of the dangers of post-factum interpretation, and make it possible to quantify data gathered by this method. Their methodological innovations are reported in Howard S. Becker, "Problems of Inference and Proof in Participant-Observation," *American Sociological Review*, vol. 23 (1958), pp. 652-660; and in Howard S. Becker and Blanche Geer, "The Analysis of Qualitative Field Data" in Richard N. Adams and Jack J. Preiss, eds., *Human Organization Research*, Homewood, Ill.: Dorsey Press, 1960, pp. 267-289. The field study in which these methods are applied is reported in H. Becker, B. Geer, E. Hughes, and A. Strauss, *Boys in White: Student Culture in Medical School*, University of Chicago Press, 1961.

able to indicate whether my generalization applies to all of the second-generation Italians in the West End, or only to certain subgroups among them.

The West Enders with whom I had the most intensive and most frequent contact were drawn more from working-class routine-seekers and mobile people than from the lower-class action-seeking population. Although I did have many opportunities to observe the latter, and to hear their actions discussed, they were harder to reach directly and therefore were reached less often in the time I had for field work. Moreover, some of the people I encountered were marginal to the peer group society, and for this reason were most cooperative with me. Conscious of the bias in my sample, and knowledgeable enough about the West End to evaluate the information I received from the marginal people, I was able to take these considerations into account when I analyzed my data. This does not, however, entirely eliminate the distortion due to lack of contact with the West Enders who are lowest on the educational and socio-economic level. Consequently, the findings should be read with the reminder that I did not report as fully about the people for whom life was hardest, and for whom the outside world was most threatening.

Finally, more of my data were gathered from and about men than women. As I noted in my description of the peer group society, communication between the sexes is much more difficult than in middle-class society. Even though my wife participated in the field work and told me about the female social gatherings, my report does tend to place greater emphasis on the male portions of the peer group society.

This, then, is not a scientific study, for it does not provide what Merton has called compelling evidence for a series of hypotheses. It is, rather, an attempt by a trained social scientist to describe and explain the behavior of a large number of people—using his methodological and theoretical training to sift the observations—and to report only those generalizations which are justified by the data. The validity of my findings thus rests ultimately on my judgment about the data, and of course, on my theoretical and personal biases in deciding what to study, what to see, what to ignore, and how to analyze the products. Properly speaking, the study is a *reconnaissance*—an initial exploration of a community to provide an overview—guided by the canons of sociological theory and method but not attempting to offer documentation for all the findings. In making this statement, I do not mean to cast doubt on the conclusions I reached—I stand behind them all—or on the methods I used. Participant-observation is the only method I know that enables the researcher to get close to the realities of social life. Its deficiencies in producing quantitative data are more than made up for by its ability to minimize the distance between the researcher and his subject of study.

Joy Browne ───

A. THE USED CAR GAME

INTRODUCTION

This study is based on field research completed as part of the requirements for a doctorate in sociology at Northeastern University. The data was
obtained by the use of participant observation; over a 16-month period, 80
used-car salesmen were interviewed and observed, largely during the course
of a two-week training seminar offered by a major car manufacturer.
Twenty-four salesmen were studied on a long-term basis *in situ,* i. e., as they
worked on a used car lot in interaction with other salesmen, the house, and
most importantly, their customers.

Participant observation was used because the nature of the "action" was
ongoing and dynamic, and because this technique permits first-hand understanding without reliance on an interpreter or informant. After some weeks, it
was possible to understand well enough that there was no need for a
translator. Since interaction was frequent and varied, symbolic interaction
seemed an especially appropriate choice of theory. The car involved, the
interchange of money, the aspects of a game, and the used car salesmen
themselves could all be seen as symbols.

As the study evolved, a number of unique factors came to light. The
used car game could be seen as an example of three-person, simultaneous
interaction—a format which does not appear elsewhere in the sociological
literature—as an example of a brokerage relationship; and as an example of
the middleman phenomenon. While Georg Simmel describes interactions in
which three parties are involved, he always reduces them to eventual
two-party interactions by allying two parties against one. The participants in
such interactions may or may not form alliances, but in the used car game all
three parties, salesman, customer, and house act independently and simultaneously.

A used car salesman acts as broker because he is one person acting as an
agent for another. There are many other examples of brokers—generals,
ambassadors, parents, and teachers, to name a few—and the conduct of
salesmen in this sense is of interest.

───────────

Source: Prepared especially for this volume.

Salesmen also act for themselves; there is something in it for them. In this sense they are middlemen who act as buffers between two other parties. Since even the simplest act an individual performs can be seen as a mediation between what he or she wants to do and what he or she thinks others expect, to a large extent it can be said that society makes middlemen of us all.

Because the used car game highlights the existence of three-person simultaneous interaction, brokerage relationships, and middlemen responsibilities, it is a crackerjack example of bargaining behavior, the compromise between what one has and what one is willing to lose in exchange for what one wants. Because bargaining is something everybody does, nobody talks about, and very few people understand, bargaining behavior has great potential impact on our understanding of the interactions of everyday life. Used car salesmen are professional bargainers.

In studying the process of bargaining it became necessary to settle for either a superficial view of the proceedings, centering on the bargain itself, or to focus on one side in order to achieve some depth of understanding of the action. For this reason, the used car salesmen were studied as the pivotal point of the interaction. It would be advantageous to see the picture that could be drawn of the game if each of the participants could be simultaneously studied in depth by each of three observers.

For the purposes of this study, however, only the used car salesmen were studied in depth. This allowed for an understanding of the interaction on three levels: (1) the used car game, a specific view of a specific bargain; (2) the middleman's perspective, a more focused view of how a bargain works in the eyes of an intermediary, or a specific sociology of the bargain; and (3) the bargain in its most generalizable format. All three are slightly different views of the same process, increasing in applicability as they decrease in specificity. Diplomats, spouses, teachers, and students all bargain, and middlemen bargain with two different groups simultaneously. Used car salesmen are the most "professional" and expert of all bargainers since there is a used car game which these salesmen play all the time. The name of this game is bargaining, and in it money is one of the least crucial commodities; trust is the most important. As in any game there are rules to be followed, but, unlike most conventional games, in this one everybody does not know or play by the rules.

THE USED CAR GAME

The used car game (see Figure 1) begins before a customer walks onto the lot. The salesmen have already determined who has the "up" or chance for this particular customer. In most operations the salesmen take turns, but, because a relatively small percentage of any salesman's business is based on these walk-ins, many consider this "cold" or unknown customer a waste of time.

FIGURE 1
The Used Car Game

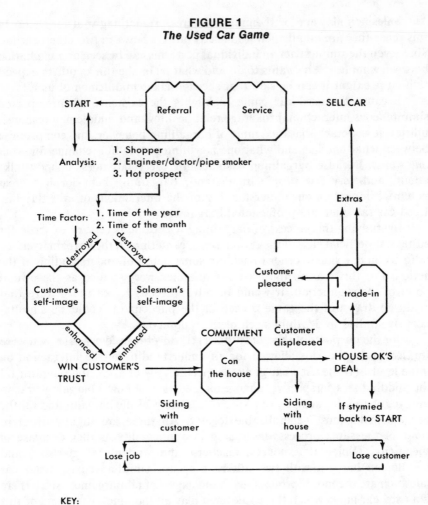

KEY:

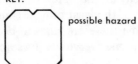   possible hazard

THE RESEARCH EXPERIENCE

The salesman's first step is to try to find out if both he and the customer have any intention of playing the same game. Through the process of sizing up he analyzes the customer: Is he or she a tire kicker, just a looker, or a hot prospect? As one salesman said:

"First thing you got to do with a customer is find out if he's legitimate. You talk to him and you find out if he's a tire kicker or a shopper and you find out in his mind, what I call 'qualify' him, whether he's serious or not."

Once the salesman has made an initial determination that the customer is not just a shopper who will waste his time but a legitimate, serious prospect, he moves to the next step, collecting more specific clues. Is the customer family-oriented, wealthy, interested in sports? What is the customer's reaction to various "pitches" likely to be? What does he or she want in terms of lifestyle, goals, and (incidentally) a car consistent with these aspirations? One car-lot philosopher said: "I've got to unconsciously weigh each factor in the total scheme in order to assist my customer in the best buy." Another salesman noted more specifically, "Hell, for every guy that comes in here, I have to find out how much assistance he needs to help him get the best buy, even though sometimes there's a conflict between extra features and his pocketbook."

The salesman finds the answers to his questions through a number of clues: the customer's appearance, present car, attitude in general. When all else fails, he asks whether the customer is in the market for a car and, if so, what kind of car. This series of moves takes place in two different directions. While the initial direction is covert, the second is more open and usually verbal. Both series of steps are used to secure information, but the second combines forward moves with the conversational relaxation of the customer. The salesman is laying the strategy for a future move of establishing intimacy.

During this process of analysis, which is called "qualifying," the salesman is aware that the customer is conducting an analysis of his own, based partially on the image the salesman is attempting to convey.[1] Because he knows he is one of the least trusted men in America, the salesman seeks to reassure the customer by being friendly, on a first-name basis, congenial, folksy, knowledgeable, and helpful. He asks about the customer's family, business, leisure pursuits, pets, hobbies, school ties, home town, and anything else that comes to mind. He tries to appear interested and informed. Appropriate and relevant moves are clued by the customer's clothing, car decals, speech patterns, and general appearance. He establishes intimacy, in order to be able to establish trust a few moves farther along. If either party decides not to continue as a result of these analyses, the game is over. If both

---

1. Interestingly enough, to the salesman the word "qualify" has two meanings: to separate the buyers from the shoppers (to find out information about the customer), and to give the customer "appropriate" information about the salesman himself.

are convinced that there is some possibility for a good game, the first go or no-go decision has been made.

The participants must balance self-images. The salesman offers the possibilities of what he can do for the customer. By his or her presence, the customer has tacitly made the bargain, "I may buy a car from you." Weighing each other's needs and desires is a crucial set of plays; if it is not handled to each party's satisfaction, the game is over. Because the game is played out in a public place, both participants need assurance not only that neither will lose but also that neither will *appear* to lose. The game has an audience of kibitzers which includes the salesman's colleagues as well as the customer's friend or family. Neither participant can afford to lose big, to lose face. Both must feel that they have a chance, an equal right to impose their will, to exert their demands. Both must feel important, powerful, and evenly matched.

Part of the trick of this set of moves centers around the salesman's image. He must achieve a balance between overcoming the customer's suspicion and hostility and saving his own face. This balancing act must reassure both the customer, who feels that the salesman is a crook, and the salesman who is convinced that the customer is out to get him. As one salesman said: "Every guy who comes in here has it in his mind that he's going to beat you." This attitude can be illustrated by an anecdote told by an ex-salesman about the need to "win" on the customer's part:

> You may not believe this, but in 1959, a woman came in here and gave me $50 right out of her pocket; she took it out and counted it out to me, to bargain with her husband, but not to let him know it. So I could cut my price by $50. He had a bad heart, and he was old and didn't get out much and he wanted to beat me, but she said, "Don't make it easy for him, but let him win." Fifty dollars.

The salesman's desire to keep from being overmatched is evidenced by a general unwillingness to deal with pipe-smoking intellectuals. Another gambit utilized by salesman is to assure themselves that their customers are coming to them for help because they know nothing about cars.

If this balancing of self-images can be handled successfully by the salesman, the most hazardous part of the game has been negotiated. In large part the destructive competition and hostility that could occur have been blunted.

The foregoing strategy has laid the groundwork for a quick succession of moves in which the salesman presents himself to the customer. He shares secrets and intimacies about himself by telling about his wife and kids, school, neighborhood, friends, car, hobbies, and boss. If asked what he was doing in this conversation, the salesman would say he was selling himself. One said, "Whether you're selling refrigerators or TV's or houses or vacuum cleaners or cars or I don't care what, the first thing you go to sell is yourself, and the product will be sold." On the other hand, some used car salesmen feel they have a special selling job to do, since "each of the men is on the defensive when a customer comes up. He has got to sell himself, make the customer like him and trust him, because the customer expects not to."

At this point in the game, the salesman displays his first commitment to the customer by letting him in on what kind of person he is: skilled, cheerful, honest, and worth dealing with. As one salesman said, "If you establish a good relationship, the customer will be willing to give you more money because you are a nice guy." In this set of moves, which is called "tying in close," a salesman obligates a customer, gets him to feel committed, appears to reciprocate the customer's trust and intimacy. A skilled veteran of the game reports occasionally offering to put $20 down for a customer who claims to be broke (the money is quickly removed from the order form the moment the customer leaves the lot). If the salesman can move beyond this step, not only is he committed to the customer (*his* customer), but the customer also becomes committed to him, since the salesman's virtues now "deserve" a reward or at least some consideration. This indebtedness allows the salesman to begin to control moves. One salesman said, "Once you create an obligation, you've got him. He'll feel guilty if he doesn't deal with you, like he's a crook or a thief. He'll also think you're a nice guy."

Once intimacy on both sides has been established, it can suffice for trust. The salesman can now begin to get down to business, the selling of the car rather than of himself. Two steps occur in tandem: the narrowing of choice to the appropriate, available cars, and the establishment of "usness," which uses the first step as a vehicle.

What the salesman sells is only partially determined by what the customer wants or thinks he wants. Sometimes there are bonuses attached to a car that has been sitting around on the lot for too long:

> . . . here's a car's been around a year and they have a sales meeting and they announce a bonus and that car's gone in three days. Tell all the salesmen they get a $50 bonus, cause everybody who comes in you show that car no matter what they say they're interested in, and sooner or later you find somebody who likes it.

On the other hand, there are cars that a salesman considers "unsafe" in a superstitious way:

> Most of the cars here are worth their price tags, but there are some here that I wouldn't touch, because, in spite of the warranty and everything, you just don't trust 'em for your customer. It's not worth it to have 'em for your customer. It's not worth it to have 'em on your neck. Every guy here feels that way about certain of the cars.

· The game has now moved into the area of trying to match what the customer wants to what the salesman has and therefore wants to sell. Most salesmen would agree that, "If you don't have what they want, then you suggest something else. I do it and I sell more cars than any other guy here."

This is the way the gambit goes for one salesman:

> Four door? Hard top sedan? An Oldsmobile? That one right behind you's got four doors. I also have a Fury in good shape, late model; and a nice little Falcon. The Fury is quite comparable to the Olds and I should have an Olds or two coming in in the next few days.

The idea is to interest the customer in an available car, since the salesman knows that a customer who "walks" without a specific car in mind is unlikely to return to finish the game.

If the salesman can match a customer with one or more possible alternatives, the game shifts into high gear. Another of the crucial points in the game has been reached: To further cement the intimate relationship, the salesman will align himself with the customer rather than his boss: "I go across the street and con the boss a little. I tell him there's a hairline fracture in the crankshaft and we should let the poor bastard have it cheap anyhow." While part of this alliance is illusion, part is real, since the salesman's livelihood is based on how many cars he sells and on a customer's willingness to return to buy another car and to send friends in to play the game. The salesman must now control the moves to the extent that he must convince the customer to move in the same direction. Suggesting that "It's the two of us against the house," the salesman indicates he is willing to side with the customer and con the house. This "we shall overcome together" approach is delineated in one salesman's patter:

> I'm giving you a good price. Now, my boss, he'll probably yell at me—but I want to sell you a car and then I want to sell you another one in a couple of years. So I gotta see you get taken care of. Maybe if I do a good job you'll even send me a friend sometime. This is how I figure to do business—sound reasonable?

Once the salesman has convinced the customer of their "usness," all that remains to be settled are the details, the customer's trade-in, any extras to be offered (the side bets and face-saving devices that can be employed before the game ends), and the final deal. One successful bargainer suggested:

> Keep something in reserve. Something free. Be willing to give up five bucks worth of floor mats on a three hundred dollar deal;[2] just pull them right out of the inventory. It will help the customer to make a decision in your favor. . . . Let the customer leave with the feeling he won.

Price becomes important at this point, but it can seldom blow the deal since the car has already been chosen, the salesman is trusted, and rapport has been established. It is more a matter of when, not if, a satisfactory price

---

2. The "three hundred dollar deal" refers to the amount of profit the house makes. The salesman makes a top figure of $25 or $30 on any car he sells initially, until bonuses are added at the end of the month based on the total number of cars he sells.

THE RESEARCH EXPERIENCE

can be reached. The game of price is more problematical, however, than would appear at first glance. As a salesman reports, this isn't a department store with inflexible price tags:

> How do I know how much I can bargain? Well, see, the house doesn't tell us how much they actually paid for the car, so we ask around on the lot to see if we can find the guy who took it in trade and after awhile you get so you can tell how much the company appraiser gave 'em for it.

Another salesman reports that, if they so desire, he or any of his colleagues can give someone a good deal on a car. Part of that move entails conning the house, but part is based on the salesman's feelings about his customer: "Sure a young couple comes in and we'll give 'em a little better deal, or sometimes one of those bearded long-haired types comes in and we give 'em a high price, take it or leave it. They're not our kind of people."

Assuming the price game has been completed and the car is sold, the salesman holds on to his hard-won customer by guiding him along the path of future service and a possible referral, until each is ready to begin the game again: "I make an appointment for the customer if there's an emergency. That way he feels like I did everything I could. He's proud of me and he buys from me and sends his friends in to buy from me." Worthy adversaries are not easy to come by, and the salesman is a professional gamesman. The advantage to him of referrals and repeat business, other than the obvious, is that the hazardous business of both parties assessing self-identity and value to one another can be partially circumvented. They know each other, so the game can begin at who "we" are against the house, the greatest part of the battle having been alleviated and bypassed.

As much as the game is ever finished, it can be said to have ended at this point. Like any good game, however, the participants' appetites should have been whetted for another match in the indefinite future. To a certain extent, it is probably this long-term perspective that allows both salesman and customer to bargain effectively, to give a little. If the game is satisfying, the salesman has a future customer, and the customer has a salesman he feels he can trust. The trust and the commitment of the game endure long after the car has been totaled and the money forgotten. It is here that the virtuosity of the salesman as gamesman can be understood and applied.

THE MIDDLEMAN'S PERSPECTIVE

The specifics of the used car game can be seen in the broader perspective of the middleman (Figure 2). In this view qualifying of a customer by the salesman as "shopper," "tire kicker," or "hot prospect" is done by a middleman analyzing the situation. The salesman confiding about his family is an attempt to balance self-images, and so it goes around the board.

The middleman's bargain starts with analyzing his prospective "part-

FIGURE 2
Middleman's View of a Bargain

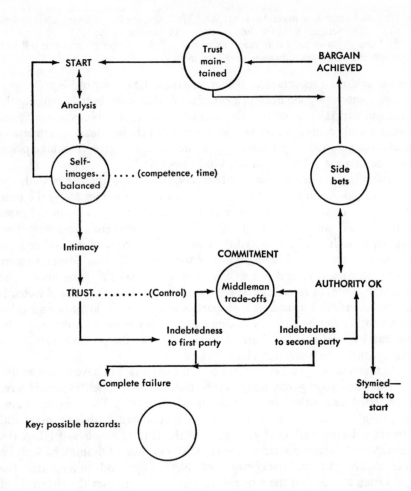

Note; The possibility for complication or failure to consummate a bargain is much greater initially; more steps are involved, with many more pitfalls. As trust is actively sought and achieved, "falling-out" becomes less and less likely. However, this trust must be balanced on both sides, or too much indebtedness to either party will also result in failure.

THE RESEARCH EXPERIENCE

ner" in the transaction. What could he conceivably want? What would he be willing to do to get it? Although presumably the middleman is strongly motivated to play, he retains the option to refuse to do so, particularly if he suspects that the game will waste his time or end unfavorably for him. One of the advantages of being a middleman is that, if the game is played at all, an unfavorable outcome for him personally is unlikely. The backer stands to win or lose the most. However, a "bad" bargain may affect the middleman's image of himself as a competent bargainer and human being and may also jeopardize his career as a middleman.

The crucial move always involves the middleman's ability to balance his goals with those of his partner without damaging the self-image of either. Having successfully achieved this, he is able to lay the groundwork for an intimate relationship, allowing his partner to identify strongly with him. It is hoped this will result in his partner's trust, which would allow the middleman maximum control of the situation. Although to a certain extent he is now committed to his partner, his partner is also committed to him.

FIGURE 3
Generalized Format of a Bargain

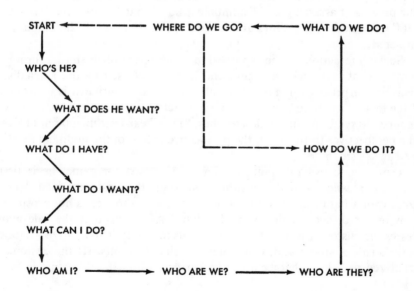

Note: In the specific case of the used car game, "he" is the customer; "I" is the salesman; "they" is the house. However, the model in this figure applies to other perspectives, other situations, and other games.

Unless he too is a middleman who must experience a dual loyalty, presumably the partner's commitment is the stronger of the two. The middleman, while maintaining a working relationship with his backer, must give the impression of a stronger, if not total, commitment to his partner rather than to his backer. Assuming he is able to accomplish this rather delicate balance, his backer allows him to continue in the game. Provided he does not jeopardize or violate his contract with the backer, the middleman is also relatively free to arrive at his own side bets with his partner.

Once the bargain is realized, trust must be maintained so that, at some future date, the whole process can be reactivated without the tedious and dangerous machinations necessary to initially establish trust and control.

Note that the middleman has two "partners," a reluctant one whose loyalty is tenuous and undependable, and a silent one, who occasionally thrusts himself upon the scene. Though referred to as a backer above, the latter is, in reality, a partner as well.

GENERALIZED FORMAT

The final generalization of the game can be seen as a basic unit of human interaction—the bargain (Figure 3). Qualifying or analysis becomes more simply "Who is he?" and "What does he want?" Balancing self-images is the process of assessing and communicating "What I have" and "What I want," culminating in "Who I am." The steps continue until the bargain is completed.

Social interaction can be expressed in its simplest (albeit sterile) form by the who, what, why, where, when, and how model used by the journalist. This is not surprising when it is remembered that the journalist is interested in "the facts," the bare bones of social interaction reported in a news story. Of course, as symbolic interaction teaches, "facts" exist within a point of view and a perspective. In this case, the perspective is that of the middleman, the used car salesman.

From the salesman's point of view of the used car game, he is first interested in who—who the customer is. Who the customer is depends primarily on what he or she wants. Is the customer a shopper, a hot prospect, family oriented, a difficult personality type? Assuming that the salesman assesses the customer as worth any effort, his next step is to analyze what he has (in terms of stock) and, consequently, what he wants. (If the customer is analyzed as a loser, either a tire kicker or an S.O.B., the game is over for both.)

What I, the salesman, have in terms of merchandise, time, motivational factors, commissions, and hours to go in the day determines what I want. Obviously, I would prefer to sell a car rather than not, or I would not be standing around. Weighing these two factors, what he wants and what I want, what can I do? This is a crucial and tricky part of the game because, if the two factors are not properly weighed, no deal can be consummated and again the game is over.

Assuming that a balance can be achieved, I, the salesman, am now ready to assert who I am to the customer: the kind of fellow who deserves to be trusted, because of my knowledgeability, skill, and general honesty. At this point the salesman first displays a commitment to the customer. By doing so, he begins the process of committing the customer to him, because presumably the used car salesman is seen as a virtuous human being.

At this point, the bargain takes on the character of we, the two of us, against the world. Who we are is defined by who we are not: we are not the house (they). We're together, on each other's side. Who they are has now been defined.

The crucial part of the bargain has now been reached. We have a basis of trust. *How* we do it is the chief problem remaining, as opposed to *do* we do it. How we do it relies heavily on who we are, both individually and jointly. Even though this must be constantly reinforced, it has already been established. What we do is accomplished, which leaves only where we go from here.

Personal Journal

B. FIELDWORK FOR FUN AND PROFIT

The excitement of the first fieldwork experience can often quickly give way to an equally intense feeling of panic when a researcher becomes aware that the process being observed is an ongoing one—the situation will not be the same again. This article is an attempt to discuss that excitement and panic and the process in ways that will be both understandable and helpful to the novice researcher.

Practical information on how to conduct research is difficult to come by. As a bridge across the gap between textbook proscriptions and finished product, this article discusses method, particularly participant observation as a research technique, in specific, applied ways. Since the preceding article is a conventional treatment of theory, method, results, and discussion, such

---

Source: Prepared especially for this volume.

information will not be repeated here. Instead, attention will be focused on how to do fieldwork for fun and profit. The compendium of helpful hints, true confessions, and grievous errors is divided into nine parts: (1) choosing a group, (2) arranging entree, (3) the bargain, (4) the field, (5) field techniques, (6) field notes, (7) analysis, (8) model building, and (9) write-up.

CHOOSING A GROUP

There are literally infinite groups to study, topics in which to be interested, and methods to employ. To my way of thinking, there are four reasons for choosing one group over another: the group should be fun, accessible, convenient, and suitable. Lest these criteria be dismissed as frivolous, let me explain. Fieldwork is exhausting, difficult, psychologically demanding, and time-consuming. The more fun and interesting the group, the greater the likelihood that your interest and commitment will be sustained. A fun group can be just as important as a dull group, and a lot easier to study.

Accessibility is crucial. A group that is physically inaccessible is an obvious stumbling block, but an emotionally or psychologically inaccessible group is equally, if more subtly, an inappropriate choice. For example, a group of nuns I chose to study via participant observation was so psychologically inaccessible that I was counting ballpoint pen clicks for lack of more relevant data. It is impossible to learn very much about a group from a long distance, whether it be physical or psychological space.

Convenience is the key to good research. The more often you can be on the scene, the more you will learn. And the more convenient the group is, the more often you can be on the scene.

Suitability is a time bomb with a long fuse. Often it is not until a study has progressed, or at least continued for some length of time, that it becomes obvious whether the group is suitable for study in terms of relevance to theory and method, personability of the researcher, and time constraints. The group of nuns was a poor choice for studying symbolic interaction by means of participant observation because they interacted very little and they allowed for no participation and precious little observation. The nuns were not an uninteresting group and could probably be profitably studied, but my choice of both method and theory was inappropriate for optimum results with such a group.

A brief word is in order here pertaining to theory and method. Quite often one or the other is predetermined by the requirements of a particular course, department, professor, grant, or proposal. The choice is also tempered by personal preference. Once the method and theory have been determined, for whatever reason, it is important to make sure that the group chosen for study is compatible with them, since the researcher should not, and probably cannot, alter the functioning of the group. In participant observation you must be able to observe without an interpreter and to participate to a limited extent. Studying a group that employs a language with which you are unfamiliar is idiocy. In the same vein, picking a group (as I did with nuns) that is in some other way uncommunicative will doom the effort to failure.

The most efficient way of avoiding such pitfalls is: (1) to understand the limitations of theory and method in specific ways, (2) to catalog what you think you know about the group before you start, and (3) to consider your own motivation—why you're there in the first place. When I undertook the used car game study, I was searching for both a used car and a thesis topic. An advisor had explained that a good research topic is one that is concise, manageable, bounded, and capable of being completed—any topic expands under scrutiny. I found a car (a 1969 Plymouth), and I thought I had found a thesis topic—the used car salesman as an example of situational paranoia. As you might have noticed, this is not the topic of study reported in the preceding article.

At this point, I had a theory, a method, a topic, and a group. I was ready to begin. To get the lay of the land, I began by hanging around a local used car lot. Since I question the morality, not to mention the validity and the possibility of doing undercover work, I decided that I would be straightforward about my intentions. I asked the salesman if it was okay if I observed him and asked questions, provided I stayed out of his way. He said it was okay with him, but I should check it out upstairs. I had to ask who "upstairs" was, even though I thought I knew. As a researcher, I learned always to ask; I could not afford the luxury of assuming that I knew. That's the advantage of being a newcomer and of studying an unknown group. You take nothing for granted, and you can learn the rules as you go along.

ENTREE

Participant observation as a field method is limited to a point of view which is relevant, ongoing, and dynamic, but limited nonetheless. The first indication that such a limitation exists is entree, the door through which a researcher must pass in order to gain access to the group. It must be arranged through someone; it is the bargain that must be made to get in. The person from whom to seek admittance is the one who might decide you were not wanted and who could prevent you from being there. You go to the person who has this power, regardless of who might be the person on the organization's chart who is supposed to be powerful. This is the first clue to the informal as opposed to stated or formalized organization of the group.

Entree is a power game, and therefore the only good ally is a powerful one. Unfortunately, it is not always initially obvious wherein the power lies. You may find out the hard way that you made the bargain with the wrong person—someone who has an axe to grind, or who can deny you information, or who is mistrusted by more useful informants. An individual may possess some or all of these "faults," but at least you gain something if the entree ally is a powerful person. On the other hand, you should not go too high; you might have to arrange again at a lower level to gain access to the relevant information. In my case, I could have gained entree through the owner of a dealership or through the consumer protection bureau, but neither would have been on the scene to "protect" me, and I would have been suspected by everyone from the salesmen to the sales manager to mechanics. I would have been considered a spy. Since the sales manager was on the scene, could have made me leave, and had control over the salesmen's time, I went to him. He was an effectively rather than a nominally powerful person.

I discerned the sales manager as my man by a combination of thought and reconnaissance. I hung around and watched the action for as long as I could without appearing suspicious, and then I asked one of the salesmen who should be consulted about staying on the lot for the duration of the study. The salesmen could have been wrong in their power analysis, and since I took their word for it early on, I could have been wrong in my analysis, but at least I had some reasons for my actions, so the odds were in my favor. Any reason is always better than no reason, and, as a sociologist, it seemed appropriate to make minimal kinds of assumptions based on what I knew about power and groups in general.

The researcher compromises with whoever is used as an entree, becoming beholden to that person. It is important to structure the entree with as few strings attached as possible and to go as high as possible, so that the compromise will only have to be made once.

THE BARGAIN

It has been established that the deal should be made with the person who has the power. The next issue is the kind of deal to be made. There are two basic rules of thumb: be honest, and tell only what is absolutely necessary, since you want to limit yourself as little as possible.

Here again, a bit of thought may help you avoid the most common mistake I know of. This is promising to show the results of the study to the entree individual. This promise may be obvious and easy, but it also implies that veto power is being offered. Since this power is seldom honored and the offer is therefore untrue, it is a mistake to make such a promise.

The reason the pact is seldom honored is that the researcher usually leaves the field before the analysis of the data is completed. The raw data are either meaningless to the entree person or could possibly compromise an informant. Raw data can be interpreted and/or misinterpreted. Since the researcher is often far removed from the field when the data are analyzed and written up, the pact may be forgotten or overlooked. A bit of thought can prevent the necessity of such a predicament. Assuring the entree person that the report can be seen at its completion on request offers cooperation but places the responsibility for affirmative action on the other's shoulders.

Assurance is the name of the game in the entree bargain. What you are trying to do is gain access by the least expensive but most direct route. In my case, I had some feelings that the salesmen were both pivotal to the action and the focal point of the study. Because they had had such a bad press, I had to assure the sales manager that I was not playing exposé games. I did this by mentioning that I was a student (I am powerless), that I was doing a study on occupations (I am legitimizing you, at least tacitly, by association), and that I was doing the work for a class (It is private study). The parenthetical statements, while unmentioned, were the obvious interpretation of my bargain. Had I said, "I'm nobody you have to be afraid of, I'm not trying to expose you, and all of my findings will remain confidential," I would have raised a negative specter with which I was unprepared to deal. (Incidentally, when the possibility of publication came up, obviously much later, I asked the salesmen for their blessings, which they gave. Essentially, I renegotiated my bargain.)

The uneasy, temporary nature of original understanding is often evidenced by the researcher's agreeing to a trial period, after which entree will be renegotiated. Agreeing to a trial period is a means by which you can reaffirm your reasonableness and the entree's ultimate power. Since the entree had the power all along and you are simply (and presumably profitably) affirming that power, neither side loses anything.

Once entree has been gained, the individual with whom it has been arranged will let the word out that it is okay for others to talk with you, either by introducing you personally or by sending around a memo or whatever is appropriate to the group. Often a researcher will find out late that what appeared to be carte blanche was only a tentative arrangement which was much more limited than it appeared. If the researcher remains in the field long enough to establish some degree of intimacy and trust, it will usually turn out that potential informants were cautioned not to tell all or to be careful what they said, as a number of salesmen gleefully reported to me later.

THE FIELD

The question of how you can be assured that events are proceeding as they would without your presence is the single most chilling, frightening, moral, methodological, and theoretical implication of participant observation or any field technique. How much are the data being influenced by your presence? The best way to guard against influencing any group is to be aware that you might do so.

It is hoped that what you are observing would have happened had you not been there and will exist after you leave. The knife-edged present, once removed for analysis, ceases to exist, but there are events leading to that moment and consequences of that action that continue as expectations. The problem for the researcher is assuring that that reality has not been unalterably affected by the research. To a certain extent, you can never be completely assured that what is going on could have happened before you arrived and could happen again, that you are studying some situation other than how a group reacts to a stranger—you.

If a rat in a maze can be affected by the body language of the researcher, then surely a human can be influenced by the expectations of the questioner or the presence of an observer. If you have ever watched the cameras pan the audience of Johnny Carson's show you have seen apparently normal, sedate people doing crazy things for the benefit of an audience, even if unknown and unseen. The televised coverage of the 1968 Democratic Convention in Chicago testified to the same phenomenon. People react in strange ways when they feel they are being observed by the communications media, the means of global communication.

In part my own wrestling with the problem was due to a remembrance of a personal experience in which I was followed around France for three days by a photographer who wanted to do a minute-by-minute account of what young women do on archeology digs. Being as camera shy as the next person, I was sure I would lose my mind, but I found to my delight and amazement that within a very short time I was quite oblivious of the guy. Also, perhaps not so surprisingly, when I stopped being aware that I was having my picture taken, the photographer got some very "me" pictures; I was giving a true impression of myself.

Given enough time, people can not only get used to anything or anyone but also can become rather oblivious of them. The first rule of fieldwork is to become familiar enough to others that your presence is taken for granted. When you are no longer a novelty, you begin to get the feeling that things are happening over and over again, in a consistent manner, without regard to your presence. (In the back of your mind, though, it is well to remember that you are always influencing the situation; it is a matter of how much, in what ways, and to what degree.)

As you melt into the woodwork and begin to discern patterns in behavior, you also develop a sense of your own irrelevancy in the situation. You begin to share a perspective that you had not previously understood and are able to predict what will happen next. You finally achieve that nonstatus to which informants respond with "Gee, I forgot you were even here." They stop asking "Did you get that all down yet?" or "Am I talking too fast for you?" As informants stop explaining, you find you do not need to ask for an explanation. They neither clean up nor dirty their language for your benefit.

FIELD TECHNIQUE

In participant observation, it is important to be more observer than participant in the early days in the field. Do not interfere. In this way you do

THE RESEARCH EXPERIENCE

not inadvertently slip into a role of leadership or importance in the group. To facilitate this nonparticipant, strictly observer role, it is wise to choose a group about whom you have little first-hand knowledge and with whom you have little in common. With familiar groups, you may be tempted to assume or to interfere.

The second big "no" is do not use a tape recorder. First, you miss more than you get, since nonverbal communication is lost. Second, tape recorders malfunction. Third, tape recorders make people nervous by continually emphasizing that they are being observed and preserved. Fourth, if you think your tape recorder is picking it all up, *you* may not. You think you will remember things, but you do not because you have not been concentrating.

The third "no" is do not take notes; listen instead. A panicky thought, perhaps, but unless you are in a classroom setting where everyone is taking notes, the note taking can be as intrusive as a tape recorder and can have the same result: paranoia or influencing the action. The subject worries whether you got everything down. To affect the situation as little as possible, just listen. But how do you remember? You learn. You learn to listen; you scribble notes and you learn to remember.

At first I listened for about five minutes and then furiously jotted down sentences. I soon progressed to key words, then kept from note taking for longer and longer periods of time. Within a month or so I was able to remember two and a half or three hours of conversation, happenings, glances and the like, without using a notebook at all. As soon as I returned home, I would write out a chronological transcript, based on scribbled key words jotted down upon leaving the field. I had to be especially careful not to talk about the events on the way home, but simply to "throw it all up" when I got there. The panic of the early days eventually gave way to a quiet confidence in the skill to remember. (It becomes a bit of an occupational hazard in that I find it difficult to relate any event simply or briefly. If someone inquires three hours later about a party I have attended, they learn what everyone wore, drank, said, meant, and implied. Bored friends notwithstanding, it is pleasant to develop the skill of effortless observation.)

In the early days, it is crucial to collect only data, not analysis. Don't interpolate or integrate—just remember. What is important or trivial is usually not evident until much later. So don't sift, just collect.

FIELD NOTES

The form of data in participant observation is field notes. Like any notes, they vary with the person who is taking them. The basic rule of thumb in note taking is: If it works, don't knock it. I found it easiest to remember events chronologically, since this gave me an obvious way of placing things in sequence. The scene unfolds logically and the dialog can be remembered because it occurs in response to questions or topics.

Initially, it is more important to evolve a style of note taking than to be overly concerned with "missing" something in the notes. You may miss things, but if they are crucial to an understanding of the group, they will reoccur or be referenced again.

Because writing is an ineffective way of listening (as described above), field notes are usually done away from the field. However, I always take pencil and paper (in some discreet form or another) into the field as a security blanket. Often the way you will learn that everything does not have to be written down is when you get interested in a situation unfolding and forget to take notes. Later you find out how much you remember. With a minimal number of key words, five-minute intervals of remembered events and conversations can be stretched to two- or three-hour intervals. It is pleasant to watch this skill develop.

As events unfold, your feelings and ideas may become interspersed with what actually happens. Both categories of events are important, but they should not be confused, confounded, or combined. The hard data of factual happenings are no more important than the soft data of interpretation, but, for obvious reasons, they must be kept separate. Since I type my field notes, I find it convenient to indent my "impressions" as opposed to what actually happens. Using different colored typewriter ribbon, capital letters, or some other form of notation are equally effective. By keeping both hard and soft data "together but separate," you can at a future time combine them in analysis without their being either tainted or lost.

Everyone has biases—preconceptions, expectations, pet theories, prejudices. For the researcher whose study offers the possibility of replication and validation, it is important to note biases so they can be teased out from the final product. Since used car salesmen have a societal image, this was fairly simple for me. At the same time, I had a slightly different perception since I had just bought a used car with which I was pleased, and I had found the salesmen to be interesting and talkative (attributes not without value for a researcher).

As I progressed with my project, it became important to note that I was a young woman. Irrelevant as it might have seemed at the outset, the fact that used car lots have little shacks which can cozily accommodate a salesman (nearly all are men, and all those I encountered were men) and a researcher (who happened to be a woman) created a methodological problem. I had to develop a method of convincing a sometimes overeager informant that I did not want to be *that* kind of participant. (The solution, as is often the case, was to leave the field for a while and let things cool off naturally rather than face a showdown and lose an informant.)

The point is that those reading a research report should have some idea of who wrote it and why. It is important for the researcher to know the same things. Notations about time of year, time of day, the state of the economy, social factors, personal factors, and other details and limitations of the study also help to place the research in perspective. My interpretation of the data is important, but it is not the same as the data itself. For instance, the mood of the researcher can dramatically affect the data. Grumpy data is often the result of a grumpy researcher. By noting both your mood and your data, you can get a clearer picture of what actually happens.

Field notes are for using, so neatness is not as important as legibility. My field notes are symphonies of typos, erasures, and x-ing out. I would have been much happier if I had made three copies of my field notes. Three is an arbitrary number, based on the assumption that it is a good idea to have one set of field notes intact forever, one set to cut and paste during analysis, and one set to hoard in some nice fireproof place. While this might seem a bit paranoid, I kept hearing horror stories of fires and floods and ruined field notes. (The most common student place for securing notes seems to be the refrigerator, but, since ours was too small to closet ice cubes, the oven seemed the second most fireproof place in the house for my *single*—yes, I was foolish!—set of notes.) There is a certain panic associated with data. Because lost data cannot be recaptured, precautions are necessary.

ANALYSIS

The major question of analysis is when it should be done. The answer is rather enigmatic; you just know when it is time to start. The warning sign is a panicky feeling about the amount of data piling up, yet you are not sure what the study is really about. As mentioned previously, it is a good idea to put off analysis for as long as possible, so that there is some feeling that the research is speaking to the researcher rather than vice versa.

When it is time for analysis, you may find lots of data but no study— just a great many people saying interesting things. There is a rich broth but no substance. Sifting through the data, you must look for abstract-able ideas that are grounded in specific data for the purpose of creating a specific model that is generalizable to other situations of human inter-action. Some specificity is necessary so that the model will fit at least one situation, with the potential for describing others. This is why data should originally be transcribed without analysis.

The process of analysis begins with rereading the data to see if they fall into categories. Between one and two dozen "readings" is a good place to start—fewer are too abstract, more are unwieldy. If the categories seem to form a picture, the first dim outline of a study appears. If you are lucky, brilliant, experienced, or some combination of these, you may well be on the way. More often the first stages of analysis are times for painful revelation. It was at this point in my research that I began to understand (with a good deal of prodding from my mentor) that the original idea of studying the used car salesman as an example of situational paranoia was in trouble.

True, I was firmly committed to the theoretical implications of symbolic interaction, and, true, I had found participant observation to be an enlightening and enjoyable experience. As far as I was concerned, this was what compatability of theory and method meant. Over a period of several weeks, however, I began to understand that my theory and method were not only incompatible but were in direct conflict, mainly because method entails research design and intent as well as field technique.

This unsettling development emerged when I discovered that, although I knew a great deal about how used car salesmen interacted with customers and about what their feelings were concerning such customers and their boss (the house), I knew nothing about the customer's feelings toward the salesman. Such information would have had to be obtained prior to the first encounter between salesman and customer. The best way to do this would have been to give the customer a questionnaire before he entered the lot. To get to the customer before he entered the situation was impossible, however, because he was not a customer until he did. By flitting back and forth between salesmen and customer, I would also have jeopardized my entree to my informants and my impartiality in their eyes. Whose side was I on? By presenting a questionnaire to a customer, I would not only have introduced but would have sponsored and encouraged distrust, thus creating a self-fulfilling prophecy. If I had asked the customer if he trusted the salesman, it would not have been surprising to find that indeed trust or the lack of it was a significant variable in the interaction.

The question then became how to be a participant and an observer yet privy to information on both sides. The answer was that it was impossible to accomplish this because I could only lose my credibility with both sides, while influencing and directing the situation—not very good research at all. Since it would have required access to the opinion of both customer and salesman, I found it necessary to abandon the concept of paranoia as a workable field theory.

Undaunted, I moved on to the idea that what I was really studying was a disputation of game theory. I was prepared to show, contrary to the tenets of game theory, that participants are seldom playing the same game by the same rules. Because game theory and its distortion had long been a pet peeve, I was cheered by the new development. My glee was short-lived. This new model required the same sort of verification as the first unworkable hypothesis. If I had been disappointed originally, I was inconsolate now. My chance for the big time had been nearly within my grasp; a chance to take on the big guys and win. Yet, it couldn't work.

After a few heartbroken weeks, I compromised by rereading my data and finding that what had become so common as to be overlooked was really a very workable, useful, usable idea. Used car salesmen bargain. So do the rest of us, only nobody had even gone to the trouble to point it out, dissect it, describe it, and define it. I was still in business, not in the way I had envisioned, but in business nonetheless. I point this out not to say that I was able to pull defeat from the jaws of victory, or the opposite, but because to some degree or another almost every researcher ends up writing about a different study than the one originally envisioned. Time often plays an important part in this phenomenon. A respite of a month or two from data collection and analysis often helps stave off boredom, panic, and ennui—and it avoids confusing the forest with the trees.

I had nearly overlooked the real value of the group I was studying. Because I came to know them so well, I made the classic mistake: I took for granted the same things they did. The things that are taken for granted are those that are the most basic and crucial and therefore, quite often, the most important. I also nearly forgot the tacit assumption of sociology that somehow people in groups act in similar fashion, whether that group be the D.A.R. or the S.D.S., the Cub Scouts or General Motors. The researcher tries to make similarities evident in the midst of seeming disparity. Otherwise there can be no value in studying any particular group, since conclusions would be applicable only to that group at a particular time and place.

Another tacit assumption is that no research, if properly conducted, is ever useless. Any group has something to offer to the study of how groups act. The point is to be open to what is in the data rather than to what you have in mind. This is another reason for keeping hard and soft data separate.

By realizing that I could not study the interaction of three groups (or even two) simultaneously, I stumbled onto a bonus. I evolved a research strategy that allowed the study of interaction between groups through studying one group in depth. This technique allows a degree of understanding that is unavailable in studying only the interaction. Although I was able to study only one of the groups, the technique makes it possible to study interaction by having a number of independent researchers study each of the involved groups in depth and to evaluate the interaction from each perspective.

ENDING A STUDY: BEGINNING A MODEL

The only hard and fast rule of model building is that everything must fit. Data cannot be discarded because they do not fit, rather, a model is discarded because it does not fit the data. There are many discussions of how to construct a model, going from the particular to the general or the opposite. I find the most effective method to be a continual sifting of data into increasingly specific categories. The moment when I feel assured that I have a study is when I have a simple title that can adequately describe pages and pages of research. From that point on, everything seems to fall into place.

Model building is an ongoing process. Because a participant-observer does not go into the field with a hypothesis, the end point of such a study is not always obvious. The construction of the model signals the end of the study, and first attempts at model building usually are made long before the researcher leaves the field. The beginning of description of the model often points out questions that are still unanswered or particles of information that ought to be pursued.

One of the advantages of this method of model building is that you can use the group's opinion for verification; that is, various participants can be queried for their opinions of the accuracy of the model. The burden of verification can thus be shared. Because any material that can elucidate can also expose, the question of ethics can also be eased by showing informants the results of their confidences.

In my own study, I had to face the possibility that my findings could be interpreted as giving the customer privileged information on how to beat the salesman. I dealt with this issue by asking the salesmen what they thought the result would be if the customer were informed of what they had told me. I was enormously relieved and reassured to be assured, as I had suspected, that the salesmen would prefer that customers have a better idea of what was going on. The salesmen would then only have to sell themselves, rather than first "unselling" themselves.

Even had this not been the case, I suspect that the salesmen would have seen some tangible benefit from my "exposé" and that the hunger for notoriety would have resulted in their enthusiastic acceptance of the study. This thirst for notoriety does not diminish the responsibility of the researcher to try for at least tacit approval when "secrets" are being made public. First, you should feel some sense of ethical responsibility to people who have been willing to confide in you. Second, you will never get any reliable information again if the word gets around that you are an unreliable, unprincipled fink. A researcher must deal with the issue of confidentiality according to conscience, and these decisions are never more evident than at the beginning and at the end of a study.

Leaving the field should be a voluntary move, based on the feeling that everything necessary for the study has been learned. It should not be forced, as it will be if you have revealed your findings or interpretations and have alienated the informants, thus eliminating the possibility of obtaining any more usable data. It is time to leave the field when a perspective is effortlessly shared, when events seem to be repeating, and when you can begin to predict with accuracy and confidence what will happen next—when the model is completed.

WRITE-UP

The hard part, for me at least, is the lonely and difficult task of finally sitting down at the typewriter and saying something. There is no place to hide, nobody to talk to, nothing to do but face myself and what I am trying to communicate. Because this is difficult for me (and for everyone I know), I try to compromise between writing on a schedule and only writing on good days. The latter situation is the more crucial of the two. Since once words exist on

THE RESEARCH EXPERIENCE

paper it is very difficult for me to destroy them, I write only when I am "up." While this may approach a neurotic point of view, I recognize it as something with which I must cope. It is much easier for me to write than to rewrite, and it is very difficult for me to give up my own prose, especially when it is the result of a strong commitment to an idea. As evidence, the research I did around the area of game theory as described in the analysis section above is included as a glossary in *The Used Car Game* (Browne, 1973). It was the best compromise I could make with myself over the inappropriateness of game theory to my study and a strong conviction that it is an important if tangential issue. Besides, it was already written.

Though it is advisable to write on "good" days, it is also important just to write. Because my writing was difficult work, I found it discouragingly easy not to have good days. After a futile period of trying to write "some" every day and writing very little and very poorly, I finally evolved what I call the intense pain vs. constant aggravation model of writing. The constant aggravation mode was one in which I felt that I constantly had to write a little bit. As I did not do this, I became more and more unhappy and antisocial. On the theory that I should be writing, I would refuse to go out, read, play, or even giggle much. If I did not write, I did not deserve to do anything at all. The problem with this rather stoic and completely unprofitable method was that it was a constant aggravation. I could learn to live with something that was constant and merely aggravating. I was not writing, but neither was I doing much of anything else.

At certain points, I would get disgusted and decide either to write for awhile and then forget it for awhile as a reward, or, more likely, just to shuck the whole thing for a while. By this, I was well on my way to intense pain. Aggravation, left untreated, tended to build up. When it became painful, and finally intensely painful, it became imperative to "do" something. Write! I would write for awhile, then stop and go about other business for awhile until the pain again became overwhelming. Using this method, I finished up the study in a fairly short time. I could learn to live with aggravation, but not pain.

The next painful topic was editing. I admire, respect, envy, and hate those people who can reread their own material and heartlessly slash inappropriate sentences, adjectives that confound, and other needless flotsam. As you may have gathered, I am not that kind of writer. Although I am slowly evolving my own style (and a sense of indignation and humility about my writing), an editor is still necessary. By editor, I simply mean someone who is willing to read my work and criticize in appropriate ways.

One of the techniques that has helped me to get over the trauma of sitting down to write and helped reduce the need for outside editing is using an inexpensive tape recorder in the writing process. I talk while I try to figure out what it is I am trying to say. My propensity to be more verbal than literate is the chief reason it seems to help me.

CONCLUSION

A final word is in order about "psyching" up for each step of a research project. Because there are new skills to be learned, each level of the study seems difficult when it is begun, whether it is picking a group, getting up nerve enough to go into the field, or learning to take notes. As each step is mastered, it is often psychologically difficult to begin the next one, to start the sometimes painful process of learning again. Each step is progressively harder but also more satisfying, until finally there is the exhilaration of having actually done research and created a study.

It is hoped this article has conveyed not only the pitfalls, pressures, and pain of the fieldwork experience but also the real delights and fun and pleasure of meeting new people, finding out new things, and explaining in yet another way how things work and how people behave.

REFERENCES

Browne, Joy. *The Used Car Game.* Lexington, Mass.: D. C. Heath, 1973.

Laud Humphreys ——————————————————————————————

A. TEAROOM TRADE: IMPERSONAL SEX IN PUBLIC PLACES

At shortly after five o'clock on a weekday evening, four men enter a public restroom in the city park. One wears a well-tailored business suit; another wears tennis shoes, shorts and teeshirt; the third man is still clad in the khaki uniform of his filling station; the last, a salesman, has loosened his tie and left his sports coat in the car. What has caused these men to leave the company of other homeward-bound commuters on the freeway? What common interest brings these men, with their divergent backgrounds, to this public facility?

They have come here not for the obvious reason, but in a search for "instant sex." Many men—married and unmarried, those with heterosexual identities and those whose self-image is a homosexual one—seek such impersonal sex, shunning involvement, desiring kicks without commitment. Whatever reasons—social, physiological or psychological—might be postulated for this search, the phenomenon of impersonal sex persists as a widespread but rarely studied form of human interaction.

There are several settings for this type of deviant activity—the balconies of movie theaters, automobiles, behind bushes—but few offer the advantages for these men that public restrooms provide. "Tearooms,"[1] as these facilities are called in the language of the homosexual subculture, have several characteristics that make them attractive as locales for sexual encounters without involvement. They are accessible, easily recognized by the initiate, and provide little public visibility. Tearooms thus offer the advantages of both public and private settings. They are available and recognizable enough to attract a large volume of potential sexual partners, providing an oppor-

---

Source: Reprinted from Laud Humphreys, *Tearoom Trade* (Chicago: Aldine Publishing Company, 1970); pp. 1-15, and 104-130; Copyright © 1970 by Laud Humphreys. Reprinted by permission of the author and Aldine Publishing Company.

1. Like most other words in the homosexual vocabulary, the origin of *tearoom* is unknown. British slang has used "tea" to denote "urine." Another British usage is as a verb, meaning "to engage with, encounter, go in against." According to its most precise meaning in the argot, the only "true" tearoom is one that gains a reputation as a place where homosexual encounters occur.

tunity for rapid action with a variety of men. When added to the relative privacy of these settings, such features enhance the impersonality of the sheltered interaction.

In the first place, tearooms are readily accessible to the male population. They may be located in any sort of public gathering place: department stores, bus stations, libraries, hotels, YMCAs or courthouses. In keeping with the drive-in craze of American society, however, the more popular facilities are those readily accessible to the roadways. The restrooms of public parks and beaches—and more recently the rest stops set at programmed intervals along super-highways—are now attracting the clientele that, in a more pedestrian age, frequented great buildings of the inner cities. My research is focused on the activity that takes place in the restrooms of public parks, not only because (with some seasonal variation) they provide the most action but also because of other factors that make them suitable for sociological study.

There is a great deal of difference in the volumes of homosexual activity that these accommodations shelter. In some, one might wait for months before observing a deviant act (unless solitary masturbation is considered deviant). In others, the volume approaches orgiastic dimensions. One summer afternoon, for instance, I witnessed 20 acts of fellatio in the course of an hour while waiting out a thunderstorm in a tearoom. For one who wishes to participate in (or study) such activity, the primary consideration is finding where the action is.

In most cases, I could only enter, wait and watch—a method that was costly in both time and gasoline. After surveying a couple of dozen such rooms in this way, however, I became able to identify the more popular tearooms by observing certain physical evidence, the most obvious of which is the location of the facility. During the warm seasons, those restrooms that are isolated from other park facilities, such as administration buildings, shops, tennis courts, playgrounds and picnic areas, are the more popular for deviant activity. The most active tearooms studied were all isolated from recreational areas, cut off by drives or lakes from baseball diamonds and picnic tables. The ideal setting for homosexual activity is a tearoom situated on an island of grass, with roads close by on every side. The getaway car is just a few steps away; children are not apt to wander over from the playground; no one can surprise the participants by walking in from the woods or from over a hill; it is not likely that straight people will stop there. According to my observations, the women's side of these buildings is seldom used at all.

VOLUME AND VARIETY

The availability of facilities they can recognize attracts a great number of men who wish, for whatever reason, to engage in impersonal homoerotic

THE RESEARCH EXPERIENCE

activity. Simple observation is enough to guide these participants, the researcher and, perhaps, the police to active tearooms. It is much more difficult to make an accurate appraisal of the proportion of the male population who engage in such activity over a representative length of time. Even with good sampling procedures, a large staff of assistants would be needed to make the observations necessary for an adequate census of this mobile population. All that may be said with some degree of certainty is that the percentage of the male population who participate in tearoom sex in the United States is somewhat less than the 16 percent of the adult white male population Kinsey found to have "at least as much of the homosexual as the heterosexual in their histories."

Participants assure me that it is not uncommon in tearooms for one man to fellate as many as ten others in a day. I have personally watched a fellator take on three men in succession in a half hour of observation. One respondent, who has cooperated with the researcher in a number of taped interviews, claims to average three men each day during the busy season.

I have seen some waiting turn for this type of service. Leaving one such scene on a warm September Saturday, I remarked to a man who left close behind me: "Kind of crowded in there, isn't it?" "Hell, yes," he answered, "It's getting so you have to take a number and wait in line in these places!"

There are many who frequent the same facility repeatedly. Men will come to be known as regular, even daily, participants, stopping off at the same tearoom on the way to or from work. One physician in his late fifties was so punctual in his appearance at a particular restroom that I began to look forward to our daily chats. This robust, affable respondent said he had stopped at this tearoom every evening of the week (except Wednesday, his day off) for years "for a blow-job." Another respondent, a salesman whose schedule is flexible, may "make the scene" more than once a day—usually at his favorite men's room. At the time of our formal interview, this man claimed to have had four orgasms in the past 24 hours.

According to participants I have interviewed, those who are looking for impersonal sex in tearooms are relatively certain of finding the sort of partner they want. . . .

> You go into the tearoom. You can pick up some really nice things in there. Again, it is a matter of sex real quick; and, if you like this kind, fine—you've got it. You get one and he is done; and, before long, you've got another one.

. . . and when they want it:

> Well, I go there; and you can always find someone to suck your cock, morning, noon or night. I know lots of guys who stop by there on their way to work—and all during the day.

It is this sort of volume and variety that keeps the tearooms viable as market places of the one-night-stand variety.

Of the bar crowd in gay (homosexual) society, only a small percentage would be found in park restrooms. But this more overt, gay bar clientele constitutes a minor part of those in any American city who follow a predominantly homosexual pattern. The so-called closet queens and other types of covert deviants make up the vast majority of those who engage in homosexual acts—and these are the persons most attracted to tearoom encounters.

Tearooms are popular, not because they serve as gathering places for homosexuals but because they attract a variety of men, a *minority* of whom are active in the homosexual subculture and a large group of whom have no homosexual self-identity. For various reasons, they do not want to be seen with those who might be identified as such or to become involved with them on a "social" basis.

PRIVACY IN PUBLIC

There is another aspect of the tearoom encounters that is crucial. I refer to the silence of interaction.

Throughout most homosexual encounters in public restrooms, nothing is spoken. One may spend many hours in these buildings and witness dozens of sexual acts without hearing a word. Of 50 encounters on which I made extensive notes, only in 15 was any word spoken. Two were encounters in which I sought to ease the strain of legitimizing myself as lookout by saying, "You go ahead—I'll watch." Four were whispered remarks between sexual partners, such as, "Not so hard!" or "Thanks." One was an exchange of greetings between friends.

The other eight verbal exchanges were in full voice and more extensive, but they reflected an attendant circumstance that was exceptional. When a group of us were locked in a restroom and attacked by several youths, we spoke for defense and out of fear. This event ruptured the reserve among us and resulted in a series of conversations among those who shared this adventure for several days afterward. Gradually, this sudden unity subsided, and the encounters drifted back into silence.

Barring such unusual events, an occasionally whispered "thanks" at the conclusion of the act constitutes the bulk of even whispered communication. At first, I presumed that speech was avoided for fear of incrimination. The excuse that intentions have been misunderstood is much weaker when those proposals are expressed in words rather than signalled by body movements. As research progressed, however, it became evident that the privacy of silent interaction accomplishes much more than mere defense against exposure to a hostile world. Even when a careful lookout is maintaining the boundaries of an encounter against intrusion, the sexual participants tend to be silent. The mechanism of silence goes beyond satisfying the demand for privacy. Like all other characteristics of the tearoom setting, it serves to guarantee anonymity, to assure the impersonality of the sexual liaison.

Participants may develop strong attachments to the settings of their adventures in impersonal sex. I have noted more than once that these men seem to acquire stronger sentimental attachments to the buildings in which they meet for sex than to the persons with whom they engage in it. One respondent tells the following story: We had been discussing the relative merits of various facilities, when I asked him: "Do you remember that old tearoom across from the park garage—the one they tore down last winter?"

> Do I ever! That was the greatest place in the park. Do you know what my room-mate did last Christmas, after they tore the place down? He took a wreath, sprayed it with black paint, and laid it on top of the snow—right where that corner stall had stood. . . . He was really broken up!

PEOPLE NEXT DOOR

Tearoom activity attracts a large number of participants—enough to produce the majority of arrests for homosexual offenses in the United States. "For some people," says Evelyn Hooker, an authority on male homo-sexuality, "the seeking of sexual contacts with other males is an activity isolated from all other aspects of their lives." Such segregation is apparent with most men who engage in the homosexual activity of public restrooms; but the degree and manner in which "deviant" is isolated from "normal" behavior in their lives will be seen to vary along social dimensions.

For the man who lives next door, the tearoom participant is just another neighbor—and probably a very good one at that. He may make a little more money than the next man and work a little harder for it. It is likely that he will drive a nicer car and maintain a neater yard than do other neighbors in the block. Maybe, like some tearoom regulars, he will work with Boy Scouts in the evenings and spend much of his weekend at the church. It may be more surprising for the outsider to discover that most of these men are married.

Indeed, 54 percent of my research subjects are married and living with their wives. From the data at hand, there is no evidence that these unions are particularly unstable; nor does it appear that any of the wives are aware of their husbands' secret sexual activity. Indeed, the husbands choose public restrooms as sexual settings partly to avoid just such exposure. I see no reason to dispute the claim of a number of tearoom respondents that their preference for a form of concerted action that is fast and impersonal is largely predicated on a desire to protect their family relationships.

Superficial analysis of the data indicates that the maintenance of exemplary marriages—at least in appearance—is very important to the subjects of this study. In answering questions such as "When it comes to making decisions in your household, who generally makes them?" the participants indicate they are more apt to defer to their mates than are those in the control sample. They also indicate that they find it more important to "get along well" with their wives. In the open-ended questions regarding marital relationships, they tend to speak of them in more glowing terms.

THE AGING CRISIS

In most cases, fellatio is a service performed by an older man upon a younger. In one encounter, for example, a man appearing to be around 40 was observed as insertee with a man in his twenties as insertor. A few minutes later, the man of 40 was being sucked by one in his fifties. Analyzing the estimated ages of the principal partners in 53 observed acts of fellatio, I arrived at these conclusions: the insertee was judged to be older than the insertor in 40 cases; they were approximately the same age in three; and the insertor was the older in ten instances. The age differences ranged from an insertee estimated to be 25 years older than his partner to an insertee thought to be ten years younger than his insertor.

Strong references to this crisis of aging are found in my interviews with cooperating respondents, one of whom had this to say:

> I suppose I was around 35—or 36—when I started giving out blow jobs. It just got so I couldn't operate any other way in the park johns. I'd still rather have a good blow job any day, but I've gotten so I like it the way it is now.

Perhaps by now there is enough real knowledge abroad to have dispelled the idea that men who engage in homosexual acts may be typed by any consistency of performance in one or another sexual role. Undoubtedly, there are preferences: few persons are so adaptable, their conditioning so undifferentiated, that they fail to exercise choice between various sexual roles and positions. Such preferences, however, are learned, and sexual repertories tend to expand with time and experience. This study of restroom sex indicates that sexual roles within these encounters are far from stable. They are apt to change within an encounter, from one encounter to another, with age, and with the amount of exposure to influences from a sexually deviant subculture.

It is to this last factor that I should like to direct the reader's attention. The degree of contact with a network of friends who share the actor's sexual interests takes a central position in mediating not only his preferences for sex role, but his style of adaptation to—and rationalization of—the deviant activity in which he participates. There are, however, two reasons why I have not classified research subjects in terms of their participation in the homosexual subculture. It is difficult to measure accurately the degree of such involvement; and such subcultural interaction depends upon other social variables, two of which are easily measured.

Family status has a definitive effect on the deviant careers of those whose concern is with controlling information about their sexual behavior. The married man who engages in homosexual activity must be much more cautious about his involvement in the subculture than his single counterpart. As a determinant of life style and sexual activity, marital status is also a determinant of the patterns of deviant adaptation and rationalization.

The second determining variable is the relative autonomy of the respondent's occupation. A man is "independently" employed when his job allows him freedom of movement and security from being fired; the most obvious example is self-employment. Occupational "dependence" leaves a man little freedom for engaging in disreputable activity. The sales manager or other executive of a business firm has greater freedom than the salesman or attorney who is employed in the lower echelons of a large industry or by the federal government. The sales representative whose territory is far removed from the home office has greater independence, in terms of information control, than the minister of a local congregation. The majority of those placed in both the married and unmarried categories with *dependent* occupations were employed by large industries or the government.

Median education levels and annual family incomes indicate that those with dependent occupations rank lower on the socioeconomic scale. Only in the case of married men, however, is this correlation between social class and occupational autonomy strongly supported by the ratings of these respondents on Warner's Index of Status Characteristics. Nearly all the married men with dependent occupations are of the upper-lower or lower-middle classes, whereas those with independent occupations are of the upper-middle or upper classes. For single men, the social class variable is neither so easily identifiable nor so clearly divided. Nearly all single men in the sample can be classified only as "vaguely middle class."

As occupational autonomy and marital status remain the most important dimensions along which participants may be ranked, we shall consider four general types of tearoom customers: (1) married men with dependent occupations, (2) married men with independent occupations, (3) unmarried men with independent occupations, and (4) unmarried men with dependent occupations. As will become evident with the discussion of each type, I have employed labels from the homosexual argot, along with pseudonyms, to designate each class of participants. This is done not only to facilitate reading but to emphasize that we are describing persons rather than merely "typical" constructs.

TYPE I: TRADE

The first classification, which includes 19 of the participants (38 percent), may be called "trade," since most would earn that appellation from the gay subculture. All of these men are, or have been, married—one was separated from his wife at the time of interviewing and another was divorced.

Most work as truck drivers, machine operators or clerical workers. There is a member of the armed forces, a carpenter, and the minister of a pentecostal church. Most of their wives work, at least part time, to help raise their median annual family income to $8,000. One in six of these men is black. All are normally masculine in appearance and mannerism. Although 14 have completed high school, there are only three college graduates among them, and five have had less than 12 years of schooling.

George is representative of this largest group of respondents. Born of second-generation German parentage in an ethnic enclave of the midwestern city where he still resides, he was raised as a Lutheran. He feels that his father (like George a truck driver) was quite warm in his relationship with him as a child. His mother he describes as a very nervous, asthmatic woman. At the age of 20 he married a Roman Catholic girl and has since joined her church, although he classifies himself as "lapsed." In the 14 years of their marriage, they have had seven children, one of whom is less than a year old. George doesn't think they should have more children, but his wife objects to using any type of birth control other than the rhythm method. With his wife working part time as a waitress, they have an income of about $5,000.

"How often do you have intercourse with your wife?" I asked. "Not very much the last few years," he replied. "It's up to when she feels like giving it to me—which ain't very often. . . . She's afraid to have sex but doesn't believe in birth control. I'd just rather not be around her! I won't suggest having sex anyway—and she just doesn't want it anymore."

While more open than most in his acknowledgement of marital tension, George's appraisal of sexual relations in the marriage is typical of those respondents classified as Trade. In 63 percent of these marriages, the wife, husband or both are Roman Catholic. When answering questions about their sexual lives, a story much like George's emerged: At least since the birth of the last child, conjugal relations have been very rare.

These data suggest that, along with providing an excuse for diminishing intercourse with their wives, the religious teachings to which most families adhere may cause the husbands to search for sex in the tearooms. Whatever the causes that turn them unsatisfied from the marriage bed, however, the alternate outlet must be quick, inexpensive and impersonal. Any personal, ongoing affair—any outlet requiring money or hours away from home—would threaten a marriage that is already shaky and jeopardize the most important thing these men possess, their standing as father of their children.

Around the turn of the century, before the vice squads moved in (in their never-ending process of narrowing the behavioral options of those in the lower classes), the Georges of this study would probably have made regular visits to the two-bit bordellos. With a madam watching a clock to limit the time, these cheap whorehouses provided the same sort of fast, impersonal service as today's public restrooms. I find no indication that these men seek homosexual contact as such; rather, they want a form of orgasm-producing action that is less lonely than masturbation and less involving than a love relationship. As the forces of social control deprive them of one outlet, they provide another. The newer form, it should be noted, is more stigmatizing than the previous one.

George was quite affable when interviewed on his home territory. A year before, when I first observed him in the tearoom of a park about three miles from his home he was a far more cautious man. Weighing 200 pounds or more, George has a protruding gut and tattoos on both forearms. Although muscular and in his mid-thirties, he would not be described as a handsome person. For him, no doubt, the aging crisis is also an identity crisis. Only with reluctance—and perhaps never—will he turn to the insertee role. The threat of such a role to his masculine self-image is too great.

Moreover, for men of George's occupational and marital status, there is no network of friends engaged in tearoom activity to help them adapt to the changes aging will bring. I found no evidence of friendship networks among respondents of this type, who enter and leave the restrooms alone, avoiding conversation while within. Marginal to both the heterosexual and homosexual worlds, these men shun involvement in any form of gay subculture. Type I participants report fewer friends of any sort than do those of other classes. When asked how many close friends he has, George answered: "None. I haven't got time for that."

It is difficult to interview the Trade without becoming depressed over the hopelessness of their situation. They are almost uniformly lonely and isolated: lacking success in either marriage bed or work, unable to discuss their three best friends (because they don't have three); en route from the din of factories to the clamor of children, they slip off the freeways for a few moments of impersonal sex in a toilet stall.

TYPE II: AMBISEXUALS

A very different picture emerges in the case of Dwight. As sales manager for a small manufacturing concern, he is in a position to hire men who share his sexual and other interests. Not only does he have a business associate or two who share his predilection for tearoom sex, he has been able to stretch chance meetings in the tearoom purlieu into long-lasting friendships. Once, after I had gained his confidence through repeated interviews, I asked him to name all the participants he knew. The names of five other Type II men in my sample were found in the list of nearly two dozen names he gave me.

Dwight, then, has social advantages in the public restrooms as well as in society at large. His annual income of $16,000 helps in the achievement of these benefits, as does his marriage into a large and distinguished family and his education at a prestigious local college. From his restroom friends Dwight learns which tearooms in the city are popular and where the police are clamping down. He even knows which officers are looking for payoffs and how much they expect to be paid. It is of even greater importance that his attitudes toward—and perceptions of—the tearoom encounters are shaped and reinforced by the friendship network in which he participates.

It has thus been easier for Dwight to meet the changing demands of the aging crisis. He knows others who lost no self-respect when they began "going down" on their sexual partners, and they have helped him learn to enjoy oral sex. Three-fourths of the married participants with independent occupations were observed, at one time or another, participating as insertees in fellatio, compared to only one-third of the Trade.

Dwight is in his early forties and has two sons in high school. The school-bound offspring provide him with an excuse to leave his wife at home during frequent business trips across the country. Maintaining a list of gay contacts, Dwight is able to engage wholeheartedly in the life of the homosexual subculture in other cities—the sort of involvement he is careful to avoid at home. In the parks or over cocktails, he amuses his friends with lengthy accounts of these adventures.

Dwight recounts his first sexual relationship with another boy at the age of "nine or ten:"

> My parents always sent me off to camp in the summer, and it was there that I had my sexual initiation. . . . I suppose I started pretty early. God, I was almost in college before I had my first woman! I always had some other guy on the string in prep school—some real romances there! But I made up for lost time with the girls during my college years.

Culminating an active heterosexual life at the university, Dwight married the girl he had impregnated. He reports having intercourse three or four times a week with her throughout their 18 married years but also admits to supplementing that activity on occasion: "I had the seven-year-itch and stepped out on her quite a bit then." Dwight also visits the tearooms almost daily:

> I guess you might say I'm pretty highly sexed [he chuckled a little], but I really don't think that's why I go to tearooms. That's really not sex. Sex is something I have with my wife in bed. It's not as if I were committing adultery by getting my rocks off—or going down on some guy—in a tearoom. I get a kick out of it. Some of my friends go out for handball. I'd rather cruise the park. Does that sound perverse to you?

Dwight's openness in dealing with the more sensitive areas of his biography was typical of upper-middle and upper-class respondents of both the participant and control samples. Actual refusals of interviews came almost entirely from lower-class participants; more of the cooperating respondents were of the upper socioeconomic ranks. In the same vein, working-class respondents were most cautious about answering questions pertaining to their income and their social and political views. Other researchers have encountered a similar response differential along class lines, and I realize that my educational and social characteristics encourage

THE RESEARCH EXPERIENCE

rapport with Dwight more than with George. Two-thirds of the married participants with occupational independence are college graduates.

Another factor may be operative in this instance: although the upper-class deviants may have more to lose from exposure (in the sense that the mighty have farther to fall), they also have more means at their disposal with which to protect their moral histories. Some need only tap their spending money to pay off a member of the vice squad. In other instances, social contacts with police commissioners or newspaper publishers make it possible to squelch either record or publicity of an arrest. Evidence must be strong to prosecute a man who can hire the best attorneys. Lower-class men are rightfully more suspicious, for they have fewer resources with which to defend themselves if exposed.

This does not mean that Type II participants are immune to the risks of the game but simply that they are bidding from strength. To them, the risks of arrest, exposure, blackmail or physical assault contribute to the excitement quotient. It is not unusual for them to speak of cruising as an adventure, in contrast with the Trade, who engage in a furtive search for sexual relief. On the whole, then, the action of Type II respondents is apt to be somewhat bolder and their search for "kicks" less inhibited than that of most other types of participants.

Dwight is not fleeing from an unhappy home life or sexless marriage to the encounters in the parks. He expresses great devotion to his wife and children: "They're my whole life," he exclaims. All evidence indicates that, as father, citizen, businessman and church member, Dwight's behavior patterns—as viewed by his peers—are exemplary.

Unlike the Trade, Type II participants recognize their homosexual activity as indicative of their own psychosexual orientations. They think of themselves as bisexual or ambisexual and have intellectualized their deviant tendencies in terms of the pseudopsychology of the popular press. They speak often of the great men of history, as well as of certain movie stars and others of contemporary fame, who are also "AC/DC." Not only do they read a great deal about homosexuality, they discuss it within their network of friends. For the Dwights there is subcultural support that enables them to integrate their deviance with the remainder of their lives, while maintaining control over the information that could discredit their whole being. For these reasons they look upon the gaming encounters in the parks as enjoyable experiences.

TYPE III: GAY GUYS

Like the Ambisexuals, unmarried respondents with independent occupations are locked into a strong subculture, a community that provides them with knowledge about the tearooms and reinforcement in their particular brand of deviant activity. This open participation in the gay community distinguishes these single men from the larger group of unmarrieds with dependent occupations. These men take the homosexual role of our society, and are thus the most truly "gay" of all participant types. Except for Tim, who was recruited as a decoy in the tearooms by the vice squad of a police department, Type III participants learned the strategies of the tearooms through friends already experienced in this branch of the sexual market.

Typical of this group is Ricky, a 24 year-old university student whose older male lover supports him. Ricky stands at the median age of his type, who range from 19 to 50 years. Half of them are college graduates and all but one other are at least part-time students, a characteristic that explains their low median income of $3,000. Because Ricky's lover is a good provider, he is comfortably situated in a midtown apartment, a more pleasant residence than most of his friends enjoy.

Ricky is a thin, good-looking young man with certain movements and manners of speech that might be termed effeminate. He is careful of his appearance, dresses well, and keeps an immaculate apartment, furnished with an expensive stereo and some tasteful antique pieces. Seated on a sofa in the midst of the things his lover has provided for their mutual comfort, Ricky is impressively self-assured. He is proud to say that he has found, at least for the time being, what all those participants in his category claim to seek: a "permanent" love relationship.

Having met his love in a park, Ricky returns there only when his mate is on a business trip or their relationship is strained. Then Ricky becomes, as he puts it, "horny,'" and he goes to the park to study, cruise and engage in tearoom sex:

> The bars are o.k.—but a little too public for a "married" man like me. . . . Tearooms are just another kind of action, and they do quite well when nothing better is available.

Like other Type III respondents, he shows little preference in sexual roles. "It depends on the other guy," Ricky says, "and whether I like his looks or not. Some men I'd crawl across the street on my knees for—others I wouldn't piss on!" His aging crisis will be shared with all others in the gay world. It will take the nightmarish form of waning attractiveness and the search for a permanent lover to fill his later years, but it will have no direct relationship with the tearoom roles. Because of his socialization in the homosexual society, taking the insertee role is neither traumatic for him nor related to aging.

Ricky's life revolves around his sexual deviance in a way that is not true of George or even of Dwight. Most of his friends and social contacts are connected with the homosexual subculture. His attitudes toward and rationalization of his sexual behavior are largely gained from this wide circle of friends. The gay men claim to have more close friends than do any other type of control or participant respondents. As frequency of orgasm is reported, this class also has more sex than any other group sampled, averaging 2.5 acts per week. They seeem relatively satisfied with this aspect of their lives and regard their sexual drive as normal—although Ricky perceives his sexual needs as less than most.

The vocabulary of heterosexual marriage is commonly used by those of Ricky's type. They speak of "marrying" the men they love and want to "settle down in a nice home." In a surprising number of cases, they take their lovers "home to meet mother." This act, like the exchange of "pinky rings," is intended to provide social strength to the lover's union.

Although these men correspond most closely to society's homosexual stereotype, they are least representative of the tearoom population, constituting only 14 percent of the participant sample. More than any other type, the Rickys seem at ease with their behavior in the sexual market, and their scarcity in the tearooms is indicative of this. They want personal sex—more permanent relationships—and the public restrooms are not where this is to be found. They find the anonymity of the tearooms suitable for their purposes, but not inviting enough to provide the primary setting for sexual activity.

TYPE IV: CLOSET QUEENS

Another dozen of the 50 participants interviewed may be classified as single deviants with dependent occupations, "closet queens" in homosexual slang. Again, the label may be applied to others who keep their deviance hidden, whether married or single, but the covert, unmarried men are most apt to earn this appellation. With them, we have moved full circle in our classifications, for they parallel the Trade in a number of ways:

1. They have few friends, only a minority of whom are involved in tearoom activity.

2. They tend to play the insertor role, at least until they confront the crisis of aging.

3. Half of them are Roman Catholic in religion.

4. Their median annual income is $6,000; and they work as teachers, postmen, salesmen, clerks—usually for large corporations or agencies.

5. Most of them have completed only high school, although there are a few exceptionally well-educated men in this group.

6. One in six is black.

7. Not only are they afraid of becoming involved in other forms of the sexual market, they share with the Trade a relatively furtive involvement in the tearoom encounters.

Arnold will be used as the typical case. Only 22, Arnold is well below the median age of this group; but in most other respects he is quite representative, particularly in regard to the psychological problems common to Type IV.

A routine interview with Arnold stretched to nearly three hours in the suburban apartment he shares with another single man. Currently employed as a hospital attendant, he has had trouble with job stability, usually because he finds the job unsatisfactory. He frequently is unoccupied.

> *Arnold:* I hang around the park a lot when I don't have anything else to do. I guess I've always known about the tearooms . . . so I just started going in there to get my rocks off. But I haven't gone since I caught my lover there in September. You get in the habit of going; but I don't think I'll start in again—unless I get too desperate.
>
> *Interviewer:* Do you make the bar scene?
>
> *Arnold:* Very seldom. My roommate and I go out together once in a while, but everybody there seems to think we're lovers. So I don't really operate in the bars. I really don't like gay people. They can be so damned bitchy! I really like women better than men—except for sex. There's a lot of the female in me, and I feel more comfortable with women than with men. I understand women and like to be with them. I'm really very close to my mother. The reason I don't live at home is because there are too many brothers and sisters living there. . . .
>
> *Interviewer:* Is she still a devout Roman Catholic?
>
> *Arnold:* Well, yes and no. She still goes to Mass some, but she and I go to seances together with a friend. I am studying astrology and talk it over with her quite a bit. I also analyze handwriting and read a lot about numerology. Mother knows I am gay and doesn't seem to mind. I don't think she really believes it though.

Arnold has a health problem: "heart attacks," which the doctor says are psychological and which take the form of "palpitations, dizziness, chest pain, shortness of breath and extreme weakness." These attacks, which began soon after his father's death from a coronary two years ago, make him feel as if he were "dying and turning cold." Tranquilizers were prescribed for him, "but I threw them out, because I don't like to become dependent on such things." He quoted a book on mental control of health that drugs are "unnecessary, if you have proper control."

He also connects these health problems with his resentment of his father, who was mentally ill:

> *Arnold:* I don't understand his mental illness and have always blamed him for it. You might say that I have a father complex and, along with that, a security complex. Guess that's why I always run around with older men. . . . Nearly all my lovers have been between 30 and 50. The trouble is that *they* always want sex —and sex isn't really what I want. I just want to be with them—to have them for friends. I guess it's part of my father complex. I just want to be loved by an older man.

Few of the Type IV participants share Arnold's preference for older men, although they report poorer childhood relationships with their fathers than do those of any other group. Many closet queens seem to prefer teenage boys as sexual objects. This is one of the features that distinguishes them from all other participant types. Although scarce in tearooms, teenagers make themselves available for sexual activity in other places frequented by closet queens. A number of these men regularly cruise the streets where boys thumb rides each afternoon when school is over. One closet queen from my sample has been arrested for luring boys in their early teens to his home.

Interaction between these men and the youths they seek frequently results in the sort of scandal feared by the gay community. Newspaper reports of molestations usually contain clues of the closet queen style of adaptation of the part of such offenders. Those respondents whose lives had been threatened by teen-age toughs were generally of this type. One of the standard rules governing one-night-stand operations cautions against becoming involved with such "chicken." The frequent violation of this rule by closet queens may contribute to their general disrepute among the bar set of the homosexual subculture, where "closet queen" is a pejorative term.

Arnold expressed loneliness and the need for someone to talk with. "When I can really sit down and talk to someone else," he said, "I begin to feel real again. I lose that constant fear of mine—that sensation that I'm dying."

STYLES OF DEVIANT ADAPTATION

Social isolation is characteristic of Type IV participants. Generally, it is more severe even than that encountered among the Trade, most of whom enjoy at least a vestigial family life. Although painfully aware of their homosexual orientations, these men find little solace in association with others who share their deviant interests. Fearing exposure, arrest, the stigmatization that might result from a participation in the homosexual subculture, they are driven to a desperate, lone-wolf sort of activity that may prove most dangerous to themselves and the rest of society. Although it is tempting to look for psychological explanations of their apparent preference for chicken, the sociological ones are evident. They resort to the more dangerous game because of a lack of both the normative restraints and adult markets that prevail in the more overt subculture. To them, the costs (financial and otherwise) of operating among street corner youths are more acceptable than those of active participation in the gay subculture. Only the tearooms provide a less expensive alternative for the closet queens.

I have tried to make it impossible for any close associate to recognize the real people behind the disguised composites portrayed in this article. But I worked equally hard to enable a number of tearoom players to see themselves in the portrait of George, and others to find their own stories in those of Dwight, Ricky, or Arnold.

My one certainty is that there is no single composite with whom all may identify. It should now be evident that, like other next door neighbors, the participants in tearoom sex are of no one type. They vary along a number of possible continua of social characteristics. They differ widely in terms of sexual career and activity, and even in terms of what that behavior means to them or what sort of needs it may fulfill.

In delineating styles of adaptation, I do not intend to imply that these men are faced with an array of styles from which they may pick one or even a combination. No man's freedom is that great. They have been able to choose only among the limited options offered them by society. These sets of alternatives, which determine the modes of adaption to deviant pressures, are defined and allocated in accordance with major sociological variables: occupation, marital status, age, race, amount of education. That is one meaning of social probability.

B. METHODS:
THE SOCIOLOGIST AS VOYEUR

In the summer of 1965, I wrote a research paper on the subject of homosexuality. After reading the paper, my graduate adviser raised a question, the answer to which was not available from my data or from the literature on sexual deviance: "But where does the average guy go just to get a blow job? That's where you should do your research." I suspected that the answer was "to the tearooms," but this was little more than a hunch. We decided that this area of covert deviant behavior, tangential to the subculture, was one that needed study.

My initial problem was one of locating the more popular tearooms. Once I could find where the "action" was, I knew that potential research subjects would be involved. This is the advantage of studying a population defined only by their participation in a specific sort of interaction. Since this is not a study of "homosexuals" but of participants in homosexual acts, the subjects of this study have but one thing in common: each has been observed by me in the course of a homosexual act in a public park restroom. This is the activity, and these are the actors, that I set out to study in 1965.

OTHER TEAROOMS—OTHER VARIABLES

There are, of course, other tearooms, not located in parks, that might have been studied. Those in the Y's and transportation facilities have

---

Source: Edited version of pp. 16-44 and 167-73 of *Tearoom Trade* (Chicago: Aldine Publishing Co., 1970).

received the greatest publicity. My study, however, has been focused upon the park facilities for two reasons. First, the latter have the greatest notoriety in the homosexual subculture. Second, I wanted to control the ecological and demographic variables as much as possible. All but two of the restrooms in which I conducted systematic observations were of the same floor plan, and all shared common environmental conditions. Of greater importance is the "democratic" nature of outdoor facilities. Parks are much more apt to draw a representative sample of the population.

Although I have made informal observations of tearoom activity in New York, Chicago, St. Louis, Kansas City, Des Moines, Tulsa, Denver, Los Angeles, and San Francisco, the greater part of the research was concentrated in one metropolitan area. One feature of the toilet stalls in the city where my research was concentrated constitutes an important variable: there are no doors on the stalls in the public parks. Signals from the stalls, therefore, are all of the bodily motion variety—gestures of the head or hands. Other variables such as climate, availability of parks, the nature of police surveillance, amount of newspaper publicity accorded offenders, or relative popularity of other sexual outlets could result in wide variations in the volume of tearoom activity. My contention, however, is that the basic rules of the game—and the profile of the players—are applicable to any place in the United States. This much may be said with certainty: there is probably no major city in the nation without its tearooms in current operation.

NEATNESS VERSUS ACCURACY

I employed the methods described herein not because they are the most accurate in the sense of "neatness" or "cleanness" but because they promised the greatest accuracy in terms of faithfulness to people and actions as they live and happen. These are strategies that I judged to be the least obtrusive measures available—the least likely to distort the real world.

My biases are those that Bruyn attributes to the participant observer, who "is interested in people as they are, not as he thinks they ought to be according to some standard of his own."[1] To employ, therefore, any strategies that might distort either the activity observed or the profile of those who engage in it would be foreign to my scientific philosophy and inimical to my purposes.

Some methods, then, have grown quite naturally from the chromosomal messages of a particular "school" of sociology. Others are mutations resulting from interaction with my research environment. As obstacles developed, means were devised to circumvent them. Unusual difficulties call for unusual strategies. Although I have employed a number of "oddball measures," as they are called by Webb and his associates, these research

1. Severyn T. Bruyn, *The Human Perspective in Sociology* (Englewood Cliffs, N.J.: Prentice-Hall, 1966), p. 18.

methods are actually only uncommon applications of such tested measures as physical traces, the running record, and simple observation.[2]

My concern in this study has been with the description of a specific style of deviant behavior and of the population who engage in that activity. I have not attempted to test any prestated hypotheses. Such an approach tends to limit sociological research to the imagery of the physical sciences. Hypotheses should develop *out of* such ethnographic work, rather than provide restrictions and distortions from its inception. Where my data have called for a conceptual framework, I have tried to supply it, sometimes with the help of other social scientists. In those cases where data were strong enough to generate new theoretical approaches, I have attempted to be a willing medium. The descriptive study is important, not only in obtaining objective and systematic knowledge of behavior that is either unknown or taken for granted, but in providing the groundwork for new theoretical development. If the social scientist is to move back and forth between his data and the body of social theory, the path of that movement should not be restricted to a set of predestined hypotheses.

The research in which I engaged, from the summer of 1965 through the winter of 1967-68, may be broken down into two distinct stages, each with its subcategories. The first was an ethnographic or participant-observation stage. This part of the research extended over two years on a part-time basis (I was also involved in graduate study at the time).

The second half involved six months of full-time work in administering interview schedules to more than one hundred respondents and in attempting to interview another twenty-seven. Another year was devoted to analysis of resulting data.

PASSING AS DEVIANT

Like any deviant group, homosexuals have developed defenses against outsiders: secrecy about their true identity, symbolic gestures and the use of the eyes for communication, unwillingness to expose the whereabouts of their meeting places, extraordinary caution with strangers, and admission to certain places only in the company of a recognized person. Shorn of pastoral contacts[3] and unwilling to use professional credentials, I had to enter the subculture as would any newcomer and to make contact with respondents under the guise of being another gay guy.[4]

---

2. Eugene J. Webb and others, *Unobtrusive Measures: Nonreactive Research in the Social Sciences* (Chicago: Rand McNally, 1966). All of these measures are described in some detail in this work.
3. While a seminarian, I was employed for two years in a parish that was known in the homosexual world as a "queen parish"—a place to which the homosexuals could turn for counsel, understanding priests, good music, and worship with an aesthetic emphasis. I soon came to know the gay parishioners and to speak their language.
4. My reticence at admitting I was a sociologist resulted, in part, from the cautioning of a gay friend who warned me that homosexuals in the community are particularly wary of sociologists. This is supposedly the result of the failure of a graduate student at another university to disguise the names of bars and respondents in a master's thesis on this subject.

THE RESEARCH EXPERIENCE

Such entry is not difficult to accomplish. Almost any taxi driver can tell a customer where to find a gay bar. The real problem is not one of making contact with the subculture but of making the contact "stick." Acceptance does not come easy, and it is extremely difficult to move beyond superficial contact in public places to acceptance by the group and invitations to private and semiprivate parties.

On one occasion, for instance, tickets to an after-hours party were sold to the man next to me at a bar. When I asked to buy one, I was told that they were "full up." Following the tip of another customer, I showed up anyway and walked right in. No one questioned my being there. Since my purpose at this point of the field study was simply to "get the feel" of the deviant community rather than to study methods of penetrating its boundaries, I finally tired of the long method and told a friendly potential respondent who I was and what I was doing. He then got me invited to cocktail parties before the annual "drag ball," and my survey of the subculture neared completion.

During those first months, I made the rounds of ten gay bars then operating in the metropolitan area, attended private gatherings and the annual ball, covered the scene where male prostitutes operate out of a coffee house, observed pick-up operations in the parks and streets, and had dozens of informal interviews with participants in the gay society. I also visited the locales where "instant sex" was to be had: the local bathhouse, certain movie theaters, and the tearooms.

From the beginning, my decision was to continue the practice of the field study in passing as deviant. Although this raises questions of scientific ethics, there are good reasons for following this method of participant observation. In the first place, I am convinced that there is only *one* way to watch highly discreditable behavior and that is to pretend to be in the same boat with those engaging in it. The second reason is to prevent distortion. Hypothetically, let us assume that a few men could be found to continue their sexual activity while under observation. How "normal" could that activity be? How could the researcher separate the "show" and the "cover" from standard procedures of the encounter?

SERVING AS WATCHQUEEN

My preliminary observations of tearoom encounters led to the discovery of an essential strategy—the real methodological breakthrough of this research—that involved mobilization of the social organization being observed. The very fear and suspicion encountered in the restrooms produces a participant role, the sexuality of which is optional. This is the role of the lookout ("watchqueen" in the argot), a man who is situated at the door or windows from which he may observe the means of access to the restroom. When someone approaches, he coughs. He nods when the coast is clear or if he recognizes an entering party as a regular.

The lookouts fall into three main types. The most common of these are the "waiters." The others are the masturbaters, who engage in autoerotic behavior while observing sexual acts, and the voyeurs, who appear to derive sexual stimulation and pleasure from watching the others.

In terms of appearances, I assumed the role of the voyeur—a role superbly suited for sociologists and the only lookout role that is not overtly sexual. Before being alerted to the role of lookout by a cooperating respondent, I tried first the role of the straight and then that of the waiter. As the former, I disrupted the action and frustrated my research. As the latter—glancing at my watch and pacing nervously from window to door to peer out—I could not stay long without being invited to enter the action and could only make furtive observation of the encounters. As it was, the waiter and voyeur roles are subject to blurring and I was often mistaken for the former.

By serving as a voyeur-lookout, I was able to move around the room at will, from window to window, and to observe all that went on without alarming my respondents or otherwise disturbing the action. Being a watchqueen enabled me to gather data on the behavioral patterns and also facilitated the linking of participants in homosexual acts with particular automobiles.

During the first year of observations—from April of 1966 to April 1967—my field research notes were made with the aid of a portable tape recorder, concealed under a pasteboard carton on the front seat of my automobile. Research efforts during this time were directed toward comprehensiveness. I attempted to survey all of the active tearooms in one city and to extend my observations, whenever possible, to other communities across the country. My concern was to observe the activity across a representative range of times and places distributing observation time throughout periods of varying activity—and in different parks and different seasons. In all, during the first year, I observed some 120 sexual acts in nineteen different men's rooms in five parks of the one city.

My purpose in this "time and place sampling" was to avoid the research errors outlined by Webb and others—particularly the danger "that the timing of the data collection may be such that a selective population periodically appears before the observer, while another population, equally periodically, engages in the same behavior, but comes along only when the observer is absent. Similarly, the individual's behavior may shift as the hours or days of the week change."[5]

SAMPLING COVERT DEVIANTS

Hooker has noted that homosexuals who lead secret lives are usually available for study "only when caught by law enforcement agents, or when

---

5. Webb and others, *op. cit.*, p. 136.

seeking psychiatric help."[6] To my knowledge, no one has yet attempted to acquire a *representative* sample of *covert* deviants for any sort of research. Following the suggestions of Lee Rainwater, who was my project director, I gathered a sample of the tearoom participants by tracing the license plates of the autos they drove to the parks. My observations had indicated that, with the sole exception of police cars, autos that parked in front of these public restrooms (which, as has been mentioned, are usually isolated from other park facilities) for a quarter of an hour or more invariably belonged to participants in the homosexual encounters. The same is true for cars that appeared in front of two or more such facilities in the course of an hour.

In September of 1966, then, I set about to gather a sample in as systematic a manner as possible under the circumstances. With the help of the tape recorder, I took the license numbers of as many cars during each half-hour period as equalled approximately 10 per cent of the average volume of "likely" autos at that time on that day of the week. At least for the largest park (which represents roughly half of the observed homosexual activity of this sort in the city), the results were fairly representative on a time basis. Random selection cannot be claimed for this sample: because of the pressures of time and possible detection, I was able to record only a portion of the license plates of participating men I saw at any one time, the choice of which to record being determined by the volume and flow of traffic and the position in which the autos were parked.

I also noted, whenever possible, a brief description of both the car and its driver. By means of frequent sorties into the tearooms for observation, each recorded license number was verified as belonging to a man actually observed in homosexual activity inside the facilities. Sometimes the numbers were taped prior to my entrance, in anticipation of what I would find inside. In most cases, however, I observed the activity, left the tearoom, waited in my car for the participants to enter their autos—then recorded the plate numbers and brief descriptions. For each of these men but one I added to the data the role he took in the sexual encounter.

The original sample thus gained was of 134 license numbers, carefully linked to persons involved in the homosexual encounters, gathered from the environs of ten public restrooms in four different parks of a metropolitan area of two million people. With attrition and additions, one hundred participants in the tearoom game were included in the final sample.

SYSTEMATIC OBSERVATION

Before leaving the account of my observation strategies to consider the archival measures employed during the first half of my research, I want to

---

6. Evelyn Hooker, "The Homosexual Community," in *Personality Research* (Copenhagen: Monksgaard, 1962), p. 169.

describe the techniques employed in "tightening up" my data. Following the preliminary observations, I developed a "Systematic Observation Sheet" on which to record my observations. This form helped to assure consistent and thorough recording of the observed encounters. This report sheet includes places for recording the time and place involved; a description of the participants (their age, attire, auto, and role in the encounter); a description of weather and other environmental conditions; a diagram on which movements of the participants could be plotted, along with location of the places of contract and fellatio; as well as a complete description of the progress of the encounters and reactions of the observer.

Such care was taken for several reasons. My first concern has been for objective validity—to avoid distortion of the data either by my presence or my presuppositions. I have also desired to make future replications and comparative studies possible, by being as systematic as possible in recording and gathering data.

Finally, I wanted to make the best of a rather unique opportunity for participant observation. The tearooms are challenging, not only because they present unusual problems for the research but because they provide an extraordinary opportunity for detailed observation. Due to the lack of verbal communication and the consistency of the physical settings, a type of laboratory is provided by these facilities—one in which human behavior may be observed with the control of a number of variables.

THE TALK OUTSIDE

The silence of these sexual encounters confounds such research problems as legitimation of the observer and identification of roles. Despite the almost inviolate silence within the restroom setting, however, away from the scenes where their sexual deviance is exposed—outside the "interaction membrane"—conversation is again possible. Once my car and face had become familiar, I was able to enter into verbal relationships with twelve of the participants, whom I refer to as the "intensive dozen."

After the initial contacts with this intensive dozen, I told them of my research, disclosing my real purpose for being in the tearooms. With the help of some meals together and a number of drinks, all agreed to cooperate in subsequent interviewing sessions. A few of these interviews were taped (only two men were sufficiently unafraid to allow their voices to be recorded on tape—and I don't blame the others) but most were later reconstructed from notes. Apart from the systematic observations themselves, these conversations constitute the richest source of data in the study.

Some may ask why, if cooperating respondents were obtained without the formal interviews, I bothered with the seemingly endless task of acquiring a sample and administering questionnaires—particularly when interviews with the intensive dozen provided such depth to the data. The answer is simple: these men are not representative of the tearoom population. I could engage them in conversation only because they are more overt, less defensive, and better educated than the average participant. Their very willingness to cooperate sets them apart from those they are meant to represent.

ARCHIVAL EVIDENCE

The unobtrusive measures of participant observation and physical traces, combined with a limited use of open-ended interviews for purposes of correction and validation, enabled me to describe the previously unexplored area of tearoom encounters. The preliminary description of the participant population, however, began only after the establishment of a verified sample. For this stage of the study, I turned to archival measures, "the running record."[7]

Identification of the sample was made by using the automobile license registers of the states in which my respondents lived. Fortunately, friendly policemen gave me access to the license registers, without asking to see the numbers or becoming too inquisitive about the type of "market research" in which I was engaged. These registers provided the names and addresses of those in the sample, as well as the brand name and year of the automobiles thus registered. The make of the car, as recorded in the registers, was checked against my transcribed description of each car. In the two cases where these descriptions were contradictory, the numbers were rejected from the sample. Names and addresses were then checked in the directories of the metropolitan area, from which volumes I also acquired marital and occupational data for most of the sample.

Geographic mobility and data gaps plague the researcher who attempts to use the city directory as a source of information. Fortunately, however, new directories had been issued just prior to my need for them. Somewhat to my surprise, I had another advantage due to residential stability on the part of the population under study. Only 17 per cent of the men in the sample were not listed in these directories. Occupational data were not given for 37 per cent of the men (including those not in the directories).

In those few cases where addresses in license registers did not correspond with those in the city and county directories, I took advantage of still another archival source: the telephone company's index of numbers by street addresses, which had been published more recently than either of the other archival sources. By the time my sample had been verified and identified, none of the archival measures employed was over a year old.[8]

---

7. Webb and others, *op. cit.*, pp. 53-87.
8. Because identification of the city in which this research was conducted might result in pressure being brought to bear on law enforcement agencies or respondents, it has been necessary for me to omit references to the archival volumes used. The name of the city, county, or state appears in the title of each of these sources.

For fear of eliminating variables that might profitably be studied at a later date, I did not scrub from my sample those for whom the archives provided no marital or occupational data. These men, I felt, might represent either a transient or secretive portion of tearoom participants, the exclusion of which would have distorted the population.

A VIEW FROM THE STREETS

Having gained addresses for every person in my sample, I spent a Christmas vacation on the streets and highways recording a description of every residence and neighborhood represented in the sample. The first purpose of this survey of homes was to acquire descriptions of the house types and dwelling areas that, when combined with occupational data gleaned from the archives, would enable me to use Warner's Index of Status Characteristics (I. S. C.) for a socioeconomic profile of my population.[9] Generally speaking, this attempt was not successful: job classifications were too vague and large city housing units too difficult to rank by Warner's criteria.

As physical evidence, however, homes provide a source of data about a population that outweighs any failure they may have as a status index. Swing sets and bicycles in the yards indicate that a family is not childless. A shrine to Saint Mary suggests that the resident is Roman Catholic in religious identification. Christmas decorations bespeak at least a nominal Christian preference. A boat or trailer in the driveway suggests love of the outdoor life. "For Rent" signs may indicate the size of an average apartment and in some cases, the price. The most important sign, however, was the relative "neatness" of the house and grounds.

OBTRUSIVE MEASURES

Realizing that the majority of my participant sample were married—and nearly all of them quite secretive about their deviant activity—I was faced with the problem of how to interview more than the nine willing respondents. Formal interviews of the sample were part of the original research design. The little I knew about these covert deviants made me want to know a great deal more. Here was a unique population just waiting to be studied—but I had no way to approach them.

About this time, fortunately, I was asked to develop a questionnaire for a social health survey of men in the community, which was being conducted by a research center with which I had been a research associate. Such interview schedules would provide nearly all the information I would want on the men in my sample: family background, socioeconomic factors, personal

9. See W. Lloyd Warner and others, *Social Class in America* (Chicago: Science Research Associates, 1949).

health and social histories, religious and employment data, a few questions on social and political attitudes, a survey of friendship networks, and information on marital relationships and sex.

With the permission of the director of the research project, I added my deviant sample to the over-all sample of the survey, making certain that only one trusted, mature graduate student and I made all the interviews of my respondents. Thus legitimized, we set out to interview. Using a table of random numbers, I randomized my sample, so that its representativeness would not be lost in the event that we should be unable to complete all 100 interviews.

None of the respondents was threatened by the interviews. My master list was kept in a safe-deposit box. Each interview card, kept under lock and key, was destroyed with completion of the schedule. No names or other identifying tags were allowed to appear on the questionnaires. Although I recognized each of the men interviewed from observation of them in the tearooms, there was no indication that they remembered me. I was careful to change my appearance, dress, and automobile from the days when I had passed as deviant. I also allowed at least a year's time to lapse between the original sampling procedure and the interviews.

This strategy was most important—both from the standpoint of research validity and ethics—because it enabled me to approach my respondents as normal people, answering normal questions, as part of a normal survey. They *are* part of a larger sample. Their being interviewed is not stigmatizing, because they compromise but a small portion of a much larger sample of the population in their area. They were not put on the spot about their deviance, because they were not interviewed as deviants.

The attrition rate for these interviews was high, but not discouragingly so. Attempts were made at securing seventy-five interviews, fifty of which were completed. Thirty-five per cent were lost by attrition, including 13 per cent who refused to cooperate in the interviews.

Because of the preinterview data obtained by the archival and observational research previously described, it was possible to learn a great deal even from the losses. As should be expected, the remaining men, with whom interviews were completed, are slightly overrepresentative of the middle and upper classes; they are suburbanites, more highly educated men. Those who were lost represent a more transient group (the most common reason for loss was that the subject had moved and left no forwarding address), employed in manual jobs. From preinterview information it was learned that the largest single occupational class in the sample was the truck drivers. Only two members of this class remained among those interviewed.

The refusals also indicated some biases. These men, when pinpointed on a map, clustered around the Italian and working class German areas of the city. Of the ten lost in this manner, three had Italian names and five bore names of distinctly Germanic origin.

Once these interviews were completed, preparations could be made for the final step of the research design. From names appearing in the randomly selected sample of the over-all social health survey, fifty men were selected, matched with the completed questionnaires on the following four characteristics: I. S. C. occupational category, race, area of the metropolitan region in which the party resided, and marital status. The loss here was not from refusals or lost addresses but from those who, when interviewed, failed to correspond with the expected characteristics for matching. Our procedure, in those cases, was simply to move on to another name in the larger sample.

There were a number of open-ended questions in the interview schedules, but the majority included a wide range of precoded answers, for the sake of ease in interviewing and economy in analysis. In addition, the interviewers were trained to make copious marginal notes and required to submit a postinterview questionnaire with each schedule. The median time required for administering the interview schedules did not differ greatly between the two samples: one hour for the deviants, fifty-five minutes for the "straights." Even the days of the week when respondents were interviewed showed little variation between the two samples: Sunday, Tuesday, and Saturday, in that order, were the more popular days.

SUMMARY

From a methodological standpoint, the value of this research is that it has employed a variety of methods, uniting the systematic use of participant observation strategies with other nonreactive measures such as physical traces and archives. The exigencies of research in a socially sensitive area demanded such approaches; and the application of unobtrusive measures yielded data that call, in turn, for reactive methods.

Research strategies do not develop *ex nihilo*. In part, they are the outgrowth of the researcher's basic assumptions. Special conditions of the research problem itself also exercise a determining influence upon the methods used. This discussion has been an attempt to indicate how my ethnographic assumptions, coupled with the difficulties inhering in the study of covert deviants and their behavior, have given rise to a set of strategies.

With the help of "oddball" measures, the outlines of the portrait of participants in the homosexual encounters of the tearooms appeared. Reactive strategies were needed to fill in the distinguishing features. They are human, socially patterned features; and it is doubtful that any one method could have given them the expressive description they deserve.

POSTSCRIPT: A QUESTION OF ETHICS

So long as we suspect that a method we use has at least *some* potential for harming others, we are in the extremely awkward position of having to weigh the scientific and social benefits of that procedure against its possible costs in human discomfort.[10]

In the article from which I have quoted, Erikson develops an argument against the use of disguises in gaining entrance to social situations to which the researcher would otherwise be denied admission. My research in tearooms required such a disguise. Does it, then, constitute a violation of professional ethics?

Antecedent to Erikson's focus on *methods,* there is a larger question: Are there, perhaps, some areas of human behavior that are not fit for social scientific study at all? Should sex, religion, suicide, or other socially sensitive concerns be omitted from the catalogue of possible fields of sociological research? At first glance, few would answer yes to this question. Nevertheless, several have suggested to me that I should have avoided this research subject altogether.

Concern about "professional integrity," it seems to me, is symptomatic of a dying discipline. Let the clergy worry about keeping their cassocks clean; the scientist has too great a responsibility for such compulsions! This is not to say that I am unconcerned about the inquirer's ethics in regard to the protection of his research subjects. Quite to the contrary, I believe that preventing harm to his respondents should be the *primary* interest of the scientist. We are not, however, protecting a harassed population of deviants by refusing to look at them.

SITUATION ETHICS

If it be granted, then, that the sociologist may commit a grave ethical violation by ignoring a problem area, we may consider the methods that should be used in such studies. Let it be noted that any conceivable method employable in the study of human behavior has at least some potential for harming others. Even the antiseptic strategies involved in studying public archives may harm others if they distort, rather than contribute to, the understanding of social behavior. Criminologists may study arrest statistics, as filtered to us through the FBI, without stirring from the safety of their study chairs, but such research methods may result in the creation of a fictitious "crime wave," a tide of public reaction, and the eventual production of a police state—all because the methods may distort reality.

As I learned during the time I administered examinations in Christian Ethics to candidates for the priesthood, questions that arise in regard to means are always relative. There are no "good" or "bad" methods—only "better" or "worse" ones. Neither interview schedules nor laboratory experiments nor participant observation can be neatly classified as involving either

---

10. Kai T. Erikson, "A Comment on Disguised Observation in Sociology," *Social Problems,* Vol. 14, No. 4 (Spring, 1967), p. 368.

"open" or "disguised" approaches. I have never known an interviewer to be completely honest with his respondents; were this so, the whole concern with constructing an "effective" questionnaire could be dropped. Neither does any researcher ever have adequate insight for a perfect representation of his identity; it is always a matter of greater or lesser misrepresentation.

The problems facing researchers, then, are of which methods may result in more or less misrepresentation of purposes and identity, more or less betrayal of confidence, and more or less positive or negative consequences for the subjects. Those who engage in the study of deviant behavior—or any behavior, for that matter—must become accustomed to the process of weighing possible social benefits against possible cost in human discomfort. Erikson describes this process as "awkward," and I shall call it "awful" in the sense of being awe-inspiring. The researcher must also keep in mind that no method can ever be completely safe for himself or his respondents, and thus must weigh it in relation to others that may be applied in any instance. The ethics of social science are situation ethics.

PROBLEMS OF MISREPRESENTATION

At the conclusion of his article, Erikson proposes two rules regarding misrepresentation of the researcher's identity and purposes:

> It is unethical for a sociologist to *deliberately misrepresent* his identity for the purpose of entering a private domain *to which he is not otherwise eligible.*
> It is unethical for a sociologist to *deliberately misrepresent* the character of the research in which he is engaged.[11]

Since one's identity within the interaction membrane of the tearoom is represented only in terms of the participant role he assumes, there is no misrepresentation of my part as an observer: I was indeed a "voyeur," though in the sociological and not the sexual sense. My role was primarily that of watchqueen, and that role I played well and faithfully. In that setting, then, I misrepresented my identity no more than anyone else. Furthermore, my activities were intended to gain entrance not to "a private domain" but to a public restroom. The only sign on its door said "Men," which makes me quite eligible for entering. It should be clear, then, that I have not violated Erikson's first canon. Although passing as deviant to avoid disrupting the behavior I wished to observe, I did not do so to achieve copresence in a private domain.

The second rule may be applied to the reactive part of my research, when I interviewed persons I had observed in the tearooms under the pretext of a social health survey. Here it should be noted that all interviews were in fact made as part of a larger social health survey, and abstracted data from

---

11. Erikson, "Disguised Observation in Sociology," p. 373. Italics mine.

my interviews are already in use in that study. The problem then may be viewed in two ways: First, I gave less than full representation of what I was doing, though without giving false representation. I wore only one of two possible hats, rather than going in disguise. Second, I made multiple use of my data. Is it unethical to use data that someone has gathered for purposes one of which is unknown to the respondent? With the employment of proper security precautions, I think such multiple use is quite ethical; it is frequently employed by anyone using such data banks as the records of the Bureau of Census.

PROBLEMS OF CONFIDENTIALITY

It should be apparent to readers of this treatise that I have taken every possible precaution to protect the identities of my respondents and the confidential nature of their communication with me. I have guarded the names and addresses in my sample and used only strategies that would safe-guard all identities. I even allowed myself to be jailed rather than alert the police to the nature of my research, thus avoiding the incrimination of respondents through their possible association with a man under surveillance.

In writing this report, I have exercised great care to conceal all identifying tags. This is not always an easy task when one is also concerned with avoiding distortion of his data, but it is an essential one. The question I have always asked in this connection is: Could the respondent still recognize himself without having any others recognize him? I may have failed in a few cases to meet the first part of this standard, but I am confident that I could not have failed to meet the second.

PROBLEMS OF CONSEQUENTIALITY

Finally, I must weigh the possible results of this research. It is not enough to plead that I am no seer, for I am a sociologist and should have some ability for prediction. If I have been honest enough in my analyses and convincing enough in their presentation, there should be no negative reaction from the forces of social control. I should hope they would have learned something. Perhaps some will move to construct and situate restrooms in such a way as to discourage the tearoom trade. Except where such activity constitutes an obvious public nuisance, I hope there will be no change in the tearoom scene. There is no need to drive this harmless activity underground. Those who deal in the sex market are resourceful, however, and I doubt that anything short of a total police state could erase the search for sex without commitment.

Others have suggested that I have produced an "operation manual for tearoom queens." If it is a good manual, perhaps I should be flattered, but that is not my purpose or concern. Those who know the game do not need a manual. As for the possibility of its use by potential deviants, I can only say that the world is filled with operation manuals, and people are selective as to which ones they use. I have little interest in manuals that would guide me in building a sailboat, and those who are not interested in engaging in homo-erotic activity will not use this manual as a rule book.

I doubt that this work will have any effect in either increasing or decreasing the volume of homosexual activity in park restrooms. I do hope it will give readers a better understanding of the activity that is already there. I have no moral or intellectual objection to what goes on in the tearooms, and only a mild aesthetic one. I do have a moral objection to the way in which society reacts to those who take part in that action. As a scientist, I must believe that any addition to knowledge, which has suffered as little distortion as possible from the methods used, will help correct the superstition and cruelty that have marked such reaction in the past.

Charles C. Moskos, Jr. _____

A. ATTITUDES TOWARD POLITICAL INDEPENDENCE

INTRODUCTION

West Indian demands for a greater measure of self-government associated with ill-defined aspirations for national independence can be traced
back to the nineteenth century. After Canada was federated in the 1860's
there was considerable popular discussion in the British Empire regarding
the possibility of establishing an Imperial Federation complete with an
imperial parliament—the forerunner of sentiments leading to the establishment of the Commonwealth—and these notions reached the West Indies.
When a staunch imperialist and anti-reform Oxford Professor of History
arrived for a visit in Trinidad in the late eighties he was dismayed to find that
popular orators "did their best to imitate the fine phrases of the apostles of
liberty in Europe."[1] After his arrival in Jamaica, he noted caustically that
Mr. Gladstone's government had recently revived representative government
in the colony and had placed the franchise so low " . . . as to include
practically every negro peasant who possessed a hut and a garden." "It is
therefore assumed and understood," he wrote with considerable exaggera-
tion of the sentiment for self-government present at that time, "to have been
no more than an initial step towards passing over the management of
Jamaica to the black constituencies."[2]

Source: Abridged from Charles C. Moskos, Jr., "Attitudes toward Political Independence,"
in Wendell Bell (Ed.), *The Democratic Revolution in the West Indies* (Cambridge, Mass.:
Schenkman Publishing, 1967), pp. 49-67.

It should be noted that I have occasionally followed the text of Wendell Bell's and Ivar
Oxaal's summary of my research in *Decisions of Nationhood: Political and Social Development
in the British Caribbean* (Denver, Colo.: Social Science Foundation, University of Denver,
1964), pp. 15-24.

1. James Anthony Froude, *The English in the West Indies*, London: Longmans, Green, and
   Co., 1888, p. 76. The British Governor in Trinidad at the time was more sympathetic, and
   Froude discovered that "responsible government" was an open topic for table talk at Government House.
2. *Ibid.*, p. 179.

Although things would not move so quickly, "the fine phrases of the apostles of liberty in Europe" had indeed taken root in the West Indies and continued to stir the nationalist imaginations of at least a few local apostles of liberty. These were chiefly middle-class men, some of whom came into their own after World War I in Trinidad where a revered local white man of Corsican descent, Captain Andrew A. Cipriani, emerged as the colony's foremost labor leader and elected politician. By 1932 an area-wide conference had been held by West Indian political reformists on the island of Dominica and a program for constitutional progress toward self-government and federation was announced. This generation of middle-class gradualists, operating on a limited franchise and without benefit of large-scale, organized, lower-class support, was overtaken by the dramatic social convulsions which rocked the West Indies in the 1930's. A fiery immigrant from the nearby island of Grenada named Uriah Butler led labor demonstrations in the Trinidad oilfields and staged a hunger march on Port of Spain. Rioting broke out on the sugar estates in British Guiana and spread up the Leeward and Windward chains. Powerful trade unions and a new set of nationalist militants appeared almost overnight in Jamaica, where Alexander Bustamante and Norman W. Manley emerged as powerful leaders. It was a time of warning from the West Indies to the Colonial Office.

The Colonial Office began to heed that warning. Although the Second World War delayed action, the end of the war emergency and the accession of Labour to power in Britain placed Dominion status for a federated West Indies within reach. As was shown earlier, the road to independence which began with the 1947 Montego Bay conference was a long one and has led—up to the present—not to political federation but to the emergence of four new nations and some uncertain "orphans" in the Leewards and Windwards.

It is by no means obvious why the major political thrust in the West Indies since the late 1930's should have been in the direction of self-government. The West Indies had been under British rule for so long, and exposed to Britain's cultural penetration to such an extent, that even such militant early nationalists as Cipriani frequently coupled their demands for political reform with sincere expressions of fealty to the Crown. There was little hatred of the British in the West Indies; indeed, many of the educated colored colonials acquired the air, manner, and accents of cultivated British gentlemen—and so they were. These celebrated "black Englishmen" who emerged in the West Indies may have struck the experienced (and biased) observer as caricatures of the real article, but they did not view themselves as such.

The black Englishman, however, was only one manifestation of a long historical process that exposed and acculturated the descendants of slaves and indentured laborers to European values. As will be shown here, Enlightenment values in the form of an interesting and felicitous mixture of bourgeois liberalism and labor radicalism had become the ideological and political master trend in the West Indies. These were the societal values which impelled the independence movement in the West Indies.[3] Moreover, these values were the motivating force not only of the independence movement *per se*, but were of the utmost importance in the discussions and calculations underlying the other big decisions of nationhood. They frequently tended to set narrow limitations on the range of policy alternatives which could be seriously entertained by the West Indian nationalists in power. That is to say, the goal of national independence was part of a general system of values which included conceptions of what constituted a proper form of government, its relationship to other institutions, the nature of a just society, and so forth.

Men and groups differ in the degree of clarity, commitment and consensus with which they adhere to such values, and it is my purpose in this chapter to show how differences in the commitment to national independence for the West Indies were correlated with differences in individual attitudes toward Enlightenment values as well as social background characteristics. I examine in this article, then, the factors that led certain members of a colonial society to question the old order and eventually to take steps that would bring about a dismantlement of an empire, and others to look on with alarm at this course of events, and still others to accept the changing order without being personally committed to it.

BASIC DATA

The data reported here are from interviews with 112 top leaders in Jamaica, Trinidad and Tobago, (then) British Guiana, and in a sample from the smaller islands: Barbados, Grenada, and Dominica.[4] All told, these six territories account for well over 90 per cent of the population and land area of the British West Indies. The leaders who were interviewed constituted, with a few exceptions, the most important decision-makers in their respective territories.

To locate such national leaders, a modified "snow ball" technique was used. Initially, persons in a cross-section of institutional sectors were selected who, on the basis of their formal roles or institutional positions, were likely to be top leaders. They were asked to identify individuals whom they considered to wield national influence. As the nominations of the national leaders accumulated, the most frequently mentioned persons were in turn asked to identify other influentials. In this way, the original positional approach gave

---

3. Space does not permit an examination of the historical process that led to the state of affairs described here. In the following discussion attention is focused on the value *outcomes* of that process.

4. This section constitutes in part a brief summary of some of the data collected by Moskos, "The Sociology of Political Independence: A Study of Influence, Social Structure, and Ideology in the British West Indies," unpublished Ph.D. dissertation, University of California, Los Angeles, 1963.

way to a reputational approach, and the list of reputed national leaders was increasingly refined. The same procedure was used in each of the territories, so that comparability between the units was insured.

None of the West Indian leaders so selected and identified refused to be interviewed and, when the field research had been completed, each leader had been questioned at some length about, among other things, the issues discussed here. These leaders were interviewed during late 1961 and early 1962, and included in each territory the Premier, the most influential Cabinet members, top leaders of the opposition party (ies), heads of labor unions, wealthy merchants, large plantation owners, and newspaper editors. Also interviewed were leading members of the clergy, educationists, leaders of voluntary organizations, prominent professionals, and high-ranking civil servants.

Although the West Indies Federation disintegrated and there are now four new or emergent nations in the British Caribbean instead of one, a similar pattern runs through them and the meanings of their "nationalisms" are much the same. Thus, West Indian nationalism here is viewed as turning upon the question of the desire for political independence *per se,* rather than upon the size of the unit—the entire West Indies or some particular territory within it—for which independence was desired.

A NATIONALIST TYPOLOGY

As might have been expected, there was considerable disagreement among these West Indian leaders over the desirability of political independence, and while that disagreement to a great extent was correlated with the basic cleavages in the social structure, it was more closely associated with the broader values of individuals regardless of social position. From a content analysis of the respondents' attitudes and activities regarding political independence, three basic types were identified: *colonialists, acquiescing nationalists,* and *true nationalists.*

Colonialists were those leaders who opposed political independence for the West Indies in the present or future and favored an indefinite continuation of colonial rule. Usually, however, they did not express such sentiment publicly because of their belief that theirs was a lost cause, that independence was inevitable and that the climate of opinion was hostile to such views. There were exceptions to this posture of colonialist political disaffiliation, particularly in British Guiana where colonialists openly espoused an anti-independence position.

Acquiescing nationalists were differentiated into three sub-types. Some were found to be *reluctant nationalists* because, while they expressed a desire for political independence as a long-range goal, they disavowed it for the near future. They temporized by saying, for example, that the West Indies were not ready for independence, that economic development should come first and that the people lacked political maturity. They were not prepared, however, to form an open opposition to the nationalist movement but expressed the notion that events were moving too quickly. Another acquiescing group were the *dutiful nationalists,* leaders motivated to aid the nationalist movement out of a sense of *noblesse oblige.* Some of these men were mavericks from the traditional upper classes who did not view political independence as desirable but who nonetheless were willing to bend with the "inevitable" by using their skills and influence to alleviate the strains of the transition from colony to independent nation-state. A third acquiescing type was identified, the *opportunistic nationalists* who, although privately opposed to independence, publicly engaged in pro-independence activity in the belief that they would gain personally by doing so.

True nationalists were defined as those leaders who favored immediate independence and who backed their expressed convictions by open support of the nationalist cause, including such activities as membership in nationalist parties, public speaking, and pamphleteering in favor of independence.

The distribution of these types among the top West Indian leaders was as follows:

Nationalist Types		Percentage
True nationalists		39
Acquiescing nationalist:		25
Reluctant	11	
Dutiful	5	
Opportunistic	9	
Colonialists		36
Total (112 cases)		100

Slightly more than one-third each of the West Indian leaders were either true nationalists or colonialists. The remainder, one-fourth of the total, were acquiescing nationalists. These findings can be viewed in either of two ways. From one perspective, much less than a majority of the West Indian elites were genuinely committed to political independence. But the apparently low number of true nationalists may be a result of the narrow definition of this type which involved private as well as open support for immediate political independence. Thus, by keeping in mind the acquiescing nationalists, it can be said that close to two-thirds of the leaders exhibited some amount of pro-independence sentiment.

From analysis not shown here, it was found that the individual configurations of background traits, attitudes, and activities relating to political independence were markedly similar among the West Indian leaders regardless of locality. For this reason, we treat the West Indies as a whole and group the various territories together in the presentation of the findings.

EFFECTS OF SOCIAL BACKGROUND CHARACTERISTICS

As one would expect, variation in three nationalist types was correlated, although never perfectly, with the social backgrounds of the West Indian leaders. The relative frequency of selected social characteristics among the nationalist types is given in Table 1.

The colonialists were generally very well off economically, being found chiefly among the more prosperous planters and merchants. Because economic status is associated with skin color in the West Indies, most whites and near whites were also found to be colonialists. In contrast to the true nationalists, colonialists were statistically likely to be older, to adhere most closely to Anglo-European styles of life, and to have been educated to the secondary-school level rather than having received more or less education. True nationalists, on the other hand, were younger, tended toward a more provincial middle-class West Indian variant of European life styles, and were

TABLE 1
Types of Nationalists by Selected Social Background Characteristics

Selected Characteristics	Percentages of West Indian Leaders Who Were:			
	Colonialists	Acquiescing Nationalists	True Nationalists	Total
Age				
60 and over	54	34	12	100 (24)
50 to 59	47	23	30	100 (36)
40 to 49	23	23	54	100 (35)
39 and under	12	23	65	100 (17)
Education				
College or higher	32	19	49	100 (37)
Secondary school	38	32	30	100 (57)
Elementary only	28	22	50	100 (18)
Personal Wealth				
Wealthy	66	21	13	100 (39)
Not wealthy	20	27	53	100 (73)
Color and Ethnicity				
White	59	23	18	100 (39)
Light brown	35	35	30	100 (20)
East Indian and Chinese	42	33	25	100 (12)
Dark brown and black	12	20	68	100 (41)
Institutional Sector				
Political or labor	6	25	69	100 (48)
Economic	76	18	6	100 (34)
Mass media	25	50	25	100 (8)
Civil service	13	50	37	100 (8)
Other*	57	14	29	100 (14)
Life Style				
Anglo-European	42	32	26	100 (62)
West Indian	27	16	57	100 (49)

*Includes religious personages, free professionals, educationists, and heads of voluntary organizations.

Note: Number of cases on which percentages are based is given in parentheses.

THE RESEARCH EXPERIENCE

likely to have either a university degree or an education not extending beyond elementary school. Moreover, the true nationalists were typically dark brown or black (and East Indian in British Guiana) and leaders of mass-based organizations such as trade unions or political parties. The true nationalists, therefore, included relatively few members of the traditional white oligarchy but at the same time their numbers were not overly reflective of a basically lower-class origin.[5]

Acquiescing nationalists tended to have intermediate background characteristics, although they were notably persons who occupied important positions in governmental service or in the mass media. Many of the opportunistic nationalists among the acquiescing type were old-style colonial politicians who apparently were not leading so much as they were following the crowd down the path toward independence.

EFFECTS OF ECONOMIC IDEOLOGIES

More highly correlated with the nationalist types than the above social background characteristics were the economic ideologies of the leaders. We classified the leaders into five categories according to their views on the proper role of the government in the economy of their territories: *reactionaries*—those who thought the state's role should be about what it was before the rise of the nationalist movements and should not extend beyond providing basic services such as a postal system, roads, police and fire protection; *conservatives*—those who wished to maintain the present situation, with the state in addition to providing basic services also being responsible for welfare schemes for the ill, aged, and unemployed, for public works, and for a general educational system, but with the reservations that taxation should be less discriminatory against the entrepreneurial class and that government should be less protective of labor union interests; *populists*—those who lacked long-range economic policies, and who were pragmatically concerned with immediate bread and butter issues, although accepting a belief in a market economy geared to the demands of labor unions or mass-based political organizations; *liberals*—those who wanted greater intervention of the government in the economy, but who did not foresee radical changes beyond the achievement of modern welfare capitalism; and the *radicals*—those who advocated fundamental changes in the present system so that the state would become the major factor in determining local

---

5. Interestingly, this was not true of the early leaders of the nationalist movement in Trinidad. Cipriani, as true a West Indian nationalist as there has been, was born into the local white elite. Uriah Butler, who came after Cipriani as the prophet of independence, was incurably proletarian in behavior and outlook. Fragmentary reports indicate, however, that most of their lieutenants were not generally unlike the profile of contemporary nationalists reported here.

economic life, with the extreme radicals seeking the abolishment of all private property.

The distribution of these economic ideologies among the nationalist types is reported below:

Economic Ideologies	Percentages of West Indian Leaders Who Were:				Number of Cases
	Colonialists	Acquiescing Nationalists	True Nationalists	Total	
Reactionaries	86	14	0	100	(22)
Conservatives	58	42	0	100	(33)
Populists	18	36	46	100	(11)
Liberals	0	28	72	100	(25)
Radicals	0	0	100	100	(21)

The above table shows an unmistakable connection between nationalist behavior and economic ideologies. Among West Indian leaders, "Left" economic ideologies went with true nationalism and "Right" economic ideologies went with support for the colonial system: all of the radicals were true nationalists, and none of the reactionaries or conservatives were. Moreover, the acquiescing nationalists tended to be concentrated in the intermediate economic ideologies.

These data illustrate what was quite evident in the interviews with the West Indian leaders: the nationalists wanted political change not so much as an end in itself, but as a means to greater economic growth and to distributional reforms by governmental action—to be controlled by the new elite. From its onset, the independence movement had been motivated not simply by a desire for political independence, but by the desire and demand for economic and social progress as well. And it was seen that this progress could not be achieved without a substantial departure from the narrow economic horizons and aspirations of the planter and merchant.

It was true, as conservative critics of the independence movement had argued, that political change in itself would not alleviate the poverty and stagnation of the West Indies economy, but for the nationalists this meant that political power had to be exercised to stimulate economic development. The only way in which the complacency of the traditional colonial economic oligarchy could be ended, it was believed, was by mass political action and by winning control of local governmental machinery. Political change and economic reform were intimately linked in the minds of the nationalists and, once they had achieved power during the terminal phases of colonial rule, they discovered that their promises of economic progress could be dis-charged—at least to a considerable degree. In the 1950's Jamaican nation-alists under Norman W. Manley stimulated a tremendous increase in economic growth, and economic indicators under the new nationalist government launched by Dr. Eric Williams in Trinidad in 1956 showed a similar sharp rise. Moreover, once in power, nationalist politicians found practical reinforcement for their electoral claims that greater local political autonomy would breed greater economic opportunities. "We became increasingly eager to end colonial rule," a Trinidad nationalist politician said, "after we had gotten into office. We repeatedly found that so many of the things we wanted to do were hampered by our political status as a colony." Thus, the West Indian nationalist movement in power found that political power was indeed instrumental to the achievement of its overall economic objectives and this provided an important fillip to bringing independence aspirations to their culmination.

EFFECTS OF ENLIGHTENMENT VALUES

It would be a mistake, however, to view the preceding table as suggesting that adherence to programmatic economic philosophies in the narrow sense was the ideological mainspring of the independence movement. For the goals of the true nationalists went far beyond increasing the role of government in the economy. In fact, the most distinctive trait among the nationalist leaders was their overwhelming commitment to reorganize West Indian society in such a far-reaching fashion as to achieve many of the higher ideals of Western civilization. Indeed, the course of nationalism in the West Indies seems to have recapitulated some of the ideological currents that brought about the rise of nationalism in Western Europe and that underlay the ethical principles of the French, American, and Russian revolutions.

To document this thesis, we use as points of reference attitudinal items which, although having roots deep in the past, were specific outgrowths of a common philosophical tradition—the Enlightenment.[6] There were, of course, many strains in the Enlightenment, not all of which were necessarily consistent, but the principal feature of the Enlightenment was its radical approach to what constituted the Good Society. Basically, the thought of the Enlightenment consisted of a belief in the possibility of progress, the use of reason, skepticism of the old order, the equality of man, the removal of inherited privilege, and a faith in men collectively to govern themselves under democratic procedures.

This general intellectual movement culminated politically in the *rights of man* embodied in the French Revolutionary slogan: *liberté, égalité,*

---

6. Since the realization that the attitudinal measures used were tapping Enlightenment values came rather late during the data collection, it was not possible to obtain data on other facets of these value patterns. Thus, the present Index of Enlightenment is limited to the rights-of-man dimension of the Enlightenment. Other dimensions could have been included such as measures of belief in progress, in the efficacy of reason, and in the potentiality of man to transform and develop himself.

fraternité. These ideals were codified in such documents as the American Declaration of Independence, the Bill of Rights in the Constitution of the United States, and the French Declaration of the Rights of Man and of the Citizen. Three of the items covered in the interviews with the West Indian leaders—attitudes toward political democracy, egalitarianism, and social inclusiveness—can be paired with their equivalents embodied in the rights of man. That is, "liberty" corresponds to political democracy, "equality" is egalitarianism, and "fraternity" comes close to our meaning of social inclusiveness.

Attitudes toward political democracy were measured by asking the leaders if they thought the democratic form of government was the best suited for their territory, the referent being a British parliamentary type of government based on universal adult suffrage with guarantees for the maintenance of civil rights. Of all the leaders interviewed, half said that they did not think the democratic form was desirable, or else expressed major misgivings about it. They were termed "non-democrats," while leaders who believed that the democratic form was most suitable for their home territories without qualification were called "democrats."

The concept of equality used here refers primarily to equality of opportunity, to the desire for a society within which each individual would be able to advance according to his capabilities. The measurement of attitudes toward equality was based on responses to a probe following the question concerning attitudes toward democracy. If the leaders revealed that equality of opportunity or the classless society were part of their images of the Good Society, then they were classified "egalitarian." If no such images, or if contrary images, were expressed, then the leaders were classified "inegalitarian." Thus, democrats and non-democrats could be either egalitarian or inegalitarian.

The concept of social inclusiveness or fraternity refers to the attitudes persons have toward interaction with other persons. It is akin to notions of low social distance and comradeship, the social inclusivist favoring contact between groups and individuals that transcend whatever barriers there may be, such as those based on racial, religious, or class differences. Social inclusiveness was operationalized by measuring the attitudes of West Indian leaders toward reducing social barriers between groups *within* their societies as compared to their attitudes toward increasing their contact with persons *outside* of the West Indies. Leaders who placed high priority on eliminating internal social barriers were termed "inclusivists." Contrariwise, persons who placed secondary emphasis on reducing internal social barriers or who favored the perpetuation of such social distinctions within their societies were designated "exclusivists."

On the basis of these three indicators of the rights of man, an Index of Enlightenment was constructed by adding together attitudes toward political democracy, egalitarianism, and social inclusiveness. Each of these attitudes was dichotomized in such a way as to separate out the most intense commitment to the Rights of Man. Democrats included only those who expressed no reservations on the suitability of parliamentary democracy and public liberties for their territory; egalitarians affirmed their desire for a society based on equal opportunities in an open-ended question; and social inclusivists gave higher priority to reducing social barriers among members of their own societies than they did to increasing external contact. Thus, a maximum score of three on the Index of Enlightenment was possible only if a West Indian leader was a democrat, an egalitarian, and an inclusivist. Similarly, a leader would obtain a score of zero on this Index if he was a non-democrat, an inegalitarian, and an exclusivist.

TABLE 2
Types of Nationalists by an Index of Enlightenment

| Index of Enlightenment* | Percentages of West Indian Leaders Who Were: | | | |
	Colonialists	Acquiescing Nationalists	True Nationalists	Total
High 3 (enlightened)	0	0	100	100 (29)
2	0	22	78	100 (18)
1	25	71	4	100 (24)
Low 0 (unenlightened)	83	17	0	100 (41)

*Based on attitudes toward political democracy ("liberty"), reducing social barriers ("fraternity"), and egalitarianism ("equality").
Note: Number of cases on which percentages are based is given in parentheses.

The data reported in Table 2 support the contention that West Indian nationalism was a manifestation of the desire to transform West Indian society into one which conformed more closely than before to some of the basic values of Western civilization, as symbolized by the Rights of Man derived from the Enlightenment.[7] As is obvious from Table 2, there is a direct relationship between adherence to Enlightenment values and true nationalism among the West Indian leaders.

At this juncture the more tough-minded reader might interpose the objection that these findings are "merely" ideological correlations and therefore do not reveal very much about the social dynamics of the independence movement. These high-flown ideals, it could be objected, might merely be altruistic rationalizations for private interests and that the individuals here identified as "true nationalists" may be nothing more than clever and articulate brothers of the "opportunistic nationalists."

Space here does not permit a full refutation of such objections. In a sense, they are really irrelevant to the demonstration at hand, which has to

---

7. The 1961-62 study of West Indian nationalism reported here confirms and elaborates the findings of an earlier study done among Jamaican leaders in 1958. See Wendell Bell, *Jamaican Leaders: Political Attitudes in a New Nation,* Berkeley and Los Angeles: University of California Press, 1964.

do with a description of what types of societal values were voiced in connection with the independence movement in the West Indies. It is difficult to see how the societal values just analyzed can be regarded as any less real in a causal sense than the undoubtedly wide range of personal rewards obtained by nationalist leaders through participation in the independence movement. The nationalist leaders were not always paragons of virtue immune to the temptations of seizing some personal advantages as these may arise from their participation in nationalist politics. All that has been attempted here is to show that those West Indian leaders who demonstrated the greatest commitment to the cause of national independence—regardless of whether some among them might be vain, alcoholics, status seekers, wife beaters, or had authoritarian personalities—were the same men who manifested the strongest belief in the ideals of the Enlightenment.

AN EXPLANATION OF THE RISE OF WEST INDIAN NATIONALISM

It is always a difficult task in social science to make causal inferences concerning human behavior. And this task is even more complex when we deal with large-scale societal issues involved in the decisions of nationhood. As has been apparent in the arrangement of the tabular data in this article, the nationalist behavior of the West Indian leaders has been conceived as being a "dependent" variable or "effect" of the diverse background characteristics and attitudinal items that have been presented. The following explanation of the development of West Indian nationalism is based on the logical and temporal priorities of the variables examined, the historical context of the British Caribbean setting, and a qualitative analysis of the West Indian leaders' own assessments of the origins of their views toward political independence.

The political independence movement in the British Caribbean was an outcome of the economic discontent of the depressed segments of West Indian society being linked with the introduction of Enlightenment values to which many middle-class West Indians had been exposed in their higher education abroad. Thus, the inchoate demands of the traditionally underprivileged social groups to improve their positions and the long-range goals of individuals adhering to Western Enlightenment values became articulated in terms of the Rights of Man. To attain these ends, it was held that the colonial order would have to be terminated. Through the establishment of a new and independent political order with enlarged control over the rest of society, it was believed, the power to achieve the desired changes could be instituted. Metaphorically, we can liken the indigenous unrest of the West Indian masses to a dry tinder which was ready to be set aflame by the spark of a Western-derived ideology.

This sociological overview of West Indian nationalism, supported by empirical evidence, leads us to interpret the bases of the drive for political independence as centering on collective efforts to attain the Rights of Man. In the words of a prominent labor union leader, "I began to realize that political independence was the only means to bring about a society with no discrimination and equal opportunity for all. I had just come back from the university in England and was filled with all those notions of social justice. After a while, I knew that real changes were possible only in an independent nation where we could control our own destiny."

Concurrently, a large number of the West Indian leaders who desired a society dedicated to liberty, equality, and fraternity saw this as being achievable only through a radical change in the existing economic order. In terms of its intellectual content and its role in the history of ideas, a radical or "socialist" economic ideology concerns instrumentalities toward structuring an economy in such a way as to facilitate the establishment of a certain kind of egalitarian society. Thus, like the desire for political independence, we regard a Left economic ideology as a "dependent" variable, while the Rights of Man have more of an "independent" nature. This line of reasoning is also supported by the interviews with the West Indian leaders. For the socialist leaders themselves explicitly regarded their economic ideology as a means to attain a more generalized version of their images of the Good Society. Hence, economic radicalism is seen here as an associative rather than a causal factor of West Indian nationalism.

SUMMARY

The West Indian nationalist movement, reflecting its Enlightenment origins, was in its fundamental meaning a combination of both nineteenth-century, middle-class liberalism and twentieth-century, working-class radicalism. The desires of the West Indian nationalist leaders to reshape their societies to conform more closely with the principles symbolized by the Rights of Man were able to materialize into major social action because the economic discontent of the West Indian masses was largely directed into support of the nationalist movement. Toward this end grass-root political organizations were formed and alliances with labor unions were made. Thus, with middle-class leadership and working-class support, it became possible for a social movement, engendered by humanistic ideals, to arise which was able to transform older notions of the legitimacy of the imperial order into a belief in the sovereignty of the West Indian people.[8]

It is too early to say how consistently the ideals documented here as underpinning the drive for political independence will be realized in the West

---

8. The argument underlying the causal explanation of West Indian nationalism is developed in detail in Moskos, "The Sociology of Political Independence," *op. cit.*

Indies. Whether "massa day done" or whether new masters will replace the traditional elite is a decision yet to be determined by the leaders and citizenry of the West Indies. Without radical reform, the new nationalist leadership will be unable to bring to fruition the hopes of the independence movement. On the other hand, fulfillment of the humanistic and egalitarian promise of the West Indian nationalists would demonstrate the far-reaching changes that are possible through a democratic revolution. Given the obvious short-comings of the more advanced societies in their progress toward these same goals, one wonders how much success can be expected of the smaller and poorer West Indian nations. But the urge to try is there, as it is for any person, group, or nation that believes in progress, reason, and the future perfectability of man.

Personal Journal ————————————————————————————

B. PERSONAL REMARKS ON SOCIOLOGICAL RESEARCH IN THE THIRD WORLD

An unsung burden of the "underdeveloped" countries of the third world (roughly defined as Latin America, Asia, and Africa) is that they have become research locales for legions of American social scientists. Graduate students writing doctoral theses, as well as established scholars, pursue their peripatetic studies in growing numbers. It is to be hoped that as the number of social scientists going abroad increases there will be an effort to report the implementation and theoretical assumptions as well as the results of their studies. In this way the interaction between theory, methods, and findings can be understood more fully. And hopefully, some of the unstated premises of much of social science can be subjected to closer scrutiny. The following account, then, deals not so much with the empirical findings of my study (1967) of West Indian nationalism, but rather with some specifics on the manner in which the research was conducted and my views on how this research is related to the ongoing sociological enterpise.

———————————————

Source: Charles C. Moskos, Jr., "Personal Remarks on Sociological Research in the Third World," in Irving L. Horowitz, *Sociological Self-Images* (New York: Sage Publications, 1969), pp. 101-16.

THE RESEARCH EXPERIENCE

My study sought to uncover the forces affecting attitudes and actions toward political independence among the top leaders of the emerging nations of the British Caribbean: Jamaica, Trinidad, Guyana, Barbados, and the smaller islands comprising the Leeward and Windward island chains. The study revealed a diversity of beliefs; a dynamic and changing system, and a problematic future within which the hopes people have and the actions that they take can affect their future in significant ways.[1] How is it that certain members of colonial society begin to question the old order and take steps towards its termination? Why is it that the other persons in the same society look on with alarm at this course of events? And why do still others acquiesce to the shift to nationhood without being personally committed to it? It was to questions of this sort that I sought answers.

Being myself a "bird of passage," as the West Indians say, candor compels me to say that I originally came to the British Caribbean because it seemed like a pleasant and interesting place to do field work. Though the anticipated pleasures of my travels were more than realized, I also became morally committed to the efforts of the West Indian peoples to try to shape their own destiny. At the same time, I was forced to confront and reappraise many of the methodological tenets and theoretical assumptions so widespread in social science as it is practised and taught in the United States. For in addition to the inevitable personal culture shock one experiences in a foreign society, there was another culture shock concerning my sociology, my *American* sociology.

Much time, too much, was spent before leaving in formulating a research design which attempted to be "theoretically significant" as that term is currently misused. Attempts to operationalize the various grand theoretical schemes so popular back home either resulted in ending up with a trivial problem, or something so abstract that there was little connection with social change in the West Indies. These formalistic approaches—so consciously trying to avoid cultural bias—paradoxically underemphasize the most important causal factors of change in the third world: modernizing ideologies; the forms of power, control, and violence; and international economic relationships. In my case, I found it necessary to abandon orthodox conceptualizations once I began to face the realities of the West Indian scene. For it is incumbent upon the inquiring mind itself to make an order out of facts, and not to force data into a priori irrelevant pigeonholes.

A related problem is that much of the training in methodology (a result of its being oriented around team research?) excessively stresses the principle of reliability (i.e., standardizing data collection by reducing inconsistencies in measurement) to the detriment of validity (i.e., getting the truth by measuring what one is looking for) in sociological research. Methodological

---

1. This approach is amplified in Wendell Bell and Ivar Oxaal (1964), and Bell (1967). For a study of our own society using a related perspective, see Raymond Mack (1967).

rituals cannot substitute for the inventiveness which the field researcher must come up with when he is out on his own. Conventions and never-to-be-deviated-from research designs can perform an important function for the growth of science, but they cannot result in the creative act on which science also depends.

THE POLITICS OF DEVELOPING INTERVIEWS
Identifying Top Leaders

An important methodological feature of the study was the procedure used to identify the top West Indian leaders—those to be eventually interviewed. In each of the societies in which research was conducted the same procedure was used. Initially, interviews were held with five persons, each located in a different institutional sector, who on the basis of their *position* ought to have been society-wide influentials. These initial interviews were with persons in: (1) the incumbent political group, (2) the political opposition, (3) major economic enterprises, (4) the civil service, and (5) the mass media. Each of these initial interviewees was asked who he thought wielded widespread influence in their society. The reason for using persons located in different institutional sectors during the early interviewing period was to reduce the likelihood of bias in the identification procedure toward particular institutional sectors. There was, however, little "halo" effect. On the whole, perhaps because of the small scale of West Indian society, there was general agreement on who were local leaders even if located in institutional sectors other than those of the respondent. Those influentials most frequently mentioned in the initial interviews were in turn interviewed, and asked to identify other society-wide influentials. Thus, the identification procedure developed into a *reputational* method.[2]

Departing from customary practise, I have reported in the published findings the actual names and rankings of the West Indian leaders so identified (though, of course, responses to questions in the interview are not identified with individual names). Such a public listing of societal leaders allows for an informed evaluation of the identification procedure by residents and observers of the West Indies.

Arranging Interviews

The period in which the field work took place (1961-62) was a particularly favorable one for interviewing. None of the leaders identified in the manner described above refused to be interviewed. There was an atmosphere of political excitement which even the casual visitor could not escape noticing. It was a time when the issue of independence was on everyone's

---

2. This method of elite identification was pioneered by Floyd Hunter (1953 and 1959).

mind; as I was to learn, it was a time when West Indians of all levels were willing to talk about where they thought their society was heading. By the time the field work was completed, I had interviewed prime ministers, cabinet members, leaders of opposition parties, heads of labor unions, wealthy merchants, large plantation owners, newspaper editors and columnists, leading members of the clergy, ethnic spokesmen, heads of voluntary organizations, prominent professionals, high-ranking civil servants, and leading intellectual and artistic figures.

An indispensable help in arranging interviews was the genuine interest of most West Indians with whom I became acquainted during my stay in the area. In every island I visited, prior introductions removed many of the obstacles I had feared. These introductions were of particular value in the smaller islands where strangers are quickly heard of and almost as quickly labeled to be helped or avoided. Many times an interview difficult to obtain was made possible by running into someone at a social gathering who was able to intervene for me. I discovered that one should not be bashful about explaining what one is trying to do. Most people are interested and if they can help they generally will. Somewhat surprisingly, I believe my relatively short stay in each island helped rather than hindered my research. Since I was leaving soon, people had to act quickly. Moreover, for those who befriended me there was no possibility that I could turn into a long-term burden.

There are occasions, however, when all available personal contacts have been used, and the interviewer himself must seek out his quarry. After some trial and error, I realized that the best procedure is simply to go to the respondent's office or home and ask to see him. If you have referred leads or letters of introduction, well and good; if not, go anyway. Rather than try to make appointments by telephone or mail beforehand, it is best to present yourself personally. The interviews themselves averaged over an hour in length and many were much longer.

Most of the interviews took place in the respondent's office, but in many cases arrangements were made to meet in other locations. Some of the more memorable interview situations were: talking to the editor of one of the West Indies' leading newspapers while a demonstration against him, bordering on a riot, was taking place outside his office; quizzing a prime minister alternately waist and shoulder deep in the Caribbean surf; passing the better part of an hour with a Roman Catholic bishop while he was waiting to officiate at a funeral; meeting a leader of a black racist cult at a political rally and then moving into the back room of a poor man's bar where the interview went on into the early hours of the morning.

The Interview Situation

At the outset of the interview, before beginning any questioning, I tried, when possible, to set a leisurely mood. Our meeting was presented as an opportunity for the respondent to take a little time off from his busy and hectic schedule to philosophize, meditate, and think aloud. I was talking to him, it was understood, because he was obviously an influential person whose views mattered. In fact, few of my interviewees displayed any false modesty concerning their importance in their society.

No attempt was made to stress anonymity, such as telling the respondent that his answers would be reduced to statistical tables. It was also made very clear, however, that any desire to keep certain remarks confidential would be honored. Indeed, excessive emphasis on anonymity may create doubts in the mind of the respondent as to the candor he should exhibit. After all, no matter what the interviewer says about impartial anonymity, the respondent correctly realizes that the interviewer can subsequently report whatever he wants. For this reason, the interview must be pitched on a level of mutual trust. One should try to establish a man-to-man relationship stressing the uniqueness and importance of what the respondent is saying. And this requires that intelligent comments be made during the interview by the interviewer himself. My natural "one-down" position was somewhat overcome by the fact that during my research I had picked up a great deal of information which was of interest to my interviewees. Because I learned that I too would be questioned, and because my own information was cumulative, I reserved my most important interviews for the terminal period during my stay in a particular island.

Because the interview itself is a rapport builder, the sequence of questions is of great importance. Particularly when one is working in a foreign society, the researcher's common sense is not always a good criterion for determining how questions vary in the anxiety they may cause among his respondents. This knowledge can be effectively gained only through pilot interviews. Once one has an idea of the anxiety various questions produce, it is possible to maximize valid responses by attempting to control anxiety levels during the interview.

I found the following sequence to be best suited for eliciting information when talking to West Indian leaders. At the start of the interview, moderately high-anxiety questions were asked. This was done to gain the respondent's attention and to remove temptations to slip into clichés. But the anxiety produced at the start of the interview must not be so high as to cause the respondent to become unduly apprehensive. After the initial set of questions, the anxiety level is reduced and rapport established as firmly as possible. In the third phase of the interview, the highest-anxiety-producing questions are asked. By this time, the respondent is usually involved in his answers and has committed himself to the interview situation. At the close of the interview, the questions are of a very low-anxiety potential. The interview should end on a pleasant note and a mood of mutual good feeling. And, as any interviewer knows, some of the significant responses come after the notebook is closed.

Confidants

Regardless of how well the interviews appear to be going, one's interpretation of them needs to be supplemented with outside opinions. It is essential to know one or more local persons with whom one can discuss the study in depth. These confidants will tend to be personal friends. Usually, but not always, they are individuals whose ideological viewpoints are close to those of the researcher. The background information these confidants can give makes it easier to piece together isolated data into a coherent picture. Frequently, such confidants are able to prevent the researcher from completely misinterpreting some finding, although one must also beware of too readily accepting interpretations which are often versions of locally accepted social myths.

Contact with confidants should be maintained even after one has left the area. In particular, published accounts of the study should be sent to persons who assisted in the gathering and interpretation of the field materials. Not only does common courtesy require that one keep in some touch with those who befriended you, but the kind of impression one leaves behind can either clear or muddy the waters for subsequent researchers. Too often I heard, "There was another chap who came down from America to do some sort of a study, but we never heard from him again."

THE PASSING OF TRADITIONAL RESEARCH METHODS

A major impression I had after completing my field work in the West Indies was that many of the principles taught to apprentice sociologists in the United States are open to question. This is not to say that our graduate programs are to be categorically damned, but it does mean that many of the standard tenets set forth in professional training are inappropriate when one does field work outside the United States, or more generally, when one's research differs from the usual social science endeavors.

A study dealing with leaders, elites, and influentials involves "upward interviewing" from the viewpoint of the researcher's status. Yet, most methodological maxims seem to be premised on "downward interviewing." (Perhaps, because so many of our subjects are housewives and college students or members of some dependent population such as prisoners, slum dwellers, old people, etc.) Attitudes of individuals are gauged by circuitous and veiled questionnaire items. My West Indian experience, however, indicated that the best questions were the most direct. Likewise, scaled or forced-choice questions proved to be uneconomical in terms of time consumption, not to mention their well-known validity problems. Yet, questions must be specific enough to allow for the comparable collection of information between persons. One must not become reconciled to "stream of consciousness" interviews just because it takes some effort to keep the questioning structured.

My study involved, along with a standard statistical treatment of the data, the utilization of a sociological method which has been variously termed "the quest for universals," "the genetic perspective," or most commonly, "analytic induction." Unlike the conventional handling of data, the analytic induction method tries to go beyond finding statistical correlations by providing explanatory theories of causal relationships. There is an assumption that the most desirable form of knowledge rests on formulating generalizations that apply to all cases of the phenomenon under consideration. Hypotheses are constructed, tested, rejected, reconstructed, and retested until a set of preconditions is found that apply universally to the phenomenon being described during the collection phase of research. Thus, this method entails an ongoing clarification of the explicit character of the data. Moreover, there is an incorporation of the negative cases, or "exceptions," by either changing the explanatory hypotheses, refining the phenomenon to be explained, or both.

Although the analytic induction method has been customarily used (see Lindesmith, 1947; Cressey, 1953; Becker, 1963) to explain types of social deviancy (e.g., drug addiction, marijuana smoking, embezzlement), this procedure may be especially suitable for certain kinds of behavior studies in the third world. Our understanding of these areas is handicapped because of the inappropriateness of the constructs developed within American social science. Analytic induction, however, is a parsimonious method which identifies behavioral variables as they reveal themselves within a particular cultural and social context. Because analytic induction possesses a kind of dialectic dynamic and is inherently fluid, much more flexibility in the field is required than is the case with conventional survey designs discussed in most methodology primers. Later, of course, these variables can be formulated into testable propositions amenable to further examination based on large-scale sampling procedures.

AMERICAN VALUES ABROAD

As severe as the problems posed in adopting a meaningful methodology are, third world studies are faced with even more profound questions of theoretical appropriateness. The epithet of ethnocentrism is one of the oldest in social science and, as is to be expected, it is a source of special controversy in the theoretical literature on underdeveloped areas. Writers on emerging nations are frequently criticized for forcing non-Western phenomena into Western-derived categories. It is proposed, however, that much of the controversy concerning ethnocentrism has been misdirected. The question is not so much the utility of general Western concepts to studies of the third world, but the more subtle one of the relevance of social science assumptions that are uniquely American.

In contrasting European with American sociology, the German sociologist Ralf Dahrendorf (1961) has listed six "missing traits" in American social analyses: violence, revolution, class, history, elites, and intellectuals. Many of these traits are also absent in the literature on the third world, even though they are especially germane in examining the social changes occurring there (and increasingly so, in the United States as well). Thus, despite the revolutionary situation in many of the emerging nations, a large number of American social scientists have focused their studies on requisites for stability; despite the far-reaching transformations in the social bases of power, we hear of psychological determinants and problems of personal identity; and despite the global historical processes that have divided the world into rich and poor nations, the consequences of international inequalities are discussed *sotto voce*. Even the terms "elites" and "intellectuals," which are widely used in the literature on emerging nations, are so watered down from their European usages as to lose much of their explanatory power. Where European theorists dealt with intraelite conflict and the forms of dominance, American social scientists speak of the elite-mass gap. Where intellectuals in the European tradition were seen as carriers of ideologies, studies on emerging nations focus on personal frustrations of Westernized individuals.

Along this same line, C. Wright Mills (1942), over a quarter-century ago, discussed the prevailing assumptions in American studies dealing with social disorganization on the domestic scene. These same tendencies have been transplanted into the literature on underdeveloped countries. One of the assumptions that Mills noted was conceiving society largely as a cultural system. In the writings on the third world, there has also been a strong emphasis on continuities in value orientations. Social determinants are placed in the realm of amorphous psychocultural entities which preclude the volitional control of social change. A second assumption pointed out by Mills was that undesirable consequences, especially the deterioration of *gemeinschaft* norms, accompany urbanization. Likewise, a persistent theme pervading much of the literature on underdeveloped areas is the supposed deleterious effects on social integration and personality arising from the rapid social change. One wonders whether American social scientists are more worried over the psychological costs of change than are the peoples they are describing. A third assumption of American sociology that Mills indicated was an emphasis upon the solution of problems through individual effort and adjustment, and a disregard for the efficacy of political action to implement structural changes. In the writings on the emerging nations as well, the role of the social scientist is rarely seen to include bringing his knowledge to bear on how problems of individuals are related to public issues which can be collectively resolved by structural alterations.

Such a comprehension of developments in the third world complements another of the persistent features in the analyses of most American social scientists—the failure to explore, if not acknowledge, the contingencies on development resulting from the gap between the rich and the poor nations of the world. Indeed, evidence points to an increasing rather than a diminishing gulf between the economically developed and underdeveloped countries, and this gap cuts across both communist and noncommunist countries. Not only are the political systems of emerging nations discussed in a vacuum with regard to global realities, but there is little consideration of the alternative courses of development which would open up in the poor countries if the structure of the international stratification was changed.[3]

Even the self-consciously "comparative" studies that have been made almost always have been *horizontal*—comparing nations at the same "stage" of development. *Vertical* comparisons—explaining how events in industrialized countries and in the third world are intermeshed—would seem mandatory, but when such studies do appear they are typically written by foreign social scientists, or by journalists, ideologues, and others on the periphery of social science in the United States.

Another feature in much of the literature on new nations is a misrepresentation of the motives behind the nationalist or revolutionary movements in the third world. To the disadvantaged of the emerging nations, invidious comparisons are drawn between their current strivings and the earlier ideologies of the West. There is a strong similarity, in the explanations of the motivating forces underlying the movements in the third world by many contemporary social scientists, with the neo-Machiavellian sociology that arose in the wake of the nineteenth-century European socialist movements. In both cases, the egalitarian, altruistic, and national components of the change-provoking movements are belittled, while the elitist, self-seeking, and irrational aspects are stressed.

Such cynical interpretations of the ideological underpinnings of the political independence movements in the emerging nations are directly contradicted by the findings of my study. The data revealed that, at least in the case of the West Indies, the movement toward independence was based on an ideology anchored in the values of the Western Enlightenment, and is to be understood as a scale-increasing movement linked with humanitarian ideals. This, of course, does not mean the future development of West Indian nationalism will remain within the humanistic mold. For in an earlier era, a turning away from the values of the Enlightenment transformed the initial humanitarian nationalism into subsequent exclusivist movements. Unfortunately, imitation may still be the sincerest form of flattery. Already there are dismaying signs that the current nationalisms of the colonial peoples may in some instances follow the road of their European and American predecessors.

---

3. A notable exception is Irving L. Horowitz (1966).

THE CIVIL SOCIAL SCIENTIST

At this stage of history, though, the meaning of the West Indian political independence movements goes beyond the spread of equality of opportunity and political rights within the emergent Caribbean nations. Rather, it is to be viewed as the working out in one particular region of the broader worldwide effort of colonial peoples to obtain dignity and improvement in their lives. Moreover, the modern-day strivings of the colonial peoples serve as a mirror by which the wealthier nations themselves can reassess the worth, consequences, and timeliness of the humanistic values which they profess to cherish—values that are now being put to new tests as they become really human in scale. No longer can the social science of the wealthier nations enjoy its accustomed splendid isolation. In the United States, both the race crisis at home and the Vietnam war—each with its colonial overtones—are indicative of the need for American social science to adopt a responsibly critical stance toward the direction of our society.

To bring my remarks to a close, then, it is perhaps appropriate that I try to indicate a few of the students of society who have strongly influenced my own thinking. Among the classic writers, the insights of Karl Marx and Max Weber have had a deep impact. The utility of Marxian analyses—its emphasis on underlying economic determinants, its focus on contradictions and social conflict, its view of ideology as both unself-conscious reflection of social conditions as well as narrow, self-interested rationalization—remains powerful even (especially?) in understanding pre- and post- as well as industrialized society. Although Weber's intellectual life can be properly considered a running battle with Marxian analyses, Weber was amazingly astute in highlighting the pervasive trends in modern history: in religion, a rationally argued ethic; in economics, rational calculation of interests; in politics, the rule of law and administration by an impersonal bureaucracy; and that only certain ideas out of a broader set may be selected in a society undergoing change because they fit the interests of certain "status groups" and such groups can shape the moral ideas of large numbers of others.

Among contemporary sociologists, the influences are more diffuse. A few have already been acknowledged, but four individuals need to be mentioned directly: Eshref Shevky, who as my teacher at UCLA, awakened me to the ramifications of the changing scale of contemporary society and the meaning of a humane social science; Wendell Bell, who as a teacher and collaborator set personal standards of scholarship and moral responsibility which continue to be a model for my own efforts; C. Wright Mills, whose practised use of the "sociological imagination" (i.e., relating facts of cultural and social structure to personal behavior within an historical framework) continues to inform and inspire; and Irving Louis Horowitz, who despite a sometimes hurried style has the rare ability to come unerringly to grips with the really significant issues of our time, of getting down—in today's vernacular—to the "nitty-gritty."

As typified by the above men—and there are many others—it is my belief that scholarly output and the social use of critical intelligence cannot be separated. When studying such issues as nationalism, the distribution of power, the drive toward equality, or the conditions of democracy, the effective researcher cannot be detached from the consequences of his work. Objective and intellectually honest, yes—but detached, no.

Indeed, an uncommitted posture will actually hamper the social scientist who is doing research in the third world. A person who is not self-conscious about the implications of his work will be looked upon with suspicion and distrust. As a step toward reducing this likelihood it may be well for us to consider some sort of "participatory sociology" in third world studies. That is, a plan of research in which the subjects themselves help define what are proper and needed avenues of investigation. (Although I have intentionally ignored here the role of the social scientist at home, the implications for domestic social science should be obvious.) The natural and correct question of people in the third world is, "What are you doing here?" Certainly the social scientist must always ask himself just what it is that he is doing. And if he cannot satisfactorily answer that question for the people with whom he is dealing, as well as for himself, his research is betraying both his humanity and his science.

REFERENCES

Becker, H. (1963). *Outsiders.* New York: Free Press.

Bell, W. [ed.] (1967). *The Democratic Revolution in the West Indies.* Cambridge, Mass.: Schenkman.

Bell, W., and I. Oxaal (1964). *Decisions of Nationhood.* Denver: Social Science Foundation, University of Denver.

Cressey, D. (1953). *Other People's Money.* Glencoe, Ill.: Free Press.

Dahrendorf, R. (1961). "European sociology and the American self-image." *Archives Européenes de Sociologie* 2: 324-66.

Horowitz, I. L. (1966). *Three Worlds of Development.* New York: Oxford University Press.

Hunter, F. (1953). *Community Power Structure.* Chapel Hill: University of North Carolina Press.

Hunter, F. (1959). *Top Leadership, U.S.A.* Chapel Hill: University of North Carolina Press.

Lindesmith, A. R. (1947). *Opiate Addiction.* Bloomington, Ind.: Principia Press.

Mack, R. W. (1967). *Transforming America.* New York: Random House.

Mills, C. W. (1942). "The professional ideology of social pathologists." *American Journal of Sociology* 49 (September): 165-80.

Moskos, C. C., Jr. (1967). *The Sociology of Political Independence.* Cambridge, Mass.: Schenckman.

EXPERIMENTS

A. *RESEARCH BY*
Philip A. Goldberg
Craig Haney,
W. Curtis Banks &
Philip G. Zimbardo
John M. Darley &
C. Daniel Batson
Weldon Johnson
Jeffrey H. Goldstein &
Robert L. Arms

B. *PERSONAL JOURNALS BY*
Philip A. Goldberg
Craig Haney
C. Daniel Batson
Weldon Johnson
Jeffrey H. Goldstein

CHAPTER 3

CHAPTER 3

EXPERIMENTS

Experiments are the method of choice when the goal of the researcher is to maximize control. As pointed out in Chapter 1, control is achieved in several ways—by manipulation of independent variables, by random assignment of subjects to treatment or control groups, and by holding constant or randomizing certain other important variables, either in the environment or in the subjects. The studies included in this section illustrate the use of these procedures in experimental research.

Philip Goldberg's study of the prejudice of women against women grew out of a general interest in the phenomenon of prejudice and out of his specific experiences as a teacher. Called upon to teach classes which were composed of either all men or all women, he observed that "women could be counted on to do the work; the men could be counted on to do the talking." His experiences suggested to him that women did not value themselves or their work as they should, and that they were generally prejudiced against other women. He set out to obtain data that would "prove" this phenomenon.

Goldberg's experimental design was simple and straightforward. The independent variable was manipulated by giving some young women copies of articles with a man's name as author, while other young women received copies of the identical article, but with a hypothetical woman's byline. No elaborate laboratory setup or equipment was required; the "lab" was a regular college classroom. Use of a questionnaire enabled Goldberg to obtain the data in a single administration. While he ultimately found support in his data for the finding that "the work of men was more highly valued than the work of women," it is interesting to note that the immediate postexperimental reaction of the women, when informed of the experiment's true purpose, was to deny that the author's sex had influenced their evaluation.

Since experiments are considered the most effective strategy for testing a causal hypothesis, the possibility of using experimental designs for other purposes is seldom considered. The experimental simulation of Craig Haney, W. Curtis Banks, and Philip G. Zimbardo is unique in this regard. It illustrates the creative (though, in this case, potentially harmful) ways in which an experiment can be used for exploratory purposes. No specific hypotheses were advanced other than the general one that assignment to the treatment of "guard" or "prisoner" would result in very different reactions in subjects as they adapted to these different and extreme institutional roles.

Here also the research "design" was a relatively simple one, involving only a single treatment variable: the random assignment to either a guard or a prisoner condition. Execution of the design was, however, much more difficult, complex, and time-consuming than in Goldberg's study. The authors were interested in exploring the effect of both situational and dispositional variables. To minimize the effects of prior social history, considerable time and energy went into screening the subjects. To maximize control of the environment, and to achieve, in so far as possible, a *functional* simulation of the "reality" of prison life, elaborate procedures were employed in arranging the laboratory setting. Much attention was given to such details as uniforms, administrative routine, and the physical aspects of the simulated prison. To introduce enough "mundane realism" into the experience, so that the role-playing participants might be able to go beyond the superficial demands of their assigned roles into the deep structure of the prisoner and guard mentality, the researchers also enlisted the cooperation of the local police department to make the unexpected arrests appear to be part of a routine raid. A local TV station even sent a cameraman to film the "arrests." Parole board meetings and visits to the prison by a Catholic priest, a public defender, and the parents, relatives, and friends of the prisoners helped to enhance realism as well.

Because of the exploratory nature of the study, much unspecified data was collected using a variety of data collection techniques: video and audio tapes were used to record interaction, and questionnaires, personality tests, and post-experimental interviews were used to determine individual reactions. From the point of view of data analysis, Haney et al. actually faced many of the problems common to fieldworkers: How does one systematically analyze and make sense of immense amounts of varied data? How does one know what the important variables are? How does one develop categories to study them? The exploratory nature of the simulation provided voluminous data— full, rich, profound—and made the organization and presentation of findings difficult and time-consuming. And, one can assume stimulating and challenging as well. Though the particular nature of the results in the Stanford Prison Study might lead one to question whether or not such research should be done (see discussion below), the strength of experimental simulations lies in the fact that they preclude explanations which are "person-blaming" (or dispositional). Further, they provide an opportunity for the uninitiated to obtain an appreciation for and an understanding of potential role demands in the situation under study. If one views "research-as-teaching," as does Haney, experimental simulation can be a very powerful research—and teaching—tool.

Field experiments attempt to strike a compromise between the naturalness of the field and the control of the experiment. Three studies in this collection employ this type of research strategy. The first, by John M. Darley and C. Daniel Batson, actually includes elements of both laboratory and field experiments. Parts of the research did take place in the laboratory, but the crucial dependent variable, helping behavior, was measured in a natural situation. As they passed through an isolated alleyway on their way from one laboratory location to another, the seminarians who served as the subjects of the study encountered an individual "sitting slumped in a doorway, head down, eyes closed, not moving." As the subject passed, "the victim coughed twice and groaned." The victim observed and recorded whether or not a particular subject stopped to help and what type of help was offered.

Like Haney, et al., Darley and Batson were also interested in distinguishing between dispositional and situational factors, in this case in terms of their effects on helping behavior. Dispositional factors were related to religiosity and were measured by a series of personality scales. The situational variable was manipulated by telling seminarians in different treatment conditions whether or not they had to "hurry" on their way to the second location. Some were told they were late (high-hurry condition); others were told they were on time (intermediate hurry); still others (low hurry) were told that they still had a few minutes more.

In his personal journal, Batson reports that "more than any other research I've conducted, this study did seem to involve a symphony of happy circumstances." He had access to money and facilities under someone else's grant; he found a congenial and supportive advisor, interested in his work and open to his ideas; he developed a significant and yet manageable research problem; he located an "ideal physical environment;" everyone cooperated, and all of the runs went smoothly. Even the alley was not turned into a park until *after* the study was completed. For once, things went pretty much as the textbook indicated. That's when doing research is "not just worthwhile, it's fun."

In contrast, Weldon T. Johnson observes that his experience in conducting a field experiment on religious revivalism "departed in some important respects from what I expected on the basis of the accounts in methods textbooks." For one thing, his research evolved not out of any high-minded theoretical interest but out of informal discussions with fellow graduate students. For another, he acknowledges the constraints imposed on his work by such mundane matters as time, money, and convenience. With patience and imagination, Johnson forged a worthwhile study out of "everyday resources."

By using participant observation in an experimental design, Johnson's study of a Billy Graham crusade challenges some of the stereotypes of a novice researcher. The independent variable, role playing, was manipulated by assigning one treatment group to "active" participant observation and another to "passive" participant observation. By not going to the rally at all, a third group served as a nontreatment comparison group. The dependent variable of religious commitment was measured at three points in time via self-administered questionnaires—once before exposure to Billy Graham and twice after, at three-week intervals.

Johnson points out one of the special problems associated with field experiments. Concomitant with minimizing artificiality is a consequent loss of control: "The real world often is not organized in a way that facilitates orderly experiments." It may not be possible to manipulate variables of interest. Opportunities for random selection and assignment of subjects may be limited. Behavior and events may be unpredictable. Despite all his advance planning, Johnson was unable, for example, to predict that the Billy Graham crusade would attract so many so early and that his observers would be unable to make their way to their assigned locations.

Jeffrey H. Goldstein feels that data from an experiment should have relevance for the development of theory and that they should be related to real and important human behaviors. Thus, he and his colleague, Robert Arms, decided to study human aggression *outside* the laboratory. Their desire "to examine the effects on observers of witnessing a fairly lengthy and realistic kind of violence in a natural setting" led them to consider using a football game as the aggressive event for the study and spectators at the game as their research subjects. Their location in Philadelphia conveniently provided such a game played on "neutral" territory, the Army-Navy game.

Aggression was the dependent variable. To measure it, Goldstein and Arms had student interviewers administer three subscales from the Buss-Durkee Hostility Inventory. Because they wanted to know if observing an "aggressive" athletic contest increased aggression in their subjects, it was necessary to have before and after measurements. With over 100,000 people, all of them in a hurry, obtaining such data on the same spectators before and after the game was impractical. They decided to have two groups of subjects, one in which aggression was measured prior to the game and one in which they measured aggression afterward. Information was also obtained on spectators' allegiances to Army or Navy, as well as on several other background factors. This information was used to determine whether the before and after groups were similar on these demographic variables. Goldstein cites one of the weaknesses of field experiments also mentioned by Johnson, the inability of the researcher to assign subjects randomly to treatment groups. To provide a control group, therefore, Goldstein and Arms studied observers at a gym meet, a nonaggressive sport, in the same way as they had the football spectators. Fortunately, Goldstein and Arms fared better than did Johnson. All of their interviewers were on time and appropriately located.

Goldstein's desire to study real-life behavior of some importance ultimately had some consequences for which he was not prepared. A year after his research was published, the public relations office at his university prepared a brief press release, summarizing his findings in nontechnical terms. Within days, the wire services were disseminating reports of his study across the country. Despite the letters from angry housewives, the inquiries from interested students, and the invitations from various talk shows, Goldstein resisted the role of expert. He does observe, however, that people seem genuinely interested in social science research "when it proves pertinent to their own lives" and that they seem willing to consider empirical findings as one factor in their decision making. He concludes that research which is meaningful to researchers and lay persons alike can be done.

Beyond their specific experimental characteristics, like manipulation of independent variables and control of other factors, all of these experiments have several other things in common. For one, all of them use students, usually as research subjects. In one case (Goldstein and Arms), the students were employed as interviewers. As pointed out by Goldberg, Batson, and Johnson, the primary reason is probably convenience. The students are there and easily accessible. With the exception of Goldberg, all of the studies also use *males only* as their subjects. This is not unusual in social science experiments, nor is it unusual that most of these males are college students. Beyond convenience, the rationale for this is usually that the experimenter is attempting to control certain variables, age and sex, which might influence the outcome of the experiment. One sometimes wonders if all our conclusions about human behavior would be challenged if, on occasion, we used females or senior citizens.

As mentioned in Chapter 1, experiments, because they usually involve the manipulation of a crucial variable, inevitably pose questions about the treatment of human subjects. Physical or psychological harm must be avoided, and subjects' rights must not be usurped. Of the contributions in this section, the prison simulation of Haney et al. presents the most serious ethical concerns. The outcome is sobering. In less than one week, the behavior of both prisoners and guards could only be characterized as antisocial and pathological. The experiment had to be terminated. Without intending to, the researchers had produced a totally negative environment. The accompanying personal journal prepared by Haney confronts some of the ethical issues raised by their research, including their own very powerful involvement in the situation.

As he points out in his personal journal, Haney feels strongly that the prison simulation study in which he was involved is important not because of any brilliant methodological insights it may provide but because of the profound questions it raises about social-psychological research and about human social life. He discusses the "politics of objectivity," and argues that, "as its political uses [have] increased, social science [has become] more apolitical in its form." Methodological precision is demanded and practitioners are expected to be dispassionate and uninvolved in the issues they address. Haney maintains that this seeming neutrality and objectivity can be used "to confer legitimacy on political decisions by cloaking them in the mantle of the scientifically compelled." It is his concern (and it should be ours) that social scientists recognize the extent to which the conduct of research is itself a *situation*—a social context capable of shaping and controlling the behavior of *all* its participants.

Haney argues that social scientists, in their roles as researchers, are, no less than others, subject to the general principles of behavior they articulate. Consequently, they may be in "an especially disadvantageous position to maintain a balanced perspective on what they do." He advocates public accountability and personal responsibility on the part of researchers; they must be sensitive to the very crucial issues involved. Consideration of "cost-benefit" ratios has become the acceptable way to confront the matter of the protection of human subjects. Haney raises important questions, however, about the researcher's ability to determine the potential risk (physical, psychological, sociological, or legal) to subjects and respondents *or* to weigh any such potential harm or discomfort against the "worth" of the study. For Haney (and for me), "informed consent" is not enough. "How much responsibility," Haney asks, "do [researchers] have to guarantee that the subjects can't make a 'bad deal,' even if they want to: Does insisting upon 'deciding for them' reflect a 'paternalistic' frame of mind?" Haney recognizes that, in the Prison Study, the ethical questions are especially compelling because in a very real sense the findings depend for their impact on negative consequences. But, research of human importance *must* be done. Haney's own experience prompts him to suggest that we examine our motives very carefully and be very selective in the research we choose to do.

In addition to questions related to the potential for harm to subjects or respondents, experiments also pose questions regarding deception: Should the subjects be told what the study is actually about? It is argued, on the one hand, that full knowledge of the research purpose would distort the behavior of subjects, making research impossible. On the other hand, deception, even minimal and trivial deception, may also violate the subjects' right of "informed consent."

In several of the experiments presented in this section the subjects were not aware beforehand of the exact nature of the study. The women in Goldberg's study thought that they were making "critical evaluations of professional literature." Darley and Batson's seminarians thought that they were participating in a study of the "vocational careers of seminary students," when in actuality Darley and Batson were studying helping behavior. The students in Weldon Johnson's study thought that they were observing attendees at a Billy Graham crusade. They did not know that they were the subjects. Johnson terms it "the little lie."

It can be argued that participants in experiments probably do not expect to be told the full truth. Whether the subjects feel "used" or "exploited" probably depends on how seriously they view the deception, and whether or not they feel that the benefits of the experiment outweigh the psychological or social costs to themselves or others. The seminarians in Darley and Batson's study seemed to feel this way about the experiment in which they participated. The reactions of students, when reading about this deception, are usually subdued, as is the case with Goldberg's study of prejudice in women. Not telling the prisoner subjects in the Haney et al. experiment that they were actually going to be arrested or not telling them where they were being taken seems to most student readers a more serious breach of trust. Reaction is mixed, however, on Johnson's "little lie."

Crucial in the reactions of both subjects and readers to such deception is the use of effective debriefing sessions by the experimenter, wherein the full nature of the experiment is disclosed, its significance is discussed, and subject reaction sought. Goldberg, Haney, Batson, and Johnson all report on their debriefing activities. Rubin, in Chapter 6, has more to say on the researcher-subject relationship.

Philip A. Goldberg ————————————————————————————————

A. MISOGYNY AND THE COLLEGE GIRL

Perhaps one of the most consistent findings in regard to sex differences cited in the literature is the fact of differential evaluation of the two sexes. Both men and women tend to value men more highly (Kitay, 1940; McKee & Sherriffs, 1957; Sherriffs & McKee, 1957; Smith, 1939).

In the study by Sherriffs and McKee, the authors find that "women are regarded as guilty of snobbery and irrational and unpleasant emotionality" (1957, p. 463). The most general finding is that there are reliably perceived sex differences, and both sexes are in substantial agreement in valuing the salient male characteristics and denigrating the salient female characteristics. Consistent with this theme is the finding by French and Lesser (1964) that "women who value intellectual attainment feel they must reject the woman's role" (p. 128).

Even such feminists as Simone de Beauvoir (1953) and Betty Friedan (1963) believe that women differ unfavorably from men on a wide variety of dimensions. But whatever the facts as to the nature and extent of true differences between the sexes, Allport (1954) makes it clear that antifeminism can function as any other prejudice to organize and distort experience and perception. Indeed, it is the very distortion of experience and evidence that is for Allport and others definitional of prejudice.

The major purpose of the present study was to investigate the operation of perceptual distortion in reflecting prejudice toward women. More specifically the focus of this study was on the prejudice of women toward women in the areas of intellectual and professional competence.

METHOD
Subjects

One hundred and forty female undergraduate students were randomly selected to participate in the study. A pre-experiment occupational rating

Source: Paper presented at the meetings of the Eastern Psychological Association, Boston, April 1967.

The author is indebted to Elizabeth Lawe, Edith Marden, and Judith Milstein for assistance in the conduct of the experiment.

scale was completed by 100 subjects, and 40 subjects took part in the experiment proper.

Procedure

In a preliminary step, normative data were obtained for a six-point rating scale which asked subjects to decide for a list of 50 occupational fields "the degree to which you associate the field with men or with women." Based on these data two occupations strongly associated with men (law, city planning), two strongly associated with women (elementary education, dietetics), and two occupations intermediate in regard to sexual association (linguistics, art history) were identified.

Six articles were selected from the professional literature of these six occupational fields.[1] The six articles were edited and abridged to approximately 1,500 words each and combined in booklets. Fictitious titles and authors' names appeared on the first page of each article. The critical experimental manipulation had to do with the name of the author. For any one article half the booklets had a male author's name, and half had a female author's name. Only the first name was altered, e.g., John T. McKay, Joan T. McKay. Each booklet had three "male" articles and three "female" articles.

The instructions to the subjects, who were all seated together in a large lecture hall, were as follows:

> In this booklet you will find excerpts of six articles, written by six different authors in six different professional fields. At the end of each article you will find several questions which are to be answered before you proceed to the next article. You are not presumed to be sophisticated or knowledgeable in all the fields. We are interested in the ability of college students to make critical evaluations of professional literature.

At the end of each article, the subjects were required to answer nine questions which were the same for all subjects and all articles. The questions were as follows, with the exception, of course, that the author's name was changed as appropriate:

1. How valuable for the general reader would you consider Mr. McKay's article to be?
   1. extremely valuable   2. moderately valuable   3. some value
   4. little value   5. no value
2. How valuable for the professional person in the field would you consider Mr. McKay's article to be?
   1. extremely valuable   2. moderately valuable   3. some value
   4. little value   5. no value

---

1. The original sources for the six articles in the fields of linguistics, law, art history, dietetics, elementary education, and city planning were, respectively, Vossler (1932), Kittrie (1964), Hunter (1956), Stare (1964), Bruner (1961), Gans (1962).

3. Quite aside from content, how effective would you judge Mr. McKay's writing style to be?
1. extremely effective 2. moderately effective 3. partially effective 4. moderately ineffectual 5. extremely ineffectual
4. Based on this article, what would you judge Mr. McKay's professional competence to be?
1. extremely competent 2. above average competence 3. average competence 4. below average competence 5. incompetent
5. To what extent did you agree with Mr. McKay's point of view?
1. complete agreement 2. great deal of agreement 3. partial agreement 4. little agreement 5. complete disagreement
6. How profound would you judge Mr. McKay's article to be?
1. extremely profound 2. moderately profound 3. somewhat profound 4. little profundity 5. not at all profound
7. Based on your reading of this article, what would you guess Mr. McKay's status in his field to be?
1. great status in the field 2. more than average status in the field 3. average status 4. less than average status 5. little or no status in the field
8. To what extent did Mr. McKay sway your opinions about the issues discussed in his article?
1. completely 2. a great deal 3. somewhat 4. very little 5. not at all
9. If you were to assign a grade to Mr. McKay's article, what would it be?
1. A 2. B 3. C 4. D 5. F

The general hypothesis was that female subjects would show a tendency to value the professional work of men more highly than the work of women, even when the work was identical, but that this tendency would be inversely related to the degree of "femaleness" associated with the particular professional field.

RESULTS

The means for the nine questions for the six pairs of articles are presented in Table 1. For each article a summary score based on the scores of all nine questions was computed. Differences between summary scores for each pair of the six articles were analyzed by means of Mann-Whitney U tests, as outlined by Siegel (1956). The results of these analyses are summarized in Table 2.

Based on this analysis, it is clear that the general hypothesis receives only very partial support. Only one statistically significant difference was obtained. That difference, consistent with the hypothesis, reveals that for a field with high male association, city planning, the male-authored article is more highly valued than the female-authored article ($U = 130.5$, $p < .05$). For the other articles, the data were generally in the predicted direction but failed to achieve conventional levels of statistical significance.

In order to determine possible differences in the sensitivity of the nine

TABLE 1
Means for the Six Pairs of Articles on the Nine Evaluative Questions

	Articles											
	(1) Linguistics		(2) Law		(3) Art		(4) Dietetics		(5) Education		(6) City Planning	
Question	Male	Female	Male	Female	Male	Female	Male	Female	Male	Female	Male	Female
1	3.15	3.65	2.25	2.70	2.65	2.15	1.95	2.25	2.10	2.10	2.30	2.65
2	3.10	3.50	2.30	3.00	2.50	2.80	3.65	3.45	2.25	2.50	2.70	2.90
3	2.65	3.05	2.50	3.05	2.55	2.30	1.50	2.05	2.15	2.20	2.10	2.35
4	2.50	2.85	2.10	2.60	2.30	2.20	2.15	2.35	1.95	2.30	2.50	3.15
5	2.70	3.15	2.15	2.65	2.55	2.40	1.65	1.75	1.70	1.65	2.55	3.45
6	3.35	3.70	2.50	2.95	2.80	2.85	3.35	3.45	2.60	2.80	2.75	3.30
7	2.80	3.55	2.30	2.95	2.50	2.85	2.70	2.80	2.25	2.65	2.70	3.30
8	3.95	4.25	3.05	3.15	3.20	3.50	3.25	3.25	3.25	3.50	3.05	3.75
9	2.75	3.00	2.05	2.55	2.30	2.05	1.85	2.10	1.95	2.05	2.45	2.45

Note: The lower the score, the more favorable the rating.

TABLE 2
Differences between Summary Scores of the Six Pairs of Articles

Article	Mean		U	p^a
	Male	Female		
Linguistics	26.95	30.70	146.0	<.07
Law	21.20	25.60	155.0	<.10
Art history	23.35	23.10	197.5	n.s.
Dietetics	22.05	23.45	173.5	n.s.
Education	20.20	21.75	165.0	n.s.
City planning	23.10	27.30	130.5	<.05

^{a}One-tailed tests.

TABLE 3
Differences between Male and Female Articles for the Nine Evaluative Questions

Question	N	z	p^a
1	36	1.50	<.06
2	36	1.50	<.06
3	35	.68	n.s.
4	32	3.00	<.001
5	37	1.64	<.05
6	34	1.19	n.s.
7	30	2.75	<.003
8	32	.002	n.s.
9	33	1.05	n.s.

^{a}One-tailed tests.

questions to evaluate sex differences, the following procedures were used: a difference score was obtained between the summed score on the male articles and the summed score on the female articles for all subjects for each of the nine questions. Differences were analyzed by means of sign tests; these are summarized in Table 3. The results of these analyses again offer partial support for the general hypotheses. For all questions the results were in the same direction, male articles were more favorably evaluated than female articles. For questions 4, 5, and 7 the differences were statistically significant, the values being, respectively, $z = 3.00$, $p < .001$; $z = 1.64$, $p < .05$; and $z = 2.75$, $p < .003$. For questions 1 and 2 the results approached statistical significance, the values being the same for each question, $z = 1.50$, $p < .06$.

The final analysis of the data evaluated the direction of the difference for all questions on all pairs of articles. Nine questions for six pairs of articles yielded 54 mean comparisons. Of the 54 mean comparisons, 3 means were tied, 7 means favored the female authors, and 44 favored the male authors. A sign test analysis yields $z = 5.04$, $p < .001$.

It is clear from these data that the hypothesis concerning the general tendency among women to evaluate more favorably the work of men than of women was confirmed. The hypothesis that this tendency would be lessened as the "femaleness" of a professional field increased was not supported.

DISCUSSION

The empirical fact of reliable sex differences across a wide range of psychological tasks and experiences is too well known to need citation. That many of these differences lend themselves to evaluative judgments of good-bad or favorable-unfavorable is also clear. In the research previously cited, it was noted that women are generally evaluated less favorably than men.

Two basic steps would seem to be involved in this evaluative process. First, the individual must make a determination as to the existence and nature of a sex difference. The second step involves a value judgment of the perceived difference. Either or both steps may involve inaccuracy. The accuracy of the perception of difference is a simple empirical matter, whatever methodological difficulties might be involved in ascertaining the relation of the perceived to the true difference.

Ascertaining the accuracy of the evaluative step in the judgmental process is clearly more complex. Nonetheless, it would seem reasonable to suggest that the accuracy of the value judgment is a function of the logical relation of the perceived difference to a given and stated set of criteria.

It would seem clear, then, that a difference can be accurately perceived and inaccurately valued. It is, however, obvious that for the entire judgmental process to be accurate, the basic perception of difference must be accurate. Much of the research in this field has been concerned with the perception of difference, irrespective of the accuracy of the perception.

In the present study, true sex-related differences were eliminated. Consequently, the basic general finding that the work of men was more highly valued than the work of women represents obvious distortion.

Further, it should be noted that there was nothing in the experimental procedure or in the instructions to the subjects that specifically directed the subjects' attention to sex differences as such. Their attention was directed specifically to the intellectual qualities of professional literature, and they were informed of the authors' sex only in an indirect and incidental manner.

The data clearly suggest that the subjects were sensitive to the sex of the author and that this logically irrelevant fact served to distort their judgments. Both the sensitivity and the distortion are characteristics of prejudice, and it seems clear that these young women did, in fact, reveal a significant prejudice against women.

It is not yet clear how pervasive are these attitudes across populations and experiences. Nor is it clear that principles derived from the study of ethnic and racial prejudice can be directly applied to these attitudes. It does seem clear, however, that antifeminism among women is a phenomenon of theoretical and social significance.

THE RESEARCH EXPERIENCE

REFERENCES

Allport, G. W. *The nature of prejudice.* Cambridge: Addison-Wesley, 1954.

Bruner, J. S. *The process of education.* Cambridge: Harvard University Press, 1961.

de Beauvoir, Simone. *The second sex.* New York: Knopf, 1953.

French, Elizabeth G., & Lesser, G. S. Some characteristics of the achievement motive in women. *Journal of Abnormal and Social Psychology,* 1964, *68,* 119-128.

Friedan, Betty. *The feminine mystique.* New York: Norton, 1963.

Gans, H. J. City planning and urban realities. *Commentary,* February 1962, pp. 170-175.

Hunter, S. *Modern French painting.* New York: Dell, 1956.

Kitay, P. M. A comparison of the sexes in their attitudes and beliefs about women. *Sociometry,* 1940, *34,* 399-407.

Kittrie, M. N. A post mortem of the Eichmann case: The lessons for international law. *The Journal of Criminal Law, Criminology and Police Science,* 1964, *55,* 16-29.

McKee, J. P., & Sherriffs, A. C. The differential evaluation of males and females. *Journal of Personality,* 1957, *25,* 356-371.

Sherriffs, A. C., & McKee, J. P. Qualitative aspects of beliefs about men and women. *Journal of Personality,* 1957, *25,* 452-464.

Siegel, S. *Nonparametric statistics for the behavioral sciences.* New York: McGraw-Hill, 1956.

Smith, S. Age and sex differences in children's opinion concerning sex differences. *Journal of Genetic Psychology,* 1939, *54,* 17-25.

Stare, F. G. Sense and nonsense about nutrition. *Harper's,* October 1964, pp. 66-70.

Vossler, K. *The spirit of language in civilization.* New York: Harcourt, Brace, 1932.

Personal Journal ———————————————————————————————

B. A PERSONAL JOURNAL

I remember in the 1950s, when I was an undergraduate, commuting to Columbia University from my home in the Bronx. It was an hour's trip either way, but I had my choice of two routes. I could take the Independent subway to 59th Street and transfer to the IRT back uptown to 116th Street, or I could take the D train to 125th Street and walk across Harlem to school. If the weather was good, I took the Harlem route.

The walk through Harlem took me past a drug store which advertised two products in its windows I had never seen or even heard of before: *hair straightener* and *skin lightener.* It was a time of innocence, perhaps cultural, perhaps personal, but in any event I was led to muse about the ultimate con-

---

Source: Prepared especially for this volume.

sequences of discrimination and persecution, the acceptance by the victim of the criteria for his or her victimization. Surely not a new idea, but it was new to me, my own private act of discovery.

I do not recall with the same exactness when it was specifically that I encountered similar examples with other people and other groups. As a general part of my experience, widely shared, I am sure, I have encountered the Jew who is flattered when told he "doesn't seem Jewish" and the woman pleased to be told that she "thinks like a man." Perhaps these examples are dated; I hope so, but they were a part of my experience growing up in America after World War II and a part of the experience that I brought with me to the study of psychology.

In graduate school I became interested in studying Jewish anti-Semitism. One methodological problem I encountered in this research was that all the available scales I could find that alleged to measure anti-Semitism seemed to me to be too obvious. I tried for a while to construct a more subtle measure of anti-Semitism using such items as:

1. Who was the greater scientist, Newton or Einstein?
2. Which is the more appropriate food symbol of the United States, ham and eggs or apple pie?

I don't know if such items were either subtle or valid. In any event, nothing much came of this research. Nevertheless, the general idea of studying self-hatred remained.

The idea took a somewhat different form and concerned a different target group after I began teaching at Connecticut College. The college, which is now coeducational, was, when I first started to teach there in the 1960s, exclusively a women's college. I remember being struck by the passiveness of the students; the women were bright, able, hard-working, but with few exceptions they lacked intellectual aggressiveness. I also remember at the end of one course reading a final exam that I thought superb by a student whose name I didn't recognize. I remember feeling sure that had this student been a male, *he* wouldn't have been anonymous.

But the incident which most sharply led me to consider the differences between male and female college students and which prompted my research on the misogynous attitudes of women was the following: I had been asked by a neighboring school to teach a course. This school was a fine, liberal arts college, very much like Connecticut College except that its students were men only. I knew these students to be similar to the students at Connecticut in intelligence, ability, and background. They were in substance the brothers of the women I taught at Connecticut, but they were very different in their classroom behavior. These male students were actively involved in the class in a way that the girls rarely were; they spoke up, they seemed enthusiastic and deeply interested, their comments and ideas were far-ranging—and it took me nearly a month to discover I was getting a first-rate snow job. These guys hadn't done ten cents' worth of reading since the course had started, a fact which their enthusiastic chatter had successfully obscured long past the time that a sensible teacher should have ferreted out their scheme.

The contrast then between these "brothers and sisters" was sharp. The girls could be counted on to do the work, the guys could be counted on to do the talking. This formulation is surely too sweeping, but it did help to sharpen some questions I had always had about my students. The more I thought about this particular incident, the more others came to mind. The only coordinated meaning I could impose on these experiences was my sense that these young women did not value themselves as they should, that because they were women they chose to participate in and compete in a different world of experience, a less good one. They denigrated themselves and other women. They were, in short, prejudiced against women.

The "hard" part of the research was now completed: The question was asked. It remained now only for me to put the question into an experimental form and to decide on certain technical questions such as sample, sample size, and measuring device.

In reading the work of other people in this general area, two facts seemed to emerge:

1. There were a lot of data that *suggested* prejudice toward women.
2. There were no data to *prove* the phenomenon.

Most of the studies simply elicited negative evaluations of women. Are men or women more generous? Such a question, whatever the answer, is not sufficient to demonstrate prejudice. What is required is the demonstration that the evaluation is not consistent with the personal experience of the subject and that the attitude is not modifiable by new and contradictory evidence.

The first task then was to devise an instrument that would provide a sample of misogynous attitudes. I do not recall now the single moment when I hit upon the idea to prepare pairs of identical articles in which the author's first name, and therefore sex, would be varied. The idea emerged, precisely how or why I don't know, other than that I was immersed in a set of questions forcing a set of experimental requirements that my idea seemed to satisfy. The mechanics of selecting the articles and fitting them together in an experimental instrument are discussed in the preceding article.

The experimental task I undertook, then, was to establish experimentally the existence of the phenomenon of prejudice toward women by experimentally controlling the relevant evaluative experience. If I had asked my subjects "Who is more likely to write a good article on city planning, a man or a woman?" the answer to such a question would leave the question of prejudice untouched. By asking subjects to evaluate *identical* articles that differ only in the *sex* of the author, the difference in evaluation can be attributed only to that experimental difference.

The next basic question with which I was confronted was the selection of subjects. Here I must admit that I was guided in large part by convenience. I taught at a women's college, so obtaining female college students for subjects was an easy thing to do. Such a sample appeared to me to be an entirely proper and experimentally conservative choice as well. I reasoned that if a bright, selective group of young women, from a setting in which they were continually being exhorted to achieve academically and in which they were provided with numerous models of women who had attained scholarly careers, demonstrated prejudicial attitudes, then women less intellectual, without the stimulation of such a favorable setting, would be even more likely to be prejudiced.

It should be noted that my reasoning that the subject sample was a good one did not settle the question. The question remained an empirical one which would ultimately be answered empirically or not at all. But all researchers must make decisions about the manner of their experiment in the absence of entirely adequate information, and I made the decision about the sample for the reasons I cite.

As noted in the report of the research, the subjects were gathered together in a large lecture hall and the data were collected in a single session. At the end of the testing, because there was no longer any reason to maintain deception, I asked the subjects what they thought was the true purpose of the experiment. A majority of the young women admitted that they thought it was as I had represented it to them: a study to determine "the ability of college students to make critical evaluations of professional literature." Others, the more skeptical ones, imagined some other purposes. None recognized the true intent of the research.

When I explained to the students what the research was all about, the first general reaction was laughter. The next reaction, pretty much shared in by all, was to deny the possibility that the authors' sex had influenced their evaluation. Indeed, a substantial number of subjects claimed that they hadn't been aware of the authors' sex when they made their evaluations. In light of the results, this reaction in itself is an interesting phenomenon.

How successfully the research dealt with the question it was intended to answer is a judgment I'd prefer not to make. But I do take this satisfaction from my work: I challenged an area of human importance. Others are doing more to answer the questions that remain and to effect social and personal change, and that's as it should be.

Craig Haney, W. Curtis Banks, and Philip G. Zimbardo ————

A. INTERPERSONAL DYNAMICS IN A SIMULATED PRISON

Although we have passed through many periods of so-called prison "reform," in which physical conditions within prisons have improved and in which the rhetoric of rehabilitation has replaced the language of punitive incarceration, the social institution of prison has continued to fail. On purely pragmatic grounds, there is substantial evidence that prisons really neither "rehabilitate" nor act as a deterrent to future crime—in America, recidivism rates upwards of 75 percent speak quite decisively to these criteria. And, to perpetuate what is additionally an economic failure, American taxpayers alone must provide an expenditure for "corrections" of 1.5 billion dollars annually. On humanitarian grounds as well, prisons have failed: our mass media are increasingly filled with accounts of atrocities committed daily, man against man, in reaction to the penal system or in the name of it.

Attempts at explaining the deplorable condition of our penal system, and its dehumanizing effects upon prisoners and guards, characteristically focus upon what can be called the *dispositional hypothesis*. Rarely expressed explicitly, it is central to a prevalent nonconscious ideology: The state of the social institution of prison is due to the "nature" of the people who administrate it, or the "nature" of the people who populate it, or both. The dispositional hypothesis has been embraced by the proponents of the prison status quo (blaming violence on the criminal dispositions of prisoners), as

Source: Abridged from Craig Haney, W. Curtis Banks, and Philip G. Zimbardo, "Interpersonal Dynamics in a Simulated Prison," *International Journal of Criminology and Penology*, 1973, *1*, 69-97.

This research was funded by an ONR grant: N00014-67-A-0112-0041 to Professor Philip G. Zimbardo.

The ideas expressed in this paper are those of the authors and do not imply endorsement of ONR or any sponsoring agency. We wish to extend our thanks and appreciation for the contributions to this research by David Jaffe who served as "warden" and pretested some of the variables in the mock prison situation. In addition, Greg White provided invaluable assistance during the data reduction phase of this study. Many others (most notably Carolyn Burkhart, Susie Phillips, and Kathy Rosenfeld) helped at various stages of the experiment, with the construction of the prison, prisoner arrest, interviewing, testing, and data analysis—we extend our sincere thanks to each of these collaborators. Finally, we especially wish to thank Carlo Prescott, our prison consultant, whose personal experience gave us invaluable insights into the nature of imprisonment.

well as by its critics (attributing brutality of guards and staff to their sadistic personality structures). The appealing simplicity of this proposition localizes the source of prison riots, recidivism, and corruption in these "bad seeds" and not in the conditions of the "prison soil." The system itself goes on essentially unchanged, its basic structure unexamined and unchallenged.

A critical evaluation of the dispositional hypothesis, however, cannot be made directly through observation in existing prison settings, since such naturalistic observation necessarily confounds the acute effects of the environment with the chronic characteristics of the inmate and guard populations. To partial out the situational effects of the prison environment per se from those attributable to a priori dispositions of its inhabitants requires a research strategy in which a "new" prison is constructed, comparable in its fundamental social-psychological milieu to existing prison systems but entirely populated by individuals who are undifferentiated in all essential dimensions from the rest of society.

Such was the approach taken in the present empirical study, namely, to create a prisonlike situation in which the guards and inmates were initially comparable and characterized as being "psychologically healthy," and then to observe the patterns of behavior which resulted and to record the cognitive, emotional, and attitudinal reactions that emerged.

No specific hypotheses were advanced other than the general one that assignment to the treatment of "guard" or "prisoner" would result in significantly different reactions on behavioral measures of interaction, emotional measures of mood state and pathology, and attitudes toward self, as well as other indices of coping and adaptation to this extreme situation.

METHOD

The effects of playing the role of "guard" or "prisoner" were studied in the context of an experimental simulation of a prison environment. The research design was a relatively simple one, involving as it did only a single treatment variable, the random assignment to either a "guard" or "prisoner" condition. These roles were enacted over an extended period of time (nearly one week) within an environment which had been physically constructed to closely resemble a prison. Central to the methodology of creating and maintaining the psychological state of imprisonment was the functional simulation of significant properties of "real prison life" (established through information from former inmates, correctional personnel, and texts).

Subjects

The 22 subjects who participated in the experiment were selected from an initial pool of 75 respondents who answered a newspaper ad asking for male volunteers to participate in a psychological study of "prison life," in return for payment of $15 per day. Those who responded to the notice completed an extensive questionnaire concerning their family background, physical and mental health history, prior experience, and attitudinal propensities with respect to any possible sources of psychopathology (including their involvements in crime). Each respondent who completed the background questionnaire was interviewed by one of two experimenters. Finally, the 24 subjects who were judged to be *most stable* (physically and mentally) were selected to participate in the study. On a random basis, half of the subjects were assigned the role of "guard," half were assigned to the role of "prisoner."

The subjects were normal, healthy males attending colleges throughout the United States who were in the Stanford area during the summer. They were largely of middle-class background and Caucasians (with the exception of one Oriental subject). Initially they were strangers to each other, a selection precaution taken to avoid the disruption of any preexisting friendship patterns and to mitigate against any transfer of previously established relationships or patterns of behavior into the experimental situation.

Procedure
Role Instructions

All subjects had been told that they would be randomly assigned either the guard or the prisoner role, and all had voluntarily agreed to play either role for $15 per day for up to two weeks. They signed a contract guaranteeing a minimally adequate diet, clothing, housing, and medical care, as well as the financial remuneration, in return for their stated "intention" of serving in the assigned role for the duration of the study.

It was made explicit in the contract that those assigned to be prisoners should expect to be under surveillance (have little or no privacy) and to have some of their basic civil rights suspended during their imprisonment. They were aware that physical abuse was explicitly prohibited. Subjects were given no other information about what to expect and no instructions about behavior "appropriate" for the prisoner role. Those actually assigned to this treatment were informed by phone to be available at their place of residence on a given Sunday, when we would start the experiment.

The subjects assigned to be guards attended an orientation meeting on the day prior to the induction of the prisoners. At this time they were introduced to the principal investigators, the "superintendent" of the prison (P.G.Z.) and an undergraduate research assistant who assumed the administrative role of "warden." They were told that we were attempting to simulate a prison environment within the limits imposed by pragmatic and ethical considerations. Their assigned task was to "maintain the reasonable degree of order within the prison necessary for its effective functioning," although the specifics of how this duty might be implemented were not explicitly detailed. To involve the subjects in their roles even before the first prisoner was incarcerated, the guards assisted in the final phases of completing the prison complex—putting the cots in the cells, posting signs on the walls, setting up the guards' quarters, and moving furniture, water coolers, and refrigerators.

The guards generally believed that we were interested primarily in studying the behavior of prisoners. Of course, we were also concerned with effects which enacting the role of guard in this environment would have on their behavior and subjective states. For this reason, they were given few explicit instructions on what it meant to be a guard and were left to "fill in" their own definitions of the role. A notable exception was the explicit and categorical prohibition against the use of physical punishment or aggression, which we emphasized from the outset of the study.

The prisoner subjects remained in the mock prison 24 hours a day for the duration of the study. Three were arbitrarily assigned to each of the three cells, and two others were on standby call at their homes. The guard subjects worked on three-man, eight-hour shifts, remaining in the prison environment only during their work shifts and going about their usual routines at other times. The one subject assigned to be a standby guard withdrew just before the simulation phase began. Final data analysis, then, is based on 11 prisoners and 10 guards.

Physical Aspects of the Prison

The prison was built in a 35-foot section of a basement corridor in the psychology building at Stanford University. It was partitioned by two fabricated walls, one of which was fitted with the only entrance door to the cell block; the other contained a small observation screen. Three small cells (6 x 9 feet) were made from converted laboratory rooms by replacing the usual doors with steel-barred doors painted black and removing all furniture. A cot (with mattress, sheet, and pillow) for each prisoner was the only furniture in the cells. A small closet across from the cells served as a solitary confinement facility; its dimensions were extremely small (2 x 2 x 7 feet), and it was unlit.

In addition, several rooms in an adjacent wing of the building were used as guards' quarters (to change in and out of uniform or for rest and relaxation), a bedroom for the "warden" and "superintendent," and an interview-testing room. Concealed video recording equipment was located in the testing room and behind the observation screen at one end of the "yard," where there was also sufficient space for several observers.

Uniforms

In order to promote feelings of anonymity in the subjects, each group was issued uniforms. For the guards, this consisted of plain khaki shirts and trousers, a whistle, a police nightstick (wooden baton), and reflecting sunglasses which made eye contact impossible. The prisoners' uniforms were loosely fitting muslin smocks with an identification number on front and back. A light chain and lock were placed around one ankle. On their feet they wore rubber sandals, and their hair was covered with a nylon stocking made into a cap. Each prisoner was also issued a toothbrush, soap, soapdish, towel, and bed linen. No personal belongings were allowed in the cells. The outfitting of both prisoners and guards in this manner served to enhance group identity and reduce individual uniqueness within the two groups.

Induction Process

With the cooperation of the Palo Alto City Police Department, all of the subjects assigned to the prisoner treatment were unexpectedly "arrested" at their residences. A police officer charged them either with suspicion of burglary or armed robbery, advised them of their legal rights, handcuffed them, thoroughly searched them (often as curious neighbors looked on), and carried them off to the police station in the rear of the police car. At the station they went through the standard booking routines of being finger-printed, having an identification file prepared, and then being placed in a detention cell. Subsequently, each prisoner was blindfolded and driven by one of the experimenters and a subject-guard to our mock prison. Throughout the entire arrest procedure, the police officers involved maintained a formal, serious attitude, avoiding answering any questions of clarification as to the relation of this "arrest" to the mock prison study.

Upon arrival at our experimental prison, each prisoner was stripped, sprayed with a delousing preparation (deodorant spray), and made to stand alone, naked, in the cell yard before being outfitted. After being given their uniforms and having an I.D. picture ("mug shot") taken, each prisoner was put in his cell.

Administrative Routine

When all the cells were occupied, the warden greeted the prisoners and read them the rules of the institution (developed the previous day by the guards and the warden). They were to be memorized and to be followed. Prisoners were to be referred to only by the number of their uniforms, in a further effort to depersonalize them.

The prisoners were served three bland meals per day, were allowed three supervised toilet visits, and were given two hours daily for the privilege of reading or letter writing. Work assignments were issued for which the prisoners were to receive an hourly wage to constitute their $15 daily payment. Two visiting periods per week were scheduled, as were movie rights and exercise periods. Three times a day all prisoners were lined up for a "count" (one on each guard work-shift). The initial purpose of the count was to ascertain that all prisoners were present and to test them on their knowledge of the rules and of their I.D. numbers. The first perfunctory counts lasted only about ten minutes, but on each successive day (or night) they were spontaneously increased in duration by the guards until some lasted several hours. Many of the preestablished features of administrative routine were modified or abandoned by the guards, and some privileges were forgotten by the staff over the course of study.

Data Collection: Dependent Measures

The exploratory nature of this investigation and the absence of specific hypotheses led us to adopt the strategy of surveying as many behavioral and psychological manifestations of the prison experience on the guards and the prisoners as was possible. The dependent measures were of two general types: (1) transactions between and within each group of subjects, recorded on video and audio tape as well as directly observed, and (2) individual reactions on questionnaires, mood inventories, personality tests, daily guard shift reports, and postexperimental interviews.

Data collection was organized around the following sources:

1. *Videotaping* Using the concealed video equipment, about 12 hours of recordings were made of daily, regularly occurring events such as the counts and meals, as well as unusual interactions such as a prisoner rebellion; visits from a priest, a lawyer, and parents; parole board meetings; and others.

2. *Audio recording* Concealed microphones recorded over 30 hours of verbal interactions between guards and prisoners in the prison yard, as well as some within the cells and in the testing-interview room.

3. *Rating Scales* Mood adjective checklists and sociometric measures were administered on several occasions to assess emotional changes in affective state and interpersonal dynamics among the guard and prisoner groups.

4. *Individual Difference Scales* Prior to the start of the simulation all subjects had completed a series of paper-and-pencil personality tests selected to provide dispositional indicators of interpersonal behavior styles—the F scale of Authoritarian Personality (Adorno, Frenkel-Brunswik, Levinson, & Sanford, 1950) and the Machiavellianism Scale (Christie & Geis, 1970)—and to isolate areas of possible personality pathology through the newly developed Comrey Personality Scale (Comrey, 1970).

5. *Personal Observations* The guards made daily reports of their observations after each shift, the experimenters kept informal diaries, and all subjects completed postexperimental questionnaires of their reactions to the experience about a month after the study was over.

Data Analysis: Video Recordings

Special analyses were required only of the video and audio material. The other data sources were analyzed following established scoring procedures.

Since the present discussion is based primarily on the videotaped material, details of this analysis are outlined here.

There were 25 relatively discrete incidents identifiable on the tapes of prisoner-guard interactions. Each incident or scene was scored for the presence of nine behavioral (and verbal) categories by two judges who had not been involved with the simulation study. These categories were defined as follows:

Question All questions asked, requests for information or assistance (excluding rhetorical questions).

Command An order to commence or abstain from a specific behavior, directed either to individuals or groups. Also generalized orders; e.g., "Settle down."

Information A specific piece of information proffered by anyone, whether requested or not, dealing with any contingency of the simulation.

Individuating Reference Positive: use of a person's real name, nickname, or allusion to special positive physical characteristics. Negative: use of prison number, title, generalized "you," or reference to derogatory characteristic.

Threat Verbal statement of contingent negative consequences of a wide variety; e.g., no meal, long count, pushups, lock-up in hole, no visitors.

Deprecation/Insult Use of obscenity, slander, malicious statement directed toward individuals or groups, e.g., "You lead a life of mendacity," "You guys are really stupid."

Resistance Any physical resistance, usually prisoners to guards, such as holding onto beds, blocking doors, shoving guard or prisoner, taking off stocking caps, refusing to carry out orders.

Help Person physically assisting another (excludes verbal statements of support); e.g., guard helping another to open door, prisoner helping another prisoner in cleanup duties.

Use of Instruments Use of any physical instrument to either intimidate, threaten, or achieve specific end; e.g., fire extinguisher, batons, whistles.

RESULTS

The results of the present experiment support many commonly held conceptions of prison life and validate anecdotal evidence supplied by articulate ex-convicts. The environment of arbitrary custody had great impact upon *the affective states* of both guards and prisoners as well as upon *the interpersonal processes* between and within those role-groups.

In general, guards and prisoners showed a marked decrease in positive affect or emotion, and their overall outlook became increasingly negative. As the experiment progressed, prisoners expressed intentions to do harm to others more frequently. For both prisoners and guards, self-evaluations were more deprecating as the experience of the prison environment became internalized.

Overt behavior was generally consistent with the subjective self-reports and affective expressions of the subjects. While guards and prisoners were essentially free to engage in any form of interaction (positive or negative, supportive or affrontive, etc.), the characteristic nature of their encounters tended to be negative, hostile, affrontive, and dehumanizing. Prisoners immediately adopted a generally passive style of responding, while guards assumed a very active initiative role in all interactions. Throughout the experiment, commands were the most frequent form of verbal behavior and, generally, verbal exchanges were strikingly impersonal, with few references to individual identity. Although it was clear to all subjects that the experimenters would not permit physical violence to take place, varieties of less direct aggressive behavior were observed frequently (especially on the part of guards). In fact, varieties of verbal affronts became the most frequent form of interpersonal contact between guards and prisoners. (See Figure 1 below.)

The most dramatic evidence of the impact of the mock prison upon the participants was seen in the gross reactions of five prisoners who had to be released from the study because of extreme emotional depression, crying, rage, or acute anxiety. The pattern of symptoms was quite similar in four of the subjects and began as early as the second day of imprisonment. The fifth subject was released after being treated for a psychosomatic rash which covered portions of his body. Of the remaining prisoners, only two said they were unwilling to forfeit all the money they had earned in return for being "paroled" from the study. When the experiment was terminated prematurely after only six days, all the remaining prisoners were delighted by their unexpected good fortune; in contrast, most of the guards seemed to be distressed by the decision to stop the experiment. It appeared to us that the guards had become sufficiently involved in their roles so that they now enjoyed the extreme control and power they exercised and were reluctant to give it up. One guard, who did report being personally upset at the suffering of the prisoners, claimed to have considered asking to change his role to become one of them—but never did so. None of the guards ever failed to come to work on time for their shift, and indeed, on several occasions guards remained on duty voluntarily and uncomplainingly for extra hours—without additional pay.

The extreme reactions which emerged in both groups of subjects provide clear evidence of the power of the social forces operating in this pathological setting. There were, however, individual differences observed in *styles* of coping with this stressful experience, as well as varying degrees of success in adaptation to it. While all were somewhat adversely affected by it, half the prisoners did "endure" the oppressive atmosphere—at least in the sense that they remained until the study was completed. Not all of the guards resorted to the overt and inventive forms of hostility employed by others. Some guards

THE RESEARCH EXPERIENCE

were tough but fair ("played by the rules"), some went far beyond their roles to engage in cruelty and harassment, while a few were passive and rarely instigated any coercive control over the prisoners. It is important to emphasize, however, that at some time during the six days *all* guards participated in what could be characterized as sadistic treatment of prisoners.

Initial Personality and Attitude Measures

Overall, it is apparent that initial personality-attitude dispositions account for an extremely small part of the variance in behavioral reactions to the mock prison environment. In a few select instances, however, such dispositions do correlate with prisoners' ability to tolerate the experimental situation.

Mean scores on the *Comrey Personality Scales* reveal no statistically significant differences between prisoners and guards on any of the eight subscales. Further, all group means fall within the 40-60 percentile range of the normative male population reported by Comrey. There were also no significant mean differences found between guards ($\bar{X} = 7.73$) and prisoners ($\bar{X} = 8.77$) on the *Machiavellianism Scale* of effective interpersonal manipulation. In addition, the Mach Scale was of no help in predicting a prisoner's ability to endure the prison milieu by remaining in the study until its termination. On the F scale (Adorno et al., 1950) designed to measure rigid adherence to conventional values and a submissive, uncritical attitude toward authority, there was no significant difference between the mean score for prisoners (4.78) and the mean score for guards (4.36).

Several suggestive trends emerged, however, when prisoners who remained in the study were compared with those five who had to be released because of their emotional reactions to the environment. Although none of the comparisons achieved statistical significance, three Comrey scales seem to be potential discriminators of those who were able to tolerate this type of confinement: Prisoners who remained scored higher on conformity ("acceptance of society as it is"), extroversion, and empathy (helpfulness, sympathy, and generosity). Stronger, however, is the relationship of tolerance for the prison environment to the F scale on authoritarianism. This intragroup comparison shows that those prisoners who remained scored more than twice as high on conventionality and authoritarianism ($\bar{X} = 7.78$) as did those released early ($\bar{X} = 3.20$). While the difference between these means also fails to reach acceptable levels of significance, it is striking to note that a rank ordering of prisoners on the F scale correlates very highly with the duration of their stay in the experiment ($r_s = .898$, $p < .005$).

Video Recordings

The characterization of our prison as an "authoritarian" milieu is substantiated by a detailed analysis of the nature of the interactions between

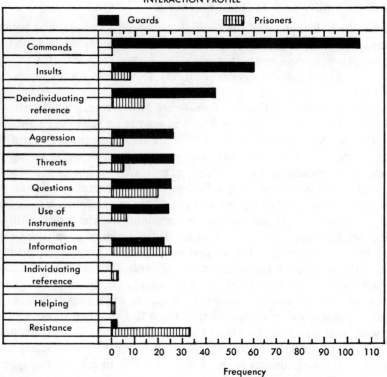

FIGURE 1
Interaction profile of guard and prisoner behavior across 25 occasions over six days in the simulated prison environment

INTERACTION PROFILE

■ Guards   ▥ Prisoners

Commands

Insults

Deindividuating reference

Aggression

Threats

Questions

Use of instruments

Information

Individuating reference

Helping

Resistance

0 10 20 30 40 50 60 70 80 90 100 110

Frequency

prisoners and guards as video recorded over 25 separate behavioral units (including counts, meals, and so on). These data are presented in Figure 1. The pattern of results which emerges is remarkably similar to that reported by Lewin, Lippitt, and White (1939) in their classic study comparing autocratic and democratic forms of group leadership. They found authoritarian role leaders were differentiated from others in the marked frequency with which they gave orders, commands, and information. Similarly, in our study there was a high degree of differentiation in social behavior between the mock guards and prisoners.

For guards, the most frequently exhibited verbal behavior was giving commands (which included orders), and their most frequent form of physical behavior was aggression. The most prevalent form of prisoners' verbal behavior was question asking, and resistance was their most commonly performed physical behavior. On the other hand, the most *in*frequent behavior engaged in overall throughout the experiment was "helping"—only one such incident was noted from all the video recordings collected. That solitary sign of human concern for a fellow occurred between two prisoners.

Although question asking was the most frequent form of verbal behavior for the prisoners, guards actually asked questions more frequently overall than did prisoners (but not significantly so). This reflects the fact that the overall level of behavior emitted was much higher for the guards than for the prisoners. All of those verbal acts which were categorized as commands were engaged in by the guards. Obviously, prisoners had no opportunity to give commands, since that behavior had become the exclusive "right" of guards.

Of a total of 61 incidents of direct interpersonal reference observed (incidents in which one subject spoke directly to another with the use of some identifying reference; e.g., "Hey, Peter," "You there"), 58 involved the use of some deindividuating rather than some individuating form of reference. (Recall that we characterized this distinction as follows: an individuating, or positive, reference involved the use of a person's actual name, nickname, or allusion to special physical characteristics, whereas a deindividuating, or negative, reference involved the use of a prison number or a generalized "you"—thus being a very depersonalizing form of reference.) Since all subjects were at liberty to refer to one another in either mode, it is significant that such a large proportion of the references noted were in the deindividuating mode ($Z = 6.9$, $p < .01$). Deindividuating references were made more often by guards in speaking to prisoners than the reverse ($Z = 3.67$, $p < .01$). (This finding, as with all prisoner-guard comparisons for specific categories, may be somewhat confounded by the fact that the guards apparently enjoyed a greater freedom to initiate verbal as well as other forms of behavior. Note, however, that the existence of this greater "freedom" on the part of the guards is itself an empirical finding, since it was not prescribed a priori.) It is of additional interest to point out that in the only three cases in which verbal exchange involved some individuating reference, it was prisoners who personalized guards.

A total of 32 incidents were observed which involved a verbal threat spoken by one subject to another. Of these, 27 such incidents involved a guard threatening a prisoner. Again, guards indulged in this form of behavior significantly more than prisoners did, the observed frequencies deviating significantly from an equal distribution of threats across both groups ($Z = 3.88$, $p < .01$).

Guards more often deprecated and insulted prisoners than prisoners did guards. Of a total of 67 observed incidents, the deprecation-insult was expressed disproportionately by guards to prisoners 61 times ($Z = 6.72$, $p < .01$).

Physical resistance was observed 34 times. Of these, 32 incidents involved resistance by a prisoner. Thus, as we might expect, at least in this reactive behavior domain, prisoner responses far exceeded those of the guards ($Z = 5.14$, $p < .01$).

The use of some object or instrument in the achievement of an intended purpose or in some interpersonal interaction was observed 29 times. Twenty-three such incidents involved the use of an instrument by a guard rather than a prisoner. This disproportionate frequency is significantly variant from an equal random use by both prisoners and guards ($Z = 3.16$, $p < .01$).

Over time, from day to day, guards were observed to generally escalate their harassment of the prisoners. In particular, a comparison of two of the first prisoner-guard interactions during the counts with two of the last counts in the experiment yielded significant differences in the use of deindividuating references per unit time:

$$\bar{X}_{t_1} = 0.0 \text{ and } \bar{X}_{t_2} = 5.40, \text{ respectively; } t = 3.65, p < .10$$

and in the incidence of deprecation-insult per unit time:

$$\bar{X}_{t_1} = .3 \text{ and } \bar{X}_{t_2} = 5.70, \text{ respectively; } t = 3.16, p < .10$$

On the other hand, a temporal analysis of the prisoner video data indicated a general decrease across all categories over time: Prisoners came to initiate acts far less frequently and responded (if at all) more passively to the acts of others—they simply *behaved less*.

Although the harassment by the guards escalated overall as the experiment wore on, there was some variation in the extent to which the three different guard shifts contributed to the harassment in general. With the exception of the 2:30 A.M. count, prisoners enjoyed some respite during the late-night guard shift (10:00 P.M. to 6:00 A.M.). But they really were "under the gun" during the evening shift. This was obvious in our observations and in subsequent interviews with the prisoners, and it was also confirmed in analysis of the videotaped interactions. Comparing the three different guard shifts, the evening shift was significantly different from the other two in resorting to command, the means being 9.30 and 4.04, respectively, for standardized units of time ($t = 2.50$, $p < .05$). In addition, the guards on this "tough and cruel" shift showed more than twice as many deprecation-insults toward the prisoners (means of 5.17 and 2.29, respectively, $p < .20$). They also tended to use instruments more often than other shifts to keep the prisoners in line.

Audio Recordings

Since we could video record only public interactions in the "yard," it was of special interest to discover what was occurring among prisoners in private. What were they talking about in the cells—their college life, their vocation, girl friends, what they would do for the remainder of the summer once the experiment was over? We were surprised to discover that fully 90 percent of all conversations among prisoners were related to prison topics, while only 10 percent were related to nonprison topics such as the above. They were most concerned about food, guard harassment, setting up a grievance committee, escape plans, visitors, reactions of prisoners in the other cells, and conditions in solitary. Thus, in their private conversations, when they might have escaped the roles they were playing in public, they did not. There was very little discontinuity between their presentation of self when under surveillance and when alone.

The prisoners were all strangers to each other to begin with, and becoming obsessed with these immediate survival concerns hindered them from comparing backgrounds and sharing information about their true identities. After days of living confined together in this tight environment, many of the prisoners did not even know the names of the others, where they came from, or even the most basic information about what they were like when they were not "prisoners."

Even more remarkable was the discovery that the prisoners had begun to adopt and accept the guards' negative attitude toward them. Half of all reported private interactions between prisoners could be classified as non-supportive and noncooperative. Moreover, when prisoners made evaluative statements of, or expressed regard for, their fellow prisoners, 85 percent of the time they were uncomplimentary and deprecating. This set of observed frequencies departs significantly from chance expectations based on a conservative binomial probability frequency ($p < .01$ for prison vs. nonprison topics; $p < .05$ for negative vs. positive or neutral regard).

Representative Personal Statements

Much of the flavor and impact of this prison experience has been unavoidably lost in the relatively formal, objective analyses outlined in this paper. The following quotations taken from interviews, conversations, and questionnaires provide a more personal view of what it was like to be a prisoner or guard in the "Stanford County Prison" experiment.

GUARDS' COMMENTS

They [the prisoners] seemed to lose touch with the reality of the experiment—they took me so seriously.

I didn't interfere with any of the guards' actions. Usually if what they were doing bothered me, I would walk out and take another duty.

. . . looking back, I am impressed by how little I felt for them.

They [the prisoners] didn't see it as an experiment. It was real and they were fighting to keep their identity. But we were always there to show them just who was boss.

I was tired of seeing the prisoners in their rags and smelling the strong odors of their bodies that filled the cells. I watched them tear at each other, on orders given by us.

Acting authoritatively can be fun. Power can be a great pleasure.

During the inspection, I went to cell 2 to mess up a bed which the prisoner had made and he grabbed me, screaming that he had just made it, and he wasn't going to let me mess it up. He grabbed my throat, and although he was laughing I was pretty scared. I lashed out with my stick and hit him in the chin (although not very hard) and when I freed myself I became angry.

PRISONERS' COMMENTS

The way we were made to degrade ourselves really brought us down, and that's why we all sat docile toward the end of the experiment.

I realize now (after it's over) that no matter how together I thought I was inside my head, my prison behavior was often less under my control than I realized. No matter how open, friendly, and helpful I was with other prisoners I was still operating as an isolated, self-centered person, being rational rather than compassionate.

I began to feel I was losing my identity, that the person I call _____, the person who volunteered to get me into this prison (because it was a prison to me, it *still* is a prison to me, I don't regard it as an experiment or a simulation . . .) was distant from me, was remote until finally I wasn't *that* person, I was 416. I was really my number and 416 was really going to have to decide what to do.

I learned that people can easily forget that others are human.

Debriefing Encounter Sessions

Because of the unexpectedly intense reactions (such as the above) generated by this mock prison experience, we decided to terminate the study at the end of six days rather than continue for the second week. Three separate encounter sessions were held, first for the prisoners, then for the guards, and finally for all participants together. Subjects and staff openly discussed their reactions, and strong feelings were expressed and shared. We analyzed the moral conflicts posed by this experience and used the debriefing sessions to make explicit alternative courses of action that would lead to more moral behavior in future comparable situations.

Follow-ups on each subject over the year following termination of the study revealed that the negative effects of participation had been temporary, while the personal gain to the subjects endured.

CONCLUSIONS AND DISCUSSION

It should be apparent that the elaborate procedures (and staging) employed by the experimenters to ensure a high degree of "mundane realism" in this mock prison contributed to its effective functional simulation of the psychological dynamics operating in "real" prisons. We observed empirical relationships in the simulated prison environment which were strikingly isomorphic to the internal relations of real prisons, corroborating many of the documented reports of what occurs behind prison walls. Most dramatic and distressing to us were the ease with which sadistic behavior could be elicited from individuals who were not "sadistic types" and the frequency with which acute emotional breakdowns could occur in persons selected precisely for their emotional stability.

Situational versus Dispositional Attribution

To what can we attribute these deviant behavior patterns? If these reactions had been observed within the confines of an existing penal institution, a dispositional hypothesis would likely be invoked in explanation. Some cruel guards might be singled out as sadistic or passive-aggressive personality types who chose to work in a correctional institution because of the outlets it provided for sanctioned aggression. Aberrant reactions on the part of the inmate population would likewise be viewed as an extrapolation from the prior social histories of these men as violent, antisocial, psychopathic, unstable character types.

The design of our study minimized the utility of trait or prior social history explanations by means of judicious subject selection and random assignment to roles. Considerable effort and care went into determining the composition of the final subject population from which our guards and prisoners were drawn. Through case histories, personal interviews, and a battery of personality tests, the subjects chosen to participate manifested no apparent abnormalities, antisocial tendencies, or social backgrounds that were other than exemplary. On every one of the scores of the diagnostic tests each subject scored within the "normal-average" range. Our subjects, then, were highly representative of middle-class, Caucasian American society, 17-30 years of age, but above average in both intelligence and emotional stability.

Nevertheless, in less than one week their *behavior* in this simulated prison could be characterized as pathological and antisocial. The negative, antisocial reactions observed were not the product of an environment created by combining a collection of deviant personalities but rather the result of an intrinsically pathological situation which could distort and rechannel the behavior of essentially normal individuals. The abnormality here clearly resided in the psychological nature of the situation and not in those who passed through it. Thus we offer another instance in support of Mischel's (1968) social-learning analysis of the power of situational variables to shape complex social behavior. Our results are also congruent with those of Milgram (1965), who most convincingly demonstrated the proposition that evil acts are not necessarily the deeds of evil men but may be attributable to the operation of powerful social forces. Our findings appear to have implications beyond these previous studies, however, in that we removed the immediate presence of the dominant experimenter-authority figure, gave our subjects-as-guards a freer range of behavioral alternatives, and involved the participants for a much more extended period of time.

Despite strong evidence favoring a situational causal analysis in this experiment, it should be clear that our research design actually minimized the effects of individual differences by use of a homogeneous middle-range subject population. It did not allow the strongest possible test of the relative utility of the two types of explanation. We cannot say that personality differences *never* have any effect on behavior in situations such as the one reported here. Rather, we may assert that the variance in behavior observed in this setting could be reliably attributed to variations in situational rather than personality variables. The inherently pathological characteristics of the prison situation itself, at least as functionally simulated in our study, were a *sufficient* condition to produce aberrant, antisocial behavior. (An alternative design which would maximize the potential operation of personality or dispositional variables would assign subjects who were extreme on preselected personality dimensions to each of the two experimental treatments. Such a design would, however, require a larger population and more resources than we had available. Moreover, it would not provide the demonstration attempted in the present study, namely the effects of prisonlike conditions on so-called "normal," average people.)

The failure of personality assessment variables to reliably discriminate the various patterns of prison behavior, guard reactions as well as prisoner coping styles, is reminiscent of the inability of personality tests to contribute to an understanding of the psychological differences between American POWs in Korea who succumbed to alleged Chinese Communist brainwashing by "collaborating with the enemy" and those who resisted (cf. Schein, 1961). It seems to us that there is little reason to expect paper-and-pencil behavioral reactions on personality tests taken under standard or "normal" conditions to generalize to coping behaviors under novel, stressful, and abnormal environmental conditions. It may be that the best predictor of behavior in situations of stress and power, as occurs in prisons, is overt behavior in functionally comparable simulated environments.

In the situation of imprisonment faced by our subjects, despite the potent situational control, some individual differences were manifested both in coping styles among the prisoners and in the extent and type of aggression and exercise of power among the guards. Personality variables, conceived of as learned behavior styles, can act perhaps as moderator variables in allaying or intensifying the impact of social situational variables. Their predictive utility would then depend upon acknowledging the interactive relationship of such learned response styles to the eliciting force of the situational variables.

Pathology of Power

In this experimental prison setting, the social status of guard carried with it a strong group identity and, above all, the freedom to exercise an unprecedented degree of control over the lives of other human beings. This control was invariably expressed through the use of sanctions, punishment, and demands and the threat of physical abuse. There was no need for the guards to rationally justify a request as they did in their ordinary life—merely to make a demand was sufficient to have it carried out. Many of the guards showed in their behavior, and revealed in postexperimental statements, that this sense of power was exhilarating.

The guards' use of power in this situation was self-aggrandizing and self-perpetuating. Initially derived from an arbitrary and randomly assigned label, it was intensified whenever there was any perceived threat from the prisoners, and this new level subsequently became the baseline from which further hostility and harassment would begin. The most hostile guards on each shift moved spontaneously into the leadership roles of giving orders and deciding upon punishments. They became role models whose behavior was emulated by other members of the shift. Despite minimal contact between the three separate guard shifts and nearly 16 hours a day spent away from the prison, the absolute level of aggression, as well as more subtle and "creative" forms of aggression manifested, increased in a spiraling function. Not to be tough and arrogant was taken as a sign of weakness by the other guards, and even those "good" guards who were not drawn as deeply into the power syndrome as the others respected the implicit norm of *never* contradicting or interfering with an action of a more hostile guard on their shift.

After the first day of the study, practically all prisoner rights (even such things as the time and conditions of sleeping and eating) were redefined by the guards as "privileges" which had to be earned for obedient behavior. Constructive activities such as watching movies or reading (previously planned and suggested by the experimenters) were arbitrarily canceled until further notice by the guards—and were subsequently never allowed. "Reward," then, became the granting of permission for prisoners to eat, sleep, go to the toilet, talk, smoke a cigarette, or wear eyeglasses, or it was reflected in the temporary and infrequent diminutions of harassment that occurred.

We wonder about the conceptual nature of "positive" reinforcement when subjects are in such conditions of deprivation, and the extent to which even minimally acceptable conditions become rewarding when experienced in the context of such an impoverished environment. We might also question whether meaningful nonviolent alternatives can exist as viable models for prisoner behavior inside real prisons. In a world where men are either powerful or powerless, one learns to despise the lack of power in others and in oneself. Control and manipulation rather than cooperation too often become necessary strategies for survival.

The "Prisoner" Syndrome

Various coping strategies were employed by our prisoners as they began to react to their perceived loss of personal identity and the arbitrary control of their lives. At first they exhibited disbelief at the total invasion of their privacy, constant surveillance, and the atmosphere of oppression in which they were living. Their next response was rebellion, first by the use of direct force and physical resistance, later through verbal insult and defiance. They then tried to work within the system by setting up an elected grievance committee. When that collective action failed to produce meaningful changes in their existence, individual self-interests emerged, kindled by subtle divisive tactics implemented by guards to foster distrust among the prisoners. The breakdown in prisoner cohesion was the start of social disintegration which gave rise not only to feelings of isolation but to deprecation of other prisoners as well.

As noted before, half the prisoners coped with the prison situation by becoming "sick"—extremely disturbed emotionally—as a passive way of demanding attention and help. Others became excessively obedient in trying to be "good" prisoners. They sided with the guards against a solitary fellow prisoner who coped with his situation by refusing to eat. Instead of supporting this final and major act of rebellion, the prisoners treated him as a troublemaker who deserved to be punished for his disobedience. It is likely that the negative self-regard among the prisoners noted by the end of the study represented a kind of "victim self-derogation"—the belief that the continued hostility they were receiving was justified because they somehow "deserved it" (Walster, 1966). As the days wore on, the modal prisoner reaction came to be one of passivity, dependence, and flattened affect.

Let us briefly consider some of the relevant processes involved in bringing about these reactions.

Loss of Personal Identity

For most people, identity is conferred by social recognition of one's uniqueness and is established through one's name, dress, appearance, behavior style and history. Living among strangers who know neither your name nor personal history (who refer to you only by number), dressed in a uniform exactly like all other prisoners, fearful of calling attention to yourself because of the unpredictable consequences it might provoke—all this led to a weakening of self-identity among the prisoners. As they began to lose initiative and emotional responsivity, while acting ever more compliantly, the prisoners indeed became deindividuated, not only in the eyes of the guards and the observers but also to themselves.

Arbitrary Control

On postexperimental questionnaires, the most frequently mentioned aversive aspect of the prison experience was being subjected to the patently arbitrary, capricious decisions and rules of the guards. In the simulated prison setting a question asked by a prisoner as often elicited derogation and aggression as it did a rational answer. Smiling at a joke could be punished in the same way that failing to smile might be. An individual acting in defiance of the rules could bring punishment to his innocent cell partners (who became, in effect, "mutually yoked controls"), to himself, or to all.

As the environment became more unpredictable, and previously learned assumptions about a "just and orderly world" were no longer functional, prisoners ceased to initiate any action whatever. They moved about only on orders and when in their cells rarely engaged in any purposeful activity. Their unemotional and passive reaction was the functional equivalent of the learned helplessness phenomenon reported by Seligman and Groves (1970). Since their behavior bore little relationship to environmental consequences, the prisoners essentially gave up and stopped behaving. Thus, the subjective magnitude of aversiveness was manipulated by the guards, not in terms of physical punishment but rather by controlling the psychological dimension of environmental predictability (Glass & Singer, 1972).

Dependency and Emasculation

The network of dependency relations established by the guards not only promoted helplessness in the prisoners but served to emasculate them as well. The arbitrary control by the guards put the prisoners at their mercy for even such daily, commonplace functions as going to the toilet. To do so required publicly obtained permission (not always granted) and then a personal escort to the toilet while blindfolded and handcuffed. The same was true for many other activities ordinarily practiced spontaneously and taken for granted, such as lighting up a cigarette, reading a novel, writing a letter, drinking a glass of water, or brushing one's teeth. These were all privileged activities requiring permission and necessitating a prior show of good behavior. These low-level dependencies engendered a regressive orientation in the prisoners. The extent of their dependency was defined in terms of the domain of control over all aspects of their lives which other individuals (the guards and prison staff) now exercised.

As in real prisons, the assertive, independent, aggressive nature of male prisoners posed a potential threat which was overcome with a variety of guard tactics. The prisoner uniforms resembled smocks or dresses, which made them look silly and enabled the guards to refer to them as "sissies" or "girls." Wearing these uniforms (without any underclothes) forced the prisoners to move and sit in unfamiliar, feminine postures. Any sign of individual rebellion or autonomy was labeled as indicative of "incorrigibility" and resulted in loss of privileges, solitary confinement, humiliation, or punishment of cell mates. Physically smaller guards were able to induce stronger prisoners to act foolishly and obediently. Prisoners were encouraged to belittle each other publicly during the counts. These and other tactics all served to engender in the prisoners a lessened sense of their masculinity (as defined by their external culture) and a waning of personal control. It followed, then, that although the prisoners usually outnumbered the guards during line-ups and counts (nine versus three), there never was an attempt to directly overpower them. (Interestingly, after the study was terminated, the prisoners expressed the belief that the basis of assignment to guard and prisoner groups was physical size. They perceived the guards were "bigger," when, in fact, there was no difference in average height or weight between the two randomly selected groups.)

Important ethical, legal, and practical considerations set limits upon the degree to which this situation could approach the conditions existing in actual prisons and penitentiaries. Necessarily absent were some of the most salient aspects of prison life reported by criminologists and documented in the writing of prisoners (as in George Jackson's Soledad letters, 1970, and Charrière, 1969). There was no involuntary homosexuality, no racism, no physical beatings, no threat to life by prisoners against each other or the guards. Moreover, the maximum anticipated "sentence" was only two weeks and, unlike some prison systems, could not be extended indefinitely for infractions of the internal operating rules of the prison. In this context, the profound psychological effects observed under the relatively minimal prison-like environment which existed in our mock prison have grave implications for conditions inside existing penitentiaries. We would hope that many will be moved to consider how terrible must be the psychic costs exacted from real prisoners and guards in their struggle to adjust to an environment far harsher than any we could have simulated.

Shortly after our study was terminated, the indiscriminate killings at San Quentin and Attica occurred, emphasizing the urgency for fundamental prison change which recognizes the dignity and humanity of both prisoners and guards who are constantly forced into one of the most intimate and potentially deadly encounters known to man.

REFERENCES

Adorno, T. W., Frenkel-Brunswik, E., Levinson, D. J., & Sanford, R. N. *The authoritarian personality.* New York: Harper, 1950.

Charrière, H. *Papillon.* Robert Laffont, 1969.

Christie, R., & Geis, F. L. (Eds.). *Studies in Machiavellianism.* New York: Academic Press, 1970.

Comrey, A. L. *Comrey Personality Scales.* San Diego: Educational and Industrial Testing Service, 1970.

Glass, D. C., & Singer, J. E. Behavioral aftereffects of unpredictable and uncontrollable aversive events. *American Scientist,* 1972, *6*(4), 457-465.

Jackson, G. *Soledad brother: The prison letters of George Jackson.* New York: Bantam Books, 1970.

Lewin, K., Lippitt, R., & White, R. Patterns of aggressive behavior in experimentally created "social climates." *Journal of Social Psychology,* 1939, *10,* 271-299.

Milgram, S. Some conditions of obedience and disobedience to authority. *Human Relations,* 1965, *18*(1), 57-76.

Mischel, W. *Personality and assessment.* New York: Wiley, 1968.

Schein, E. *Coercive persuasion.* New York: Norton, 1961.

Seligman, M. E., & Groves, D. P. Nontransient learned helplessness. *Psychonomic Science,* 1970, *19*(3), 191-192.

Walster, E. Assignment of responsibility for an accident. *Journal of Personality and Social Psychology,* 1966, *3*(1), 73-79.

Personal Journal ─────────────────────────────────

B. THE PLAY'S THE THING: METHODOLOGICAL NOTES ON SOCIAL SIMULATIONS

Craig Haney

> *The Father* [mellifluously]: Oh sir, you know well that life is full of infinite absurdities, which, strangely enough, do not even need to appear plausible, since they are true.
> *The Manager:* What the devil is he talking about?
> *The Father:* I say that to reverse the ordinary process may well be considered a madness: That is, to create credible situations, in order that they may appear true. But permit me to observe that if this be madness, it is the sole *raison d'etre* of your profession, gentlemen.
> —Luigi Pirandello, *Six Characters in Search of an Author*

ON SIMULATING REALITY

Because things are not always as they seem, we have devised a variety of oblique strategies to better know "reality." It is not uncommon, in science as

Source: Prepared especially for this volume.

well as drama, for the most unnatural of arrangements to provide a window onto the "natural" order of things, or for the unreal to be used as a vehicle to arrive at valuable insights into the real. Indeed, the methodologies of social science are best viewed as precisely this: a myriad of indirect, seemingly circuitous paths to arrive at better approximations of "truth" than might be attained from the direct confrontation of our experience.

The problem with our naive experience—which necessitates our being devious rather than direct—is that it is inherently relative, yet has an unmistakably absolutist "feel" to it. It provides us with neither the historical nor the intersubjective perspectives that would allow us to understand whence it came or the degree to which it is shared by others. It is naive of us to think, however, that research methods automatically purge us of our biases or "objectify" our experience. Indeed, the danger is that research, especially for its practitioners, comes also to acquire the noncontingent "feel" of direct experience. We come to lose sight of the fact that objective-appearing, experimental truth is, itself, a perspective, not *necessarily* more or less true than subjective personal knowledge.

At its very best, research is an act of teaching, an attempt at instructive communication. Through its unusual perspective or "angle" it seeks to isolate from the buzz of experience patterns and relationships that the complexities of everyday life may have masked or rendered imperceptible. Unlike more arcane physical sciences, there are few "inventions" or genuine "discoveries" in the social sciences. At most, social science research generally effects changes in people's expectancies or "prior probabilities" about the world and the way it works. (In this sense, the social scientist's preoccupation with counterintuitive findings is not misplaced.) Our revolutions are shifts in the way people perceive already existing phenomena.

A view of research-as-teaching should sensitize us to requirements of cogency and credibility in experimental design. Of the many "valid" ways to study a topic, those that are likely to be understood and believed by the intended audience are most preferred. Especially where social change is our ultimate goal, we wish to avoid the state of affairs which now characterizes some areas of applied research, namely production of "knowledge which is better by any scientific standard, [but] no more authoritative by any political standard and often more mystifying by any reasonable public standard" (Cohen & Garet, 1975, p. 33). In laboratory research we too often opt for abstract operationalizations that seem to leave us less methodologically vulnerable, but more open to questioning and skepticism by nonscientists. Realism has public value—which is not to underestimate the sophistication of the public. In fact, the current popularization of social science promises that increasing numbers of people will be familiar with fundamental research methods. If science has indeed become the "religion of modernity," then large numbers of the lay public are rapidly being initiated into the priesthood. This suggests that more people are likely to understand rather than be awed by empty ritual. The more general point, of course, is that the form of the research should be governed by its intended use.

What, then, can be the rationale for a methodology so implausible as the laboratory simulation of a complex institutional environment? Largely it is in terms of explanations effectively precluded. Specifically, studies of the pernicious effects of "real" social institutions are susceptible to the challenge that the people studied were somehow "different" beforehand. The impact attributed to social structural variables is then minimized by speculation about how fundamentally different kinds of people distribute themselves throughout the system. Behavioral pathology comes to be explained in personal rather than systemic terms.

However, laboratory research allows screening of those persons about whom individual pathology could be alleged, and random assignment of the remaining people to different treatment conditions. The resulting outcomes can only be a function of the different conditions to which equivalent groups of people have been exposed. The "person-blamers" are deprived of their most potent explanatory device—persons who can be credibly blamed.

The experimental simulation of institutional reality becomes less far-fetched when the institutional nature of laboratory settings is acknowledged. In fact, experimental control might be viewed merely as a subset or variety of institutional control. Researcher preoccupation with surveillance, impersonality, and procedure certainly rivals that of longer term institutions. Whatever the methodological justifications—and there are many—this may say something about the social control inclinations of many social scientists (whose motto, after all, is "explanation, prediction, and *control*"). It may also explain the virtual absence of research on freedom or liberty—such studies would be seriously hampered by the inherent incompatibility of methodology and subject matter.

Ironically, studies of the reactive effects of research may tell us much about behavior in "real" contexts increasingly seen and experienced as inauthentic—a measure, to be sure, of the artificiality of "natural" environments rather than the realism of experimental settings. Especially during the initial stages of institutional socialization, a mood of unreality and uncertainty prevails. On the other hand, the highly socialized may simply *expect* institutional manipulation rather than finding it foreign or discrepant. Laboratory contrivance or pretense may produce no more reactivity in them than would occur "naturally" in other contexts. (Thus the ease with which our simulated prison environment came to represent "reality" for the college student participants may be more a function of the unreality of their everyday lives, rather than of our ingenuity as experimenters.)

Compatibility of institutional and experimental forms exists also on another level. Social institutions are themselves "grande experiments"—by no means the only or even the most desirable way of partitioning societal reality. Their awesome and imposing presence conveys a permanence not intended by their originators, who saw them as temporary solutions to transitory problems. There is much propriety to the recent suggestion that politicians and social planners begin to regard their institutional "reforms as experiments" (Campbell, 1969), for it asks them to admit what we have too long forgotten—social reforms are tentative and contingent, or should be, and their continuation should depend upon favorable public evaluation.

But substantial commitment of resources results in the creation of "separate realities"—institutional domains with a "psycho-logic" of their own. Rather than depending upon input from their public constituents, they eschew it. In the name of efficiency and professionalism these realities are closed to the "inexpert," which too often means anyone who does not have a vested interest in system self-maintenance. (Here is another justification for simulation, since methods of direct and participant observation depend ultimately for their validity upon the access to the innermost corners of real institutions which is often denied to "outsider" social scientists.)

This gap between institutional ideal and reality is bridged by a working ideology which reconciles institutional agents to their tasks. Localizing problems within patients and prisoners sanctions their extraordinary, often inhumane, treatment. Thus encapsulated, the victims are thought to require, deserve, and be less adversely affected by their victimization. Simulations which employ role reversals undercut this working ideology by forcing participants to adopt the reality of the "other" (e.g., Orlando, 1973).Exposing the controllers to the perspective of the controlled is to be distinguished from therapeutic role playing, which acts as a palliative, mending personal disjunctions created by external conditions that are self-contradictory and brutalizing. Where such contradictions exist, role reversal should intensify them and represent the managerial reality as, at best, partial. An incidental but not insignificant consequence of simulations is that formerly uninitiated participants can obtain an appreciation of potential role demands and of their potency. It may be possible to employ such "inoculation" procedures as part of training programs to counteract the dehumanizing tendencies of institutions by enabling the forewarned to become psychologically forearmed.

THE POLITICS OF OBJECTIVITY

The origins of academic social science in America were in a discipline known as "moral philosophy." Fine (1956) reports that the first volume of the *American Journal of Sociology* was dedicated by its editor in 1895 to the support of "every wise endeavor to insure the good of men" (p. 265). And among the expressed goals of the American Social Science Association, founded in 1865, was "to learn patiently what *is*—to promote diligently what *should* be" (*Id.*, 348). How far we have come.

Wolin (1975) has noted a quickening in the pace of Western political life beginning in the 19th century, and the decline of "deliberative politics."

Social science analysis crept gradually into the vacuum once occupied by the reflective political actor-philosopher. The conceptual and methodological decisions of social scientists about a problem or phenomenon came to have implications for political "reality": they both embodied as well as affirmed "a political decision about what matters" (p. 15).

But as its political uses increased, social science became more apolitical in its form. As a profession it demanded not only methodological precision but also practitioners who appeared more dispassionate and uninvolved in the issues they addressed. This seeming neutrality and objectivity could be used to confer legitimacy on political decisions by cloaking them in the mantle of the scientifically compelled. (Not unlike the way "the Law" was invoked to "impartially" dictate decisions—blind justice weighing equities on a scale to reach the just result, as if by some mechanical or physical law.)

One commentator has called political beliefs the "master scale of biases in social science" (Myrdal, 1944, p. 1038). It is possible, however, for the politics of an entire discipline to be badly skewed. It may regularly employ assumptions which implicitly incorporate a biased view of people and problems. A predilection for the measurement of individual deviance and deficiency is an implicit political statement which has implications far beyond the pages of a social science textbook (e.g., Caplan & Nelson, 1973). Since certain research methods can be adapted to only certain kinds of questions, methodological preferences (or imperatives) mean that some things simply will not be studied.

Social psychology's laboratory methods, for example, have not been useful in studying the effects of social structural and institutional variables on individuals. The potentially powerful tool of randomization has been ineffective in application, due largely to compromises in other aspects of design. Ubiquitous "one-hour treatment effects"—the length of most psychological experiments—are ill-suited for the measurement of gradually accruing or long-term change. Thus the range of potential subject matter—and possible findings—is constricted at the very outset. Since institutional conditions are more chronic than acute, they are necessarily neglected.

Conventional methods limit themselves further by the choice of variables employed. Aronson and Carlsmith (1968) recite the traditional litany when they write: "We want as few extraneous differences as possible between treatments. We want to specify as precisely as possible the exact nature of the treatment we have administered" (p. 12). Such precision is most often obtained at the expense of the richness and complexity in experimental conditions which would be required to operationalize more global institutional and social structural variables. The increasing importance of these institutional variables in determining social behavior, as against our inability to contribute to an understanding of them, may explain the malaise which seems currently to pervade the field—we sit waiting for some methodological Godot to make us relevant again.

Constant narrowing and abstracting of issues often refines them out of functional existence. Labels which appear neutral and remote can defuse and distance the thinking of both reader and writer. A colleague strongly suggested we entitle our prison work, "Behavior in Extremely Cruel Environments" so that we would "avoid petty debates and misunderstandings." Research which refers directly to its real-life analogs is thought to be cheapened in the process. It also forces its authors to take a stand vis-à-vis the real-world setting of which it speaks. In 1973, *Scientific American* commissioned an article from us about our prison simulation. Although they were highly complimentary of the manuscript they received, their editorial board refused to publish the paper because, as they put it, it was "too strong stuff." This is the same *Scientific American* which received a 1974 National Magazine Award. The category? "Public Service."

The degree to which social science technology is actually "objective" or value-free may be largely irrelevant, given the strong value commitments of those who are in a position to use and apply it. For example, see Baritz (1960) for a carefully documented study of the applications of social science, especially psychology, in industry during the first half of this century. He points to the prevalent use of industrial "counseling" and more indirect forms of psychotherapy on workers and explains that "[m]anagement hoped through this process of adjusting people to situations rather than situations to people, [that] grievances, tensions, absenteeism, turnover, low production, and militant unionism would be avoided" (p. 105). Note that, to the extent any correlation exists between the presence of a professional class of social scientists in a society and that society's ability to effect political and social change, it appears to be negative. In fact, the country that offers the greatest example of continuing institutional transformation, the People's Republic of China, seems to have *no* influential group fairly analogous to Western professional social scientists. Is there something about the perspective of social science, once it has become institutionalized and professionalized, which necessitates its (at best) innocuous relationship to social change and the status quo?

SIZING UP THE SITUATION

Some time ago, Lewin (1951) observed that "[i]f one has to derive behavior from the situation at that time, a way has to be found to determine the character of the situation at that time" (p. 48). That satisfactory ways have not been found is both a cause and consequence of our tendency to view people rather than situations as the causal locus of behavior.

Because our intention in the Stanford Prison Study was to simulate the existing social environment of prison, it was high in what Aronson and Carlsmith (1968) have labelled "mundane realism" or what the Germans call "Lebensmähe"—literally, a "closeness to life." Although we attempted to maintain as much fidelity as possible to the social ecology of the institutional environment, a number of ethical and pragmatic considerations greatly constrained the degree to which a *literal* replication of "real" prison details or standard operating procedures could be achieved, or would even be attempted. Rather our emphasis was on a *functional* simulation of the prison environment—we attempted to introduce into the situation the psychological equivalents of the specific conditions which we had learned (and hypothesized) existed in real prisons.

We did this by first making an intensive conceptual analysis of the variables involved in the prison situation after spending hundreds of hours in discussions with ex-convicts, parole officers, and correctional personnel, and after reviewing much of the existing literature on prisons and concentration camps. We then formulated a set of procedures to operationalize these variables so they would be maximally effective, given the limitations and constraints of the setting available to us. We tried to introduce enough "mundane realism" into the experience so that the role-playing participants might be able to go beyond the superficial demands of their assigned roles into the deep structure of the prisoner and guard mentality. This was accomplished in part through the cooperation of the local Police Department, who made the unexpected arrests appear as part of a routine raid. A local TV station sent a cameraman to film the "arrests," which furthered the illusion of a newsworthy event actually taking place and encouraged the arresting officers to act their roles convincingly. Realism was enhanced by a visit to the prison from a Catholic priest who had been a prison chaplain; by a public defender, who discussed bail and trial procedures with the prisoners; and by parents, relatives, and friends during several scheduled visitors' hours. There were parole board meetings, as well as disciplinary meetings headed by an ex-convict and staffed by "adult authorities" who were strangers to the prisoners. Small details, such as stationery imprinted with the name of the prison, also helped to carry some of the burden of realism.

In a sense, the notion of "functional simulation" is analogous to the more general process of operationalization which takes place in all laboratory research, with the exception that in functional simulation particular attention is given to preserving the exact configuration of variables which characterize the situation being simulated. A concern for replicating the precise social ecology of an environment may be contrasted with the standard laboratory method of varying unitary dimensions (or multiple variables orthogonally) between conditions. This aspect of functional simulation was given explicit statement initially by Egon Brunswik (1950), in the development of his concept of "representative design." He wrote,

> One may demand that the "order", or pattern, of research "ideas", or design, should be the same as the pattern of the "things" studied, which in our case is behavior. Research may be said to have reached an adequate, functional

. . . level of complexity only if it parallels, and is thus capable of representing, behavior in all its essential features. . . . One may adopt Boring's admonition to "tap" the organism at the right places and augment it by pointing out that the environment—both spatial and temporal—must be tapped at the right places. (p. 25)

But Brunswik's concept of representative design has not reached fruition in contemporary social psychology. There still exists no well developed statistical, methodological, or analytic tool for measuring the representativeness of laboratory design, and, by implication, the extent to which a simulation functionally replicates a real phenomenon. Theorists like Mischel (1971) believe this to be the result of our overconcern with "tapping" the organism to the neglect of the environment. It is a tendency in psychology which has resulted in "the existence of literally hundreds of tests designed to infer dispositions and almost none to measure situations." Yet, it is upon this very ability to measure and compare situations that a sophisticated simulation methodology will ultimately stand or fall. Until we have developed a method of assessing the representativeness of design, there is simply no way to accurately judge the adequacy of simulations like the Stanford study.

The dilemma of not being able to determine how "good" or representative the simulation variables are of the matrix of real-world social forces has given rise to the additional problem of being "right for the wrong reasons." That is, it is possible that a simulation might produce behavior which resembles its real-world counterpart or "target" but is the actual product of forces other than those the experimenter intended to replicate. Abelson (1968) expresses the difficulty when he asks,

> If a simulation could be "right for the wrong reasons," that is, fit the data by virtue of compensating errors, then in what sense can a good fit be regarded as support for the theory underlying the simulation model? . . . If the outcome variables of the model are few while the number of parameters to be judged is great, there can always be the lingering suspicion that a good fit was too easy to achieve and thus not strongly supportive of the model. (pp. 343-344)

Thus, since the *same* behavior may have a variety of different causes, we cannot be sure that our simulated environment produced a specific behavior or syndrome for the same reasons that the actual conditions under study produce it. This is particularly true in the simulation of institutional behavior, where the array of potential forces which might operate in any situation is enormous and their combinations exceedingly complex. At this point, the only method an experimenter can employ to accommodate this dilemma is to provide for a large number and a wider range of dependent measures. In this sense, the evaluation of a simulation differs little from the same process which takes place in other varieties of research: multiple measures and "remote outcroppings" (Webb, et al., 1966) can be used to triangulate in on phenomena—the greater the number of predictions that are confirmed, the more plausible becomes the simulation, and the less likely one is to be "right for the wrong reason."

A SOCIAL PSYCHOLOGY OF SOCIAL PSYCHOLOGISTS

Perhaps a growing awareness of the power of situational forces will increase our concern over the extent to which the conduct of social science research is itself a *situation*—a social context capable of shaping and controlling the behavior of *all* its participants. In our roles as researchers, we are no less subject to the general principles of behavior we articulate. "Demand characteristics" (Orne, 1962) and the like are not conveniently confined to only our "subjects," not ourselves.

This suggests that social scientists may be in an especially disadvantageous position to maintain a balanced perspective on what they do, perhaps underscoring the need for their accountability to those less situationally controlled. Invoking the claim of "expertise" to disdain public accountability then seems only to enhance the irony. (Indeed, if we cannot justify what we do to the very people we study, by what justification do we do it?)

Questions of accountability raise others concerning more specific effects of the research "situations." Note, for example, that the *act* of behavioral research is an explicit use of people as means rather than ends in themselves. What kind of psychological consequences await those too long exposed to this exploitive style of social interaction? Does spending much of our professional time "running subjects" mean that we will come to see people merely as subjects to be run?

Or consider some recent experimental evidence suggesting that when persons are placed in "observer" roles—where they watch rather than act—they are more likely to explain the behavior of others in dispositional or trait terms (Jones & Nisbett, 1971). The relevance for social psychologists, whose occupation demands incessant observation, should be obvious. It may explain the intransigence of dispositionalism in a field where experiment regularly substitutes for experience, observation for action.

There are other aspects to the "observer-syndrome." Sontag (1973) notes that "[t]he person who intervenes cannot record; the person who is recording cannot intervene" (p. 60). Perhaps it is the "situation" of social science research which has created a corps of observer-recorders increasingly reluctant to act or intervene in the human affairs they study. This may be why we are so maladroit at providing strategies for social action; they would require us to use social science to transform reality rather than merely describe its transformations. Since we make our living from describing the empirical world, do we have an incentive to "let it be"?

Consider also the extent to which, as social scientists, we are subject to the "law of the instrument" (colloquially described as "give a small child a hammer and everything begins to look like a nail"). Are there many occasions in which we feel compelled to apply our techniques to problems where social science research is not only uncalled for but untoward? Purely technical or empirical proofs of moral propositions have a way of changing the nature of the debate. (For example, isn't there something *morally* wrong about the intentional segregation of black and white schoolchildren per se, or is it wrong only if blacks can be shown to suffer measurable decrements in learning?) Facile technical solutions tend to drive out weightier moral ones because they permit us to ignore underlying conflict. Recognition of this may moderate the generalized admonition to "get involved" by reminding us to regularly ask "toward what end and to what effect?"

The quest for rigorous objectivity in research may further the alienation of the social scientist from social reality. What are the personal psychological consequences of the attempt to purge oneself of values and politics while studying the very contexts in which these things most fully and forcefully operate? [Shils (1961) tells us that "whatever else sociology might be, it is the cultivation of detachment . . ." (1425)] But if "objectivity" is thought to be enhanced by distancing, here the separation must be from most basic and intimate spheres of social life. Perhaps, then, the occupational alienation of the psychologist is far greater than for most workers, for it is from people as well as from his labor that he is alienated.

At another level entirely, social scientists are influenced by an even larger "situation" than the laboratory or field setting. Because the model we have emulated has been that of physical science, we have sought immutable patterns, relationships, and laws. But concern for experimental replication and a search for *the* laws of behavior are reflections of a kind of dispositional fallacy—belief that there really is a fundamental "human nature" which is, or should be, constant over time and across situations. If, on the other hand, human nature is malleable and responsive to situational conditions, rapidly changing social environments will produce behavioral forms which are truly protean. Traditional notions of "fixed" laws of behavior and those who hold them may be among the casualties of "future shock," as the historical specificity of social science—situational control on a grande scale—intensifies.

But this applies to the notion of situational control itself. Research findings like those of the Stanford Prison Study must also be seen as historically contingent. In an era dominated by powerful institutional forces and mechanisms of social control, modal personalities *will* be situationally controlled. But it is not hard to imagine sociohistorical conditions where social situations are less potent and people account for far more of the variance in behavior. Indeed, the "formative era" of both American social science and law—the 19th century—was just such a period, perhaps explaining the highly dispositional and individualistic assumptions of both enterprises (Haney, 1975).

AN ETHICAL EPILOGUE TO THE PRISON STUDY

Certain research designs are convincing, despite the absence of explicit control groups. The Milgram (1965) obedience paradigm and the Prison Study are salient examples and might be regarded more as "demonstrations" than formal experiments. They are compelling because of the *implicit* control group, in the form of our own intuition or expectations, which we impose upon them. "People—others and ourselves—just don't behave that way," we say. When presented with evidence that, in fact, they do, we are unsettled, shocked, appalled.

But notice that the same social conditioning history which has created these cognitive expectations has also created the behavioral susceptibilities which violate them. Thus we have been taught to think one way and act another. (The psychological debate over when attitudes and behavior *can* be separated here seems less politically significant than the observation that regularly they *are*.) Individuals unaware of their potential to brutalize will have little incentive to safeguard against it—or protest vehemently against those conditions likely to elicit such behavior.

These "demonstrations" have established the troublesome proposition that we are simply not very good at predicting how we or others will act in a given situation. Generally, of course, we tend to discount the power of certain situational forces and rely too much on personal capacity to resist or withstand them. This applies to researchers as well as their subjects, which raises a difficult ethical problem. Aronson and Carlsmith (1968) recognize that "one cannot easily quantify discomfort caused by an experimental procedure," but nonetheless they counsel researchers that "the amount of discomfort should be weighed against the worth of the experiment" (p. 33). But if we are notoriously inept at predicting the effects of certain kinds of conditions, how can we possible estimate both the "discomfort" and eventual "worth" of an experimental outcome? (Indeed, if researchers could be completely confident about the outcome of a study, one might reasonably ask the justification for doing it at all.)

I have had a number of heated discussions with people who believe that "informed consent" is a sufficient ethical precaution in research—that volunteers who are provided requisite information and still "freely choose" to enter an experiment should be permitted to do so, whatever its nature. Although (and perhaps, because) they are social scientists themselves, they seem unwilling to be persuaded that the entire experimental setting is a powerful situation in which ethical imperatives may preclude the creation of certain experimental conditions, no matter how many people agree to participate in them. In a sense, our discussion recapitulates the classical positions in respect to the individual versus situational control. Is there an experimental "contract" such that whoever of sound mind accepts its apparent terms must also accept its unlikely but not inconceivable consequences? How much responsibility do the experimenters have to guarantee that subjects cannot make a "bad deal," even if they want to? Are some experimental agreements "unconscionable" on their face? Legally, contracts may be invalidated when it can be shown that one party's "will" was overborne in the making of the agreement. But isn't the overbearing of subjects' wills what many experiments are all about anyway? What consolation (and protection) may we then derive from the fact that subjects "decided" to remain in an experiment until its completion? Does insisting upon "deciding for them" reflect a "paternalistic" frame of mind? (Insofar as it dwells on real or imagined differences in the ability of some people to tolerate situational stresses, our social science seems as much elitist as paternalistic. Coupled with a perhaps endemic blindness to the "situation" of social science, commentaries on the plights of others by those impliedly above—or at least beside—the struggle will always seem paternalistic. Here is another sense in which the appreciation of situational relativism in social science seems not only valid but salutary.)

Research like the Prison Study puts the ethical question much harder because in a very real sense it depends for its impact upon negative consequences. To the *extent* that the effects on subjects were painful, the lesson about institutional conditions was made more expressly and convincingly. In words which could as easily apply to such social science, Sontag (1973) writes of photography:

> ... To take a picture is to have an interest in things as they are, in the status quo remaining unchanged (at least for as long as it takes to get a good picture), to be in complicity with whatever makes a subject interesting, worth photographing, including, when that's the interest, another person's pain or misfortune. (p. 60)

But while the ethically tenuous decision for the photographer is merely to photograph and not to intervene or prevent, for the social scientist it is sometimes to actually *create* the conditions which result in "pain or misfortune." How much greater must be the justification, or lesser the potential harm risked? Indeed, can such an undertaking *ever* be justified?

Without answering such a question, we can look to several ironies which it suggests. It seems disturbing and perverse that we might refrain from engaging in the kind of research which is needed to effectively demonstrate the dehumanizing effects of certain social environments and rebut the localization of pathology within individuals, because the necessary research is itself too dehumanizing. It seems equally ironic that persons moved by a deep concern over the effects of dehumanizing environments on people would engage in research which is similarly harmful in kind if not degree. For me personally there is a paradox in the recognition that now my own sensitivity to these issues might well preclude performing the research which produced it.

On the other hand, this concern for human "subjects"—those inside research laboratories or in society's at large institutional experiments—can be easily perverted. A short time ago, the Chancellor of the University of California issued a policy statement which contained guidelines for "the protection of human subjects." It admonished social scientists to avoid research "procedures that may place the reputation or status of a social group or an institution in jeopardy." The statement then cautioned that "an institution, such as a church, a university, or a prison must be guarded against derogation," for many people may be affiliated with, or employed by the institution, and pejorative information about it would injure their reputation and self-esteem (*San Francisco Chronicle*, August 19, 1973). Thus, in the name of protecting people, an attempt is made to preclude critical analysis of those environments which may be most harmful to them. But if social scientists cannot challenge the role of certain institutions, document their excesses and the nature of their harm, and seek techniques by which individuals may begin to fight back, who can?

Such dilemmas are not to be facilely solved in this or any essay, but are meant uniquely for personal and individual decision. However, it will not do to take refuge behind our professional roles, to ignore such "subjective" and political issues by pointing to a mandate for objectivity or the implicit instruction "not to reason why." Acting out an assigned role in a given occupation or profession, be it psychologist or prison guard, can serve as the ultimate self-deception procedure. It permits you to assert a difference between what is experienced as the "real" you and the "role-playing" you. Thus you may engage in behaviors contrary to your "private" values— perhaps to manipulate, degrade, or depersonalize other people—while abdicating personal responsibility in the name of role-instigated behavior. Of course, eventually it becomes difficult for the actor to know where the role ends and the self begins. Is it this to which the poet Matthew Arnold adverted when he wrote, "Such a price the gods exact for a song/ To become what we sing." At the very least it suggests we examine our personal motives very carefully and be terribly selective in the "songs" we choose to sing.

REFERENCES

Abelson, R. Simulation of social behavior. In Lindzey, G., & Aronson, E. (Eds.). *The handbook of social psychology*, Vol. II. Reading: Addison-Wesley, 1968.

Aronson, E., & Carlsmith, M. Experimentation in social psychology. In Lindzey, G., & Aronson, E. (Eds.). *The handbook of social psychology*. Vol. II. Reading: Addison-Wesley, 1968.

Baritz, L. *The servants of power: A history of the uses of social science in American industry*. New York: John Wiley & Sons, 1960.

Brunswik, E. The conceptual framework of psychology. In Neurath, O. (Ed.). *International encyclopedia of unified science*. Chicago: University of Chicago Press, Vol. I, Number 10, 1950.

Campbell, D. Reforms as experiments. *American Psychologist*, 24, 1969, 409-429.

Caplan, N., & Nelson, S. On being useful: The nature and consequence of psychological research on social problems. *American Psychologist*, March, 1973, 199-211.

Cohen, D., & Garet, M. Reforming educational policy with applied research. *Harvard Educational Review,* *45*(1), February, 1975, 17-43.

Fine, S. *Laissez-faire and the general welfare state: A study in conflict in American thought, 1865-1901.* Ann Arbor: University of Michigan Press, 1956.

Haney, C. Social change and the ideology of individualism in psychology and law. Paper presented at the Annual Meeting of the Western Psychological Association, April, 1975.

Jones, E., & Nisbett, R. The actor and the observer: Divergent perceptions of the causes of behavior. In Jones, E., *et al.* (Eds.). *Attribution: Perceiving the causes of behavior.* Morristown, N.J.: General Learning Corporation, 1971.

Lewin, K. *Field theory in social science: Selected theoretical papers.* New York: Harper & Row Inc., 1951.

Milgram, S. Some conditions of obedience and disobedience to authority. *Human Relations,* 1965, *18*(1), 57-75.

Mischel, W. The construction of personality: Some facts and fantasies about cognition and social behavior. Address of the Chairman, Section III, Division 12, American Psychological Association, Washington, D.C., September 3, 1971.

Myrdal, G. *An American dilemma: The Negro problem and modern democracy.* New York: Harper, 1944.

Orlando, N. The mock ward: A study in simulation. In O. Milton & R. Wahler (Eds.). *Behavior disorders: Perspectives and trends.* Philadelphia: Lippincott, 1973.

Orne, M. T. On the social psychology of the psychology experiment: With particular reference to demand characteristics and their implications. *American Psychologist,* 1962, *17,* 776-783.

Ryan, W. *Blaming the victim.* New York: Vintage Books, 1971.

Shils, E. The calling of sociology. In Parsons, T. (Ed.) *Theories of society.* New York: The Free Press, 1961.

Sontag, S. Photography. *New York Review of Books,* October 18, 1973, p. 60.

Webb, E., Campbell, D., Schwartz, R. & Sechrest, L. *Unobstrusive measures: Nonreactive research in the social sciences.* Chicago: Rand McNally, 1966.

Wolin, S. Looking for "reality." *New York Review of Books,* February, 1976, pp. 15-20.

John M. Darley and C. Daniel Batson

A. "FROM JERUSALEM TO JERICHO": A STUDY OF SITUATIONAL AND DISPOSITIONAL VARIABLES IN HELPING BEHAVIOR

Helping other people in distress is, among other things, an ethical act. That is, it is an act governed by ethical norms and precepts taught to children at home, in school, and in church. From Freudian and other personality theories, one would expect individual differences in internalization of these standards that would lead to differences between individuals in the likelihood with which they would help others. But recent research on bystander intervention in emergency situations (Bickman, 1969; Darley & Latané, 1968; Korte, 1969; but see also Schwartz & Clausen, 1970) has had bad luck in finding personality determinants of helping behavior. Although personality variables that one might expect to correlate with helping behavior have been measured (Machiavellianism, authoritarianism, social desirability, alienation, and social responsibility), these were not predictive of helping. Nor was this due to a generalized lack of predictability in the helping situation examined, since variations in the experimental situation, such as the availability of other people who might also help, produced marked changes in rates of helping behavior. These findings are reminiscent of Hartshorne and May's (1928) discovery that resistance to temptation, another ethically relevant act, did not seem to be a fixed characteristic of an individual. That is, a person who was likely to be honest in one situation was not particularly likely to be honest in the next (but see also Burton, 1963).

The rather disappointing correlation between the social psychologist's traditional set of personality variables and helping behavior in emergency

Source: John M. Darley and C. Daniel Batson, "From Jerusalem to Jericho": A Study of Situational and Dispositional Variables in Helping Behaviors, *Journal of Personality and Social Psychology*, 1973, *27*, 100-108.

For assistance in conducting this research thanks are due Robert Wells, Beverly Fisher, Mike Shafto, Peter Sheras, Richard Detweiler, and Karen Glasser. The research was funded by National Science Foundation Grant GS-2293.

situations suggests the need for a fresh perspective on possible predictors of helping and possible situations in which to test them. Therefore, for inspiration we turned to the Bible, to what is perhaps the classical helping story in the Judeo-Christian tradition, the parable of the Good Samaritan. The parable proved of value in suggesting both personality and situational variables relevant to helping.

"And who is my neighbor?" Jesus replied, "A man was going down from Jerusalem to Jericho, and he fell among robbers, who stripped him and beat him, and departed, leaving him half dead. Now by chance a priest was going down the road; and when he saw him he passed by on the other side. So likewise a Levite, when he came to the place and saw him, passed by on the other side. But a Samaritan, as he journeyed, came to where he was; and when he saw him, he had compassion, and went to him and bound his wounds, pouring on oil and wine; then he set him on his own beast and brought him to an inn, and took care of him. And the next day he took out two dennarii and gave them to the innkeeper, saying, 'Take care of him; and whatever more you spend, I will repay you when I come back.' Which of these three, do you think, proved neighbor to him who fell among the robbers?" He said, "The one who showed mercy on him." And Jesus said to him, "Go and do likewise." (Luke 10: 29-37 RSV)

To psychologists who reflect on the parable, it seems to suggest situational and personality differences between the nonhelpful priest and Levite and the helpful Samaritan. What might each have been thinking and doing when he came upon the robbery victim on that desolate road? What sort of persons were they?

Once can speculate on differences in thought. Both the priest and the Levite were religious functionaries who could be expected to have their minds occupied with religious matters. The priest's role in religious activities is obvious. The Levite's role, although less obvious, is equally important: The Levites were necessary participants in temple ceremonies. Much less can be said with any confidence about what the Samaritan might have been thinking, but, in contrast to the others, it was most likely not of a religious nature, for Samaritans were religious outcasts.

Not only was the Samaritan most likely thinking about more mundane matters than the priest and Levite, but, because he was socially less important, it seems likely that he was operating on a quite different time schedule. One can imagine the priest and Levite, prominent public figures, hurrying along with little black books full of meetings and appointments, glancing furtively at their sundials. In contrast, the Samaritan would likely have far fewer and less important people counting on him to be at a particular place at a particular time, and therefore might be expected to be in less of a hurry than the prominent priest or Levite.

In addition to these situational variables, one finds personality factors suggested as well. Central among these, and apparently basic to the point that Jesus was trying to make, is a distinction between types of religiosity. Both the priest and Levite are extremely "religious." But it seems to be precisely their type of religiosity that the parable challenges. At issue is the motivation for one's religion and ethical behavior. Jesus seems to feel that the religious leaders of his time, though certainly respected and upstanding citizens, may be "virtuous" for what it will get them, both in terms of the admiration of their fellowmen and in the eyes of God. New Testament scholar R. W. Funk (1966) noted that the Samaritan is at the other end of the spectrum:

> The Samaritan does not love with side glances at God. The need of neighbor alone is made self-evident, and the Samaritan responds without other motivation (pp. 218-219).

That is, the Samaritan is interpreted as responding spontaneously to the situation, not as being preoccupied with the abstract ethical or organizational do's and don'ts of religion as the priest and Levite would seem to be. This is not to say that the Samaritan is portrayed as irreligious. A major intent of the parable would seem to be to present the Samaritan as a religious and ethical example, but at the same time to contrast his type of religiosity with the more common conception of religiosity that the priest and Levite represent.

To summarize the variables suggested as affecting helping behavior by the parable, the situational variables include the content of one's thinking and the amount of hurry in one's journey. The major dispositional variable seems to be differing types of religiosity. Certainly these variables do not exhaust the list that could be elicited from the parable, but they do suggest several research hypotheses.

Hypothesis 1 The parable implies that people who encounter a situation possibly calling for a helping response while thinking religious and ethical thoughts will be no more likely to offer aid than persons thinking about something else. Such a hypothesis seems to run counter to a theory that focuses on norms as determining helping behavior because a normative account would predict that the increased salience of helping norms produced by thinking about religious and ethical examples would increase helping behavior.

Hypothesis 2 Persons encountering a possible helping situation when they are in a hurry will be less likely to offer aid than persons not in a hurry.

Hypothesis 3 Concerning types of religiosity, persons who are religious in a Samaritanlike fashion will help more frequently than those religious in a priest or Levite fashion.

Obviously, this last hypothesis is hardly operationalized as stated. Prior research by one of the investigators on types of religiosity (Batson, 1971), however, led us to differentiate three distinct ways of being religious: (a) for what it will gain one (cf. Freud, 1953, and perhaps the priest and Levite), (b) for its own intrinsic value (cf. Allport & Ross, 1967), and (c) as a response to and quest for meaning in one's everyday life (cf. Batson, 1971). Both of the latter conceptions would be proposed by their exponents as related to the more Samaritanlike "true" religiosity. Therefore, depending on the theorist one follows, the third hypothesis may be stated like this: People (*a*) who are religious for intrinsic reasons (Allport & Ross, 1967) or (*b*) whose religion emerges out of questioning the meaning of their everyday lives (Batson, 1971) will be more likely to stop to offer help to the victim.

The parable of the Good Samaritan also suggested how we would measure people's helping behavior—their response to a stranger slumped by the side of one's path. The victim should appear somewhat ambiguous—ill-dressed, possibly in need of help, but also possibly drunk or even potentially dangerous.

Further, the parable suggests a means by which the incident could be perceived as a real one rather than part of a psychological experiment in which one's behavior was under surveillance and might be shaped by demand characteristics (Orne, 1962), evaluation apprehension (Rosenberg, 1965), or other potentially artifactual determinants of helping behavior. The victim should be encountered not in the experimental context but on the road between various tasks.

METHOD

In order to examine the influence of these variables on helping behavior, seminary students were asked to participate in a study on religious education and vocations. In the first testing session, personality questionnaires concerning types of religiosity were administered. In a second individual session, the subject began experimental procedures in one building and was asked to report to another building for later procedures. While in transit, the subject passed a slumped "victim" planted in an alleyway. The dependent variable was whether and how the subject helped the victim. The independent variables were the degree to which the subject was told to hurry in reaching the other building and the talk he was to give when he arrived there. Some subjects were to give a talk on the jobs in which seminary students would be most effective, others, on the parable of the Good Samaritan.

Subjects

The subjects for the questionnaire administration were 67 students at Princeton Theological Seminary. Forty-seven of them, those who could be reached by telephone, were scheduled for the experiment. Of the 47, 7 subjects' data were not included in the analyses—3 because of contamination of the experimental procedures during their testing and 4 due to suspicion of the experimental situation. Each subject was paid $1 for the questionnaire session and $1.50 for the experimental session.

Personality Measures

Detailed discussion of the personality scales used may be found elsewhere (Batson, 1971), so the present discussion will be brief. The general personality construct under examination was religiosity. Various conceptions of religiosity have been offered in recent years based on different psychometric scales. The conception seeming to generate the most interest is the Allport and Ross (1967) distinction between "intrinsic" versus "extrinsic" religiosity (cf. also Allen & Spilka, 1967, on "committed" versus "consensual" religion). This bipolar conception of religiosity has been questioned by Brown (1964) and Batson (1971), who suggested three-dimensional analyses instead. Therefore, in the present research, types of religiosity were measured with three instruments which together provided six separate scales: (a) a *doctrinal orthodoxy* (D-O) scale patterned after that used by Glock and Stark (1966), scaling agreement with classic doctrines of Protestant theology; (b) the Allport-Ross *extrinsic* (AR-E) scale, measuring the use of religion as a means to an end rather than as an end in itself; (c) the Allport-Ross *intrinsic* (AR-I) scale, measuring the use of religion as an end in itself; (d) the *extrinsic external* scale of Batson's Religious Life Inventory (RELI-EE), designed to measure the influence of significant others and situations in generating one's religiosity; (e) the *extrinsic internal* scale of the Religious Life Inventory (RELI-EI), designed to measure the degree of "driveness" in one's religiosity; and (f) the *intrinsic* scale of the Religious Life Inventory (RELI-I), designed to measure the degree to which one's religiosity involves a questioning of the meaning of life arising out of one's interactions with his social environment. The order of presentation of the scales in the questionnaire was RELI, AR, D-O.

Consistent with prior research (Batson, 1971), a principal-component analysis of the total scale scores and individual items for the 67 seminarians produced a theoretically meaningful, orthogonally rotated three-component structure with the following loadings:

Religion as means received a single very high loading from AR-E (.903) and therefore was defined by Allport and Ross's (1967) conception of this scale as measuring religiosity as a means to other ends. This component also received moderate negative loadings from D-O (—.400) and AR-I (—.372) and a moderate positive loading from RELI-EE (.301).

Religion as end received high loadings from RELI-EI (.874), RELI-EE (.725), AR-I (.768), and D-O (.704). Given this configuration, and again following Allport and Ross's conceptualization, this component seemed to involve religiosity as an end in itself with some intrinsic value.

Religion as quest received a single very high loading from RELI-I (.945) and a moderate loading from RELI-EE (.75). Following Batson, this component was conceived to involve religiosity emerging out of an individual's search for meaning in his personal and social world.

The three religious personality scales examined in the experimental research were constructed through the use of complete-estimation factor score coefficients from these three components.

Scheduling of Experimental Study

Since the incident requiring a helping response was staged outdoors, the entire experimental study was run in 3 days, December 14-16, 1970, between 10 A.M. and 4 P.M. A tight schedule was used in an attempt to maintain reasonably consistent weather and light conditions. Temperature fluctuation according to the *New York Times* for the 3 days during these hours was not more than 5 degrees Fahrenheit. No rain or snow fell, although the third day was cloudy, whereas the first two were sunny. Within days the subjects were randomly assigned to experimental conditions.[1]

Procedure

When a subject appeared for the experiment, an assistant (who was blind with respect to the personality scores) asked him to read a brief statement which explained that he was participating in a study of the vocational careers of seminary students. After developing the rationale for the study, the statement read:

What we have called you in for today is to provide us with some additional material which will give us a clearer picture of how you think than does the questionnaire material we have gathered thus far. Questionnaires are helpful, but tend to be somewhat oversimplified. Therefore, we would like to record a 3-5 minute talk you give based on the following passage. . . .

Variable 1: Message   In the task-relevant condition the passage read,

With increasing frequency the question is being asked: What jobs or professions do seminary students subsequently enjoy most, and in what jobs are they most effective? The answer to this question used to be so obvious that the question was not even asked. Seminary students were being trained for the ministry, and since both society at large and the seminary student himself had a relatively clear understanding of what made a "good" minister, there was no need even to raise the question of for what other jobs seminary experience seems to be an asset. Today, however, neither society nor many seminaries have a very clearly defined conception of what a "good" minister is or of what sorts of jobs and professions are the best context in which to minister. Many seminary students, apparently genuinely concerned with "ministering," seem to feel that it is impossible to minister in the professional clergy. Other students, no less concerned, find the clergy the most viable profession for ministry. But are there other jobs and/or professions for which seminary experience is an asset? And, indeed, how much of an asset is it for the professional ministry? Or, even more broadly, can one minister through an "establishment" job at all?

---

1. An error was made in randomizing that increased the number of subjects in the intermediate-hurry conditions. This worked against the prediction that was most highly confirmed (the hurry prediction) and made no difference to the message variable tests.

THE RESEARCH EXPERIENCE

In the helping-relevant condition, the subject was given the parable of the Good Samaritan exactly as printed earlier in this article. Next, regardless of condition, all subjects were told,

> You can say whatever you wish based on the passage. Because we are interested in how you think on your feet, you will not be allowed to use notes in giving the talk. Do you understand what you are to do? If not, the assistant will be glad to answer questions.

After a few minutes the assistant returned, asked if there were any questions, and then said:

> Since they're rather tight on space in this building we're using a free office in the building next door for recording the talks. Let me show you how to get there [draws and explains map on 3 x 5]. This is where Professor Steiner's laboratory is. If you go in this door [points at map], there's a secretary right here, and she'll direct you to the office we're using for recording. Another of Professor Steiner's assistants will set you up for recording your talk. Is the map clear?

Variable 2: Hurry In the high-hurry condition the assistant then looked at his watch and said, "Oh, you're late. They were expecting you a few minutes ago. We'd better get moving. The assistant should be waiting for you so you'd better hurry. It shouldn't take but just a minute." In the intermediate-hurry condition he said, "The assistant is ready for you, so please go right over." In the low-hurry condition he said, "It'll be a few minutes before they're ready for you, but you might as well head on over. If you have to wait over there, it shouldn't be long."

The Incident When the subject passed throught the alley, the victim was sitting slumped in a doorway, head down, eyes closed, not moving. As the subject went by, the victim coughed twice and groaned, keeping his head down. If the subject stopped and asked if something was wrong or offered to help, the victim, startled and somewhat groggy, said, "Oh, thank you [cough]. . . . No, it's all right. [Pause] I've got this respiratory condition [cough]. . . . The doctor's given me these pills to take, and I just took one. . . . If I just sit and rest for a few minutes I'll be O.K. . . . Thanks very much for stopping though [smiles weakly]." If the subject persisted, insisting on taking the victim inside the building, the victim allowed him to do so and thanked him.

Helping Ratings The victim rated each subject on a scale of helping behavior as follows:

> 0 = failed to notice the victim as possibly in need at all; 1 = perceived the victim as possibly in need but did not offer aid; 2 = did not stop but helped indirectly (e.g., by telling Steiner's assistant about the victim); 3 = stopped and asked if victim needed help; 4 = after stopping, insisted on taking the victim inside and then left him.

The victim was blind to the personality scale scores and experimental conditions of all subjects. At the suggestion of the victim, another category was added to the rating scales, based on his observations of pilot subjects' behavior:

> 5 = after stopping, refused to leave the victim (after 3-5 minutes) and/or insisted on taking him somewhere outside experimental context (e.g., for coffee or to the infirmary).

(In some cases it was necessary to distinguish Category 0 from Category 1 by the postexperimental questionnaire and Category 2 from Category 1 on the report of the experimental assistant.)

This 6-point scale of helping behavior and a description of the victim were given to a panel of 10 judges (unacquainted with the research) who were asked to rank order the (unnumbered) categories in terms of "the amount of helping behavior displayed toward the person in the doorway." Of the 10, 1 judge reversed the order of Categories 0 and 1. Otherwise there was complete agreement with the ranking implied in the presentation of the scale above.

The Speech   After passing through the alley and entering the door marked on the map, the subject entered a secretary's office. She introduced him to the assistant who gave the subject time to prepare and privately record his talk.

Helping Behavior Questionnaire   After recording the talk, the subject was sent to another experimenter, who administered "an exploratory questionnaire on personal and social ethics." The questionnaire contained several initial questions about the interrelationship between social and personal ethics, and then asked three key questions: (*a*) "When was the last time you saw a person who seemed to be in need of help?" (*b*) "When was the last time you stopped to help someone in need?" (*c*) "Have you had experience helping persons in need? If so, outline briefly." These data were collected as a check on the victim's ratings of whether subjects who did not stop perceived the situation in the alley as one possibly involving need or not.

When he returned, the experimenter reviewed the subject's questionnaire, and, if no mention was made of the situation in the alley, probed for reactions to it and then phased into an elaborate debriefing and discussion session.

Debriefing

In the debriefing, the subject was told the exact nature of the study, including the deception involved, and the reasons for the deception were explained. The subject's reactions to the victim and to the study in general were discussed. The role of situational determinants of helping behavior was explained in relation to this particular incident and to other experiences of the subject. All subjects seemed readily to understand the necessity for the deception, and none indicated any resentment of it. After debriefing, the subject was thanked for his time and paid, then he left.

RESULTS AND DISCUSSION

Overall Helping Behavior

The average amount of help that a subject offered the victim, by condition, is shown in Table 1. The unequal-N analysis of variance indicates that while the hurry variable was significantly ($F = 3.56$, $df = 2/34$, $p < .05$) related to helping behavior, the message variable was not. Subjects in a hurry were likely to offer less help than were subjects not in a hurry. Whether the subject was going to give a speech on the parable of the Good Samaritan or not did not significantly affect his helping behavior on this analysis.

Other studies have focused on the question of whether a person initiates helping action or not, rather than on scaled kinds of helping. The data from the present study can also be analyzed on the following terms: Of the 40 subjects, 16 (40%) offered some form of direct or indirect aid to the victim (Coding Categories 2-5), 24 (60%) did not (Coding Categories 0 and 1). The percentages of subjects who offered aid by situational variable were, for low hurry, 63% offered help, intermediate hurry 45%, and high hurry 10%; for helping-relevant message 53%, task-relevant message 29%. With regard to this more general question of whether help was offered or not, an unequal-N analysis of variance (arc sine transformation of percentages of helpers, with low- and intermediate-hurry conditions pooled) indicated that again only the hurry main effect was significantly ($F = 5.22$, $p < .05$) related to helping behavior; the subjects in a hurry were more likely to pass by the victim than were those in less of a hurry.

Reviewing the predictions in the light of these results, the second hypothesis, that the degree of hurry a person is in determines his helping behavior, was supported. The prediction involved in the first hypothesis concerning the message content was based on the parable. The parable itself

TABLE 1
Means and Analysis of Variance of Graded Helping Responses

	Means			
		Hurry		
Message	Low	Medium	High	Summary
Helping relevant	3.800	2.000	1.000	2.263
Task relevant	1.667	1.667	.500	1.333
Summary	3.000	1.818	.700	

Analysis of Variance				
Source	SS	df	MS	F
Message (A)	7.766	1	7.766	2.65
Hurry (B)	20.884	2	10.442	3.56*
A X B	5.237	2	2.619	.89
Error	99.633	34	2.930	

Note: $N = 40$.
*$p < .05$.

TABLE 2
Stepwise Multiple Regression Analysis

Help vs. No Help

Step	Individual Variable		Overall Equation	
	r^a	F	R	F
1. Hurry[b]	−.37	4.537*	.37	5.884*
2. Message[c]	.25	1.495	.41	3.834*
3. Religion as quest	−.03	.081	.42	2.521
4. Religion as means	−.03	.003	.42	1.838*
5. Religion as end	.06	.000	.42	1.430

Graded Helping

Step	Individual Variable		Variable Equation	
	r	F	R	F
1. Hurry	−.42	6.665*	.42	8.196**
2. Message	.25	1.719	.46	5.083*
3. Religion as quest	−.16	1.297	.50	3.897*
4. Religion as means	−.08	.018	.50	2.848*
5. Religion as end	−.07	.001	.50	2.213

Note: $N = 40$. Helping is the dependent variable. $df = 1/34$.
[a]Individual variable correlation coefficient is a point biserial where appropriate.
[b]Variables are listed in order of entry into stepwise regression equations.
[c]Helping-relevant message is positive.
*$p < .05$.
**$p < .01$.

seemed to suggest that thinking pious thoughts would not increase helping. Another and conflicting prediction might be produced by a norm salience theory. Thinking about the parable should make norms for helping salient and therefore produce more helping. The data, as hypothesized, are more congruent with the prediction drawn from the parable. A person going to speak on the parable of the Good Samaritan is not significantly more likely to stop to help a person by the side of the road than is a person going to talk about possible occupations for seminary graduates.

Since both situational hypotheses are confirmed, it is tempting to stop the analysis of these variables at this point. However, multiple regression analysis procedures were also used to analyze the relationship of all of the independent variables of the study and the helping behavior. In addition to often being more statistically powerful due to the use of more data information, multiple regression analysis has an advantage over analysis of variance in that it allows for a comparison of the relative effect of the various independent variables in accounting for variance in the dependent variable. Also, multiple regression analysis can compare the effects of continuous as well as nominal independent variables on both continuous and nominal dependent variables (through the use of point biserial correlations, r_{pb}) and shows considerable robustness to violation of normality assumptions (Cohen, 1965, 1968). Table 2 reports the results of the multiple regression analysis using both help versus no help and the graded helping scale as dependent measures. In this table the overall equation Fs show the F value of the entire

THE RESEARCH EXPERIENCE

regression equation as a particular row variable enters the equation. Individual variable Fs were computed with all five independent variables in the equation. Although the two situational variables, hurry and message condition, correlated more highly with the dependent measure than any of the religious dispositional variables, only hurry was a significant predictor of whether one will help or not (column 1) or of the overall amount of help given (column 2). These results corroborate the findings of the analysis of variance.[2]

Notice also that neither form of the third hypothesis, that types of religiosity will predict helping, received support from these data. No correlation between the various measures of religiosity and any form of the dependent measure ever came near statistical significance, even though the multiple regression analysis procedure is a powerful and not particularly conservative statistical test.

Personality Difference among Subjects Who Helped

To further investigate the possible influence of personality variables, analyses were carried out using only the data from subjects who offered some kind of help to the victim. Surprisingly (since the number of these subjects was small, only 16) when this was done, one religiosity variable seemed to be significantly related to the kind of helping behavior offered. (The situational variables had no significant effect.) Subjects high on the religion as quest dimension appear likely, when they stop for the victim, to offer help of a more tentative or incomplete nature than are subjects scoring low on this dimension ($r = -.53$, $p < .05$).

This result seemed unsettling for the thinking behind either form of Hypothesis 3. Not only do the data suggest that the Allport-Ross–based conception of religion as *end* does not predict the degree of helping, but the religion as quest component is a significant predictor of offering less help. This latter result seems counterintuitive and out of keeping with previous research (Batson, 1971), which found that this type of religiosity correlated positively with other socially valued characteristics. Further data analysis, however, seemed to suggest a different interpretation of this result.

It will be remembered that one helping coding category was added at the suggestion of the victim after his observation of pilot subjects. The correlation of religious personality variables with helping behavior dichotomized between the added category (1) and all of the others (0) was examined. The correlation between religion as quest and this dichotomous helping scale was

---

2. To check the legitimacy of the use of both analysis of variance and multiple regression analysis, parametric analyses on this ordinal data, Kendall rank correlation coefficients, were calculated between the helping scale and the five independent variables. As expected τ approximated the correlation quite closely in each case and was significant for hurry only (hurry, $\tau = -.38$, $p < .001$).

essentially unchanged ($r_{pb} = -.54$, $p < .05$). Thus, the previously found correlation between the helping scale and religion as quest seems to reflect the tendency of those who score low on the quest dimension to offer help in the added helping category.

What does help in this added category represent? Within the context of the experiment, it represented an embarrassment. The victim's response to persistent offers of help was to assure the helper he was all right, had taken his medicine, just needed to rest for a minute or so, and, if ultimately necessary, to request the helper to leave. But the *super* helpers in this added category often would not leave until the final appeal was repeated several times by the victim (who was growing increasingly panicky at the possibility of the arrival of the next subject). Since it usually involved the subject's attempting to carry through a preset plan (e.g., taking the subject for a cup of coffee or revealing to him the strength to be found in Christ), and did not allow information from the victim to change that plan, we originally labeled this kind of helping as rigid—an interpretation supported by its increased likelihood among highly doctrinal orthodox subjects ($r = .63$, $p < .01$). It also seemed to have an inappropriate character. If this more extreme form of helping behavior is indeed effectively less helpful, then the second form of Hypothesis 3 does seem to gain support.

But perhaps it is the experimenters rather than the super helpers who are doing the inappropriate thing; perhaps the best characterization of this kind of helping is as different rather than as inappropriate. This kind of helper seems quickly to place a particular interpretation on the situation, and the helping response seems to follow naturally from this interpretation. All that can safely be said is that one style of helping that emerged in this experiment was directed toward the presumed underlying needs of the victim and was little modified by the victim's comments about his own needs. In contrast, another style was more tentative and seemed more responsive to the victim's statements of his need.

The former kind of helping was likely to be displayed by subjects who expressed strong doctrinal orthodoxy. Conversely, this fixed kind of helping was unlikely among subjects high on the religion as quest dimension. These latter subjects, who conceived their religion as involving an ongoing search for meaning in their personal and social world, seemed more responsive to the victim's immediate needs and more open to the victim's definitions of his own needs.

CONCLUSION AND IMPLICATIONS

A person not in a hurry may stop and offer help to a person in distress. A person in a hurry is likely to keep going. Ironically, he is likely to keep going even if he is hurrying to speak on the parable of the Good Samaritan, thus inadvertently confirming the point of the parable. (Indeed, on several occasions, a seminary student going to give his talk on the parable of the Good Samaritan literally stepped over the victim as he hurried on his way!)

Although the degree to which a person was in a hurry had a clearly significant effect on his likelihood of offering the victim help, whether he was going to give a sermon on the parable or on possible vocational roles of ministers did not. This lack of effect of sermon topic raises certain difficulties for an explanation of helping behavior involving helping norms and their salience. It is hard to think of a context in which norms concerning helping those in distress are more salient than for a person thinking about the Good Samaritan, and yet it did not significantly increase helping behavior. The results were in the direction suggested by the norm salience hypothesis, but they were not significant. The most accurate conclusion seems to be that salience of helping norms is a less strong determinant of helping behavior in the present situation than many, including the present authors, would expect.

Thinking about the Good Samaritan did not increase helping behavior, but being in a hurry decreased it. It is difficult not to conclude from this that the frequently cited explanation that ethics becomes a luxury as the speed of our daily lives increases is at least an accurate description. The picture that this explanation conveys is of a person seeing another, consciously noting his distress, and consciously choosing to leave him in distress. But perhaps this is not entirely accurate, for, when a person is in a hurry, something seems to happen that is akin to Tolman's (1948) concept of the "narrowing of the cognitive map." Our seminarians in a hurry noticed the victim in that in the postexperiment interview almost all mentioned him as, on reflection, possibly in need of help. But it seems that they often had not worked this out when they were near the victim. Either the interpretation of their visual picture as a person in distress or the empathic reactions usually associated with that interpretation had been deferred because they were hurrying. According to the reflections of some of the subjects, it would be inaccurate to say that they realized the victim's possible distress, then chose to ignore it; instead, because of the time pressures, they did not perceive the scene in the alley as an occasion for an ethical decision.

For other subjects it seems more accurate to conclude that they decided not to stop. They appeared aroused and anxious after the encounter in the alley. For these subjects, what were the elements of the choice that they were making? Why were the seminarians hurrying? Because the experimenter, *whom the subject was helping,* was depending on him to get to a particular place quickly. In other words, he was in conflict between stopping to help the victim and continuing on his way to help the experimenter. And this is often true of people in a hurry; they hurry because somebody depends on their being somewhere. Conflict, rather than callousness, can explain their failure to stop.

Finally, as in other studies, personality variables were not useful in predicting whether a person helped or not. But in this study, unlike many previous ones, considerable variations were possible in the kinds of help given, and these variations did relate to personality measures—specifically to religiosity of the quest sort. The clear light of hindsight suggests that the dimension of kinds of helping would have been the appropriate place to look for personality differences all along; *whether* a person helps or not is an instant decision likely to be situationally controlled. How a person helps involves a more complex and considered number of decisions, including the time and scope to permit personality characteristics to shape them.

REFERENCES

Allen, R. O., & Spilka, B. Committed and consensual religion. A specification of religion-prejudice relationships. *Journal for the Scientific Study of Religion,* 1967, *6,* 191-206.

Allport, G. W., & Ross, J. M. Personal religious orientation and prejudice. *Journal of Personality and Social Psychology,* 1967, *5,* 432-443.

Batson, C. D. Creativity and religious development: Toward a structural-functional psychology of religion. Unpublished doctoral dissertation, Princeton Theological Seminary, 1971.

Bickman, L. B. The effect of the presence of others on bystander intervention in an emergency. Unpublished doctoral dissertation, City College of the City University of New York, 1969.

Brown, L. B. Classifications of religious orientation. *Journal for the Scientific Study of Religion,* 1964, *4,* 91-99.

Burton, R. V. The generality of honesty reconsidered. *Psychological Review,* 1963, *70,* 481-499.

Cohen, J. Some statistical issues in psychological research. In B. B. Wolman (Ed.), *Handbook of clinical psychology.* New York: McGraw-Hill, 1965.

Cohen, J. Multiple regression as a general data-analytic system. *Psychological Bulletin,* 1968, *70,* 426-443.

Darley, J. M., & Latané, B. Bystander intervention in emergencies: Diffusion of responsibility. *Journal of Personality and Social Psychology,* 1968, *8,* 377-383.

Freud, S. *The future of an illusion.* New York: Liveright, 1953.

Funk, R. W. *Language, hermeneutic, and word of God.* New York: Harper & Row, 1966.

Glock, C. Y., & Stark, R. *Christian beliefs and anti-Semitism.* New York: Harper & Row, 1966.

Hartshorne, H., & May, M. A. *Studies in the nature of character.* Vol. 1. *Studies in deceit.* New York: Macmillan, 1928.

Korte, C. Group effects on help-giving in an emergency. *Proceedings of the 77th Annual Convention of the American Psychological Association,* 1969, *4,* 383-384. (Summary)

Orne, M. T. On the social psychology of the psychological experiment: With particular reference to demand characteristics and their implications. *American Psychologist,* 1962, *17,* 776-783.

Rosenberg, M. J. When dissonance fails: On eliminating evaluation apprehension from attitude measurement. *Journal of Personality and Social Psychology,* 1965, *1,* 28-42.

Schwartz, S. H., & Clausen, G. T. Responsibility, norms, and helping in an emergency. *Journal of Personality and Social Psychology,* 1970, *16,* 299-310.

Tolman, E. C. Cognitive maps in rats and men. *Psychological Review,* 1948, *55,* 189-208.

B. LATENT ASPECTS OF "FROM JERUSALEM TO JERICHO"

C. Daniel Batson

Freud contended that dreams include both a manifest or surface meaning and a deeper and more personally significant latent content. The same might be said of a research project. The published version of a piece of research is the manifest meaning, but there is much which lies unsaid behind the published report. And like a psychoanalyst the task here is to probe behind the manifest to the more latent aspects of the research—or, in the language of Chapter 1 of this volume, to probe behind the context of justification to the context of discovery. The psychoanalyst is convinced that all behavior is sensible once one understands the motivations or whys behind it. In parallel fashion, I shall attempt to answer two why questions: Why did we do this research? Why did we do it the way we did?

WHY DID WE DO THIS RESEARCH?

At a most obvious level the answer may seem apparent: I was a graduate student at the time and people were beginning to mumble, "When is he going to get his ass in gear and do something?" In a more positive but equally crass vein, as a student I had access to both money and facilities for running a study on someone else's grant. At an institution where one must pay subjects for participation in research, available funds can be a more real incentive than the threat of flunking out. But neither of these rather cynical pat answers shed light on the question of why *this* research. And since in the case of this particular study the desire to do *this* research was much stronger than the sense of necessity to do *some* research (a sequence which is all too often reversed), I would like to focus attention on that question. There are, of

───────────

Source: Prepared especially for this volume.

course, still a number of answers which could be given; some are scholarly reasons, others are more serendipitous.

Scholarly Reasons

One would like to think that each piece of research he does lies at a nexus where competing explanations of some aspect of social behavior come head to head. For the present research such a nexus was assured, in terms of biases, at least, if not well-formulated scientific theories.

John Darley had been working for five or six years on bystander intervention in emergencies (cf. Latané & Darley, 1970). He came to that research with a fairly strong bias toward the importance of factors in the social environment, as opposed to dispositional or personality characteristics in determining social behavior. John's bias was grounded largely in Festinger's (1954) theory of social comparison, on which he did considerable work during his graduate training at Harvard. His research on bystander intervention added to the conviction that situational factors are far more salient than dispositional ones in determining social behavior. Examining the circumstances under which a person will offer to help in a possible emergency, he and Bibb Latané consistently found variation of the social situation had strong effects on subjects' responses. Specifically, the number of other bystanders and whether they were known or not significantly affected the speed and frequency of bystander intervention. Persons alone tended to respond to the possible crisis most frequently, those with friends less frequently, and those with strangers least frequently. This was found regardless of whether the bystanders could see and talk with one another (Latané & Rodin, 1969) or not (Darley & Latané, 1968). A person seems both to cue on the response (or lack of response) of others in determining whether the situation is in fact an emergency and also to diffuse responsibility for acting in an emergency to others.

The presence or absence of others when a possible emergency arises is a situational variable. But what about dispositional variables, the personality characteristics of the bystander; should these not also affect his response? Even if one's bias runs toward the greater importance of situational determinants of helping, as John's did, one must also consider the other possibility, that who the helper is is at least as important as who else is present. John did consider this possibility by having persons who had been subjects in one of his emergency studies fill out several personality scales. As is frequently done in probing for personality determinants of social behavior, John administered a barrage of scales, all those he thought might predict helping or not helping. He used the Berkowitz and Daniels Social Responsibility Scale, the Marlowe-Crowne Need for Approval Scale, and Christie's revision of the F scale (measuring authoritarianism), Christie's anomia scale, and Christie's Machiavellianism scale.

But all of these personality scales failed to predict helping. The best any of the scales could do in explaining the data was to account for only a minor amount of the variance (4 percent) beyond that attributable to the situational determinants. John concluded: "In general, we found our failure to demonstrate personality correlates of helping somewhat discouraging, although, of course, further research may well uncover other variables which are more effective, or other situations in which more effects occur" (Latané & Darley, 1970, p. 115).

It was fortunate for me that John maintained an open mind toward "other variables" and "other situations." For while he was finding strong effects for situational factors in determining helping and was getting his fingers burned on what seemed to be plausible personality predictors, I had been spending several years at Princeton Theological Seminary trying to develop a new personality measure which I felt should relate to helping behavior. The measure attempted to distinguish three styles or ways of being religious: as a *means* to some other end, as an *end* in itself, and as an ongoing *quest.* The first two styles I borrowed from Allport and Ross (1967), though I sought to elaborate upon and extend them a bit. The third was my own addition, an attempt to tap what I considered a more mature, flexible type of religiosity than the other two.

As virtually all religious leaders will argue, one reason religion is important is that it calls for changes in the way people act. The believer is admonished to love his neighbor (and even his enemy), to turn the other cheek, and so on. Religion is supposed to make a difference in behavior. But almost all studies in the psychology of religion simply relate a person's responses on one questionnaire (e.g., doctrinal orthodoxy) to his responses on another questionnaire (e.g., racial prejudice), or perhaps to such factors as his religious affiliation, race, or sex. I, too, had been doing correlational studies of this sort but had become increasingly dissatisfied with them. If we are to find out whether religion makes a difference in behavior, we must look at behavior. It was with this motivation that I applied to Princeton University to do graduate work in experimental social psychology.

I arrived at Princeton carrying my new personality measure, which I was anxious to test in a behavioral setting, to find that John, although open to the possible importance of dispositional determinants of helping, was far more prone to look toward situational variables. Obviously, there was a study we both wanted and needed to do, comparing the relative power of the religious personality variables and situational variables in a helping situation. To do so, we needed a helping context for which it was clear that religious belief and training should be relevant. But after looking around, none of the contexts that had been used previously seemed quite appropriate.

Fortunately, Jesus showed us the way—with his parable of the Good Samaritan. Not only did the parable suggest a helping context, it also contained a relevant and more complex configuration of variables than we had originally conceived. First, the parable pointed to a distinction between types of religiosity, that of the scribe and Pharisee and that of the Samaritan. Second, it suggested a relevant situational variable, social status or importance, of which we adopted only one aspect, hurry. Further, the fact that the parable was told at all suggested a third variable which might affect helping—having such exemplary stories among one's mental furniture to serve as a guide to right action. Thus, thanks to the parable of the Good Samaritan, we found ourselves with a rich research design, one which focused simultaneously upon the effects of religious style and training (disposition) and on the hurry (situation) of the potential helper.

We had our design. But further, the richness of the parable of the Good Samaritan convinced us of the immense potential value of parables, fables, and other literary lore for the social science researcher. Presumably, such literature is maintained in the culture because it rings true in behavior, and often with a sophistication and subtlety far beyond that of any of our present psychological or sociological theories. The scientist of human behavior may, it seems, do well to listen to the poet, the prophet, and the sage in conceptualizing his research problems.

Serendipitous Reasons

These somewhat rational scholarly reasons are only part of why we did this study at this time. Let me mention a few more serendipitous reasons. The list is by no means exhaustive, but it should illustrate the more accidental aspects of research.

First, although I was acquainted with and interested in John's work on helping in emergencies, I did not plan to study or collaborate on research with him when I decided to do graduate work in social psychology at Princeton. I chose Princeton because I had explicit plans to work with another professor there. But between the time I accepted Princeton's acceptance of me for graduate study in the spring and when I entered the program in the fall, the other professor left Princeton. Casting about for another advisor, John and I both, somewhat guardedly, I think, decided to take a chance on one another.

A second serendipitous factor: if one is to do research comparing different types of religiosity, one must first have people who are religious. This means that the standard college sophomore subject pool may be less than totally appropriate. Fortunately, while doing my graduate work at Princeton University, I was also teaching part time at Princeton Theological Seminary. Virtually all the seminary students considered themselves religious in *some* way, and they presented a rather wide range of conceptions and styles of being religious, at least within Protestantism. Therefore, the religious personality scales "made sense" to them (indeed, they had originally been developed on an earlier sample of Princeton Seminary students). Some agreed strongly and some disagreed strongly with almost every item, but as a group they seemed to find the items relevant to their experience. Thus it appeared legitimate to speak of different styles of religiosity in a sample drawn from these seminarians.

Third, as we began to play with the idea of attempting to simulate some of the aspects of the parable of the Good Samaritan under experimental control, an ideal physical environment presented itself. We knew what we wanted. First we felt it was necessary to set the scene outside of the laboratory or, indeed, any place associated with the psychology department, for all of the seminarians were college graduates and aware of the possible deviousness of psychologists in the lab. Second, we wanted a moderately sinister "road from Jerusalem to Jericho"—not one frequented by robbers and cutthroats, perhaps, but also not without some element of uncertainty and possible threat. We also had to be able to control traffic in the area. One of the major difficulties in taking an experimental design into the real world is to maintain some semblance of control of extraneous variables so that different subjects will experience the same situation. Finally, logistically we needed a place either close to the psychology department or where we could get free office space to make the cover story, our explanation to the subject of why the research in which he was participating required that he "take a walk," plausible.

"You don't ask for too much," you may say. Agreed, but we found the spot. A short dead-end alley ran between the building which housed the psychology department and a partially condemned old building in which some members of the sociology department had their offices. The only people who used the alley regularly were these sociology faculty members, some of their students, a secretary, and various service trucks. We asked the faculty members to help us by taking a longer route to their offices which avoided the alley. They graciously complied. We ran the study when classes were not meeting so student traffic was minimal. Not only did the secretary agree to avoid the alley, she served as part of the cover story, efficiently referring subjects to "the office being used for Professor Steiner's research" when they appeared.

Service traffic was harder to control because it was sporadic. One morning, about ten minutes before the first subject was to be sent through the alley, we found a telephone truck sitting squarely in the middle of the alley, with no phone men in sight. A frantic search produced one of the service men, who rather quizzically but amiably moved his truck out of sight. The janitor also presented a problem. On the second day of running, just as a subject entered the alley, he came out of a side door and cheerily called over to our "victim" huddled ready and waiting, "Feeling better today?" One subject's data, $2.50, and over an hour of experimenter time evaporated.

But on the whole, the alley served admirably as a research context. It was dim, dingy, and drab. Traffic was comparatively light, and it was very close at hand. A footnote, however, on an additional danger of using a field setting for experimental research: The alley did prove to have one major drawback. It disappeared. While we were busily planning some follow-up studies using this same general research paradigm, an environmental beautification program at Princeton turned our sinister alley into a park! Instead of asphalt, trash cans, and puddles, it now contains ivy, a winding walk, a bench, and even a tree. Everyone agrees that it is a much prettier place, and of course it is. But it's hard not to regret the loss of a beautiful sinister alley.

A final serendipitous contribution to the design of this study came when I presented our plans to a graduate research seminar. John and I had originally planned simply to record whether a subject stopped to offer aid or not as the major dependent measure. Another graduate student suggested, however, that we should at least code different types of helping responses. This we did, arranging them on an admittedly crude scale of the amount of help offered (including the "super-helper" category added after running a number of pilot subjects). This coding of *how* a person helped as well as *whether* he helped proved extremely important. Not only did it provide a vehicle for interpreting the differential effects of situational and personality variables in the present study, it also provided the stimulus for a whole new research program concerning variables affecting how a person helps, given that he helps. Although it may cost a bit in strain on one's ego, it certainly pays to bounce research designs off of others who have not been involved in developing the design *before* being irrevocably committed to the particular design (i.e., before the data has been collected).

WHY DID WE DO THE RESEARCH THE WAY WE DID?

I have already referred to some of the whys behind the particular experimental procedures we employed. Let me simply restate and expand briefly upon them. We wanted to move outside of the laboratory, where a subject fears he's being watched and evaluated. We thought this evaluation apprehension might be a particular problem with seminary students, our religious and moral leaders of the future, when faced with a possible helping situation. But once you move outside the laboratory, two problems arise.

One is that you must give the subject plausible and impactful reasons why he is doing what you are asking him to do, for if he doesn't follow instructions (as by traveling an alternate route) you are lost. Both plausibility and impact are important. The former is necessary if the subject is to buy your initial explanation of why he is doing what he is doing, the latter if he is to be involved enough while doing it that he doesn't have second thoughts and begin to get suspicious.

In the present study, the cover story was built around a research project on the ministry as a profession in ferment. The seminarians were all well aware that the ministry is a profession in ferment—this is one of the few consensus items on seminary campuses today—so such a study seemed plausible. Further, specific names of people, places, and organizations were used to increase plausibility. For impact, the seminarians were asked to give a three- to five-minute impromptu talk. As aspiring preachers this was something they would not only consider possible but also would want to do well. It was an ego-engaging task. Most subjects busily scribbled notes before they were sent to give their talks. To reduce the chance of suspicion, the procedure of sending a subject to the other building through the alley was purposely not introduced until after he had a chance to think about and was "into" the topic on which he was about to speak.

The second problem is that control of extraneous variables making it possible to compare different subjects' responses on the experimental variables is far more difficult outside the laboratory. I have already mentioned the difficulties in controlling traffic in the alley, but such subtle factors as variation in temperature and light must also be taken into account. A dark alley at night is quite a different place from the same alley at noon. Also, a young man slouched in a doorway in freezing weather is quite different from the same scene on a balmy summer day. In an attempt to control for such variation, we ran the entire experiment between 10 A.M. and 4 P.M. on three consecutive days in December. Luckily, weather conditions were fairly constant. Further, we tried to balance the number of persons in each experimental condition run on different days and at different times of day.

To control for possible experimenter bias (Rosenthal, 1966) in recording subjects' helping responses, the victim was "blind," or unaware of the experimental condition and personality scores of the subjects. Indeed, he was literally blind, for he kept his eyes closed unless he was approached and spoken to. This led to one snafu in which the victim, having been signaled that a subject was coming, got in position, heard footsteps approach, coughed, heard the footsteps pass by, and went back inside—at which point the real subject rounded the corner and hurriedly walked through the empty alley.

Moving from the particularities of the research design itself, I must comment about the importance of the debriefing in this study. We allotted approximately 30 minutes to the debriefing of each subject, roughly twice as long as the subject spent in the experiment procedure itself. Why? First, as is true in any study, the subject deserves to know exactly what the research is about and why it is being done. Second, our subjects had been deceived. They were told we were studying one thing when in fact we were studying another. No one likes to have one put over on him, and breaking that news is a delicate process (cf. Aronson & Carlsmith, 1968, for a sensitive analysis of how this might be done). Third, the behavior actually being studied was of great importance to most of the seminarians. Most thought it was important to help people in need, and there was the possibility that some of those who did not stop would be inclined to blame themselves. Therefore, it was extremely important to make clear that we were studying the conditions under which a person will be more or less likely to offer aid and were not passing judgment on any individual's behavior. We focused upon the social forces operative in the situation rather than the rightness or wrongness of a given subject's response. Further, we encouraged subjects to express their feelings and reactions during the experiment, as well as their present feelings. As is true in almost any study, such comments are extremely helpful both in suggesting weaknesses in the research design (manipulations which may not be working, etc.) and in suggesting variables for further study.

The debriefing in any deception study is a bit ticklish. In this study it was particularly so. It is to the credit of the seminarians who served as subjects that all took the deception with good grace. Indeed, many encouraged us to continue such research and showed intense interest in the results.

Finally some things I had recently learned about data analysis affected the way we went about the study. Traditionally, psychologists are given to using analysis of variance (ANOVA) for testing statistical significance in experiments and using correlations on personality data. If personality variables are included within an experimental design, it is through the use of medians or some other centile splitting of the continuous personality variable into discrete levels. This means that a great deal of information contained in the personality data is systematically obliterated. Further, to add three-factor analytically created personality variables (as was the case in the present research) to an ANOVA design would make it extremely complex. It would be difficult to find a computer program to handle the analysis. But, on the other hand, to resort to a correlational analysis of the personality variables would not allow us to compare their strength relative to the situational (hurry) and normative (message) variables.

All these difficulties are nicely overcome by a rather sophisticated statistical technique, long known to the sociologist but rather new to the psychologist—multiple regression analysis (MRA). A more general analysis of which ANOVA is a special case, MRA allows the combination of continuous personality and discrete-level experimental variables in the same analysis, and it provides a clear picture of the amount of variance in the dependent variable accounted for by each.

There are both positive and negative aspects to the power one's available techniques for data analysis may hold over the way one collects the data. On the one hand, it is essential that one give thought to how one plans to thrash the data before reaping the harvest. Otherwise, it may not be possible to separate wheat from chaff, the result being bushels of trash. On the other hand, there is the danger of limiting the areas one explores to those for which clear procedures of analysis are available (indeed, these usually are the procedures in vogue wherever one received his undergraduate or graduate training). The social researcher, caught up with the flush of discovering exciting and relevant new things, may find it difficult to leave the field long enough to do some reading in recent journals of applied statistics. But it may be time well spent, for it can enable him to tackle exciting and relevant problems in far more relevant and significant ways.

This review of the latent whys behind the "From Jerusalem to Jericho . . ." study may leave the psychoanalyst invoked at the outset disgruntled and suspicious. It all seems to fit together too, too nicely; a symphony of happy circumstances. I agree, but I'm afraid that's the way I feel about this particular study.

Certainly, it has its problems. I could wish that we had been able to run more subjects, particularly in the high- and low-hurry conditions, both to give additional strength to our findings and to improve the balance of the design. Also, although I was pleased to obtain the results we did with the religious personality scales, I wish either that these scales had more general applicability (they seem limited to those with clear involvement in Christianity, and perhaps even to American Protestants) or that we had had available scales which possibly could tap ethical styles which are less overtly religious but lie behind the religious differences found. These difficulties raise questions about the generality of the study's findings. And a satisfactory answer to this question must await further research, on other subject samples and in other contexts.

True, the study has its problems, but more than any other research I've conducted, this study did seem to involve a symphony of happy circumstances. It was enjoyable throughout—from the discovery of the general research design in the parable of the Good Samaritan, through the creation of the cover story, observation of the responses of individuals in a controlled but complex and "real" social situation, and talking with the subjects afterward in the debriefing, to a challenging data analysis and intriguing pattern of results. I'm well aware the world isn't usually that pretty. But it is sometimes. That's when doing social psychological research is not just worthwhile, it's fun.

REFERENCES

Allport, G. W., & Ross, J. M. Personal religious orientation and prejudice. *Journal of Personality and Social Psychology,* 1967, *5,* 432-443.

Aronson, F., & Carlsmith, J. M. Experimentation in social psychology. Chapter 9 in G. Lindzey and E. Aronson. *The handbook of social psychology,* 2nd Edition, Volume II. Reading, Mass.: Addison-Wesley, 1968, pp. 1-79.

Darley, J. M., & Latané, B. Bystander intervention in emergencies: Diffusion of responsibility. *Journal of Personality and Social Psychology,* 1968, *8,* 377-383.

Festinger, Leon. A theory of social comparison processes. *Human Relations,* 1954, *7,* 117-140.

Latané, B., & Rodin, J. A lady in distress: Inhibiting effects of friends and strangers on bystander intervention. *Journal of Experimental Social Psychology,* 1969, *5,* 189-202.

Rosenthal, R. *Experimenter effects in behavioral research.* New York: Appleton-Century-Crofts, 1966.

Weldon T. Johnson ——————————————————————————

A.   THE RELIGIOUS CRUSADE: REVIVAL OR RITUAL?

Religious behavior, as a topic of scientific inquiry, has a peculiar status in sociology as (1) an independent variable whose influence and effects are unclear, and perhaps unknown; and (2) as a dependent variable whose conditions and causal factors are seldom investigated. In regard to the first variable, there is a body of literature inconsistent with Lenski's (1961) findings that the religious factor is a useful predictor variable.[1] In regard to the second variable (i.e., the impact of secular factors upon religious behavior) there is increasing evidence that the traditional church-sect typology is no longer a useful approach to organizational analysis (Goode 1967; Demerath 1967; Eister 1967).[2]

The literature which deals with the conditions of religious revivalism is equally inconsistent (Lipset 1959; Lang and Lang 1960; Glock and Stark 1965; Elinson 1965). A number of descriptive studies (Niebuhr 1929; Holt 1940; Pope 1942, 1948; Goldschmidt 1944; Sweet 1920; Boisen 1955) directed attention to the sociological character of religious revivals at the turn of the century, and interpreted revivalism, variously, as a social-psychological response to cultural shock, economic distress, and social frustration. More recent research suggests that contemporary religious crusades of A. A. Allen, for example, provide a religious solution to problems of illness,

Source: Weldon T. Johnson, "The Religious Crusade: Revival or Ritual?" *American Journal of Sociology,* 1971, 76, 873-890.

This research was conducted while I was a trainee of the Behavioral Sciences Training Branch of the National Institute of Mental Health Training Grant program (MII 07827-06). Grateful acknowledgment is made for this support. I also wish to express appreciation to Otto N. Larsen at the University of Washington, who supervised this research.

1. There is disagreement as to whether religious behavior is an accurate predictor of voting patterns (Petersen 1962), fertility (Glick 1960; Freedman, Whelpton, and Campbell 1959), marital interaction patterns (Moberg 1962, p. 365), educational aspiration and performance (Greeley 1963; Greeley, Rossi, and Westhoff 1964; Bressler and Westoff 1963), and social class (Lazerwitz 1964, pp. 426-39; Demerath 1965, 1967; Goode 1966; Dillingham 1967). Research in the area of religious behavior reflects frequently contradictory findings because of the absence of available national statistics (Petersen 1962; 1964, pp. 248-70) and methodological problems in the measurement of religious behavior (Demerath 1965).
2. The most commonly cited contemporary studies of the church-sect typology are Yinger (1957), Wilson (1959), Dynes (1955), Glock and Stark (1965), Johnson (1957, 1961, 1963), and Demerath (1965).

poverty, and status deprivation (Elinson 1965). On the other hand, the revivalistic crusades of Billy Graham have been interpreted as mechanisms which crystallize personal identity of middle-class Protestant believers (Lang and Lang 1960, pp. 415-27), or as religious ritual for the already religiously socialized (Whitam 1965).

Whatever the social and ecological circumstances of revivalism, and they have probably changed since the time of Moody and Sunday, considerable ambiguity remains in the sociology of religion literature concerning the effects of revivalism.

Does exposure to revivalism produce change, that is, is revivalism a condition of religious change? Two current methodological practices in the sociology of religion have probably slowed the development of acceptable answers to this question, as well as to others. First, much of the current literature in this area carelessly slides from discussions of belief to practice, or ritual, as indices of religiosity. Thus, there is conspicuous inconsistency in the nominal and operational definitions of the religious factor. A recent review of this literature concluded that "religiosity is apparently not a single dimension. It has various facets which are given various emphases by various social classes" (Demerath 1965). A number of studies have found that the relationship between, for example, religious beliefs and practices is not only complicated, but may be negatively correlated (Demerath 1965). This belief-practice distinction is related to the more general problem of defining the relationship between verbal and nonverbal behavior.

A second practice in the sociology of religion pertains to treatments of religious change. Change in belief has not often been distinguished from change in practice, and all too often investigators have accepted *religious definitions* of change, such as conversion, as the central measure of religious change. Sociologically, however, conversion may be regarded as the "emergence of a new role, outlook, belief, group identification, character or personality" (Moberg 1962). This conception of religious change directs attention to the more general topics of attitudinal and behavioral change, and the social-psychological and social-structural mechanisms which produce such change.

The central concern of the research reported here was to test and specify some conditions under which persons differentially experience certain consequences after exposure to persuasive religious communication in a revivalistic setting. A methodology was incorporated which permits us to distinguish religious belief from practice, and which conceives of religious change in sociological terms. Lang and Lang's (1960) study of a Billy Graham revival meeting generated the initial interest in such a study.

STUDY OF GRAHAM REVIVALISM BY LANG AND LANG

Lang and Lang (1960) employed forty-four college students to collect descriptive data at a Billy Graham crusade in New York in 1957. The purpose of the study was to describe *"who* the persons were whom Graham attracted and *how,* or by which technique, he appealed to them." Their findings are relevant to the descriptive literature in the area of religious behavior. More important for the present study was a methodological problem they experienced by the unanticipated "mortality" of student observers. Several of their observers failed to complete the observational tasks when they became involved religiously in the meeting and pursued their own spiritual interests. Lang and Lang (1960, pp. 424-25) reported:

> Two observers among our own group, who made their decision during the Crusade had been long-time churchgoers. . . . J, the one genuine "convert," i.e., life-changer . . . was so shaken by her experience that no report was forthcoming. J went to the meeting feeling that he [Graham] would have no effect on her. . . . She kept notes during the proceedings. Her notes were primarily concerned with Graham's sermon. She said she gave him her undivided attention. Somewhere in the course of the sermon she decided to step forward. She cannot remember exactly when. The next thing she knew was that she had risen and was hurrying to the main floor to declare herself [a believer]. She felt that this was "right." . . . Her primary reaction was one of fright. . . . The next morning—Sunday— she called two Unitarian churches, intending to attend services; the services had been called off for the summer months.
>
> Two weeks later J felt that she had stepped forward merely out of "curiosity," laughed when she received follow-up literature from the Crusade, and began to view the whole affair as a "lark."

The Langs' interpretation (1960, p. 426) of this development, as well as for thousands of other persons who participated in Graham's meetings as "decision makers" or "inquirers," was that

> unlike other campaigns, what is at stake here is not some specific evil to be fought with palliatives, but personal salvation . . . the dramatization evidently plays on certain tendencies, making it effective for some kinds of people. The middle-class person, torn between the simpler, old-fashioned religious prescriptions and the need to accommodate to a mobile society, is unsure of his identity . . . the declaration of faith, the decision to take Christ into one's heart, is somewhat akin to a ritual confession and ritual atonement.

An alternative explanation, particularly for the observers' behavior, might have focused on the dynamics of participation and on how the definition of the situation affected susceptibility to persuasion. That is, are there circumstances of participation which function as a sufficient condition for susceptibility to persuasive appeals? A small body of research suggests that such circumstances do exist and operate, under certain mediating conditions, to increase the likelihood of persuasion. Klapper (1961, p. 80), for example, notes: "The conversion [change] potential of persuasive communication appears to be intensified under conditions of audience participation, and particularly among persons who are required, regardless of their actual feelings, to assume a role sympathetic to the point of view expressed."

To pursue this explanation, the Langs' observational procedures and directives were examined. The crucial question concerned the extent to which the Langs's observers were "required, regardless of their actual feelings, to assume a role sympathetic to the point of view expressed." It was found that the Langs did indeed prescribe a definite mode of participation. Observers were asked to "talk to them [members of the audience] as if you were there just like everybody else. Don't forget to take along a Bible or equivalent thereof. . . . Keep to your assignment to record behavior."[3]

Given the observer mortality in the Lang study, and the implications concerning the impact of role playing upon persuasion susceptibility, the consideration of differential mediating or intervening social influences suggests the following questions: (a) What are the effects of role playing in a potentially persuasive situation, and (b) What social factors operate to mediate the persuasive appeals for some persons and not others?

ROLE PLAYING AND PERSUASIVE COMMUNICATION

The dynamics of persuasion include the influence of processes which operate both inside and outside the communication context. Role playing may be regarded as an "inside" variable in persuasive communication, and a body of literature suggests that role playing is sufficient for attitude change under certain conditions. In several experiments conducted during World War II, Lewin (1958, pp. 197-211) and others found that food habits were more easily changed under conditions of group discussion than exposure to lectures. Various observers have reported impressions that role playing changed the behavior of American soldiers. Myers observed that a number of "chronic kickers" at an Army camp showed improved morale by participating in public speaking courses where they created speeches favorable to Army life (Janis and King 1954).

Currently, there is a sizable social-psychological literature which documents the assertion that "if a person is forced to improvise a speech supporting a point of view with which he disagrees, his private opinion moves toward the position advocated in the speech" (Festinger and Carlsmith 1959). There is, however, considerable disagreement as to the explanation. Two alternative explanations have been suggested. One formulation draws from Festinger's theory of cognitive dissonance and asserts that if a person can be induced to behave publicly in a manner that is inconsistent with his private attitudes, he will experience cognitive dissonance. Dissonance may be reduced or eliminated by a change in private attitudes. The pressure to reduce dissonance is considered to be a function of the magnitude of the dissonance (Festinger and Carlsmith, 1959). There is some support for this

---

3. The students who participated in the Lang study were not instructed to heed Graham's call to step forward, but were asked to "blend with the audience" (Kurt Lang, personal communication).

THE RESEARCH EXPERIENCE

explanation (Kelman 1953; Festinger and Carlsmith 1959; Cohen, Brehm, and Fleming 1958; Cohen 1962).

An alternative explanation follows an incentive (or reinforcement) formulation. It asserts that high rewards or incentives for role playing produce changes in opinions and attitudes, and there is also some support for this explanation (Janis and Gilmore 1965; Rosenberg 1965; Harvey and Beverly 1961). A more recent study concludes that the dissonance explanation is accurate when subjects are permitted to pursue alternatives to the role-playing requirement, and that incentive (reinforcement) theory pertains only to those situations in which compliance is forced (Linder, Cooper, and Jones 1967).

Extension of these experimental studies to the naturalistic situation observed by the Langs requires some interpretation. First, the subjects' mode of participation in role-playing experiments has been restricted primarily to verbal behavior, such as writing an essay or giving a speech. Nonverbal role playing requires considerably more behavioral commitment, and thus may be more powerful in its generation of persuasion suggestibility. Second, application of incentive or dissonance theory to naturalistic settings requires consideration of conditions and variables operating outside the communication context—behavioral history, predispositions, and salience and effect of group norms. The role-playing interpretation of religious change may be extended to include these "outside" influences as "mediating factors" (Klapper 1961). For example, there appear to be distinguishable expectations for religious behavior according to age and sex roles. Women are more religious than men on all criteria of religiosity, and children and the elderly are more highly involved in belief behavior than adolescents or the middle-aged (Argyle 1958). There is also a large literature which suggests that conditions of social deprivation (Yinger 1957; Herberg 1955), ill health (Argyle 1958; Moberg 1962), fear of death (Stouffer 1949; Allport, Gillespie, and Young 1948), and economic deprivation (Holt 1940; Boisen 1955; Pope 1942, 1948; Goldschmidt 1944; Catton 1957; Demerath 1965) are sufficient for religious change. All of these variables may be taken as conditions which define both the dissonance and incentives in role playing.

The research reported here defined two modes of nonverbal, behavioral role playing, and attempted to test the following hypothesis in a replication of the Langs' study:

HYPOTHESIS: *The more active the role playing, the greater the positive effect of persuasive appeals for increasing religious commitment in belief and practice, particularly under conditions where* (a) persons were more religiously involved at an earlier time in their life than at the present; (b) persons perceive close friends and relatives to support positive change in religious commitment; and (c) persons perceive themselves to be relatively underprivileged in economic and physical status.

PROCEDURE

The methodology of this study may be viewed as a replication of the Langs' study with one central exception—student observers served unknowingly as experimental subjects. The study design utilized two experimental groups and a control group, each with forty-six subjects. One experimental

TABLE 1
Inter- and Intracorrelations of All Indicators of Religious Commitment (Pearsonian r)

Indicators	Self-Concept A	B	C	D	E	F	G	Devotion-alism H	I	Asso-ciation-alism J	Com-munalism K	L
Self-concept:												
A	1.00	.408	.444	.481	.446	.422	.488	.387	.438	.488	.172	.269
Doctrinal orthodoxy:												
B		1.000	.682	.709	.506	.546	.637	.566	.584	.387	.066	.248
C			1.000	.788	.602	.642	.697	.522	.635	.500	.062	.343
D				1.000	.636	.597	.674	.674	.707	.539	.076	.368
E					1.000	.691	.708	.470	.484	.445	.070	.435
F						1.000	.687	.365	.503	.525	.054	.405
G							1.000	.462	.503	.532	.107	.324
Devotionalism:												
H								1.000	.685	.475	.016	.239
I									1.000	.536	.104	.375
Associationalism:												
J										1.000	.038	.252
Communalism:												
K											1.000	.304
L												1.000

Note: These correlations are taken from responses to the first questionnaire: A = Self Concept (TST), B = There is a God, C = God is like, D = God answers, E = Life after death, F = When they are able, G = Jesus was, H = How often pray, I = Decisions, J = Attend, K = close friends, and L = Spouse.

TABLE 2
Religious Preference of Experimental Subjects

Religious Group	Active %	Active N	Passive %	Passive N	Control %	Control N	Total %	Total N
Presbyterian	11	5	17	8	17	8	15	21
Methodist	17	8	20	9	7	3	14	20
Catholic	17	8	13	7	4	2	12	17
Lutheran	4	2	17	8	13	6	12	16
Congregational	17	8	4	2	11	5	10	15
Episcopal	7	3	9	4	11	5	9	12
Baptist	4	2	4	2	4	2	4	6
Jew	4	2	0	0	4	2	3	4
Other Protestant	15	7	13	6	17	8	15	21
None or no response	1	1	0	0	11	5	4	6
Total		46		46		46		138

group received verbal instruction for active participant-observation (role playing) at a Graham revival meeting. A second experimental group was instructed to passively participate during observation (role playing). The control group was not involved in participation or attendance at Graham's meeting, but served as a nontreatment comparison group.

All subjects' "religious commitment" was measured at three points in time via self-administered questionnaires—once before exposure to Graham, and twice after exposure at three-week intervals. Lenski's (1961) conceptual and operational definitions of doctrinal orthodoxy, devotionalism, associationalism, and communalism were adopted and modified to a five-point Likert scale, although scale values were not summed for an overall scale score. The Twenty Statements Test (TST) was used to measure the salience of religious identification for self-concept. Table 1 shows the intercorrelations between all indicators of the dependent variable.[4]

Each experimental group was composed of students from introductory sociology classes at the University of Washington who were invited to participate in an observational study of Graham's revival. Members of the control group, also sociology students from an introductory social psychology course, were unaware of the study and of their participation as experimental controls. All experimental subjects met for an orientation lecture and were told of the sociological relevance of the study and of the importance of their ability to follow instructions for participant-observation. At the close of the orientation lecture, volunteers were assigned randomly to one of the two experimental groups which subsequently met independently for the "treatment" instructions. Volunteers were not told that they were the subjects of the study; nor were they told of the different instructions for the two experimental groups.

Experimental and control subjects were well matched in terms of age, sex, father's occupation, previous exposure to Billy Graham, and religious preference. Between 61 percent and 67 percent of each group was under twenty-one; about one-third of all subjects were male, and over two-thirds of each group reported father's occupation as professional or managerial. Between 89 percent and 98 percent of these students had never attended a Graham meeting. The religious preferences of the students are summarized in Table 2.

---

4. Some of the interitem correlations displayed in Table 1 are noteworthy. The belief (doctrinal orthodoxy) items (i.e., B, C, D, E, F, and G) have values of relatively the same magnitude and are high (from .50 to .78). The three dimensions of religious practice (devotionalism, associationalism, and communalism) are associated with each other and with belief items to varying degrees. In particular, it may be noted that frequency of church attendance (J) is about as strongly related to other dimensions of religious practice as to belief items. The third general dimension of religious commitment, salience of religious identification for self-concept, shows moderate correlations with all other indicators (from .38 to .48) except for the communalism indicators.

Observer Role Playing

At the second orientation session, volunteers met independently but at the same hour. At this session, volunteers were "trained" to be observers at the Graham meeting. Active participant-observers met with one supervisor; passive observers met with another. Although the instructions for each group were different, the training procedure was similar—research questions were reviewed, observers' questionnaires were distributed and discussed, instructions for observation were given, and a twenty-minute tape recording of selected segments of previous Graham meetings was played so that all observers would be familiar with the format and style of the Graham meeting.

Active Role Playing

The important difference in the training sessions of the two groups was in their instructions for participation. Active observers were instructed to be "totally involved" in the Graham meeting. They were instructed to participate in the progression of the revival meeting and to "play the role of the typical audience member." They were told:

> You should freely participate in the singing, praying, and whatever Graham asks you to do. . . . When Graham asks the audience to stand and pray—take the role of the typical member in the audience.
>
> Your role will be defined by Graham. When he asks the audience to bow their heads—bow your head. When he asks the members of the audience to get up and walk forward—you should get up and walk forward. It is very important that you be able to comply with this aspect of the meeting.
>
> If you do not feel that you can carry through with your participant-observation, please tell us now. But understand, that without maximum participation, we will be unable to answer questions about the sociological and psychological processes operative here.

Passive Role Playing

In another room, passive participant-observers were instructed to restrict their activity at the Graham meeting to quiet and unobtrusive observation. They were asked to refrain from involvement in the singing, prayers, and in the "decision making" at the close of the meeting. The role of the passive observer was defined as follows:

> You are asked to merely sit and watch, recording information on your questionnaire as you are asked . . . so that other things will not interfere with your ability to record accurate and objective information, we are asking you to refrain from any active involvement in any aspect of the meeting such as singing, prayer, or going forward at the end. . . . When Graham appeals to the members of the audience to come forward, your instructions still hold: *Observe.*

After attending the Graham meeting, all observers were asked to report on their own participation. Responses to three questionnaire items constituted a

TABLE 3
Observer Participation

Answers	Active		Passive	
	%	N	%	N
To what extent did you participate in the following phases of the Graham meeting:				
Audience singing	76	35	17	8
Prayer	70	32	24	11
Going forward at the end of the meeting	65	30	0	0

Note: Subjects estimated the degree of their involvement on a five-point scale.

TABLE 4
F-Ratios for Experimental Groups and Time Comparisons on All Indicators of Religious Commitment (two-way analysis of variance)

Indicators	Between Treatments (df, 2/135)	Between Times (df, 1/135)	Interaction (df, 2/135)
Salience of self-concept:			
Self-concept	0.546	0.716	0.775
Doctrinal orthodoxy:			
There is a God	0.474	0.252	0.256
God is like	1.092	22.194*	3.717**
God answers	0.235	0.750	0.480
There is a life	1.391	0.089	0.089
When they are	1.022	1.990	0.124
Jesus was	0.476	4.117*	2.728
Devotionalism:			
Frequency pray	2.264	3.439	0.000
Decisions	1.036	4.628*	1.157
Associationalism:			
Attendance	0.871	7.256*	0.151
Communalism:			
Close friends	0.927	0.016	2.930
Spouse agree	3.432*	0.384	1.897

*$p < .05$.
**$p < .001$.

measurement of the relative success in creating the active and passive roles. Table 3 indicates that most active and passive role players did in fact engage in the appropriate nonverbal behaviors.

FINDINGS

The experimental design of the study facilitated before-after comparisons between all three groups on the dependent variable, religious commitment. Individual subjects within each experimental group were assigned a "change score" on each indicator of religious commitment. The three measures in time permitted analysis of both short-term (one day) and long-term (three weeks) effects.

Table 4 summarizes the overall differences between experimental groups on all indicators of religious commitment and between short-term

TABLE 5
Proportion of Positive, Negative, and No Change on All Indicators
of the Dependent Variable over Time

	Active			
	Short		Long	
	%	N	%	N
Plus change	10.8	60	11.0	61
Minus change	15.4	85	15.8	87
No change	73.7	407	73.2	404
	Passive			
	Short		Long	
	%	N	%	N
Plus change	13.4	74	11.7	65
Minus change	15.0	83	20.1	111
No change	71.6	395	68.1	576
	Control			
	Short		Long	
	%	N	%	N
Plus change	10.3	57	8.6	48
Minus change	12.3	68	15.6	86
No change	77.4	427	75.7	418

Note: Number of Ss in each group: 46.

TABLE 6
Subjects' Assessment of Own Belief-Behavioral Responses to Graham

	Active				Passive			
	Belief		Behavior		Belief		Behavior	
	%	N	%	N	%	N	%	N
No effect	73.9	34	84.7	39	71.7	33	84.7	39
Reinforced	21.7	10	8.7	4	21.7	10	6.5	3
Created	4.3	2	6.5	3	6.5	3	8.7	4
N		46		46		46		46

TABLE 7
Subjects' Assessment of Own Self-Concept Response to Graham Exposure

	Active		Passive	
	%	N	%	N
No effect	56.6	26	80.0	37
Slight change	34.1	16	19.5	9
Great change	8.9	4	0.0	0
N		46		46

Note: Responses to: How has it affected the way you think of yourself?

and long-term differences. On only one indicator is there a statistically significant difference between experimental groups. On four of the twelve items there are statistically significant differences between short- and long-term effects. The data in Table 4 show practically no differences between groups, and the hypothesized relationship between degrees of role playing and change in religious commitment is not supported.[5]

The use of multiple indicators of religious commitment facilitates an examination of patterns of change without regard for statistical significance. A simple enumeration of the direction of changes (i.e., positive, negative, and no change) is shown in Table 5.

The data show that disproportionately more positive changes occurred for both short-term and long-term effects among members of the passive group. Active role players showed more positive changes than members of the control group. When negative change (lessened religious commitment) is examined, the data indicate that active observers experienced a greater proportion of negative change than passive observers, and passive observers more than members of the control group. When negative changes in long-term effects are examined, however, the pattern corresponds to the regularities observed in positive changes—passive observers show proportionately more negative change then either active role players or members of the control group.

These differences, however, are exceedingly small. The data indicate that the most common consequence of exposure to Billy Graham was neither positive nor negative change, but no change.

SELF-REPORTED CHANGE: PERCEIVED CONSEQUENCES

Three weeks after exposure to Graham, experimental subjects were asked to assess the consequences of their attendance at the revival. Student observers were still unaware of their "subject" role in the experiment. They were asked to indicate the extent to which exposure to Graham had an effect on their own beliefs, religious practices, and self-concept (Tables 6, 7). Table 6 shows that most treatment subjects judged Graham to have had no effect on religious beliefs and practices. The subjects' own reports tend to corroborate the questionnaire data—no effect.

An examination of observers' written reports indicated additional consequences of exposure to Graham. A few observers felt that their participation facilitated religious goals. One observer wrote to the experimenter: "I know Jesus Christ as my personal savior and I'm so thrilled that our Soc.

---

5. Experimental subjects were also subdivided on the variables of relative orthodoxy of religious background, the extent to which peer groups supported religious change, and perceived high and low physical and economic deprivation. Analysis of variance, not shown here, produced fewer statistically significant differences than would have been expected by chance.

class has this assignment so that many souls can hear about the Lord's saving grace. It is truly an answer to Prayer. Thank you so much for the assignment."

Some observers reported that their mode of participation at the Graham meeting influenced the extent to which Graham might have "moved" them. One observer complained that his passive role prevented expression of genuine religious sentiment. He said: "I felt if I hadn't been restricted I may have gone up to be saved." On the other hand, some active observers expressed the same sentiment—that their participation interfered with the generation of serious religious sentiments. One observer reported: "I was not moved. The difference in feeling was because I had to muster the guts to get up there." Several observers, however, reported that they were in fact "moved" by Graham's appeal. The reports of two observers characterize the experiences of several and are reminiscent of observer experiences in the Langs' study. An active observer reported:

> At the meeting itself, I felt it would be very embarrassing to walk down in front of these people. Although I was instructed to do so, I think I would have anyway just to affirm my own belief in God.

TABLE 8
Observers' Reactions to Graham

	Active		Passive		Totals	
	%	N	%	N	%	N
I consider the meeting to have been a rewarding and uplifting experience	15.0	7	15.0	7	15.0	14
I was emotionally stirred	7.0	3	9.0	4	8.0	7
I was not particularly stirred, but it was an interesting experience	67.0	31	61.0	28	64.0	59
I was totally bored	2.0	1	4.0	2	3.0	3
My reaction to the meeting is negative. I resent what Graham is trying to do	9.0	4	11.0	5	10.0	9

Note: Answers to: Which statement best describes your own feelings and experiences as you participated in the meeting?

TABLE 9
Observers' Interest to See Graham Again

	Active		Passive		Total		Significance*
	%	N	%	N	%	N	
Definitely or probably yes	9.0	4	15.0	7	12.0	11	No $z = 0.890$
Possibly	24.0	11	13.0	6	18.0	17	No $z = 1.37$
Probably or definitely no	67.0	31	72.0	33	70.0	64	No $z = 0.521$

Note: Answers to: If you had the opportunity, would you go to see and hear Billy Graham again—for personal rather than for sociological or other reasons?
*Difference between proportions test; $a = .05$ (one-tail test).

THE RESEARCH EXPERIENCE

When returning to the dormitory, I told some of my friends of my participation and my actual feelings and they laughed about it. I was actually offended at the time and defending the cause and becoming quite heated. After a few days of not talking to them, I apologized and thought my actions quite silly.

After returning from the Graham meeting, all observers were asked to check a statement which best described their reaction to the Graham meeting, and to indicate whether they would go to see and hear Billy Graham again, for personal rather than observational purposes. Table 8 indicates, for example, that 64 percent of all observers were "not particularly stirred but thought it was an interesting experience." The differences in reaction between active and passive observers in this table are not statistically significant; the pattern of responses for both groups of observers is similar.

When observers were asked if they would attend a Graham meeting in the future, passive observers were more likely to indicate both yes and no. Table 9 indicates that active observers were more likely than passive observers to view future attendance as a possibility. Again, the differences between active and passive observers are small, and all observer responses contribute to an overall pattern of reaction—mostly negative.

CONCLUSIONS AND DISCUSSION

The principal findings of this study indicate that (1) the hypothesized relationship between nonverbal role playing and persuasion was not demonstrated; (2) regardless of other variables (e.g. religious background, the existence of group norms prescribing reli us change, and perceived deprivation of health and economic statuses), the Graham meeting was ineffectual in changing religious beliefs, behaviors, or religious self-concepts; and (3) when change did occur among student observers, religious commitment was attenuated.

There are at least three alternative interpretations for the findings of this study. First, the findings may be misleading insofar as they suggest that Graham revivals are ineffectual in changing religious behavior. It may be that college populations, such as the one studied here, are (a) unsocialized to the style of Protestantism which Graham presents and are, hence, unable to respond religiously to the "make a decision for Christ" approach (these students may make their religious decisions, if they make them at all, in some other context); and (b) college students may be sufficiently areligious so that exposure to Graham or anyone else has no pronounced effect upon either their verbal or nonverbal religious behavior.

A second interpretation is that Graham does in fact generate religious changes in his audiences, but that the instruments employed in this study were insensitive to them. Systematic measurement remains a core problem in sociology, and the pitfalls which stem from the use of verbal reports of nonverbal events are well known (Deutscher 1966). In this study, measurement of the dependent variable and independent variables (i.e., role playing, religious background, etc.) was accomplished through verbal reports.

A third interpretation—and one favored by me—is that exposure to Graham revivalism does not produce changes in religious behavior, but rather, normatively prescribed "religious experiences" for certain individuals already socialized into this form of religious expression. In the present study, nine students indicated to the investigator that they "made a decision for Christ" at the meeting. An examination of their religious backgrounds revealed that, in each case, they had been exposed either to Billy Graham meetings in the past, or had attended those Protestant churches which support the Graham movement and incorporate his style of conversion. An examination of the questionnaire data for these subjects showed that there were no changes in the salience of religious identification for self-concept, nonverbal religious behaviors, or in the number and intensity of religious beliefs. This study, like the research of Zetterberg (1952), Tamney (1962), and Whitam (1965), views revivalism of the style practiced by Billy Graham as subcultural tradition whose norms define and prescribe ritualistic religious "conversions," without changing either verbal or nonverbal religious behavior.

REFERENCES

Allport, G., J. M. Gillespie, and J. Young. 1948. "The Religion of the Post-War College Student." *Journal of Psychology* 25: 3-33.
Argyle, M. 1958. *Religious Behavior.* London: Free Press.
Boisen, A. 1955. *Religion in Crisis and Custom.* New York: Harper & Row.
Bressler, M., and C. Westhoff. 1963. "Catholic Education, Economic Values and Achievement." *American Journal of Sociology* 69 (November): 225-33.
Catton, W. R., 1957. "What Kind of People Does a Religion Cult Attract?" *American Sociological Review* 28 (October): 562-66.
Cohen, A. R. 1962. "An Experiment on Small Rewards for Discrepant Compliance and Attitude Change." In *Explorations in Cognitive Dissonance,* edited by J. W. Brehm and A. R. Cohen. New York: Wiley.
Cohen, A. R., J. W. Brehm, and W. H. Fleming. 1958. "Attitude Change and Justification for Compliance." *Journal of Abnormal and Social Psychology* 56 (September): 276-78.
Demerath, N. J., III. 1965. *Social Class in American Protestantism.* Chicago: Rand McNally.
_____. 1967. "Comment: In a Sow's Ear." *Journal for the Scientific Study of Religion* 6 (April): 77-84.
Deutscher, I. 1966. "Words and Deeds: Social Science and Social Policy." *Social Problems* 13 (Winter): 235-54.
Dillingham, H. C. 1967. "Rejoinder to 'Social Class and Church Participation.'" *American Journal of Sociology* 73 (July): 110-14.
Dynes, R. 1955. "Church-Sect Typology and Socio-economic Status." *American Sociological Review* 20 (October): 555-60.
Eister, A. 1967. "Toward a Radical Critique of Church-Sect Typologizing." *Journal for the Scientific Study of Religion* 6 (April): 85-90.
Elinson, H. 1965. "The Implications of Pentecostal Religion for Intellectualism,

Politics, and Race Relations." *American Journal of Sociology* 71 (January): 403-15.

Festinger, L., and J. Carlsmith. 1959. "Cognitive Consequences of Forced Compliance." *Journal of Abnormal and Social Psychology* 58 (March): 203-10.

Freedman, R., P. Whelpton, and A. Campbell, 1959. *Family Planning, Sterility, and Population Growth.* New York: McGraw-Hill.

Glick, P. 1960. "Intermarriage and Fertility Patterns among Persons in Major Religious Groups." *Eugenics Quarterly* 7 (March): 31-38.

Glock, C., and R. Stark. 1965. *Religion and Society in Tension.* Chicago: Rand McNally.

Goldschmidt, W. 1944. "Class Denominationalism in Rural California Churches." *American Journal of Sociology* 49 (January): 248-55.

Goode, E. 1966. "Social Class and Church Participation." *American Journal of Sociology* 72 (July): 102-11.

———. 1967. "Some Critical Observations on the Church-Sect Dimension." *Journal for the Scientific Study of Religion* 6 (April): 69-76.

Greeley, A. 1963. "Influence of the 'Religious Factor' on Career Plans and Occupational Values of College Students." *American Journal of Sociology* 68 (May): 658-71.

Greeley, A., P. Rossi, and C. Westhoff. 1964. *The Social Effects of Catholic Education.* Report 99-A. Chicago: National Opinion Research Center.

Harvey, O. J., and G. Beverly. 1961. "Some Personality Correlates of Concept Change through Role Playing." *Journal of Abnormal and Social Psychology* 37 (July): 125-30.

Herberg, W. 1955. *Protestant, Catholic, Jew.* New York: Anchor Books.

Holt, J. 1940. "Holiness Religion: Cultural Shock and Social Reorganization." *American Sociological Review* (October): 740-47.

Janis, I., and B. Gilmore. 1965. "The Influence of Incentive Conditions on the Success of Role Playing in Modifying Attitudes." *Journal of Personality and Social Psychology* 1 (January): 17-27.

Janis, I., and B. King. 1954. "The Influence of Role Playing on Opinion Change." *Journal of Abnormal and Social Psychology* 49 (April): 211-18.

Johnson, B. 1957. "A Critical Appraisal of the Church-Sect Typology." *American Sociological Review* 22 (February): 88-92.

———. 1961. "Do Holiness Sects Socialize in Dominant Values?" *Social Forces* 39 (May): 309-16.

———. 1963. "On Church and Sect." *American Sociological Review* 28 (August): 539-49.

Kelman, H. 1953. "Attitude Change as a Function of Response Restriction." *Human Relations* 6 (August): 185-214.

Klapper, J. 1961. *The Effects of Mass Communication.* Glencoe, Ill.: Free Press.

Lang, K., and G. Lang, 1960. "Decisions for Christ: Billy Graham in New York City." In *Identity and Anxiety,* edited by M. Stein et al. Glencoe, Ill.: Free Press.

Lazerwitz, B. 1964. "Religion and Social Structure in the United States." In *Religion, Culture and Society,* edited by L. Schneider. New York: Wiley.

Lenski, G. 1961. *The Religious Factor.* New York: Doubleday.

Lewin, K. 1958. "Group Decision and Social Change." In *Readings in Social Psychology.* 3d ed., edited by E. Maccoby, et al. New York: Holt, Rinehart & Winston.

Linder, D., J. Cooper, and E. Jones. 1967. "Decision Freedom as a Determinant of the Role of Incentive Magnitude in Attitude Change." *Journal of Personality and Social Psychology* 6 (July): 245-54.

Lipset, S. 1959. *Political Man.* New York: Doubleday.

Moberg, D. 1962. *The Church as a Social Institution.* Englewood Cliffs, N.J.: Prentice-Hall.

Niebuhr, H. R. 1929. *The Social Sources of Denominationalism.* New York: Holt.

Petersen, W. 1961. "Religious Statistics in the United States." *Journal for the Scientific Study of Religion* 1 (Spring): 165-79.

––––––. 1964. "Religious Statistics in the United States." In *The Politics of Population,* edited by W. Petersen. New York: Doubleday.

Pope, L. 1942. *Millhands and Preachers.* New Haven, Conn.: Yale Univ. Press.

––––––. 1948. "Religion and Class Structure." *Annals of American Academy of Political and Social Science* 256 (March): 84-91.

Rosenberg, J. J. 1965. "When Dissonance Fails: On Eliminating Evaluation Apprehension from Attitude Measurement." *Journal of Personality and Social Psychology* 1 (January): 28-42.

Stouffer, S. A., et al. 1949. *The American Soldier: Combat and its Aftermath.* Vol. 2. New York: Wiley.

Sweet, W. 1920. *The Rise of Methodism in the West.* Nashville, Tenn.: Smith & Lamar.

Tamney, J. 1962. "An Exploratory Study of Religion Conversion." Ph.D. dissertation, Cornell University.

Whitam, F. 1965. "Adolescence and Mass Persuasion: A Study of Teen-age Decision-Making at a Billy Graham Crusade." Ph.D. dissertation, Indiana University.

Wilson, B. 1959. "An Analysis of Sect Development." *American Sociological Review* 24 (February): 3-15.

Yinger, J. M. 1957. *Religion, Society, and the Individual.* New York: Macmillan.

Zetterberg, H. 1952. "The Religious Conversion as a Change of Social Roles." *Sociology and Social Research* 26 (February): 159-66.

Personal Journal ───────────────────────────────

B. RESEARCHING THE RELIGIOUS CRUSADE: A PERSONAL JOURNAL

This study was conducted in 1965 while the author was a graduate student in the Department of Sociology at the University of Washington, Seattle. The research ultimately resulted in a master's thesis and the published article reprinted above. Like many graduate thesis projects, this research provided the intended initial experience with study design, ques-

───────────

Source: Prepared especially for this volume.

tionnaire construction, data collection and analysis. It also, of course, involved a series of concrete encounters with the full range of situational and practical problems associated with such research. Through this experience, I learned that the research enterprise actually entails a series of decision points which often allow for limited solution options and which frequently necessitate regrettable compromises. My experience confirmed Bachrach's First Law: "People don't usually do research the way people who write books about research say that people do" (Bachrach, 1965).

THE IDEA EVOLVES: WOULDN'T IT BE INTERESTING!

The impetus to this research was unpretentious. The study was not generated by theoretical or conceptual questions alone. Like much research, this project was literally hatched in a bull session attended by several weary students at the end of a long day of studying. These informal and free-wheeling chats occurred at different times and irregular intervals; participants were drawn from whoever was around at the time. The usual topics of conversation were faculty members, graduate education, pure sociology, and functionalism. All of these were discussed with an odd mixture of irreverence, cynicism, and humor.

It was during one of these early morning events that I first amused my colleagues by recounting the unusual methodological problem encountered in a study I had recently read (Lang & Lang, 1960). The research found that, during an observational study of a religious crusade, several observers had lost sight of their research assignments when they got involved in the meeting. I cannot now recall what generated this discussion, except that earlier we had been amused at having found an article that one of our professors had written on the need for research on prayer, entitled "Can Science Improve Praying?" (Dodd, 1961). In any event, the Langs' observer problem also was discussed, with tempered seriousness, as an unusual instance of what the methods textbooks called "subject mortality." What followed was some speculation about a nontheological interpretation of the Langs' problem. For tenable interpretations, we pooled our knowledge of the research literature on persuasive communications. Ultimately, the important consequence of our discussion was not the effort to interpret the Langs' problem but the suggestion of another student who said: "Wouldn't it be interesting . . . to take a bunch of people and *experimentally* send them to a Billy Graham meeting!" We speculated for a few minutes about how such an experiment might be performed before we packed our books and left. As a group, we never talked about the idea again, but I pondered it privately for several weeks.

My interest in this matter, including the Langs' study, stemmed from prior reading in the sociology of religion literature. During undergraduate studies, I had written several papers on religious fundamentalism, and I spent one entire summer reading Weber, Parsons, Durkheim, and Malinow-ski. After a year and a half of graduate school, I was looking for a suitable thesis topic within this area.

Some months after the graduate student discussion described above, I read in a Seattle newspaper of the impending visit to the city of Billy Graham. He would be coming in the summer for a one-day crusade. At about the same time, I discovered a reference to an obscure passage from Huxley's *The Devils of Loudun:*

> . . . no man, however highly civilized, can listen for very long to African drumming, or Indian chanting, or Welsh hymn singing, and retain intact his critical and self-conscious personality. It would be interesting to take a group of the most eminent philosophers from the best universities, shut them up in a hot room with Moroccan dervishes or Haitian Voodooists and measure with a stop-watch, the strength of their psychological resistance to the effects of rhythmic sound. Would the Logical Positivists be able to hold out longer than the Subjective Idealists? Would the Marxists prove tougher than the Thomists or Vedantists? What a fascinating, what a fruitful field for experiment.

Although the Graham crusade did not contain all of Huxley's variables, I shared his curiosity about this general phenomenon. I was now excited about the actual *opportunity* to perform the study we had talked about casually months before. I began to think more seriously about how the study could be conducted and about the theoretical principles in the area of persuasive com-munications that could be tested. I was concerned, however, about the aca-demic respectability of the project, something which, in general, the sociology of religion had not yet been fully granted. The study obviously was a little kinky, and although this appealed to me, I worried about the faculty's response to my prospectus.

The months that followed were devoted to designing the research and doing additional reading in the area of persuasive communications. By con-ception, the research was to involve a field experiment. I could find no such studies in the area of religion, and I was puzzled by Argyle's contention that such studies were "unsuitable not only because it is undesirable to change people's attitudes or beliefs on such fundamental matters, but because the effects would be minimized under the artificial conditions of experiments" (Argyle, 1959, p. 13). I was well aware of both the appropriateness and artificiality issues, but I wanted to postpone my concern with them until after the study, which I did. I was more taken with the analytic assets of field experiments. I argued in my prospectus that the field experimental design would have some of the advantages of both controlled experiments and survey research. It would be possible to control certain variables through random assignment of subjects to treatment groups; to clarify the direction of relationships, both experimentally and statistically; to select the control variables so that confounding variables could be excluded; and to avoid the artificiality issue by conducting the experiment in a natural setting. I acknowledged that my experiment was not technically an experiment insofar as it was not possible to control or manipulate the stimulus (Graham's persuasive appeal). My prospectus also outlined a list of hypotheses, drawn from the appropriate bodies of literature, and I promised to follow a nine-cell factorial design with 50 observations in each cell. My concern about an unfavorable faculty response to the prospectus was unwarranted; the project was approved, and I proceeded to work out additional design and procedural matters.

THE IDEA DEVELOPS: DECISIONS AND COMPROMISES

In addition to the considerations outlined above, this research was designed around certain practical considerations—time, money, and convenience. First of all, since the day of data collection was literally scheduled by the Graham organization, the time frame for the study was absolutely inflexible. Thus, instrumentation and the pretesting of questionnaire items had to be accomplished without delay. Second, the absence of funds, except for a small mimeographing allocation, forced the decision concerning selection of subjects. As in so many other studies, the availability of students facilitated this decision. I was aware that probably most of the previous research on persuasive communication also had used college students as subjects and that this was sometimes a criticism of them. Even the growing literature on religious beliefs and behavior had a disproportionate number of student samples, but here the traditional hypotheses about the salience of religion among the young as a point of awakening or, more recently, secularization seemed to justify student samples. I had no special interest in age as a variable or a condition, and the main criterion for sample selection was accessibility. Using students, however, may have carried with it some substantive import in that the college-age sample may have facilitated conservative main effects to which older samples would not have contributed. Though this consideration was not recognized explicitly at the time the subjects were selected, sample characteristics (i.e., their youth) may have made it more difficult for the "treatment" to take.

The population of students from which the sample was drawn ultimately was defined as three sociology courses taught during the summer session. I was not then teaching, but I persuaded three instructors to help me. The study design called for three groups of 50 subjects, two treatment groups and a control group. The study also called for one pretest and two posttest measures of religious commitment. Once the agreement with the instructors was reached, I moved immediately to preparation for the administration of the pretest measure. The instructors agreed to invite their students to participate in the study and not to disclose the nature of that participation until later. Thus, on the first day of class, the project was mentioned to the students, and they were told that they could get term paper credit for subsequent participation. During the first week of summer school instruction, the pretest instrument was administered. The procedure was straightforward; I simply arrived in each class at a designated hour and distributed the questionnaires, with the following explanation:

> The Institute for Sociological Research is doing a study of student opinion about basic beliefs. This is the first step in preparing an instrument for a larger study which will be conducted this summer.
>
> We need your answers to these questions, as they are asked as a basis for making assignments to the observation tasks that you will participate in later.
>
> We can't give you much more information about the study now, but you will learn the whole story later.
>
> It is important that you fill out the whole questionnaire, and put your name on the last page as it is requested. You should understand that your name will be known only to me and that it will be converted into a code number for statistical analysis on a computer.

Once the pretest data were collected, I turned to the problem of recruiting volunteers. Again, I persuaded the course instructors to encourage participation, and I asked each instructor to read the following memorandum to the class:

> The Institute for Sociological Research in this Department is recruiting student volunteers to assist in data collection for a current project. All of the students in this class are qualified to participate, and participation will constitute work equivalent to the term paper assignment.
>
> The total number of hours involved will range from eight to twelve; a short written report of the research experience will be expected at the end of the quarter.
>
> I am encouraging you to volunteer your time and interest to this valuable learning experience.
>
> If you are interested, you may sign your name on the sheet of paper at the end of the hour today and tomorrow.

Nearly all students volunteered, and I listed all of them because I anticipated some participant mortality.

Initially, I intended to assign students randomly to one of the three groups. Certain practical problems encouraged me to modify that plan slightly. Although students from three courses were available, I decided that it would be difficult if not impossible to control interstudent conversation about the project. I was particularly concerned that control group subjects would learn of the treatment groups' activity and, hence, of their own role as controls. A decision was made to designate one entire class as the control group, a judgment which also complicated subsequent analysis: members of the control group were generally older than treatment group subjects. Otherwise, the intended assignment procedures were followed such that volunteers were randomly assigned on the basis of a prior measure of religious commitment to one of two treatment groups. Thus, after administering the religious commitment pretest, student volunteers from two courses were classified as high or low on religious commitment, and then students from both lists were assigned randomly to each treatment. This resulted in an equal distribution of highs and lows in each treatment group.

THE LITTLE LIE: WHO WAS STUDYING WHOM

Preparation of subjects for participation in this research involved the construction of a disguise. Students had to be recruited to participate in the study and to be given a purpose for their participation, but without disclosing at this point that they were *the* subjects of the study. It was decided that if students were recruited to observe at the Graham meeting, as the Langs had done, the legitimacy of their involvement would be established. Such a procedure could also produce additional observational data of the sort collected by the Langs. Creation of the participant-observer role was critical to the broader aims of the study, and considerable effort was directed to this dimension of the project. A general orientation meeting was held, and one additional "treatment" lecture was conducted.

The orientation meeting began with a short presentation by a distinguished faculty member who already was familiar to the students as a coauthor of their textbook. The sole purpose of this appearance was to legitimize the students' participation in the study. After this brief and warm welcome to the research business, I spoke with the students about the purpose and importance of the research. I told them that the study was to investigate a particular kind of social movement, and I spoke briefly about the nature of sociological interest in collective behavior and social movements. My presentation moved to a consideration of reform movements, using religious movements as an example. I mentioned several historical examples of religious movements, such as those associated with John Calvin, Jonathon Edwards, and Billy Sunday, and I summarized some of the sociological literature which purported to explain such phenomena. In this context, I introduced the religious crusades of Billy Graham and formulated for the students a series of questions about the Graham crusades of interest to sociologists. I then announced that the principal research task of our project would be to answer some of the questions through observation of a Billy Graham crusade.

I emphasized that the theoretical and substantive interests underlying the project came from two areas of sociological literature. First, the earlier Lang study (I did not report on the Langs' problem with observers) was discussed, and I told them that we would attempt to replicate that study. Secondly, I mentioned sociological interest in collective dynamics, the emergence and development of collective excitement, unrest, tension, and atmosphere that are thought to take place in such meetings. Finally, I indicated that this project called for a particular kind of data collection procedure, participant observation of a Billy Graham Crusade meeting on

Sunday, July 11, in the Seattle Coliseum. I discussed participant observation briefly and cited several examples of prior studies in other areas. I presented the argument that the central methodological problem in participant observation is the issue of observer objectivity, and I outlined two ways to handle the problem: first, to ask the observer simply to try hard to be objective, or second, to control for observer bias by independently measuring observers' interest and disinterest in the phenomenon observed. I said that we would follow the latter procedure.

The orientation session ended with an announcement that we all would meet again on the following day for specific instructions (this was the "treatment" lecture), and for this meeting we would break up into smaller groups to facilitate discussion. At this point, lists of student volunteers were distributed. The lists contained two columns of names with a room number and a meeting time at the top. Again, I should emphasize that volunteers were not told at this point that they were *the* subjects of the study, nor were they told of the nature of the treatment groups to which they had been assigned. On the following day, prior to the next meeting, two students who had volunteered to participate in the study came to my office to report that after describing the project to their parents, they wanted to withdraw from the study. Both cited religious conflicts as the reason for their decision, although the nature of the conflicts was rather different. In each case, parental guidance had indicated that the daughter's participation would be inappropriate because of their faith—Jewish in one case and Baptist in the other.

The second session was designed to create passive and active observational roles through explicit verbal instructions and other procedures. In each training session, students were first reminded of the two concerns of the research—to replicate the Langs' study and to collect additional information on the social processes of emotional contagion, excitement, and so on. Students were told that two specific research questions were to be addressed: *Who* are the persons whom Billy Graham attracts (the Langs' question) and *how*, or by what techniques, does Graham appeal to these people (the social process question). At this point, each training group received very different instructions. The passive group was told that it was concerned only with the *who* question, and the active group was told that its exclusive concern was with the *how* question. In each group it was emphasized that the purpose of the study was not to evaluate the truth or falsity of God, religion, or Billy Graham.

The specific instructions to passive and active observers are described in the preceding paper. In addition to the participant-observer role instructions, certain other procedures important to creating the observer role were followed at this session. A packet of written instructions, and a paper-and-pencil recording instrument were distributed to each observer. These items were designed to further legitimize and structure the observer role. The

THE RESEARCH EXPERIENCE

instructions summarized the specific behavioral expectations which were discussed earlier. The pocket-sized recording instrument ($3\frac{1}{4}$ x $4\frac{1}{2}$ inches) was designed to be both convenient and inconspicuous. To reinforce the respective roles, two versions of the recording instrument were prepared, one for each treatment group. The instrument given to passive observers contained questions about the demographic composition of the audience and a variety of other questions about the meeting's "atmosphere."[1] The active observer questionnaire contained only questions pertaining to "atmosphere." Four time points of observation were designated; these were identified as: (1) the first ten minutes of the meeting, (2) Graham's entrance, (3) midway through Graham's presentation, (4) and Graham's closing.[2] The instrument required that the exact time of these observations be recorded to ensure uniformity. Observers actually made recordings on the instrument at only four points in time so that their recording activity would not interfere with full exposure to the meeting and to Graham.

Recording procedures were discussed in detail, and each item on the instrument was examined and explained. At this point in the training session, an audio tape recording of a prior Graham meeting was played to familiarize the observers with the Graham crusade format and to sensitize them further to the observation requirements. As the tape played, I guided the observers through a "dry run" on the recording instrument.

Finally, students were asked to find their own transportation to the Coliseum, and they were assigned seating locations so that the observations could be evenly distributed, eliminating the formation of observer groups at the meeting. A seating map of the Coliseum was used to randomly assign observers to the general seating sections. Observers were asked to arrive at the Coliseum 30 minutes before the scheduled start of the crusade. They were instructed to complete the observations required by the recording instrument during the meeting, to avoid interviewing audience members, and to deposit the completed instrument with me after the meeting at a designated adjoining location. Above all, observers were asked to remain unobtrusive in their activity and to follow the role definitions.

Our final training session adjourned, and I felt confident about the students' preparation and motivation and about how thoroughly we had reviewed the instructions and made explicit the expectations. I was satisfied that all aspects of the study had moved along comparatively smoothly to this point, and I was relieved to know that the hard work was over. I did not then know that the major crisis was yet to strike.

---

1. The term "atmosphere" was meant to carry its consensual definition. Its measurement involved a magnitude estimation technique adapted from Catton (1957).
2. Data from the observers' paper-and-pencil recordings are not presented in either the earlier paper or here, but they are reported in the thesis (Johnson, 1966).

METHODOLOGICAL SIN AND SUBJECT IMMORTALITY

The morning of the crusade meeting began as a typically gloomy July day in Seattle, and although the weather improved by early afternoon, the sun did not shine on our research that day. Twenty thousand people filled the Coliseum long before 2:30—a half hour before the meeting was to begin and the time at which observers were to secure their seats. I had not anticipated that the Coliseum would fill so early and so quickly. At about the time the students were to arrive, an overflow crowd of several thousand had already assembled outside. I worried about whether the observers had found seating. The Graham organization, obviously educated to attendance patterns, had constructed seating facilities outside the Coliseum, and loudspeakers carried the audio content of the meeting taking place inside. I wanted to find the students and help them locate their seats, but I could not get past the fire marshals at the door. I briefly entertained a theological explanation for what I could see happening to my research.

I found a quiet corner of grass outside the Coliseum, where I remained throughout the meeting. None of the observers was in sight. In disbelief, I reflected on what now seemed to be an unending number of sources of "observer mortality." My thoughts turned to salvation of the study and to the redemption of a lost master's thesis. The meeting seemed to take a long time, and I reluctantly moved toward the area where I had agreed to meet the observers after the meeting closed.

Gradually, observers began to filter out of the crowd and one by one they reported as planned, with completed recording instruments in hand. Nearly all of the observers, it seemed, said that they had not secured assigned seating—or even an inside location. Later, I found that 60 percent of the observers had not gained entrance to the Coliseum. They did not, however, leave the area; all of them stayed, independently securing points of observation outside among the overflow crowd. As the students deposited their observations, they looked glum, and many apologized for the departure from plan. Feeling guilty, I reassured them that the error was mine and congratulated them for completing the task in a confusing situation. Until I examined their recording instruments, I did not know how loyal the students had felt toward the project. Virtually all of the observers who had been unable to secure inside seating found, on their own, other locations which they then mapped on the cover of the instrument, identifying their location in the crowd.

On the day following Graham's meeting, all observers and members of the control group were asked to complete the first of two posttest questionnaires. As in the pretest, students completed a self-administered inventory pertaining to religious commitment. A third and final questionnaire was administered to treatment and control groups three weeks later. A final session was held for all subjects, at which time their actual role as subjects was disclosed. The purpose of the experiment and expected findings were discussed with the participants at that time. Only one student reported prior suspicion that "we are probably the guinea pigs in this study!"

Our unanticipated seating contingency had the consequence of depressing enthusiasm about the study. Whether or not it in fact affected the quality of the data collected, however, was yet to be determined. That is, the data collection activity produced a new variable that had to be introduced into the data analysis: the effect of inside vs. outside seating on the hypothesized relationships. Thus, active and passive observers would now be dichotimized into inside and outside active and passive groups, and this additional division threatened to produce the statistical complications associated with small cell size. Subsequent analysis indicated, however, that the inside-outside variable did not confound the results of the study.

Immediately after the Graham meeting, I anticipated that outside observers might be less susceptible to Graham's persuasive appeal than inside observers. But when active and passive groups were subdivided according to location, the anticipated differences were not found. None of the inside-outside differences was statistically significant. The only inside-outside difference found was with regard to the time points at which observations were recorded; outside observers entered their observations somewhat later than inside observers. This difference also did not, however, interact with main effects. Thus, what began as apparent disaster did not ultimately affect the study's findings, except in making the data collection procedures somewhat less elegant and uniform than planned or preferred (Johnson, 1966).

IN RETROSPECT AND SUMMARY

The findings of the study, their implications, and their relationship to the areas of religious behavior and persuasion are discussed in the article reprinted above. Several other conclusions regarding the methods employed in the study may be noted, however. I have already discussed the informal and unpretentious origin of this research. I have also described the important influence of mundane matters such as time, money, and convenience on the study's procedures and have recounted our anticipated field problem during data collection. One other factor is characteristic of this study and it, too, should be stressed. In keeping with the Protestant focus of the study, the factor is best designated as *hard work*. My experience with this research as well as with survey design, involving both face-to-face interviews and self-administered questionnaires, and with laboratory experimentation has led me to conclude that the field experiment is among the most difficult study designs employed in sociological research.

I noted earlier that my experience with this study departed in some important respects from what I expected on the basis of the accounts in methods textbooks. I think this applies to all of the points mentioned above: the frequency with which research is generated informally, the importance of everyday resources, the problem of unpredictability, and the need for hard work. I, for one, never picked this up in my methods courses.

The other point to be emphasized concerns the special problems associated with field experiments, and their gravity may explain why such studies are so seldom attempted. The chief problem is probably best termed *control,* control not only of unknown and unmeasured sources of variance, but, more importantly, control over the resources that are required to perform these studies properly. The real world often is not organized in a way that facilitates orderly experiments. The variables of interest often are not experimentally manipulable. The preferred procedures of random selection and random assignment of subjects ordinarily are not possible, except within narrow limits. And even the well-designed experiment always is susceptible to complications produced by unpredictable events.

These characteristics of the sociological field experiment also are seldom addressed in our textbooks or research articles. Not even the guy who originally suggested "Wouldn't it be interesting . . ." could have told me to get the students to the Coliseum on time.

REFERENCES

Argyle, Michael. *Religious behaviour.* London: Free Press, 1959.
Bachrach, Arthur J. *Psychological research: An introduction.* New York: Random House, 1965.
Catton, William R., Jr. What kind of people does a religious cult attract? *American Sociological Review* 1957, *22,* (5) 561-566.
Dodd, Stuart C. Can science improve praying? *Darshana,* I 1961, (4) 1-16.
Johnson, Weldon T. Role playing and religious commitment: An experimental study in mass persuasion. Unpublished master's thesis, Department of Sociology, University of Washington, Seattle.
Lang, Kurt, and Lang, Gladys Engel. Decisions for Christ: Billy Graham in New York City. In Maurice Stein, et al. (eds.), *Identity and anxiety: Survival of the person in mass society.* Glencoe: Free Press, 1960.

Jeffrey H. Goldstein and Robert L. Arms ─────────────

A. EFFECTS OF OBSERVING ATHLETIC CONTESTS ON HOSTILITY

In May, 1964, a riot, precipitated by a referee's decision, erupted at a soccer match in Lima, Peru, killing a number of spectators; the war between El Salvador and Honduras has been traced to a soccer match between those two countries (Lever, 1969); and additional outbreaks of violence have occurred at soccer matches in Great Britain and at boxing matches in New York's Madison Square Garden.

Of course, where large numbers of people gather for public events many of the preconditions for collective behavior exist (cf. Milgram & Toch, 1969; Turner & Killian, 1957; Zimbardo, 1969). Nevertheless, the nature of such competitive and aggressive sports may, in itself, increase spectators' predispositions to engage in violent behavior. The present study examines the arousal of hostility among spectators at athletic contests.

Although a number of laboratory studies have examined hostility and aggression as a function of observing violence (e.g., Bandura, Ross & Ross, 1963; Berkowitz, Corwin & Hieronimus, 1963; Feshbach, 1961; Geen & O'Neal, 1969), the natural setting contains many characteristics not present in such situations. Spectators at a sports event are likely to be more involved than laboratory subjects since school ties and ego identity increase their stake in the outcome of the event. Observers are apt to be more committed in the field setting since they must pay a price for admission. The observed event in the natural setting differs from that typically used in laboratory studies; a sports event, such as a football or soccer game, is a sanctioned and carefully regulated form of interaction in which penalties are imposed for the violation of rules and in which some kinds of violence are condoned. In laboratory experiments the observed aggression is usually a film of an overt aggressive act

Source: Jeffrey H. Goldstein and Robert L. Arms, "Effects of Observing Athletic Contests on Hostility," *Sociometry,* 1971, *34,* 83-90.

This study was supported by a grant to the first author from the Bolton Research Fund, Temple University. We thank the Department of Recreation, Philadelphia, for their cooperation. The assistance of Jerry Suls and the comments of Robert Lana, Thomas Ostrom, and Ralph Rosnow on an earlier draft of this paper are greatly appreciated.

which cannot usually be interpreted as justifiable. Given these several differences between the laboratory and field settings, a priori predictions concerning changes in hostility among observers at athletic contests are not possible. However, an examination of theoretical interpretations of aggression leads to several mutually exclusive hypotheses.

Recently a number of books have appeared which suggest that the observation of competitive aggressive sports will serve to reduce hostility among spectators (Ardrey, 1966; Lorenz, 1966; Storr, 1968). This type of vicarious hostility catharsis has been reported in only a few laboratory experiments (cf. Bramel, 1969; Feshbach, 1955, 1956, 1961). If observation of aggressive sports does result in a hostility catharsis, then spectators' post-game hostility should be less than pre-game.

Most laboratory experiments on the observation of aggression report that observers are likely to be more aggressive after viewing violence than before. Frustration-aggression theories (Dollard, Doob, Miller, Mowrer & Sears, 1939; Berkowitz, 1969) suggest that aggression is most likely to occur in observers who are angry, frustrated, or whose goal-directed behavior has been thwarted. If watching one's preferred team lose a game can be regarded as frustrating, then observers whose preferred team loses should be more aggressive than those whose preferred team wins and than those who have no team preference.

Other approaches to aggression are not dependent upon a prior state of frustration and suggest that witnessing violence may reduce the strength of inhibitions against aggressive behavior (Bandura & Walters, 1963). Thus, all spectators at an aggressive athletic contest, regardless of their team preferences, should show an increase in hostility.

To determine the relative merits of these theoretical positions, a field study was conducted in which spectators at a football game were interviewed before or after the game. As a control condition, spectators were also interviewed at a competitive, though nonaggressive sport. The interview was designed to assess hostility, team preference, and additional demographic data.

METHOD

Interviews were conducted at the 1969 Army-Navy football game and also at an Army-Temple gymnastics meet held during the same month. The Army-Navy football game was chosen for study because it is played on "neutral" territory (Kennedy Stadium, Philadelphia), thus assuring a relatively even split among observers' team preferences. The Army-Navy game is more than just a "game" to most spectators; it is a traditional rivalry and emotional involvement in its outcome is quite high.

Interviewers (*I*s) were 13 paid undergraduate students who, several weeks prior to the game, received detailed instructions concerning interview procedures. Each *I* memorized a prepared introductory speech to be presented to each subject. The speech explained the study as a survey of spectators' attitudes at various intercollegiate athletic contests conducted by Temple University. Pairs of *I*s were randomly assigned to entrances of the Kennedy Stadium and were to conduct interviews only with subjects about to enter their assigned gates. The subjects consisted exclusively of adult males.

Immediately after arrival at the assigned entrance, *I* was to interview the first adult male approaching that gate. After completing an interview, *I* was to approach the very next eligible subject. This procedure was employed to eliminate any systematic factors which may have biased subject selection. The *I*s also recorded the number of people who refused to be interviewed.

The interview began with the introductory speech. All subjects were assured that the interviews would be anonymous. A number of demographic questions were then asked. These items served two purposes: to check on the equivalence of the various groups in the study and to engage the subject's involvement in the interview. The questions concerned distance traveled to the game, frequency of attendance at football games, cost of tickets, and number of other people accompanying the subject. Subjects were also asked to indicate their preferred team, if any, and in the former case, how upset they would be if their preferred team lost the game.

Following these items were three scales taken from the Buss-Durkee inventory, designed to measure hostility (Buss & Durkee, 1957). Hostility was used as the dependent variable in the study because it was felt to be sensitive to influence by situational factors. Hostility is used here as one index of overt aggression. Each hostility scale consists of a number of statements to be answered "true" or "false" by the subject. The scales employed were the indirect hostility (9 items), resentment (8 items), and irritability (11 items) scales, each of which was found to have satisfactory reliability in a number of independent investigations reported by Buss (1961). Included among these 28 hostility items were eight filler questions concerning football, placed at random intervals throughout the hostility portion of the interview schedule. These items were designed to minimize suspicion about the true nature of the study.

Following completion of the hostility items, subjects were asked to state their reactions to the study and to indicate what they felt the study was about. Subjects were then thanked for their cooperation and dismissed. The total time required for each interview was approximately 10 minutes. The post-game interview was identical to the pre-game interview, except that the tense was changed in a few items where that was appropriate.

In the control condition, five *I*s were employed at the Army-Temple gym meet. They were to interview only male spectators and the interview schedule was nearly identical to that employed at the Army-Navy football game. The only difference between the two interviews was that gymnastics items were inserted for football items on the appropriate questions.

RESULTS

Comparability of Groups

Football Game Data

Before the game, 59 eligible subjects refused to be interviewed from a total of 156 subjects approached (37.8%). There were 44 post-game refusals of the 97 approached (45.5%). A chi-square with 1 df was not significant. A total of 150 subjects completed the interview, 97 pre- and 53 post-game.[1]

A 2×3 analysis of variance was computed for each dependent measure, the factors being Time of Interview (pre- or post-game) and Preferred Team (Army, Navy, or no preference). Since unequal ns resulted, an unweighted means solution was used. Analysis of demographic data revealed no significant differences among any of the six groups, for distance traveled, frequency of attendance at football games, cost of tickets, or number of companions. Thus, the six experimental samples were considered to come from the same population. The subjects' comments about the interview indicated no suspicion of the true purpose of the study.

Gymnastics Meet Data

Because the gymnastics meet was not held on "neutral" territory as the football game was, over 90% of the subjects favored the home team (Temple). Because of the small number of subjects who had no team preference or who preferred Army, these groups were combined and only before-after comparisons were made.

A total of 49 pre- and 32 post-game interviews were completed. Only 4% of the subjects approached refused to be interviewed, and there were no differences in refusal rate for the before and after groups. The higher refusal rate at the football game may have been due to the difficulty encountered in getting into and out of the stadium, which placed a greater premium on time at that event.

There were no differences between the before and after gym meet groups on distance traveled, age of subjects, or number of companions with subjects. However, pre-meet subjects attended gym meets significantly more often than post-meet subjects ($t = 2.84$, $df = 79$, $p < .01$). This may reflect the fact that the less involved (those who attend meets less frequently) left the gym meet earlier and were, therefore, overrepresented in the post-meet sample. On the whole, the pre- and post-meet groups are considered to be equivalent.

---

1. This difference reflects the greater variance in arrival time than in departure time. Subjects began arriving for the game as much as two hours prior to its scheduled starting time. Nearly all subjects left the stadium within 30 minutes of the termination of the game.

Comparability of Football and Gym Meet Groups

The before and after subjects at the football game and the gymnastics meet were compared on distance traveled to attend the event, frequency of attendance at such events, age, and number of companions with the subject, in 2 x 2 unweighted means analyses of variance. These results indicate no differences among any of the four groups on distance traveled or number of companions. Subjects attending the football game, however, were significantly older than those at the gymnastics meet ($p < .01$) and they attended football games significantly more often ($p < .05$). The only interaction obtained was for frequency of attendance, in which post-gym meet subjects attended meets less than pre-meet subjects, and this finding has been discussed above. Taken as a whole, the pre-post football and pre-post gym meet subjects are considered equivalent.

Hostility Data

Football Game

Group means for each of the three hostility subscales from the Buss-Durkee inventory were highly intercorrelated, and separate analyses for each subscale lead to similar findings. Therefore, a single score, the sum of the three subscales, was computed for each subject. The possible range of hostility scores was from 0 to 28, with the higher figure representing maximum hostility.

The mean hostility scores by group are presented in Table 1. Analysis of these data indicate that, regardless of subjects' preferred team, post-game hostility was greater than pre-game ($F = 5.29$, $df = 1/144$, $p < .025$). Neither the main effect for Preferred team ($F < 1.0$) nor the interaction effect ($F < 1.0$) was significant.

Gymnastics Meet

As with the football game hostility data, the three Buss-Durkee subscales were combined into a single hostility score. The pre-meet hostility

TABLE 1
Mean Football Game Hostility Scores by Condition

	Preferred			
	Army (winning team)	Navy (losing team)	No preference	Total
Pre-game	n = 38 10.42[a]	n = 47 11.72	n = 12 11.67	11.20
Post-game	n = 18 13.33	n = 30 13.17	n = 5 15.00	13.40

[a]The higher the score, the greater the hostility.

mean (12.00) was not significantly different from the post-meet hostility mean (12.71, $t = .66$, $df = 79$, $p < .20$). Thus, hostility did not significantly increase as a result of observing the gymnastics meet.

DISCUSSION

Hostility data collected at the football game indicates that, regardless of team preference and the outcome of the game, subjects were significantly more hostile after observing the game than before. A number of alternative explanations for this finding may be eliminated on the basis of data obtained at the gymnastics meet. The gym meet includes many similarities to the football game: subjects are seated for two to three hours in a large and compact crowd where outbursts of cheering and applause occur. Therefore, the relative increase in hostility found at the football game, but not at the gym meet, cannot be attributed to any of these factors, although it should be borne in mind that the spectators at the football game were slightly older and attended football games more often than their counterparts at the gym meet. In addition, there was a slight, though nonsignificant, increase in hostility among the gymnastics spectators. There are a number of differences between the two events, however, which cannot be eliminated as possible explanations for the present findings: the absolute number as well as the density of others was greater at the football game; norms for expressive behavior at a football game differ from those at a gym meet, where the crowd is usually less vociferous, and where the general activity level is lower owing to the absence of vendors, bands, and cheerleaders. It seems, however, that one major difference between the nature of the two events is that a football game involves multiple players in direct physical contact with one another, while a gym meet involves individual performances in which no contact can occur. It seems likely, therefore, that the increase in hostility is due to the nature of the observed event; watching an aggressive sport leads to an increase in hostility among spectators.

One methodological difficulty in the present study is the possibility of a subject selection bias: it may be that more hostile observers are attracted to a football game than to a gymnastics meet. This may be indicated by the higher refusal rate at the football game. However, it might be reasonably assumed that subjects who refuse to be interviewed are more hostile than those who are cooperative, and thus the differential refusal rate would lead one to expect fewer hostile responses at the football game among the cooperative subjects.

No support for a catharsis effect is obtained in the present study, contrary to the many popular notions (Ardrey, 1966; Lorenz, 1966; Storr, 1968) that such an effect would occur. Elicitation of hostility catharsis, if it does occur, may require more intense or more direct aggression than that present in a football game.

The failure to find an interaction of preferred team and game outcome seems to support a general disinhibition notion. That is, the act of observing an aggressive sport may reduce subjects' inhibitions against aggression and result in increased hostility. Whether disinhibition is a result of an increase in aggressive drive or is due to the heightened salience of hostility cannot be determined from the present data.

REFERENCES

Ardrey, R. *The territorial imperative.* New York: Dell, 1966.

Bandura, A., Ross, Dorothea, & Ross, Sheila. Imitation of film-mediated aggressive models. *Journal of Abnormal and Social Psychology,* 1963, *66,* 3-11.

Bandura, A., & Walters, R. H. *Social learning and personality development.* New York: Holt, Rinehart & Winston, 1963.

Berkowitz, L. The frustration-aggression hypothesis revisited. In L. Berkowitz (ed.), *Roots of aggression.* New York: Atherton Press, 1969, pp. 1-29.

Berkowitz L., Corwin, R., & Hieronimus, R. Film violence and subsequent aggressive tendencies. *Public Opinion Quarterly,* 1963, *27,* 217-229.

Bramel, D. The attraction and reduction of hostility. In J. Mills (ed.), *Experimental social psychology.* New York: Macmillan, 1969, pp. 33-63.

Buss, A. H. *The psychology of aggression.* New York: Wiley, 1961.

Buss, A. H., & Durkee, Ann. An inventory for assessing different kinds of hostility. *Journal of Consulting Psychology,* 1957, *21,* 343-348.

Dollard, J., Doob, L., Miller, N., Mowrer, O. & Sears, R. *Frustration and aggression.* New Haven: Yale University Press, 1939.

Feshbach, S. The drive reducing function of fantasy behavior. *Journal of Abnormal and Social Psychology,* 1955, *50,* 3-11.

Feshbach, S. The catharsis hypothesis and some consequences of interaction with aggressive and neutral play objects. *Journal of Personality,* 1956, *24,* 449-462.

Feshbach, S. The stimulating versus cathartic effects of a vicarious aggressive activity. *Journal of Abnormal and Social Psychology,* 1961, *63,* 381-385.

Geen, R. G., & O'Neal, E. C. Activation of cue-elicited aggression by general arousal. *Journal of Personality and Social Psychology,* 1969, *11,* 289-292.

Lever, Janet. Soccer: Opium of the Brazilian people. *Trans-action,* 1969, 7(2), 36-43.

Lorenz, K. *On aggression.* New York: Harcourt, Brace & World, 1966.

Milgram, S., & Toch, H. Collective behavior: Crowds and social movements. In G. Lindzey and E. Aronson (eds.), *Handbook of social psychology.* 2nd. ed. Reading, Mass.: Addison-Wesley, 1969.

Storr, A. *Human aggression.* New York: Atheneum, 1968.

Turner, R. H., & Killian, L. M. *Collective behavior.* Englewood Cliffs, N.J.: Prentice-Hall, 1957.

Zimbardo, P. G. The human choice: Individuation, reason, and order versus deindividuation, impulse, and chaos. In W. J. Arnold and D. Levine (eds.), *Nebraska Symposium on Motivation.* Lincoln: University of Nebraska Press, 1969.

B. CONDUCTING FIELD RESEARCH ON AGGRESSION: NOTES ON "EFFECTS OF OBSERVING ATHLETIC CONTESTS ON HOSTILITY"

Jeffrey H. Goldstein

ORIGINS OF THE STUDY

Human aggression is both a fascinating and an important topic, and as a psychologist I have been interested in it since my days as a graduate student. There were no courses taught on human aggression when I was a student at Ohio State, and there are few offered in it now around the country, so the student who wants to learn something about the psychology of aggression must devote some of his spare time to reading the literature on his own. I was particularly interested in the effects of violence in television and movies and in sports and humor. Much of what I had read in the professional journals failed to provide satisfactory answers to my questions about aggression, and I began to suffer from the feeling that many freshmen experience upon taking their first course in psychology. I was curious about problems that seemed pertinent to my experiences and interests only to discover that most psychologists spent their time running rats and studying what appeared to me then, at least at first glance, to be trivial phenomena. Although there are philosophical, historical and practical reasons for this tendency—and people should, after all, be free to study what they wish—still it seemed that my questions were amenable to study by scientific means. Yet the psychological and sociological literature was quite meager on this subject. Either the research was too artificial, making it difficult to generalize beyond the laboratory to the real world, or it was theoretically empty, with no hint of the underlying dynamics of aggression.

I have always felt that data from an experiment must serve two functions: first, they must test, build, or revise theory; and second, they must relate, as closely as possible, to real and important human behaviors. In other words, research should serve to provide explanations, and not merely descriptions, of behavior. I also believe, though many of my colleagues do

Source: Prepared especially for this volume.

not share this view, that the behavior under study must be one of some consequence. A good deal of human behavior, though it may follow discoverable and empirical principles, is simply too trivial to study. For example, it may be that each person puts on the same shoe first every day; if one put on his left shoe first this morning, he is likely to put the left shoe on first every morning. Now this could quite easily be studied, and I suppose that some sort of abstract explanation could be built and tested around this observation. But the behavior has no consequences for other actions and is in this sense "unconnected" to other behaviors and, therefore, trivial. A behavior worth spending time and energy studying must be one with both theoretical implication for and some "connectedness" or interrelation with one or more other behaviors. The study of human aggression is connected to such issues as war, crime, prejudice, hatred, and less directly to political and economic behavior, and it is this connectedness which makes it a nontrivial and worthwhile phenomenon to study.

The available research in the journals suffered primarily from the unconnectedness of the behavior studied in the laboratory to real-life behaviors and was also, for the most part, theoretically unimportant as well. In the course of discussing this state of affairs with Robert Arms, then a graduate student at Temple University and now a member of the psychology faculty at the University of Lethbridge, we decided to conduct an aggression experiment outside the laboratory. We sought to test aggression theory using real episodes of violence rather than contrived situations. Our primary interest was in determining, first, whether the results obtained in the laboratory could also be obtained outside the laboratory, using a real aggressive episode. Second, we wanted to study a fairly subtle but pervasive kind of violence rather than the type used in laboratory research. In most laboratory research on aggression, subjects are exposed to an excerpt from a movie, usually of only a few minutes' duration, which is either extremely violent or (for subjects in control groups) totally benign. What would happen if researchers used an entire aggressive film, such as *Clockwork Orange* or *Straw Dogs,* rather than a brief excerpt?[1] Would they still discover that watching violence leads to an increase in aggression among observers? What would happen if the violence were not quite so intense?

PARING DOWN THE ALTERNATIVES

Our interest was essentially to examine the effects on observers of witnessing a fairly lengthy and realistic kind of violence in a natural setting.

---

1. A study recently completed and submitted for publication was designed to answer this question (Jeffrey H. Goldstein, Ralph L. Rosnow, Tamas Raday, Irwin Silverman, & George D. Gaskell). Punitiveness in response to films varying in content: A cross-sectional field study of aggression, and an unpublished study just called to my attention has also sought to answer it (Martin, Gray, Smoke, & Wilson).

We expected, in the absence of substantial laboratory evidence to the contrary, that observers would show an increase in aggressiveness after watching an aggressive event. This hypothesis is consistent with the bulk of laboratory research on the effects of witnessing violence. However, there were theories of aggression which made quite different predictions, and so we were able to test these theories at the same time, most notably those of Ardrey, Lorenz, and Storr (see the article reprinted above).

After considerable discussion with several of our colleagues (once you obtain a Ph.D. your friends mysteriously turn into "colleagues"), we decided to use a football game as the aggressive event for the study and to use spectators at the game as our research subjects. We next had to decide which football game to use. We thought it would be ideal to find a game where half the fans were partisan toward one team and the remaining half toward the other; in this way we could get some subjects whose preferred team won and others whose preferred team lost the game. We felt this would be desirable because the effects of the game might well depend upon whether subjects were pleased or disappointed over the outcome of the game. A football game played on "neutral" territory would certainly satisfy this requirement. As it turns out, one of the rare advantages of living in Philadelphia is that it is the site of the annual Army-Navy football game. We expected that, since Philadelphia is about halfway between West Point and Annapolis, nearly half the fans would be pro-Army and half pro-Navy.

At this point we knew only that we wanted to measure aggression as a result of watching the Army-Navy game. With over 100,000 people expected at the game, we knew we would have to use an easily administered measure of aggression, since our subjects would probably be in a hurry to get to their seats on the way into the game and back to their cars on the way out. We also knew that it would be impractical to measure aggression in the same spectators both before and after the game, so we decided to have two groups of subjects, one in which we measured aggression prior to the game, and one in which we measured aggression afterwards. These two groups could then be divided into subgroups according to whether they wanted Army or Navy to win, or whether they didn't care about the outcome. Deciding on the measure of aggression to use was more difficult. Of course, we could have asked each subject how aggressive he felt, but that is a vague and not too meaningful question. We eventually decided to use three subscales from the Buss-Durkee Hostility Inventory. This measure has several advantages: it can be administered verbally, so subjects don't have to fill out any forms; its reliability and correlation with other measures of aggression are known; and, by using three subscales rather than the whole inventory, the measure could be administered in only a few minutes.

By now, the study was beginning to take shape. We knew what we wanted to do and how we wanted to do it; aggression would be measured in spectators using the Buss-Durkee inventory before and after the Army-Navy

THE RESEARCH EXPERIENCE

game. What if the subjects interviewed after the game were different in aggressiveness from those interviewed before the game? Well, of course, we would want to attribute the difference to the violent nature of the game itself. But it was possible that those who would agree to be interviewed after the game might differ in some major way from those who agreed to be interviewed before the game, and this uncontrolled factor might have caused our difference in aggressiveness, and not the football game. That was a realistic possibility, and to help eliminate it we decided to ask all subjects a number of questions, such as their age, place of residence, and so on, in order to determine whether the before and after groups were similar on these demographic variables. If the mean age, occupation, residence, and other variables were the same for all groups of subjects, we could say with some confidence that the groups came from the same population. Then, if a before-to-after change in aggression were found, it could more safely be attributed to the football game.

Or could it? Although it didn't seem likely, it was possible that people who went to a football game were different from other people, and that they were more likely to become aggressive as a result of watching a game than others. It was also plausible that not just football, but *any* game—even a chess match—might cause people to become more aggressive. Clearly a control group was needed which might help eliminate these possible alternative explanations for an increase in aggression at the football game. The same week as the Army-Navy game, an Army-Temple gymnastics meet was scheduled at Temple University, and we decided to measure aggression before and after the gym meet among spectators as a control group. A gym meet is clearly a nonaggressive sport, and, if an increase in aggression were found at the football game but not at the gym meet, it was likely to be caused by the violence of the football game.

While the questionnaires for the study were being typed and mimeographed, we asked undergraduate psychology students if they would like to serve as interviewers for our study. About a dozen students agreed to participate, and a meeting was arranged with them. Because the study was scheduled for Thanksgiving vacation, students would have to interview during their free time, and so we wanted to compensate each interviewer for his time and expenses. I applied for, and graciously received, a small grant from Temple University to meet these expenses.

At the meeting, we explained in considerable detail how the interviews were to be conducted, and went over the entire interview with the students, discussing possible difficulties that might arise: what they were to do if someone decided not to complete the interview once he had begun, for example, or what should be recorded if more than one person answered a question directed to a particular respondent. Of primary importance was who should be selected as subjects for the study. We feared that our interviewers might tend to approach spectators in such a way as to systematically eliminate (or systematically include) only those who appeared least aggressive; in other words, they might selectively choose whom to interview, and this nonrandom selection would bias our results. In order to minimize this possibility, interviewers were instructed to approach the very first male spectator entering the stadium (or leaving it, for postgame subjects) and then to interview the first male they saw as soon as the previous interview had been completed. Finally, interviewers were told to keep an accurate count of the number of people approached who refused to be interviewed.

It should be clear from the above that we anticipated several possible problems before they ever arose and had decided (though sometimes rather arbitrarily) what to do about each of them. I think that any piece of research can be improved considerably by trying to anticipate every conceivable problem that can arise. In the case of our study, such considerations led us to add the Temple-Army gym meet as a control group, to determine the comparability of our groups by use of demographic questions, to keep a tally of the refusals for each condition of the study, and to specify rules for the selection of subjects. We also decided to restrict our subjects to male spectators, since females at a football game are generally accompanied by a male, and it is unclear whether they are there by choice or coercion. One additional bit of trouble that could arise was that the police might object to interviewers at the football game. So we wrote to the Philadelphia Department of Recreation, caretakers of the J. F. Kennedy Stadium, site of the Army-Navy game, and obtained permission to conduct the study.

With seating diagrams in hand, we randomly assigned our interviewers to entrances of the JFK Stadium and to entrances of the Temple gymnasium, where the Army-Temple gym meet would be held. After arming them with an introductory speech about the study, we waited for the day of the football game.

THE DATA AND DATA ANALYSIS

Interviewers arrived at JFK Stadium about two hours before game time and began interviewing as soon as they arrived and until the game began. This resulted in 97 completed pregame interviews. As soon as the final gun sounded, they began the postgame interviews, and a total of 53 completed interviews were obtained. A few days later, five interviewers collected 49 pre- and 32 post-gym-meet interviews.

We now had 150 interviews from the football game and 81 from the gym meet, each of which contained demographic information about the respondent, his preferred team, and answers to 28 true-false hostility questions. We coded the questionnaires by indicating on each interview whether the respondent was at the football game or gym meet, whether he was interviewed before or after the event, and which team, if any, he wanted to win. We then recorded all this information, plus the respondent's age, residence, cost of tickets, and number of companions, onto IBM punch cards, along with the total hostility score from the Buss-Durkee inventory. The analysis of the data was fairly simple and straightforward; we wanted to know whether subjects showed any change in hostility as a result of watching the football game or the gym meet, and we wanted to know whether any of the groups in the study differed from the others on any of the demographic variables. These analyses were done by computer but could easily have been done by hand.

The data analysis revealed that those at the football game were more aggressive after the game, whereas there was no statistically significant change in level of aggression for those at the gym meet. Since the results were not unexpected, we didn't have to spend a great deal of time in reanalysis of the data trying to find out what did happen to spectators' levels of aggression. The data made sense and were consistent with previous research on the effects of witnessing violence. The final task was to write up the study in the form of a journal article, have several colleagues comment on the manuscript, and, after making some suggested changes,[2] submit the paper for publication. Since my training in social psychology was both in psychology and in sociology, my choice of journal was *Sociometry,* the social-psychology journal of the American Sociological Association.

THE IDEAL STUDY

It should be obvious that the study has several weaknesses, some of which are mentioned in the paper itself and some of which are implied above. Its major shortcoming is that it is open to at least two alternative explanations: first, that the subjects interviewed before and after the football game and gymnastics meet may not have been equivalent on their pregame levels of hostility, and second, that the excitement inherent in a football game, and not the violence of the game, caused the obtained increase in hostility. The ideal study would involve random assignment of subjects to the various groups in the study; that is, people would be randomly assigned to watch either a football game or a nonviolent sport which was equivalent to the football game in excitement. In this way it could be assumed that, prior to these two events, all groups of subjects were equivalent in aggressiveness. This would permit assessment of aggression after the two events, with no need for a before measure. Then if the post-football-game hostility were greater than the post-control-game hostility, the difference between the two could be confidently attributed to the violence of the football game.

One difficulty with all aggression research is the measurement of aggression. Laboratory research tends to rely heavily on the administration of shock

---

2. Helene Feinberg, Louise Kidder and Ralph Rosnow were kind enough to comment on a draft of this paper as well, and I am grateful to them for their suggestions.

by subjects to another person as a measure of aggression, while field research relies on fairly lengthy interviews or questionnaires. What is needed is a brief interview or easily observable behavior which is reliable and is correlated highly with aggression in naturalistic situations.

A NOTE ON INDIVIDUAL DIFFERENCES

It is obvious to any psychologist that, while observing violence may lead to an increase in subjects' levels of aggression, it leads to greater increases in some subjects than in others. There may even be some people who show a decline in aggressiveness after watching violence. The problem I am raising here is generally referred to under the heading of "individual differences." As a *social* psychologist, my interest is in studying general effects of social variables; that is, dealing with factors which have an influence on people in general, or on most people. It is a perfectly legitimate enterprise to study characteristics of people which make them respond differently to a situation than others do. However, there are two disadvantages to this type of study, from my point of view. First, personality traits can be *measured,* but they often cannot be experimentally *manipulated;* thus, individual-difference studies tend to be correlational rather than experimental. Second, even if a particular trait were found which enabled the researcher to determine who responded aggressively to observed violence and who did not, such a finding would not in itself provide an explanation for this effect. In other words, such correlational studies are often descriptive, but only rarely explanatory.

EXPLANATION AND DESCRIPTION

The data from our study tell us what happened, but they do not tell us, to any great extent, why it happened. The study indicates that aggressiveness increased as a result of watching a football game but not as a result of a gymnastics meet. It is also clear that the catharsis effect predicted by Ardrey, Lorenz and Storr failed to occur; watching a violent sport did *not* lower observers' aggressiveness. But why does watching a football game increase aggressiveness? The article above contains a brief discussion of several possible explanations: (1) there could be a general reduction of inhibitions against aggressing as a result of watching aggression on the playing field; (2) watching aggression might increase the strength of observers' aggressive drives; (3) watching aggression might lead to a general increase in spectators' levels of arousal, and the arousal in turn may lead to increased aggression; (4) the general excitement of the football game might cause the increased aggression, and not necessarily the violence of the game; and (5) watching violence might make aggression more salient to observers, and the salience could cause the increase in aggressiveness.

Since I have come to believe that there is no such thing as an aggressive "drive," the most plausible explanations to me are the arousal and salience interpretations. An increase in observers' arousal might well account for the increased aggression, and there is some experimental evidence which supports this explanation (Zillmann, 1971). Support also has been generated for the notion that increasing the salience of a topic leads to a preference for that and related topics (Goldstein, 1972; Goldstein, Suls, & Anthony, 1972). Since these explanations seem the most likely, I have been engaged in further research on them for the past three years to find out more precisely why we obtained the results we did (Goldstein, Davis & Herman, in press; and the Goldstein, Rosnow, Raday, Silverman & Gaskell study cited in footnote 1 above).

There is one other interpretation of the data which occurred to me only after the study was published, based on the well-known work of Bandura and his associates (1971, 1972). If you will examine the means in Table 1 of the study, you will notice that the smallest increase in hostility at the football game occurred among those whose preferred team lost. For the Navy fans, there was an increase of only about 1.5 points, though for the Army fans the increase was nearly twice that. Surely this is an unexpected finding; one might expect that those whose preferred team lost the game would be more upset and, therefore, more frustrated and aggressive. If it can be argued that both Army and Navy players were aggressive on the field, and that winning the game was a reward for Army's aggression while losing was a punishment for Navy's aggression, then this finding can be explained. The vicarious punishment served to inhibit the aggressiveness of pro-Navy spectators, while the vicarious reward served to increase the aggressive level of pro-Army spectators. This interpretation is based on that developed by Bandura, Ross and Ross in their 1963 study in which aggressive models were either rewarded or not rewarded for aggression. Observers were more aggressive when they had seen the model rewarded than when they had seen the model punished.

THE AFTERMATH

The study reprinted above appeared in *Sociometry* in the Spring of 1971, and after its appearance there were the usual inquiries and requests for reprints from people in the social sciences. Over a year later, the public relations office of Temple University prepared a brief press release which was a summary in nontechnical terms of the study and its findings. Two days later I was contacted by the Associated Press and other news sources which were preparing stories about the study.

Since that time I have been invited to appear on talk shows and have received letters from scores of people around the country inquiring about the study. I have been besieged by letters from wives who are angry that their husbands spend too much time watching football on TV, by jocks of every description wondering whether they should give up their sport, by people writing term papers or theses for physical education, sociology, psychology, or health. I am asked questions about topics from child rearing to the massacre at the 1972 Munich Olympics.

I have neither the physical nor intellectual resources to answer all these questions, and so I have generally responded by sending a reprint of the paper along with a note of apology at my inability to offer much practical advice. But there are some lessons to be learned from this experience. People are genuinely interested in psychological research when it proves pertinent to their own lives; they seem willing to consider empirical findings as one factor in their decision making. It seems possible to conduct psychological research which is meaningful both to other researchers and to laymen. I must confess that I was surprised at the level of sophistication of questions asked by both journalists and laymen concerning aggression. Obviously one doesn't have to be a trained social scientist to be interested in, or to know a good deal, about human behavior. There were, of course, some exceptions, such as the sports magazine article which reported the study as comparing reactions at a football game with those of people at the movie *Bambi* and which implied that hostility increased at the football game because spectators were interviewed *during* the game. But generally the journalists reported the study accurately, and peoples' questions about aggression were psychologically meaningful.

No one study is able to provide very many answers to practical questions, but I think research can be done which is theoretically meaningful and of value to other professionals and at the same time "connected" enough to everyday experience to be of interest, and perhaps of some use, to all of us. Certainly this should come as no surprise to anyone, least of all to social psychologists, who are generally familiar with Kurt Lewin's concept of "action research." But if Lewin could survey the bulk of contemporary social-psychological research, he would surely ask where the action was. By conducting theoretically meaningful studies in field settings, the action can be put back into action research, and we can then pay more than lip service in our debt to Lewin. Steps in this direction are being taken, if slowly, by social psychologists, and there are now enough such studies to have warranted an anthology (Bickman & Henchy, 1972; see also Webb, Campbell, Schwartz, & Sechrest, 1966).

SOME CONCLUDING NOTES

Although the discussion above indicates in a fairly specific fashion why the Army-Navy game study was done in the manner in which it was, I have not made much mention of research as a whole. I would not spend the better part of my days engaged in research if it weren't personally satisfying. First, systematic inquiry is the *only* way I know that enables one to find the answer to a previously unanswered question, and to retain some confidence in the answer. Short of divine revelation, the supply of which seems to have run out in the 18th Century, empirical research can provide answers to questions available by no other means. Most important, if others doubt your answer, they are free to repeat the research for themselves.

Second, I find that doing research is fun and challenging. A study may begin with an observation, with a problem for which there is no known solution, or with a question derived from a theory. Regardless of its origin, I begin with some abstract idea which can usually be stated in the form of a hypothesis without much difficulty. From then on, I am free to devise what seems the best test of that hypothesis, given my limitations of time, money, research assistants, subjects, and patience. Although the practical tasks of questionnaire construction, data collection, and analysis are less interesting than the creation of the experimental design, they are, of course, indispensable to the overall project. Once the data have been collected and analyzed, I have already seen an idea develop from a mere thought to a tangible set of findings. If the data fail to support the hypothesis, there is the frustrating but challenging problem of making maximum sense of that data.

However, regardless of the results, conducting a study is a demanding and creative enterprise, not unlike painting a picture or taking a photograph, hobbies in which I engage with considerable enthusiasm if not talent. In each case, one starts with an idea and the raw materials of the craft. The challenge is to translate the idea, given the usually severe limitations of the tools, into a concrete form. The results cannot always be anticipated in advance, as witness some of my paintings, photographs, and research, but the act in itself provides the real enjoyment.

REFERENCES

Albert Bandura. *Social learning theory.* Morristown, N.J.: General Learning Press, 1971.
Albert Bandura. *Psychological modeling.* New York: Atherton, 1972.
Albert Bandura, Dorothea Ross, & Sheila A. Ross. Vicarious reinforcement and imitative learning. *Journal of Abnormal and Social Psychology,* 1963, *66,* 601-607.
Leonard Bickman & Thomas Henchy. *Beyond the laboratory: Field research in social psychology.* New York: McGraw-Hill, 1972.
Jeffrey H. Goldstein. Preference for aggressive movie content: The effects of cognitive salience. Unpublished manuscript, Temple University, 1972.
Jeffrey H. Goldstein, Roger Davis, & Dennis Herman. The escalation of aggression: Experimental studies. *Journal of Personality & Social Psychology,* in press.
Jeffrey H. Goldstein, Jerry M. Suls, & Susan Anthony. Enjoyment of specific types of humor content: Motivation or salience? In J. H. Goldstein & P. E. McGhee (Eds.) *The psychology of humor.* New York: Academic Press, 1972. Pp. 159-171.
J. D. Martin, L. N. Gray, G. L. Smoke, & F. D. Wilson. Mass media violence and overt behavior: A natural experiment. Unpublished manuscript, Washington State University.
Eugene J. Webb, Donald T. Campbell, Richard D. Schwartz, & Lee Sechrest. *Unobtrusive measures: Nonreactive research in the social sciences.* Chicago: Rand McNally, 1966.
Dolf Zillmann. Excitation transfer in communication-mediated aggressive behavior. *Journal of Experimental Social Psychology,* 1971, *7,* 419-434.

SURVEYS

Howard Schuman
H. Edward Ransford
Stella B. Jones
Joseph J. Lengermann

B. PERSONAL JOURNALS BY
Howard Schuman
H. Edward Ransford
Stella B. Jones
Joseph J. Lengermann

CHAPTER 4
CHAPTER 4

SURVEYS

In surveys, one's primary concern is usually with representativeness and with being able to generalize one's findings to a larger population of units (individuals, or cases, or settings). To ensure representativeness, random sampling procedures are necessary. All of the studies in this chapter employ a "cross-sectional" survey research design, and random sampling procedures are used in each of them. There are some variations, however, in the purposes for which the studies were undertaken, as well as in the techniques of data collection employed.

Howard Schuman and H. Edward Ransford both used interviews to obtain their responses. In Schuman's work the interview was less structured and used open-ended questions, whereas Ransford relied primarily on more structured questions and scales to obtain measures of his variables. A structured questionnaire was the data collection technique chosen by both Joseph Lengermann and Stella Jones.

Since opinion polls are the type of survey research with which most individuals are familiar, there is a tendency to assume that surveys have a descriptive purpose. Schuman's work is instructive in this regard. In his study of differences in attitudes toward the Vietnam War, his purpose was largely exploratory.

Initially, Schuman had "no intention of becoming involved in research on war attitudes." He first began searching through various related polls when, given his doubts about the effect of mass demonstrations on the broader public, he chose not to accompany family and friends to an antiwar demonstration in Washington. His alternative activity that weekend, however, led to a three-year avocational involvement and, ultimately, to research on and publication of an article about antiwar attitudes in a mass-circulation magazine. His attempts to discover which background factors—sex, race, age, education—were correlated with opposition to the war and his efforts to distinguish between "moral" and "pragmatic" opposition led him ultimately to include open-ended questions related to these factors in the 1971 Detroit Area Study. The use of such open-ended, unstructured questions in a survey instrument is quite unusual; their successful incorporation in Schuman's study suggests that such questions can provide a creative and fertile source of data in survey research. Though both Ransford and Jones also included open-ended questions in their survey instruments (an interview and a questionnaire, respectively), neither researcher utilized them as a central part of the investigation, and both report difficulties in dealing with them. Ransford found wide variations among coders' interpretations of his open-ended questions; and Jones reports that the very complex coding schemes she had developed for some of her open-ended questions proved to be "quite unwieldy." Schuman's "Two Sources" article is unique methodologically, because of its emphasis on, and analytic use of, an open-ended question. He cautions, however, that the "approach does make analysis more difficult" and suggests that "it probably should be used only where the question under consideration is quite important and where the analyst has some experience in working with complex data."

In contrast to a number of the other contributors to this book, Schuman had access to rather sophisticated and comprehensive resources for conducting his research. He was an established researcher connected to a survey research organization of considerable reputation. His position made it possible for him, for example, to incorporate his "antiwar" questions in a large-scale survey he was planning. In such a context, too, it can be assumed that experienced interviewers and coders—graduate students and permanent staff of the research organization—were also more readily available. As reflected in his personal journal, most of Schuman's research concerns were related either to whether or not antiwar attitudes were an appropriate subject for research or to working out appropriate categories for the data. Once the decision was made to do the research, Schuman did not seem to have to worry about where to find or how to pay for the necessary resources for executing it. It should be noted, however, that even experienced researchers do not always have control over circumstances. Because of limitations of time and other resources, Schuman was not able to allow for proper sampling design in his "contrast" student sample.

Ransford's research also dealt with an area of vital concern to society: the potential consequences of feelings of isolation and powerlessness experienced by a racial minority. It was not the study he set out to do. The initial project was concerned with what in 1965 were "new" forms of militant protest: sit-ins, boycotts, mass demonstrations. Theoretically, Ransford was interested in the concept of alienation and its relationship to these phenomena. He had already begun the preliminary stages of his research in Los Angeles in the summer of 1965 when the Watts riot "broke." Ransford soon realized that his original conception of "militancy" had to be expanded to include the "raw anger of riot violence" and that he and his research team were in the unique position of being able to gather historical data. They were in the field[1] before others—even the government commission appointed to investigate the causes of the riot—could begin to think about being there. In a very real sense, Ransford had to deal with the unpredictabilities of social research.

The seriousness of this unexpected and tragic social event meant that others, like the McCone Commission, were interested in Ransford's data and were willing to provide money and facilities to expedite analysis. But Rans-

---

1. Students should recognize that, although Ransford and his interviewers were in the "field" (i.e., doing their interviews in the community), they were not doing a *field study* in the sense outlined in Chapter 1. Ransford's emphasis was *not* on the "system character of the context" (as in the studies included in Chapter 2), but rather on *representativeness,* and on being able to generalize his findings to the populations from which his samples were drawn. He was doing *survey* research.

ford faced other dilemmas. He recognized that after the riot, some people might be more open in interviews; others, however, might be more frightened and might suspect that the interviewers were police in disguise. It was possible as well that those who were frightened were likely to refuse to be interviewed at all.

Ransford also had to deal with other practical problems. Time limitations and the complexities of mapping geographic areas for sampling forced "a retreat from the ideal of representativeness." Suspicion-arousing interview schedules with different handwriting or changes from ink to pencil, and doubts about the honesty of interviewers he trusted, produced for Ransford one of those "famous dissertation nightmares." Tedium and deadlines created similar problems in the coding phase. Fatigue meant "goofing" and often inaccurate coding, even by conscientious and trusted associates. All of this meant repetition of time-consuming activities. But there were high points and good experiences as well. Students who have never done any work on the computer (even those who might be "afraid" of it) should keep in mind that they might well have reactions very much like those of Ransford:

> Even learning how to call out a "canned program" was a nightmare at first, but I finally caught on and even began to enjoy it. When I was able to see what the computer could do with my data, I became so engaged that I often spent 10 to 12 hours a day at the computer center.

After he finally "got through" (i.e., completed his dissertation), Ransford had a common graduate student reaction. For six months he was so tired of the study he "couldn't even look at it, let alone think about publishing." Fortunately this feeling usually passes, as it did for Ransford. As is obvious from the article reprinted here, Ransford reworked his ideas on powerlessness and peripherality into an article which was subsequently published.

To generalize to all the women moved by a particular company during a particular year, Jones obtained responses from a representative sample on a structured questionnaire. A general interest in adult socialization, combined with the serendipitous availability of both funds and a population for study, determined the choice of her research problem. The situation fit with her "expedient" orientation regarding her dissertation research: "Decision: Pursue the question for which there was a relevant population available and for which the financial costs would be the least." When a van line agreed to finance her study and to provide a list of persons who had been recently moved by the company, Jones's research problem was "chosen." Though her decision was somewhat expedient, the problem did fit well into her theoretical area of interest. Her experience illustrates the powerful influence of the personal and pragmatic considerations mentioned in Chapter 1.

Though funds were fortuitously made available by the van line, Jones notes that her inexperience caused her, in several places, to underestimate costs. Because she was located in a small, teaching-oriented college, she was isolated from other researchers and from adequate research facilities. Consequently she faced a series of annoying procedural problems—administering research funds, securing "competent auxiliary help," finding suitable computer programs—that are not likely to be encountered by those, like Schuman, working in more sophisticated research environments. Further, though she developed and sustained "a fine rapport" with van line personnel, she had not anticipated the large investment of time required to do so.

Public interest in the topic she was studying meant that Jones was given considerable media coverage and was approached to give lectures and to participate in meetings. As in Goldstein's case, the unexpected publicity resulted in demands being placed on her to play the role of "expert," an unusual position for a graduate student who has not yet completed her comprehensive examinations. Giving lectures and participating in meetings distracted her from her main concern, completing her dissertation, and put her in a position for which she was not totally prepared.

In a somewhat circuitous fashion, Lengermann's interest in professional autonomy in organizations led him to a study of CPAs. Initially, his interest was as much personal as theoretical. As a sociologist, he was himself having to face questions of his own professional autonomy within the context of the religious order to which he then belonged. Had he remained in the priesthood, he very likely would have studied professional autonomy within the substantive context of sociology of religion, with emphasis on changes within religious orders. As an alternative, he developed "the same basic interest within the substantive context of the sociology of occupations and formal organizations, with emphasis on the possibilities for autonomy among professionals in bureaucratic organizations." Because he ultimately did not have the necessary time, money, and/or expertise, Lengermann was unable to conduct his "ideal" study. His research on CPAs emerged out of his decision "to focus on one profession which had representatives in organizations of various types and sizes."

Like Jones, Lengermann also used a structured questionnaire, and, like hers, his personal journal is a very useful step-by-step account of the procedures and problems involved in survey research. Both authors discuss many of the kinds of "nitty-gritty" points not usually covered in conventional methods textbooks. They provide details of some of the kinds of "compromises" researchers are faced with and some of the limitations that can be imposed on them if they do not have appropriate kinds or adequate amounts of time or money or expertise. For Lengermann, for example, precious months spent preparing grant proposals only partially paid off. Jones found that accepting support from the van line meant committing more of her time than she had anticipated. Both of them considered several different research problems before settling, for largely practical reasons, on the ones that were to form the bases for their respective dissertations.

Both Jones and Lengermann also deal with some of the pedestrian and practical activities commonly faced by novice researchers—securing and handling funds, minimizing sample loss, finding competent help, wording questions, printing questionnaires, using statistics and computers. (Students should be aware that both Jones and Lengermann were doing their research before statistical packages, like SPSS, were widely available.) Both mention the difficulty of cutting the questionnaire down to manageable size and the strange fascination and attachment the researcher develops for specific (irrelevant?) questions. Both voice concern with maximizing response rates. Lengermann acknowledges that after failing to heed warnings that his questionnaire was too long, he "then became purist in resorting to every possible printing, packaging, and mailing detail that might add a touch of personal appeal or professional status" in order to increase the response rate. He admits, too, that "the attention to so many variables resulted in my not giving sufficient attention to developing first-rate measures for my most important variables." He realized too late that appropriate data analysis requires appropriate data collection.

Lengermann comments that one of the things his research experience most impressed on him was "the incredible amount of clerical work required in survey research." Normally such clerical work adds to budget cost. For most students, who lack both sufficient time and money, much of this activity must be undertaken, and the costs absorbed, by the researchers themselves. Even Jones (and Ransford), who theoretically had some money available, ran into trouble in this area. Money can buy someone else's time but not necessarily their commitment. (Though Ransford and Jones both report difficulties in this area, such was not the case for Lengermann. He had a "reliable" coder—me! MPG) Students should recognize how much of even the most exciting research project can be taken up with routine and tedious clerical tasks. Certainly, in mailed questionnaire surveys, much of this activity is related to selecting a random sample and subsequently trying to secure responses from that sample. Jones and Lengermann both deal with unforeseen difficulties in this area. Composing letters, addressing envelopes, and stamping letters in the early stages and coding and keypunching data later on are some of the other routine, tedious, and often boring tasks which must be carried out by the lone, inexperienced researcher. That these pressing activities do not deter these researchers from completing their projects is a tribute to their seriousness and to their involvement in the research experience.

Finally, Lengermann discusses the question of "taking up a teaching position before having completed one's dissertation." Graduate students are usually advised to have the Ph.D. "in hand" before seeking a job. Lengermann feels that he made a mistake in not heeding this advice and in not realizing that, given the unpredictables in social research, one can easily fall behind on optimistic schedules. (Students in any situation who have ever overextended themselves should see the parallels.) The demands of a new position or other responsibilities may leave little time or energy for work on the research project. The "technical advice and emotional support" of one's professors and peers are forfeited. Like a number of other contributors, Lengermann found that, having taken so long to complete his research, his interests had shifted and he was writing about a topic on which his perspectives had changed and for which he had lost some of his initial enthusiasm.

Howard Schuman

A. TWO SOURCES OF ANTIWAR SENTIMENT IN AMERICA

Two distinct measures of opposition to American involvement in Vietnam can be traced over the seven-year period from 1965-1971. One is the intensity and scope of college-related protests against the war. The other comprises the results of Gallup polls and similar opinion surveys based on cross sections of the entire American adult public. Both measures show increasing disenchantment with the war over time, and it is easy to treat them as simply two aspects of the same thing. There is some truth to this, but even more error. The college-based protest focused on moral objections to the use of American military power in Vietnam. The general public disenchantment, however, seems to have been largely practical, springing from the failure of our substantial military investments to yield victory. Confusing these two sources of opposition to the war leads to serious miscalculations about the relationship between mass opinion and presidential action in matters of war and peace.

THREE DIFFERENCES BASED ON PAST SURVEY FINDINGS

The first major campus protest occurred in March 1965 at the University of Michigan. A handful of faculty members and students created the "teach-in" as a way of arousing opposition to the recently initiated bombing of North Vietnam. Several thousand members of the university community attended the all-night series of lectures and discussions about the war, concluding on an emotional note with songs and oratory. Above all, there was a strong tone of moral indignation in the teach-in. The main issue

Source: Edited version of "Two Sources of Antiwar Sentiment in America," *American Journal of Sociology*, 1972, *78*, 513-536.

This paper draws on data collected in the 1971 Detroit Area Study, carried out in collaboration with Otis Dudley Duncan, and supported by funds from the Russell Sage Foundation and from the University of Michigan. I am indebted to Elizabeth Fischer and Sunny Bradford, who helped in the development of the Vietnam codes, and to Mark Tannenbaum, who aided in the analysis.

presented was not whether the United States could win the war but rather the devastation that such a victory would entail. Similar protests spread rapidly in the next months to other major campuses. Later, they expanded beyond the campus and led to massive demonstrations in Washington, New York, and other cities. This expansion was characterized by the same moral emphasis seen in the first teach-in.

It is commonly assumed that the public slept until awakened by the college protests. Public opinion is then thought to have moved in much the same direction, though more slowly, and with uncertainty and occasional backtracking. This movement of national opinion can be traced by the one question that the Gallup organization repeated regularly during this period. "In view of the developments since we entered the fighting, do you think the United States made a mistake in sending troops to fight in Vietnam?"[1] Results for this question show a large and unmistakable trend in growth of opposition to the war over the seven-year period. In August 1965, only 24% of the population believed our intervention a mistake; by May 1971 that figure had climbed well past a majority to 61%.

So far it appears that public opinion followed much the same course as the college protest. But a closer look at dates and events reveals some important differences. The first teach-in, for example, was created to protest a major new employment of military force by the United States—the bombing of North Vietnam. The countrywide campus strikes in May 1970 were directed in good part against still another example of expanding American military power—the thrust into Cambodia. These two examples reflect the fact that university protests were provoked primarily by anger and dismay over *offensive* military actions by the United States.

When we search the polls for similar turning points in the trend of general public opinion, we find them at different locations. The most dramatic change in survey trends on the war is best reflected by a "hawk-dove" question that Gallup administered at several points in 1968 and 1969: "People are called 'hawks' if they want to step up our military effort in Vietnam. They are called 'doves' if they want to reduce our military effort in Vietnam. How would you describe yourself—as a hawk or a dove?" Just before the Tet attacks in January 1968, with American leaders confidently predicting victory, the number of self-described hawks outnumbered doves by two to one. But two months after Tet the proportion of doves in the country slightly exceeded that of hawks, and by the end of the same year, doves outnumbered hawks by nearly two to one. The shift in a space of just 60 days represents probably the largest and most important change in public

---

1. These and other Gallup findings appear in the monthly publication *Gallup Opinion Index*. Further descriptive analysis of these results and of related data from the University of Michigan Survey Research Center and other sources can be found in Converse and Schuman (1970), Davis (1970), and Mueller (1971).

THE RESEARCH EXPERIENCE

opinion during the entire war.[2] (The "mistake" question quoted above also reveals a sharp drop in support for the war over the first eight months of 1968; the slope is less precipitous, probably because the question was less fitted to immediate policy directions.) These transformations came, it will be noted, not in reaction to expanding American power but in response to a widely advertised American defeat.[3] It is almost as though a sizeable number of Americans had suddenly concluded that the war was not about to be won by being "stepped up," and that hence the only alternative was to step it down. More generally, the curve of broad public disenchantment with the war seems to reflect not offensive actions but news of defeats, casualties, and frustrations.[4]

A second divergence between campus-related protests and general public opinion appears in the reaction of the public to antiwar demonstrators. The gathering of more than a quarter million people in Washington in November 1969 drew heavily from colleges and universities but was intended as evidence of the extent of opposition across the country to the administration's prolongation of the war. Great pains were taken to keep the demonstration peaceful, so that it would appeal to the public at large. Yet the following month the Gallup Poll showed a 6% *rise* in public approval "of the way President Nixon is handling the situation in Vietnam." The president's speech a few days before the march undoubtedly had some influence in rallying the public opinion to his side. But there is also reason to think that the demonstration itself had a negative effect on parts of the public unhappy with the war but even unhappier with demonstrators.

---

2. The figures for several key dates are:

	Hawks	Doves	No Opinion	Total
(a) January 1968	56	28	16	100
(b) March 1968	41	42	17	100
(c) April 1968	41	41	18	100
(d) November 1969	31	55	14	100

The Tet Offensive occurred between the (a) and (b) measurement points, while President Johnson's announcement of a partial bombing halt (and his decision not to seek reelection) occurred between (b) and (c). Thus the decisive change in early 1968 seems attributable to the offensive itself, rather than to the presidential policy announcements. The subsequent decline in number of hawks over the next year and a half is no doubt more complicated and represents the basic acceptance by both political parties of the bombing halt, the Paris talks, and later the troop withdrawals. By the end of 1968, almost all political leaders had become "doves," at least in rhetorical expression.
3. Oberdorfer (1971) offers a persuasive case for the official American interpretation of Tet as a military defeat for the Viet Cong and North Vietnamese. But he also documents graphically the way in which the Communist offensive was interpreted by the American public as new and dramatic evidence that the war was far from over and far from being won.
4. Mueller (1971) suggests that both the Korean and the Vietnam wars can best be explained in terms of an initial "rally round the flag" enthusiasm, followed by a drop in support as the costs, frustrations, and length of each war became clear. The Chinese intervention in Korea had an impact even greater than Tet in shattering expectations of a quick and decisive victory. Mueller seems to argue against the importance of any single similar traumatic event for the Vietnam war, but he does not deal explicitly with Tet, or with the hawk-dove question we have reviewed here.

Poll data show clearly that open protest against the war was not well regarded by the great majority of American adults. In 1968 the University of Michigan Survey Research Center asked a national sample to indicate their "feelings" toward "Vietnam war protesters" on a scale ranging from zero (very unfavorable) to 100 (very favorable), with a neutral midpoint of 50. It is perhaps no great surprise that seven out of every 10 adults placed protesters on the negative half of the scale. What may seem strange is that extreme dislike of war protesters was shown by many people who on other questions indicated their own opposition to the war. For example, one question in the survey asked "Which of the following do you think we should do now in Vietnam?" Three alternatives were given:

1. Pull out of Vietnam entirely.
2. Keep our soldiers in Vietnam but try to end the fighting.
3. Take a stronger stand even if it means invading North Vietnam.

Of those who chose the first response, calling for unilateral withdrawal, more than half nevertheless placed "Vietnam protesters" on the negative side of the feeling scale. One out of four of these extreme doves placed protesters at the absolute bottom of this 100-point scale. These findings raise serious questions about the effect of the massive antiwar demonstrations. When the television cameras focused on the protesters themselves, rather than on the object of protest, Vietnam, the demonstrations probably led many people who were against the war toward support for the president.

One more important set of findings from national surveys points to the divergent types of antiwar sentiment. As we have already noted, the most forceful dissent over Vietnam came from students and faculty in leading universities. These articulate opponents of the war tended to assume that their potential allies in the general public were the most educated and informed segments of the population. Such is indeed the case on many issues—for example, questions involving civil liberties—where the universities provide forward positions which then find public support in direct proportion to the education of those questioned (Stouffer 1955).

Contrary to common belief, however, this was not the case with the Vietnam war. Analysis of poll data shows more educated sections of the public to have generally provided the greatest support for continuing American involvement. In February 1970, for example, Gallup asked its national sample: "Some U. S. Senators are saying that we should withdraw all our troops from Vietnam immediately—would you favor or oppose this?" Of those having an opinion, more than half the grade-school-educated adults favored immediate withdrawal, about two-fifths of those with high school backgrounds, and only 30% of those with at least some college. This was not a fluke. In May 1971, 66% of those college-educated persons with opinions claimed that the war was a mistake, but the figure rose to 75% among the grade-school-educated. In general, a careful review of public opinion data over the seven-year period shows that on most war-related issues, the greatest opposition to continued American involvement in Vietnam came from the least educated parts of the population.[5]

A related finding is that on the issue of Vietnam, the "generation gap," at least in a simple form, was largely a myth. Age differences in the general public were neither great nor consistent. On the question about immediate withdrawal mentioned above, those under 30, those 30-49, and those over 50 all showed much the same pattern of responses. Later, young people did call for a faster rate of withdrawal, but older people continued to be more likely to regard the war as a mistake.

What sense can we make out of these poll results, especially when they contradict reports about the intensity of antiwar feeling among youth on college campuses? The first thing to realize is that college students comprise less than half the college-age population in the United States. More particularly, it would have been quite possible to have had every student in the major universities in complete opposition to the war, yet find the total college-*age* population showing strong support. To this we must add the obvious but easily forgotten fact that in national surveys, "college"-educated persons are primarily adults who are well past college age at present, so that we cannot expect them to reflect recent changes on campuses.

Once we realize that students (and faculty) at Columbia, Michigan, or Berkeley could not have told us much about the degree of public opposition to the war, we must also recognize a more subtle point: the *basis* for disenchantment with Vietnam need not have been the same in the general population as on the campus. Why, indeed, was there public opposition to the war? This is such a simple-minded question that it may seem absurd even to raise it. The fact is, however, that we do not know the answer. Gallup and other polls documented well the growing negative sentiments on the war, over time, but almost no effort was made to explore the reasons behind those sentiments. Such exploration would have required open-ended questions asking people to state in their own words why they held a particular policy position.[6] Questions of this sort, however, are expensive to include in interviews and complex to analyze and report. Unfortunately, their omission

---

5. The socioeconomic findings from survey data are supported by the results of census tract analysis using cities and towns that have carried out referenda on the Vietnam war (Hahn 1970). More detailed analysis *within* the college category reveals that opposition was great in high-quality college groups, exactly as one would expect from the fact that the protest movement began at such places as Columbia, Harvard, and Michigan (see Converse and Schuman 1970; Robinson and Jacobson 1969).

6. The other alternative is structural analysis of a large set of interrelated closed questions, as is done insightfully by Modigliani (1972) on poll data from the Korean War period. Ideally both approaches should be used. In the present case, where we are attempting to discover basic frames of reference, it seems to me, as it did to Robinson and Jacobson (1969), essential to be able to draw on relatively unprompted verbalizations by respondents. Of course, both these approaches deal with overt "reasons" and "goals," and still further analysis of social and psychological motives is possible; some steps in this direction are indicated later.

TABLE 1
Reasons against U.S. Intervention: Major Themes Coded
(with percentages for Detroit sample)

Theme	%
I. U.S. Not Winning War	
0. Theme not mentioned	66
1. The war is unwinnable	10
Example: "It can't be won militarily; it's guerrilla warfare, not like World War II or Korea."	
2. We are not trying to win the war	8
"Win or get out."	
3. We are not winning (stated as a fact with no additions)	1
"We're just getting beat like crazy."	
4. The war is not ending (low priority relative to 1, 2, 3)	16
"The war just goes on and on."	
Total	101
N	(1,263)
II. People Killed or Injured by the War	
0. Theme not mentioned	58
1. American soldiers killed or injured	28
"So many boys being killed."	
2. American soldiers hurt in other ways	2
"All those soldiers getting the dope habit."	
3. People killed or injured: identity ambiguous	7
"So many innocent lives have been taken."	
4. Both Americans and Vietnamese explicitly mentioned; objections to all war	3
"I hate violence." "Too many Americans and Vietnamese killed."	
5. Vietnamese killed or injured (includes references to any Vietnamese, on either side, either civilian or soldier)	0
"Thousands of Vietnamese killed by the mass bombing."	
6. Vietnamese people hurt in other ways	1
"We make racketeers out of the people and prostitutes out of the women."	
Total	99
N	(1,263)
III. Loss of U.S. Resources	
0. Theme not mentioned	80
1. U.S. resources wasted: no mention of alternative social uses	9
"It's ruined our economy."	
2. U.S. resources wasted: explicit mention of alternative social uses	3
"We send money there and there's poverty here."	
3. War causes polarization in U.S.	4
"All the young people are turning against the country."	
4. We have enough problems of our own to take care of (vague; low priority)	4
"Enough problems here at home."	
Total	100
N	(1,263)

TABLE 1 (Continued)

Theme	%
VII. Vietnam War Is Internal Conflict	
0. Theme not mentioned	54
1. It is a civil war (codes only clear references to *civil* war)	5
2. Vietnamese don't want us there	5
"The Vietnamese don't care who wins, just want to be left alone."	
3. The war is the Vietnamese responsibility, not our war	16
"Let them fight their own war."	
4. Our intervention worsened the conflict (low priority)	1
"We changed a small war into a bigger one."	
5. Shouldn't meddle in other people's business (low priority)	19
"Too messed up . . . we should not get involved in other people's troubles."	
Total	100
N	(1,263)
VIII. U.S. Goals Morally Questionable	
0. Theme not mentioned	89
1. U.S. motives wrong or questionable	3
"Our efforts at world domination are subject to question."	
2. We shouldn't force our way of life on Vietnam	6
"Who are we to say what is the right way there."	
3. North Vietnamese or Vietcong justified	1
"North Vietnamese form of Communism is the best way for them."	
4. The war is immoral or wrong; no further explanation (low priority)	1
Total	100
N	(1,263)

may have a more dangerous effect than simply leaving us ignorant, for in the absence of knowledge of public opinion we all have a tendency to project our own views onto the population as a whole. This is particularly true when one tries to interpret the reasons behind a position with which one agrees. If one feels that American involvement in Vietnam was a mistake and then reads that two-thirds of the population also says that it was a mistake, it is quite natural to assume the reasons are the same in both cases. But of course this need not be true, any more than it is true that votes for a Democratic presidential nominee by Mississippi whites and New York blacks spring from the same motives and concerns.

A BROAD HYPOTHESIS AND SOME RELEVANT DATA

Let us summarize in the form of a general hypothesis the argument developed thus far. We have seen that public opinion was turned against the war mainly by reversals such as the Tet offensive. It is also clear that a good part of the public opposed to the war was also opposed to the antiwar protests and presumably, the beliefs that they symbolized. Finally, we have found that the larger public opposition to the war included a substantial proportion of people who were low in education, not very interested in the war, and about as likely to be older as to be younger. What these several pieces of evidence suggest is that much of the disenchantment with the war registered in public opinion polls—as against student protests—was of a purely pragmatic character, with little or no concern over the morality of employing American power in Vietnam. It is this hypothesis that we examined, using open-ended response data gathered in 1971.

From April through August 1971, the Detroit Area Study interviewed an area probability cross-section sample of 1,881 persons, 21 years old and over, in the metropolitan Detroit area.[7] The interview included the Gallup "mistake" question discussed earlier; it was followed by open probe questions to those who said they thought our sending troops to Vietnam was a mistake. The probes were simply: "Why would you say it was a mistake?" and "Is there any other reason why you think it was a mistake?" The instruction to interviewers was to be completely nondirective but to encourage full responses. The resulting verbal data from the 1,263 respondents who said "yes" to the closed question were coded in terms of 10 broad themes developed partly on the basis of theoretical expectation and partly after carefully reviewing 100 responses chosen at random. In the final coding, each of the 1,263 responses was coded zero for a particular theme if that theme was not mentioned; if the theme was mentioned, the response was further categorized in terms of the way the theme was treated. Table 1 presents the five themes that are most relevant for our analysis, along with the marginal percentages for the metropolitan Detroit sample.[8] The themes were not mutually exclusive; hence a response could be coded other than zero on as many of the 10 themes as were appropriate, although *within* a given theme a response could be coded in one subcategory only.

The Detroit marginal percentages in Table 1 can be inspected in light of the theoretical expectations developed earlier in this paper. Content analysis

---

7. A report on the sampling design for the 1971 survey can be obtained from the Detroit Area Study, University of Michigan, Ann Arbor. The geographic area covered is the Detroit Standard Metropolitan Statistical Area (SMSA), minus the city of Pontiac and the outlying semirural areas of the three-county area; it includes about 85% of the SMSA population.
8. The remaining five themes, and percentage coded as mentioning each, were: IV. Vietnam Not Important to American Interests, 28%; V. Okay to Intervene, But Handling of War Incorrect, 15%; VI. Entry into War Not Procedurally Correct, 15%; IX. The War Is Confusing, 11%; X. Problems with South Vietnamese Government or People, 6%. In general, these themes tend either to duplicate or to provide additional support for the results presented in the text. A copy of the complete set of coding instructions for all 10 themes, together with the results of check coding, can be obtained from the Detroit Area Study. Coding was carried out by professional Survey Research Center coders.

THE RESEARCH EXPERIENCE

of speeches and writings by antiwar protest leaders would also be useful as a basis for comparison. For our present purposes, however, we make use of responses to the same closed and open questions by students in three sociology classes at the University of Michigan: an introductory class consisting almost entirely of freshmen; the same course but with a majority of sophomores; and a more advanced concentration course for juniors. The combined sample (initial $N = 278$, reduced to 236 who answered "yes" to the closed question), while obviously not an adequate representation of the university, provides a useful contrast, as we will see. In one sense it is too conservative a sample, since it seriously underrepresents juniors, seniors, and graduate students who were most fully exposed to the prevailing university views on the war.[9] Exactness is not absolutely essential here because we use the sample mainly to bring out broad differences between the general population and at least a core of students at the university. It can safely be assumed that the students and faculty members who actually engaged in antiwar protests would have shown more sharply the same trends as our classroom samples.

It would be misleading to proceed as though the open-ended responses and code summaries can provide a definitive, completely objective, or simple test of the moral-pragmatic distinction I have proposed. Instead we use the data in Table 1 on an exploratory basis both to evaluate important aspects of that distinction and to illuminate public thinking about the war. Let us begin with the evaluative emphasis, looking at the themes that provide an indication of the degree of moral concern about the war in the general (Detroit) population. The results for the student and Detroit samples on the three most relevant themes are summarized in Table 2.[10]

COMPARISONS OF GENERAL POPULATION AND STUDENTS

Theme II, People Killed or Injured by the War, was one of the two most frequently mentioned by both samples, perhaps partly because of the wording of the original closed question, but even more likely because of the

---

9. All the variables reported below that have been examined *within* the student sample show an accentuated difference for the more advanced classes. This is also reflected in answers to the initial "mistake" question: 85% of the freshman class regard the war as a mistake, 88% of the mainly sophomore class, and 98% of the junior class. On Theme VIII, the percentages offering moral criticisms of the United States are 22%, 38%, and 49%, respectively, for the three classes.

10. We should note that the student responses differ in several other ways from the Detroit interviews. They were obtained at the beginning of 1972, in self-administered form in classrooms, without the context of other questions, and at the request of a faculty member (rather than a more neutral interviewer). It is doubtful that any of these differences affected the *content* of the responses seriously, though the differences may account for the greater quantity. We will see below that the main Detroit vs. student differences are replicated to a significant degree *within* the Detroit sample when younger college-educated respondents are singled out for attention. Other checks on the results will also be presented.

TABLE 2
Comparisons of General (Detroit) and Student Samples on Three Themes

Themes	Students (%)	Detroit (%)
A. Theme II: Identity of People Killed or Injured		
Americans only (1, 2)	15	73
Both (3, 4)	75	24
Vietnamese only (5, 6)	10	3
Total	100	100
N	(147)	(525)
B. Theme VIII: U.S. Goals Morally Questionable		
Theme not mentioned (0)	65	89
Theme mentioned (1-4)	35	11
Total	100	100
N	(236)	(1,263)
C. Theme VII: Vietnam as Internal Conflict		
They cause us trouble (3, 5)	43	84
We cause them trouble (2, 4)	57	16
Total	100	100
N	(90)	(518)

Note: For full description of themes, see Table 1. Note that A and C here are based only on those who mention a particular theme, while B compares those who mention a theme and those who do not. All three panels show relationships statistically significant at $p < .001$, using χ^2 and 3, 2, and 2 df, respectively.

salience of the theme to any question about the war. Students showed this concern to a greater degree than did the general public (62%-42%, $\chi^2 =$ 34.6, 1 df, $p < .001$), but the more important differences have to do with the types of mention, as shown in Table 2, topic A. A primary focus of the college-related antiwar movement was on the destruction wrought on Vietnam and the Vietnamese by American military technology. Even those moral critics of the war who granted some legitimacy to American political goals argued that the costs to the Vietnamese had long since exceeded any possible gain to them. From this standpoint, the American military effort was well symbolized by a U.S. officer's explanation at Ben Tre during Tet in 1968: "It became necessary to destroy the town to save it" (Oberdorfer 1971, p. 184). Our research question, then, is the extent to which concern for Vietnamese suffering showed up in the answers of those members of the general public who opposed the war. We see in Table 2, topic A, that, of those Detroit respondents who opposed the war and who mentioned lives lost or injured as a reason for their opposition, nearly three-quarters referred *only* to American soldiers. The students, on the other hand, were much more likely to refer to both Americans and Vietnamese and also more likely to refer to Vietnamese only. Again we must note that even the students reflected only imperfectly the emphasis of the humanitarian part of the antiwar movement. But they reflected it to a much greater degree than did the general public.

Theme VIII covers a more political type of antiwar criticism, one which centers not on the destructive nature of the war, but rather on the motivations for, and goals of, American policy in Vietnam. The category includes accusations of imperialism, support for the North Vietnamese, and more general criticisms of the war as "immoral." We would not expect anything approaching consensus on this among students, but in fact more than a third did touch on such a theme, as shown in Table 2, topic B. In the Detroit sample, however, only one out of nine persons gave a response classified anywhere under this theme. For the general public, opposition to the war seldom entailed a political-moral criticism of American goals in Vietnam.

Theme VII provides a more subtle distinction between moral and pragmatic concerns. The theme as a whole deals with emphasis on the Vietnam war as an internal conflict, but there are two ways of looking at this. The one represented by categories 3 and 5 focuses on our staying out of "their troubles." "Let them fight their own wars" is the epitome of this outlook. The other point of view, categories 2 and 4, carries the assumption that either the Vietnamese do not want American involvement or such involvement only makes the war worse for Vietnam. (Category 1, "civil war," probably belongs with the second point of view, but we omit it as somewhat ambiguous.) In other words, the first perspective on the war is strictly in terms of American interests and concludes that "they cause us trouble"; the second perspective is at least partly in terms of Vietnamese interests and concludes that "we cause them trouble." Summarized under these rubrics, Table 2, topic C shows that Detroiters who mention this theme at all do so overwhelmingly in terms of "they cause us trouble." Students, however, are much more likely to place the emphasis on "we cause them trouble."

Thus on all three of these themes we find sharp differences between the general population and the student sample. If we are correct that a sample of students who actually participated in antiwar demonstrations would be still more different from the Detroit population, we begin to get some measure of the gap between the campus-based protests and the public disenchantment with the war reflected in national surveys. It is interesting that this gap itself is validated in a sense by our code, as can be seen from Theme III, category 3: "War causes polarization in U.S." This category was mentioned infrequently by the general population (4%), but 16% of the students referred to the fact that the war created polarization within America.[11] Perhaps for much of the Detroit population polarization was not salient because protesters were perceived as deviants rather than dissenters. Students, on the other hand, personally experienced the conflict between the university climate of opinion and that in their homes or hometowns.

---

11. This category against all others (including zero) yields a χ^2 of 49.8, 1 df, $P < .001$, for students vs. Detroit. Unlike the comparisons in Table 2, this comparison is strictly post factum, but its significance is so high as to make replicability likely.

Some modifications in the moral-pragmatic distinction are required by findings on other themes. Theme I, U.S. Not Winning War, represents the pragmatic position in perhaps its purest form, namely, that the war was a mistake because we were not winning it, could not win it, or had not tried to win it (see Table 1).[12] Approximately a third of the Detroit respondents give this response, three times more than offered a specifically moral critique (Theme VIII), it is true, but still far less than unanimity. Morever, 29% of the students are also coded in Theme I categories, indicating that students were nearly as likely to give such a pragmatic response as were members of the general population. It is probable that this is the case generally: what were distinctive were moral types of responses, while pragmatic reasons were given by all groups who opposed the war. Only when the two positions were incompatible within a particular theme did students and the general population differ greatly. One other theme given frequently by *both* students and general public was Theme IV-4: "We gain nothing from the war" (not shown in a table). This was coded for 20% of the students and for 22% of the Detroit sample, indicating the general lack of clarity about American aims and purposes in Vietnam. Finally, an unexpected finding occurred with Theme X-1: "Negative characteristics of South Vietnamese government" (not shown in a table). We had expected this to be mentioned with some frequency by the general population, since it was often referred to in the mass media, but in fact it was hardly mentioned at all (3%). Students were significantly more likely to focus on negative characteristics of the South Vietnam government (10%), suggesting that this complaint about our involvement tended to appeal mainly to those influenced by a general political-moral criticism of the war.

ANALYSIS WITHIN THE GENERAL POPULATION: SEX, RACE, AND SES

The Detroit sample can be further broken down in several useful ways. As was mentioned earlier, public opposition to the war in surveys over the seven-year period was associated with lower education and to some extent with older age. Opposition was also more characteristic of women than of men by a small degree, and of blacks than of whites by a substantial margin.

---

12. The subthemes obviously differ greatly both in their sophistication and in their implications for action. "The war is unwinnable" includes the type of judgment finally made by those Pentagon officials and advisers who, having first participated in the escalation of the war, later sought to deescalate it (see Hoopes 1969). "We are not trying to win the war," on the other hand, is a pure hawkish response identified with the military's push for more extreme bombing and related measures. The remaining two categories suggest less a policy point of view than a matter-of-fact if weary observation. Despite these important differences, all four categories must be described as pragmatic in terms of our present frame of reference.

TABLE 3
Percentage Believing the United States Made a Mistake in Sending
Troops to Vietnam, by Sex, Race, Education, and Age

	Gallup National Results (May 1971) (N = 1,500 +)	Detroit Area Study Results (April-August 1971) (N = 1,881)
Sex		
Male	65	66
Female	72	72
Race		
White	67	68
Black*	83	82
Education		
College	66	70
High school	67	68
Grade school	75	73
Age		
21-29	63	68
30-49	67	66
50 and over	73	74
Total	68	69

Note: Percentages calculated after removing missing data (11% reported by Gallup, 3.3% by Detroit Area Study).
*Includes other nonwhites for Gallup only.

As Table 3 shows, both the Gallup national data of May 1971 and our Detroit sample of summer 1971 displayed these sex and race relationships with almost identical percentages. Gallup also shows small but clear age and education relationships, while our Detroit sample reveals less consistent associations for both these variables.[13] In any case, it is useful to know how all four of these basic background characteristics related to reasons for being against the war.[14] At least three, it may be noted, identify groups excluded from political dominance: blacks, women, and low-educated persons.

---

13. When race is controlled, the Detroit sample reveals the same relationship to age for whites that Gallup reports for the nation as a whole. This is a reasonable control, since the percentage of blacks in our Detroit sample is twice that at the national level and therefore prevents an exact comparison. (From this the reader will infer correctly that the relationship of age to opposition to the war is reversed for blacks: younger blacks in the Detroit sample are more likely than older blacks to regard our intervention as a mistake.) However, with or without the control for race, we do not obtain for Detroit the usual (or any other) association between support of the war and education.

14. There are slight differences in the average number of codable (nonzero) responses given by different population subgroups. At the extreme, those with grade school education (0-8) give an average of 2.16 nonzero responses; those with some college (13+) give an average of 2.44 nonzero responses—a ratio of only 1.1. This difference is too slight to affect the results presented below. Black-white, male-female and age differences are even smaller on this response count.

TABLE 4
A. Percentage Mentioning U.S. Motives Morally Questionable
(Theme VIII) by Education and Age

Age	Education (years)				
	0-8	9-11	12	13-15	16+
21-29	...(5)	4 (28)	3 (67)	12(49)	28(36)
30-49	0(21)	4 (75)	8(147)	17(76)	24(66)
50+	8(90)	5(100)	12 (89)	13(47)	21(38)

B. Percentage Mentioning American Soldiers Killed or Injured
(II-1, 2) by Education and Age

Age	Education (years)				
	0-8	9-11	12	13-15	16+
21-29	...	50	40	14	17
30-49	38	28	35	21	20
50+	40	33	26	25	26

Note: Results are for whites only. The figures in parentheses indicate the base *N* on which each percentage is based. The same bases apply in both panels of the table. The cells based on only five cases are omitted as unstable; the frequencies are zero in A and one in B.

Let us begin with education and age, two variables that are usefully treated together, and with the focus on the white subsample where the number of cases is large enough to allow for more detailed analysis. The main findings here, as shown in Table 4, fit well with those reported earlier for students versus the general population. For example, Theme VIII, U.S. Goals Morally Questionable, produces a strong positive relationship to education, with a quarter of the college graduates voicing some moral criticisms of U.S. motives or actions, but decreasing proportions doing so at lower educational levels. Age may act as a conditional factor here, with the gap in mention of this moral theme somewhat greater between high- and low-educated for the young than for the old. That is, among young people 21-29 who opposed the war, those with college education were fairly likely to do so in terms morally critical of government actions, while those with less than high school education were very unlikely to do so. Complementing this, we find that on Theme II, People Killed or Injured, those young opponents of the war without college education were considerably more likely to mention American soldiers being killed or injured (and less likely to mention Vietnamese) than were those with at least some college training—perhaps reflecting the fact that there is not only a social class difference in sensitivity to moral issues but also a social class difference among young men in the risk of entering the army and being sent into combat. These data support our earlier finding of a gulf between college students and the general population in their reasons for opposing the war, and also reinforce the point sometimes made that the gulf was not only between young and old but also between those young people with college education and those without it.[15] We are also reminded that moral reasons for having opposed the war (as well as for having given principled support to it) may have been easier to elaborate when one was not directly in the line of fire.

The less educated, therefore, and especially less educated youth, were particularly likely to interpret their opposition to the war in terms of the danger to American lives. Since older Americans tend to be low in education, this also helps explain the special opposition to the war of older people. However, age as such is associated with still another type of opposition, labeled earlier as "they cause us trouble" (Theme VII-3, 5). This stance should perhaps be relabeled "traditional isolationism," for it focuses on the avoidance of intervention into troubles elsewhere. The percentage giving this response is directly associated with age, but in a single-step threshold fashion:

		Age in Decades			
20-29	30-39	40-49	50-59	60-69	70 and Over
32%	29%	31%	42%	40%	42%

Those over 50 are a third again as likely as younger persons to have voiced this sentiment, but there is little variation within either of the age categories created by the division at 50. The relationship continues to hold when education is controlled, except that the rejection of isolationism is strongest in the 30-49 age range. This is exactly the generation that came to maturity between the beginning of World War II and the beginning of serious frustration over Vietnam—that is, the generation most exposed to what might be called successful "military internationalism" on the part of the United States. Presumably it is this age group that found especially resonant ad-

---

15. The methods developed by Goodman (1969, 1972; Davis, 1972) for analysis of multivariate contingency tables were applied to the results in Table 4B. For full table (including the five cases omitted in percentaging), only the relationship between education and mention of American soldiers is significant ($\chi^2 = 21.2$, 4 df, $p < .001$; with age partialed out, $\chi^2 = 32.5$, 4 df, $p < .001$). Age is not significantly related to mention of American soldiers ($\chi^2 = 0.8$, 2 df), nor is there a significant three-way interaction ($\chi^2 = 11.6$, 8 df, $p < .10$). However, since the interaction expected on the basis of our earlier student versus Detroit findings was specified in terms of young college-educated persons, the problem was run again with age and education each reduced to two categories. The table below presents the observed percentages on the basis of this specification, along with, in brackets, those expected on the hypothesis of no three-way interaction. (The appropriate base N's can be constructed from Table 4.)

	Education (years)	
Age	0-12	13 and Over
21-29	42 [36]	15 [22]
30 and over	33 [34]	22 [20]

The predicted interaction does occur ($\chi^2 = 4.7$, 1 df, $p < .03$ for rejection of two-variable model). The largest discrepancies between observed and expected frequencies of mention of American soldiers are located among those 21-29 years old, indicating that the young college-educated differ not only from the rest of the population generally but especially from the noncollege portion of their own cohort.

ministration appeals referring to "Munich" and to the early episodes of the Cold War. In any case, whether or not this generational interpretation is correct, we see that the *older* age groups that were disproportionately opposed to the war were often drawn to that position on the basis of traditional isolationist sentiments. We assume that the failures of intervention in Vietnam reinforced these sentiments, although we lack trend data to demonstrate such reinforcement.[16]

The persistence of both sex and race differences in poll data on the war over the seven years has been interpreted as evidence that at least two groups—blacks and women—had special reasons for their opposition. It is easy to hypothesize that these reasons fit under the several categories that operationalize moral reservations or criticisms. In the case of women this could involve a less aggressive and greater humanitarian attitude. Black opposition, on the other hand, could reflect disenchantment with American society generally and therefore a greater willingness to criticize the war in moral or ideological terms. We find some support for both these expectations in our thematic data, but important qualifications are needed as well.

TABLE 5
Percentages by Sex on Selected Antiwar Themes and Subthemes

Themes	Men (N = 535)	Women (N = 728)	Difference
Theme I: U.S. Not Winning War			
We are not trying to win the war (2)	11	5	6*
The war is not ending (4)	13	18	−5*
Theme II: People Killed or Injured	33	48	−15**
Americans only (1 and 2)	22	37	−15
Both (3 and 4)	9	10	a
Vietnamese only (5 and 6)	2	1	a
Theme VIII: U.S. Goals Morally Questionable	15	7	8**

aLess than 2% difference.
*$p < .05$, using χ^2 for category I-2 versus remainder of Theme I ($df = 1$); $p < .01$ for category I-4 versus remainder of Theme I ($df = 1$).
**$p < .001$, using χ^2 for zero versus nonzero categories ($df = 1$].

Considering sex differences first, Table 5 shows that women were more likely than men to mention people killed or injured as a reason for opposing the war, but that this difference is entirely accounted for by the "Americans only" category. Men and women did not differ at all with regard to mention of Vietnamese deaths or suffering. Thus the greater concern of women for the pain of war seems to have been channeled wholly along national lines. On other themes, our general finding is that men were more critical of the war

---

16. One other result involving education that is worth noting is a positive association between number of years of schooling and belief that the war is "unwinnable" (I–1). Percentages coded into the latter category are: 4% (grade school), 7% (some high school), 10% (high school graduates), 15% (some college or above). The finding supports our earlier note about the sophistication of this point of view. The association involves only education and not age.

effort in *all* ways, both moral and pragmatic. Men were more likely to complain that "we are not really trying to win the war"—a "hawk" type of response—but men were also more likely than women to question the morality of U.S. motives and actions in Vietnam.[17] Women were more apt to phrase their opposition in more passive ways, for example, that "the war goes on and on" (I-4). These findings help explain why the sex difference in opposition to the war never seemed to translate well into political actions. Despite their concern for American lives lost in war, Detroit women were less rather than more critical of the policies that supported and guided the war effort.

The black-white difference on the basic "mistake" question is the largest in Table 3, and this finding of greater black opposition held consistently over the course of attitude surveys on the war. Moreover, a number of student responses, self-identified as black, offered criticisms of the war in clear racial terms: that the war was racist and genocidal, that the money should have been spent at home on urban problems, etc. Despite this indirect evidence that blacks may have been ideologically more opposed to the war than whites, the Detroit black sample of adults gives only a little evidence of having been more highly motivated by moral sentiments than were whites. As Table 6 shows, blacks as a group did not differ from whites in their distribution of responses to Theme II, People Killed or Injured, or to Theme VIII, U.S. Goals Morally Questionable. They also did not differ significantly on a theme (III-2) which concerned alternative social uses of

TABLE 6
Percentages by Race on Selected Antiwar Themes and Subthemes

Themes	Black (N = 322)	White (N = 941)	Difference
Theme I: U.S. Not Winning War (1-4)	20	39	−19*
Theme II: People Killed or Injured	42	42	a
Americans only (1 and 2)	31	30	a
Both (3 and 4)	10	10	a
Vietnamese only (5 and 6)	1	2	a
Theme III: Loss of U.S. Resources	22	20	a
Explicit mention of alternative uses (2)	4	3	a
Theme VII: Vietnam War Is Internal Conflict	52	44	6
They cause us trouble (3 and 5)	42	32	10*
We cause them trouble (2 and 4)	5	7	a
Theme VIII: U.S. Goals Morally Questionable	10	11	a
Theme IX: The War Is Confusing (1 and 2)	18	6	12*

a Less than 2% difference.
* $p < .001$, using χ^2 for categories shown versus all other categories of same theme ($df = 1$ in each case).

---

17. These conclusions are *not* changed when age and education are controlled. For example, considering only the youngest and most educated respondents—those 21-29 with 13 or more years of school—26% of the 53 men question U.S. motives or actions (Theme VIII), as against only 6% of the 32 women.

money and resources being spent in Vietnam, although this was a point often made by black leaders. Blacks did differ, however, quite substantially on Theme I, U.S. Not Winning War, with 19% *fewer* responses here than reported by whites, the reduction being distributed evenly over categories 1, 2, and 4. In other words, blacks were much less concerned than whites about the lack of "victory" in Vietnam, and therefore in this sense black opposition to the war seems to have been less pragmatically based than was the case for whites. But this deemphasis on pragmatic opposition does not appear to have been translated into a more positive critique of the war. The 19% difference on Theme I was not compensated for elsewhere in any single category; it generally appears to be reversed in the categories we called, "They cause us trouble" (Theme VII-3, 5), as well as on other categories indicating confusion over what the war was about (especially Theme IX). Together these findings suggest a picture of the war as a distant and unclear set of troubles belonging to someone else—an isolationist trend of thinking based on low interest in the war, rather than on conscious moral opposition to it.

DISCUSSION

When the evidence from both past opinion surveys on Vietnam and the 1971 Detroit study is drawn together, the broad distinction between moral and pragmatic types of opposition to the war remains a persuasive one. The college-based protest was led almost entirely by spokesmen presenting the moral critique, but much of the public opposition to the war flowed from quite different sources. These had to do primarily with the long and frustrating nature of the war but also draw on other closely related themes, of which the two most important were probably the costs in American lives and the lack of clarity about the goals of the war. A very pragmatic current of isolationism was also involved, symbolized by the phrase: "Let them fight their own war."[18]

18. One must expect emphases to change somewhat over time as the impact of the war itself changes. Several months after our main field interviewing, we conducted brief telephone reinterviews with a random subsample of 198 respondents. Nine of the 10 themes showed a drop in mention, perhaps merely a function of the telephone context, but one showed a rise. This was Theme VII: Vietnam as an Internal Conflict, and especially the subthemes (3 and 5) we have labeled "they cause us trouble" or traditional isolationism, which increased from 32% to 46% for the relevant reinterview subsample ($N = 119$). The largest single drop in mention (from 42% to 27%) occurred for Theme II: People Killed or Injured. Since the salience of the war itself was decreasing at that point (for example, U.S. casualties had declined to a relatively tiny number), it makes sense that such specific objections were disappearing and being replaced by a hardening of general isolationist sentiment toward a more and more remote "nuisance." These findings reinforce the value of the broad abstractions "moral" and "pragmatic"; the distinction carries the danger of oversimplification, but it also points to more enduring stances toward the war than do most of the specific themes and subthemes.

The moral-pragmatic distinction does not, of course, correspond exactly to the difference between major universities and the rest of the population. One finds both types of opposition in both settings—though, as we have shown, their proportions differ sharply. Nor is it necessary or wise to assume that the distinction represents characterological differences between the campus and the city. We are dealing here with ideology, not with personality. While it is probably true that some of the leaders and participants in the college-based protest movement were motivated by deeply held ethical principles, it would obviously be a mistake to infer individual character directly from verbal reasons for opposition to the war. College students provided moral criticisms primarily because they were exposed to, and learned, such criticisms on campus. In addition, they were intellectually equipped to elaborate their sense of dissatisfaction with the war, and to turn personal concern about participating in it into a critical examination of its goals—what Weber meant by rationalization, which is far more than merely "explaining away" something distasteful. Our aim here has been an analysis of the content and social bases of antiwar sentiments and ideology, not an attempt at delineation of personality differences.

From a policy standpoint, the main overall implication of our argument is that the president never had much to fear directly from the college antiwar movement, because the latter did not speak the same language as the general public. Public disillusionment with the war grew despite the campus demonstrations, not because of them. The president's primary enemy was the Viet Cong and the North Vietnamese, for it was their resilience and success that undermined larger public support for the war. The antiwar movement was not wholly ineffective: it influenced commentators and columnists, who in turn (but in different words) influenced the public. And it provided energy and money in political campaigns. But attempts by moral spokesmen against the war to proselytize the general public directly were probably unsuccessful and perhaps even counterproductive unless carried out with more skill and less righteousness.

There is another long-term implication to the moral-pragmatic distinction. Our Detroit questionnaire included a question on a possible future Communist-inspired revolution in South America (preceding the Vietnam question by several items). As might be expected, those who regarded the Vietnam war as a mistake were more likely to resist intervening in such a future situation. But our thematic code proves useful in distinguishing further. Of those who were opposed to the Vietnam intervention simply because we were not winning (Theme I), 50% would still intervene in a new South American war. But of those who criticized the Vietnam war on moral grounds (Theme VIII), only 25% would intervene in a new war. The *reasons* people gave for thinking the Vietnam war a mistake were linked to their willingness to become involved in future wars of the same general type. We need not pretend to be entirely clear on cause and effect here, but we can insist on the value of understanding more thoroughly not only pro and con positions, but also the reasons for them.

REFERENCES

Converse, Philip E., and Howard Schuman. 1970. " 'Silent Majorities' and the Vietnam War." *Scientific American* 222 (June): 17-25.

Davis, James A. 1970. "American Opinion on the Vietnam War: March, 1966-March, 1970." Multilith.

_____. 1972. "The Goodman System for Significance Tests in Multivariate Contingency Tables." National Opinion Research Center, University of Chicago.

Gallup Opinion Index. 1965-current. Princeton, N.J.: International.

Goodman, Leo. A. 1969. "On Partitioning χ^2 and Detecting Partial Association in Three-way Contingency Tables." *Journal of the Royal Statistical Society,* ser. *B* (Methodological), 31 (3): 486-98.

_____. 1972. "A Modified Multiple Regression Approach to the Analysis of Dichotomous Variables." *American Sociological Review* 37 (February): 28-46.

Hahn, Harlan. 1970. "Correlates of Public Sentiments about War: Local Referenda on the Vietnam Issue." *American Political Science Review* 54 (December): 1186-98.

Harris Survey Yearbook of Public Opinion, 1970: A Compendium of Current American Attitudes. 1971. New York: Harris.

Hoopes, Townsend. 1969. *The Limits of Intervention.* New York: McKay.

Hyman, Herbert. 1954. *Interviewing in Social Research.* Chicago: University of Chicago Press.

Modigliani, Andre. 1972. "Hawks and Doves, Isolationism and Political Trust: An Analysis of Public Opinion on Military Policy." *American Political Science Review,* in press.

Mueller, John E. 1971. "Trends in Popular Support for the Wars in Korea and Vietnam." *American Political Science Review* 65 (June): 358-75.

Oberdorfer, Don. 1971. *Tet!* New York: Doubleday.

Robinson, John, and Solomon Jacobson. 1969. "American Public Opinion about Vietnam." In *Vietnam: Some Basic Issues and Alternatives,* edited by Walter Isard. Cambridge, Mass.: Schenkman.

Stouffer, Samuel A. 1955. *Communism, Conformity, and Civil Liberties.* New York: Doubleday.

B. PERSONAL ORIGINS OF "TWO SOURCES OF ANTIWAR SENTIMENTS IN AMERICA"

In November of 1969 my wife and 14-year-old son prepared for an overnight bus trip to join what turned out to be the largest protest ever held in Washington against the Vietnam war. Many of my friends and colleagues were also traveling to the capitol for the same purpose. I shared their opposition to the war and felt the pull to participate in the demonstration, but at the same time I had vague doubts about the effect of such a mass demonstration on the broader public.

The doubts were not then based on any systematic look at "data." But I had a sense that my friends might be overestimating the extent to which the larger public felt the same depth of opposition to the war.[1] More important, they very likely underestimated the extent to which a complacent country would pay careful attention to the medium rather than the message of the protest. On the contrary, the general public might well be upset by images of strange bearded protesters and frightened by the more militant fringes certain to be highlighted by television. There was evidence that this had happened at the Democratic convention in Chicago in 1968, and my own research on racial attitudes suggested that much the same thing occurred in the area of civil rights protest.[2] More generally, nearly a decade of experience in cross-section survey research had convinced me that one should be very cautious indeed about assuming that actions perceived in a certain light by one's own intellectual community would be seen that same way by others coming from different backgrounds and with different preconceptions and preoccupations.

The upshot of these considerations—plus the quite practical need for someone to take care of our two younger children—was that I stayed home. I wished my wife success and promised to spend the time trying to locate data that would cast some light on how effective mass demonstrations were. So I

Source: Prepared especially for this volume.

1. In the one limited study I had participated in at an earlier point, it was sobering to learn that even my own university colleagues were far from united in opposing the war: Howard Schuman and Edward O. Laumann, "Do Most Professors Support the War?" *Trans-Action*, November 1967, pp. 32-35.

2. In a 1968 study for the National Advisory Commission on Civil Disorders, we found that more than a third of the population denied that any real difference existed between "nonviolent marches and demonstrations" and "riots."

spent the period of the Washington demonstration watching children, looking at television coverage of the protest, and rummaging through old files for survey data on public attitudes toward the war. I had no intention of becoming involved in research on war attitudes, but in fact that avocational work provided the start for the article reprinted above, which appeared some three years later.

The first step was to review Gallup polls and a few other scattered sources of opinion on the war. These immediately revealed some interesting facts about public opposition to the war, such as the then unexpected finding that opposition to continued American involvement seemed stronger among the oldest and least educated citizens—those furthest in lifestyle from the college campus. These Gallup data had the advantage of offering answers to a variety of questions asked over a period of time, but they were frustrating because it was not possible to do more detailed analysis with "controls." Since age and education are negatively correlated in the American population, their effects are easily confused; any relationship involving one is more fully understood if the other can be held constant or controlled statistically. I recalled that the Survey Research Center had asked questions on Vietnam in its 1968 election study and began in my spare time some analysis of those national data. The results of this analysis, plus the earlier review, led to an informal set of notes which formed the basis for a talk on public attitudes toward the war. The talk traced the history of public opinion on the war and spelled out some unexpected correlations between attitudes and such background factors as age, education, and interest. Only indirectly did it attempt any general interpretation.

At that point I became aware that Philip Converse, one of the primary investigators in the 1968 Survey Research Center study, had separately developed somewhat similar conclusions, and I talked with him about somehow preparing a piece for general distribution. Our idea was partly scholarly, but equally practical—the two were not in any conflict here. We felt that those who actively opposed the war and wanted to do something about it would benefit by knowing more about the nature of mass opinion on this issue.

Together Converse and I prepared an article and sent it to the widely circulated magazine *Scientific American,* which seemed a suitable location for a serious but non-technical discussion of public opinion on the war. The piece was accepted, revised, and published in June 1970, some eight months after the Washington demonstration.[3] It stresses the history and demographic correlates of Gallup-type questions about the war, but the last paragraphs adumbrate a more general emphasis that had begun to seem to me more significant than any of the specific findings. This was that the

---

3. Philip E. Converse and Howard Schuman, "Silent Majorities and the Vietnam War," *Scientific American,* June 1970, pp. 17-25.

THE RESEARCH EXPERIENCE

important fact about general public opposition to the war was its practical character, in contradistinction to the moral indignation I saw among my friends and colleagues. Later that summer, on a vacation in Maine, I tried to set down this conclusion in a more straightforward way, writing in effect what turned out to be the basis for the first seven pages of the "Two Sources" article. My goal was now even more clearly practical—to get across to antiwar leaders a fact not then much realized: If they hoped to lead larger public opposition to the war, they would have to learn to appeal to the public in its own terms. In particular, broad sentiment against the war was not coupled, as it was on campus, with criticism of the United States, its goals, or its actions, and such criticism tended to arouse defensive support of the President. I sent this popular summary to several magazines that reach the nonscientific intellectual public, but none of these evinced any great enthusiasm for publishing it. (Despite my attempts at simplification, one editor commented that the piece had too many "figures.") Somewhat sadly I filed the short paper away and turned to other matters.

But the basic idea stayed with me, and I occasionally talked about it to others. As I did so, I realized that the evidence for the "moral"–"pragmatic" distinction was too indirect, and that additional data were really needed. By now it was spring of 1971, and I was involved in the planning of a large survey of the Detroit population. At almost the last minute it proved possible to include an open question on Vietnam about the reasons people gave for opposition to the war—to let them speak in their own words. Useful as are "closed questions" for survey analysis, at times it is essential to capture more directly and with less preconception the thinking of the general public. To anchor this inquiry to some national standard, I made it a "why" follow-up to a Gallup question on American involvement in Vietnam that had been repeated a number of times over the course of the war. (In retrospect, it might have been better to have asked a more straightforward question about support or opposition to the war, followed by "Why do you feel that way?" But the Gallup question did have advantages in allowing comparison of the Detroit data with past and current findings on the total U.S. population.)

Over that summer the data that form the basis for much of the "Two Sources" article were gathered. Coding the open-ended responses, however, proved to be very difficult. On the one hand, we[4] wanted to include all possible reasons that could exemplify "moral" or "pragmatic" objection to the war, if only to test the hypothesis that the moral categories would turn out to be essentially empty. On the other hand, we did not wish to impose this framework arbitrarily on the data. We therefore read a large sample of responses to make certain that categories "natural" to the respondents were

---

4. "We" because two University of Michigan graduate students, Elizabeth Fischer and Sunny Bradford, worked with me to develop these codes.

created, whether or not they fit the moral-pragmatic distinction.

The standard overall code that resulted from these combined goals proved much too long (over a dozen categories), and we soon despaired of being able to categorize responses with the necessary reliability. Moreover, use of nondirective probes in the original "why" question had added to the common problem of open inquiries: the occurrence of more than one codable response in the same answer, usually with no clear order of importance among such points. For a time it looked as though there was no way to reduce this mass of rich verbal material to a set of categories that could be summarized and analyzed quantitatively.

At this point we abandoned the attempt to create a single set of exhaustive and mutually exclusive categories into which each answer (or the "first" or "most important" response in each answer) could be coded. It seemed better, and certainly more feasible, to allow each total answer to be coded for all relevant points it contained, without worrying about which was more important to the respondent or whether one point was consistent with another. This led to the set of "thematic codes" reported in the article, and they did indeed prove much more easily and reliably coded. Each answer was examined in terms of each theme and coded for the absence or presence of the theme. If the theme was judged to be present, we allowed further sub-coding into several mutually exclusive categories, but the ten overall themes themselves were not treated as mutually exclusive. This plan not only simplified the task of the coders, it had the additional advantage of not forcing my own version of consistency onto the respondents. Thus, in the article it is noted that students and the general population do not differ greatly in frequency of mention of "pragmatic" themes, though they do differ in frequency of mention of "moral" themes. Such a finding could not have appeared had we constrained moral and pragmatic codes to be mutually exclusive.

The large set of thematic codes finally employed presented some difficulties. They prevented any neat summary of results, contained some unnecessary redundancy, and generally made the analysis and presentation of the data more complex. At one point I experimented, for purposes of hypothesis testing, with a summary score for each respondent of the number of moral themes mentioned. While this worked reasonably well, it did not seem to add a great deal to the analysis and risked too simplistic a view of the moral-pragmatic dichotomy. All in all, the thematic approach to coding this complex open material turned out to be a good way to combine the goals of richness of summary with reliability of procedures. The approach does, however, make analysis more difficult, and it probably should be used only where the open question under consideration is quite important and where the analyst has had some experience in working with complex data.

At the end of the coding operation, it occurred to me that the general population responses could be evaluated more clearly if they were contrasted with antiwar student responses. Unfortunately time and other resources did not allow for proper sampling design in this case, so that the classroom samples used for the article are much less adequate than that for the general population. But the general point here is worth noting: a set of survey data can often be illuminated as much by contrast with an external reference standard as by internal analysis.

The article itself was written in the early months of 1972, with some sense of time pressure because I still saw it as having some small practical effect on efforts to end the war. In fact it probably had none at all and must be justified on intellectual grounds as any other sociological paper. In this sense, its main contribution is probably methodological: emphasis on, and analytic use of, an open-ended question. The fair success in working with such data certainly reenforced my own interest in this approach to the measurement of attitudes and beliefs, as against the more common reliance on simple closed attitude items.

Beyond its concern with question and coding methodology, however, the analysis raised questions about the nature of antiwar sentiments in America, and I remain persuaded of the soundness of the basic argument, though perhaps not of every part. On the latter score, consideration of the consequences of the antiwar demonstrations must take account of more than their immediate effects on mass opinion. Their consequences for both participants and onlookers were many and varied, manifest and latent, and these deserve a more rounded treatment than they receive in this article. While I like to think that my decision to stay home in November 1969 was a useful one, the decision of my wife and others to journey to Washington had, I imagine, positive effects as well.

One final point can be made about the relation between personal values and scientific method. As John Dewey liked to stress, it is appropriate, often useful, and perhaps inevitable that one's personal values play an important role in defining problems for investigation. At the same time, scientific methods offer the means for carrying out an investigation objectively; they provide tools for performance and analysis, and a framework which permits disconfirmation as well as confirmation of preferred hypotheses. The actual connections between values and methods, however, are not always as simple as this conceptualization suggests: thus the article "Two Sources of Antiwar Sentiments in America" provides one example of an attempt to balance the two in a way that is complementary and fruitful, rather than antagonistic or subverting. Whether it was a successful attempt is for the reader to judge.

H. Edward Ransford ——————————————————————————

A. ISOLATION, POWERLESSNESS, AND VIOLENCE: A STUDY OF ATTITUDES AND PARTICIPATION IN THE WATTS RIOT

Since the summer of 1965, it is no longer possible to describe the Negroes' drive for new rights as a completely non-violent protest. Urban ghettos have burst at the seams. Angry shouts from the most frustrated and deprived segments of the Negro community now demand that we recognize violence as an important facet of the Negro revolution.

In attempts to understand the increase in violence, much has been said about unemployment, police brutality, poor schools, and inadequate housing as contributing factors.[1] However, there are few sociological studies concerning the characteristics of the participants or potential participants in racial violence.[2] Little can be said about which minority individuals are likely to view violence as a justifiable means of correcting racial injustices. It is the purpose of this paper to identify such individuals—specifically, to identify those Negroes who were willing to use violence as a method during a period shortly after the Watts riot.

A THEORETICAL PERSPECTIVE

Studies dealing with political extremism and radical protest have often described the participants in such action as being isolated or weakly tied to the institutions of the community.[3] Kerr and Siegel (1954) demonstrated this

Source: Reprinted, with permission of the author and publisher, from the *American Journal of Sociology*, 1968, 73, 581-591. Copyright © 1968 by The University of Chicago Press.

The author acknowledges his debt to Melvin Seeman and Robert Hagedorn for helpful comments and advice on earlier drafts of this paper. This is a revised version of a paper presented at the annual meetings of the Pacific Sociological Association, Long Beach, Calif., April, 1967.

1. See, e.g., report of the Governor's Commission on the Los Angeles Riots (1965).
2. One of the very few studies of the potential participants in race violence was conducted by Kenneth B. Clark, shortly after the Harlem riot of 1943 (see Clark, 1944; Humphrey, 1943).
3. See, e.g., Kornhauser (1959); Lipset (1960); Kerr and Siegel (1954).

relationship with their finding that wildcat strikes are more common among isolated occupational groups, such as mining, maritime, and lumbering. These isolated groups are believed to have a weak commitment to public pressures and the democratic norms of the community. Thus, when grievances are felt intensely and the bonds to the institutions of the community are weak, there is likely to be an explosion of discontent (the strike) rather than use of negotiation or other normative channels of expression.

More recently, mass society theory has articulated this relationship between isolation and extremism (Kornhauser, 1959; Bramson, 1961). The mass society approach sees current structural processes—such as the decline in kinship, the increase in mobility, and the rise of huge bureaucracies—as detaching many individuals from sources of control meaning, and personal satisfaction. Those who are most isolated from centers of power are believed to be more vulnerable to authoritarian outlooks and more available for volatile mass movements. Indeed, Kornhauser instructs us that the whole political stability of a society is somewhat dependent upon its citizens being tied meaningfully to the institutions of the community (Kornhauser, 1959). He suggests that participation in secondary organizations—such as unions and business groups—serves to mediate between the individual and the nation, tying the individual to the democratic norms of the society.

The relationship between structural isolation and extremism is further accentuated by the personal alienation of the individual. Isolated people are far more likely than non-isolated people to feel cut off from the larger society and to feel an inability to control events in the society.[4] This subjective alienation may heighten the individual's readiness to engage in extreme behavior. For example, Horton and Thompson find that perceived powerlessness is related to protest voting (Horton & Thompson, 1962; Thompson & Horton, 1960). Those with feelings of political powerlessness were more likely to be dissatisfied with their position in society and to hold resentful attitudes toward community leaders. The study suggests that the discontent of the powerless group was converted to action through the vote—a vote of "no" on a local bond issue being a form of negativism in which the individual strikes out at community powers. This interpretation of alienation as a force for protest is consistent with the original Marxian view of the concept in which alienation leads to radical attack upon the existing social structure (Fromm, 1962).

In summary, there are two related approaches commonly used to explain participation in extreme political behavior. The first deals with the degree to which the individual is structurally isolated or tied to community institutions. The second approach deals with the individual's awareness and

---

4. E.g., Neal and Seeman found that isolated workers (non-participants in unions) were more likely to feel powerless to effect outcomes in the society than the participants in unions (Neal and Seeman, 1964).

evaluation of his isolated condition—for example, his feeling a lack of control over critical matters or his feeling of discontent due to a marginal position in society. Following this orientation, this research employs the concepts of racial isolation, perceived powerlessness, and racial dissatisfaction as theoretical tools for explaining the participation of Negroes in violence.

STUDY DESIGN AND HYPOTHESES

In the following discussion, the three independent variables of this study (isolation, powerlessness, and dissatisfaction) are discussed separately and jointly, as predictors of violence participation.

Racial Isolation

Ralph Ellison has referred to the Negro in this country as the "invisible man" (Ellison, 1952). Although this is a descriptive characterization, sociological studies have attempted to conceptualize more precisely the isolation of the American Negro. For example, those studying attitudes of prejudice often view racial isolation as lack of free and easy contact on an intimate and equal status basis.[5] Though the interracial contact may be frequent, it often involves such wide status differentials that it does not facilitate candid communication, nor is it likely to give the minority person a feeling that he has some stake in the system. In this paper, intimate white contact is viewed as a mediating set of relationships that binds the ethnic individual to majority-group values—essentially conservative values that favor working through democratic channels rather than violently attacking the social system. Accordingly, it is reasoned that Negroes who are more racially isolated (by low degrees of intimate contact with whites) will have fewer channels of communication to air their grievances and will feel little commitment to the leaders and institutions of the community. This group, which is blocked from meaningful white communication, should be more willing to use violent protest than the groups with greater involvement in white society.

Powerlessness and Racial Dissatisfaction

In contrast to structural isolation, powerlessness and racial dissatisfaction are the subjective components of our theoretical scheme. A feeling of powerlessness is one form of alienation. It is defined in this research as a low

---

5. Many studies have brought forth the finding that equal status contact between majority and minority members is associated with tolerance and favorable attitudes. For the most recent evidence of the equal status proposition, see Williams (1964). For an earlier study, see Deutsch and Collins (1951).

THE RESEARCH EXPERIENCE

expectancy of control over events.[6] This attitude is seen as an appropriate variable for Negroes living in segregated ghettos; that is, groups which are blocked from full participation in the society are more likely to feel powerless in that society. Powerlessness is also a variable that seems to have a logical relationship to violent protest. Briefly, it is reasoned that Negroes who feel powerless to change their position or to control crucial decisions that affect them will be more willing to use violent means to get their rights than those who feel some control or efficacy within the social system. For the Negro facing extreme discrimination barriers, an attitude of powerlessness is simply a comment on the society, namely, a belief that all channels for social redress are closed.

Our second attitude measure, racial dissatisfaction, is defined as the degree to which the individual feels that he is being treated badly because of his race. It is a kind of racial alienation in the sense that the individual perceives his position in society to be illegitimate, due to racial discrimination. The Watts violence represented an extreme expression of frustration and discontent. We would expect those highly dissatisfied with their treatment as Negroes to be the participants in such violence. Thus, the "highs" in racial dissatisfaction should be more willing to use violence than the "lows" in this attitude. In comparing our two forms of subjective alienation (powerlessness and racial dissatisfaction), it is important to note that, although we expect some correlation between the two attitudes (a certain amount of resentment and dissatisfaction should accompany the feeling of powerlessness), we propose to show that they make an independent contribution to violence.

UNIFICATION OF PREDICTIVE VARIABLES

We believe that the fullest understanding of violence can be brought to bear by use of a social-psychological design in which the structural variable (racial isolation) is joined with the subjective attitudes of the individual (powerlessness and dissatisfaction).

In this design, we attempt to specify the conditions under which isolation has its strongest effect upon violence. It is reasoned that racial isolation should be most important for determining participation in violence (a) when individuals feel powerless to shape their destiny under existing conditions or (b) when individuals are highly dissatisfied with their racial treatment. Each of the attitudes is seen as a connecting bridge of logic between racial isolation and violence.

For the first case (that of powerlessness), we are stating that a weak attachment to the majority group and its norms should lead to a radical

---

6. This definition of subjective powerlessness is taken from the conceptualization proposed by Seeman (1959).

break from law and order when individuals perceive they cannot effect events important to them; that is, they cannot change their racial position through activity within institutional channels. Violence, in this instance, becomes an alternative pathway of expression and gain. Conversely, racial isolation should have much less effect upon violence when persons feel some control in the system.

For the second case (racial dissatisfaction), we believe isolation should have a far greater effect upon violence when dissatisfaction over racial treatment is intense. Isolation from the society then becomes critical to violence in the sense that the dissatisfied person feels little commitment to the legal order and is more likely to use extreme methods as an outlet for his grievances. Statistically speaking, we expect an interaction effect between isolation and powerlessness, and between isolation and dissatisfaction, in the prediction of violence.[7]

METHODS

Our hypotheses call for measures of intimate white contact, perceived powerlessness, and perceived racial dissatisfaction as independent variables, and willingness to use violence as a dependent variable. The measurement of these variables, and also the sampling techniques, are discussed at this time.

Social Contact

The type of social contact to be measured had to be of an intimate and equal status nature, a kind of contact that would facilitate easy communication between the races. First, each Negro respondent was asked if he had current contact with white people in a series of situations: on the job, in his neighborhood, in organizations to which he belongs, and in other situations (such as shopping). After this general survey of white contacts, the respondent was asked, "Have you ever done anything social with these white people, like going to the movies together or visiting in each other's homes?" (Williams, 1964). The responses formed a simple dichotomous variable: "high" contact scores for those who had done something social (61 per cent of the sample) and "low" contact scores for those who had had little or no social contact (39 per cent).[8]

---

7. In contrast to the mass society perspective, in which structural isolation is viewed as a cause of subjective alienation, we are viewing the two as imperfectly correlated. For example, many Negroes with contact (non-isolates) may still feel powerless due to racial discrimination barriers. We are thus stressing the partial independence of objective and subjective alienation and feel it necessary to consider both variables for the best prediction of violence.

8. As a further indication that this measure was tapping amore intimate form of interracial contact, it can be noted that 88 per cent of those reporting social contact with whites claimed at least one "good friend" ("to whom you can say what you really think") or "close friend" ("to whom you can talk over confidential matters"). Only 10 per cent of those lacking social contact claimed such friendships with white people.

Powerlessness

Following the conceptualization of Melvin Seeman, powerlessness is defined as a low expectancy of control over events (Seeman, 1959). Twelve forced-choice items were used to tap this attitude.[9] The majority of items dealt with expectations of control over the political system. The following is an example:

☐ The world is run by the few people in power, and there is not much the little guy can do about it.

☐ The average citizen can have an influence on government decisions.

After testing the scale items for reliability,[10] the distribution of scores was dichotomized at the median.

Racial Dissatisfaction

The attitude of racial dissatisfaction is defined as the degree to which the individual feels he is being treated badly because of his race. A five-item scale was developed to measure this attitude. The questions asked the Negro respondent to compare his treatment (in such areas as housing, work, and general treatment in the community) with various reference groups, such as the southern Negro or the white. Each of the five questions allows a reply on one of three levels: no dissatisfaction, mild dissatisfaction, and intense dissatisfaction. Typical of the items is the following: "If you compare your opportunities and the treatment you get from whites in Los Angeles with Negroes living in the South, would you say you are much better off—a little better off—or treated about the same as the southern Negro—?" After a reliability check of the items, replies to the dissatisfaction measure were dichotomized into high and low groups.[11] The cut was made conceptually, rather than at the median, yielding 99 "highs" and 213 "lows" in dissatisfaction.[12]

Violence Willingness

The dependent variable of the study is willingness to use violence. Violence is defined in the context of the Watts riot as the willingness to use

---

9. The powerlessness scale was developed by Shephard Liverant, Julian B. Rotter, and Melvin Seeman (see Rotter, 1966).
10. Using the Kuder-Richardson test for reliability, a coefficient of .77 was obtained for the twelve items.
11. Kuder-Richardson coefficient of .84.
12. With a cut at the median, a good many people ($N = 59$) who were mildly dissatisfied on all five items would have been placed in the "high" category. It was decided that a more accurate description of the "high" category would require the person to express maximum dissatisfaction on at least one of the five items and mild dissatisfaction on the other four.

direct aggression against the groups that are believed to be discriminating, such as the police and white merchants. The question used to capture this outlook is, "Would you be willing to use violence to get Negro rights?" With data gathered so shortly after the Watts violence, it was felt that the question would be clearly understood by respondents.[13] At the time of data collection, buildings were still smoldering; violence in the form of looting, burning, and destruction was not a remote possibility, but a tangible reality. The violence-prone group numbered eighty-three.

A second measure of violence asked the person if he had ever used violent methods to get Negro rights.[14] Only sixteen respondents of the 312 reported (or admitted) that they had participated in actual violence. As a result of this very small number the item is used as an indicator of trends but is not employed as a basic dependent variable of the study.

SAMPLE

The sample was composed of 312 Negro males who were heads of the household and between the ages of eighteen and sixty-five. The subjects responded to an interview schedule administered by Negro interviewers. They were chosen by random methods and were interviewed in their own homes or apartments. Both employed and unemployed respondents were included in the sample, although the former were emphasized in the sampling procedure (269 employed in contrast to 43 unemployed). The sample was drawn from three major areas of Los Angeles: a relatively middle-class and integrated area (known as the "Crenshaw" district) and the predominantly lower-class and highly segregated communities of "South Central" and "Watts." The sample could be classified as "disproportional stratified" because the proportion of subjects drawn from each of the three areas does not correspond to the actual distribution of Negroes in Los Angeles. For example, it was decided that an approximate fifty-fifty split between middle- and lower-class respondents would be desirable for later analysis. This meant, however, that Crenshaw (middle-class) Negroes were considerably overrepresented, since their characteristics are not typical of the Los Angeles Negro community as a whole, and the majority of Los Angeles Negroes do not reside in this, or any similar, area.

---

13. As an indication that the question was interpreted in the context of participation in violence of the Watts variety, it can be noted that our question was correlated with approval of the Watts riot ($\phi = .62$).

14. The question, "Have you ever participated in violent action for Negro rights?" was purposely worded in general terms to avoid accusing the respondent of illegal behavior during the Watts violence. However, racial violence in the United States was somewhat rare at that time, so it is likely that most of the sixteen resondents were referring to participation in the Watts violence.

THE RESEARCH EXPERIENCE

RESULTS

We have predicted a greater willingness to use violent methods for three groups: the isolated, the powerless, and the dissatisfied. The data presented in Table 1 confirm these expectations. For all three cases, the percentage differences are statistically significant at better than the .001 level.

The empirical evidence supports our contention that Negroes who are more disengaged from the society, in the structural (isolation) and subjective (powerlessness and racial dissatisfaction) senses, are more likely to view violence as necessary for racial justice than those more firmly tied to the society.

It is one thing to establish a relationship based on action willingness and quite another thing to study actual behavior. Unfortunately, only sixteen of the 312 respondents (5 percent) admitted participation in violent action for Negro rights. This small number did, however, provide some basis for testing our hypotheses. Of the sixteen who participated in violent action, eleven were isolates while only five had social contact. More impressive is the fact that fifteen of the sixteen "violents" scored high in powerlessness, and thirteen of the sixteen felt high degrees of dissatisfaction. Even with a small number, these are definite relationships, encouraging an interpretation that those who are willing to use violence and those who reported actual violent behavior display the same tendency toward powerlessness, racial dissatisfaction, and isolation.

The next task is to explore the interrelationships among our predictive variables. For example, we have argued that powerlessness has a specific meaning to violence (a low expectancy of changing conditions within the institutional framework) that should be more than a generalized disaffection; that is, we expected our measures of powerlessness and racial dissatisfaction to have somewhat unique effects upon violence.

TABLE 1
Percentage Willing to Use Violence, by Social Contact, Powerlessness, and Racial Dissatisfaction

Variables	Not willing (%)	Willing (%)	Total (%)
Social contact[a]			
High	83	17	100 ($N = 192$)
Low	56	44	100 ($N = 110$)
Powerlessness[b]			
High	59	41	100 ($N = 145$)
Low	84	16	100 ($N = 160$)
Racial dissatisfaction[c]			
High	52	48	100 ($N = 98$)
Low	83	17	100 ($N = 212$)

[a]$\chi^2 = 24.93$, $P < .001$.
[b]$\chi^2 = 22.59$, $P < .001$.
[c]$\chi^2 = 30.88$, $P < .001$.
Note: In this table and the tables that follow, there are often less than 312 cases due to missing data for one or more variables.

TABLE 2
Percentage Willing to Use Violence, by Social Contact Controlling for Powerlessness and Racial Dissatisfaction

	Percentage Willing to Use Violence			
	Low power-lessness (%)	High power-lessness (%)	Low dissatis-faction (%)	High dissatis-faction (%)
Low contact ...	23 ($N = 31$)	53 ($N = 78$)	23 ($N = 47$)	59 ($N = 63$)
High contact ..	13 ($N = 123$)	26 ($N = 66$)	15 ($N = 158$)	26 ($N = 34$)
χ^2	$p < .20$	$p < .01$	$p < .20$	$p < .01$

Note: The interaction χ^2 between powerlessness and contact: $P < .05$. The interaction χ^2 between dissatisfaction and contact: $P < .01$.

The data indicated an interaction effect (interaction $\chi^2 = 7.85$; $P < .01$)[15] between the two attitudes. The feeling of powerlessness is a more relevant determiner of violence for the highly dissatisfied or angry Negro. Similarly, racial dissatisfaction is far more important to violence for those who feel powerless. In sum, the data suggest that the powerless Negro is likely to use violence when his feelings of powerlessness are accompanied by intense dissatisfaction with his position. It can be noted, however, that, even among those who were relatively satisfied with racial conditions, powerlessness had some effect upon violence (a 13 per cent difference, $\chi^2 = 5.41$; $P = .02$). Presumably, a low expectancy of exerting control has a somewhat unique effect upon violence.

As a second way of noting an interrelationship between our predictive variables, we turn to the more crucial test of the isolation-extremism perspective in which the effect of racial isolation upon violence is controlled by powerlessness and dissatisfaction.[16] It will be recalled that we expected the isolated people (with a lower commitment to democratic norms and organized channels) to be more violence-prone when these isolated individuals perceive they cannot shape their destiny within the institutional framework (high powerlessness) or when they perceive differential treatment as Negroes and, as a result, are dissatisfied. It is under these subjective states of mind that a weak attachment to the majority group would seem to be most important to extremism. Table 2, addressed to these predictions, shows our hypotheses to be strongly supported in both cases.

15. The χ^2 interaction test is somewhat analogous to the interaction test in the analysis of variance. A total χ^2 is first computed from the two partial tables in which all three variables are operating. Second, χ^2 values are obtained by cross-tabulating each possible pair of variables (e.g., χ^2AB, χ^2AC, and χ^2BC). These three separate χ^2 values are then summed and subtracted from the total χ^2. The residual, or what is left after subtraction, is the interaction χ^2. It can be viewed as the joint or special effect that comes when predictive variables are operating simultaneously. For a further description of this measure, see DuBois and Gold, (1962).
16. The independent variables are moderately intercorrelated. For isolation and powerlessness, the ϕ correlation is .36, $P < .001$; for isolation and dissatisfaction, the ϕ is .40, $P < .001$; for powerlessness and dissatisfaction, the ϕ is .33, $P < .001$.

THE RESEARCH EXPERIENCE

TABLE 3
Percentage Willing to Use Violence, by the Combined Effect of Social Contact, Powerlessness, and Racial Dissatisfaction

	Not willing (%)	Willing (%)	Total (%)
Ideal-type alienated (low contact, high powerlessness, and high dissatisfaction)	35	65	100 (N = 51)
Middles in alienation	76	24	100 (N = 147)
Ideal-type non-alienated (high contact, low powerlessness, and low dissatisfaction)	88	12	100 (N = 107)

Note: $\chi^2 = 49.37$; $P < .001$ (2 d.f.).

Among the powerless and the dissatisfied, racial isolation has a strong effect upon violence commitment. Conversely, the data show that isolation is much less relevant to violence for those with feelings of control in the system and for the more satisfied (in both cases, significant only at the .20 level).[17]

The fact that isolation (as a cause of violence) produces such a small percentage difference for the less alienated subjects calls for a further word of discussion. Apparently, isolation is not only a stronger predictor of violence for the people who feel powerless and dissatisfied, but is *only* a clear and significant determiner of violence for these subjectively alienated persons. For the relatively satisfied and control-oriented groups, the fact of being isolated is not very important in determining violence. This would suggest that a weak normative bond to the majority group (isolation) is not in itself sufficient to explain the participation of the oppressed minority person in violence and that it is the interaction between isolation and feelings of powerlessness (or racial dissatisfaction) that is crucial for predicting violence.

A final attempt at unification involves the cumulative effect of all three of our predictive variables upon violence. Since it was noted that each of the three predictive variables has some effect upon violence (either independently or for specific subgroups), it seemed logical that the combined effect of the three would produce a high violence propensity. Conceptually, a combination of these variables could be seen as ideal types of the alienated and non-alienated Negro. Accordingly, Table 3 arranges the data into these ideal-type combinations.

The group at the top of the table represents the one most detached from society—individuals who are isolated and high in attitudes of powerlessness and dissatisfaction. The group at the bottom of the table is the most involved in the society; these people have intimate white contact, feelings of control, and greater satisfaction with racial conditions. The middle group is made up of those with different combinations of high and low detachment. Note the dramatic difference in willingness to use violence between the "ideal-type"

17. The .05 level is considered significant in this analysis.

alienated group (65 percent willing) and the group most bound to society (only 12 percent willing). The "middles" in alienation display a score in violence between these extremes.

SPURIOUSNESS

It is possible that the relationship between our predictive variables and violence is due to an intercorrelation with other relevant variables. For example, social class should be related both to violence and to our isolation-alienation measures. In addition, we could expect a greater propensity toward violence in geographical areas where an extreme breakdown of legal controls occurred, such as the South Central and Watts areas (in contrast to the Crenshaw area, where no rioting took place). In such segregated ghettos, violence may have been defined by the inhabitants as a legitimate expression, given their intolerable living conditions, a group definition that could override any effects of isolation or alienation upon violence. In short, it seems essential to control our isolation-alienation variables by an index of social class and by ghetto area.[18]

Because of the rather small violent group, it is necessary to examine our predictive variables separately in this analysis of controls. Table 4 presents the original relationship between each of the independent variables and violence, controlled by two areas of residence: the South Central Watts area, at the heart of the curfew zone (where violence occurred), and the Crenshaw area, on the periphery (or outside) of the curfew zone (where violent action

TABLE 4

Percentage Willing to Use Violence by Contact, Powerlessness, and Racial Dissatisfaction, Controlling for Two Geographical Areas and Education

Independent variables	Neighborhood		Education	
	South Central Watts	Crenshaw	Low (high school or less)	High (some college)
Low contact	53^b (N = 62)	33^b (N = 45)	52^b (N = 77)	24^a (N = 33)
High contact	27 (N = 83)	10 (N = 109)	26 (N = 86)	10 (N = 105)
Low powerlessness	22^b (N = 73)	11^a (N = 88)	19^b (N = 67)	14 (N = 93)
High powerlessness	55 (N = 77)	25 (N = 68)	51 (N = 100)	18 (N = 45)
Low dissatisfaction	26^b (N = 81)	12^b (N = 130)	22^b (N = 96)	12 (N = 114)
High dissatisfaction	53 (N = 68)	39 (N = 28)	59 (N = 73)	17 (N = 24)

$^a P < .05.$
$^b P < .01.$

Note: Interaction χ^2 between contact and neighborhood: P is not significant. Interaction χ^2 between powerlessness and neighborhood: $P < .02$. Interaction χ^2 between dissatisfaction and neighborhood: P is not significant. Interaction χ^2 between contact and education: P is not significant. Interaction χ^2 between powerlessness and education: $P < .02$. Interaction χ^2 between dissatisfaction and education: $.05 < P < .10$.

18. Age was also considered as a control variable but was dropped when it was discovered that age was not correlated with violence or the independent variables. The r's ranged from .04 to .09.

was rare). In addition, Table 4 includes a control for education as a measure of social class.[19]

When the ghetto residence of the respondent is held constant, it appears that our independent variables are important in their own right. Education (social class), however, proved to be a more powerful control variable. Among the college educated, only isolation persists as a predictor of violence; powerlessness and racial dissatisfaction virtually drop out. Yet each variable has a very strong effect upon violence among the high school (lower-class) group. In other words, we do not have an instance of spuriousness, where predictive variables are explained away in both partials, but another set of interaction effects—attitudes of powerlessness and dissatisfaction are predictors of violence only among lower-class respondents. These results may be interpreted in several ways. Persons higher in the class structure may have a considerable amount to lose, in terms of occupational prestige and acceptance in white society, by endorsing extreme methods. The college educated (middle class) may be unwilling to risk their position, regardless of feelings of powerlessness and dissatisfaction. These results may further indicate that middle-class norms favoring diplomacy and the use of democratic channels (as opposed to direct aggression) are overriding any tendency toward violence.[20] An extension of this interpretation is that middle-class Negroes may be activists, but non-violent activists, in the civil rights movement. Thus, class norms may be contouring resentment into more organized forms of protest.

CONCLUSIONS

In an attempt to locate the Negro participant in violence, we find that isolated Negroes and Negroes with intense feelings of powerlessness and dissatisfaction are more prone to violent action than those who are less alienated. In addition, isolation has its strongest effect upon violence when individuals feel powerless to control events in the society or when racial dissatisfaction is intensely felt. For those with higher expectations of control or with greater satisfaction regarding racial treatment, isolation has a much smaller and non-significant effect (though in the predicted direction) upon violence. That is, a weak tie with the majority group, per se, appeared insufficient to explain wide-scale participation in extreme action. This study indicates that it is the interaction between a weak bond and a feeling of powerlessness (or dissatisfaction) that is crucial to violent participation.

---

19. For this sample, education was believed to be superior to other indexes of class. It is an index that is freer (than either occupation or income) from the societal restrictions and discrimination that Negroes face. Also it was discovered that Negro occupations in the more deprived ghetto areas were not comparable to the same occupations listed in standardized scales, such as the North-Hatt or Bogue scales.
20. For a discussion of class norms, see Lipset (1960).

Viewed another way, the combined or tandem effect of all three predictive variables produces an important profile of the most violence-prone individuals. Negroes who are isolated, who feel powerless, and who voice a strong disaffection because of discrimination appear to be an extremely volatile group, with 65 percent of this stratum willing to use violence (as contrasted to only 12 percent of the "combined lows" in alienation).

Ghetto area and education were introduced as controls. Each independent variable (taken separately) retained some significant effect upon violence in two geographical areas (dealing with proximity to the Watts violence) and among the less educated respondents. Powerlessness and dissatisfaction, however, had no effect upon violence among the college educated. Several interpretations of this finding were explored.

Applying our findings to the context of the Negro revolt of the last fifteen years, we note an important distinction between the non-violent civil rights activists and the violence-prone group introduced in this study. Suggestive (but non-conclusive) evidence indicates that the participants in organized civil rights protests are more likely to be middle class in origin, to hold considerable optimism for equal rights, and to have greater communication with the majority—this represents a group with "rising expectations" for full equality (Searles & Williams, 1962; Ransford, 1966; Gore & Rotter, 1963). In contrast, this study located a very different population—one whose members are intensely dissatisfied, feel powerless to change their position, and have minimum commitment to the larger society. These Negroes have lost faith in the leaders and institutions of the community and presumably have little hope for improvement through organized protest. For them, violence is a means of communicating with white society; anger can be expressed, control exerted—if only for a brief period.

REFERENCES

Bramson, L. *The Political Context of Sociology.* Princeton: Princeton University Press, 1961.

Clark, K. B. "Group Violence: A Preliminary Study of the Attitudinal Pattern of Its Acceptance and Rejection: A Study of the 1943 Harlem Riot." *Journal of Social Psychology,* 1944, *19,* 319-337.

Deutsch, M., & Collins, M. E. *Interracial Housing.* Minneapolis: University of Minnesota Press, 1951.

DuBois, P. H., & Gold, D. "Some Requirements and Suggestions for Quantitative Methods in Behavioral Science Research." In N. F. Washburne (ed.), *Decisions, Values and Groups.* Vol. 2. New York: Pergamon Press, 1962. Pp. 42-65.

Ellison, R. *Invisible Man.* New York: Random House, 1952.

Fromm, E. "Alienation under Capitalism." In E. Josephson, & M. Josephson (Eds.), *Man Alone.* New York: Dell Publishing Company, 1962. Pp. 56-73.

Gore, P. M., & Rotter, J. B. "A Personality Correlate of Social Action." *Journal of Personality,* 1963, *37,* 58-64.

Horton, J. E., & Thompson, W. E. "Powerlessness and Political Negativism: A Study of Defeated Local Referendums." *American Journal of Sociology,* 1962, *67,* 483-493.

Humphrey, Norman D. *Race Riot.* New York: Dryden Press, 1943.

Kerr, C., & Siegel, A. "The Interindustry Propensity to Strike—An International Comparison." In A. Kornhauser, R. Dubin, and A. M. Ross (eds.), *Industrial Conflict.* New York: McGraw-Hill, 1954. Pp. 189-212.

Kornhauser, W. *The Politics of Mass Society.* New York: Free Press, 1959.

Lipset, S. M. *Political Man: The Social Bases of Politics.* Garden City, N.Y.: Doubleday, 1960.

Neal, A. G., & Seeman, M. "Organizations and Powerlessness: A Test of the Mediation Hypothesis." *American Sociological Review,* 1964, *29,* 216-226.

Ransford, H. E. "Negro Participation in Civil Rights Activity and Violence." Unpublished doctoral dissertation, University of California, Los Angeles, 1966.

Rotter, J. B. "Generalized Expectancies for Internal vs. External Control of Reinforcements." *Psychological Monographs,* 1966, *80* (1, Whole No. 609).

Searles, R., & Williams, J. A., Jr. "Negro College Students' Participation in Sit-Ins." *Social Forces,* 1962, *40,* 215-220.

Seeman, M. "On the Meaning of Alienation." *American Sociological Review,* 1959, *24,* 783-791.

Thompson, W. E., & Horton, J. E. "Political Alienation as a Force in Political Action." *Social Forces,* 1960, *38,* 190-195.

Williams, R., Jr., Dean, J. P., & Suchman, E. A. *Strangers Next Door.* Englewood Cliffs, N.J.: Prentice-Hall, 1964.

Personal Journal ————————————————————————————

B. ON "ISOLATION, POWERLESSNESS, AND VIOLENCE"

During the summer of 1965, I was beginning to gather data for my doctoral dissertation, "Negro Participation in Civil Rights Activity," at UCLA. I was interested in the new forms of militant protest, such as sit-ins and demonstrations, which, at that time, seemed outside of the mainstream of politics. It appeared that, for the first time, black Americans were building up an independent power base and coercing the white majority into concessions by means of economic boycotts and demonstrations that called attention to discriminating institutions. I was eager to find out who these more militant civil rights activists were, the people who were picketing and even willing to go to jail. I was interested in the most militant behavior that existed at that time.

I felt there must be certain personal characteristics and certain struc-

---

Source: Prepared especially for this volume.

tural circumstances that would be conducive to militant outlooks and behavior. In studying protest potential, I became increasingly interested in the concept of alienation. Melvin Seeman was the one person in the department who had written extensively on this concept. Seeman also had the reputation for being a very fair guy, a real human being, and easy to work with in spite of unyielding high standards. I asked him to be the chairman of my committee. He and I worked out two kinds of theoretical perspectives to apply to my dissertation interests: powerlessness and peripherality. It seemed that if power was a key variable, those who felt more control over their own lives and social institutions would be the activists in a kind of militant civil rights thrust. It also seemed that militant activists would be those who were freer from the dominant society's controls, that is, freer from constraints and white reprisals that would channel their behavior into more traditional tracks. This second approach was labeled the peripheral perspective.

For a pretest, I hired a black interviewer who was recommended by a fellow graduate student. He and I began interviewing in South-Central Los Angeles and discovered very quickly that blacks were much more willing to agree with a black interviewer on items such as "Sometimes I hate white people" and "Would you be willing to . . . (do these militant things) . . . ?" This difference in responses to two key variables, hostility and militance, was further accentuated by many of the residents' reactions to a white man in their neighborhood. I frequently had residents question my activity. Some were fearful: "Anything wrong, Officer?" Others accused me of being a plainclothesman or member of the vice squad. It became obvious that my presence in South Central Los Angeles meant just one thing—I was an agent of the system, either a social worker or a cop. I certainly got a feel of the separation that exists between blacks and whites in our society.

We then hired a team of black interviewers. (My interviews were eliminated from the sample.) The four interviewers were young (18-26) and of varied socioeconomic backgrounds. Three held white-collar jobs: a high school teacher, a real estate agent, and a graduate student/part-time engineer. One of these middle-class persons grew up in the South-Central ghetto and was able to establish very good rapport with lower class respondents. The fourth interviewer was a student, also from a lower-class background. In an attempt to establish social class rapport, the two persons from lower-class backgrounds interviewed in the lower- and working-class South-Central and Watts area. Two interview training sessions were held. We discussed wording of items (changing those that were difficult to understand or that might be offensive), and practiced interviewing one another.

After examining about 85 interviews, it was clear that there was a very militant mood; about one-third of the respondents said they would be willing to use violence to get Negro rights. This seemed like an incredibly high proportion to me. I wondered if my questions were worded correctly to convey the meaning that I intended. Also, responses seemed to indicate far

THE RESEARCH EXPERIENCE

more hostility toward whites and willingness to participate in organized demonstrations (even with the threat of jail) than I or anyone else might have predicted. Prior to 1965, urban ghettos had been fairly quiet, except for demonstrations in the South. In fact, I had originally hoped that my dissertation research might uncover some clues as to why Los Angeles had been so quiet. Why so few demonstrations? Was Los Angeles so much better off? Then the Watts Riot broke! Son of a bitch! The whole South-Central area exploded into flames, sirens, and looting. After the first day and night of rioting, things appeared to be subsiding and I drove back to the sample area. Ahead of me on the road I saw some young black men jumping up and down on a car. I pulled a fast U turn and returned to the West side.

After a few panicky days it seemed to me that the study was not ruined but had to be changed, that is, extended. Militance, as I had originally conceived it—a kind of programmed, organized demonstration—had to be expanded to include the raw anger of riot violence. The whole study, then, took on an air of excitement. We felt as if we had a chance to gather historical data, since we were in the field so fast in the aftermath of a riot and were studying both civil rights militance and riot violence. I had some rough hunches that the original theory, dealing with powerlessness and involvement with the white majority group (the peripherality framework), was not lost, and those variables would probably have a great deal to do with the violent activist or the person who said he would be willing to use violence. So we added to the interview schedule some questions like "What were your reactions to the riot?" and "What do you think caused the riot?" These were open-ended questions because I didn't know what people were going to say, and I felt I might lose some valuable responses if the schedule were entirely structured. There were also some questions concerning "How well do you think you're represented by leaders in this area?" I held onto the question that was actually on the interview before the riot: "Would you be willing to use violence to get Negro rights?" So, with a slight addendum to the interview, we returned to the field immediately after the area quieted down and the National Guardsmen let us back in.

The study really became remarkable. Here were a group of trained interviewers, familiar with an interview schedule, used to gaining rapport with the respondents, going into the immediate aftermath of a riot three to six months before any other studies were approaching the field. For these reasons, the McCone Commission (which had been appointed to investigate the causes of the riot) offered to purchase the results of my findings and, to speed up the coding and card punching, they made available to me $1,000, some members of their staff, and free computer time.

Even with all the excitement and the great time and financial boost from McCone Commission resources, the riot aftermath bothered me a little. Of course it bothered me personally: I don't like to see people killed, and I was very angered by the mayor and police chief's explanation of outside agitators and communists as the sole cause of the riot. Such comments made me more eager to get an accurate pulse reading of the people. The riot aftermath was also bothersome to me as a researcher, yet I was intrigued by it. I expected people, in some cases, to express themselves more freely in the aftermath; there might be a lot of suppressed rage that would be openly expressed. On the other hand, people might be frightened in general and more fearful that interviewers were really the police in disguise. In fact, one of the interviewers said that he often had to drink with the respondents to indicate that he was one of the community and not a plainclothesman. In sum, there were plusses and minuses to conducting the research in the aftermath of the riot: It promised the spontaneous, raw expression of emotion that survey research often misses, but also held the disadvantage of people being afraid.

The aftermath of the riot could also have polarized the types of respondents, so that those who were eager to speak in a more militant vein would be expecially likely to agree to be interviewed, whereas those who were extremely fearful and viewed this outbreak as the worst possible disaster might be unlikely to do so. It is possible that I oversampled the most militant, though at the time I remember thinking that everyone seemed to appreciate the opportunity to express his opinion. Even now when I'm troubled by the current critique of surveys as being new ways to exploit black people and the charge that academics are engaging in intellectual colonialism and are raping the minds of minority people for no results or results that only feed the status quo, I am reminded that this was not the attitude of the black respondents in the summer of 1965. People seemed glad to have a chance to be interviewed. They seemed to have an image of UCLA as an objective, impersonal institution with researchers who had no vested interests in the data turning out in a particular way. They had hopes that a true pulse reading of the black people in this community might be felt. Prior to the riot, many politicians had been insensitive—they had never visited Watts and certainly had never asked opinions of the residents. Many respondents seemed delighted that their complaints were being recorded and might be heard at last. (I'm sorry to say that the McCone Commission report let them down. Disillusionment with the mayor and other elected officials never hit the press, and problems with the police were considerably watered down.) In sum, the special after-riot climate was difficult to assess, but the advantages of interviewing during that time seemed to outweigh the disadvantages.

The study, then, was not abandoned but was extended or expanded to include not only civil rights militance but also riot violence. Of course I had some thoughts about the two being quite different. It seemed to me that the civil rights militance that I knew from CORE meetings, for example, involved groups of people with a fairly high degree of education, people who were engaging in programmed, organized activity such as "I'll meet you tomorrow at 8 a.m. and we'll picket this store and then move on to city hall." It was a highly disciplined movement. I felt that Watts, however, would be

THE RESEARCH EXPERIENCE

representative of more spontaneous, at most semiorganized activity—though there was *some* order to the whole thing, such as first destroying stores that sold rancid meat. I was curious about how peripherality and powerlessness would actually work with the two kinds of militance. Watts was the first major riot, and it introduced violence as a new mode of expression. I found I was challenged by this turn of events and looked forward to a dissertation that would be really meaningful and not just a painful required exercise.

To back up a little, I should mention how the mode of sampling changed when the riot began. I had to think fast. First, I decided I did not want to mix the preriot and postriot samples. That is, Watts was such a profound explosion that many responses could have changed between the two time periods. Beginning a postriot sample with limited funds, I was under much more constraint to plan my sampling strategy carefully. That is, the riot forced me to define strategic areas for sampling: the lower-working-class, highly segregated South-Central Watts area, and the middle-class, integrated Crenshaw area. I decided about half of all the respondents should come from South-Central Watts so I could tap the pile-up of frustrations due to police treatment, consumer exploitation, government neglect, and so on which presumably led to the riot. Because I had the civil rights militance idea in mind, because I was very interested in variables dealing with contact and integration, and because I wanted to see how concepts like powerlessness varied from low to high, I thought that the integrated, middle-class Crenshaw area would be a very good contrast group. What I left out was a fairly sizable upper-working-class area in between these extremes.

Second, I had money for just about 300 interviews (the actual total was 312 after the riot), and I wanted 150 from South-Central Watts and 150 from the Crenshaw area. This meant that if I continued to choose random blocks from the entire black sector of L.A., I would not have enough middle-class blacks to look at as a separate group. So I oversampled from the Crenshaw area. I assigned two interviewers to South-Central Watts and two to the Crenshaw area, and they were pulling equal amounts of interviews. Yet, in fact, half of all blacks in L.A. do not live in the Crenshaw section (or in comparable middle-class areas). Thus I got what you would call a disproportional stratified random sample. I was stratifying by area and over-sampling from Crenshaw to give me the case base I needed to test hypotheses. This means of course, that I can generalize to the two areas taken separately but I cannot put the two areas together and generalize to the entire black community without weighting down the Crenshaw sector.

I found I had to make another sampling concession. Ideally, I thought I could carve out a large section on an aerial map, such as South-Central Watts, and then pick random blocks from this area. Next I would go to the actual block to be sure it was not a vacant lot and number the total dwellings or house units on that block. Finally, I would randomly choose households to be interviewed from the mapped blocks. But as I was climbing up trees and over fences, I found that my ideal goal was impossible. Many of the old houses had units in back (with addresses such as 653½, 653¼), and some garages had been converted to homes. It was taking too many hours to map out even a few blocks. So I retreated somewhat from the ideal pattern and used a technique whereby each corner of the block was given a random choice (two coins were flipped: heads-heads—you proceed from the NE corner, heads-tails—SE corner, etc.). In effect, I was still picking random blocks from a universe total area. Once having reached the randomly chosen block, the interviewer was to start from a randomly picked corner and proceed to at least eight units in that block. After eight, he was to switch to another block. This was not allowing every single person an equal probability of getting into the sample. A person could pick up eight interviews in the first eight dwellings and the remaining three-fourths of the block's residents would not be given the same opportunity of getting into the sample. So it was a retreat from the ideal of representativeness, but it was one of those practical decisions that seemed necessary.

There were other problems, too. Toward the end I had a feeling of sloppiness. There were a couple of suspicious interviews in which there was a change from pencil to ink, as if the interviewer had filled in missing items at a later date. There were some interviews with different handwritings. I heard through a graduate student that one of the interviewers had, on one occasion, passed out some of the interviews to friends or to a group of people. If interviewing was a group activity, respondents could have influenced one another. I was really disappointed to learn that the person I had worked with at first, the man who was so careful at the beginning, was the very person I felt was showing sloppiness toward the end. It was one of those famous dissertation nightmares. I removed all of his interviews at one point, which cut the sample size down to about 175, to see if the main relationships still held. They did, but I finally eliminated the most questionable interviews anyway. Everything worked out all right, except that I felt I never regained the same rapport with the interviewer after I had confronted him with my doubts.

There seemed to be genuine interest in the study on the part of the interviewers, especially at first. Right after the riot they seemed to be even more enthusiastic about gathering the first data on what was bound to become an historical event, and one so personally close to them. However, interviewing is exhausting work, and all the interviewers became tired and slightly less thorough (missing a few items) toward the last of the data gathering period. Yet all this present talk about black interviewers feeling they are oppressing their own people, taking their time for something that ultimately will do the black community not much good, was a later ideological stand that developed around 1967. The interviewers with whom I worked seemed as curious as I was to hear peoples' explanations about this event. After several hundred opinions, however, even the most curious person becomes satiated and bored. I think this may be a problem to watch for in any large study.

Other similar personnel problems cropped up at coding time. With the $1,000 from the McCone Commission study, I was able to hire eight to ten people for the tedious, exacting job of sifting and resifting through every interview, sorting responses into appropriate categories (according to my master code book) and marking the correct column on IBM code sheets. Even though I hired fellow UCLA graduate students, some who were personal friends of mine and all conscientious workers from whom I expected utmost care and interest, a certain amount of goofing (similar to the interviewers') developed as they too became tired. Because of the McCone Commission's deadline, the coding sessions were very intense, and normal problems were probably exaggerated. Toward the end of this phase there was a detectable loss in accuracy, especially in the case of open-ended responses. I found wide variations among coders' interpretations. My wife and I had to recode all the open-ended responses and, with the help of a friend or two, we checked and corrected all the others.

Once fieldwork and coding had been completed (and a brief summary report was handed to the McCone Commission) the next big job was my own analysis and writing of the dissertation. I had never done any work with the computer but felt that my multivariate analysis needed more than just the counter-sorter other students had been able to get by with. One of the graduate students familiar with the computer gave me a few quick lessons to get my data going. Even learning how to call out a "canned program" was a nightmare at first, but I finally caught on and even began to enjoy it. When I was able to see what the computer could do with my data, I became so engaged that I often spent 10 to 12 hours a day at the computer center. Because I had such a fragile set of factors that I was pulling together for the first time, and I had to concentrate so hard, many times I went down to the basement of the UCLA Med Center at midnight when there were very few people and all the machines were available. In actuality, I got all of my analyses completed in four or five weeks, which is considered fairly good time. I have to say that among the best advice my chairman gave me was to "get dirty in your data." Even now I do my own computer work, wrestle with that data until it is so familiar to me I am able to see all sorts of relationships that otherwise would very likely remain buried.

After the computer work came the painstaking chapters, reporting the findings, smoothing the theory. Obviously, the whole dissertation story had a happy ending—I did get through. For six months after completion, however, I was so tired of the study I couldn't even look at it, let alone think about publishing. Very gradually my interest picked up. Converting what I considered some of the most important messages from my dissertation into article form is another, briefer tale. Basically, the two main theories, powerlessness and peripherality, remained the same. I saw them as two good representatives of the basic theoretical traditions available to me at the time.

First was a Marxian orientation in which powerlessness fit beautifully. Political protest was seen as a rational response on the part of those (in my case, working- and lower-class blacks) who lacked social access to power. The other major tradition was that of an order model in which participants in deviant action (like violence) are seen as those who often have weakest ties to the majority group. I borrowed from this tradition with the peripherality-isolation framework. I was interested in a structural or behavioral measure that would indicate the degree to which the person was isolated from or engaged with white society in terms of its norms and its values and the constraints that white society could place on the person. In the dissertation, ghetto residence was used as the measure of isolation. However, the ghetto stood for so many things besides amount of contact and involvement in white society (poor schools, police harassment, consumer exploitation, etc.) it seemed to me that contact with whites on an equalitarian basis was a cleaner, more direct measure of a weak normative bond with white society. I reasoned that the black person who lacked equalitarian contact with whites, who saw whites only as employers, social workers, and agents of the system above him, was likely to be more distrustful of white society and was less likely to feel constraint to abide by the white man's system of law and order.

Let me mention two things that have led to unhappy misinterpretations of the isolation variable. A person "isolated" by my measure was not necessarily separated from the black community; he could have been highly involved in black organizations or friendships. That is, I was not talking about persons isolated from all primary group contacts (as some have implied). Secondly, I made no value judgments about the psychological health of the "isolated" person. Such a person is just as likely to have ego strengths as one with white social contact. I was not talking about "misfits," as some have suggested. In order to prevent such misinterpretations, these two points might have been made more clear in the published article.

The powerlessness scale was transplanted from the dissertation to the article without any major changes. However, at the time I was writing the article there was developing, for the first time, a distinction between personal and social powerlessness. In the planning stages of the dissertation I had a rough hunch that powerlessness in the ghetto was not so much a function of fate and luck and chance (individual powerlessness) but rather that it was probably a realistic response on the part of the ghetto residents to tangible barriers and blocked mobility. For this reason, I used Seeman's Swedish scale, which incorporated mainly social- or societal-type items ("The world is run by the few people in power, and there's not much the little guy can do about it") rather than other previous scales that had about 50-50 or even a preponderance of the more individual fate-luck-chance items ("Most of the unhappy things in my life have been due to bad luck"). I regret that I did not make it crystal clear in the article that my scale leaned heavily toward social powerlessness.

In addition to powerlessness, there was another attitudinal variable: feelings of deprivation due to racial discrimination. There were, then, two attitudinal variables (perceived powerlessness and feelings of unjust deprivation) and one structural or behavioral variable (degree of equalitarian contact with whites). I anticipated that combinations of two of these variables and even interaction of all three would produce the greatest propensity to use violence. For a long time, I had thought interaction effects were extremely interesting. We often overlinearize social action with our two variable relationships (the higher the X, the higher the Y, etc.), when in fact many social occurrences are a result of three, four, ten variables interacting dynamically, feeding on each other, producing more than the sum of their parts. Yet so often, statistical interaction has been viewed only as a residue after linear effects are accounted for. I was seeking a level of explanation beyond this. For example, I attempted to explain *why* isolation might only predict violence when combined with feelings of discrimination or feelings of political powerlessness.

If I were doing the article again I would make many changes. For example, I would stretch out my variables from the crude low/high dichotomies to a more sensitive breakdown such as quartiles. I would place much more emphasis on strength of association rather than statistical significance.

Also in retrospect, I would have included at least one more riot measure besides just "Would you be willing to use violence . . . ?" I had another measure of riot reaction, but there were about 75 people who did not answer the question in terms of the coding categories that I had developed (approval of the riot, mixed feelings, disapproval of the riot): To eliminate the 75 would have dropped the case base so low that I would not have been able to do the same analysis. However, the study would have had a much stronger riot context if I had used additional dependent variables that *were* measured, such as: "What was your reaction to the recent riot in Los Angeles?", "What do you think caused the riot?", and an action ideology question that asked respondents to choose among four action strategies to liberate black people (from negotiation to violence). The problem was that inclusion of all of these items would have made the article so complex that I could not have held on to the same distortion-free theory. Instead, the research would have splintered in many directions and would have been difficult to wrap into as neat a package. My demand for order and integration in my own writing and my interest in interaction effects among variables forced me to make a choice: a "together" piece with one dependent variable and clear theoretical linkage or a much looser and more descriptive analysis with a number of riot questions. I decided on the former.

In summary, I feel that conducting social research by way of survey interview techniques can be a very challenging, rewarding, but often frustrating experience. No matter how well the study is planned, there are bound to be unanticipated problems, tough decisions to be made, and compromises along the way. One has to live with the knowledge that there is a degree of error at every step. If the study is carried out with reasonable care, survey research (with interviews) has advantages over other techniques. For example, one can assess the unique significance (and combined effects) of particular variables—variables that may be especially important as a test of a theory or a contribution to policy. Additionally, survey results can be generalized to larger populations with a known degree of accuracy. However, I'm becoming more and more convinced that, at best, survey research illuminates a piece of reality through one prism. Ideally, the topic under investigation should be studied with a combination of methodologies. In particular, the survey method usually falls short in uncovering process and change, deeper meanings, and social patterns *between* groups and individuals. There is a real need to round out survey techniques with more qualitative methods such as participant observation, in-depth interviews, and case studies.

Stella B. Jones ——————————————————————————————

A. GEOGRAPHIC MOBILITY AS SEEN BY THE WIFE AND MOTHER

The recent publication of Vance Packard (1972) can be criticized from the perspective of sound sociological research (Gans, 1972), but it does indicate the current relevance of a discussion of geographical mobility and the American family. Packard is not alone in suggesting that moving can be a disruptive experience for family members. A clinician (Seidenberg, 1972) has suggested that a company executive should reevaluate his own striving after success in terms of what this might do to the wife if she is forced into a geographical move. In the sociological literature the most frequently quoted study on the effects of moving is the 1927 publication of Thomas and Znaniecki. This study of Polish immigrants to America describes the function of an ethnic enclave in softening the effects of geographical mobility, but the main thrust of the study is in depicting the social disorganization attendant upon the moving process. Pauline Young portrays a similar scene and processes in a work based upon her study of Russian immigrants (1932).

Sociological theory in general has been biased in favor of stability, order, and balance on the organizational and individual levels. This bias is expressed, for example, in the social system approach of Talcott Parsons and in many interpretations of symbolic interaction. More recently there has been a growing interest in processes of social change, in the ubiquitous nature of social conflict, and in the functional value of disorder. This is evident, for example, in the approach which Richard Sennett takes in his analysis of city life today (1970). Within the contemporary sociological imagination there is thus a growing ability to discuss with objectivity the pros and cons of, and the conditional factors surrounding, the moving process for individuals and family units.

———————
Source: Stella B. Jones, "Geographic Mobility as Seen by the Wife and Mother," *Journal of Marriage and the Family,* May 1973, pp. 210-218.

This research was made possible by a grant from Allied Van Lines. The data on which this paper is based were generated from a mail-out questionnaire in March 1972. This is a revision of a paper delivered at the Symposium on Moving and The Wife sponsored by Allied Van Lines, Chicago, and the Department of Sociology, Indiana University–Purdue University at Indianapolis.

BACKGROUND

The available literature specifically on geographical mobility is best summarized in terms of general focus and relevant variables which have been explored rather than in terms of accumulative theory. Some of the studies on mobility are primarily focused upon demographic and/or ecological factors. In such studies the city rather than the individual is often used as the unit of analysis (*e.g.*, Reiss & Kitagawa, 1953-54). There has been considerable work in the development of models to explain voluntary geographical mobility (Sabagh, Van Arsdol, & Butler, 1969). This kind of model building, however, has not focused on the generation of a model of adjustment when the move is considered as a given. Social class mobility has received considerably more attention in the literature than geographical mobility. When the adjustments made by individuals involved in geographical mobility are given attention there is a tendency for the focus to remain upon the adjustments of marginal groups such as southern migrants to northern urban centers (Killian, 1953-54). Research on the moving process has generated some descriptive material regarding the impact of specific variables. Length of residence, age, level of education, and the presence of relatives are associated with high "adjustment scores" in a new community (Omari, 1956-57). Migrants change and adjust to the norms of a new community (Killian, 1953-54). Families who move frequently have been able to settle into new communities quickly and without apparent difficulties (Landis & Stoetzer, 1966). The presence of a kin group in the area of destination facilitates the adjustment process (Scharyweller & Seggar, 1967). Extended family relations can be maintained despite geographical mobility (Litwak, 1960). The movement of older people into retirement communities does not cut them off from family contact (Bultena & Marshall, 1970). Parents have more difficulty adjusting to a new community than do their children (Smith & Christopherson, 1966).

The present research assumes that the wife-mother role is important in the process of family relocation. Questionnaires completed by a sample of women who moved with their families are used to describe the structural contingencies in the moving process when this process is viewed from the perspective of status passage and adult socialization. Socialization occurs throughout the life cycle (Brim & Wheeler, 1966). As people face the demands of new situations they change and adjust through the learning mechanisms available in these situations. From this perspective personality is seen as a dynamic, ever-changing phenomenon and not as an entity which was permanently molded during the early years of life. Geographic mobility is one of the channels through which new situations and role demands are confronted by the individual. Obviously the greater the change in the social situation, the greater will be the requirements for new role learning and thus personality modification. Given that geographic mobility (one type of status passage, but one which may simultaneously involve multiple status passages) produces changes in the individual's or family's location in social space, changes in behavior, attitudes, values, and goals will follow. The specific processes and mechanisms through which adult personality transformations occur with status passage need to be explored. This paper is a preliminary report focusing on significant aspects of the moving process as perceived by the wife-mother, and her perception of changes in her behaviors, attitudes, emotionality and information levels as a result of her experiences with geographic mobility.

RESEARCH PROCEDURE

A simple random sample of 500 was drawn from a total population of families moved by a major van line during the previous year (about 200,000). Questionnaires were mailed to 462 current addresses from the list of 500. This questionnaire was sent to the wife in each case. Specific items in the questionnaire were designed to tap such areas as basic satisfaction in former community, satisfaction in present community, sources of information available to the family prior to the move, behavioral and emotional changes associated with the moving process, sources of assistance in the process of adjusting to the new community, and basic information on such factors as age, education, income, and number of children. In responding to some of these items recall was necessary on the part of the respondent, and this poses a problem in terms of accuracy (Rossi, 1955). Some of this problem may have been reduced by the fact that the study involved a sample of fairly recent movers.

The response to the mail-out questionnaire was most gratifying. The normal problems in working with a mailing list were encountered (wrong addresses, incorrect inclusion in the sample, post office error, etc.). In spite of these mechanical problems in getting the questionnaires to the proper persons, 55 per cent (256) of the target population (462) returned completed questionnaires.

DESCRIPTION OF THE SAMPLE

Neither the sample employed in this study, nor the population from which it was drawn, can be taken as representative of all families who move during the course of any given year in the United States. The educational and income statuses of the sample are higher than the national averages. Sixty-two per cent (158) of the women and 83 per cent (213) of the husbands have at the least some college education. Work on the graduate level is reported by 9 per cent (24) of the women, and 27 per cent (69) of the women report that their husbands have done graduate work. When college graduates and those who have attended graduate school are grouped together, 32 per cent (73) of the women and 63 per cent (160) of the husbands are in this high educational category. This same skewedness in the distribution is reflected in the reported total monthly family income. Some 30 per cent (77) of the women report monthly incomes for the family of $1,000 to $1,500, and 45 per cent (115) of the respondents indicate that the family's monthly income exceeds $1,500 per month. There are only eight respondents (three per cent) reporting incomes for the month of less than $500.

The modal response category for the occupation of the husband is managerial (101, or 39 per cent). The next most popular occupation for the husband is professional (69, or 27 per cent). Twelve per cent (32) of the respondents are best described as lower white-collar workers. This is followed by those who are retired (9 per cent, or 24) and then by those who are in positions which can be described as "craftsmen and operatives" (8 per cent, or 22). The lower blue-collar occupations are conspicuous by their absence in this population. Only 1 per cent (three) of the respondents indicate that their husbands are employed in occupations fitting into this general category. In terms of length of time with the employing company, there is a decided preponderance of people who are fairly new with their current company (42 per cent, or 108, of the respondents indicate they have been with their current firm less than two years). In 30 per cent (77) of the cases the move itself was related to a change of employers. Some 85 per cent (218) of the wives report having worked full time at some point in their lives. However, only 19 per cent (50) are currently employed either full- or part-time. Most of the women (52 per cent, or 114) who indicate some prior working experience indicate that they have worked in clerical positions. The second most frequently mentioned employment category for the women was that of professional (31 per cent, or 68).

In terms of age, the modal category of the respondents is 30 to 39 years (34 per cent, or 88, are in this category). Nineteen per cent (48) indicate that they are in the 40 to 49 age category, while 9 per cent (24) state that they are over 60 years of age. There is no obvious clustering in terms of the number of years married. The sample contains a fairly even representation of categories based upon length of time married from 2 years up through and including 28 years. Very few respondents fall in the extreme categories on this dimension. The distribution on the number of children is skewed toward the small family, with the modal category being two children (29 per cent, or 75), followed by one and then three children in terms of number of respondents in each category. There are few families with four children (9 per cent, or 22) and only seven respondents in the total sample with five or more children.

FREQUENCY OF MOVING

In many of the studies on moving, all "movers," regardless of the number of moves, are treated as a single category. This is true, for example, in the classical research on migratory groups. In contrast this study uses a population in which moving itself is a variable. The advantage of this is that it allows for a discussion of specific variables as they are associated with the number of times which the family has moved.

Considerable geographical mobility typifies these families. The modal category for number of times moved is five to six ("move" was operationalized as a change in residence either intra- or intercity). In terms of total number of family moves, 15 per cent (39) of the sample report 11 or more moves. In intercity or long distance moving 32 per cent (82) of the respondents report moving five or more times. There was no opportunity for the respondents to indicate the distance of each of their moves, but if their most recent move is an adequate reflection of previous moves, it would seem that much moving is within a fairly limited geographical area. The modal response category for distance of the most recent move is 500 miles or less.

The occupational positions of the wife and the husband are related to the frequency of moving. The stronger the tendency for the wife to assume full-time employment, the greater are the chances that the family unit has moved often. (Forty per cent of the women who are presently working full time say that they have moved nine or more times, whereas only 20 per cent of those who are not employed or who are working only part time indicate this much moving.) The husband's employment and frequency of moving is important in that there is a disparity between salary increases and expanded work responsibilities with more moves. The most immediate move is described by the respondents as resulting in an increase in salary for a majority of the husbands (60 per cent, or 153). The data reveal, however, that there is not a linear relationship between the number of times moved and salary increases. Through the third move the husband is reported to have received an increase in salary. From the fourth move on there is less likelihood that the move will result in a salary increase. From the wife's perspective, however, the husband is seen as assuming more job responsibility with the move, regardless of the number of times the family has moved. This provides a basis for some disillusionment about the moving process on the part of the wife.

There is a strong tendency for the women in this sample to express the conviction that "the wife is the key person in establishing the home and making the move successful." In the total sample 78 per cent (199) responded in the affirmative to this item. The tendency to see the wife's role as central in the moving process increases with the number of times moved. Some 60 per cent (18) of those respondents who have moved once or twice respond in this way. In families characterized by 11 to 15 moves 80 per cent (20) see the role of the wife as pivotal. This percentage increases to 85 per cent (12) for those who have moved 16 or more times.

The respondents see no necessary diminution of social relationships with increases in the number of times moved. There is no significant relationship between the total number of times moved and agreement with the statement that the respondent is "unable to develop intimate friendships." In fact, most of these wives express the conviction that they have grown in their skills to meet people and form friendships. On the dimension of extended family relationships, there is a strong tendency for the wife to report that families on the move can maintain close ties with relatives. This conviction is more firmly expressed as the number of moves by the family increases. At the same time the importance placed on living near relatives declines with the number of moves which have been made ($\chi^2 = 110.12$; $p < .01$).

There is a subjective dimension to the "frequency of move" situation. In contrast to the objective data, which reveal geographical mobility, there is a strong propensity for the respondents to see themselves as fairly stable in terms of location and as nonchangers in terms of life styles. In response to a question regarding the relative permanence of the present place of residence some 50 per cent (129) indicate that they "see no move in the foreseeable future." In spite of the objective reporting of salary increases and changes in position within the company 56 per cent (143) of the wives see no change in life style for the family.

THE WIFE IN THE PLANNING STAGE

The involvement of the wife during the planning phase of the moving process becomes a critical consideration in the analysis of other dimensions of the move. The data reflect a pattern of husband and wife working together in the making of major decisions surrounding the move. A majority of the respondents report that the decision to move was a "joint decision" (58 per cent, or 148). When there was an opportunity for the family to select the moving company this was also generally a joint decision. There were some 145 respondents reporting some kind of participation on the part of the family in the selection of the moving company. Of these 64 per cent (93) reported that the decision was a joint husband-wife affair.

The happiness of the wife in the new community is related to the degree of her involvement in the planning stages of the move. In 10 per cent (25) of the families in this study the decision to move was made by the husband alone. (In a number of cases the wife felt that neither she nor her husband made the decision, since the move was company directed.) When the husband made the decision unilaterally, 64 per cent (16) of the wives report that they are happy in the new community. Within the category of those who report a joint decision-making process, 79 per cent state that they are happy in the new place of residence. Some 19 of the women indicate that they were consulted by their husband's firm prior to the move. In this category of respondents 84 per cent (16) say that they are happy in the new community.

The availability of information regarding the new community prior to the move and the making of exploratory trips before the final move are important in the anticipatory part of the moving process. The respondents who reported that they are unhappy in the new city were much more likely to also say that they had no information about the city prior to the move. The sources of information which are most strongly related to a high happiness rating are friends and exploratory trips. In those cases where an exploratory trip was made, 83 per cent (160) list the present city as a good place to live. In most cases where such a trip was made the wife accompanied the husband. Those who are unhappy consistently state that they could have used more information in the planning stages of the move. There is, however, no consistent pattern reflecting the kinds of information which they believe would have been most helpful. Regardless of the adjustment in the new community, for example, all respondents suggest that information about schools and the cost of living are very important.

GENERAL ORIENTATION OF RESPONDENTS TO MOVING

The women in this study indicate definite attitudinal positions with respect to statements regarding specific aspects of moving. This general orientation is summarized below in terms of those positions which are expressed by at least 70 per cent of the respondents.

The wives in this sample strongly agree that informal learning mechanisms are more important than formal mechanisms in the preparation for moving. They agree that the best source of learning how to cope with the problems of moving is the actual experience of moving. They feel there is little training in early life or college which helps in the adjustment to moving or preparing them to cope with the many demands and problems faced by a family which is caught up in the moving process. What training is there for selling the family home and purchasing a new one all at the same time? They report that they are less threatened by the prospects of a move now than when they faced a move for the first time.

A strong social mobility orientation is apparent in the sample. The women agree with the statement that it is "better to accept an opportunity for transfer rather than damage chances for upward mobility." They feel that the necessity to live at a distance from relatives should not deter a family from accepting a good job. There was general agreement that a person's position in life depends on his own efforts but they strongly disagree with the statement that it is necessary to sacrifice convictions in order to get ahead.

The respondents place a strong value on friendships and feel that the moving process need not impede the formation of intimate, close friendships. They disagree with the statement that they are unable to develop intimate friends due to moving. They feel that they are *not* rootless, with no community to call "home." They are in agreement with the notion that it is better to have a small number of good, intimate friends rather than a large number of acquaintances who are liked but not well known. They suggest that their children are able to adjust to the moving process. Only 12 per cent (31) report that their children have had difficulty because of the necessity to change schools with frequent family moves.

There is a general positive pattern with respect to the growth potential in the moving experience. The respondents report that (1) they have grown in their ability to cope with stress as a result of their experiences in moving; (2) they have become more flexible and adaptable; (3) they have broader ranging interests; (4) they have developed skills in meeting people and making friends; and (5) they are more understanding of and accepting of other people, cultures, and customs. A few of the respondents have written telling how they have become more religious and developed "finer character" (less selfish and less materialistic) due to the moving experience.

TABLE 1
The Moving Process as It Affects the Wife's Allocation of Time to Selected Roles (N = 256)

Wife Reports Considerable Time Devoted To:	Typically in Former Community	Two Weeks Prior to Moving	During First Two Weeks Here	Currently in This Community
Routine housekeeping	56%	47%	60%	57%
Visiting with neighbors	21	31	8	15
Visiting with friends outside of the neighborhood	27	31	6	16
Visiting with relatives	20	23	13	8
Entertaining husband's business associates	10	4	1	8
Being entertained by husband's business associates	5	12	4	5
Doing volunteer work (Scouts, hospital, etc.)	12	3	0	6
PTA, Room Mother, other school activities	10	2	1	5
Attending meetings of clubs or organizations	25	8	2	19
Attending church-related activities.	30	16	8	24
Chauffeuring children to their activities	21	15	12	19
Pursuing her own hobbies and interests	34	6	5	34
Writing letters to friends	19	8	20	25
Writing letters to relatives	26	9	21	30
Reading newspapers, magazines, books	45	12	16	45
Watching TV	27	19	12	25
Helping entertain children's friends	18	9	6	19
Relaxing "at home" with husband (just the two of you)	45	20	32	46
Participating in family games, recreation, picnics, etc.	30	11	12	30
Going out with husband to dinner, movies, theater, etc.	39	24	23	33
Giving emotional support to husband	51	47	48	45
Giving emotional support to children	35	39	41	35

THE RESEARCH EXPERIENCE

BEHAVIORAL CHANGES IN THE MOST RECENT MOVING EXPERIENCE

When moving is seen in terms of socialization, changes in the role demands upon the wife can be expected to produce changes in her normal activities. Changes in the way that she spends her time or in the apportionment of her time among various activities affect in turn her self-concept, attitudes, relationships with her family and others, and her emotional life. This study shows that a definite change in behavior occurs in terms of the amount of time allocated to specific activities during the moving process. Table 1 shows that quite predictable changes occur, for example, in the amount of time spent visiting friends and neighbors, doing volunteer work, pursuing personal hobbies and interests, and reading. These changes are clearly indicated by the time sequence analysis used. In the questionnaire the respondents were asked to specify how much time they devoted to selected activities at four different time periods (typically in former community, two weeks prior to the move, two weeks after the move, and currently in the present community).

EMOTIONALITY DURING THE MOVING PROCESS

The changes in demands placed upon the wife by the moving process have an impact upon the emotional dimension of her life. These changes are summarized in Table 2 in a time sequence format similar to the presentation of the data on behavioral changes. As this table reveals, there are marked changes in the percentage of respondents reporting they experienced specific emotions during the different phases of the moving process. For the most part these changes reflect a condition of stress or anxiety during the actual relocation. Only a few of the trends are summarized below.

TABLE 2
The Impact of the Moving Process on the Wife Emotionally (N = 256)

Wife Reported She Frequently:	Typically in Former Community	Two Weeks Prior to Moving	During First Two Weeks Here	Currently in this Community
Felt excited or exhilarated	33%	60%	51%	33%
Felt lonely or remote from other people	19	16	33	20
Felt depressed or quite unhappy ..	15	18	24	13
Had moments when cried	10	14	15	5
Felt anxious	18	42	34	13
Felt irritable, became annoyed	14	24	24	11
Had trouble with headaches	12	16	15	7
Felt nervous or "on-edge"	14	34	28	20
Had trouble sleeping	8	19	25	9
Couldn't get going to take care of things	8	8	10	8
Had time on her hands	16	4	7	16

A marked increase in feelings of excitement or exhilaration is reported in the total sample during the two weeks before and the two weeks after the move. The women who are in the "empty nest" stage of the family cycle are the most likely to indicate feelings of excitement (in the 50 to 59 age category 81 per cent, or 13, of the women respond in this direction).

The feeling of being lonely or remote from other people is more likely to occur during the first two weeks in the new community. Age is significant in relation to these feelings ($\chi^2 = 60.7$; $p < .01$). The older the woman the less likely she is to express feelings of being lonely in relation to the move. The women who are in the 20- to 29-year age category are the most likely to say that they feel lonely or remote from other people during the two weeks prior to the move and immediately after the move. There is also a significant relationship between the amount of education and feelings of loneliness ($\chi^2 = 146.2$; $p < .01$). The decisive cutting point here is between college graduates and those with some college work or less. Those with less formal education are more likely to say that they feel lonely and remote from others during the actual moving period. It is of interest to note that there is a significant relationship when the wife's education is used but that the relationship does not hold when the husband's education is used.

As Table 2 reveals, there is a slight increase in feelings of depression or unhappiness two weeks prior to the move and a further increase during the first two weeks in the new community. In terms of age the most unhappy and depressed group in the sample is the 40 to 49 age category. The greater the reported formal education the *less* the tendency to report feelings of depression or unhappiness during the first two weeks in the new community ($\chi^2 = 151.8$; $p < .01$). The wife experiences more difficulty in adjustment if her husband is employed in the categories of clerical and kindred workers or craftsmen and kindred workers.

An interesting variable in the area of emotionality is the item regarding "moments when I cried." The proportion of the sample reporting that they cried often is *not* large, but the crying which is reported is definitely related to phases in the moving process. There is an increase in crying behavior during the two weeks before the move and in the first two weeks after the move to the new community. Age is the most important single predictor of crying behavior during the first two weeks in the new community ($\chi^2 = 54.2$; $p < .05$). In the 60 and older category none of the respondents report crying. The 40 to 49 age group is characterized by a larger proportion who report that they cry often during the moving process than any of the other age categories.

MECHANISMS USED IN THE ADJUSTMENT TO THE NEW COMMUNITY

The mechanisms which facilitate adjustment to the new community are indicated in rank order according to their perceived importance in Table 3.

TABLE 3
Mechanisms Facilitating Adjustment to a New Community (N = 256)

Mechanism	Helpful	Not Helpful	Not Relevant or No Contact
Arrival of furniture and other familiar objects	86%	4%	7%
Return to "normal" schedule	75	6	14
Neighbors in the new neighborhood	70	14	14
Newspapers	62	17	15
Familiar chain stores, restaurants, brands	60	17	19
Favorite family TV programs	56	17	25
Real estate agents	56	24	27
Letters from friends	55	10	31
Letters from relatives	53	10	34
Husband's co-workers	48	16	31
Friends in new community known prior to moving here	48	4	45
Presence of family pets	41	5	49
Church and church activities	40	14	42
Firm's personnel office	26	17	55
School teacher or school guidance counselor	26	11	55
Minister, rabbi, or priest	24	15	56
Relatives living in the new community	21	2	72
National organizations in which membership was transferred	16	5	75

Note: Percentage on any single item may be less than 100% due to nonresponse.

Those specific mechanisms which are reported as most helpful are (1) the arrival of furniture and other familiar objects; (2) the return to a "normal" schedule; (3) the neighbors in the new neighborhood; (4) familiar chain stores and restaurants; (5) favorite family TV programs; and (6) real estate agents.

If the wife works full time in the new location this reduces the amount of help which she receives from the neighbors in the adjustment process. There is a significant relationship between the perceived helpfulness of neighbors and reported monthly income ($\chi^2 = 147.4$; $p < .01$). The less the monthly income, the greater the propensity to indicate that there is either no contact or that neighbors are not relevant in the adjustment. This research brings into sharp relief the vital role played by neighbors and other casual friendship contacts in the adjustment process of the wife and family in their new home. Of all interpersonal contacts, neighbors are the most significant. If the neighbors are seen as unfriendly, there is a much greater tendency to report unhappiness in the new city.

Notions held regarding interpersonal relationships are one of the factors which make for a strong tendency for the respondents to select the summer months (especially June) as the time to move. This selection changes to March, April, or May for those who are 50 or older. The most frequent reason given for the selection of the summer months or other months characterized by having "good weather" is that friendships will be easier to develop at this time of the year as people are inclined to be out in their yards, etc. The shift in preference to months other than June after the school-age children are out of the home suggests the belief that casual neighboring patterns leading to friendship formation among adults easily develop during any of the "good weather months." Women value casual, informal occasions for meeting people. Whether or not friendship formation is in reality facilitated by arrival in the new community between June and August is questionable, as a larger proportion of the neighbors are away on vacation during the summer months than at any other time during the year.

SUMMARY

The topic of family geographical mobility can be understood within the general perspective of socialization. Individual members of the family such as the wife-mother are often called upon to undergo changes in status and to learn new roles when the family moves. Adjustment to moving is dependent in part upon the mechanisms which are available to assist individual family members as they go through status passages attendant on the moving process.

In this study the data reveal that women are able to make a positive adjustment in most cases. There is, however, indication of severe strain at specific stages in the moving process. This strain is more pronounced within specified categories on the dimensions of age, education, and income.

As in the case of other socialization experiences, the involvement of the person undergoing socialization (the wife-mother becoming active in planning for the move), familiarity with new role demands (prior experiences with moving), and peer associations (friendly neighbors) are all important in easing the trauma of status passage. There are some unique features of moving which make it different from other socialization processes. One of these is the importance of material artifacts (chain stores, newspapers, familiar brand names) and personal possessions (furniture and other household items) in the moving process. This dimension has received only limited attention in the sociological studies of socialization. Status degradation ceremonies generally involve a stripping away of personal possessions. In other situations the accumulation of possessions or the maintenance of given objects becomes part of the socialization experience and merits further attention.

REFERENCES

Brim, Orville, & Stanton Wheeler. *Socialization After Childhood*. New York: Wiley, 1966.
Bultena, Gordon L., & Douglas G. Marshall. "Family patterns of migrant and non-migrant retirees." *Journal of Marriage and the Family*, 1970, 32 (February): 89-93.
Canan, Ruth S. *The American Family*. New York: Thomas Y. Crowell, 1963.
Gans, Herbert J. "Stimulus response: Vance Packard misperceives the way most American movers live." *Psychology Today*, 1972, 6 (September): 20-26.

Killian, Lewis. "The adjustment of southern white migrants to northern urban norms." *Social Forces*, 1953-54, 32: 66-69.

Landis, Judson, & Louis Stoetzer. "Migrant families: an exploratory study of middle class migrant families." *Journal of Marriage and the Family*, 1966, 28 (February): 51-53.

Litwak, Eugene. "Geographic mobility and extended family cohesion." *American Sociological Review*, 1960, 25 (February): 385-393.

Omari, Thompson Peter. "Factors associated with urban adjustment of rural southern migrants." *Social Forces*, 1956-1957, 35: 47-53.

Packard, Vance. *A Nation of Strangers*. New York: David McKay, 1972.

Reiss, Albert J., & Evelyn Kitagawa. "Demographic characteristics and job mobility of migrants of six cities." *Social Forces*, 1953-1954, 32: 70-75.

Rossi, Peter H. *Why Families Move: A Study in the Social Psychology of Urban Residential Mobility*. Glencoe: The Free Press, 1955.

Sabagh, George, Maurice Van Arsdol, & Edgar Butler. "Some determinants of intra-metropolitan residential mobility: conceptual considerations." *Social Forces*, 1969, 48: 88-98.

Schwaryweller, Harry K., & John Seggar. "Kinship involvement: a factor in the adjustment of rural migrants." *Journal of Marriage and the Family*, 1967, 29 (November): 662-671.

Seidenberg, Robert. "Dear Mr. Success: Consider your wife." *The Wall Street Journal* Monday, February 7, 1972.

Sennett, Richard. *The Uses of Disorder*. New York: Vintage Books, 1970.

Smith, Ramona, & Victor A. Christopherson. "Migration and family adjustment." *Journal of Home Economics*, 1966, 58 (September): 670-671.

Thomas, William, & Florian Znaniecki. *The Polish Peasant in Europe and America*. New York: Knopf, 1927.

Young, Pauline. *The Pilgrims of Russian-Town*. Chicago: University of Chicago Press, 1932.

Personal Journal ————————————————————————————————

B. PERSONAL REFLECTIONS ON THE RESEARCH IN PROCESS

While returning home from a speaking engagement which came as a result of my research on the effects of moving upon the wife-mother, I reflected on the process of doing the initial study, and it seemed natural to think of the research experience as analogous to a journey across the country. The process of doing research can be an experience with many serendipitous turns. Given the transportation and research sophistication available today, there is a temptation to think of both as nonproblematic. In reality the traveler and the researcher alike find that the best laid plans must frequently be altered

---

Source: Prepared especially for this volume.

in transit. Unexpected delays occur, last-minute changes in routing are sometimes necessary, and more time and money may be needed than originally planned. Such unexpected factors may add to or detract from the total travel or research experience.

POINT OF DEPARTURE

Unless you want to stay where you are (there have been times when I have wondered why I did not leave well enough alone), the first step in getting a research project underway is the selection of a problem. By this I do not mean to imply that all kinds of problems are lying around waiting to be "selected" from a problem cafeteria.

Prior to the selection of this specific problem, I spent an extended time reading in the area of adult socialization, with a direct focus upon status passage. This study was summarized in a paper which became the final step in my Ph.D. prelims in the summer of 1972. From this work I became very interested in the effects status passage has upon the adult personality, and this interest gradually was more narrowly defined as I considered the adult female and her traditional wife-mother role. Possible research areas which seemed feasible at this stage included (1) the personality changes resulting from a change in status from married to widowed and (2) the personality changes resulting from geographical mobility which may or may not be accompanied by changes in social status. Both of these general problem areas aroused my curiosity and flowed directly out of the theoretical concerns I had been pursuing extensively in the literature.

Being quite pragmatic about the whole thing—I had to have a dissertation, and the sooner the better—I started exploring the availability of a population for study. Decision: Pursue the question for which there was a relevant population available and for which the financial cost would be the least. A contact was made with the local department of health which resulted in the information that a listing of males dying in accidents, as well as the wife's name and address, could be obtained. Most encouraging. I had yet to develop any ideas relative to the procedures I might follow in obtaining a relevant population for the geographic mobility study. The questions I wished to ask on geographic mobility required a national sample. That would be expensive, and no funding was in sight. Obviously, the expedient thing to do was to look at the passage of women into the status of widowhood.

At this preliminary stage in the process of problem selection and development, the sociology department in which my husband has a position (which I will call City University) began planning a symposium on the effects of geographical mobility upon the wife-mother. This symposium was to be funded by a major van line. It occurred to me (at the suggestion of my husband) that I might generate some input for this occasion. I assumed that being female would be helpful to my cause. The symposium format called for the presentation of original research, and, as it turned out, all of the other participants in the symposium were men. This format meant that I would need to develop a research design, get funding from the van line, and gain acceptance as part of the symposium. Practically overnight, I drew up a request for funding in which it was proposed that a mail-out questionnaire be sent to a random sample of the families moved by this van line during the previous year. In return I offered to present a paper reporting the research findings at the symposium scheduled for the following May or June. It was then the middle of December!

Frequent conversations via long distance telephone with the chairman of my dissertation committee were held throughout the process of problem selection and development. He was totally in accord with submitting the research proposal to the van line for funding, despite the extremely limited time that would be available for the development of an instrument and carrying out the research. In order to facilitate the research, he suggested that the final rewriting of my paper on adult socialization be set aside until after the symposium. Thus, interestingly, I conducted the research for my dissertation before completing the requirements for doctoral candidacy. A real mistake at this point was my failure to discuss with my chairman the proposed research budget that I submitted to the van lines. Much later in the game, when it became painfully evident that I had underestimated certain costs, I thought back to a course in study design taught by the chairman. He had warned of the tendency to underestimate research costs and had outlined procedures to be followed in developing budget proposals to compensate for this tendency. I charge the mistakes in underestimating costs to the time pressures I was under at this point. If a funding proposal was to be submitted, it had to be done without delay. There was simply no time for thinking or consulting. Fortunately, I had been advised to allow for a consulting fee for my work on the project (as evidence of my naiveté, I was quite resistant to this when first proposed), and this more than covered the unexpected additional expenses.

IN FLIGHT

The van line was most receptive to the research proposal. The relative ease of access to funding and a mailing list was a complete surprise to me, given the understanding I had of how difficult it can be to gain access into organizations to do research. (Much attention had been devoted to the art of gaining access to organizations in methods courses in graduate school. Also, I had experienced near failure in securing access on a previous research project.)

The research proposal and other details of the symposium were discussed at one lengthy meeting with van line personnel in January. The van line approved the proposed research project at this meeting, without my having to do any kind of a selling job. I now look back on my naiveté with great amusement, as they knew far better than I what was in such a research project for them. It was not until months later that I slowly came to see the practical returns this research had for the moving industry.

The meeting in January was followed by a number of telephone contacts and a visit to the campus by van line representatives before the time of the symposium. The campus was about 200 miles from the main offices of the van line. I soon found these meetings required quite an investment of my time; in addition to the actual meeting time, there was the time required to prepare for the meetings and the travel time. At the January meeting, which was held in the company offices, I was very impressed with the personnel from the van line and their public relations firm—vice-presidents of large corporations had not been my daily associates nor obviously had they been for the other two sociologists present.

Prior to the January meeting, I had decided that I would like a simple random sample of all the families moved by the van line in 1971 within the United States (Alaska and Hawaii included). The total sample was to include 500 names and addresses of families. The funding agency assured me that they had a computer program using a table of random numbers with which to select the cases. Further, their program would print out the cases on gummed address labels on 8½" x 14" sheets. (They assumed that I would want to use these labels on the envelopes for mailing out the questionnaires, saving all that typing of addresses.) The van line person responsible for drawing the sample assured me that he would have this job scheduled for immediate attention. There would be no problem in having the sample lists to me by the first of February. Just simple routine for them.

Once I had secured funding of the project and had worked out the details for drawing the sample, there was one other thing I desired of the van line at the time of the January meeting—a letter, formulated by the van line on their letterhead and supporting the research, to accompany the question-naire. I felt that such a letter, in addition to the one I would generate and send on a university letterhead, would definitely increase the legitimacy of the research and thus the response rate. This suggestion was negatively received, but most politely. Given their experience in doing research, they were confident that the response rate would be much higher if there were no obvious connection with any van line. I was surprised by their response, but if they did not wish to supply the letter, it seemed the better part of wisdom not to press the matter further. Later, when questionnaires started coming in and I read the spontaneous comments that respondents wrote in so freely, I thought back to this meeting. Obviously, the thinking of the van line people was quite correct. My failure to gain the desired letter had contributed to the success of the project.

Overall, the January meeting was most valuable. Not only were some of the details concerning the drawing of the sample worked out, but a very fine

THE RESEARCH EXPERIENCE

rapport was developed which has continued to the present time. I came away from the meeting assured of the van line's interest in the success of the project and their complete cooperation. There was a general understanding that they would have the opportunity to suggest specific questions for the questionnaire; but as it turned out, they did not actually contribute to its construction. I also learned at this meeting that a large corporation does not just hand an individual researcher a check made out to her. The first thing I had to do upon returning to my campus was to obtain an account number so that the van line could send me its check. It really seemed that the research project was off the ground, and at this point I envisioned no real hang-ups. Indeed, I was most optimistic.

Before proceeding further with the actual research story, a brief note on my situation while conducting the research seems in order. Many of the events I have chosen to discuss seem peculiar even to me. Certainly they are not the type of thing I have found discussed at length in research methods texts. But doing research when you are a member of the faculty of a small college with a teaching emphasis is a very different thing from doing research in a major university, with all of its resources at your immediate disposal. Or so it has been in my experience. Not only might the facilities for doing research at a certain institution leave much to be desired, but its value system may give very low priority to the conduct of research by its faculty. I was caught up in this particular scene as my husband had completed his program in sociology some two years earlier and accepted a position with a university in the midwest—some 2,500 miles from the department in which I was completing my graduate work. Fortunately, my interest in doing research and the dissertation pressures were great enough that, despite my immediate situation, I became involved in this study. It proved to be a rather unique research experience in that I received mass media coverage and speaking assignments which do not normally follow from a dissertation project.

Admittedly, this unanticipated fallout did not occur because of the sociological sophistication of the design and the conduct of the research. It was due strictly to the timeliness of the research problem; there is currently considerable interest in a number of circles in the problems faced by the wife-mother as she moves across country with her vagabond family.

My first inkling of the role my particular situation was to play in the conduct of this piece of research came upon my return to campus. The first day back I asked a colleague about the procedure for having an account number set up to handle the research funds. Armed with this information, I set off to see the dispenser of such account numbers. Much to my surprise (in fact, great dismay) the institution had no system for handling such funds, and I was informed that it would be quite impossible to even consider setting one up. I returned with this smashing bit of news and discussed it with an interested colleague, whose interest was immediate because he had a $25,000 research grant pending. He had been with the institution for five years (I had been there less than five months), and he knew more people and had more angles to pursue than I did. He proved to be of invaluable assistance as, for two weeks, we met with administrative types to explain the great fallout that accrues to an institution when its faculty does research. It was finally decided that the risk would not be too great, and I received the needed account number, and the handling of the funds went smoothly from that point on.

Our expectations to the contrary, however, this did not result in the establishment of a procedure which would be automatic whenever a faculty member received a research grant. My colleague later spent over six months negotiating with the institution after his grant application had been approved before it agreed to administer his grant funds. Currently, I have funds for another small study available whenever I have time to go ahead with the research. I have no idea what the reaction of this institution would have been to administering these funds (I say "would have been" as I have now joined the faculty of another institution). This whole question of whether or not to administer research funds was about as unexpected as anything could have been. Certainly the only discussion of the institution and the administration of research funds I had ever heard in methods classes was concerning the advisability of allowing for the percentage charged by the institution ("overhead") in setting up the budget for the research project.

Personnel

Throughout the course of this research it was difficult to secure competent auxiliary help. The short-term nature of the project contributed both to the urgency of getting specific tasks completed and to the problem of obtaining people who wanted only temporary work. Time pressures were intense from the moment the project was undertaken. There were only five months between the date of the meeting in January at which final approval and funding of the project were granted and the symposium in June. During these five months, a questionnaire had to be developed, printed, mailed out, completed and returned, data had to be coded, punched on cards, and analyzed, and a research report had to be written and presented.

In the final stages of the project, keypunching became a crucial issue. To the best of my knowledge there was not an agency in the city set up to do small jobs of this type on contract. The computer center at my institution was too busy and lacked the equipment to do the job the way I wanted it done. At City University it would have been at least three weeks before they could start the job. The research report was scheduled to be read in four weeks! At that point my husband remembered the head of the educational computer center located on the university's north-end campus. We had met him at a party a few months previously and a contact was made which produced two key punchers who wanted work. Because they competed with each other for the lion's share of the work, they were motivated to put in very long hours each evening after finishing their regular duties. Fortunately, they were also very competent. A random check of their work produced no errors which could be attributed to them. Instead errors were the result of unclear codes. Lesson learned: When coding, slow down and write more legibly. Later I learned that the very complex coding schemes I had developed for some of the open-ended questions were quite unwieldy (except for the open-ended questions, the questionnaire was precoded). I really got carried away with preserving information, which meant an expenditure of additional time on my part and additional use of computer time in order to revise the coding into a usable form.

With exactly three weeks to go until the day of the symposium, I met the consultants in the computer center at City University. The computer facilities on my campus were totally inadequate, and I had arranged to use those at City University. This was inconvenient, since I had to drive through the downtown area every time I went to the computer center from my campus. The computer consultants proved to be friendly and very cooperative, but we were new to each other and had different styles of working. In time, we came to understand each other and to work well together. During the data analysis for this research report, the SPSS program was not available (it became available three months later!) nor was any computer program of similar capabilities. Therefore, it was necessary to run the data on two different and very limited programs in order to produce frequency distributions and then cross tabulations. I had to learn to work with two new programs—fortunately, they were simple, but this simplicity proved extremely frustrating in the end, as their capacities were unbelievably limited. It took four passes to generate the frequency distributions, and I lost track of the number of passes required to generate the desired cross tabulations.

It came as a shock to learn that the computer center was closed each evening and at noon on Saturdays for the weekend. I had anticipated working the late evening hours (as I had always done) when few people are using the equipment and the turn-around time is a matter of minutes. Certainly I needed to work at night, as I was in the process of winding up my teaching responsibilities for the year and the crunch of papers and exams had begun. Basically, the computer center personnel were cooperative and really tried to be helpful. The very limited time period out of each 24 hours that the consultants and equipment were available greatly extended the time required to complete the data runs and meant I had to spend a great deal of time driving back and forth from my campus to the computer center—two and sometimes three trips a day.

The last computer run was completed with only four days remaining in which to analyze the output and write the research report. This was totally contrary to everything I had learned about writing research reports. First, you do not write a research report when you are only in the preliminary stages of data analysis, and I do consider frequency distributions and bivariate cross tabulations the preliminary steps in the data analysis process. Second, it takes time (a lot of it) to go through mountains of computer output. Third, research reports are not something the researcher can sit down to a typewriter and peck out—and that's it. Not at all. Papers are written the first time so that they can be rewritten and probably rewritten again before presentation. My consolation, since I had no choice except to come up with something to read four days hence, was that the paper's audience would be very limited and that, among those present, there would be very few sociologists. Fortunately for my feelings at that moment, I had no inkling whatever that, later, that very paper would be published practically verbatim in a professional journal.

Sample

Personnel was not the only area in which I encountered unanticipated problems and hang-ups. At the meeting in January the funding agency agreed to draw a simple random sample from all the families moved by their company in 1971 (universe of 200,000). It was further agreed to draw the sample using a computer program which utilizes a table of random numbers for selecting the cases. At the time of that meeting they anticipated getting the sample list to me in approximately two weeks (by February 1).

Immediately following the formal part of the January meeting, a discussion of the procedural details for drawing the sample was initiated by the van line employee charged with this responsibility. All was not quite as simple as it had seemed earlier in the meeting. He explained that for a sample of 500 cases, which I had set, they should draw a random sample of 2,000. It seemed that such a safety margin was necessary since many of the cases would not have the family name but the employer's name (i.e., General Electric). Also, in some cases addresses would be incomplete. Obviously this would reduce the true randomness of the sample, but since this was the best available, it seemed that I would have to work with it.

Early in February the sample list still had not been received. When I chatted with my contact person I learned that they did not have a computer program for selecting cases using a table of random numbers after all. (They had been quite sincere in thinking they did.) It would be too time-consuming to develop the program at this point. They did have available a program which would select the first case randomly and then every nth case thereafter. I was now quite agreeable to the use of this program.

It was the end of February before the sample list of 2,000 names and addresses on gummed labels was received. I went through the sheets and eliminated all listings for which there was (1) no name, (2) only the firm's name, or (3) an obviously incomplete address—like no city. In doing this I discovered that single individuals had been included on the list (contrary to specifications), along with families. Consequently, the list was checked again and all obvious singles were eliminated. From those left, apparent families with complete addresses, a simple random sample of 500 was drawn using a table of random numbers.

I failed to anticipate the errors in these "complete addresses," and it was not until after the mailing of the questionnaires that I was to learn how grossly inaccurate they were. They came back stamped by the post office with messages such as "unknown at this address," "no such post office in state," "no such street." The inaccuracies were due to a number of factors. First, this was a mobile population, and a number had already moved on without leaving a forwarding address. This had been anticipated, and replacement sampling had been planned to meet this contingency. Second, many errors had occurred because the van line's records had been generated from carbon copies of their agents' bills of lading. By the time these copies got to key punchers in the home office, they frequently were not altogether legible. This resulted not only in errors in addresses but also in gross misspelling of customers' names. The third problem in getting questionnaires to the people on the sample list grew out of post office error. My awareness of the failure of the post office to deliver the questionnaire to the addressee arose from the postal system's inconsistency in the ways it handled multiple items addressed to the same individual. When questionnaires were not returned by either the post office or the subject, a follow-up letter was mailed, and then the follow-up letter might be returned by the post office as undeliverable. In some cases the post office was so slow in returning the questionnaire as undeliverable that a follow-up letter was sent out before the questionnaire came back—but the follow-up letter was never returned. For those cases in which there was no response to the mailings and nothing returned by the post office, a third mailing (remailing the questionnaire) was sent. In a few instances this third mailing was returned by the post office as undeliverable. Whatever happened to the first two mailings to those individuals remains a mystery. Some error on the part of the postal system is to be anticipated, but the extent of the error uncovered in this study seems unreasonable.

As a result of the inaccuracies in the sample list and the failures of the postal system to function efficiently, a much larger replacement sample was necessitated than originally planned. Obviously, this added to the costs—additional stamps and postal cards had to be purchased. But it also added to the demands on my time. I was now doing all the typing, with some help from my husband; we got very good at addressing envelopes. Despite the attempt to maintain the sample at 500 through replacement sampling for those questionnaires that were not deliverable, the sample size was reduced to 462. It was assumed that in cases in which no completed questionnaire had been received and none of the three mailings had been returned by the post office as undeliverable, it was a case of simple nonresponse. The subject did not wish to participate or was unable to do so for some reason.

A rather interesting source of error in the sample which resulted in people being included who did not meet the criteria was quite unanticipated.

There were at least ten women who received the questionnaire but responded that they had not moved in 1971 or, for that matter, not in the last 5, 10, or even 15 years. The first two questionnaires returned uncompleted with no comment other than this really blew my mind—a new way to refuse to participate in a study! Fortunately, others went into more detail: "I only received a shipment of furniture from my parents," or "I inherited some furniture from an estate." Later I discussed this with the funding agency, and they indicated that a considerable percentage of their moving business is of this type; no people are involved in the move—just furniture. There is no way to tell from their files which cases are of this type. Next time I will aniticipate this source of sample loss and make allowances for it.

There was also loss in the sample as originally drawn due to the death of subjects. This was unusually high, given that this was a one-shot study (such mortality is not uncommon in a longitudinal study). Death was a factor in this study because 9 percent of the sample was retired, and by the time the questionnaire was in the mail, a lapse of 15 months from the date of the actual move was possible. I had not thought of this factor in planning the study, as I had not anticipated nearly this proportion of elderly people in the sample. This also came as a surprise to the moving company, which was not aware that such a large percentage of their business came from the retired segment of society.

It was gratifying throughout the project to learn how interested people are (on the whole) in helping out a stranger; we have read so extensively of the opposite. Sometimes, however, they are so helpful they can foul you up. One lady had not moved in 25 years (she had merely inherited some furniture from an estate), but, after reading the questionnaire and cover letter, she decided a friend fit the demands perfectly. She wrote that she had passed the questionnaire along to a friend and indicated how sorry she was that she could not help by completing the questionnaire—she just did not remember the details of her move 25 years ago well enough! Actually this created no serious problem, since the friend included a letter indicating how she had gotten the questionnaire and her pleasure in participating, and I was able to select out the questionnaire. While I have frequently mentioned the unanti-cipated in terms of problems (and indeed this has great practical value), just as unanticipated was the very warm response of many of the respondents to the study. There were also some responses of the other variety, which I expected. But I did not expect women to take out time to write long letters sharing their experiences with me for the expressed purpose of encouraging me in what I was attempting to do. This was an unexpected bonus from the research.

Questionnaire Construction

The questionnaire was a product of ideas gained from extensive reading of research reports on geographic mobility. Out of this survey of the literature I developed a tentative instrument which hopefully would test certain hypotheses I had formulated and would explore areas I assumed to be relevant. This tentative instrument was long, tedious, and redundant. To my surprise, my biggest problem in constructing the questionnaire was *cutting down* on the number of questions to be included. I had decided to limit the questionnaire to 12 pages, including one page for instructions, and there were literally pages which had to be cut from the instrument. Since I was a full week behind schedule, I submitted copies of the proposed questionnaire to my dissertation chairman and conducted a pilot test of the instrument simultaneously. Both sources of help became very involved with the questionnaire and proved to be of invaluable assistance.

Without a doubt, the single factor in the process of this research that I remember with the greatest amusement is the question I developed on sexual behavior. My naiveté, a firm belief that "nothing is too sacred or mundane for the sociologist to study," and probably an insatiable desire to peek through the keyholes of life—some blend of these factors and I have no idea of what else—prompted me to include a question on the frequency of sexual intercourse with the mate at four different phases in the moving process. This really upset almost everyone reviewing the questionnaire. My first awareness of this possible reaction to the question came from the pilot study, which was conducted in my evening classes. Instead of just leaving the questionnaires in a stack on my desk, each student sought me out individually to return the instrument. Each in turn explained to me that *she* had no hesitation in answering such a question but felt confident that the *average* woman would. I discounted this as being typical of the conservatism of the Midwest. Only a flicker of a doubt crossed my mind: What if a number of the participants were of this "conservative set"? The death blow to the question came from my dissertation advisor. He was concerned that this one question might seriously depress the response rate and asked what was the rationale for including the question. If the question was an important indicator tied into the theoretical scheme, I might feel the risk worth it. Actually, I had no well-thought-out rationale—mostly just some suspicions that I thought would be interesting to pursue. Result: One question on sexual intercourse eliminated. Since the completion of the research I have presented papers on six different occasions, literally across the country, and in all the discussions following each of these presentations and in all the letters received from organizations involved in transferring people frequently, never have I been asked anything about the moving process and the frequency of sexual intercourse. I have been asked repeatedly about the female menstrual cycle and moving, though, and could provide no answers because no questions were asked in this study.

In looking back on the process of finalizing the instrument, I am amazed that I could become so involved with specific questions. But I did, and the cutting of many of the questions from the instrument was difficult. The dissertation chairman was particularly helpful in suggesting where the blue pencil should be applied and where changes in wording or format would aid clarity. This assistance was of inestimable value.

The printing of the questionnaire was the other area of difficulty in this regard. There had not been time in developing the research budget to get cost estimates, and when I started checking print shops I discovered printing was much more costly than I had anticipated. Finally, after much checking around and bargaining, I was able to work it out that the campus print shop would print the questionnaire at cost. They did a beautiful job, but I had to wait for them to work it in when they had nothing else to do. This threw the project considerably behind schedule, and the questionnaire was mailed a full three weeks later than originally planned. Unfortunately, some subjects received the questionnaire during the spring vacation period. This could have been avoided if my budget estimates had been more in line with current printing costs and I then could have had the questionnaire done by a commercial printer.

Inadequate funds (due to my underestimating expenses) were a problem throughout the project. They also exacerbated the time pressures, since I had to do considerably more of the nitty-gritty work (such as typing) than I had planned in the beginning. I certainly learned in the course of this project that money buys time. Next time around I will make more adequate allowance for both time and costs.

ARRIVAL

There are obviously many ways in which the overly simple model of a journey does not fit the realities of the research process. The matter of the arrival stage is probably the most difficult to describe. In fact, this research is still in the process of reaching closure. All of the planned computer runs have not been made. I suppose the most vivid memory I have of the arrival stage in this research project is the experience of utter exhaustion as I read a 20 page paper at the symposium in June after having worked on the final draft until after midnight the night before the symposium. To top it off, the symposium started with an early-morning breakfast for the participants!

Because of the topic and the setting in which the results of the study were first presented, I was given far more media coverage than is normal for such a limited research project. In the months immediately following the presentation, I was asked to participate in other meetings, was interviewed by a number of national publications, and was generally inundated with requests for copies of the research report. Fortunately, the funding agency assumed the responsibility for handling these requests. All of this fallout from the research was totally unanticipated, and, certainly, there was nothing in my background to prepare me for playing the role of the "expert," but this was what was suddenly being asked of me. Actually, the mass media and consulting demands tended to detour me from my main goal. Possibly this detour could have been avoided if I had anticipated some of this fallout and developed plans for handling it in advance. Certainly, no final sense of closure on this project is conceivable until the dissertation is completed, as this was the specific purpose of the whole research endeavor.

Joseph J. Lengermann ─────────────────────────────

A. EXCHANGE STRENGTHS AND PROFESSIONAL AUTONOMY IN ORGANIZATIONS

The appropriateness of an "exchange strength" theoretical perspective for understanding the conditions that affect the possible presence and the extent of professional autonomy in bureaucratic organizations is the subject of this article. As Kornhauser (1962) has emphasized, "the theme of autonomy versus integration . . . is the central problem posed by the interdependence of professions and organizations." By "autonomy" we mean the ability of the participant to influence his mode of participation within the group or organization. By "professional autonomy," more specifically, we mean the ability of the professional to exercise his own judgment, according to his professional body of knowledge, in carrying out his work activities within the organization.

Most discussions of the incompatibilities between bureaucratic and professional modes of directing activity (e.g., Blau & Scott, 1962; Francis & Stone, 1956; Kornhauser, 1962; Scott, 1966), though motivated by a greater concern for professional than for organizational priorities, pessimistically assume that professional rather than bureaucratic principles are more likely to be compromised. More recent empirical research (Engel, 1970; Lengermann, 1971; Miller & Wager, 1971) has produced data too complex to support any simplistic pessimism about the fate of professional autonomy in organizations. Even these studies, however, have not examined the professionals' resources for maintaining professional autonomy.

This article seeks to examine some of these resources through a perspective that stresses the exchanges and dependencies central to the relationships between professionals and organizations. The thrust of this perspective is that considerable professional autonomy is possible within large organizations not only because professionals have high expectations for professional autonomy but also because professionals are far more likely than most organizational participants to enjoy an advantageous position on the exchange conditions affecting power and independence in the organi-

─────────────────────────────

Source: Prepared especially for this volume.

zational hierarchy (Blau, 1964: 118; Gouldner, 1959: 254 ff.; March & Simon, 1958: 83 ff.; Thibaut & Kelley, 1959: 121).

Once viewed in terms of exchange conditions, the basic structural and attitudinal characteristics of professionalism (Greenwood, 1966: 9-19; Hall, 1969: 99; Wilensky, 1964: 138-140) can be seen not simply as values which are in conflict with bureaucratic principles but as resources for effective resistance against bureaucratic control and for resolution of such conflict in favor of professional priorities.

Research with life insurance salesmen (Taylor & Pellegrin, 1959), military personnel (Lang, 1964; Zald & Simon, 1964), and social workers (Blau & Scott, 1962) and a number of other studies not only demonstrate that professional characteristics produce strain and conflict for professionals in organizations but also suggest that professionalization has an advantageous impact on the exchange relationships between professionals and their organizations.

This becomes more evident when the structural and attitudinal characteristics of professionalism are assessed in terms of the professional community's monopolistic control over its area of expertise (especially where protected by licensing and title laws) and its considerable influence over the communication and contact network leading to job alternatives. Thus job alternatives are likely to depend upon involvement in and favorable judgment by the community of professional peers rather than the organizational hierarchy. Miller (1967) has concluded that a variety of research evidence supports the argument that important professionals can get their desired rewards by marketing their skills in other organizations and, because of this bargaining power, can therefore exercise influence in their employing organizations. In short, a review of the literature on professional characteristics and experience, in terms of the conditions theoretically affecting power and dependence in exchange relationships, suggests that professionals are likely to be in a particularly favorable position to influence their mode of organizational participation so as to safeguard their important prerogative of professional autonomy.

In our own conception of the exchanges and dependencies involved in maintaining professional autonomy in organizations, five elements are considered most relevant:

1. *High value for professional autonomy* as part of a set of professional values and norms created during a professional socialization or training period.
2. *Identification and involvement with a professional community,* which provides peer group and professional association reinforcement of initially internalized professional values, a professional reference group whose approval remains important in self-identity, and an across-organizations network within which a professional reputation can be rewarded

both by esteem and by contact recommendations for attractive job alternatives.

3. *High value of the professional's activity* as a contribution to the employing organization.

4. *Great difficulty in replacing the professional,* because of relatively high demands for those skills or because of the ability of the professional to mobilize negative judgment within the professional community about the position or employing organization.

5. *Realistic job alternatives for the professional,* in terms of both being wanted by other work organizations and viewing alternative organizations as attractive.

Because the first two elements, high value for professional autonomy and professional community identification (referred to as "V.P.A." and "P.C.I.," respectively), are closely associated with basic professional characteristics, they will be present to the extent that an occupation is well advanced along the professionalism continuum and specific individuals are indeed involved members of that occupation. Interprofession and intraprofession variations on these conditions are considerable, however, and need to be taken into account in testing our exchange-strength perspective. The last three elements, high value to the organization, difficulty of replacement, and realistic job alternatives, we call exchange strengths (referred to as E.S.). These form the core of our perspective on professional autonomy (referred to as P.A.). We hypothesize that, *given the presence of the first two elements— value for professional autonomy and professional community identification —the possession of the three exchange strengths—value to the organization, difficulty of replacement, and realistic job alternatives—will be positively associated with the possession of professional autonomy.* Exchange strengths are considered more important to professional autonomy than value for professional autonomy and professional community identification, whose relationship to professional autonomy is considered to be secondary—i.e., they are important preliminary conditions whose fulfillment is necessary before advantageous exchange strengths can be fully utilized for attaining professional autonomy. Since other factors such as size of organization, type of organization, and a professional's position level within an organizational hierarchy can also be expected to affect the possibilities for professional autonomy, these need to be taken into account as important controls.

DESCRIPTION OF THE STUDY

To examine empirically the hypothesized relationship between exchange strengths and professional autonomy, data were collected as part of a larger study of one specific profession, Certified Public Accounting. Apart from providing descriptive information about a profession which is growing rapidly in status and importance among present-day U.S. occupations (c.f. Carey, 1965; Edwards, 1960; Montagna, 1971), data on Certified Public Accounting is particularly appropriate to our interest in professional autonomy for three reasons: First, most CPA work is carried out in organizational settings, and "professional vs. organizational" issues figure prominently in the current development of the profession (Carey, 1965; Sorensen, 1967). Second, there is considerable variation in CPA organizational settings, from sole-practice offices, to professional CPA firms (ranging drastically in size and complexity), to non-CPA organizations. Third, there is likely to be considerable variation in the extent to which characteristics (such as professional values and professional community identification) and resources (such as exchange strengths) are present among CPAs. This variation in organizational setting, in adherence to professional characteristics, and in possession of exchange strengths is necessary to assess the importance of these various elements in the maintenance of professional autonomy.

In our particular study of CPAs, data were collected by means of an extensive questionnaire completed by 373 respondents from a stratified random sample of New York State CPAs (including prospective CPAs[1]) working in sole-practice offices, local and regional firms, national "Big Eight" firms, and non-CPA organizations. The response rate of 49 percent is more representative than it may initially seem, because telephone follow-up procedures indicated that a high proportion of nonrespondents were no longer in CPA practice.

Since questionnaire data represent the self-reported judgment of respondents, our measures involve the CPAs' own assessment of their level of professional autonomy, degree of value for professional autonomy, relative identification with their organization or profession, and relative standing on each of the exchange strengths. More specifically our primary measure of professional autonomy is the respondent's rating of his work situation as "poor," "average," or "excellent" in terms of the extent to which it allows him "freedom to exercise his own professional judgment in carrying out his professional work."[2] With this measure our focus is on the respondent's overall sense of the extent to which professional autonomy is possible for him in his work situation, as determined by his reported frustration or satisfaction on this dimension rather than by some "objective" count of the times he acts independently from or in deference to his organizational superiors. This

---

1. "Prospective CPAs" refers to employees in CPA firms who are working toward the CPA certificate but have not yet fulfilled all residency and examination requirements.
2. Two secondary measures of professional autonomy were also analyzed: (1) a negative measure indicating whether it is more necessary to please superiors than clients or professional peers to receive important rewards in one's work, and (2) a negative measure indicating the presence of discrepancy between the value placed on professional autonomy and its actual realization in one's work experience. Since these three measures produced basically similar results, we focus here on the more direct primary measure.

personal evaluation of his work situation in terms of professional autonomy prerogatives is a crucial aspect of the professional's experience and vitally affects his assessment of himself as a professional.

Value for professional autonomy was measured dichotomously. From a list of 18 reward factors, the respondent was asked to rank his five most desired rewards. He was considered to have a high value for professional autonomy if he included "freedom to exercise own professional judgment in carrying out one's work" as one of his five top-ranked rewards. This measure proved more discriminating than the respondent's direct evaluation of professional autonomy as "not very important," "somewhat important," "or very important." Our primary measure of professional community identification is also a dichotomous variable: the indication of primary loyalty preference either to the CPA profession as such or to the respondent's present firm or organization (if somehow conditions should force such a choice).[3]

Our measure of exchange strengths is based on the simultaneous possession of three specific exchange strength components: value to firm, difficulty of replacement, and realistic job alternatives. Only those individuals who were in the highest categories on each of the three individual components were rated as having exchange strengths (i.e., a strong total set of exchange strengths). Our measures of the three exchange strength components are as follows:

1. Value to firm—the respondent's judgment of his superior's evaluation of his contribution to the goals of his firm or organization.
2. Difficulty of replacement—the respondent's judgment of his superior's evaluation of the difficulty of replacing him.
3. Realistic job alternatives—in a *broad* sense of "being-wanted" alternatives (the respondent indicating any of seven different job situations to be "very realistic" in terms of his being wanted in that work situation) or in a more *strict* sense of "attractive being-wanted" alternatives (the respondent indicating any of seven different job situations to be "very realistic" in the sense of simultaneously being wanted by that work situation and personally viewing it as attractive or appealing).[4]

---

3. Two secondary measures of P.C.I. were also examined, one dealing with "primary reward source" and the other with "direction of career track." Since all three measures yielded basically similar results, we rely here on the primary measure.
4. In the case of the value to firm and the difficulty of replacement variables, the three initial response categories of "low," "medium," and "high" were reduced to a dichotomous breakdown of "low" (low and medium) and "high." In the case of the realistic job alternatives variable, the seven job situations listed were: (1) move to office of (another) sole practitioner as member of staff; (2) move to start own sole-practice office; (3) move to (another) local firm as staff or partner; (4) move to (another) regional firm as staff or partner; (5) move to (another) national firm as staff or partner; (6) move to (another) industry or non-CPA organization and do accounting work; (7) move to (another) industry or non-CPA organization and do other than accounting work.

We shall rely primarily on a strict measure of exchange strengths which uses the "attractive being-wanted" alternatives as its third component. However, since "being wanted" alternatives can be attractive if dissatisfaction becomes too great, we shall include data on a broad measure of exchange strengths which uses the broader "being-wanted" alternatives as its third component. It should be noted that these measures of exchange strengths are based on the respondent's perception rather than on some totally objective assessment. It can be argued, however, that the professional's estimation of his exchange strengths is in fact a more important influence upon his decision making and influence attempts than his objective exchange strengths.

RESULTS

Because, in previous research (Lengermann, 1971), type of organization and position level within organization (but not size of professional firm) were found to relate to the professional autonomy of CPAs, we must take these factors into account. We shall list our data on the relationship between value for professional autonomy (V.P.A.), professional community identification (P.C.I.), exchange strengths (E.S.), and professional autonomy (P.A.), not only for CPAs as a whole but also for the various organization- and position-level subgroups. [5]

TABLE 1
Presence of Value for Professional Autonomy, Professional Community Identification, and Exchange Strengths among CPA Groups (in percents)

CPA Groups and Subgroups	Value for Professional Autonomy %	Professional Community Identification %	Exchange Strengths (strict) %	Exchange Strengths (broad) %
All CPAs	34 (349)	42 (337)	14 (329)	23 (349)
All in professional firms ..	30 (229)	41 (22)	12 (225)	19 (229)
Lowers in firms	29 (109)	51 (107)	13 (107)	17 (109)
Highers in firms	35 (113)	31 (108)	11 (118)	22 (113)
All in non-CPA organizations	48 (68)	52 (66)	17 (65)	32 (68)
Lowers in non-CPA organizations	48 (29)	50 (28)	20 (29)	41 (20)
Highers in non-CPA organizations	47 (39)	47 (38)	14 (36)	28 (39)
Sole-practice CPAs	39 (51)	38 (48)	24 (33)	39 (33)

Note: Figures in parentheses represent the Ns on which percentages are based.

---

5. The major position levels in CPA firms are "junior," "senior," "manager" (or "supervisor") and "partner." In using position level as a control variable, the first two positions are collapsed and referred to as the "lower" position group, while the latter two are collapsed and referred to as the "higher" position group. The lower position includes some "prospective CPA's" who have not yet passed all the examinations for their certificates. For CPAs in non-CPA organizations, our higher and lower position groups are equivalent to managerial and nonmanagerial.

TABLE 2
Percentage with Excellent Professional Autonomy among CPA Groups, According to Presence of Value for Professional Autonomy, Professional Community Identification, and Exchange Strengths

CPA Groups and Subgroups	(1) Total CPA Group	(2) CPAs with V.P.A.	(3) CPAs with P.C.I.	(4) CPAs with E.S (strict)	(5) CPAs with E.S. -(broad)	(6) CPAs with E.S. (strict) & V.P.A.	(7) CPAs with E.S. (strict) & P.C.I.	(8) CPAs with E.S. (broad) & V.P.A.	(9) CPAs with E.S. (broad) & P.C.I.
All CPAs	64 (349)	74 (120)	60 (141)	78 (46)	74 (80)	88 (16)	90 (19)	85 (27)	83 (35)
All in professional firms	65 (229)	73 (69)	63 (92)	74 (27)	75 (44)	83 (6)	92 (12)	83 (12)	90 (19)
Lowers in firms	50 (109)	48 (31)	51 (55)	57 (14)	58 (19)	67 (3)	86 (7)	75 (4)	82 (11)
Highers in firms	83 (113)	92 (38)	85 (33)	92 (13)	88 (25)	100 (3)	100 (5)	88 (8)	100 (8)
All in non-CPA organizations	53 (68)	72 (32)	47 (32)	91 (11)	70 (23)	100 (6)	86 (7)	90 (10)	77 (13)
Lowers in non-CPA organizations	35 (29)	50 (14)	29 (14)	83 (6)	50 (12)	100 (3)	75 (4)	75 (4)	60 (5)
Highers in non-CPA organizations	67 (39)	89 (18)	61 (18)	100 (5)	91 (11)	100 (3)	100 (3)	100 (6)	88 (8)
Sole-practice CPAs	77 (51)	85 (20)	72 (18)	75 (8)	77 (13)	75 (4)	100 (8)	80 (5)	67 (3)

Note: Figures in parentheses represent the Ns on which the percentages are based.

First we present data on the extent to which CPAs do in fact possess the factors whose relevance to P.A. we wish to examine—the extent of V.P.A., P.C.I., and E.S. These are summarized in Table 1.

The percentages indicated fall below our theoretical expectations, suggesting that variation on these variables among CPAs is not as great as

TABLE 3
Gamma Measures of Association: Exchange Strengths and Professional Autonomy among CPA Groups, with Controls by Value for Professional Autonomy and by Professional Community Identification

CPA Groups and Subgroups	(1) E.S. [s] & P.A.	(2) E.S. [b] & P.A.	(3) E.S. [s] & P.A. by V.P.A.	(4)	(5) E.S. [s] & P.A. by P.C.I.	(6)
			Present	Absent	Present	Absent
All CPAs	.42a	.35a	.51a	.39a	.77a	.16
All in professional firms	.25a	.31a	.39	.24b	.79a	−.11
Lowers in firms	.12	.16	.40b	.04	.75a	−.44a
Higher in firms	.52a	.33b	1.00	.51	1.00b	.32
All in non-CPA organizations	.85a	.54a	1.00a	.84a	.85a	1.00a
Lowers in non-CPA organizations	.89a	.56a	—*	—*	—*	—*
Highers in non-CPA organizations	1.00a	.78a	—*	—*	—*	—*
Sole-practice CPAs	.17	.28	—*	—*	—*	—*

*Results not reported for these control situations because N consistently < 30.
aStatistical significance <.05.
bStatistical significance >.05 <.10.

TABLE 4
Gamma Measures of Association: Value for Professional Autonomy, Professional Community Identification, and Professional Autonomy among CPA Groups, with Controls by Exchange Strengths

CPA Groups and Subgroups	(1) V.P.A. & P.A.	(2) V.P.A. & P.A. by E.S. (strict]	(3)	(4) P.C.I. & P.A.	(5) P.C.I. & P.A. by E.S. (strict)	(6)
		Present	Absent		Present	Absent
All CPAs	.30a	.44a	.33a	−.11b	.57a	−.18a
All in professional firms	.21a	.35	.20a	−.04	.76a	−.14b
Lowers in firms	−.08	.29†	−.06	.07	.88a†	−.09
Higher in firms	.52a	1.00†	.48a	.13	1.00†	.03
All in non-CPA organizations	.62a	1.00b†	.64a	−.24a	−1.00†	−.34
Lowers in non-CPA organizations	.51a	—*	—*	−.41b	—*	—*
Highers in non-CPA organizations	.80a	—*	—*	−.16	—*	—*
Sole-practice CPAs	.34a	—*	—*	−.09	—*	—*

*Results not reported for these control situations because N consistently <30.
aStatistical significance <.05.
bStatistical significance > .05 < .10.
†Gamma based on < 30.

anticipated. Analysis is thus more difficult because the number of CPA respondents who are strong on the major variables is disproportionately small. This is especially true for the most crucial independent variable, possession of strong exchange strengths.[6] This is another reason data based on a broad as well as a strict measure of E.S. will be considered, since doing so provides a larger N in the control tables. Comments as to why this particular profession produces the low percentages on the variables shown in Table 1 can be reserved until after we examine our data on the relationship between these variables and P.A.

After looking at percentage figures, we turn to measures of association. Table 2 shows the variation in the percentage of CPAs with "excellent" (rather than "average" or "poor") P.A. by V.P.A., P.C.I. and/or E.S. Columns 4 and 5 of Table 2 show that the percentage of CPAs with excellent P.A. is consistently and considerably higher among CPAs who have excellent E.S. than among CPAs as a whole (column 1). This is true both for CPAs in professional firms and for CPAs in non-CPA organizations, both for lower position CPAs as well as for higher position CPAs. It should also be noted that the P.A. percentages are in almost every instance higher for those CPAs with E.S. (columns 4 and 5) than for CPAs with P.C.I. (column 3) or for CPAs with V.P.A. (column 2). The highest percentages, however, occur among those CPAs who combine strong E.S. with either V.P.A. (columns 6 and 8) or with P.C.I. (columns 7 and 9). Thus these summary percentage data already provide some support for a positive relationship between E.S. and P.A.

We now examine the data further by means of summary tables of gamma measures of association.[7] In Table 3 the gamma measures of association between E.S. and P.A. are positive for every CPA group and thus supportive of our general hypothesis. The relationships are especially strong for the non-CPA organization groups, both at the lower and higher position levels.

Though they are positive for all CPA groups, gamma values in Table 4 show that the relationship between V.P.A. and P.A. is not as strong as that between E.S. and P.A. The relevance of E.S. is further demonstrated by their positive interaction effects with V.P.A., as seen in the control columns of Tables 3 and 4. Neither the V.P.A.-P.A. (Table 4) relationship nor the

---

6. Relatively few CPAs possessed a total set of exchange strengths, although many were strong on the individual exchange strength components. Those CPA groups that tended to be high on the first two components (the higher position group) tended to be low on the realistic alternatives component; those CPA groups that tended to be "high" on this third component (the lower position group) tended to be low on the first two components of value to firm and difficulty of replacement.

7. Because the Ns consistently fell below 30, control results are not reported for the sole-practice group, the lowers in non-CPA organization group and the highers in non-CPA organization group, despite the fact that those results follow the pattern of our overall interpretation. Tau partials (through the third order) were computed as a further check against spuriousness and also bear out our interpretation. In the few instances where reported gamma values are based on N of < 30, this is so indicated in the table.

E.S.—P.A. (Table 3) relationship washes out as spurious when we control for the other.[8] Rather, each factor adds some strength to the other.

With regard to P.C.I., gamma values (Table 4, column 4) indicate that it either is not related or else is negatively related to P.A.[9] However, there is a strong positive interaction effect when P.C.I. is combined with E.S., such that both the P.C.I.-P.A. (Table 4, columns 5 and 6) and the E.S.-P.A. (Table 3, columns 5 and 6) relationships are considerably strengthened for all CPA groups. It seems that the fulfillment of a primary orientation toward one's profession rather than one's organization results in the more direct and effective utilization of E.S. for maintaining P.A. This is especially important in the case of CPAs in firms. Among CPAs in non-CPA organizations this explicit orientation does not seem quite as necessary, since the distinction between professional and organizational concerns already is sufficiently clear to encourage the application of E.S. towards maintaining P.A.

It should be noted that possession of E.S. seems especially valuable to two CPA groups which otherwise fare rather badly on P.A., namely CPAs in non-CPA organizations and lower-level CPAs in CPA firms. For the former group, the E.S.-P.A. gamma association (Table 3, column 1) is extremely strong (.85) and the percentage with excellent P.A. rises from 53 percent to 91 percent (Table 2, columns 1 and 4) once E.S. are present. Within this group, the E.S. resource can almost entirely make up for the lack of that other P.A. resource, high position level. If P.A. is to be excellent within non-CPA organizations, E.S. are needed by both position-level groups; and the advantages to P.A. that do come with higher position level can be almost equalized by E.S. among the lower position group.

In the professional firm, however, position level remains an extremely potent resource for P.A.,[10] and its strength is never equalized by E.S. alone. For the higher position levels in the professional firm, E.S. are not really necessary, since high position level itself (especially if combined with V.P.A.) assures P.A., whether or not E.S. are present. But for those in lower position levels in professional firms, E.S. become especially important as the only

---

8. Lack of spuriousness is also indicated by a Tau partialing procedure. For the total CPA group and the CPA organizational subgroups, the zero-order tau values for the E.S.—P.A. relationship remain the same or increase slightly as first-, second-, and third-order partials when we control for V.P.A and/or P.C.I. and/or position level. The V.P.A.—P.A. relationship zero-order tau values either remain the same or decrease very slightly (.09 to .08, .36 to .33) as first- and second-order partials when we control for E.S. and/or position level.
9. This is also borne out by a tau partialing procedure.
10. For further details on the position–P.A. relationship, see Lengermann (1971). Apropos of the possible threat to continuing professional orientation and concern for professional autonomy in a situation where professional autonomy depends so strongly on hierarchical position level, we should note that in all three measures of professional community identification, the data show a move away from identification with the profession toward greater identification with the firm or organization as position level increases. Among the partners, *after* the reward system of the firm has been successfully achieved, there is some evidence of a renewed involvement in and identification with the profession.

resource likely to increase their P.A. To some extent, E.S. are such a resource in themselves (V.P.A. and P.C.I. are not). But only if they are combined with explicit adherence to V.P.A. or P.C.I. do they significantly offset the disadvantages of low position level. Table 3 shows that, for Lowers in Firms, the direct E.S.-P.A. gamma association of .12 increases to .40 and .75, when we control for the presence of V.P.A. and P.C.I. respectively, and decreases to .04 and —.44 when we control for the absence of these factors, respectively. At the same time, as seen in Table 4, the direct V.P.A.-P.A. gamma association of —.08 changes to a positive .29 when we control for the presence of E.S., while remaining negative at —.06 when we control for its absence. The direct P.C.I.-P.A. gamma association of .07 increases to .88 when we control for the presence of E.S., while decreasing to —.09 when we control for its absence.

SUMMARY AND CONCLUSION

To a convincing degree, our data support the general hypothesis that exchange strengths are positively related to professional autonomy within organizations, more so than either value for professional autonomy or professional community identification. Given the presence of either of these latter two factors, exchange strengths relate still more positively to professional autonomy. In turn, given the presence of exchange strengths, these other factors also relate more positively to professional autonomy. Within professional firms, however, organizational position level does relate more strongly to professional autonomy than do exchange strengths.

It is especially important that our hypothesis is most strongly supported among those CPA groups for whom professional autonomy is otherwise threatened, namely those in non-CPA organizations and those in lower position levels within professional firms. Exchange strengths are seen to be helpful and necessary resources for professional autonomy among professionals in nonprofessional organizations, no matter what their position level. In professional organizations, the issue of professional autonomy can resolve itself at the upper position levels through the increased decisional prerogatives that come with high organizational position. However, if the important professional principle of professional autonomy depends exclusively on the bureaucratic phenomenon of advancement to higher organizational position, the result can be a gradually increasing insensitivity among professional-firm higher level CPAs to the problematic nature of professional autonomy. This can be to the detriment of both the lower level CPAs, who come to be treated too casually as bureaucratic "employees," and the larger client society which should be served by the professional autonomy principle. Exchange strengths, however, are resources for professional autonomy which are linked more directly to the wider professional association than to the organization's position levels. For the CPAs studied, exchange strengths were positively linked to such activities as participation in professional conferences, extensive professional readings, intensive specialization, and the spreading of one's work experiences over multiple CPA work experiences.

Theoretically, such activities are open to and engaged in by all members of a profession, whether in professional organizations or not, whether in high position levels or not. Thus, theoretically, all members of a profession have access to exchange strengths as resources for professional autonomy. However our data have indicated that relatively few members of the CPA profession either possess exchange strengths or engage in these professional activities. In our opinion two major structural characteristics of the CPA profession operate to reduce such activities, and, subsequently, to reduce exchange strengths and professional autonomy: the CPA practice of within-firm socialization (presently required for certification), and the tradition of a "one-firm" concept which effectively discourages mobility of CPAs from one firm to another. Both these structural characteristics lead to an identification of one's own firm and its organizational traditions with the CPA profession itself. Some CPAs currently wish to replace the within-firm apprenticeship requirement with a university-based training program. Our theoretical approach and our findings suggest that this structural change would considerably enhance the professional autonomy of CPAs, because it would very likely encourage a more direct identification with the profession as such and develop a network of peer group contacts which might increase the acceptability and the possibility of interfirm mobility.[11]

According to our analysis of the relevance of an exchange strength perspective for understanding professional autonomy in organizations, the interaction of four types of variables needs to be taken into account:

1. The structural conditions of the profession (touched on briefly in this concluding section).
2. The structural conditions of the employing organization (e.g., position level, type of organization).
3. The value orientations of the individual professionals (e.g., value for professional autonomy, professional community identification).
4. The exchange strengths of the individual professionals (e.g., being valuable to the organization, being difficult to replace, and having realistic job alternatives).

---

11. Of course it is quite another question as to whether or not CPAs who control the profession from within or key groups who influence it from the outside (e.g., client industries) really want such changes or really would find increased concern for and resources for professional autonomy beneficial to their present interests. Though it is not our purpose to examine them here, such vested interests in preventing such changes must be acknowledged. Their relevance stresses again the importance to professional autonomy of variables (such as exchange strengths) other than the variables of values, size, or inherent incompatibility between bureaucratic and professional principles.

Some approaches have stressed one or the other of the first three types of variables and have attempted to understand professional autonomy almost exclusively in terms of that one selected variable. Here we have emphasized the importance of the fourth type of variable, but in doing so we have also considered the relevance to professional autonomy of the other three by examining how they lead to, combine with, or are offset by exchange strengths.

Though actual job market conditons may minimize exchange strengths (they have obviously decreased, and then increased, among engineers recently), the possibility for exchange strengths is generally better among professional groups than among most other occupational groups. Greater control over work activities is linked to this higher level of exchange strengths. What make a professional autonomous is that he or she has the power to insist on autonomy if desired. Except where autonomy derives from hierarchical authority in professional firms, basic exchange strengths are the ultimate supports for this power and therefore for the prerogative of professional autonomy. In some respects, this point may seem obvious enough. After all, we would expect basic exchange strengths to be helpful to any person or group seeking to control its mode of participation within any organization. But this point needs to be made explicit in regard to professional autonomy, especially since so much literature on professionals in organizations has stressed the strains and incompatibilities between professional and bureaucratic principles, while overlooking the considerable means available to professionals for resolving much of this strain and incompatibility in their own favor.

REFERENCES

Blau, Peter. *Exchange and power in social life.* New York: Wiley, 1964.

Blau, Peter, & Richard Scott. *Formal organizations.* San Francisco: Chandler, 1962.

Carey, John C. *The CPA plans for the future.* New York: American Institute of Certified Public Accoutants, 1965.

Edwards, James D. *History of public accounting in the United States.* East Lansing: Michigan State Bureau of Business and Economic Research, 1960.

Engel, Gloria V. Professional autonomy and bureaucratic organization. *Administrative Science Quarterly,* 1970, *15,* 12-21.

Francis, R. G., & R. C. Stone. *Service and procedure in bureaucracy: A case study.* Minneapolis: University of Minnesota Press, 1956.

Gouldner, Alvin. Reciprocity and autonomy in functional theory. Pp. 241-270 in Llewellyn Gross (ed.), *Symposium on Sociological Theory.* New York: Harper & Row, 1959.

Greenwood, Ernest. Attributes of a profession. Pp. 10-22 in Howard Vollmer and Arnold Mills (eds.), *Professionalization.* Englewood Cliffs, N.J.: Prentice-Hall, 1966.

Hall, Richard H. *Occupations and the social structure.* Englewood Cliffs, N.J.: Prentice-Hall, 1969.

Kornhauser, William. *Scientists in industry: Conflict and accommodation.* Berkeley: University of California Press, 1962.

Lang, Kurt. Technology and career management in the military establishment. Pp. 39-81 in Morris Janowitz (ed.), *The new military.* New York: Russell Sage Foundation, 1964.

Lengermann, Joseph J. Supposed and actual differences in professional autonomy among CPAs as related to type of work organization and size of firm. *The Accounting Review,* 1971, *46,* 665-675.

March, James, & Herbert Simon. *Organizations.* New York: Wiley, 1953.

Miller, George A. Professionals in bureaucracy: Alienation among industrial scientists and engineers. *The American Sociological Review,* 1967, *32,* 755-768.

Miller, George, & L. Lesley Wager. Adult socialization, organizational structure and role orientation. *Administrative Science Quarterly,* 1971, *16,* 151-163.

Montagna, Paul D. The public accounting profession. In Eliot Freidson (ed.), The professions in contemporary society, *American Behavioral Scientist,* 1971, *15,* 475-491.

Scott, W. Richard. Professionals in bureaucracies: Areas of conflict. Pp. 265-275 in Howard Vollmer and Donald Mills (eds.), *Professionalization.* Englewood Cliffs, N.J.: Prentice-Hall, 1966.

Sorensen, James E. Professional and bureaucratic organization in the public accounting firm. *The Accounting Review,* 1967, *42,* 533-565.

Taylor, M. Lee, & Roland Pellegrin. Professionalization: Its functions and dysfunctions for the life-insurance occupation, *Social Forces,* 1959, 110-114.

Thibaut, John, & Harold Kelley. *The social psychology of small groups.* New York: Wiley, 1959.

Wilensky, Harold. The professionalization of everyone? *The American Journal of Sociology,* 1964, *70,* 137-158.

Zald, Mayer, & William Simon. Career opportunities and commitments among officers. Pp. 257-285 in Morris Janowitz (ed.), *The new military.* New York: Russell Sage Foundation, 1964.

Personal Journal ————————————————————————————

B. REFLECTIONS ON A DISSERTATION STUDY: PROFESSIONAL AUTONOMY AMONG CPAs

DEVELOPMENT OF THE TOPIC AND THE PERSPECTIVE

Quite often I am asked why I ever decided to study Certified Public Accountants. There was nothing in my background to associate me with their world, nor was I particularly interested in them as a specific occupational group. I decided to study them because they seemed (at the time) to be a

Source: Prepared especially for this volume.

particularly appropriate group through which to study the topic issue that really did interest me: the professional autonomy of professionals working in large bureaucratic organizations. Because of the trend for more and more professionals to carry out their work in large organizational settings and because of the supposed incompatibility between basic professional and bureaucratic principles, this has become, during the past decade, an issue of considerable interest to many sociologists in the fields of formal organizations and occupations. For me it has also been an issue which can be tied closely to the more basic issue of the autonomy of the individual in any social group: from a dyadic relationship to a friendship group, a kinship group, a voluntary association, or a total society.

But personal history also influenced considerably my interest in this sociological issue. What especially interested me initially in professional autonomy as a sociological issue was that it touched on an important personal problem for me at the time. During my second year of graduate work at Cornell, I was in the process of extricating myself from what supposedly had been a lifelong commitment to the priesthood in a Catholic religious order. Developing an interest in sociology as a secular independent professional discipline, while simultaneously developing a friendship group and job alternatives within that frame of reference, helped weaken the value ties to and authority controls by that religious order. Seminarians who had received specialized training in some profession had another set of assumptions and concepts with which to define any given situation and meaningful outside relationships to support such definitions, and it was an easier task requiring less heroic risk for them to resist the outlooks and prescriptions of Church and religious order superiors. In the summer of 1965 I presented a paper to the American Catholic Sociological Convention which dealt with the system effects of this "specialization" within religious orders (as well as within the military), especially in terms of the increased demand for autonomy and its attainment by such specialists.

Had I remained in the priesthood, I very likely would have studied professional autonomy within the substantive context of the sociology of religion, with emphasis on changes within religious orders. My decision to leave the priesthood in January 1966 pretty much ruled out any chance of getting the access to and cooperation from religious orders which would have been necessary to collect such research data. This influenced me to develop the same basic interest within the substantive context of the sociology of occupations and formal organizations, with emphasis on the possibilities for professional autonomy among professionals in bureaucratic organizations. Readings in sociological theory as well as in the sociology of the professions helped to organize my ideas. Most crucial at this stage was my recognition of the close compatibility between my thinking and the perspectives of exchange theory (Blau, 1964; Gouldner, 1959; March & Simon, 1958; Thibaut & Kelley, 1959).

The issue of professional autonomy in bureaucratic organizations, approached in terms of exchange theory, therefore, came to be the general topic and perspective around which I hoped to develop my dissertation research. Though sharing the antibureaucracy and proprofessionalism bias evident in much of the literature, I felt that most sociological treatments dwelt too exclusively on the incompatibility between bureaucratic and professional modes of activity and on the "inevitable" compromises and pressures experienced by the professional. This outlook failed to recognize the increasing advantages professionals were beginning to develop in terms of controlling the exchange relationships between themselves and employing organizations. Professionals had at least some bargaining strength with which to insist on maintaining their professional autonomy. In the circles that most directly controlled their status and rewards, it might even be beneficial rather than sacrificial to do so.

THE RESEARCH EXPERIENCE

How my general topic got to be bound up with the collection of considerable substantive information about CPAs has more to do with my experience in developing a suitable research design. The first research plan I developed called for interview and questionnaire data on several different types of professionals ("established . . . ," "new . . . ," "semi . . . ," and "marginal . . .") engaged in several types of organizations (government, industry, research, academia). I submitted a grant application to the National Institute of Mental Health. Both the refusal of N.I.M.H. to fund this proposal and the patient advice of Gordon Streib, my committee chairman at Cornell, convinced me that I did not have the time, the money, or the expertise to carry out research on such an ambitious scale.

Thus came the first of a series of "compromises" which often become necessary in translating a research idea into a research reality. Somewhat reluctantly, I decided to focus on one profession which had representatives in organizations of various types and sizes. Gradually, after much reading and discussing and worrying, I settled on CPAs as an appropriate professional group for my research, for reasons listed in the accompanying research article. Apart from their appropriateness in providing variation on my major theoretical variables, my selection of the CPAs was also influenced by the scarcity of research on this particular profession (only two previous studies) and by the convenience of being able to draw an adequate sample within New York State—because of the predominance of New York City as a national finance center, more than 14,000 CPAs are registered in the state. The above factors outweighed certain cautions I received, most having to do with the fact that CPAs, despite their being acknowledged in their own literature and in certain sociological literature as a full-fledged profession, may have only marginal professional status. By the time I was fully launched into the study (and again during data analysis), I came to realize that these cautions had considerable merit and that I had selected a group which would make exploration and confirmation of my theoretical ideas somewhat difficult.

During the fall of 1966 I began to work out the specifics. I read everything I could on CPAs; I talked to accounting faculty at Cornell; I brazenly asked for a series of background interviews in national CPA firms with branch offices in nearby Syracuse, New York. Gradually I began to work up a questionnaire, guided by my new information on the specifics of the CPA profession and by several sets of diagrams which attempted to list and relate the major variables and subvariables in my theoretical approach. By this time I had become fully committed to doing a survey, partially because I had developed a bias toward this approach and partially because I felt that, at this stage, it was important to get preliminary data on a broad range of items from CPAs in a variety of work settings. This meant, of course, that my research would cost a good bit of money—more than a graduate student could easily count on. Nevertheless, I worked on the assumption that I would somehow get the money, and after a good deal of time and effort, I eventually did. I was somewhat at a disadvantage because my committee chairman was in Ireland for a year. Though we had agreed on the general orientation, we had worked out few of the specifics before he left. In his absence, Professor Wayne Thompson agreed to work with me, and he provided crucial help, both in preparing the questionnaire and in securing funds.

The first piece of financial support came in the form of a Cornell Faculty-Student Grant for $500. Conveniently, Professor Thompson had been a member of the committee which evaluated such proposals. On the basis of this $500 seed money, I committed myself to the expenses of the entire study, even as I was still applying for additional money. A great deal of time was spent preparing several drafts of a National Science Foundation proposal and getting it through various Cornell administrative channels. A Cornell—N.S.F. disagreement as to the legitimacy of computer funds as part of the budget delayed submission until late February. By the time N.S.F. officially agreed to support my proposal (for $1,300), I was already drawing on meager personal funds (accumulated by devoting scarce time to outside teaching) to pay the several hundred dollars required in postage to mail the questionnaires.

Apart from providing the needed financial assistance, the N.S.F. proposal served to clarify, organize, and establish priority among my research ideas. At least I thought so then. Looking back at that proposal today, I marvel at the naive but eloquent self-confidence of its ambitious intentions and promises. The general hypothesis of the study was that:

> sufficiently satisfactory alternatives are available for the better professionals in large organizations to the point that such professionals enjoy rather strong strategies in their exchange relationships with their organizational superiors and

that they therefore are in a position to maintain professional autonomy and resist the tendency of the organizational system to control entirely their professional work.

The support of a professional peer group, was, furthermore, considered important for successful development and utilization of such strategy advantages. Though that general hypothesis did express my basic orientation, until it was broken down into a series of subhypotheses it was not very helpful, either in operationalizing variables or in analyzing data. The diagrams I drew up to map the variables relevant to my theoretical orientation grew more and more complicated as I related them to the specifics of the CPA profession. The questionnaire became longer and longer. Even after it had reached 20 tightly packed pages, and Professor Thompson had warned me that I would never use most of this information and that I would seriously damage my response rate, I kept insisting that there was a reason for every question.

Not surprisingly (in retrospect), the attention to so many variables resulted in failing to give sufficient attention to developing first-rate measures for my most important variables—professional autonomy and exchange strengths. But this inadequacy did not really come home to roost until I began serious data analysis. In the meantime, I began the work of pretesting the questionnaire. During March 1967 I distributed ditto copies of the preliminary questionnaire to about 20 lower and higher level CPAs in small and large firms. I then interviewed most of them. On the basis of this pretest, I revised the questionnaire thoroughly, intending at the same time to shorten it. The final copy, however, still came to 24 pages, which I estimated would take about 75 minutes to complete. Perhaps some did complete it in that time range, but many scrawled messages at the end of the completed questionnaires complaining of two or even three hours of work.

One of the things this research experience was to impress on me was the incredible amount of clerical work required in survey research. Normally such clerical work adds tremendously to budget costs, but this was avoided because I did almost all of it on my own time. Much of this routine clerical work had to do with preparation of the sample. I carefully drew 600 sets of random numbers with which, in subsequent days, I selected one by one my sample of 600 CPAs from the *New York State Directory of Certified Public Accountants*, by finding first the page number, then the column, then the rank in the column indicated by each set of random numbers. It was a purist approach. Each name was recorded with a home and office address on a 3" x 5" file card and categorized according to work situation (sole practice, local or regional firm, national "Big Eight" firm, or non-CPA organization). Since the *New York State Directory* gave only home addresses, work affiliation had to be looked up separately in the directory of the New York State Society of CPAs, to which about 75 percent of New York CPAs belong. Developing a sample of 200 "prospective CPAs" (professional accounting staff who had not yet passed all four parts of the CPA exam) proved even more time-consuming. There was no existing list. I had to "make do" by randomly selecting and writing some 55 small and large firms to request either a list of their prospective CPAs (from which I then could randomly select a few names) or else a promise to randomly distribute a designated number of questionnaires to their own staff. Eventually this worked, but it was a slow and drawn-out process.

Other tasks which involved considerable clerical work were the typing of 800 letter and envelope addresses to announce the study to the sample and the preparation of the questionnaire packets, some 16 separate tasks being required for each packet. It was only by putting in long days and weeks of this sort of clerical work that the entire batch of 800 questionnaires was finally mailed out in early May 1967. Established researchers generally can simply turn all this kind of work over to graduate assistants and secretaries. In most graduate student dissertations, it is done by the researcher alone.

Because survey research requires the cooperation and time of the respondents, much attention and effort needs to be focused on details that will add to the subjective appeal of the questionnaire. Miscalculation about the respondent's assessment can be disastrous to a study, even if the questionnaire itself is objectively an excellent one. This factor contributed considerably to my anxiety, especially since my questionnaire was unusually long and my respondents unusually busy professionals already wary of social science research. Concern over motivation and response rate is reflected in my decision to do a rather expensive photo offset printing of a booklet-type questionnaire on bond paper rather than a stapled mimeograph version on rag paper. The result was a smart looking booklet that itself looked impressively professional. This same concern also reflected itself in a thousand worries about even the clerical details. Looking back on the whole operation, much of it seems quite routine. But at the time each decision was agonized over: whether or not to insist on using an electric carbon ribbon typewriter (which I was free to use only at night); whether to mimeograph, Xerox, or individually type the 800 announcement letters; whether or not to put an identification number on the questionnaires; whether to put an individual postage stamp on each questionnaire packet envelope and return envelope or have them machine stamped by the Post Office—the list could go on and on. Usually it was a question of money or time costs versus response rate probabilities. Inevitably, I favored a concern for response rate.

After having been willing to take very serious risks on response rate rather than cut the length of the questionnaire, I then became purist in resorting to every possible printing, packaging, and mailing detail that might add a touch of personal appeal or professional status. I also spent considerable time composing the important announcement letter, cover letter, and follow-up letters. I played subtly on CPAs' insecurity about the full professional status of their occupation by suggesting that being subjected to

THE RESEARCH EXPERIENCE

social science research (as lawyers and doctors had often been) was itself an indication of their increased status and importance. I then appealed strongly to their professional pride in suggesting that their cooperation in this study was important to their profession. One mistake I did make in the matter of maximizing response motivation was my timing of the several follow-up efforts. I waited too long before sending out the two mailed follow-up requests. Fortunately, the N.S.F. money allowed for one more follow-up effort, which consisted of patient telephone calls from a hotel room in New York City. Besides producing another batch of completed questionnaires, this effort was especially valuable in terms of the many personal discussions which added flavor and detail to my understanding of the CPA world and its reaction to my questionnaire.

Eventually, all these careful efforts were to produce a response rate of 49 percent, with many of the nonrespondents being those who had already left public accounting. Although I had initially hoped for more, this was a good response rate, considering the formidable length and detail of the questionnaire. It is a tribute to both the professional dedication and the meticulous nature of CPAs that so many of them completed the questionnaire so carefully. Their thoroughness was remarkable. For example, of all the respondents who completed the section of 80 Likert-type agree-disagree statements dealing with professional and bureaucratic orientations, only five people left even as many as two or three items unanswered.

The completed questionnaires continued to trickle into my mailbox thoughout the summer. This slow return, coupled with my inability to get absorbed in writing up the background and theoretical chapters of the dissertation while still absorbed with details of getting the data, slowed my initial schedule considerably. Fortunately, the N.S.F. money enabled me to pay for the data to be transferred from the questionnaires onto coding sheets and then keypunched onto IBM cards. Although most of the questionnaire was precoded, the coding was still a very complex and time-consuming task. By the middle of August, the trickle of returns had almost stopped and the coding, punching, and verifying of the data had caught up with the supply of questionnaires. By the end of August, as I left Cornell to begin a teaching position at the University of Maryland, I was able to close out the data collection, coding, and keypunching phase of the study. I took with me my collected data punched onto IBM cards, with 373 respondents and nine cards of information on each respondent. This progress was far short of my original schedule.

THE ANALYSIS EXPERIENCE

Taking up a teaching position before having completed one's dissertation is a mistake. I had always resolved to have my Ph.D. in hand before taking a teaching position but during the winter months of 1966-67 I expected to be so near completion by the end of the summer that I accepted a position at Maryland. Although school in retrospect seems an almost ideal lifestyle in terms of stimulation, casualness, and freedom, I had become anxious to move on. I immediately found that the demands of a teaching position (including student advising, departmental meetings, committee work, as well as class preparation and lectures) left little time and energy for work on the dissertation. I also missed the opportunity for regular discussions with my chairman and dissertation committee. Even more I missed the technical advice and emotional support of my graduate peer group at Cornell. Mistakenly, I hesitated to seek or accept help from the Maryland faculty because I felt somewhat guilty about not having come to them with the degree completed. During the fall semester I accomplished little. It was not until the Christmas vacation and semester break that I was finally able to finish up the four background and theoretical chapters.

During the Spring semester, progress again ground to a virtual halt. I accomplished certain "busy work" (cleaning up my data and getting it on computer tape), but I now began to experience a sense of paralysis as to what exactly I should do with all this data. This disturbed my self-confidence a great deal at the time, though I have since learned that this "paralysis" is not uncommon at this stage. The problem came down to this: I had too much information and a too complex, all-inclusive theoretical orientation for someone with limited experience to handle. My general hypothesis was too complex to be easily broken down into subhypotheses with which I could be satisfied to deal separately. As I pursued the logical implications of my diagrams, they led to an unworkable number of hypotheses. Controlling for all major variables at once was not possible because of my limited N (373). Regression analysis and path analysis were appropriate for my line of argument but not to my level of data, at least according to the more strict statistical approach I was inclined to follow. I decided to carry out the analysis in terms of cross classification percentages, chi square measures of statistical significance, and gamma measures of association. I also decided to limit myself to certain major questions which could be considered quite separately but which at the same time would add up to some sort of exploration and test of my major hypotheses about professional autonomy, large organizations, exchange strengths, and professional community involvement. Eventually this organization worked well enough, but initially I was reluctant to follow it because it meant that I ignored large sections of my questionnaire data.

Selection of the precise operational measures of the major variables also required more time than anticipated. Two separate aspects of this problem can be mentioned here, one having to do with the selection of the most satisfying measure among several already existing measures and the other with constructing a composite measure from a series of submeasures. The first type of problem is illustrated by the measure for professional autonomy.

THE RESEARCH EXPERIENCE

My questionnaire had a number of questions which touched on aspects of professional autonomy, but it came as a shock to realize at this late stage that, while making such an effort to tap so many related but nonessential variables, I had not been careful enough about constructing really good direct measures for professional autonomy itself. I now saw some drawbacks in my intended primary measure of professional autonomy in that it relied on the respondent's own assessment. Consequently, in the analysis, I decided to examine two secondary measures as well. These measures usually led to results similar to those on the primary one and added to the strength of my data, but they tripled the amount of computer output without adding proportionately to the basic information or to the complexity of the theoretical argument.

Development of a measure for the variable of total exchange strengths is one example of the need to combine results from several questions into one composite measure. Value categories for total exchange strengths were constructed from combinations of value categories for (1) value to firm, (2) difficulty of replacement, and (3) realistic job alternatives. A measure for the latter variable was itself constructed from two separate questions, one having to do with being wanted by other work situations and the other with finding other work situations attractive. Construction of such composite variables was not simply a question of which items to combine into a meaningful measure, it also involved finding or developing a computer program to carry out the operation effectively. I spent a good deal of the summer of 1968 preparing programs to carry out the kind of data transformations I wanted—transformations which could not be done by existing programs. (Packaged programs, like SPSS, were not then available.) Not only did this take considerable time, it also was the kind of busy work which always seemed to distract me from the hard task of actual writing and analysis.

By the end of the summer I finally completed the construction of the composite measures. The number of data cards per respondent had jumped from 9 to 13. At this time I finally gave up all intentions of carrying out a second data gathering phase of my study. The N.S.F. grant included money for in-depth interviews with knowledgeable CPAs representative of major position and organization types. My intention had been to do this after I had completed preliminary analysis of my data results. Unfortunately, that preliminary analysis had now fallen way behind schedule, and so the interview phase was never carried out.

In the fall of 1968 I tackled the analysis in a systematic and efficient fashion. Now in my second year of teaching, I gave priority to the dissertation and learned to take advantage of my Tuesday-Thursday teaching schedule by working without interruption at home the other five days. By February of 1969, despite considerable complexity in the data and despite the sheer quantity of computer output, a rough write-up of the analysis was finally complete.

Unfortunately, the results did not easily fall into a pattern which directly confirmed or disproved my major theoretical expectations. Even before looking at computer output, I had enough of a feel for what the questionnaires contained to know that the data would not provide an easy answer to my questions. This forced me to be much more cautious and detailed in examining the data. The biggest problem was not so much that hierarchical position was so positively related to professional autonomy as the fact that very few CPAs of any kind possessed a strong total set of exchange strengths. Those strong on value to firm and difficulty of replacement tended to be higher position CPAs who felt they had few job alternatives. On the other hand, those who felt they had job alternatives tended to be lower position CPAs who did not feel strong on the first two exchange strengths. And at first glance it even seemed that those with a strong set of exchange strengths were no better off than others in terms of professional autonomy. Informal norms among CPAs for strong identification with one's firms and against mobility from firm to firm seemed to vitiate the possession of exchange strengths and their applicability to maintaining professional autonomy. In other words, the old pessimism about the subordination of professional to bureaucratic principles seemed to be borne out by my data, despite my anticipations to the contrary.

Checking the data, however, I found very low percentages of CPAs with a professional identification, the presence of which had been a key assumption in my thinking about professionals and exchange strengths. Once I controlled for the presence of this professional community identification factor, the data on exchange strengths and professional autonomy did support my initial theroretical expectations. In some respects then, this complex set of results, which forced me to tie in my underlying assumptions, gave stronger support to my major hypothesis and theoretical framework than if the basic relationships had been supported simply and directly. They also led me to recognize the importance of the structural aspects of a profession. Differences both between and within professions had to be taken into account. My data results also confirmed earlier cautions I had been given at the beginning of the study about the appropriateness of CPAs on the grounds that they simply are not a sufficiently "professional" occupation.

As indicated above, the bulk of my analysis work was completed by February 1969. I learned a great deal about interpreting data and had developed some facility for condensing vasts amounts of data into summary charts of manageable proportion. During the Spring, I did touch-up work and waited for the evaluation of my committee, which turned out to be favorable. The official defense of the dissertation report was completed in May 1969 and the final bound copy handed over to the Cornell graduate school in August—two years after I had left Cornell with my boxes of keypunched data.

A reflective piece such as this has raised the question for me of whether the dissertation, or a journal-type article, or this article itself is a more accurate statement of my thinking pattern and my data results. Unfortunately, part of our reporting art consists in making the actual process and results conform to the ideal model, with the emphasis almost entirely on the logic of verification rather than on the context of discovery.

FINAL REFLECTIONS: WHERE TO GO FROM HERE

Looking back on the whole experience of this research project, I can see some problems and mistakes, but I am pleased that I did carry out, from start to finish, a dissertation study which was very much my own thing. At times I envied the convenient advantages enjoyed by dissertation researchers who either based their work on a secondary analysis of previously collected data or inserted a few questions of their own into a larger project already organized by an experienced researcher who not only made all the major decisions but also had already received financial support, established necessary contacts, and organized an appropriate staff. Good as such apprentice training may be, the first-hand experience I gained in every feature of a fairly involved research project prepared me well for subsequent research.

To date, despite the production of several book chapters, convention papers, and M.A. theses, in addition to the dissertation itself, most of the data collected in the study have not yet been analyzed. That this problem is common in survey research does not entirely excuse me, since Professor Thompson had warned me of this beforehand. There is still a great deal of substantive information in the data which would contribute to a more detailed description of the CPA profession as well as provide a testing ground for other aspects of the theoretical relevance of an exchange approach to professional autonomy and the compatibility of professional and bureaucratic principles. The study could also lead to several follow-ups. One might be a panel study which in five years would resubmit portions of the original questionnaire to the same lower level CPAs to see how much changes in their professional and bureaucratic orientations were related to initial strength of such orientations, divergent role pressures, or possession of exchange strengths. Another follow-up effort might be a replication of this study several years after the CPA profession drops its traditional requirement of within-firm apprenticeship in favor of a university-based educational program leading directly to the CPA certificate, as it is now contemplating doing. Such a change would broaden the CPA's network of professional contacts and increase the ease of interfirm job mobility. Changes on these dimensions would constitute an excellent further test of my theoretical stress on exchange strengths and professional community identification.

Neither these follow-up possibilities nor the detailed description of the CPA profession are, however, likely to be carried out. One reason is simply that I have never become all that interested in the substantive description of the CPA profession in its own right. Another reason is that my interest in the underlying issue of professional autonomy has itself been somewhat modified. At the time of the study's conception, my own bias included a number of positive assumptions about professions and professionalism which many of us are more hesitant about today. We now see dangers in professional specialization as well as in bureaucratic organization. We are hesitant not only about the control exercised over us by the rules and reward systems of our bureaucratic organizations, but also about the control exercised over us by the priorities and reward systems of our specialized professions. I continue to see professions as providing the individual with exchange strengths and resources for increasing personal autonomy from the employing organization. But, in developing these exchange strengths, the individual has in fact submitted to and become dependent upon the profession and its system of values, rewards, approval, and authority. Where the profession is very much under the control of a dominant orthodoxy, this can even threaten one's professional autonomy in areas of professional activity. In any case, it is more likely to affect personal autonomy by influencing one's lifestyle—success goals, political activities, dress, and consumer purchases of "appropriate" sets of status symbols and satisfactions.

In one sense, this change in my own assumptions about professions has lessened my interest in pursuing research on professions and professional autonomy. In another sense, however, my theoretical perspective and my research results on exchange strengths and professional autonomy are still consistent with my present more negative bias about professions and their own power to control. They fit in nicely with the thrust of Eliot Freidson's work (1970b) on "professional dominance" and his stress on professional autonomy as the most crucial characteristic of professional status. He speaks of professional autonomy, which is based on power or dominance over related occupations and work activity and which can be used not strictly for ensuring quality performance of central professional functions but often for convenient advantageous gain for the professional association itself. The issue, in other words, is not so much the incompatibility of professional and bureaucratic principles but which societal values, priorities, and elite groups professional and bureaucratic principles are utilized to benefit.

My own current view is that professional and bureaucratic principles are not in fact all that different. Both groups (most professionals and most bureaucrats) have operated within the context of fairly similar sets of assumptions about major financial distributions, status rewards, lifestyles, and consumer goals. Bureaucracy is one phase and professionalism is simply a subsequent phase in the same general industrialization process based on rational specialization. But now, whether because of an energy crisis, or because of counterculture dissatisfaction with industrial success, or because industrialization's own inner logic leads to the emergence of a quite different postindustrial phase, we are involved in a painful process of redefining what our basic individual and societal goals, assumptions, and interests need be. As these newly needed priorities slowly emerge we may need to be more concerned about professional accountability than professional autonomy. The present order of priorities and reward systems must give way to something we can gradually come to see as more appropriate. The concern is that the principle of professional autonomy should not be utilized to preserve the benefits and vested interests professionals have come to enjoy under the old order, but rather to contribute to those new priorities which professional expertise may indicate are most appropriate in the service of the entire society.

BIBLIOGRAPHY

Blau, Peter. *Exchange and power in social life.* New York: Wiley, 1964.

Carey, John C. *The CPA plans for the future.* New York: American Institute of Certified Public Accountants, 1965.

Freidson, Eliot. *Profession of medicine: A study of the sociology of applied knowledge.* New York: Dodd, Mead & Co., 1970.(a)

_____. *Professional dominance: The social structure of medical care.* New York: Atherton, 1970.(b)

Gouldner, Alvin. Reciprocity and autonomy in functional theory. Pp. 241-270 in Llewellyn Gross (ed.), *Symposium on sociological theory.* New York: Harper & Row, 1959.

Lengermann, Joseph. The autonomy of professionals employed in bureaucratic organizations: a study of certified public accountants. Unpublished Ph.D. dissertation, Cornell University, 1969.

_____. Supposed and actual differences in professional autonomy among CPAs as related to type of work organization and size of firm. *The Accounting Review,* 1971, *46,* 665-675.

_____. Professional autonomy in organizations: The case of CPAs. In Muriel Cantor and Phyllis Stewart (eds.), *Varieties of work.* New York: Schenkman, 1974.

March, James, & Simon, Herbert. *Organizations.* New York: Wiley, 1958.

Thibaut, John W., & Kelley, Harold H. *The social psychology of groups.* New York: Wiley, 1959.

USING
AVAILABLE DATA

A. *RESEARCH BY*
James A. Banks
Jack Levin &
James Spates
John D. Kasarda
Allan M. Schwartzbaum,
Robert A. Rothman &
John H. McGrath III
Roberta Rovner-Pieczenik

B. *PERSONAL JOURNALS BY*
James A. Banks
James L. Spates &
Jack Levin
John D. Kasarda
Allan M. Schwartzbaum,
Robert A. Rothman &
John H. McGrath III
Roberta Rovner-Pieczenik

CHAPTER 5

CHAPTER 5

USING AVAILABLE DATA

This section pulls together a number of research approaches that use "what's available." Included here are content analyses, secondary analyses, and a case study. As pointed out in Chapter 1, it is difficult to say whether these are strategies in their own right or simply variations on other, more common research strategies. There are, for example, many parallels between the principles underlying survey research and the steps involved in it and those involved in content analysis and secondary analysis.

Content analysis is a strategy which has been developed to facilitate systematic study of public and private documents. The major difference between survey research and content analysis is that in the latter the units of study are not human. Once the population—whether passages in history books or underground newspapers, song lyrics or court records—is defined, the same principles of random sampling must be used to select cases as are used in survey research. Care must be exercised to ensure that units are "representative." Further, as in framing questions for surveys, much attention is given in content analysis to developing categories and coding procedures. In fact, many of the difficulties surrounding content analysis are related to formulating appropriate and workable categories for analysis. Because it does not require securing the cooperation of respondents or subjects, whose awareness of being studied might actually affect their behavior, content analysis is often cited as a nonreactive or "unobtrusive" research strategy.

As with others represented in this book, the study by James A. Banks of the black American in textbooks was not the study he first started out to do. Time and money were important limiting factors for Banks, as they were for several other contributors. His first idea, related to his interest in ethnic studies and urban education, was to focus on the attitudes, beliefs, and behavior of teachers in urban schools. Difficulty in securing the cooperation of a large urban school district, combined with the omnipresent problems of inadequate funds and insufficient time, caused him to abandon this idea. He decided instead to consider the effects of school textbooks on students' racial attitudes, self-concepts, and beliefs.

Specifically, Banks chose to do a content analysis of the black American in elementary history textbooks. Because he wanted to do a systematic, quantitative analysis, as opposed to the more impressionistic, qualitative approaches used in previous studies, he faced several unique practical problems. As Banks notes, content analyses have been more commonly used by communication specialists in studies of the media. His content was just different enough so that he had "few models to emulate." Translating theoretical discussions into appropriate and workable categories which could be used to classify themes about blacks in American history textbooks presented a formidable challenge. The difficulty of locating all of the textbooks in his sample was an unanticipated and time-consuming minor annoyance. Compromises on the size of his validation jury and on the number of coders used to establish reliability were forced, again, by constraints of time, money, and availability of personnel.

Conceptualizing the study and formulating the design were "very intellectually demanding but exciting" tasks for Banks. Doing the statistical analysis and analyzing the findings were "enjoyable." Actually reading the textbooks and classifying the themes, however, was "time-consuming, tedious, and boring." Poor indexes and the fact that much of the material was not very well written made it even more so. Though there are some aspects Banks feels might have been improved and about which he makes some suggestions, overall he seems satisfied with his "modest attempt to describe, scientifically, how one ethnic minority group was treated in a sample of elementary American history textbooks that were used widely in schools throughout the United States." He would like to see similar attempts to study the images of other ethnic minority groups in such textbooks.

The study by Jack Levin and James Spates of the underground press is a more typical content analysis than Banks's because the content it uses is more typical of the content on which such analyses are usually done. Unlike Banks, they had few problems in conceptualizing and formulating appropriate categories for analysis. At the time, they had both just completed a course which encompassed relevant theoretical discussions, and Levin had had previous experience in doing content analysis. Further, they were able to borrow from and build on the work of others who had developed systematic techniques for analyzing values in the way they had chosen. Consequently, their data collection and analysis went rather smoothly.

In their personal journal, then, Spates and Levin focus on the personal and theoretical origins of their study. They reveal how the hippies "happened" to them, as sociologists and as people, and on their own reactions to the encounter. The journal is of special interest because it contrasts the differing perspectives of two authors on a joint project. Certainly, throughout, Spates seems to be more personally attracted to the hippies than Levin does, and thus he experiences more ambivalence. In fact, Spates became so involved that his doctoral dissertation consisted of a replication and extension of the research reported here, with Levin acting as faculty consultant.

Basically, in the study reprinted here, Levin and Spates found that "the hippies were committed, as they claimed, to an alternative (expressive) system of beliefs." It was an exciting finding. Perhaps, they thought, "'the alternative' was viable after all." As they comment, however, this was hope on Jim's part and curiosity on Jack's. They really had no evidence that such was the case. The authors discuss the findings of their subsequent research, much of it done by Spates alone, which indicates that the counterculture, if it existed, was not an enduring phenomenon. They then consider these findings in the context of their own search for identity, as persons and as sociologists.

Secondary analysis is also very closely related to survey analysis. The basic difference between survey research and secondary analysis is that, in the latter, the data have been collected by someone else for some other purpose. This means that the researcher has little control over the nature of the data or of the data collection process. As a result, it is sometimes difficult to formulate appropriate operational definitions because the data have not been collected in the appropriate form. On the other hand, it can be argued that secondary analysis frees researchers from the responsibility and the time and the expense of collecting and coding their own data.

Use of national census data, a common example of this approach, is exemplified here by the work of John D. Kasarda. As he points out, the U.S. Census is probably the largest, most diverse, and most important set of secondary data available. Certainly it makes available to many researchers data far more complete and comprehensive than they could secure for themselves. Using what is available allows the researcher to concentrate on conceptualizing and developing problems and on analyzing data.

Kasarda's interest in the influence of suburban population growth on central city services grew out of a seminar on human ecology, an area of study which is concerned with "the size, composition, and distribution of particular populations," and which takes a "geographically delimited population" as its unit of analysis. For his study, Kasarda chose to use the Standard Metropolitan Statistical Area (SMSA), as established by the Bureau of the Census, as the unit of analysis.

In the context of his seminar, Kasarda developed two research hypotheses related to the theory of ecological expansion: "Ecological expansion is a two-fold process involving, first, a movement of people outward from a center of settlement without their losing contact with that center; and, second, a development of service functions in the center to sustain activities throughout the expanded system." Kasarda thus sought to determine whether or not central cities' service functions increase at a disproportionate rate as the suburban population increases in size and, further, whether or not increased expenditures for such services were also related to the use made of them by the expanding suburban population.

To test these hypotheses, Kasarda used several of the different U.S. Censuses, those on populations, businesses, and governments. Since the census provides data on most variables at different periods of time, Kasarda was able to test his hypotheses both cross-sectionally (i.e., at one common point in time) and longitudinally (i.e., at a number of different points in time).

Because Kasarda was another student researcher with limited time and money, he did much of the work himself. Secondary analysis may spare the researcher the time and cost of data collection and tabulation, but analysis can still be complex and frustrating. The size of his sample and, especially, the number of variables in his study necessitated use of a computer. This meant keypunching the data onto IBM cards and "many tedious evenings" in the computation center. In the later extension of the study, a small grant made it possible for Kasarda to hire an assistant to do this work.

To analyze his data Kasarda used a very convenient and increasingly popular canned computer program called SPSS (Statistical Package for the Social Sciences). For the first phase, Kasarda carried out only "basic cross-tabular and correlation analyses." In the later expansion, he attempted to solve several methodological problems by including all SMSAs as of 1950, increasing the number of variables, and introducing several controls intended to minimize the possibility of spurious relationships. Kasarda also chose, in the expanded analysis, to use path analysis to determine statistically "the strength of relationship between two variables when controlling for other theoretically relevant variables." Kasarda's clear presentation of this procedure in the research article and his helpful explanation in the personal journal should make it easier for students to understand a statistical procedure which may seem formidable.

Kasarda's research is clearly in an area that has direct policy implications. While he deals with related issues in his research report, in his personal journal he also quite honestly admits his later misgivings ("I now feel that I speculated beyond the evidence of my data") and goes on to discuss his present views on the subject and his ideas for improving the study.

The research by Allan Schwartzbaum, Robert Rothman, and John H. McGrath III meets one of the criteria for secondary analysis—the data are analyzed for a purpose other than that for which they were collected. The data in this case, however, were not collected by someone else but by the authors themselves. The secondary analysis actually emerged out of a larger study of resistance to change among a group of physicians. During the analysis of questionnaire data obtained from the physicians, the authors became aware that their fixed-alternative questions obscured some of the intensity of feeling apparent in the doctors' "write-in" responses. Fixed-alternative response categories had been used to minimize the amount of time required and to maximize response rate, and Schwartzbaum, et al. were surprised at the number of doctors who added comments. They decided "to examine differences between respondents who volunteer comments . . . and those who do not." It occurred to them that these write-ins represented "an additional and potentially valuable source of data."

Having decided to do a secondary analysis of write-ins, the authors struggled with developing several measures of write-in behavior. The simplest distinguished only between those who commented and those who did not. An imaginative but tedious approach measured total output by counting every single letter of commentary.

While the authors believe that "adequate social science research requires the use of a theoretical framework," their own search for and choice of such a framework was not achieved through systematic and thoughtful

THE RESEARCH EXPERIENCE

deliberation but rather was the result of the fortuitous and serendipitous recognition by Schwartzbaum that there "might be a possible connection between the motives behind voluntary write-ins and small-group communication." It was a creative and useful insight. Utilizing Stanley Schacter's framework, Schwartzbaum and his associates predicted that those doctors involved in a reference group opposed to merger would be more likely to write in comments. Because theirs was a post hoc analysis, Schwartzbaum and his associates were unable to operationalize their variables as Schacter had in his original study. This limitation weakened their study and caused the authors to describe their research as "exploratory."

As have other contributors, Schwartzbaum et al. mention the temptation to collect more information than is needed, thus winding up with much unanalyzed data. Joint authorship was one of the important factors in making it possible for this particular, very unusual, study to be done. While "the two other members of the research team devoted their full energies to the main research topic of organizational change," Schwartzbaum was able to concentrate on "the interesting but less pressing question of 'voluntary write-in' behavior." In addition to the advantages in time expenditure, collaboration also made possible the implementation of a research design which "none of us could have produced individually" and the "division of labor with respect to the tasks of the research." Despite the inherent advantages, the authors conclude that "such elements as the compatibility of personalities and the complementarity of skills and experiences play an important role" in determining the efficiency and the quality of joint projects.

Roberta Rovner-Pieczenik's case study of an urban court involved several phases and utilized several means of data collection—participant observation, in-depth interviews, and a content analysis of court records (the type of "triangulation" suggested by several other authors in this collection). Like many other social scientists, Rovner-Pieczenik did not do the study she started out to do. For various reasons, her initial interest in studying some aspect of police operations gave way to her second choice, a study of the defense attorney. She soon discovered much had already been written on this role, and topic two was put aside. Other fears and fantasies eliminated the criminal and the judge as possible research topics, and "by default" her "path stopped at the door of the prosecuting attorney." Though she began by focusing on this topic, at still a later stage in her research she decided to study the adjudication of felony cases in the court. The prosecuting attorney thus became one of several legal actors in an organizational context.

In both the observation and interview phases of her research, Rovner-Pieczenik had few problems gaining access. Her decision "to seek an affiliation with the prosecutor attached to Metrocourt" was made largely for pragmatic reasons:

> The office I selected was close to my residence. I could be there in ten minutes and travel against rush-hour traffic. Both the head prosecuting attorney and his

chief assistant were friendly and encouraging. Lastly, . . . I felt comfortable with the office and the men. The majority of prosecutors were familiar in type: they were of similar social class and religious background and of similar political persuasion.

During the exploratory-observation phase, "establishing credibility as a researcher was more difficult" than Rovner-Pieczenik had anticipated. The 100 or so assistant prosecutors had decided she was a "spy" from "up front." She also comments on some of the peculiar problems related to being *both* "female" and "serious researcher." The apparent role confusion existed not only in the minds of court personnel but also in her own.

To study "bargain justice," which became the focus for her research, Rovner-Pieczenik decided to collect statistical information about the processing and outcome of a large number of individual cases. The research article included in this chapter is based largely on the analysis of court records which constituted this second phase of her research. To obtain the appropriate information from court files, Rovner-Pieczenik drew a stratified random sample from several different universes, from cases closed in the Lower Court through cases closed in Superior Court after Grand Jury indictment. Using available data for content analysis may be less reactive than asking questions directly of respondents, but it does not necessarily eliminate data-gathering "overkill." Like many survey researchers, Rovner-Pieczenik obtained and recorded far more data from the court files than she needed or could ever hope to analyze. This very tedious, and often boring, task provided much of the critical information for her analysis. Later she realized that her observations and interviews were "not only important for file data interpretation and speculation but also a source of information significant enough to warrant expansion and formalization."

Rovner-Pieczenik enjoyed her liaison with the court so thoroughly she was reluctant to return to being a graduate student and writing up her data. At that point, however, she had no idea how long she would remain in this position. Rovner-Pieczenik is a classic example of a person who left the disciplined and supportive environment of the university too soon. Even though her academic advisors had warned her "from the first day of entering the doctoral program" that she should remain a full-time student at the university until her degree was in hand, she failed to heed their advice. The six years it took her to complete the writing of her dissertation provide the type of material of which graduate student "horror stories" are made.

James A. Banks ——————————————————————————

A. A CONTENT ANALYSIS OF THE BLACK AMERICAN IN TEXTBOOKS

INTRODUCTION

The urgent racial crisis in our nation has evoked considerable concern among educators about the roles of the school and teaching materials in intergroup education. Research indicates that teaching materials *do* affect youngsters' racial attitudes. Trager and Yarrow found that a curriculum which emphasized cultural diversity had a positive influence on children's racial attitudes.[1] Research by Johnson indicated that courses in black history could help black children feel better about themselves and their race.[2] Litcher and Johnson investigated the effects of multiethnic readers on the racial attitudes of second-grade white pupils and concluded that ". . . use of multiethnic readers resulted in marked positive change in the subjects' attitudes toward Negroes."[3] Since textbooks, which comprise the core of the social studies curriculum, can influence racial attitudes, it becomes imperative to evaluate carefully the content of textbooks with a view toward ascertaining the contributions which they might be making toward helping youngsters clarify their racial attitudes, self-perceptions, and value orientations. The careful study of textbooks is especially urgent in this time of high racial tension and polarization.

Source: James A. Banks, "A Content Analysis of the Black American in Textbooks," *Social Education,* December 1969, pp. 954-957.

This article is based on "A Content Analysis of Elementary American History Textbooks; The Treatment of the Negro in Race Relations," unpublished Ph.D. dissertation, Michigan State University. Copyright © 1969 by James A. Banks. The author is grateful to Professor William W. Joyce, Michigan State University, for his assistance and guidance during the duration of this research endeavor.

1. Helen G. Trager and Marian R. Yarrow, *They Learn What They Live* (New York: Harper and Brothers, 1952).
2. David W. Johnson, "Freedom School Effectiveness: Changes in Attitudes of Negro Children," *The Journal of Applied Behavioral Science, 2,* 325-330, 1966.
3. John H. Litcher and David W. Johnson, "Changes in Attitudes of White Elementary School Students After Use of Multiethnic Readers," *Journal of Educational Psychology, 60,* 148-152, 1969.

THE PROBLEM

The purpose of this study was to analyze the content of a selected sample of elementary American history textbooks in terms of major themes used to discuss the Negro and race relations. A review of the literature revealed the need for a current, scientific, and comprehensive study of the black American in textbooks.

In recent years, a number of researchers have studied the image of the black American and other minority groups in textbooks. While these studies are significant contributions to the literature on race relations,[4] none utilized a content analysis technique which met the criteria of scientific content analysis as promulgated by researchers such as Berelson, Budd, Thorp and Donohew, Kerlinger, and Borg. These writers maintain that a scientific content analysis must be *objective, systematic,* and *quantitative.*[5] To satisfy these criteria, a study must have well delineated categories, a measure of reliability, clearly formulated data gathering procedures, and research hypotheses which can be tested by analyzing the data gathered during the investigation.

The study reported here was designed to utilize a scientific content analysis technique to illuminate the dominant themes (major ideas) used to discuss the Negro and race relations in a sample of 36 American history books for use in grades 4, 5, 6, 7, and 8. A sub-sample of six books was used to compare the frequency of selected theme units in books published in 1964 and in 1968.[6]

---

4. A partial list of these studies includes: Committee on the Study of Teaching Materials in Intergroup Education, *Intergroup Relations in Teaching Materials* (Washington, D.C.: American Council on Education, 1949); Lloyd Marcus, *The Treatment of Minorities in American History Textbooks* (New York: Anti-Defamation League, 1961); Kenneth M. Stampp, W. D. Jordan, L. W. Levine, R. L. Middlekeuff, C. G. Sellers and G. W. Stocking, "The Negro in American History Textbooks," *Integrated Education,* 2, 9-24: October-November 1964; Department of Public Instruction, *A Report on the Treatment of Minorities in American History Textbooks* (Lansing, Michigan: Michigan Department of Education, 1968).

5. See Bernard Berelson, *Content Analysis in Communication Research* (Glencoe: The Free Press Publishers, 1952); Richard W. Budd, Robert K. Thorp, and Lewis Donohew, *Content Analysis of Communications* (New York: The Macmillan Company, 1967); Fred N. Kerlinger, *Foundations of Behavioral Research: Educational and Psychological Inquiry* (New York: Holt, Rinehart & Winston, Inc., 1966); and, Walter R. Borg, *Educational Research: An Introduction* (New York: David McKay Company, Inc., 1963).

6. The six books were: Orrel T. Baldwin, *The Story of Our America* (New York: Noble & Noble Publishers, Inc., 1964); Richard C. Brown, Arlan C. Helgeson, and George H. Lobdell, *The United States of America: A History for Young Citizens* (Atlanta: Silver Burdett Company, 1964); Mabel B. Casner and Ralph H. Gabriel, *Story of the American Nation* (New York: Harcourt, Brace and World, Inc., 1964); Stephen H. Bronz, Glenn W. Moon, and Don C. Cline, *The Challenge of America* (New York: Holt, Rinehart & Winston, 1968); Harold H. Eibling, Fred M. King, and James Harlow, *History of Our United States* (River Forest, Illinois: Laidlaw Brothers, 1968); Jerome R. Reich and Edward L. Biller, *Building the American Nation* (New York: Harcourt, Brace and World, Inc., 1968).

PROCEDURES

Unit of Analysis

A technique called *thematic analysis* was used in this study. According to Budd, Thorp, and Donohew, a theme is a major idea or single thought unit. A sentence may contain one or more theme units. The sentence, "John is handsome and intelligent," contains *two* themes or ideas. They are, "John is handsome," and "John is intelligent."[7] The total number of themes in *each* sentence analyzed was ascertained and reported in this study.

Formulation of Categories and Coding Sheet

Theme units were classified under one of eleven categories (described below). Initially, theme units were selected from a sample of elementary American history textbooks, and the categories developed on the basis of the content of these theme units, recommendations made by social scientists and educators (studies on minority groups in textbooks were analyzed for the major ideas which were recommended for inclusion in textbooks by these researchers), and reading in black history by the investigator. Sample theme units were added and some minor modifications made in category definitions during the analysis, since, as Budd, Thorp, and Donohew noted, ". . . because it is virtually impossible to anticipate every situation that will arise during the coding, each category definition should allow for expansion. . . ."[8]

Validity of the Coding Sheet

The "jury method" was used to ascertain the validity of the procedures in this study. In this method, ". . . experts are asked to judge relevant parts of the methodology . . . or measuring instruments."[9] Four experts in the teaching of black history, one historian and three social studies educators, were identified and asked to serve on the panel of jurors to validate the instrument.[10] These individuals were selected because of their publications and reputations in the area of race relations and black history. Each juror was asked to judge whether the theme units from the initial sample of books were *appropriately* or *inappropriately* categorized. All four jurors judged 89% of the theme units to be *appropriately* categorized. *All* theme units were judged appropriately categorized by at least two jurors.

---

7. Richard W. Budd, Robert K. Thorp, and Lewis Donohew, *op. cit.*, pp. 44-46.
8. *Ibid.*, p. 28.
9. *Ibid.*, p. 69.
10. The jurors were: Dr. Nancy Arnez, Professor of Education, Northeastern Illinois State College; Dr. Dewitt Dykes, Professor of American History, Michigan State University; Miss Astrid C. Anderson, Research Associate, the Lincoln Filene Center for Citizenship and Public Affairs, Tufts University; and Mr. Irving J. Sloan, author of books on the black American and Social Studies Teacher, Scarsdale (New York) Junior High School.

Reliability of the Procedures

The reliability of the coding procedure was established by having two coders independently code the theme units in five books randomly selected from the total sample.[11] The coder proportion of agreement was .64.

Formulation of Hypotheses

Each hypothesis stated a predicted relationship between the frequencies of two theme categories. *The investigator assumed that the categories selected for comparison had a high degree of comparability, importance, and the greatest potential for yielding meaningful information.* For example, the theme unit frequencies in the categories "Racial Harmony" and "Racial Violence and Conflict" were compared because they had contrasting definitions and because previous researchers had reported that authors frequently employ units in the former category and rarely in the latter. "Racial Harmony" and "Principal Discrimination" theme unit frequencies were compared for similar reasons. The purpose and scope of this study did not warrant that all possible comparisons between categories be made.

All hypotheses were stated in the null form. The hypotheses stated that there was no difference in the frequencies of theme units in the categories compared. The .05 level of significance was selected as sufficient to reject the null hypothesis. Chi-square was used in the analysis.

Categories and Examples

Explained Discrimination Theme units which state reasons for differential treatment based on race but make no attempt to distinguish moral issues and causal issues. Such theme units are susceptible to being interpreted as *justifications* for discrimination.

Example: Negroes could withstand the hot Southern climate much better than whites.

Principal Discrimination Theme units which describe deliberate differential treatment based on race in which no attempt is made by the writer to explain the discriminatory practices depicted.

Example: The Plessy vs. Ferguson Decision upheld segregation.

---

11. The five books were: Orrel T. Baldwin, *The Story of Our America* (New York: Noble and Noble Publishers, Inc., 1964); Herbert H. Gross, Dwight W. Follett, Robert E. Gabler, William L. Burton, and Ben F. Ahlscwede, *Exploring Regions of the United States* (Chicago: Follett Publishing Company, 1966); Rembert W. Patrick, John K. Bettersworth, and Ralph W. Steen, *This Country of Ours* (Austin: The Steck Company, 1965); John A. Rickard and Rolor E. Ray, *Discovering American History* (Boston: Allyn and Bacon, Inc., 1965); and, Clarence L. Ver Steeg, *The Story of Our Country* (New York: Harper and Row Publishers, 1965).

Non-Violent Resistance to Discrimination Theme units which describe acts or words which *did not* involve violence but were designed primarily to resist discriminatory practices based on race.

Example: The NAACP worked to end discrimination.

Deliberate Desegregation Theme units which describe deliberate behavior on the part of majority groups or established institutions which ended or intended to end racial discrimination or segregation.

Example: The Brown Decision of 1954 prohibited segregation in the public schools.

Expedient Desegregation Theme units which describe behavior by majority groups or established institutions which resulted in ending segregation or discrimination but had other dominant objectives, such as political or social advancement of individuals, groups or a nation.

Example: Lincoln freed the slaves to weaken the Confederacy.

Racial Violence and Conflict Theme units which describe acts of violence which were caused in part or whole by factors involving racial confrontation and racial antagonism.

Example: The Ku Klux Klan committed violent acts against Negroes.

Deprivation Theme units which describe the physical and psychological poverty of black Americans.

Example: Slaves were poorly fed.

Stereotypes Theme units which describe conventional, fixed, and unverified characteristics of Negroes.

Example: Slaves were happy.

Prejudice Theme units which describe unfavorable racial attitudes which are held or were held in disregard of facts.

Example: Southern whites felt that the Negro was innately inferior.

Racial Harmony Theme units which describe peaceful and friendly relations between Negroes and whites, or events or acts which contributed to good race relations.

Example: Some masters freed their slaves.

Achievements Theme units which describe the accomplishments of Negroes in literature, music, art, science, industry, sports, entertainment, education and in other fields.

Example: Booker T. Washington was a famous scientist.

SUMMARY OF MAJOR FINDINGS

Theme units to be classified in the eleven categories were selected from the 36 American history textbooks used in the main analysis by checking the table of contents and index of each book and reading those parts of the book which discussed the Negro or race relations. The following comparisons of the resulting frequencies of theme units are of particular interest:

"Principal Discrimination" theme units had a higher frequency than "Racial Violence and Conflict" theme units.

"Explained Discrimination" theme units had a higher frequency than "Racial Violence and Conflict" theme units.

"Principal Discrimination" theme units had a higher frequency than "Racial Harmony" theme units.

"Racial Harmony" theme units and "Racial Violence and Conflict" theme units had equal frequencies.

"Achievement" theme units had a higher frequency than "Deprivation" theme units.

TABLE 1
Total Unit Frequencies by Category

Theme Category	Total Unit Frequency
Achievements	367
Principal discrimination	279
Deliberate desegregation	261
Explained discrimination	206
Non-violent resistance to discrimination	165
Racial harmony	164
Racial violence and conflict	140
Deprivation	82
Prejudice	25
Stereotypes	19
Expedient desegregation	14

TABLE 2
Minimum and Maximum Frequencies of Theme Units

Theme Category	Minimum units in any book	Maximum units in any book
Achievements	4	80
Principal discrimination	14	40
Deliberate desegregation	3	28
Explained discrimination	8	12
Non-violent resistance to discrimination	3	16
Racial harmony	10	24
Racial violence and conflict	5	18
Deprivation	3	12
Prejudice	0	5
Stereotypes	0	3
Expedient desegregation	0	4

"Non-Violent Resistance to Discrimination" theme units and "Racial Violence and Conflict" theme units had equal frequencies.

"Principal Discrimination" and "Deliberate Desegregation" theme units had equal frequencies.

"Deliberate Desegregation" theme units had a higher frequency than "Expedient Desegregation" theme units.

"Racial Harmony" theme units had a higher frequency than "Prejudice" theme units.

"Stereotypes" and "Prejudice" theme units had equal frequencies.

Theme units which referred to achievements, racial violence and conflict, peaceful resistance to discrimination, and deliberate acts of discrimination occurred more frequently in books published in 1968 than in 1964.

DISCUSSION OF FINDINGS

While textbook authors often attempt to explain or rationalize racial discrimination, they more frequently discuss discrimination without either explaining or condemning it. This finding supports that of other researchers who have suggested that textbook writers "avoid taking a moral stand."[12]

The authors of elementary history textbooks do not frequently depict racial violence. They seek to explain discrimination more frequently than they mention incidents of racial violence and conflict. However, authors refer to racial violence as often as they relate peaceful and friendly relations between blacks and whites. This finding conflicts with those of Stampp[13] and other writers who suggest that authors emphasize harmonious race relations and neglect discussion of racial conflict. The authors in this study also mentioned racial violence as frequently as they referred to peaceful resistance to discrimination.

Other findings in this study suggest that authors do not emphasize harmonious race relations. The authors referred to deliberate acts of discrimination much more often than they related incidents of racial harmony. However, they mentioned racial harmony more frequently than they did racial prejudice.

The textbook writers mentioned deliberate acts of discrimination as often as they related deliberate acts of desegregation. However, they referred to deliberate acts of desegregation more frequently than they mentioned acts which lead to desegregation but were expedient gestures.

The authors depicted the achievements of black Americans in literature, music, art, science, industry, sports, entertainment, education and in other fields much more frequently than they referred to any other events which

---

12. Department of Public Instruction, *A Report on the Treatment of Minorities in American History Textbooks* (Lansing: Michigan Department of Education, 1968).
13. Kenneth M. Stampp *et al., op. cit.,* pp. 9-24.

relate to the black man and race relations. For example, the physical and psychological deprivations of black Americans were rarely discussed. Thus, the achievements of individual black heroes were emphasized rather than the plight of the majority of black people in this country.

The authors of textbooks rarely used theme units which could be characterized as "stereotypes." This finding does not support the often heard contention that textbooks frequently describe Negroes in a stereotypic fashion.

A comparison of books published in 1964 and in 1968 revealed that significant changes had occurred in the frequency of several types of theme units used to discuss the Negro and race relations. Theme units which referred to achievements, violence and conflict, peaceful resistance to discrimination, and deliberate acts of discrimination occurred more frequently in books published in 1968 than in 1964. This finding indicates that textbook authors have responded, to some degree, to the demand for more comprehensive coverage of the black American in textbooks, and to the black American's increasingly active role in American life.

CONCLUSIONS AND RECOMMENDATIONS

1. This study indicates that authors rarely take a moral stand when discussing such issues as racial discrimination and racial prejudice. Those who maintain that one of the major goals of the social studies is to inculcate democratic racial attitudes will find reason here to ask for a reevaluation of the textbook author's role in intergroup education.

2. Theme units which refer to racial violence and conflict have low frequencies in elementary American history textbooks. Since racial violence and conflict are currently pervasive in our nation, a greater frequency of these units in textbooks appears necessary if that part of the curriculum is to reflect reality accurately.

3. Racial prejudice theme units appear infrequently in elementary American history textbooks. A greater number of these units might provide a context for helping children to deal with racial prejudice and conflict more intelligently.

4. This study indicates that most textbooks have "integrated" by extolling the virtues of "selected" black heroes. While both black and white youngsters need black heroes with whom they can identify, they need to know the plight of the masses of black people even more. Children cannot be expected to grasp the full significance of the black experience in America unless they are keenly aware of the social and historical factors which have kept the black man at the lower rungs of the social ladder.[14]

---

14. James A. Banks, "The Need for Positive Racial Attitudes in Textbooks" in Robert L. Green (editor), *Racial Crisis in American Education* (Chicago: Follett Publishing Company, 1969).

5. While the findings of this study support some of those of other researchers, they conflict with others. This suggests that more extensive and careful research is needed before we can derive conclusive statements regarding the treatment of the black American in teaching materials.

B. COMMENT ON "A CONTENT ANALYSIS OF THE BLACK AMERICAN IN TEXTBOOKS"

CHOICE OF RESEARCH PROBLEM

This study was done to help fulfill the requirements for my Ph.D. degree at Michigan State University, where I specialized in elementary education with particular emphasis on social studies programs for ethnic minority youths. Because of my interest in ethnic studies and racial problems, I took quite a few courses in black studies, urban education, and sociology. My career objective was to become a specialist in training teachers to teach social science in urban schools, and I felt that my Ph.D. dissertation should be directly related to my interest in ethnic studies and urban education.

I was very concerned about how the learning environment of students could be changed to increase their academic achievement and to help inner city youths, in particular, relate more positively to public school instruction. My knowledge of the sociology of schools convinced me that of all the factors that influenced student behavior, the classroom teacher was the most significant. Thus I thought that the best way to improve the learning environment for urban students was to modify the attitudes, beliefs, and behavior of their teachers. Studies by such researchers as Gottlieb (1964), Clark (1965), and Davidson and Lang (1960) indicated that teachers often have negative attitudes toward poor and minority group students.

My first idea for a Ph.D. research project was to study the effects of an experimental training program on the attitudes and beliefs of teachers in

---

Source: Prepared especially for this volume.

urban schools. I had to abandon this idea for several reasons. First, it was necessary that I complete my study *within* a one-year period, and it was unlikely that I would have been able to design and implement the kind of study I had in mind within those limitations. Second, I needed the coopera- tion of a large urban school district and numerous teachers to conduct the study, and the initial response I received from one large city school district convinced me that it was unwilling to cooperate with me in implementing the study. Third, the study would have been quite expensive to conduct, and I did not have the funds needed to finance this type of research project.

Although I was disappointed because I was unable to implement my "ideal" study, I did not despair. I realized that although the classroom teacher is the most important factor in the child's learning environment, there are other variables that influence student mastery of content and acquisition of attitudes. Of these other variables, the textbook was perhaps the most important. After reading Hillel Black's *The American Schoolbook* (1967), I became aware of the extent to which teachers relied upon the text- book for both content and methods of teaching.

Other studies, such as those by Trager and Yarrow (1952) and Litcher and Johnson (1969), revealed that teaching materials such as textbooks significantly influence students' racial attitudes, self-concepts, and beliefs. Studies by Lloyd Marcus (1961) and Kenneth Stampp et al. (1964) illumi- nated the ways in which black Americans were being omitted from textbooks written for elementary and high school students. Previous studies had estab- lished that textbooks are important tools in learning and that Black Americans had been largely left out of American history books for children. I was interested in determining whether the image of the Black American in textbooks had changed since the other studies had been conducted and whether a study that used a different technique of analysis would confirm or refute earlier studies.

The existing studies were somewhat dated; none had used a sample I considered adequate, and all employed a *qualitative* method of analysis. I wanted my study to fill in what I saw as serious gaps in the analysis of Black Americans in textbooks. I felt that I could do this by using a larger sample than had been used in previous studies, by analyzing more recent books, and by using a *scientific* content analysis technique.

CHOICE OF METHOD

Before I undertook the present study, several popular and professional articles and one book had focused on the treatment of minority groups in teaching materials. However, none of these studies had used a *content analysis* technique as defined by Berelson (1952), and other content analysts (Budd, et al., 1967). These researchers state that a scientific content analysis must be *objective, systematic,* and *quantitative.* Previous researchers had used a qualitative method of analysis. My department at Michigan State University was highly quantitatively oriented, and both my thesis committee and I felt that my study would be much more significant if I used a more scientific method to analyze the content of textbooks than had been used by other researchers. We made no attempt to minimize the importance of qualitative and impressionistic analyses of teaching materials; rather, we felt that there was less need for more studies of that type.

SAMPLE

The sample was limited to elementary American history textbooks both because of my interest in history and elementary education and because time and resources did not permit me to analyze other kinds of elementary social studies textbooks, such as those for geography and sociology. Because I wanted to keep the sample manageable, and because I was primarily interested in recently published books for the middle and upper grades, the sample was limited to books listed under "American history" in the 1968 edition of *Textbooks in Print,* to books recommended for use in grades 4, 5, 6, 7, and 8, and to books published during the period 1961 to 1968.

DIFFICULTIES ENCOUNTERED

My greatest problem was to conceptualize the design. Often a researcher who identifies a problem and decides on the basic method to be used to study it can rely heavily upon previous studies to give him directions for refining and detailing his design. All of the studies on the treatment of ethnic minorities in textbooks I reviewed used qualitative rather than quantitative methods, however, and consequently they were of little help to me while I was formulating my design.

In surveying the professional literature, I discovered that scientific analysis was an infrequently used method in the field of education. Most scientific content analysis studies had been conducted by communication specialists and were confined to studies of the media. Although I read the studies by communication researchers, they were of minimal help to me because the content they analyzed was, in every case, quite different from the content of elementary history textbooks.

With few models to emulate, I was faced with the difficult task of translating an idea into a workable design. I had to rely primarily upon theoretical discussions of content analysis for directions, and even these were limited to a few books and articles. Of the sources I studied, these two were most helpful: Richard W. Budd, Robert K. Thorp, and Lewis Donohew, *Content Analysis of Communications* (1967) and Bernard Berelson, *Content Analysis in Communication Research* (1952). Since the printed page is such a cogent variable in the learning process, I was puzzled that educational researchers had given so little attention to the scientific study of instructional materials.

My first major task was to formulate *categories* which I could use as a guide to analyze the sample of books. Because I had a rather sophisticated knowledge of the history of Black Americans, I was aware of the basic events in Black history that might be treated in elementary history textbooks and some of the major issues that might be highlighted. I first thought of formulating categories around historical periods but quickly abandoned this idea because I felt that such categories would be only indirectly related to the central problem in the study. I decided to formulate categories which could be used to classify statements or "themes" about Blacks in American history textbooks.

To identify possible categories, I started reading a sample of elementary American history textbooks and noting the statements that dealt with Black Americans. As I read, I tried to note, with a word or phrase, how various statements might be classified. For example, when I read a statement such as "W. E. B. DuBois was a famous civil rights leader," I noted that this statement or theme was an example of "Achievement." I continued this process until I formulated a number of tentative categories.

Once I had identified the tentative categories, my next major task was to construct an instrument listing the categories, with sample themes (or statements) given under the appropriate categories. I carried out this task by reference to a number of elementary history books. Several problems arose when I attempted to categorize statements using the tentative categories; some of the statements did not seem to belong to any of the categories, and others seemed to belong to more than one of them. The categories were neither exhaustive nor mutually exclusive (Selltiz et al., 1959: 392).

An attempt to resolve these problems resulted in major revisions in the preliminary categories. Some were modified, others were deleted, and some new ones were established. This major revision resulted in the 11 categories that were finally used in the study. This major revision and new set of categories helped to reduce the problem of classifying themes in the study, but it was never totally eliminated. Throughout the study the problem of theme classification continued to rise.

In addition to the conceptual problems I experienced in the study, a number of procedural problems arose. I found it very difficult to find all of the 36 books that constituted the sample I had identified. This was a problem I had never anticipated because of the ample references located in the Michigan State University Instructional Materials Center and in the local schools and public libraries. Nevertheless, this problem was resolved only after much frustration and searching. In several instances books had to be ordered directly from their publishers. This was both time-consuming and expensive.

CHANGES MADE AS RESEARCH PROGRESSED

Like almost every other graduate student, I wanted to create a "perfect" study. I felt that establishing the *validity* and *reliability* of my instrument and procedures was especially important. I had originally planned to have a validation jury of 20 experts; instead, I had 4 jurors. Discussions with several professors convinced me that having 20 jurors was both impractical and unnecessary. Although such a large jury was not practical, I still feel that a larger jury would have increased the value of the study.

Almost every researcher who uses a survey instrument experiences problems in getting the instruments returned from the respondents. I had a similar "return" problem. My case was unique because I had a validation jury of only four people, and it was absolutely essential that I get a 100 percent return before I could complete the study. After several follow-up letters and phone calls, I finally received all of the instruments. However, my study was considerably delayed because I could not proceed with it until my instrument had been validated.

To establish coder reliability, I had originally planned to have at least three individuals use the instrument to read and analyze the books. I was unable to carry out this plan because of the tremendous expense involved and because it was difficult to find people who were willing and able to perform the task. I established coder reliability by having two coders independently code the theme units in five books randomly selected from the total sample. This method was adequate and scientifically sound, but it was a compromise with my original plan for establishing coder reliability.

PERSONAL INVOLVEMENT

The conceptualization of the study, the formulation of the design, the structuring of the categories, the statistical analysis, and the derivation of the findings were the most rewarding parts of the study. Conceptualizing the study and formulating the design and categories were very intellectually demanding but exciting tasks because I was involved in the process of creating. Since I had few models of research to emulate I was, in a very real sense, free to explore and to search for novel ways to design and implement the study. Doing the statistical analysis and deriving the findings were enjoyable because I was intrigued with using mathematics to study social science content in children's books. In deriving the findings it was suspenseful to watch to see if the data would support the relationships I had predicted.

The actual reading and analysis of the textbooks was very time-consuming, tedious, and boring. These tasks were especially dull because most elementary history textbooks at that time were pedantic and traditional, and many were not very well written. Even when a book was readable, I was so busy trying to accurately identify and categorize the themes within it that I was unable to enjoy the events being described. This task was also tedious because it was often very difficult to find in the textbooks the information that dealt with Black Americans. Frequently the indexes, which were my primary guide to related content, were extremely poor. Some textbooks had very little information in them about Black Americans, and that information was thinly spread throughout the text. It often took an undue amount of time to locate the few sentences about Blacks in the book.

IMPROVEMENT OF THE STUDY

I believe that this study is significant because it was one of the first to use a scientific content analysis technique to analyze the treatment of a topic in elementary school textbooks. The thematic categories that were structured in the study can be used to ascertain the dominant themes used in elementary social studies textbooks to discuss other ethnic minority groups, such as Asian Americans, Puerto Rican Americans, Mexican Americans and American Indians. The treatment of these groups could be compared with the treatment of Black Americans in textbooks as revealed in this study.

Despite the significance of this study, it could have been substantially improved in several ways. Only four jurors were used to validate the instrument. I would have felt much more comfortable if the jury had been much larger, and if I could have explained the study to the jurors in person rather than in a letter. Because the jury worked with me through the mails, I am not sure that each of them interpreted the directions in the same way or in the way I had intended. I wish that they had had the opportunity to ask me questions about parts of the directions and the instrument they might have found ambiguous.

I would have liked to have had a coder reliability near .90; it was .64. I believe that coder reliability would have been improved if the categories had been more extensive and precise, and if standardized training sessions had been developed for the coders. The study was fully explained to the coders, to establish reliability, but they were not trained in a formal setting. I also believe that coder reliability might have been improved if more books had been used in the sample of books the coders analyzed.

This study was a modest attempt to describe, scientifically, how one ethnic minority group was treated in a sample of elementary American history textbooks that were being used widely in schools throughout the United States. Because textbooks influence children's attitudes and perceptions, they are important tools which merit serious study by educators and social scientists. I hope that this study has revealed both the feasibility of and the necessity for studying books children use in the schools.

REFERENCES

Berelson, Bernard. *Content analysis in communication research.* Glencoe, Ill.: Free Press, 1952.

Black, Hillel. *The American schoolbook.* New York: William Morrow, 1967.

Budd, Richard W., Robert K. Thorp, and Lewis Donohew. *Content analysis of communications.* New York: Macmillan, 1967.

Clark, Kenneth B. *Dark ghetto.* New York: Harper & Row, 1965.

Davidson, Helen H., and Gerhard Lang. Children's perceptions of their teachers' feelings toward them related to self-perception, school achievement, and behavior, *Journal of Experimental Education,* 1960, *29,* 107-118.

Gottlieb, David. Teaching and students: the views of Negro and white teachers, *Sociology of Education,* 1964, *27* (Summer), 245-353.

Litcher, John H., and David W. Johnson. Changes in attitudes of white elementary school students after use of multiethnic readers, *Journal of Educational Psychology,* 1969, *60,* 148-152.

Marcus, Lloyd. *The treatment of minorities in American history textbooks.* New York: Anti-Defamation League of B'nai B'rith, 1961.

Selltiz, Claire, Marie Jahoda, Morton Deutsch, and Stuart W. Cook, *Research Methods in Social Relations.* New York: Holt, Rinehart & Winston, 1959.

Stampp, Kenneth M., W. D. Jordan, L. W. Levine, R. L. Middlekeuff, C. G. Sellers, and G. W. Stocking. The Negro in American history textbooks, *Integrated Education,* 1964, *2* (October-November), 9-24.

Trager, Helen G., and Marian R. Yarrow. *They learn what they live.* New York: Harper & Bros., 1952.

Jack Levin and James L. Spates ────────────────────

A. HIPPIE VALUES: AN ANALYSIS OF THE UNDERGROUND PRESS

There is little doubt by this time that the hippie phenomenon of the late 1960s is a social movement of some consequence for American society (see Yablonsky, 1968: 290 ff.). Whatever its greater significance, the movement has already contributed to a revolution in modern dress, hairstyles, music, art, and youth culture.

Since 1966, the mass media have analyzed, scrutinized, supported, and condemned the movement, so that almost all Americans, whether or not they have had direct experience with the hippies, presently hold some opinion regarding the merits of this group of young people.

Why have the hippies attracted so much attention? It is doubtful that the answer lies solely in the number of hippies: percentagewise, they are a very small proportion of the American population—numbering, at highest estimate, only 200,000 full-time participants (Yablonsky, 1968: 36). Nor does it seem likely that the concern is a direct product of the much publicized generation gap. Despite ample evidence that most hippies are young (under thirty) and that most of their critics are "old" (over thirty), support for the movement ranges far beyond age lines: many of the hippies' most ardent admirers, if not participants, are over thirty; many of their detractors, under thirty.

After this widespread popularization, social scientists have recently attempted to account for the American reaction to the hippie phenomenon (see Berger, 1967; Davis, 1967; Simon and Trout, 1967; Brown, 1969; Marks, 1969; Yablonsky, 1968). Some have specifically focused upon the value gap between the hippies and the middle class—a gap which has been characterized as an attempt by the hippie movement to substitute a viable alterna-

Source: Jack Levin and James L. Spates, "Hippie Values: An Analysis of the Underground Press," *Youth and Society,* 1970, 2, 59-72.

We wish to especially thank Herbert J. Greenwald for his many helpful suggestions. We are also grateful to Stephen R. Marks, Kingsley H. Birge, and William F. Macauley for their critical review of earlier versions of this paper and we gratefully acknowledge the coding assistance of Ann MacConnell, Kenneth Sweezey, and Marilyn Thomas.

tive in place of the traditional American value pattern (see Marks, 1969). From this standpoint, the hippie problem becomes distinctly ideological, being directly related to those values or ideals which serve as the most general guidelines for action within society (such as the general American ideal that everyone, in order to be an American in good standing, must achieve individual success through his own occupational efforts).

The value argument raises an important aspect of the problem—that of conflict between different values as an expression of the basic gap between the hippie and middle-class views of life. Values are the most general directives for action in society, in that they are the most generally shared ideas about the correct way to behave. A challenge to the values of a social system is therefore regarded by the members of that system as a basic threat to the very raison d'être of their social structure. Hence, one might expect the expression of strong concerns regarding the challenging elements of the hippie phenomenon.

THE MIDDLE-CLASS PATTERN

The hippie mode of existence cannot be understood apart from the value structure of American society as a whole. More specifically, hippie culture has arisen directly out of the middle-class value system within which the majority of hippies were initially socialized. It has been estimated that over seventy percent of all hippies come from this middle- (or upper-) class orientation (Yablonsky, 1968: 26).

Characteristically, middle-class values tend to specify acts which are oriented to the future and normally require the individual to inhibit emotional expression in order for his resources to be fully directed toward the cognitive or rational solution to life tasks (see Parsons, 1951; Parsons and White, 1964: 196 ff.).

In the American case, the middle-class pattern typically manifests itself in the pursuit of economic concerns—that is, in rationally constructed efforts to increase economic production, profits, and occupational status by means of extended formal education and hard work. The achievement dimension of this pattern cannot be overemphasized: the middle-class value structure places major demands upon each individual to achieve occupational success, not merely in terms of personal wealth, power, or status, but as a moral obligation to contribute to the building of the good society (Parsons and White, 1964: 196). In other words, middle-class achievement cannot be purely utilitarian: a person cannot use any means to a particular end, but must use instead socially legitimized (normatively sanctioned) means to ends. Basic success, then, is defined in social as well as personal terms, and rewards are commensurate. Thus, from the middle-class perspective, the hard-working businessman who makes $10,000 a year is much more respectable than the gangster who makes ten times that amount, and, all things being equal, it is the businessman who will be given the upstanding position in the society.

These essential features of the middle-class pattern, that is, its economic, cognitive, and achievement dimensions, all of which denote the goal-oriented nature of activity within the system, can be summarized for convenience under the term "instrumentalism" (see Parsons and White, 1964: 196 ff.; Zelditch, 1955: 309-312).

THE HIPPIE PATTERN

The hippies contend that their subculture offers a radical departure from the dominant American value structure which they see as thoroughly materialistic, dehumanizing, inauthentic, and alienating (Yablonsky, 1968: 361-366). This point of view is reflected in the hippies' "almost total rejection of economic individualism and the 'dog eat dog' or 'do unto other before they do unto you' attitude that is seen by them as the driving force behind contemporary American society" (Yablonsky, 1968: 358). The following responses (Yablonsky, 1968: 350, 351, 358, 365) are illustrative of the hippies' rejection of middle-class values:

> [A hippie drop-out since 1960] To me, dropping-out means to reject the dominant moral, economic, and social values of one's society. I dropped out because the values in our society have become obsolete. . . . Our society is simply full of internal contradictions between its values and the reality of what people actually think and do. . . . Forty percent of America is terribly poor and yet we have tried to hide this from ourselves and the world because the dominant American middle-class has interests in perpetuating the myth.
>
> [A hippie] In order to act with freedom, one must not be constrained by the oppressive systems of orientation and the selfish meaningless goals that were learned while a member of the uptight, plastic society.
>
> [A 23-year-old hippie] We [America] have reached a high level of material development, many people have become hypnotized and obsessed with a desire for material good. There is a strong feeling of "us" and "them." . . . This is a negative part of contemporary American life and is blocking people from seeing the essence of one another.

In sum, then, it would appear that the hippie views the instrumental values of American society, whatever their original purpose, as presently generating dehumanized life styles, even to the point where human beings themselves, in the active quest for success, have become objects of manipulation to one another.

Such a negative reaction to his own society's dominant values (and to his own original values) has led the hippie to form a life style that is quite at odds with the typical American ideal of the hard-working, self-denying, rational businessman or professional. Yablonsky (1968: 29-31) has set forth what he sees as the basic elements of the ideal hippie: he is a philosopher who claims to be "tuned-in to the cosmic affinity of man"; he thus loves all men (the love ethic); "he has achieved this insight, at least in part, from the use of drugs [marijuana, LSD] as a sacrament"; he is a role model for new hippies

THE RESEARCH EXPERIENCE

to look up to; he is creative; he does not work in the traditional sense of American culture, rather preferring to do his own thing, whatever that may be; he is, in a word, "totally dropped out of the larger society," which he regards as plastic, and is actively engaged in "fostering another mode of existence."

This other mode of existence is, for the hippie, an alternative which completely deemphasizes the economic and achievement criteria of American society, and focuses instead upon all objects and actions as ends in themselves, as valuable and necessary foci of immediate gratification and present (rather than future) time orientation. More specifically, rather than attempting to deal with their affairs on a cognitive-rational level, or in terms of economic value, the hippie's ideals (see Greeley, 1969: 14-28) stress nonmaterial or spiritual concerns (such as participation in cosmology, mysticism, and the occult), as well as the search for love and intimacy in human relationships (Yablonsky, 1968: 358, 366). In addition, the achievement aspects of the middle-class pattern are replaced by the quest for self-expression as experienced in the immediate ongoing situation (that is, by grooving on or getting into music, art, psychedelic drugs, and the like). Whereas the middle-class individual is rewarded for following socially legitimized paths to achievement, the hippie is expected to follow his own personal path to wherever it leads him. That is, whatever his thing is, he does it.

The essential components of the hippie value pattern—as indicated by self-expression, affiliation, concern for others, and religious philosophical interests—can be conveniently characterized under the term "expressivism" (see Zelditch, 1955: 311).

The value gap between the hippies and the middle class, though often suggested by previous investigations of the hippie phenomenon, has, for the most part, lacked systematic, quantitative substantiation.[1] For this reason, it was the central purpose of the present study to test the hypothesis that, *contrary to the middle class pattern, hippie values stress expressive concerns and deemphasize instrumental concerns.*

METHOD

To delineate the value structure of the hippie movement, a sample was taken from Underground Press Syndicate (UPS) periodicals published in 1967 and 1968—a recent period during which hippie literature was available. The UPS (1969: 17-18) has an estimated, combined circulation of one million

---

1. See Berger (1967), Davis (1967), Simon and Trout (1967), Brown (1969), Marks (1969), and Yablonsky (1968). One major exception is Yablonsky, whose methods include lengthy participant observation and a questionnaire approach (n = 600). However, the study has been severely criticized on methodological grounds, particularly in its participant observations aspect—see, for example, Berger (1969).

and, as self-described, consists of an "informal association of publications of the 'alternative press' . . . produced in storefronts and basements by feelthy hippies, distributed by unorthodox channels and free-thinking bookstores and from curbs." Ron Thelin, the editor of a representative underground newspaper, has expressed the purpose of his publication in the following manner (UPS Directory, 1969: 143-144):

> [to] provide an organ for the hip community, an evolution of communications consciousness and group consciousness to reflect the universal spirit and the miracles of light in this community [Haight-Ashbury]. . . . To show that LSD provides a profound experience. . . . To provide communication of the historical and ancient discoveries that are coming out of the hip culture, to spread the word, to get everyone to turn on, tune in, and drop out.

Most hippie underground papers appeared in the mid-sixties, many of them after the publicity of 1967, and many of them were short-lived. But their common components were an emphasis on hippie argot, psychedelic lettering and art, the glorification of folk rock, flower power, and love-ins— all, as Thelin says, in an attempt to describe the hip experience to their readers.

To obtain a representative sample of underground newspapers, the following most widely circulated periodicals were selected from major centers of . . . hippie activities, including both eastern and western regions: *Avatar* (Boston), *Distant Drummer* (Philadelphia), *East Village Other* (New York), *Los Angeles Free Press, San Francisco Oracle,* and *Washington Free Press.* A single issue of each UPS periodical from every second month in the period from September 1967 to August 1968 was selected on a random basis. Every second nonfictional article appearing in this sample of issues, excluding poetry and letters to the editor, was subjected to analysis ($n = 316$).

To provide a comparable sample of articles representative of middle-class values, an analysis was also conducted of concurrently published issues of the *Reader's Digest,* selected for its variety of middle class articles from diverse sources (see Ginglinger, 1955: 56-61). Excluding fiction and poetry, each article appearing in every other issue of *Reader's Digest* was studied ($n = 162$).

The major value-theme of articles in both samples was coded by means of a modified version of Ralph K. White's *Value Catalogue* (1951). All materials were coded using a detailed set of definitions of the value-themes and appropriate coding sheets.

The central hypothesis regarding expressive and instrumental values was tested in the following manner. On the basis of the theoretical discussion above, the categories Self-Expression, Concern for Others, Affiliation, and Religious-Philosophical were treated as aspects of Expressivism, while the categories Achievement, Cognitive, and Economic became the basis for Instrumentalism. Categories of the value analysis are listed below.

Instrumental

a. Achievement: Values which produce achievement motivation for the individual in terms of hard work, practicality, or economic value are often expressed by means of contributions to society through occupation and high regard for ownership.

b. Cognitive: These represent the drive for learning as an end in itself as well as the means for achieving success, welfare, or happiness.

c. Economic: Economic values are at the collective level (such as, national state, industrial), thus differing from individual goals such as achievement.

Expressive

d. Self-expressive: This area includes all the self-expressive values and goals. The main ones are humor, play, and fun in general, relaxation, or exciting new discoveries, and travel. Art and beauty are included as well as other creative-expressive activities.

e. Affiliative: These may be the product of social conditioning, or a result of the need to belong to a group, to affiliate with another person. This category focuses upon the gregariousness of individuals and the friendships which they develop. These affiliative aims may be expressed as conformity, loyalty to the group, friendship, or other-directedness.

f. Concern for others: Concern for others does not depend upon a drive to interact. Unlike the affiliative values, this category focuses upon attitudes and feelings toward particular groups or toward humanity in general. Therefore, this category tends to include more abstract objectives than those associated with affiliation.

g. Religious-philosophical: This category includes goals dealing with ultimate meaning in life, the role of deity, concerns with after-life, and so on.

Other

h. Individualistic: This category is concerned with values which stress the importance of the individual, the development of his unique personality, individual independence, and the achievement of individualized personal fulfillment including rebellion.

i. Physiological: These are goals created by simple physiological drives such as hunger, sex, physical health, and physical safety.

j. Political: This category includes collective goals (such as, state, community, national, international objectives) in their central reference to group decision-making processes.

k. Miscellaneous: Any other goals not covered above (such as, hope, honesty, purity, modesty, and manners).

The reliability of the value analysis was tested by having three coders independently code thirty articles from both the UPS and the *Digest* samples. Using a two-out-of-three criterion (that is, where two of three coders agreed), agreement reached 90%. Total agreement was 78%.

RESULTS AND DISCUSSION

Results obtained in an analysis of UPS and *Reader's Digest* value-themes suggest that expressivism occupies a central position in the hippie value structure, whereas instrumentalism occurs only peripherally. As shown in Table 1, expressive concerns accounted for 46% of the value-themes in the underground press, while instrumental concerns were the major focus of only 10% of the articles. In sharp contrast, instrumental concerns represented the major value-theme in the *Reader's Digest* sample (42%), while expressive concerns were substantially less important (23%).

Within the expressivism of the hippie sample, the dominant emphasis appeared to be Self-Expression (28%). For example, typical articles in the underground press dealt with the mind-blowing psychedelic properties of drugs, the relationship of early rock and roll music to contemporary rock groups (such as the Beatles and the Rolling Stones), the influence of such figures as Ken Kesey, Timothy Leary, and Lenny Bruce on the hippie movement.

TABLE 1
Value-Themes in the Underground Press and Reader's Digest

Value-Theme	Underground Press		Reader's Digest	
Expressive	46%	%	23%	%
Self-expressive		28		9
Concern for others		8		6
Affiliative		4		3
Religious-philosophical		6		5
Instrumental	10		42	
Achievement		3		28
Cognitive		5		7
Economic		2		7
Other	44		35	
Individual		20		10
Political[a]		19		12
Physiological[b]		4		12
Miscellaneous		1		1
Total		100		100
(n = 478)		(316)		(162)

Note: A chi-square analysis was conducted by comparing the Underground Press and Reader's Digest on the two major value-themes, Expressive and Instrumental ($\chi^2 = 61.17$, $df = 1$, $p < .001$).

[a]The distribution of political values reveals an important aspect of the nature of the underground press: a secondary appeal of these newspapers is often to politically radical or New Left types, though most of the material is designed for hippie consumption (see Wolfe, 1968: 135-144)—a group known for its apolitical stance (see Yablonsky, 1968).

[b]In the *Reader's Digest*, this category consisted primarily of health-related topics such as methods of weight reduction, physical diseases such as cancer, and aging. In the Underground Press, it contained references to physiological sex.

THE RESEARCH EXPERIENCE

In the *Reader's Digest* sample, Achievement was the dominant component of instrumentalism, representing 28% of all value-themes. Typically, *Reader's Digest* articles emphasized methods for occupational achievement, including business enterprises created by college students, advice concerning financial investments and taxes, the careers of well-known persons who had achieved occupational success, and so on.

An independent analysis of a random sample of underground press advertisements appearing in our sample yielded the following supportive data: almost 90% of the hippie advertisements focused on expressive-related products, that is, on products which are designed either for expressive behavior or expressive consumption, such as music (rock, folk, blues, soul, and the like), movies, plays, psychedelic shops, clothing (mod), and coffee and tea houses. The most important of these expressive categories contained music-related products such as concerts, records, recording artists, and stereophonic equipment; these products accounted for 25% of all hippie advertisements. These results lend support to the suggestion that expressive concerns are a staple of great magnitude for the readers of the underground press, and more generally for the hippie movement as a whole.

An examination of the relationship of individualism to the expressive-instrumental dichotomy may shed additional light on the above findings. As is well-known, social scientists have long been concerned with the position of individualism in the American value structure. In the middle-class case, individualism has the major task of locating responsibility for contributions to the building of the good society. Thus, each individual must actively strive to accomplish those objectives which society has defined as legitimate concerns.

Similarly, the hippies show a characteristic American concern for the individual. As shown in the present study, 20% of the articles appearing in the underground press contained an individualistic value-orientation. However, the hippie version may indicate an individualism of a different order: an individualism closely tied to the expressive value-orientation. It is here that the hippie phrase, "Do your own thing!" has particular relevance, in that it essentially directs attention to the immediate gratification of needs by means of creative self-expression—an expressive individualism which stands in sharp contrast to the dominant middle-class pattern (Marks, 1969).

The hippies form a unique phenomenon in contemporary America—a large-scale movement which has arisen out of the mainstream of American life to form a contraculture within its societal boundaries. Results obtained in the present study support the contention that the hippies are attempting to stress values of an expressive nature—values which they feel have been neglected by the highly instrumental middle class.

From the sociological point of view, this is where the concern of Americans about the hippies comes home to roost: a way of life is being criticized, and sides are being taken. The ideology of the hip movement attempts to cut to the core of the instrumental view of things. The middle-class ideology, the hippies are saying, neglects the personal needs of the individual to be a human being; it neglects his need to be affective, loving, and trustful of other people; it neglects his need for self-realization by following his own individual needs; in a word, it neglects his need to be expressive.

Yet, how expressive can a social system be? There is increasing evidence that the strongly reactive nature of the hippie value system may in large part account for the general failure of the movement to form viable communities or other social structures.[2] The perceived overemphasis of the middle class on instrumentalism seems to have been matched by a similar overemphasis by the hippies on pure expressivism. In structural terms, extreme expressivism poses a significant problem for long-term, stable patterns of interaction—that is, the basic tasks of maintaining the system are not performed on a regular basis, which, in the extreme, can result in social disorganization and decay. Indeed, the literature on the hippies is replete with examples of community and group termination because food was not taken in, rent was not paid, and so on. Clearly, for a stable society, everyone doing his own thing has its limitations.

It is just this system dissolution that the middle-class American intuitively—and, we think, rightly—feels may be a consequence of a purely expressive mode of existence. Knowing this, he, like the hippie, takes a stance in defense of his life style. Though the ideological stance of each group often becomes a battle of ego defenses (that is, "My way of life is right because it is *my* way of life"), there seems to be objective merit in both positions; extreme instrumentalism does appear to neglect the necessities of personality and organismic expression, while extreme expressivism appears to neglect the requirements of stable social systems. For this reason, it may well be that neither the expressive nor instrumental value structures may come to be dominant in this ideational conflict. Rather, the solution may be in the form of systems which combine elements of both these systems—systems which are already in the process of formulation.

It already appears that the hippie's purely expressive solution to life is considered too radical as a viable solution for the society as a whole. Very few people completely drop out (which the totally expressive solution necessitates). But there is evidence that fewer and fewer people are taking the straight life in its extreme sense as their life style either. Rather, some sort of balance is apparently being worked out on both sides of the fence.

---

2. Because of harassment by various agencies of the dominant culture, a significant number of hippies have literally taken to the woods to form communes. While some of these social systems have existed for a number of years, their long-term stability has not yet been confirmed. In addition, even if successful, the price of their success may be more instrumentally oriented behavior. Such groups are in the minority if one takes the hippie population as a whole: most hippies still reside in major urban centers and exist in extremely loose confederations. See Brown (1969: 37).

THE RESEARCH EXPERIENCE

From a more general perspective, the hippie emphasis on expressive values could be regarded as partially illustrative of a process of widespread balancing in American society as a whole, whereby the social system, being pushed more and more to an instrumental extreme, is reintroducing various modes of expressivism at all levels of its structure. If this is the case, then the societywide trend toward expressivism, exemplified in its most extreme form by the hip movement, could be seen as part and parcel of other strong trends in contemporary America—civil rights, freedom of speech, representation, life style, and the like. Though the end result will most likely not be the extreme expressivism found dominant in many hip subcultures, it may very well be, over time, that an expressivism suitable to all age levels and classes of American society will become part of the American ideology. It is in this sense that the hippie movement may have its most profound influence on the character of the American value system.

REFERENCES

Berger, B. M. (1967). "Hippie morality—more old than new." *Trans-action* 5, 2 (December): 19-27.

Berger, B. M. (1969). "Sociologist on a bad trip." *Trans-action* 6, 4 (February): 54-56.

Brown, M. E. (1969). "The persecution and condemnation of hippies." *Trans-action* 6, 10 (September): 33-46.

Davis, F. (1967). "Why all of us may be hippies someday." *Trans-action* 5, 2 (December): 10-18.

Ginglinger, G. (1955). "Basic values in Readers Digest, Selection, and Constellation." *Journalism Quarterly* 32, 1 (Winter): 56-61.

Greeley, A. M. (1969). "There's a new time religion on campus." *New York Times Magazine* (June 1): 14-28.

Marks, S. R. (1969). "The hippies and the organism: a problem for the general theory of action." Department of Sociology, Boston University (unpublished)

Parsons, T. (1951). *The Social System.* New York: Free Press.

Parsons, T., and W. White (1964). *Social Structure and Personality.* New York: Free Press.

Simon, G., and G. Trout (1967). "Hippies in college—from teeny-boppers to drug freaks." *Trans-action* 5, 2 (December): 27-32.

Underground Press Syndicate (1969). *Directory.* Phoenix: Orpheus.

White, R. K. (1951). *Value-Analysis: The Nature and Use of the Method.* New York: Society for the Psychological Study of Social Issues.

Wolfe, B. H. (1968). *The Hippies.* New York: Signet.

Yablonsky, L. (1968). *The Hippie Trip.* New York: Pegasus.

Zelditch, M., Jr. (1955). "Role differentiation in the nuclear family: a comparative study," pp. 309-312 in T. Parsons and R. F. Bales et al., *Family: Socialization and Interaction Process.* New York: Free Press.

B. THROUGH THE LOOKING GLASS OF TIME: PERSONAL REFLECTIONS ON RESEARCHING THE HIP COUNTERCULTURE

James L. Spates and Jack Levin

Sociologists, like everyone else, are products of their times. Each "self" is a unique configuration: a delicate coupling of individual development and needs with present concerns in a social structure shaped by the circumstantial forces of history. In some cultures and epochs the merging of these personal and social threads is a relatively effortless process, producing personalities at home in their social order, secure in the answers to the questions of "Who am I?" and "What should I be doing?" During periods of flux, however, particularly when social change is rampant in the general society, for many the process does not proceed so easily. Because society itself is altering so rapidly, the old answers concerning the proper relationship between the individual and society seem inappropriate. Hence, new relationships have to be forged. But, the directions as to how to go about this are decidedly lacking. In such periods it then becomes the principal task of the personality to create for the self a meaningful lifestyle, a stable identity, in the midst of the ongoing change.

Ours is an age of such change. The authors of this paper grew up in the 1940s and 1950s and went to college in the early 1960s. Consequently, we experienced either directly or indirectly the effects of the tremendous socio-historical events of this period: the huge postwar economic boom, the Korean War, the terror of the Cold War, massive technological and industrial expansion, the space race, the assassination of a President, the civil rights upheavals, and so on.

Probably because of the all-pervasive nature of these events in our lives, as well as our basically liberal, upper-middle-class upbringing, we focused directly on our relationship as individuals to the society at large as one of the most meaningful problems of our development. At the very least, we clearly found our society, at least in its present form, wanting. We felt America, with its unbounded demand for achievement via the unrelenting procure-

---

Source: Prepared especially for this volume.

ment of the symbols of "success"—wealth, prestige, and power—was more often than not highly destructive of the needs and lifestyle of the individual as a fully developed human being: A mechanized society demanded mechanized people. On the other hand, we did not know, given this ideological perspective, what we could do to alleviate the situation, either culturally or personally. None of the traditional life roles (i.e., those from our family histories) particularly appealed to us, and no viable "alternative mode of existence" existed at the time we were supposed to make "life decisions"— i.e., when we graduated from college.

Yet, even given these common sociohistorical experiences—the common experiences that form a generation—there were a great many significant life encounters we did *not* share which contributed greatly to making us unique as individuals even within our generational context. For example, we grew up in different parts of the country (Jim Spates was raised in the North; Jack Levin in the South), had different religious heritages (Jim was brought up in the Protestant faith; Jack in the Jewish), different families, of course, and many different friends and acquaintances both before and after we met in graduate school. Thus it was that, when we found we were very interested in working together on a study of hippie culture, we were differently motivated in our reasons for wanting to do so.

In a paper that is this personal in nature, it might be interesting for the reader to see just what our different motivations and reasons for undertaking this particular sociological study were. Therefore we have chosen to adopt for the following section three formats: Jim's personal reflections, Jack's personal reflections and both of our observations together.

WHY WE DECIDED TO STUDY HIPPIE VALUES

Jim Spates

After college, in the midst of some confusion and frustration regarding the identity issues mentioned above (who I was, what I could do that was personally meaningful in my society), I decided to attend graduate school in sociology in Boston. Such a decision was made for a number of reasons. First, it allowed me to continue doing professionally something I had enjoyed doing for some time—thinking about the social order and, particularly, my own personal relation to it. Second, it provided me with expert training in a discipline in the event I wanted to make it a career. Third, it made it possible for me to avoid going into the military immediately after college. (People were still being drafted immediately after college in those days, and, while I was not sure about what I *did* want to do, I was sure I did not want to do *that*.) But, fourth and most importantly, it bought me time, in a manner that was both palatable to me and respectable to others: time to find the right answers for my self. It was into this mental set that the hippies dropped.

The hippies "happened" to Boston—and to me—in late 1967. It went something like this. A small group of us (myself, Jack, other graduate students and friends) had become aware, via virtually omnipresent mass media saturation, that there was a "bizarre" group of young people "out there" somewhere (in far-away, radical San Francisco and Los Angeles) preaching incessantly about the dawning of a "new age" based on "love, peace, freedom, and happiness." Suddenly, we found that these people were not out there at all, but in fact were within our very midst, alive and well and living in Cambridge and Roxbury. Our discovery came through no action of our own (after all, as a graduate student, I was supposed to be the epitome of rationality and respectability!) but as a consequence of the Herculean efforts by Boston's latently Puritanical Founding Fathers to *keep* us from finding out about "them." This group was comprised of various personages, city officials, politicians, and police who, in adopting their perceived role as pro-tectors of the society, had taken it upon themselves to protect the city from this latest scourge of a disintegrating social order by stopping, at what seemed any cost, the publication of the area's first underground paper, *Avatar*. ("Filth!" "Lies!" "Garbage!" were some of the milder epithets hurled at it.)

These efforts began shortly after the paper's initial appearance in October 1967, and, as is usually the case with such repressive tactics, they backfired significantly. First, as might have been expected in the prevailing liberal atmosphere of the courts in the late 1960s, the extensive legal case against the paper, charging obscenity, was dismissed: *Avatar* was declared to have redeeming social value.[1] Second, and more importantly, because of the immense public furor created by the obscenity action and its attendant con-frontations (seizure of papers, conflicts with local police, and politicians, etc.), everyone in Boston became either painfully or joyously (depending on their point of view) aware of the fledgling hippie communities in the area.

To those who adopted the latter perspective, mainly young people in the 15-30 age group (I was 24), this windfall exposure bordered on the revelatory. It became apparent not only that the hippies were *real* (i.e., more than just another case of "media sensationalism"), but also that they were, in their own jargon, Here! Now! Before long, literally thousands of young people, quite oblivious to the warnings and constraints of their social superiors (parents, teachers, and the Founding Fathers), started adopting the newly discovered *actual* role models about them and tuned in by degrees, both intellectually and emotionally, to the hippie lifestyle. As they did so, they adopted its myriad symbols of membership (long hair, hip jargon, psyche-

---

1. As indeed it had: At the height of the controversy surrounding it, as an indication of its own comprehension of the ludicrousness of the proceedings, *Avatar* published, in true icono-clastic fashion, a centerfold, *à la Playboy*, with four four-letter words printed in huge letters across it.

THE RESEARCH EXPERIENCE

delic drugs, distinctive music and clothes) and beliefs (self-expression, a concern for the welfare of others, affiliation and "mysticism"). From this point, the "hippie revolution," that very "personification of decadence" so feared by the Founding Fathers, was on in Boston.

I became a member of this newly hip group—at least in spirit. I say in spirit because, in my role as a graduate student, I was in a particularly ambivalent position regarding the whole hippie scene. On the one hand, I had ostensibly decided on a professional academic career for myself and was being trained in its techniques. This decision had already resulted in a good deal of time, money, and effort being expended on the sociological enterprise. I had become, *ipso facto,* committed! On the other hand, I felt a very strong affinity for the hippie position. To me, they were young people, much like myself, engaged in the search for a meaningful identity in a social structure gone sadly, perhaps madly, awry. In fact, the hippies were much more extreme in their criticism of American culture than I: They adamantly insisted that it was categorically impossible to "coexist" *within* the system (one would always "sell out" or be crushed in one's humanity in the end). They therefore concluded that the only way to *really* live your own life was to "drop out," find "your own thing" and "groove"—anything less was meaningless "games."

Obviously, taking the hippies as seriously as I did, and being as attracted to their lifestyle as I was, this was an ultimatum of some magnitude. Were they right? Was their alternative (the only widespread alternative to have appeared in America in 30 years) the one I had been looking for, if quietly? If I dropped out, I risked all the training I had accrued so far, the opprobrium of many who meant much to me, and, not least, my own inner guilt feelings at having been escapist, leaving the problems of society to others. If I stayed, I risked the catalog of ills of modern society which the hippies had so succinctly pointed out. Needless to say, I internally debated this point incessantly in the next few months, and my inability to come to a satisfactory conclusion only increased my frustration.

Jack Levin

Like Jim, I attempted to resolve (or postpone resolution of) my identity problems by attending graduate school in the social sciences. I began my graduate education by pursuing a *terminal* master of science degree in communication research, a program that combined training in both mass communication and research methods and would prepare me to work in some area of *applied* social science research. I served a short internship in consumer research, however, and soon realized that it was not for me. I would not be satisfied carrying out research that had been defined and designed by others (for example, to determine how to sell more detergent or how to effectively advertise soap). From a personal standpoint, I sincerely believed (and still believe) that much of the excitement of research involves testing research questions of some *personal* significance or interest. (My research interests have ranged widely over the last few years, leading to studies of such diverse phenomena as bathroom graffiti, prejudice, sex roles, assimilation of Chinese-Americans, and lovelorn advice columns, to mention a few). To this day, I have tremendous difficulty getting actively involved in a research project designed by others or consulting on a study whose objectives are not directly related to my immediate interests.

In contrast to Jim, however, my interest in the hippies was more conceptual and methodological than personal and ideological. Though I was sympathetic to many of the avowed goals of the hip counterculture, by late 1967 I was in a less ambivalent position than Jim regarding where I was going. By that time, many of my worst conflicts had been more or less resolved. I viewed myself as committed to the scientific method and regarded positively the possibility of a career in college teaching. In fact, it was because of these commitments that I had decided to continue my education by pursuing a Ph.D. in sociology.

Jim Spates and Jack Levin

While, for some time, during our continuing discussions on the subject, the possibility of studying the hippies sociologically had occurred to us, neither of us knew exactly how to go about it. The only real possibility appeared to be participant observation, but that was ruled out for a variety of reasons (time, degree of involvement necessitated, "courage" to risk our advanced professional involvement). One evening, while sitting around looking over a number of back issues of the *Avatar* (and related underground papers from other cities that Jim had been avidly collecting), we were lamenting the lack of any good empirical data on the hippies when Jack suddenly said: "Let's do a content analysis of the underground press!" And that, essentially, was that.

For both of us, on a personal level, the decision was perfect. For Jim, it provided the opportunity to become directly and personally involved in all the elements of the hip style without the full-blown commitment demanded by dropping out. He felt he would be able to study the hippies sociologically, thereby satisfying his professional interests (doing direct research of an ongoing social movement, and writing a paper, perhaps of publishable quality, from such work) as well as his personal desire to find out if the hippies were really, as they claimed, "where it's at" for him as an individual. Though he was aware that, to some extent, he was trying to have his cake and eat it too and that, in the long run, a decision would have to be made between the two poles (the hip life vs. the sociologist's life), it was, nevertheless, the

THE RESEARCH EXPERIENCE

right solution at the time.

For Jack, a content analysis of the underground press provided an opportunity to bring together systematically several of his substantive interests in mass communication as well as the sociology of youth. During his master's training in communications research he had taken a course in content analysis from Francis E. Barcus and written a thesis on the portrayal of minority and majority characters in black and white fiction. Thus he had become very familiar with the method and was convinced that, despite its idiosyncratic weaknesses, it was an effective, unobtrusive method in the research repertoire of the sociologist.

Sociologically, the fit was also ideal. Both of us had just completed a course in the theories of Talcott Parsons, taught by Parsons's associate Gerald Platt, and both of us had become convinced of the importance of general idea systems of "the desirable" (i.e., values) in influencing social life. More directly relevant, Jim had recently had long discussions about the hippies, from a theoretical point of view, with another graduate student at Boston University, Stephen Marks. Marks, who had taken the course in Parsonsian theory with us, had produced a paper (final version, 1969) applying to the hippies the "expressive" half of Parsons's paradigm of instrumental vs. expressive action. From this it was just a short theoretical step to conceptualize the main thrust of the hippie *value* system as expressive in contradistinction to that of the American middle class, which had already been conceptualized by Parsons and others as predominantly instrumental.

On a methodological level, content analysis was also a very useful tool for studying as dispersed a phenomenon as the hippies. As we suspected, and were later to find out from the problems encountered by Lewis Yablonsky (1968) in his participant observations of hip culture, getting an adequate "person" sample of this highly mobile group was virtually impossible. In contrast, content analysis provided a means for sampling the only written (hence, permanent) and continuing (hence, regular) product of the hippie culture, its press. In addition, unlike participant observation, it also had the advantage of consuming relatively little time and money, and it did not necessitate a host of personal contacts for its success.

Just as important, Jack, from his previous experiences with the technique, knew where to look in the literature for guidelines as to how we might construct our own research tool. It was with this objective in mind that we examined, updated, and modified the systematic value analysis technique of Ralph K. White (1951). From that point, it was relatively easy. We had, upon making the decision to do the content analysis, sent away immediately for subscriptions to six underground papers from around the country, procuring from them not only current but also back issues. With our sample thus in hand, we trained a group of students and friends as coders, performed our reliability check one afternoon, and proceeded to collect the data. The rest is reported in the original paper.

WHAT WE FOUND AND WHAT WE DID SUBSEQUENTLY

What did we find upon completing the study? Basically, as reported, strong evidence that the hippies were committed to, as they claimed, an alternative (expressive) system of beliefs. Since nothing like this had appeared in the sociological literature, it was an exciting finding. It became even more exciting as the 1960s began to draw to a close and the hip culture seemed to be spreading to most of the Western world. Perhaps, we thought, "the alternative" was viable after all.

But this last really was hope on Jim's part and curiosity on Jack's: We really had no evidence from our study that such was the case. It was at this point that the limitations of our original work began to take on much greater importance than we had originally thought. While our content analysis provided initial evidence for the hippie value structure being oriented in a specific (expressive) way, it could in no way indicate whether this alternative belief system was something that had lasted or could last through time. In this respect, it will be remembered that the sample was drawn from only a single year. Thus, we really had no way of knowing whether we had tapped a stable, continuing set of value priorities or we had inadvertently hit upon a set of unknown variables that made September 1967 to August 1968 (the time period sampled) in some way "abnormal." Furthermore, there were the limitations of sample size—we sampled only a total of 478 articles (316 from the underground press, 162 from *Reader's Digest*)—and of "representativeness." While the underground press sample was relatively adequate in terms of number and distribution of titles examined, the middle-class sample decidedly was not; we used only one title and took from it only about half the number of articles we had taken from the underground press. While we sampled as we did out of necessity (we had no money for the study, little time, and no outside assistance of any kind), such limitations meant that we lacked definitive evidence on which to make generalizations about either the underground or the middle-class press. Given the apparent growth of the hippie culture during the late 1960s and its relationship to the society as a whole, further study seemed imperative.

Hence, two follow-up analyses were undertaken. The initial replication and extension began as Jim's doctoral dissertation, with Jack as faculty consultant (Jack had received his Ph.D. in the interim between the studies), and was later written up by both (Spates & Levin, 1972).

To improve the research design as a whole and to increase the possibilities of making generalizations, we expanded the sample to cover two time periods of three years each—1957-59, chosen for comparison purposes because of the hippies' ideological ties to the beat movement, and 1967-69. We also sampled a much larger raw number of items—a total of 1,512 paragraphs,[2] 648 from the underground press (216 from 1957-59, where only one

2. We switched to coding paragraphs instead of whole articles because we felt that much more specificity in value categorization could be attained using this smaller unit of analysis.

THE RESEARCH EXPERIENCE

title was available for sampling, New York's *Village Voice*) and 864 from the middle-class literature. Finally, we expanded to six the number of middle-class titles used for this latter portion of the sample, adding to *Reader's Digest* the magazines *Life, Look, True, Redbook,* and *Cosmopolitan.*

The following were the main areas of interest and their results. First, we wanted to see whether the values of the underground press were relatively stable—i.e., unchanging—over time. This was strongly suggested in the results, which indicated that, focusing on the expressive-instrumental dichotomy only,[3] both the beats (1957-59) and the hippies (1967-69) devoted approximately three-quarters of their attention to expressive concerns and only one-quarter to instrumental ones. This was a particularly interesting finding, as it indicated not only the stability we had been looking for but also continuity between two countercultural units over time.

Second, in the interim period between the first and second study, as the counterculture spread, there appeared a number of claims, most clearly articulated by Theodore Roszak (1969) and Charles Reich (1970), that hippie culture was so significant an event as to portend major changes in American society at large. In the terms of our dichotomy, this suggested that American culture should be observably shifting from its dominant commitment to an instrumental ideology toward a more expressive one. Needless to say, if this were the case, it was a very important claim for which to obtain good empirical evidence. While our method, as developed, did not afford us a means of testing directly this purported "effect" of the counterculture on the American value system, we felt we could obtain an indirect indication of the counterculture's pressure by looking at the pattern of dominant American values over the two time periods sampled. If the change predicted was occurring, we felt it would be observable in a value shift from 1957-59 to 1967-69: The earlier period would be more instrumental and less expressive, and the latter the reverse.

Our results flatly contradicted this expectation. They indicated that virtually *no change* had occurred in American value preferences from 1957-59 to 1967-69 at all. The middle-class magazines sampled held their dominant instrumental preference in almost identical fashion in each time period: 1957-59—instrumental = 73 percent, expressive = 27 percent; 1967-69—instrumental = 78 percent, expressive = 22 percent.[4] While, sociologically speaking, this was a most significant finding, suggesting that the Roszak-Reich hypothesis of "the greening of America" was untenable, personally it was more difficult to deal with.

---

3. For purposes of simplicity in this and the remainder of the discussion, we have omitted reference to the "Other" category. The reader interested in this information can find it in Spates, 1971, and Spates, 1974.
4. These figures are taken from the third study (Spates, 1974) for reasons of clarity. In the second study, extraneous factors, too complex to be discussed here, intervened. For an explanation, see Spates and Levin, 1972.

Since we had been from the start in sympathy with the type of values that were being proffered by the hip culture and consequently were hoping that they would indeed help reorient American priorities in some fashion, it was quite disappointing to find no significant difference in middle-class values over this time span. It suggested that, rhetoric and cant to the contrary, the counterculture, except perhaps for a few representatives, wasn't "working."

Not willing to say die until the conclusion was inescapable, we reasoned that there was still a chance that our findings were spurious. After all, the sociological literature clearly maintains that values, once solidly established in a social structure, are exceedingly difficult to alter in other directions. Change, if it is to come, takes time. Hence we hoped that 1967-69 was "too soon" to be sure whether the counterculture had really affected American values. Thus it was to see what changes, if any, had occurred in later years that the second follow-up study (Spates, 1974) was conducted.

This analysis, undertaken by Jim alone, only served to confirm the results of the prior work. The sample of literature from the "dominant culture" showed, once again, no shift along the instrumental-expressive continuum from 1967-69 to 1970-72 (the "later" time period analyzed). The preference remained 78 percent instrumental, the remainder expressive. These results are all the more significant because once more, in order to be sure that this time there would be no doubt about the results due to sampling deficiencies, the sample was again expanded, in terms of both numbers—4,690 items were analyzed, 1913 from the underground press and 2,777 from the dominant culture—and representational titles. To provide a cross-cultural perspective of the counterculture *vis-à-vis* English-speaking Western society in general, an identical sample was drawn from both Canada and England. In both of these additional countries, the results of the dominant-culture data, time period by time period, were the same: no change.

Nor was this all. The real *coup de grace* concerning our high hopes for the counterculture came in the underground press figures themselves. These indicated that a major value priority shift had occurred within the counter-culture *itself*. In 1967-69 the underground press had devoted a full 70 percent of its instrumental-expressive material to expressive concerns, with 30 percent going to the instrumental side. In the following three years, this percentage had changed dramatically, to 45 percent expressive and 55 percent instrumental. The counterculture, the very center of the "do your own thing" and "Now!" ethics, had become predominantly characterized by the very values that, a few short years before, they had so vociferously repudiated! This finding, moreover, was no fluke. It was borne out everywhere in the data. In each country examined separately, in each individual title examined separately, the pattern was the same: From 1967-69 to 1970-72, expressive concerns faded immensely.

These results indicated two major conclusions. First, the stability we

THE RESEARCH EXPERIENCE

had perceived from 1957-59 (beat) to 1967-69 (hippie) was fleeting: By 1970-72, value priorities had altered dramatically. Therefore, the counter-culture could *not* be regarded as a *stable* social structure with a clearly defined value system of an "alternative" nature with which people could identify if they so desired. Second, the shift from 1967-69 to 1970-72 was *so* radical as to make hip culture virtually unrecognizable in the original terms its members had professed and which had so attracted us. In fact, since the group now preferred instrumental values to expressive ones, even though with less intensity than the dominant culture itself, there was no longer any sound reason to invest it with the rubric of "counterculture" at all. It was more like an "expressively oriented" *sub*culture which bore resemblance ideologically to the Bohemian and artistic subcultures that had existed for some time in America. Certainly, this subculture did not have the "power," speaking in terms of social structures, to significantly alter the values of the dominant culture within which it existed. In short, for all intents and pur-poses it seemed that hip culture, as an "alternative mode of existence," was dead.

This conclusion was also supported by other evidence (e.g., Kunen, 1973) which indicated strongly that even the most dedicated members of hip culture were not staying within its boundaries past a certain age (usually the late twenties or early thirties). They were "dropping" back "*in,*" becoming lawyers, businessmen, artisans, and the like. It was as though the whole thing had been a dream, as though the counterculture had never really been a *serious* alternative for these people in terms of *lifelong* commitment at all (though none in the throes of the movement in the late 1960s would have been aware of or admitted to this). Rather, it was as if the hip experience had been a way station, a sort of resting place in the life cycle at which these young people could pause for a while and articulate a position against society, and by so doing they could clarify their *own* individual positions and personal life plans independent of the dominant culture's "interference." Then, having done this in their own good time, they could eventually return to the culture that had spawned them (which they had never *really* left), secure in the knowledge that the answers they had forged to the questions of "Who am I?" and "What should I be doing?" were their own. It was as though an entire generation had concocted the counterculture for the single purpose of helping them form their own identity within a dominant culture which, changing incredibly rapidly, had not provided such a structure for them.

Jim Spates

Clearly, in retrospect, this is one of the principal ways in which I, simultaneously an aspiring sociologist *and* a young person seeking resolution of intense identity questions in the moment of sociohistorical time known as the late 1960s, had myself used the counterculture. I had been intensely involved in the literature and forms of this culture in one manner or another for three or four years and had become aware of the huge number of "bad trips" being experienced by many counterculturalists. Thus I slowly and reluctantly decided, despite the high-sounding rhetoric still being produced by and in the name of hip culture, that the hip lifestyle was not a viable alternative for me. As I became more proficient in my discipline as a result of these studies (as well as other significant sociological encounters), I realized that one of the great intellectual qualities of the sociological enterprise was that it afforded me the unique opportunity to be both *of* the society in which I was living and, at the same time, *outside* of it—analyzing it, comparing it with other cultures and being, in my own *personal* fashion, a *self*-generated critic if I chose. Jack, of course, because he came to the studies with a somewhat different "head" (as explained above), had already realized this for some time.

Jim Spates and Jack Levin

It is inescapable, however, that our individual commitments to the sociological lifestyle have been very deeply shaped by our encounter with hip culture and, more specifically, by its values. We sincerely believed in the human legitimacy of much of the expressive orientation proposed by the hippies, and from our own experiences, we were well aware that such concerns were decidedly played down in American culture. The hippies, by articulating clearly something that bothered us deeply, gave us each the means of conceptualizing our own individual concerns. Henceforth, we have the ability to work out, and even demand, a more meaningful balance between the instrumental and expressive poles in our personal lives and in our relationship to society. In short, the hippies changed *us* significantly, even if their overall effect on the dominant culture was negligible.

But perhaps such an "effect" is really not so negligible after all. Though it is a good deal more subtle than massive, immediate realignments of value priorities and social structures would be, it is nonetheless an effect that will endure in us. Moreover, this effect will hopefully be passed on by us, and others of our generation, to upcoming generations of Americans in the manner in which we live our lives and do our work. In each subsequent generation, of course, our direct influence, like that of generations before us, will have to be mediated through the personal needs and historical pressures that are relevant to these "new" people. In such a process this influence will be altered markedly, becoming in the long run so restructured it will be completely unrecognizable as having come from the period of the late 1960s and hip culture at all. But then that is really the point of the looking glass of time. Only by reflecting intensely upon what we find in our unique portion of sociohistorical time can we find the answers to the problem of our own

identity and learn from our own experiences—even our research experiences
—who we are and what we should be doing.

REFERENCES

Kunen, James S. The rebels of '70: Confessions of a middle-class drifter. *New York Times Magazine,* October 28, 1973, pp. 22-23, 67 ff.

Marks, Stephen R. The hippies and the organism: A problem for the general theory of action. Unpublished paper, Boston University, 1969.

Reich, Charles A. *The greening of America.* New York: Random House, 1970.

Roszak, Theodore. *The making of a counter culture: Reflections on the technocratic society and its youthful opposition.* Garden City, N.Y.: Anchor Books, 1969.

Spates, James L. Structures and trends in value systems in the 'hip' underground contraculture and the American middle class, 1957-59, 1967-69. Unpublished Ph.D. dissertation, Boston University, 1971.

Spates, James L. The braking of a counterculture: The values of hip and dominant culture in cross-cultural perspective. Unpublished paper, Hobart and William Smith Colleges, Geneva, N.Y., 1974.

Spates, James L., & Levin, Jack. Beats, hippies, the hip generation and the American middle class: An analysis of values. *International Social Science Journal,* 1972, *24,* 326-353.

Yablonsky, Lewis. *The hippie trip.* New York: Pegasus, 1968.

White, Ralph K. *Value-analysis: The nature and use of the method.* New York: Society for the Psychological Study of Social Issues, 1951.

John D. Kasarda ————————————————————————————————

A. THE IMPACT OF SUBURBAN POPULATION GROWTH ON CENTRAL CITY SERVICE FUNCTIONS

Since World War II, dynamic yet disproportionate growth has been occurring in our metropolitan areas. Between 1950 and 1970, the standard metropolitan statistical areas (SMSAs) accounted for approximately 80% of the national increase in population. Almost all the metropolitan growth, however, has occurred in the suburban rings surrounding the central cities, while most central cities have grown very little and many have experienced a decline in population. As a result, for SMSAs as a whole, more people are now residing in the suburban rings than in the central cities.

Concurrent with this population redistribution has been a significant alteration in the social morphology of our urban areas. The compact urban community of nineteenth-century America has been replaced by the diffuse metropolitan area as entire communities have become territorially specialized and dependent on one another. This new entity consists of a large central city nucleus and a plethora of politically autonomous but functionally dependent suburban populations serviced by the central city. As a specialized service center, the city's facilities are utilized intensely by a large part of the suburban population for employment, shopping, recreation, professional services, and other needs.

This study examines the central city as a service center for the suburban population. More specifically, it addresses two issues: (1) does the size of the suburban population have a significant impact on service functions performed in the central city, and (2) what effect, if any, have recent increases in the suburban population had on public services provided by central city

———

Source: John D. Kasarda, "The Impact of Suburban Population Growth on Central City Service Functions," *American Journal of Sociology,* 1972, *77,* 1111-1124.

I wish to thank Amos Hawley and H. M. Blalock, Jr. for their useful comments on an earlier draft of this manuscript. Any shortcomings, of course, are my responsibility.

governments? Primary attention is given to the latter issue and its implications for central city planning and metropolitan reorganization.

DATA AND METHOD

The metropolitan communities to be examined are all SMSAs as of 1950 ($N = 168$). Data representing four broad, but distinct, categories of service functions performed in central cities were obtained from the 1948, 1958,and 1967 Censuses of Business and the 1950, 1960, and 1968-69 Compendia of City Government Finances (U.S. Bureau of the Census). The categories are: (1) retail trade, (2) wholesale trade, (3) business and repair services, and (4) public services provided by central city governments. Sales and receipts for central city retail trade, wholesale trade, and business and repair services are used as indicators of the magnitude of these three categories of service functions, whereas annual operating expenditures for noneducational services provided by central city governments are used as indicators of the magnitude of the public service functions. For cross-sectional analysis, the sales, receipts, and operating expenditures are expressed in terms of "amount per central city resident"; for longitudinal analysis, these data are converted to constant dollars and expressed in terms of first differences.

Demographic data were obtained from the 1950, 1960, and 1970 censuses of population. The suburban population is defined as all population residing outside the central city but within the metropolitan area for those SMSAs that contain a single central city, and as all population residing

FIGURE 1

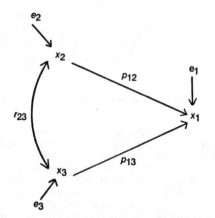

Key: X_1, central city service variable; X_2, central city population size; X_3, suburban population size; p_{12} and p_{13}, path coefficients; r_{23}, zero-order correlation coefficient; e_1, e_2, and e_3, error terms.

outside the largest central city but within the metropolitan area of SMSAs that contain more than one central city.[1]

The primary method used is path analysis, which provides an algorithm for decomposing the total correlation between the dependent and independent variables so that the direct effects of each independent variable on the dependent variables may be ascertained. For example, if central city service functions vary with both the size of the central city population and the size of the suburban population, then a path model mapping the relationship appears as shown in Figure 1.

In a multivariate path model such as this, the zero-order correlation between an independent variable and the dependent variable is the sum of its direct effect via the path from that independent variable to the dependent variable and its *indirect effect*[2] through its correlation with the other independent variable (Land 1969, pp. 12-15). In terms of the coefficients,

$$r_{12} = p_{12} + r_{23} p_{13},$$
$$r_{13} = p_{13} + r_{23} p_{12}.$$

The path coefficients (p_{12} and p_{13}) measure the variance in X_1 for which each independent variable (X_2 or X_3) is *directly* responsible, while the other

TABLE 1

Path Coefficients between per Capita Measures of Central City Service Functions and Population Size (Log) of Central Cities and Suburban Areas, 1960 and 1970

	Central City Service Functions			
Population Size	Retail Trade (1958)	Wholesale Trade (1958)	Business and Repair Services (1958)	Public Services (1960)
1960:				
Central city	—.76*	.33*	.11	.01
Suburban	.83*	.27*	.54*	.39*
Population Size	Retail Trade (1967)	Wholesale Trade (1967)	Business and Repair Services (1967)	Public Services (1969)
1970:				
Central city	—.83*	.16	.04	.06
Suburban area	.61*	.36*	.53*	.41*

*Significant at .001.

1. Since much of the detailed data analyzed in this study were available for only the largest central city of those SMSAs that contain two or more central cities, the largest city was considered the nucleus, and the other cities were treated as suburban to that nucleus. There are two exceptions to this rule. Both the twin cities of Minneapolis–Saint Paul and San Francisco–Oakland, because of their size and the availability of data for all four cities, were taken as single centers by summing the data for each respective pair.
2. Blalock (1971) provides a convincing argument that, whenever the direction of causation between exogenous (independent) variables is ambiguous, we cannot reliably estimate indirect effects through those variables. This being the case with our models, we shall restrict our analysis to the direct effects of each independent variable on the dependent variables.

independent variable is held constant.[3] Therefore, by computing path coefficients, we will be able to determine the direct effect of variation (or change) in both the central city and suburban populations on each central city service function as well as the direct effects of other independent variables.

FINDINGS

Does the size of the suburban population have any bearing on service functions performed in the central city? Table 1 presents the path coefficients between each of the four general categories of central city service functions and the population sizes of the central city and suburban areas.[4]

Looking first at the direct effects of central city size on the central city service functions, we observe that only central city wholesale trade in 1958 exhibits a significant positive relationship with central city size. Business and repair services along with public services show little relationship with central city size. Also interesting is that, when suburban population size is held constant, a strong inverse relationship emerges between retail trade per capita in the central city and the population size of the central city.[5]

TABLE 2

Path Coefficients between Changes in Central City Service Functions and Changes in the Population Size of Central Cities and Suburban Areas, 1950-60 and 1960-70

	Central City Service Functions			
Population Change	Retail Trade (1948-58)	Wholesale Trade (1948-58)	Business and Repair Services (1948-58)	Public Services (1950-60)
1950-60:				
Central city	.54**	.41**	—.15	—.18
Suburban area	.47**	.71**	.69**	.65**
Population Change	Retail Trade (1958-67)	Wholesale Trade (1958-67)	Business and Repair Services (1958-67)	Public Services (1960-69)
1960-70:				
Central city	.74**	.27**	.22*	.11
Suburban area	.31**	.62**	.51**	.45**

* Significant at .01.
** Significant at .001.

---

3. In simple recursive models such as ours, the path coefficients are equivalent to standarized partial regression coefficients.
4. For cross-sectional analysis, the logs of the size of the central city and suburban populations were regressed on the per capita service measures, since a preliminary plotting of these per capita measures with central city size and suburban size showed a slight bending effect at the upper ends of the distributions.
5. This, of course, does not mean that central city retail trade declines with increases in central city size but rather that, controlling for the effects of the suburban population, increments in central city population are associated with less than proportionate increases in central city retail trade.

On the other hand, all four categories of central city service functions exhibit highly significant positive relationships with the size of the suburban population, both in 1960 and 1970. Moreover, with the exception of wholesale trade at the former point in time, suburban population has a larger direct (positive) effect on every category of central city service functions than does central city population.

Having noticed the close association cross-sectionally between central city service functions and population size of the suburban areas, the question now becomes, To what extent are changes over time in these service functions influenced by, or related to, changes in the suburban population size? This is determined in Table 2 which shows the path coefficients between changes in the four categories of central city service functions and changes in the population of central cities and suburban areas during the two most recent decades.

The longitudinal results indicate that changes in the size of the suburban population have had highly significant direct effects on all four categories of central city service functions. The proportion of variance in the four service categories for which changes in the suburban population were directly responsible ranged from 22% to 51% during the 1950-60 decade, and from 10% to 38% during the 1960-70 decade.[6] It is again important to observe that changes in the suburban population exerted much larger direct effects on every central city service category, with the exception of retail trade, than did changes in the central city population.

The path coefficients presented in Tables 1 and 2 clearly indicate that the suburban population has a strong influence on central city service functions. Perhaps the most notable finding is that virtually no relationship exists between noneducational public services provided by the central city government and its population, either cross-sectionally or longitudinally, while positive and strong relationships exist both cross-sectionally and longitudinally between increases in the suburban population and central city public services. The obvious and important inference suggested by this finding is that the suburban population has at least as great an impact on public service provided by central city governments as does the central city population itself. The remainder of the study will examine this issue in more detail.

THE PUBLIC SERVICE ISSUE

One of the most serious problems facing our central cities in recent years has been the growing service-resource gap that has developed from a dis-

---

6. The squared path coefficients measure the proportion of variance (or change) in the dependent variable for which the determining variable is directly responsible (Land 1969, p. 10). The zero-order correlations between changes in central city and suburban populations were .11 during the 1950-60 time period and —.27 during the 1960-70 time period.

proportional increase in public services provided by central city governments over that of their resources. Either explicit or implicit in most discussions addressing this problem has been the suggestion that the major force behind the increasing demand for public services is the changing composition of the central city population. Much less emphasis has been given to the increased demand for public services in the central cities created by the rapidly expanding suburban populations.

It would be difficult to deny that the changing composition of the central city population has increased the need for certain municipal services, such as public welfare and housing. However, we should not overlook the fact that increases in suburban populations have created a large demand for many other central city services. For example, the suburban population makes regular use of central city streets, parks, zoos, museums, and other public facilities; its routine presence in the central city increases problems of the sanitation department and contributes to the costs of fire protection; the daily movement in and out of the central city of the large commuting population requires services that constitute a large portion of the operating budget of both the police and highway departments (Hawley 1957, p. 773). These are only some of the costs experienced by central city governments as a result of services they provide to their suburban neighbors. Just what has been the relationship between growth of suburban populations and services commonly provided by the central city?

In Table 3 are presented the path coefficients between the sizes of the central city and suburban populations and the annual per capita expenditures for six common central city service functions.[7] We see that the suburban population exhibits a higher positive relationship with every central city service function than does the central city population. Moreover, while the direct effects of the suburban population are significant at the .001 level on every central city service function, except highway services in 1960, not a single significant positive relationship exists between the central city population and the central city service functions when suburban population size is held constant. These data provide support, in the cross-sectional case,

---

7. Police service includes police patrols and communications, crime-prevention activities, detention and custody of persons awaiting trial, traffic safety, vehicular inspection, and the like. Fire-prevention services include inspection for fire hazards, maintaining fire-fighting facilities such as fire hydrants, and other fire prevention activities. Highway services include maintenance of streets, highways, and structures necessary for their use, snow and ice removal, toll highways and bridge facilities, and ferries. Sanitation services include street cleaning, collection and disposal of garbage and other waste, sanitary engineering, smoke regulation, and other health activities. Recreation facilities and services include museums and art galleries, playgrounds, play fields, stadiums, swimming pools and bathing beaches, municipal parks, auditoriums, auto camps, recreation piers, and boat harbors. General control includes central staff services and agencies concerned with personnel administration, law, recording, planning and zoning, municipal officials, agencies concerned with tax assessment and collection, accounting, auditing, budgeting, purchasing, and other central finance activities (source: U.S. Bureau of the Census 1970, pp. 64-67).

to the contention that increases in the size of the suburban population are a major contributor to increased expenditures for common service functions performed by central city governments.

The next step is to examine the direct effects of changes (over time) in the size of the central city and suburban populations on changes in expenditures (in constant dollars) for the six central city services. Table 4 lists the path coefficients between changes in each service function and changes in the central city and suburban populations during the 1950-60 interval and during the 1960-70 interval.

We observe that the impact of the suburban population on the six central city service functions is even larger longitudinally than was true cross-sectionally. The percentage of change in these service functions for which changes in the suburban population are directly responsible range from 26% to 64% during the 1950-60 interval and from 26% to 38% during the 1960-70 interval. Only during the 1960-70 interval do we find changes in

TABLE 3
Path Coefficients between per Capita Expenditures for Common Central City Service Functions and Population Size (Log) of Central Cities and Suburbs, 1960 and 1970

Central City Service Function	Population, 1960		Population, 1970[a]	
	Central City	Suburb	Central City	Suburb
Police	.15	.56**	.09	.61**
Fire	—.22*	.43**	—.35**	.57**
Highway	—.19*	.11	—.28**	.25**
Sanitation	—.01	.31**	—.15	.56**
Recreation	—.12	.24**	—.03	.37**
General control	.06	.33**	—.02	.41**

[a] Central city service data for 1969.
* Significant at .01.
** Significant at .001.

TABLE 4
Path Coefficients between Change in Expenditures (in Constant Dollars) for Common Central City Service Functions and Change in the Central City and Suburban Populations, 1950-60 and 1960-70

Central City Service Function	1950-60		1960-70[a]	
	Central City	Suburb	Central City	Suburb
Police	—.12	.74**	.13	.56**
Fire	.01	.79**	.17	.54**
Highway	—.13	.61**	.17	.51**
Sanitation	—.03	.72**	.18	.62**
Recreation	—.10	.80**	.23*	.54**
General control	—.10	.51**	.20*	.58**

[a] Central city service function change 1960-69.
* Significant at .01.
** Significant at .001.

THE RESEARCH EXPERIENCE

central city population size exhibiting consistent positive relationships with changes in the city services. Even during this time period, however, the direct effects of changes in the suburban population were much larger than the effects of changes in the central city population.[8]

OTHER CAUSAL FACTORS

Having demonstrated through both static and dynamic analyses that the growth of common central city service functions is strongly related to population increases in suburban areas, we now test for the possibility that some third variable or combination of variables are responsible for the strong relationships between suburban populations and central city public services. First, we must account for the effects of the age of the city. We know that suburban populations in the older SMSAs are generally larger than those in younger SMSAs. It has also been found that "older cities bearing the stamps of obsolescence, high density, high industrialization, and aging inhabitants, generate higher expenses than their size alone might have led one to suspect" (Vernon 1960, p. 172).

Another important variable is personal income of central city residents. Cities whose residents have higher personal incomes are usually able to provide more and better quality services than those whose population has lower personal incomes. It has also been long known that city-to-suburb migration is closely related to personal income of central city residents. Residents with higher incomes have a much larger choice of residential locations than do low income residents who are often economically and socially confined to the inner city.

Finally, we must control for the racial composition of the central city. One may suspect that certain municipal expenditures are either directly or

TABLE 5
Zero-Order Correlation Coefficients between Selected Characteristics of Central Cities and per Capita Operating Expenditures of Central City Governments and Size of Suburban Population, 1960

| | Central City Characteristic | | |
	Age	Per Capita Income	Non-white (%)
Per capita operating expenditures in central city (all services)	.43*	.14	.17
Size of suburban population (log)	.65*	.16	.28*

* Significant at .001.

8. Cross-sectional and longitudinal analysis was also carried out, controlling for suburban population annexed by central cities between 1950 and 1960. With this control instituted, the direct effects of the suburban population on all service functions remained positive and strong cross-sectionally and actually increased in the longitudinal analysis.

indirectly related to the racial composition of the central city population. At the same time, the "flight to the suburbs" has been greatest in those cities that have experienced the largest influx of nonwhite migrants in the past 25 years.

To discover if each of the above three variables were positively related to both per capita operating expenditures for services provided by central city governments and population size of suburban areas, zero-order correlations were computed.[9] As may be observed in Table 5, all relationships are positive. Per capita operating expenditures for central city services were found to be positively related at the .001 level of significance to the age of the central city, but positively related at only the .05 level of significance to per capita income of central city residents and percentage nonwhite in the central city population. Similarly, the size of the suburban population was found to be positively related at the .001 level of significance to both the age of the central city and the percentage nonwhite in the central city population, but less so ($p = .05$) to per capita income of central city residents.

These results raise an important question: what is the relationship between suburban population size and per capita operating expenditures for central city public services when we control, not only for central city size, but also for age of the central city, per capita income of the central city residents, and the percentage nonwhite in the central city population? In addition, we might ask: what is the relationship between per capita expenditures for central city services and each of the three central city variables (age, income, percentage nonwhite) when the remaining two central city variables, as well as central city size and suburban size are held constant? Table 6 answers these questions.

The crucial finding in Table 6 is that the impact of the suburban population remains strong and in the hypothesized direction when controls are introduced for central city size, age, per capita income, and percentage nonwhite. With these variables held constant, the direct effects of the size of the suburban population on the central city service functions are all positive, with significance at the .001 level for every service function except highway services.

Central city size exhibits a negative relationship to all service functions except sanitation services when the other variables are held constant. The significant negative relationships found between central city size and a number of the services indicate that economies of scale may operate in the provision of these services.

Examining the direct effects of central city age, per capita income, and

9. The correlation and path coefficients presented in Tables 5, 6, and 7 apply to 157 SMSAs in 1960 for which complete data were available on central city age (operationalized as the number of decades since the central city first attained a population size of 50,000 or more), per capita income of central city residents, percentage nonwhite in the central city, and the number of suburban residents who commute to work in the central city.

THE RESEARCH EXPERIENCE

percentage nonwhite on the service functions, we observe that age has a substantial direct effect on the total operating expenditures and on expenditures
for fire and highway services, as well as on general control. Also as expected,
personal income of the central city residents exerts a positive effect on all
services, with significant direct effects on fire and highway services. Percentage nonwhite exerts significant direct effects on sanitation services and
general control but, in contrast to the effects of age and personal income,
exhibits essentially no relationship with fire and highway services.

In sum, Table 6 indicates that size of the suburban population, rather
than size or composition of the central city population, is the most important
determinant of central city expenditures for public services. It may also be
inferred from Table 6 that, *ceteris paribus,* the overall per capita operating
expenditures for central city services increase with the age of the central city
and decline with increases in its size.

THE COMMUTING POPULATION

In an effort to refine the above analysis and determine the impact on
central city public services of suburban residents who utilize central city

TABLE 6
Path Coefficients between per Capita Expenditures for Central City Services and Selected Variables, 1960

	Central City Population (log)	Suburban Population (log)	Age	Per Capita Income	Non-white (%)
All services	—.24**	.38**	.34**	.10	.09
Police	—.04	.60**	.02	.15	.16
Fire	—.51**	.45**	.30**	.20*	—.03
Highway	—.29**	.08	.19*	.19*	—.04
Sanitation	.05	.28**	—.19*	.14	.27**
Recreation	—.19*	.27**	.04	.10	.12
General control	—.22*	.33**	.23*	.18	.22*

* Significant at .01.
** Significant at .001.

TABLE 7
Path Coefficients between per Capita Expenditures for Central City Services and Selected Variables, 1960

	Central City Population (log)	Commuters (log)	Age	Per Capita Income	Non-white (%)
All Services........	—.23*	.35**	.35**	.11	.08
Police	—.02	.52**	.06	.17	.16
Fire	—.52**	.44**	.32**	.21*	—.04
Highway	—.40**	.28**	.14	.18	—.08
Sanitation	.02	.31**	—.18	.14	.26**
Recreation	—.18	.24**	.03	.11	.12
General control	—.21*	.28**	.25**	.20*	.22*

* Significant at .01.
** Significant at .001.

services daily, data were obtained from the journey to work reports of the 1960 Census of Population on the total number of people in each SMSA who reside in the suburbs and commute to work in the central city. Path coefficients were again computed, substituting the number of commuters for suburban population size in the least-squares equations. The results are presented in Table 7.

We observe that the number of suburbanites who commute to work in the central city has a direct impact at the .001 level of significance on the total per capita operating expenditures for central city services as well as on per capita expenditures for each individual central city service. Recalling that highway services was the only central city function to which size of the suburban population was not significantly related (Table 6), it is noteworthy that, when number of commuters is used as the independent variable, a highly significant positive relationship emerges.

The fact that the overall results in Table 7 are so similar to those in Table 6 indicates that the number of suburban residents who commute to work in the central city corresponds closely with the size of the suburban population. When the zero-order correlation between size of the suburban population and the number of suburban residents who commute to the central city was computed, it was found to be .95. Regression analysis showed the unstandardized slope between suburban size and number of commuters to be .105. In other words, an almost perfect linear relationship exists between suburban population size and the number of suburban residents who commute daily to the central city, with each increase of 1,000 suburban residents leading to an additional 105 commuters. Furthermore, the ratio of suburban residents who work in the central city to the central city resident population increases with the size of the suburban population. A correlation coefficient of .46 exists between suburban population size (log) and the ratio of commuters to central city residents. Thus, as the size of the suburban population increases, not only do larger numbers of suburban residents daily utilize central city public services, but, more important, the proportion of suburban residents relative to central city residents who utilize city services also increases. On the average, there are 132 commuters using central city services per 1,000 central city residents. These findings, along with the results provided in Tables 3 through 7, offer empirical support to the argument that the rapid growth of suburban populations has contributed greatly to the increased demand and, hence, increased expenditures for common central city public services.

SUMMARY AND IMPLICATIONS

This study examined the relationship between suburban population growth and service functions performed in central cities of 168 SMSAs. While most sociologists acknowledge that the suburban population influences the service structure of central cities, the degree of that influence has often been underestimated. Both cross-sectional and longitudinal analysis demonstrate that the suburban population has a large impact on central city retail trade, wholesale trade, business and repair services, and public services provided by central city governments. More detailed examination of the public sector shows that the suburban population in general, and the commuting population, in particular, exerts strong effects on police, fire, highway, sanitation, recreation, and general administrative functions performed in the central cities. The impact of the suburban population remains strong when controls are introduced for central city size and age, annexation, per capita income of central city residents, and percentage of the central city population that is nonwhite.

What implications do these results have for the present and future planning of the metropolitan community? First, the findings indicate that central city officials and planners should be particularly attentive to trends in the population growth of their outlying areas when projecting future demands for central city services. As long as area specialization continues to increase within the metropolitan community, we can expect the impact of the suburban population on central city facilities and services to grow.

A second implication is that the suburban population, by its daily use of central city facilities, substantially raises the costs of municipal services. While suburban residents do partially reimburse central cities in some SMSAs through employment and sales taxes, it is not likely that these "user charges" generate sufficient revenue to cover the additional costs.[10] A strong case can therefore be made for consolidating the politically autonomous suburban units with the central city in the form of a metropolitan-wide government. With a single jurisdiction controlling the services and resources, not only would the tax load for the provision of municipal services be spread in a more equitable fashion throughout the metropolitan area, but economies of scale might also be realized. Heavy resistance from suburban populations to political reorganization, however, makes the outlook for consolidation in the near future quite pessimistic. For the time being, then, the only recourse

---

10. A recent study (Neenan 1970) of benefit and revenue flows between Detroit and six of its suburban municipalities, representing both residential and industrial suburbs, shows that the suburban communities enjoy a considerable net gain from the public sector of Detroit. Neenan's analysis indicates that the net subsidy from Detroit ranges from $1.73 per capita for the low-income industrial suburb (Highland Park) to $12.58 per capita for the high-income residential and commercial suburb (Birmingham). Although not specifically analyzed in the present study it should also be noted that many central cities indirectly subsidize their suburban areas by having to pay an unfair share of the metropolitan area's welfare services. Through zoning restrictions and discriminatory practices, the suburban populations have been able to insure that most of the low-income, poorly educated, and chronically unemployed people in the metropolitan area are confined in the central cities. Suburban residents are therefore able to avoid the costs of public housing, public health, and other welfare services, which often impose a heavy burden on the operating budget of central cities.

open to the central city is increased financial assistance for the provision of municipal services. Perhaps suburban resistance to consolidation will only recede when the circuitous flow of taxes from suburb to Washington to central city increases to an extent that the service-resource gap begins to favor the central city.

REFERENCES

Blalock, Hubert M. 1971. "Path Analysis Revisited: The Decomposition of Unstandardized Coefficients." Unpublished research note. Department of Sociology, University of Washington, Seattle.

Hawley, Amos H. 1957. "Metropolitan Population and Municipal Government Expenditures in Central Cities." In *Cities and Society*, edited by Paul K. Hatt and Albert J. Reiss. New York: Free Press.

Land, Kenneth. 1969. "Principles of Path Analysis." In *Sociological Methodology 1969*, edited by Edgar Borgatta. San Francisco: Jossey-Bass.

Neenan, William. 1970. "The Suburban-Central City Exploitation Thesis: One City's Tale." *National Tax Journal* 23 (June): 117-39.

U.S. Bureau of The Census. 1970. *City Government Finances in 1968-69*. Washington, D.C.: Government Printing Office.

Vernon, Raymond. 1960. *Metropolis 1985*. Cambridge, Mass.: Harvard University Press.

Personal Journal ──

B. THE USE OF CENSUS DATA IN SECONDARY ANALYSIS: THE CONTEXT OF ECOLOGICAL DISCOVERY

THE CENSUS AS A SOURCE OF SECONDARY DATA

There is no larger or perhaps more important set of secondary data available for social research than censuses tabulated by the U.S. Bureau of the Census.[1] While the largest and most diverse single source of secondary data is the decennial (ten-year) Census of Population and Housing, the

---

Source: Prepared especially for this volume.

1. Secondary data may be defined simply as information on people, places, or topics drawn from sources initially assembled by somebody else. Analysis of these data, which is referred to as secondary analysis, usually focuses on issues other than those for which the data were originally assembled. For an excellent discussion of the principles, procedures, and potentialities of secondary analysis, the student may wish to refer to Herbert Hyman's recent book, *Secondary Analysis of Sample Surveys* (New York: Wiley, 1972).

Bureau also conducts quinquennial (five-year) Censuses of Business, Manufacturing, Agriculture, Mineral Industries, Construction, Transportation, and Governments. These censuses provide a broad base of social science information ranging from the number of female-headed households in Albuquerque, New Mexico (Census of Population and Housing) to expenditures for police protection in Scranton, Pa. (Census of Governments). Data may be obtained to analyze educational attainment, ethnic and racial segregation, poverty, labor force participation, urban expansion, discrimination in employment and housing, commuting patterns, public services, marriage and divorce, fertility, migration, social mobility, and feminine careerism, to mention a few. So extensive are the data provided in the various censuses that opportunities for secondary analysis seem to be limited only by the imagination of the researcher.

What makes census data particularly useful for secondary analysis is that most variables are available not only cross-sectionally (i.e., at one common point in time) but also on a longitudinal basis (i.e., at a number of different points in time). This enables researchers to measure particular social relationships and examine their trends historically. For example, one may compare socioeconomic characteristics of different ethnic or racial groups over ten year intervals to determine if gaps in their socioeconomic status are widening or declining; or one may examine the suburbanization of industrial activity since World War II and analyze its impact on minority unemployment in the central cities. Most census data are now available for at least three points in time, with some comparable data extending as far back as 1790, the year of the first U.S. Census of Population.

Virtually all U.S. census data are tabulated on a geographic summary basis. This means that the data are aggregated (summed) for particular geographic areas, such as cities or counties. Population and housing data are tabulated for numerous and various geographic areas, ranging from separate residential blocks to the entire nation. The most commonly utilized geographic summary areas are blocks, census tracts, towns, cities, counties, metropolitan areas, regions, and states.

The fact that census data have generally been tabulated on a geographic summary basis has often precluded using individuals or households as units of analysis. In 1964, however, the Bureau of the Census made available on computer tape and punch cards separate records (information files) on 180,000 individuals drawn from the 1960 Census of Population and Housing. This sample included detailed information on one out of every 1,000 individuals in the United States. To ensure confidentiality, the names, addresses and other information that might possibly identify a particular individual were not included. In 1972 data were released from the 1970 Census of Population and Housing on approximately 2 million individuals (a 1 percent sample of the entire population). Again to avoid disclosure, all personal identifying information was removed from the records. These massive samples of detailed social and economic data on individuals and households provide an extremely rich source of secondary data that is just beginning to be tapped by social researchers.

A fundamental advantage of using census data for social research is that the investigator is spared the time and cost involved in survey design, collection, and tabulation of data. The Bureau of the Census carries out these initial steps, enabling the researcher to proceed almost directly to the analysis stage. Furthermore, sampling and measurement errors in U.S. censuses are among the lowest of all sources of survey data. Census data are tabulated by an experienced staff of Bureau personnel who strive to achieve a high degree of completeness and accuracy for all data reported. Nevertheless, human and mechanical errors do occur which reduce the accuracy of some reported data. In the words of the Bureau of the Census:

> Such errors include failure to obtain required information from respondents, obtaining inconsistent information, recording information in the wrong place or incorrectly, and otherwise producing inconsistencies between entries or inter-related items on the field documents. Sampling biases occur because some of the enumerators fail to follow the sampling instructions. Clerical coding and editing errors occur, and errors occur in electronic processing. . . .[2]

To mitigate these errors, Bureau of the Census personnel review enumerators' work, verify the manual coding and editing, check the tabulated figures, and utilize statistical techniques such as ratio estimation of sample data to control totals in the complete count.[3] Through such efforts, errors in the printed reports are usually kept at an acceptably low level so that secondary analysis of these data will not generally yield misleading results.

Perhaps the major shortcoming of census data for social research is that many variables of interest to sociologists are not reported in the censuses. For example, no information is collected about sentiments, attitudes, values, or beliefs. Researchers interested in social-psychological studies must therefore look elsewhere for secondary sources of data or conduct their own field studies or experiments.

On the other hand, demographers and human ecologists find the information provided in the censuses most appropriate for their research needs. Their studies rely on broad bases of data on social, economic, and demographic characteristics of population groups and geographic areas. In fact the nature, scope, and completeness of data utilized in most demographic and ecological studies are such that they could never be reproduced by the individual researcher.

Census data are particularly well suited for the ecological approach in sociology. The basic unit of analysis in this approach is a geographically

---

2. U.S. Bureau of the Census, *U.S. Census of Population: 1960, United States Summary, Characteristics of the Population,* Vol. 1, pt. 1, p. lxxxv. (Washington, D.C.: Government Printing Office, 1964.)
3. Ibid.

delimited population. The population being studied may include those living in given census tracts, cities, counties, metropolitan areas, states, regions, nations or any other defined subarea. Like demography, human ecology is concerned with the size, composition, and distribution of particular populations. Human ecologists, however, focus primarily on environmental, structural, and technological factors affecting given populations and the consequences of population size, composition, and distribution for social organization. My analysis of the impact of suburban population growth on central city service functions is an example of an ecological study utilizing census data to examine one organizational consequence of the size, composition, and distribution of population in metropolitan America. Let me briefly chronicle the evolution of ideas and events in my research experience to illustrate how census data can be used for social research.

THEORETICAL BASIS AND INITIAL DESIGN

My interest in the influence of suburban population growth on central city service functions grew out of a seminar on human ecology that I took in 1969 under Amos Hawley at the University of North Carolina. The focus of the seminar was on theoretical issues in human ecology, though we also spent a good deal of time discussing methodological techniques for empirically grounding ecological theory. The issue that particularly attracted my interest is the theory of ecological expansion. In short, ecological expansion is a twofold process involving, first, a movement of people outward from a center of settlement without their losing contact with that center; and, second, a development of service functions in the center to sustain activities throughout the expanded system. The expansion process produces a diffuse community having two loci: an inner locus, or city, in which service functions are concentrated, and an outwardly advancing periphery, or suburb, which complements the city by routinely drawing on its services.

For my seminar project, I decided to examine the theory of ecological expansion empirically. My first step in formulating a research strategy was to select appropriate units of analysis. Two criteria seemed important to me. First, I felt that the units of analysis should be conceptually linked to the territorial system characterized by the theory and, second, that relevant data on these units should be available to test empirical propositions derived from the theory. Standard Metropolitan Statistical Areas (SMSAs) as established by the Bureau of the Census clearly satisfied both criteria.

The Bureau of the Census defines an SMSA as an economically and socially integrated territorial system with a large population nucleus, i.e., a central city of at least 50,000 inhabitants. The boundaries of SMSAs are delimited by the county containing the central city and all contiguous (adjoining) counties that are urban in character and economically and socially integrated with the county containing the central city. The inner locus of SMSAs is geographically delimited by the central city and the outer locus by the suburban ring, which is that area outside the central city but within the SMSA boundaries. Since the Bureau of the Census provides comparable social, economic, and demographic data for both the central city and the SMSA, it is usually possible to derive data on the suburban ring by simply subtracting the appropriate central city data from the SMSA data.

Having chosen SMSAs as my units of analysis, I directed my efforts towards examining the central city as a service center for the suburban population. In so doing I hoped to show that metropolitan growth is a special case of ecological expansion. Two rather closely related hypotheses were derived from the theory of ecological expansion. The first followed from the proposition that population growth in the peripheral areas of a territorial system will be matched with an increase in service functions in the nucleus to sustain the enlarged system. The research hypothesis I derived from this proposition is that service functions performed in central cities will increase at a disproportionate rate as the size of the suburban population becomes larger.

My second research hypothesis followed from the proposition that in an expanding system, people move out from the center of settlement without losing contact with that center. If metropolitan growth is a special case of metropolitan expansion, then suburban population growth should lead to larger numbers of people who reside outside the central city but maintain direct contact with the central city through their daily use of its facilities and services. In turn the daily use of the central city by larger numbers of suburbanites creates an increased demand for public services in the city. I therefore hypothesized that a major cause of increased expenditures for central city services such as police, fire, highway, sanitation, and recreation is the expanding suburban population which makes routine use of these services while in the central city.

DATA AND ANALYSIS

My next step was to gather data to test my two research hypotheses. A perusal of recent censuses showed that data were available on the size, composition, and distribution of populations in central cities and SMSAs from Censuses of Population, that data on central city and SMSA retail, wholesale, and business service activity were available from the Censuses of Business, and that detailed data on public services provided in the central cities were available from the Censuses of Governments and annual Compendia of City Government Finances. Combining secondary data from these sources over different time periods enabled me to empirically test my hypotheses both cross-sectionally and longitudinally.

Because my time and budget were limited, I restricted my initial sample to those SMSAs that had a central city population of at least 100,000

($N = 91$). Still, with a sample size of 91 SMSAs and almost 20 variables for each unit, analysis by hand or desk calculator seemed out of the question; the computer became a necessity. This meant, however, that I had to keypunch the data from the various census volumes onto machine-readable cards (i.e., IBM punch cards). I can recall quite well the many tedious evenings I spent at the computer center in Chapel Hill keypunching and verifying the data. I must admit that at times I questioned the value of such efforts, particularly since I was not certain that anything meaningful would result in the final analysis. After about six weeks of coding, keypunching, and verifying, my data were ready to be analyzed.

In the analysis stage, I relied on a very useful canned computer program called SPSS (Statistical Package for the Social Sciences). This program enabled me to carry out basic cross-tabular and correlation analyses of all the dependent and independent variables I had coded. One of the most satisfying phases of the research project was discovering that the results of the analysis strongly supported both my research hypotheses. I wrote my findings up as a term paper, which I presented the following summer at the annual meetings of the American Sociological Association under the title "The Impact of Suburban Population: An Analysis of Ecological Correlates."

Encouraged by the results from my analysis of a sample of SMSAs, I presented a research proposal for financial support to expand the study to the Department of Sociology at the University of North Carolina. In the summer of 1970 I was awarded $600, which I used to hire a research assistant to code, keypunch, and verify additional census data. The data collection was extended to include all SMSAs as of 1950 ($N = 168$), recently released 1970 census data, and other data which I felt were essential for statistical control.

There were two methodological problems in my original analysis that I hoped to solve, in part, with the expanded data base. First, I had been using sales, receipts, and expenditure data (measured in dollars) as indicators of service activity in the central cities. Since the value of the dollar substantially changed between 1950 and 1970, it was essential to transform the sales, receipts, and expenditures into constant dollars. In transforming these data, I utilized the consumer price index to deflate retail sales and business service receipts, the wholesale price index to deflate wholesale sales, and the purchasing power of the dollar to deflate expenditures for public services.

The second methodological problem that became apparent was that although I had previously demonstrated a strong correlation between suburban population growth and central city services, the two factors were not necessarily functionally related. It is entirely possible for two variables to be highly correlated yet functionally (or causally) unrelated. When this occurs we have what statisticians term a "spurious" relationship. A spurious relationship between two variables emerges whenever some third variable or set of variables causes two functionally unrelated variables to co-vary in a systematic manner. A commonly cited spurious relationship is that between ice cream sales and crime rates. A strong positive relationship exists between these two factors because both vary systematically with weather conditions, rather than one factor being the cause of the other.

To guard against possible spurious relationships I found it necessary to control for other variables that may affect both the size of the suburban population and central city service functions. My review of the literature and preliminary correlation analysis suggested three variables that may result in a spurious relationship between the size of the suburban population and expenditures for central city services. As discussed in the article, these variables are the age of the central city (measured in terms of the number of decades passed since the city attained a population of 50,000 or more), the per capita income of central city residents, and the percent of nonwhites in the central city. If, after controlling for these variables, a strong relationship remains between the size of the suburban population and central city service functions, then it is quite likely that a "real" rather than a "spurious" relationship has been discovered.

How, though, does one determine the strength of relationship between two variables when controlling for other theoretically relevant variables? The method that I chose was path analysis, which is no more than basic regression analysis including a number of theoretical assumptions about linearity, additivity, and causality.[4] A path coefficient is simply a standardized regression coefficient which is often referred to as a "Beta weight" in the research literature. It indicates how much variance in the dependent variable (e.g., public service expenditures) is produced by a standardized change in one of the independent variables (e.g., suburban population size) when all other independent variables under analysis are held constant. Through path (regression) analysis I was able to determine the direct effects of not only suburban population size but also the direct effects of the age of the central city, percent nonwhite in the central city, and the per capita income of central city residents.

My analysis of the direct effects of all these variables indicated that the suburban population has by far the most pervasive impact on expenditures for public services in central cities. Of course I was pleased that the results supported my contention that the size of the suburban population is at least as important a factor influencing central city service expenditures as is the population composition of the central city itself. However, the article's concluding remarks reflect my feeling that the results were even more important from a standpoint of public policy. While I still believe the findings imply that central city planners and officials should be more cognizant of popula-

---

4. For a straightforward overview of path analysis see Kenneth Land, "Principles of Path Analysis" in Edgar F. Borgatta, ed., *Sociological Methodology 1969* (San Francisco: Jossey-Bass, 1969), pp. 3-37.

THE RESEARCH EXPERIENCE

tion trends in their suburban areas when projecting future demands for central city services, I now feel that I speculated beyond the evidence of my data by implying that the suburban population may be exploiting the central city with respect to public services.

No doubt the results suggest that the suburban population increases the costs of public services for the central cities. But to accurately infer exploitation I would also have to demonstrate that these costs are greater than the revenue the suburban population generates for the central cities. The suburban population makes contributions to the central city resource base other than commuter taxes, sales taxes, or other "user charges." For example, suburbanites' employment in downtown office buildings indirectly improves the central city tax base by increasing property values. Moreover, many central city business establishments could not survive without the large number of suburbanites who purchase their goods and services. The whole issue of central city-suburban exploitation remains a problem yet to be definitely resolved in the research literature.

FURTHER REFLECTIONS ON THE STUDY

When a researcher completes a study, he often looks back and asks himself what he would do differently to improve the study. There are two changes that I feel would make my analysis more convincing and important from a policy standpoint. First of all, I would add more independent (control) variables to my path models. The one criticism frequently heard about path (regression) analyses such as mine is: "But would your results have been the same if you had controlled for X?" For example, including a measure of the quality of public services in the central cities would have improved the analysis. Perhaps public service expenditures are higher in central cities with larger suburbs, but their services are also of better quality. Here the possibility of spuriousness is again raised. Another important variable that I would now include in the analysis is federal and state financial aid to the central cities. Recent research suggests that expenditures for some city services are quite sensitive to the amount of extralocal subsidies the cities receive.

A second step that I would take to improve the study would be to conduct a cost-benefit analysis of the use of central city services and facilities by the suburban population. This would involve computing estimates of the economic contribution that suburbanites make to the resource base of the central city along with estimates of the marginal costs they create in making use of central city services. Regression analysis of data from the Censuses of Population, Business, and Governments is one method that could be used to estimate the costs and benefits that accrue to the central cities as a result of their use by the suburban population.

Allan M. Schwartzbaum, Robert A. Rothman, and
John H. McGrath III ―――――――――――――――――

A. VOLUNTARY QUESTIONNAIRE WRITE-INS AND RESPONDENT ATTITUDES

Survey research stands as an important form of data collection in the social sciences. Mailed questionnaires are frequently used in surveys because they have certain advantages over other techniques. Considerations of time, cost, and broad geographic coverage are paramount (Goode and Hatt, 1952: 170-183; Wallace, 1954). However, mailed questionnaires also have a number of shortcomings, such as lack of response and the inability to check responses given (Parten, 1950:391-402). Consequently, a number of studies have attempted to abstract secondary data on respondents from the questionnaires. This article explores the possible uses of a neglected source of information—voluntary write-ins—in the survey research process.

The analysis presented here resulted from a larger study of resistance to change among a group of physicians (Schwartzbaum et al., 1969; Rothman et al., 1971). During the analysis it became apparent that placing respondents in categories such as "resistant to change" on the basis of fixed alternative questions obscured significant internal variations in intensity of feeling. Strong resistance was evident in the write-ins, and was also evident in the larger medical community. Therefore, this study was undertaken with the following specific aims in mind: (a) to examine differences between respondents who volunteer comments on the questionnaire and those who do not, (b) to explore the utility of employing certain models of communicative behavior within small groups for the interpretation of survey research results, and (c) to discuss possible implications of the systematic use of voluntary write-ins.

Source: Allan M. Schwartzbaum, Robert A. Rothman, and John H. McGrath III, "Voluntary Questionnaire Write-ins and Respondent Attitudes," *Rural Sociology*, 1972, *37*, 445-453.

This study was partially financed by a University of Delaware Faculty Research Grant. The authors wish to acknowledge the assistance of Melissa Huber, Jerrilyn Jones, and Joy Kiger. An earlier version of this paper was read at the AKD Research Symposium at Virginia Commonwealth University on April 17, 1971.

RESEARCH ON RESPONDENT ATTITUDES

Previous research has suggested that those who respond are markedly different from those who do not, and that scope and intensity of respondent interest is an important differentiating factor. Katz and Cantril (1937) report that a disproportionate number of mailed returns in public opinion polls come from people with intense opinions rather than from those who are uncommitted or undecided. Findings in studies conducted by Stanton (1939) and Reid (1942) were similar.

Returns from a series of repeated questionnaire mailings have shown that responders to the second and third waves have very different characteristics from responders to the first. Suchman and McCandless (1940) conducted two studies of radio listening. Their results indicate that "first wave" returns are related to familiarity with the topic, personal experience with the problem, and importance of the subject to the respondent. Pace (1939), among others, reported that characteristics of late returners were more comparable to the characteristics of nonreturners than to those of early returners. Another measure of involvement was examined by Pearlin (1961) who compared the general characteristics of signers and nonsigners of a questionnaire. His data were drawn from 1,119 returns from a self-administered questionnaire distributed to nursing personnel who were given a free option to sign or not sign their questions. Pearlin found that nonsigners had significantly less enthusiasm for their work than did signers.

Blum and Downing (1964) drew from their data conclusions about respondents' reactions to change. Using the number of returns as an index of concern about administrative innovations, they concluded that salaried professional staff were more concerned with the innovations than were volunteers. Blum and Downing also used the number of respondents who failed to identify themselves as "a simple measure of felt threat and distrust" (p. 1233).

Our working hypothesis was therefore that voluntary write-ins on questionnaires are not simply a response to questionnaire content but are also an action reflecting a particular orientation toward the subject matter under study. We used the research of Schachter (1951) on the origins of pressure to communicate within small groups as a general theoretical framework for predicting write-in behavior. Schachter found that the pressures to communicate will rise with increasing difference of opinion, increasing group cohesiveness, and increasing relevance of issue. In addition, pressures to communicate are directly related to "dependence," that is, the extent to which a person relies on the group to establish social reality.

Utilizing Schachter's framework, we predicted that respondents would be more likely to volunteer write-in comments when (1) the issues covered by the questionnaire were of great relevance to them, (2) the respondents reported high cohesiveness with an appropriate reference group, (3) the issues covered by the questionnaire uncovered large differences of opinion between the respondents and "significant others," and (4) the respondents felt a great dependence on members of a reference group concerned with the issue.

RESEARCH PROCEDURE

Data reported here were obtained from a study of patterns of resistance to the merging of three formerly independent hospitals into a single administrative unit. In June of 1968, a 40-item fixed-alternative questionnaire was mailed to all physicians affiliated with the recently combined facilities. The overall return was 64 percent (302 of 475), but unusable questionnaires reduced the final number to 265 or 56 percent.

The question of representativeness was examined by comparing the characteristics of respondents with certain data on the demographic characteristics of all physicians which were available from the local medical society. This comparison revealed that respondents did not differ significantly from nonrespondents in age, medical school, place of birth, or medical specialty, although surgeons and general practitioners were somewhat underrepresented. In addition, respondents' support of or opposition to the merger closely approximated the proportions in the official vote of the entire medical staff.

Of the total sample of 265 physicians, 172 or 65 percent volunteered written remarks on items that were closed response in nature. At the upper

TABLE 1
Write-in Behavior by Relevance of Issues (percent volunteering comments)

Write-ins	Years in Local Area		Holding of Administrative Posts		Number of Administrative Posts Held		
	1 to 5 (N = 44)	6 or more (N = 213)	No (N = 91)	Yes (N = 161)	0 (N = 91)	1 (N = 74)	2 or more (N = 86)
Yes	45%	69%	54%	72%	54%	68%	76%
No	55	31	46	28	46	32	24

Years in local area, chi square = 8.895, 1 $d.f.$, p < .01; holding of administrative posts, chi square = 8.523, 1 $d.f.$, p < .01; number of posts held, chi square = 9.453, 2 $d.f.$, p < .01.
Note: Variation in N's is attributable to lack of response to particular items on the questionnaire.

TABLE 2
Write-in Behavior by Perceptions of Impact of Merger on Individual Physician (percent volunteering comments)

Write-ins	Perceived Impact of Merger		
	Little or None (N = 95)	Moderate (N = 87)	Significant (N = 61)
Yes	69%	60%	79%
No	31	40	21

Chi square = 6.026, 2 $d.f.$, p < .05.

THE RESEARCH EXPERIENCE

extreme, 3 physicians commented on more than 9 items; at the lower extreme, 67 physicians commented on single items. The mean number of comments for those who volunteered remarks was 2.2, with a standard deviation of 1.3.

Hypotheses derived from Schachter were examined by a secondary analysis of the data. The choice of measures to operationalize variables was obviously limited because of the post hoc nature of the analysis. However, it should be noted that the purpose of this study was to explore the utility of this framework rather than to provide definitive support for the hypotheses.

FINDINGS

Relevance

The concept of relevance as suggested by Schachter was measured by length of residence in area and administrative involvement. These measures were based on the assumption that merger would be more relevant to those who would be most likely to have their practice or their professional position affected by the change.

Table 1 shows that physicians who had lived in the local area for more than six years wrote in significantly more often than physicians with shorter tenure. It also shows that physicians who held administrative positions in the merged hospitals were more likely to write in than physicians who did not occupy such positions, and that physicians who occupied several administrative posts were the most likely to provide voluntary comments.

Table 2 shows that physicians who reported that their practice had been significantly affected by the merger were more apt to write in than physicians for whom the merger had had only limited consequences. Contrary to our hypothesis, physicians who perceived little or no personal consequences associated with merger wrote in more often than physicians who were moderately affected. Physicians who opposed the merger were most likely to perceive changes in the medical system as a result of the merger; those who supported it were least likely to perceive any impact. Thus, the curvilinear relationship may, in part, show that those who had been most opposed to the change wrote in the most comments, that those who had been most supportive wrote in the next most comments, and that those in the middle wrote in the fewest comments.

Cohesiveness

Cohesiveness was measured by using self-reported frequency of professional and interpersonal contacts with colleagues. Write-in behavior was positively associated with frequency of contact with colleagues outside one's

TABLE 3
Write-in Behavior by Frequency of Interaction with Physicians Within and Outside of Own Specialty (percent volunteering comments)

	Frequency of Interaction Within Specialty		
Write-ins	Often (N = 222)	Occasionally (N = 55)	Seldom (N = 9)
Yes	64%	49%	66%
No	36	51	33

Chi square = 4.48, 2 d.f., p < .2.

	Frequency of Interaction Outside Specialty		
Write-ins	Often (N = 190)	Occasionally (N = 84)	Seldom (N = 11)
Yes	68%	49%	45%
No	32	51	55

Chi square = 10.77, 2 d.f., p < .01.

TABLE 4
Perceptions of Consequences of Merger by Write-in Behavior (percent volunteering comments)

	Write-ins	
Perceived Consequences	Yes (N = 172)	No (N = 93)
Improvement	14%	15%
No change	55	54
Decline	22	14
No answer	9	18
Total number of responses	(1720)	(930)

Note: This table was developed by totaling the number of responses to ten items cited in the text on the consequences of the merger.

TABLE 5
Write-in Behavior by Dependence on Physicians Within and Outside of Own Specialty (percent volunteering comments)

	Dependence upon Physicians Within Specialty		
Write-ins	High (N = 64)	Moderate (N = 138)	Independent (N = 80)
Yes	72%	62%	52.5%
No	28	38	47.5

Chi square = 5.64, 2 d.f., p < .10.

	Dependence upon Physicians Outside Specialty		
Write-ins	High (N = 122)	Moderate (N = 152)	Independent (N = 13)
Yes	70.5%	55%	46%
No	29.5	45	54

Chi square = 7.94, 2 d.f., p < .02.

own specialty (Table 3), but not with frequency of interaction with physicians within one's specialty. This seems consistent with our general line of reasoning, because *cohesiveness* as used by Schachter refers to total group cohesiveness, not to subgroup cohesiveness, and specialty interaction would reflect subgroup cohesiveness.

Difference of opinion

Schachter (1951:175-176) used the *difference of opinion* to refer to "the phenomenological difference between two people rather than to the absolute difference between two points on a scale." In this study, we take the second person to be a particular "generalized other" or reference group, namely the administrative and medical sponsors of merger who forecast improvements and "played down" others' predictions of decline. For example, the medical director of the Medical Center wrote (Cannon, 1961:286) that "the advantages of a merger of the three hospitals into a medical center are so numerous and so overpowering that it is difficult to know where to commence their enumeration." Therefore, this variable was operationalized by using ten statements which described positive consequences which, it had been predicted, would result from the merger.[1]

In Table 4, respondents are differentiated first on the basis of whether or not they volunteered comments and then in terms of the number of areas in which they saw "improvement," "decline," or "no change" as a result of the merger. This treatment of the data was necessitated by the failure of some physicians to respond to some of the ten items, and our resultant inability to categorize respondents meaningfully in terms of a predominant type of response.

Respondents who wrote comments in were, as predicted, more likely to perceive decline (22 percent of the items versus 14 percent) and thus to be in disagreement with the leaders of the medical community. These respondents were also less likely to exhibit indecision, if no answer can be so interpreted. These data seem consistent with our hypothesis.

Dependence

Dependence was defined as the degree of dependence on colleagues (within and outside one's specialty) for services such as consultation, re-

---

1. The items involved the following issues: (1) overall quality of patient care, (2) availability of specialized equipment needed in one's specialty, (3) patients' evaluation of medical services in the community, (4) control over the care of out-patients using the hospitals, (5) the status of local medical facilities in relation to those comparable in other communities, (6) professional standing in the national medical community, (7) satisfaction with personal status in the local medical community, (8) individual physician's ability to operate as an autonomous professional within the medical community, (9) administration of individual facilities, and (10) utilization of all health personnel.

search, and referral. In the original study, separate questions were developed in order to distinguish between *dependence* as conceptualized here, and *interaction* as used in the section on cohesiveness. The hypothesized association between dependence and voluntary comments is supported by the data presented in Table 5.

DISCUSSION

The results suggest that certain principles derived from small-group theory may provide an appropriate model for interpreting aspects of the survey research process. It is clear from the small-group literature that there are pressures toward uniformity of behavior and attitude among members of most groups. If differences of opinion exist within a group, forces will arise to restore uniformity.

The theory of Schachter (1951) presents four factors influencing the magnitude of pressure toward uniformity: increasing relevance of issue, cohesiveness, dependence, and difference of opinion. These have been found to be positively related to communicative behavior in small groups, and also generally in our questionnaire survey. Write-in behavior did, however, show somewhat mixed findings on cohesiveness and relevance.

A major difficulty in applying principles derived from communications models used in small groups to an interpretation of write-in behavior is the difference in the visibility of recipients in each case. In the small-group situation, the recipient of a communication is usually either a specific group member or the group as a whole. The recipients of questionnaire write-ins are generally a set of personally unknown researchers. Schachter's theory assumes that the communicator expects his message to have an effect upon the recipient and that future communicative behavior will be dependent upon the degree of change in the recipient. Can we make the same assumptions about the questionnaire respondent? Is it realistic to believe that the respondent expects his write-in comments to increase uniformity in a manner analogous to that in the small-group situation? The answers to these questions are dependent upon the circumstances governing the distribution of the questionnaire. If one can establish that subjects perceive that the results of the survey will reach an audience of "significant others" beyond the researchers, one can argue that questionnaire communicative behavior is subject to many of the same principles that are operative in small groups. Certain features of the study reported here support the contention that respondents expected their comments to reach such an audience. The Staff Council Committee of the merged Medical Center publicly announced its endorsement of the study. In addition, the cover letter accompanying the questionnaire stated that the findings of the study would be published in the regional medical journal.

Festinger (1950:190) made a distinction between instrumental communication, where "the force to communicate depends upon the effect of the communication on the recipient," and consummatory communication, "in which the reduction of the force to communicate occurs as a result of the expression and does not depend upon the effect it has on the recipient." The instrumental aspects of write-in behavior would seem to vary from study to study and from respondent to respondent. According to Schachter (1951: 179), "the more irrelevant an issue, the greater the number of communications that have sources other than pressures to uniformity."

Therefore, the results found here may have limited applicability in a broadly based survey. However, the approach may be useful in studies which focus on a particular issue, such as the introduction of innovations, or deal with specific groups, such as extension agents. Thus, this approach could be used in conjunction with other research which has demonstrated that saliency of the issue tends to increase responses (Slocum et al., 1956; Tallent and Reiss, 1959), if questionnaires could be designed so as to maximize the perceived communication potential.

Questionnaire write-ins may also merit more extended analysis. Questionnaire surveys are frequently constrained to proceed without being able to tap the respondent's interest or involvement in the issues being investigated. Degree of involvement may obviously influence the perceptions of situations and the responses which are elicited. For example, in the original study, positive or negative predispositions toward merger were associated with differential perceptions of the impact of the merger. Therefore, some measure of involvement might allow the researcher to weight responses, or to control for the possibly distortive impact of involvement. A quantitative or qualitative analysis of write-ins could be the basis for an index of involvement.

Another potential source of secondary data is the length of the write-ins. Research by Mehrabian (1965) concludes that the underlying state of the subject can be revealed by the number of words written in an experimental task. Subjects asked to write letters about people whom they "liked" and "disliked" wrote more words per letter about persons they disliked. Such findings extrapolated to survey research suggest that the amount of written commentary on a questionnaire could be used to develop an index of the respondent's basic orientation to the subject.

Voluntary write-ins may also provide qualitative data about the respondent's attitudes and sentiments. Systematic analysis of these data could be the source of new hypotheses or new interpretations of the data. At present, analysis of write-ins seems to be limited to the pretest stage of the design.

REFERENCES

Blum, R. H., and Joseph J. Downing. "Staff response to innovation in a mental service." *American Journal of Public Health,* 1964, 54 (August): 1230-40.
Cannon, N. L. "The case for hospital merger." *Delaware Medical Journal,* 1961, 33 (October): 281-290.

Festinger, L. "Informal social communication." Pp. 182-191 in Dorwin Cartwright and Alvin Zander (eds.), *Group Dynamics*. 3rd ed. New York: Harper and Row, 1950.

Goode, William J., and Paul K. Hatt. *Methods in Social Research.* New York: McGraw-Hill, 1952.

Katz, D., and H. Cantril. "Public opinion polls." *Sociometry* 1 (October): 155-179, 1937.

Mehrabian, A. "Communication length as an index of communication attitude." *Psychological Reports,* 1965, 17 (April): 519-522.

Pace, R. C. "Factors influencing questionnaire returns from former university students." *Journal of Applied Psychology,* 1939, 23 (June): 388-397.

Parten, Mildred. *Surveys, Polls, and Samples.* New York: Harper and Row, 1950.

Pearlin, Leonard I. "The appeals of anonymity in questionnaire response." *Public Opinion Quarterly,* 1961, 25 (Winter): 640-647.

Reid, S. "Respondents and non-respondents to mail questionnaires." *Education Research Bulletin,* 1942, 21 (April): 87-96.

Rothman, R. A., A. Schwartzbaum, and J. McGrath, III. "Physicians and a hospital merger: Patterns of resistance to change." *Journal of Health and Social Behavior,* 1971, 12 (March): 46-55.

Schachter, S. "Deviation, rejection, and communication." Pp. 165-181 in Dorwin Cartwright and Alvin Zander (eds.), *Group Dynamics*. 3rd ed. New York: Harper and Row, 1951.

Schwartzbaum, A., R. Rothman, and J. McGrath, III. "The reactions of physicians to merging of Wilmington hospitals: An initial report." *Delaware Medical Journal,* 1969, 41 (April): 113-117.

Slocum, W. L., L. Empey, and H. Swanson. "Increasing response to questionnaires and structured interviews." *American Sociological Review,* 1956, 21 (April): 221-225.

Stanton, F. "Notes on the validity of mail questionnaire returns." *Journal of Applied Psychology,* 1939, 23 (February): 95-104.

Suchman, E. A., and B. McCandless. "Who answers questionnaires?" *Journal of Applied Psychology,* 1940, 24 (December): 758-769.

Tallent, M. and W. Reiss. "A note on an unusually high rate of return for a mail questionnaire." *Public Opinion Quarterly,* 1959, 23 (Winter): 579-581.

Wallace, D. "A case for and against mail questionnaires." *Public Opinion Quarterly,* 1954, 18 (Spring): 40-52.

B. PERSONAL JOURNAL: THE CONTEXT OF DISCOVERY

The research report preceding this journal is unusual in that it represents more than simply a case of unexpected findings or unexpected difficulties encountered in the research process. Rather, it is a case of the discovery and development of an unexplored and previously unused research tool. The original study was undertaken to examine responses to organizational change (Rothman, Schwartzbaum & McGrath, 1971). Once the data collection was underway, however, our work took an unanticipated turn as we examined the data. This personal journal traces the evolution of this research technique.

One research problem every sociologist experiences concerns soliciting real or sincere cooperation from the subjects in the study. When questionnaires are administered, the subject is asked to commit a portion of his time to an activity in which he normally would not engage and which he may perceive as having little direct payoff for him. The problem of cooperation is especially critical when one is dealing, as we did in our research, with an extremely busy and preoccupied group of subjects. Physicians normally have very heavy schedules and responsibilities, and others must contend with many competing demands for their time. Thus, during the formulative stages of our research project, we were quite concerned with the amount of cooperation and the response rate we would manage to elicit from our subjects.

Our questionnaire was deliberately designed to include only fixed-alternative response possibilities in order to minimize the time required to complete items. Thus, for each question the subject had only to check which one of the four or five alternative answers best represented his position. The only exception to the fixed-alternative items were some questions on age, year of graduation, and medical school attended which required the subject to write out responses.

As we received the completed questionnaires we were surprised that many subjects, in addition to checking a given response alternative, added their own comments and observations to the questionnaire. These comments were termed "voluntary write-ins" in our research report because they were not directly solicited by any of the instructions found on the questionnaire. These voluntary write-ins, which in some cases were quite lengthy, represented an expenditure of time and energy significantly beyond that required to answer the fixed-alternative items.

Source: Prepared especially for this volume.

Most of the volunteered commentary was devoted to the recent administrative merger of three previously independent hospitals. Examples of some of the various shades of opinion represented by the write-ins follow:

The highly negative and disillusioned:

> In the parlance of my children, we were given a snow job, and a first-class one, by the high-priced upper-echelon superplanners.

The optimists and apologists:

> Merger came at the same time as Medicare and the insecurity and fears of the physician were transferred to merger. I think things will change and improve as time goes on.

The fatalists:

> Many M.D.'s were against Merger. Today, I feel most are against it. However, it is here and we must make it a success.

These additional contributions were all the more unexpected because they were volunteered by physicians. As previously stated, we expected that they especially would have difficulty in finding sufficient time to respond to the fixed-alternative items on the questionnaire. These write-ins represented an additional and potentially valuable source of data which could be employed to supplement our primary measures.

Once the decision was made to analyze write-in responses, the next step was to decide on a way of quantifying these data. First, we employed a simple dichotomy, comparing subjects who volunteered comments with those who did not. The difficulty with this approach was that it overlooked differences within the write-in group itself. Some physicians, for example, only volunteered remarks on one question or item, while others commented on as many as nine items. By simply combining subjects into a single write-in group we were ignoring the evidently large differences in extra effort within the write-in group.

We then developed a ratio scale running from no write-ins to one, two, three, and so forth, until the upper limit of nine write-ins. However, there also was a problem with this method. If we merely counted the number of separate write-in entries we would overlook the length of the commentary. Thus some respondents only wrote very brief comments consisting of three or four words, while others wrote lengthy statements containing several paragraphs. Our initial interest in write-ins developed because this behavior seemed to represent an unexpected extra contribution of time and energy from a very busy and time-pressured group. If we were to logically pursue this line of reasoning we would need to develop some gauge or measure of effort or energy expenditure. The mere counting of entries did not take into account the total amount of writing or extra effort contributed by subjects.

Hence a new measure was derived by taking all the written commentary of a subject and counting every letter of this commentary.[1]

In the end, then, we had three related but separate ways of dealing with write-in data:

1. A discrete dichotomy between those who voluntarily wrote in and those who did not.
2. A ratio measure indicating the total number of items or questions commented on.
3. A score for each subject based on total writing output calculated by counting each letter of the subject's total voluntary commentary.

We had hypothesized that examination of write-in behavior might provide researchers with a useful tool for ascertaining differences among subjects. If the procedure for using and quantifying such data proved too cumbersome, tedious, and time-consuming, however, its practical utility for the researcher would be very limited. Would the extra information gained about respondents be worth the effort involved in counting items or every letter of voluntary commentary? If we found that the first and simplest method of handling write-in data yielded the same information and highlighted the same differences about subjects as the other, more burdensome approaches, we probably would be justified in recommending that the most direct and efficient technique (the simple dichotomy) be employed.

Analysis of the data revealed that all the methods provided the same general pattern of results. The differences between subjects who voluntarily commented on only one item and those who commented on several, as well as the differences between subjects who wrote only a small volume of words and those who wrote a great deal, were not beyond what one would expect by chance. Differences between subjects who volunteered no remarks and those who volunteered comments, regardless of frequency or amount, were, however, often statistically significant.

To this point in our research, then, all we had achieved was the identification of differences between subjects through examination of their voluntary write-in behavior. What our research still lacked was some theoretical basis for exploring *why* some respondents volunteered comments and others did not. Adequate social science research requires the use of a theoretical framework which helps interpret findings and relates one's own findings to those of other studies. The choice of theoretical framework in our study was not the result of deep reflection or the slow outcome of long hours of literature review and library research. At the same time the senior author was analyzing the write-in data he was also teaching an undergraduate

---

1. It is important that students who will soon embark on their own research careers understand that there may be aspects of the research process that are tedious and dull. The counting of each letter of a subject's total voluntary write-in output was clearly a boring and uninteresting task.

course in small groups. One of the required readings in this course was Schacter's article on pressures to communicate in small groups (Schacter, 1951). The realization that there might be a possible connection between the motives behind voluntary write-ins and small-group communication must be considered the result of an unplanned but fortunate convergence of two un-coordinated activities. This is an example of the role coincidence, accident, or serendipity can play in the research process.

One of the contributions of our research is that it demonstrates the scope and elasticity of social science theory. Small-group theory was success-fully employed in explaining and interpreting behavior (physicians' re-sponses), which at first thought would appear to have no connection with small-group phenomena.

While the use of small-group theory proved very valuable, it also created a special problem. The post hoc nature of our study, along with its different subject matter, made it impossible to operationalize our variables as Schacter did in his original study. Thus we had to develop our own opera-tional definitions for such variables as relevancy and cohesiveness which, in some cases, were only partially related to the original concept. This problem to some extent weakens our study, and thus we have described our work as basically exploratory in nature rather than a time replication of Schacter's work.

It may be useful to return briefly to one of the points raised earlier in this personal journal: The difficulty of obtaining cooperation from subjects. This problem usually limits the number of times researchers can realistically re-administer questionnaires in order to obtain additional information. This fact tempts many social scientists to collect more information than they need to test their main hypotheses or complete the stated objectives of their research. Frequently only a fraction of all the data collected in a study are analyzed and interpreted. This is in large part due to the fact that social scientists must often conduct their research under pressures of time and must contend with various deadlines. The contemporary academic scene creates many incentives to publish quickly. In addition, there may also be con-siderable pressure from subjects or sponsoring groups to get some rapid feed-back concerning the study's findings. Such factors make it quite difficult to fully digest and examine all the data collected by a given survey. With respect to our specific research report, it was only because the two other members of the research team devoted their full energies to the main research topic of organizational change that attention could be devoted to the interesting but less pressing question of voluntary write-in behavior.

Such a situation often results in a wealth of available but unanalyzed data. Students just beginning to launch their careers in social science often believe that in order to conduct research, they must first design their own data collection instruments, choose a sample, and personally administer their own questions. This approach overlooks the possibility of secondary analysis. There is considerable precedent for secondary analysis in sociology, and such studies have yielded many important insights and findings (e.g., Zelditch, 1964). Typically, secondary analysis has referred to the analysis of data collected not by oneself but by other researchers. The term also implies that the secondary or subsequent analysis focuses on problems and questions not envisaged by the individuals responsible for the initial data collection. Use of national census data is a common example of this approach. Our research article corresponds to the second element of the term but is somewhat unique in that the secondary analysis was carried out by the same researchers who designed the original study.

Our research report also suggests the role that documents may play in social science investigation. Essentially there are two categories of documents. The first class comprises personal documents, in which the authors subjectively describe events in which they participated or indicate their personal beliefs and attitudes. The second group includes public or official written accounts of social activity. John Madge (1965) comments that

> in its narrow sense the personal document is a spontaneous first-person description by an individual of his actions, experiences, and beliefs. This definition does not require that the document should be entirely unsolicited, or even the choice of topics should be left entirely to the discretion of the subject (pp. 77-78).

This definition does exclude the interview and questionnaire, and especially the structured interview and the fixed-alternative item whereby subjects' responses are completed, channeled, and blinkered by the researcher's guidance. Voluntary questionnaire commentary clearly fits Madge's definition, but personal documents also include a wide range of material such as autobiographies, diaries, letters and any other documents which offer insight into the subject's attitudes, values, experiences, and beliefs. Thomas and Znaniecki's landmark work *The Polish Peasant in Europe and America* (1927) is perhaps the most famous instance of the use of personal documents in sociological research.

The major defect of personal documents as a source of data is the strong possibility of distortion attributable to the author's desire to justify, promote, defend, or challenge a particular point of view. Such propagandist elements, even if they are unconscious, undermine the objectivity of the material. Our research minimizes this problem by deliberately omitting the *content* of voluntary comments from consideration. Instead, our analysis simply takes the *act of writing* itself as the significant variable.

Some mention should be made in this personal journal concerning the fact that the research report was a product of three authors. Cooperative projects are a common occurrence in social science. Students should be aware, however, of some of the advantages and disadvantages of collaboration.

We found certain advantages in collaborative research which deserve specific mention. The presence of three researchers with different backgrounds and interests seemed to increase the quality of the study through interaction and mutual cooperation. Our diverse interests in organizational behavior (AMS), medical sociology (JHM), and occupations and organizations (RAR) combined to produce a research design which none of us could have produced individually. There was also a division of labor with respect to the tasks of the research. Different people were able to assume primary responsibility for various tasks (questionnaire construction, administrative details, liaison with medical community, etc.) in which they had special abilities. These advantages are in addition to those previously mentioned in regard to time expenditures.

Many factors influence the effectiveness and quality of collaborative work. Such elements as the compatibility of personalities and the complementarity of skills and experiences play an important role in determining the success of joint projects. Some researchers find that they always prefer to work alone, while others are stimulated and motivated by the assistance of colleagues. Some cultures tend to promote independent work, while others foster team efforts. One approach is not inherently superior to the other. Each researcher must choose the pattern that is personally most comfortable and suitable. Our experience has suggested that under some circumstances three collaborators may be superior to two. In addition to the obvious bonus of an extra "head" or "input," an odd-numbered group has the advantage of more easily forming majorities, and this tends to prevent disagreements from developing into impasses and deadlocks.

It is very difficult to offer an unbiased and objective evaluation of one's own research and work. If pressed, we might, in conclusion, offer our study as an example of a genuine sociological perspective—a perspective which seeks patterns and relationships overlooked by others, which sees in the obvious the not so obvious, and which is limited only by the ingenuity of the investigator.

REFERENCES

Madge, John. *The tools of social science.* New York: Doubleday & Co., 1965. Pp. 77-78.

Rothman, R. A., Schwartzbaum, A., and McGrath, J. III. Physicians and a hospital merger: Patterns of resistance to organizational change. *Journal of Health and Social Behavior,* 1971, *12,* 46-55.

Schacter, Stanley. Deviation, rejection, and communication. *Journal of Abnormal and Social Psychology,* 1951, *46,* 190-207.

Thomas, W. I., & Znaniecki, F. *The Polish Peasant in Europe and America.* New York: Alfred A. Knopf, 1927.

Zelditch, Morris, Jr. Role differentiation in the nuclear family: A comparative study, in T. Parsons and R. F. Bales, *Family socialization and interaction process.* London: Routledge & Kegan Paul, 1964. Pp. 307-352.

Roberta Rovner-Pieczenik

A. LABELING IN AN ORGANIZATIONAL CONTEXT: ADJUDICATING FELONY CASES IN AN URBAN COURT

In the study of criminal deviance the labeling perspective represents a shift in focus from the classification and analysis of deviant forms of behavior to the delineation of the processes by which individuals come to be defined deviant by others (Kitsuse, 1962; Becker, 1963; Schur, 1971). This shift in focus has resulted in theoretical and research emphasis being placed on the criminal justice system and on those individuals who conceptualize, formulate, and apply the deviant label. From the labeling perspective, the burden of explanation for criminal behavior shifts from the accused to the accuser, from the deviator to the reactor, from the labeled to the labeler.

Interest in the following questions has been generated by this perspective:

1. Who applies the deviant label to whom?
2. What consequences does the application of the deviant label have for the person labeled?
3. Under what circumstances is the deviant label applied? In short, the term "criminal" is no longer a quality which resides in a type of behavior or within an individual committing that behavior, "but in the interaction between the person who commits an act and those who respond to it" (Becker, 1963:32).

It is our assumption that an understanding of the application of the criminal label by the court and its authorized officials is facilitated by an understanding of organizational behavior. Schur (1971: Ch. 4) has noted the importance of informal organizational structures in shaping the experience of individuals undergoing formal processing by social control agencies. We would argue that these informal structures also shape the experiences of the individuals and agencies that process the deviant.

The existence of informal organizational agreements in court has been commented upon by Sudnow (1965) in his account of the manner in which

---

Source: Prepared especially for this volume.

the public defender prepares and conducts a defense: ". . . the P.D. (public defender) and the D.A. (district prosecuting attorney) have institutionalized a common orientation to allowable reductions." Blumberg (1967), demythologizing the adversary nature of the court, posits a version of adjudication in which institutionalized evasions of due process under law arise from informal agreements reached between representatives of all concerned parties (i.e., defense, prosecution, bench).[1] According to Blumberg, accused individuals come and go in court, ". . . but the [court] structure and its personnel remain to carry on their respective career, occupational, and organizational enterprises" (Blumberg, 1967:47).

The data presented in this article are relevant to an understanding of the labeling of criminally deviant behavior within the organizational constraints of the criminal court. To answer the question of under what circumstances the deviant label is applied, the statistics of case adjudication (that is, case flow through the criminal courts) are utilized as a base from which to comment upon the informal agreements which result in such screening and dispositional statistics.

RESEARCH PROCEDURES

The statistical information for this article was drawn from closed case files of accused felony offenders in a large northeastern city (Metrocourt). The search of case files was preceded by a period of observation of the daily routine of the court and followed by formal interviews with attorneys and judges.

The researcher spent approximately three months observing the daily operations of Metrocourt and its authorized officials. While observation in the first month was "shotgun" in its attempt to comprehend all, observation in the later period focused on the interaction of judge, prosecution, and defense in decision making.

The file data on which the statistics are based were taken from a randomly selected sample of closed criminal court cases. Two criteria for case inclusion were established: the case must have come to the court's attention charged as a felony, and it must have reached final disposition during 1967. Four samples were drawn, each representing the court stage of final disposition: (1) 100 cases adjudicated in the Lower Court without Grand Jury presentation; (2) 100 cases presented to the Grand Jury after arraignment in the Lower Court and dismissed by the Jury; (3) 100 cases presented to and returned by the Grand Jury for disposition in the Lower Court; and (4) 200 cases presented to and indicted by the Grand Jury and sent for disposition to the Superior Court. Deliberate caution was exercised in choosing

---

1. The defendant is noticeably absent in most of the interchanges among defense attorney, prosecution, and bench.

THE RESEARCH EXPERIENCE

FIGURE 1
Adjudicatory Flowchart for Metrocourt with Dispositional Alternatives

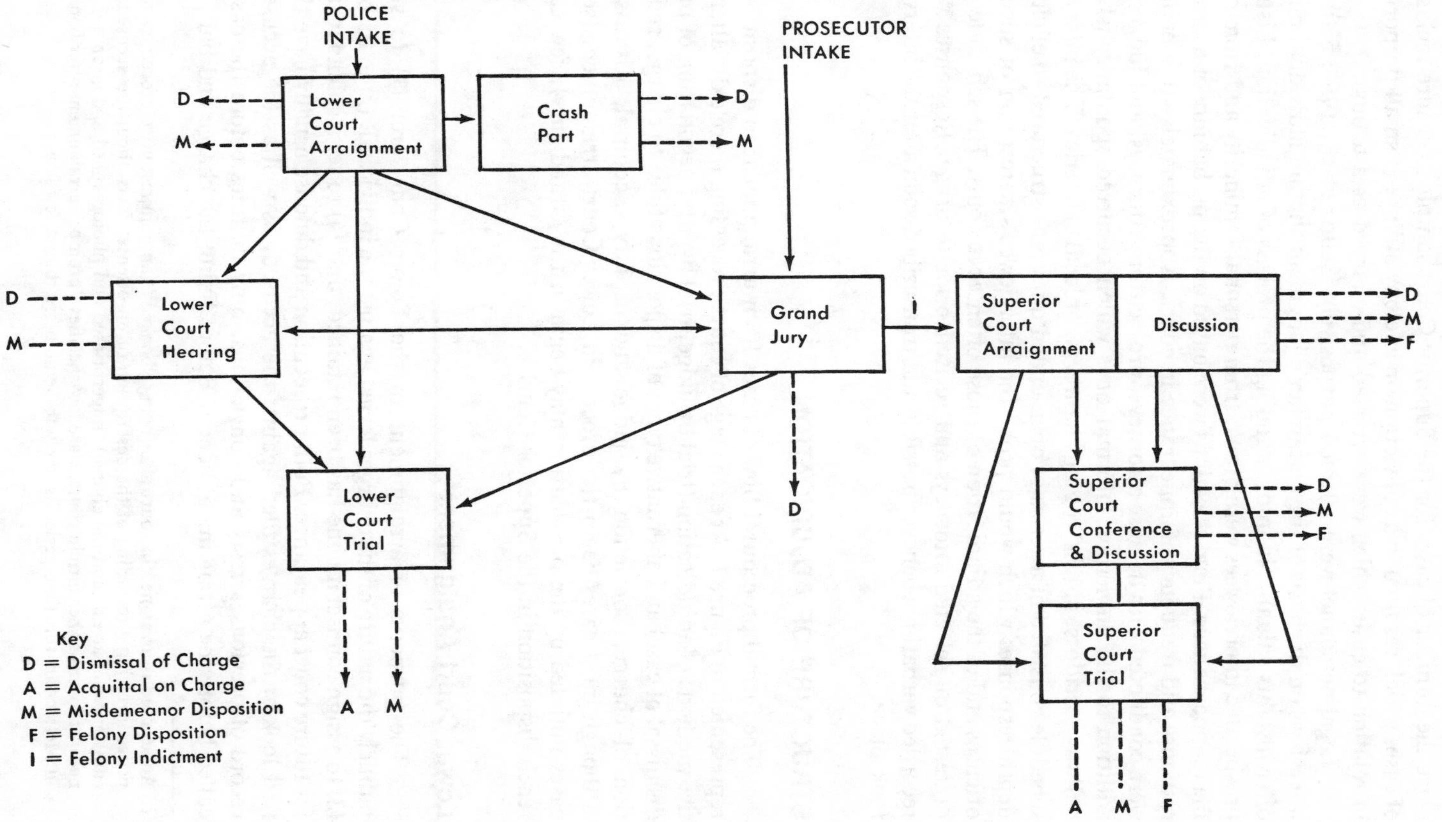

Key
D = Dismissal of Charge
A = Acquittal on Charge
M = Misdemeanor Disposition
F = Felony Disposition
I = Felony Indictment

twice the number of cases for the Superior Court sample to ensure inclusion of cases which resulted in a conviction on a felony offense (a small proportion in relation to cases which were arrested and charged as a felony).

Legal personnel were selected purposively (Selltiz et al., 1959: 520) for interviews on the basis of the researcher's judgment that an individual might offer insights valuable in understanding the process of adjudication. Lists of prospective interviewees were drawn from personal familiarity and from case file reappearances. Final selections were based on the probability of a candid response and frequency of appearance in court. Approximately 40 interviews were conducted with defense attorneys, prosecuting attorneys, and judges, in addition to the numerous informal ones which occurred spontaneously in hallway corridors, judges' robing chambers, or local cafeterias. The interview schedule consisted of a series of open-ended questions structured to elicit in-depth responses which would probe the interviewee's perception of specific offenses and of the adjudication of those offenses in court. The schedule was pretested on selected attorneys and revised prior to usage. Responses were recorded verbatim whenever possible and transcribed soon after the interview took place.

STRUCTURE OF ADJUDICATION

The formal procedural flow of cases from arraignment to disposition is represented in Figure 1. At each stage of court processing there exist alternative methods of adjudication (trial by judge, trial by jury, negotiation of plea, dismissal of case) and alternative types of dispositions (plea to charge, reduction of charge, conviction by judge and/or jury, acquittal, dismissal). Although most cases begin the process in Lower Court arraignment (some cases initiated by the prosecution may begin in the Grand Jury), few cases reach disposition in the Superior Court.

Lower Court Arraignment[2]

The purposes of arraignment in the Lower Court are: (1) to state publicly the nature of the charges levied against the individual, (2) to fix bail, (3) to assign counsel if none has been retained, and (4) to set a calendar date for future court appearance. Both prosecution and defense usually have their first look at the charges filed against the accused, as well as the accused's record of previous arrests and convictions, only minutes before the case is called before the arraignment bench. Before fixing the charge and bail, the

---

2. An accused is arraigned in court after being "booked" (an administrative procedure of the police involving a recording of the description of an offense, facts about the accused, circumstances of arrest, and the charge), fingerprinted and photographed and given a docket number for his or her turn in court. Case law specifies "prompt" arraignment after booking. In Metrocourt this time period is likely to be no more than a few hours.

judge at the bench appraises the complaint affidavit,[3] the facts of the case as recorded by the arresting officer, the prior arrest/conviction record of the defendant and the statement made by the defense counsel on behalf of the defendant.

When a defense attorney makes a special request for bail, the case and the proposed amount of bail are discussed by judge, defense attorney, and prosecutor. While the formal role of the prosecutor is to advise the court on bail this is usually done only when the prosecutor disagrees with the sum fixed by the judge. If the defendant is indigent, court assignment of counsel is made shortly before the defendant is arraigned. The majority of defendants is represented by Legal Aid attorneys—of all those claiming indigency, the Legal Aid Office turns down only 15 percent on the grounds that their income is not below the regulated poverty standard. After the statement of charge and the fixing of bail a calendar date is set for the next court appearance.

Lower Court Hearing

The hearing part (and process) of the Lower Court consists of a pretrial examination by a judge in which the goals are to establish (through *prima facie* evidence)[4] that a crime, in fact, has been committed and that there are "reasonable grounds" to believe the defendant committed the crime. Although the burden of proof remains on the prosecution, both the defense attorney and the defendant are present to question the prosecutor's witnesses.

In essence, the hearing determines not only whether or not further legal proceedings will be undertaken against the accused, but also the nature of those proceedings. A decision may be made to reduce the felony charge to a misdemeanor (which is then sent to trial if a nonguilty plea is maintained or negotiated if a plea of guilty is offered), dismiss it, or send it to the Grand Jury for felony indictment. Bail may be altered at the hearing, following a request by the defense for a reduction of bail or by the prosecutor for its elevation.

In establishing a *prima facie* case, the prosecution is often forced to open some of its evidence to the defense. Thus the hearing is often used by the defense attorney as a "fishing expedition" in attempts to discover the case the prosecutor is building and the kind of evidence the prosecutor has.

---

3. An affidavit is a written statement made on oath, usually before a court officer.
4. *Prima facie* evidence is, in the judgment of the law, sufficient to establish a given fact constituting the party's claim and which if not rebutted or contradicted will remain sufficient. Each stage of adjudication carries with it a different "burden of proof" standard necessary for continued prosecution. In the hearing stage it is "reasonable grounds"; in the Grand Jury there is an indictment when all evidence, taken together, "unexplained and uncontradicted" would be sufficient to warrant conviction by trial; in the trial in the Superior Court it is whether evidence establishes the defendant's guilt "beyond a reasonable doubt."

Grand Jury

The Grand Jury has the power to indict the accused felon,[5] dismiss the case, or advise the prosecutor to return it to the Lower Court as a misdemeanor. The Jury's decision is based upon a review of the legal evidence against the accused, presented in closed sessions by the prosecutor. Both defense counsel and judge are absent from the sessions, although the defendant can ask to appear before the Jury and give evidence in his or her own behalf.

The role of the prosecutor is to present evidence to the Jury, to instruct the Jury as to the law, and to ask the Jury to apply evidence to law and reach a finding. The prosecutor, in assuring that no illegal evidence is presented to the Jury and in respecting the legal rights of the defendant, is called upon to act in the capacity of both judge and defense attorney in addition to filling the prosecutorial role. If the defense attorney believes the clients' rights have been violated, a motion to read the sealed minutes of the Grand Jury is made. If the motion is heard, the minutes of the Jury are read by a judge who then grants or denies the motion for inspection by the defense attorney.

In 1967 about 75 percent of the original felony caseload arraigned in the Lower Court of Metrocourt was screened out before reaching the Grand Jury.

Superior Court Arraignment

A defendant who has been indicted as a felon by the Grand Jury is then arraigned in Superior Court. At this time, the charges or "counts" of the indictment are read aloud, bail is set (or reset), and the case is marked for further court action. If the submission of a guilty plea is being considered, the defense can request an immediate conference (the afternoon of the morning arraignment) and can set a date for the "conference and discussion" part of the court, or reject both options in favor of a jury trial.

Conference and Discussion

The conference and discussion part of the Superior Court serves to legitimize negotiations as a form of discussion. Prosecution, defense, and bench (judge)—again, not the defendant—discuss each case informally (off the record) and explore whether or not a specific plea of guilty is acceptable to all parties. The acceptance or rejection of a plea is often contingent upon the promise of a sentence by the judge. The following description captures the format of this court part:

---

5. The accusation of the Grand Jury is called an "indictment," "bill of indictment," or "true bill." The "information" is another form of accusation, made by the prosecutor to the Lower Court when a Grand Jury indictment is not forthcoming and adjudication as a misdemeanor is advised.

THE RESEARCH EXPERIENCE

Defendant A, female, 36 years old, indicted for Assault I (felony) and Possession of Dangerous Weapon (misdemeanor). During a brawl, the defendant shot and wounded the man with whom she had been living out of wedlock. The prosecutor, upon hearing the facts of the case as presented by the defense attorney, offered to accept a plea of guilty to Assault II (a lesser felony carrying a lesser sentence). The defense counsel rejoined with an offer to plead to Assault III (a misdemeanor), citing the fact that the defendant had no prior record, a child to support and should not be imprisoned for this type of crime. The facts of the case were again discussed. This time the judge asked the defense attorney pointed questions about the defendant. After some three-way discussion, and with the prodding of the judge, the prosecution agreed to accept a plea to Assault III, with a sentence of probation "understood." The defendant was then invited into the room, for the first time, to tell her story. Before the story ended, the judge, apparently feeling his judgment confirmed, stopped the defendant and asked the defense attorney to withdraw the defendant's earlier plea of not guilty and enter a plea of guilty to Assault III to cover all charges. The judge then asked the defendant to repeat her version of the facts of the case, this time "for the record," while the court stenographer took down the information and the plea. Before the defendant left the room the judge informed her that she would be returning for sentencing at a later date and that if the probation report had "good things to say" she would not receive a jail sentence.

Many factors were of concern when the three legal agents considered the above case: the seriousness of the offense, the likely outcome of the case if it went to trial, and the possibility of the complaint being withdrawn. The success of the conference and discussion part depends largely upon the consensus which can be reached by the differing interests.

Trial

Those felonies that are not adjudicated by negotiation in the conference and discussion part go to trial in the Superior Court. In 1967, Metrocourt conducted 245 such trials, representing 10 percent of all cases indicted as felonies. Of these cases, 53 percent were heard before a jury. In 47 percent of the cases the defendant waived his or her right to a jury trial and was tried before the court (one judge finding the facts and deciding upon them).

FINDINGS

Screening Felony Cases

Abraham Blumberg (1967:51) refers to the dropout of felony cases at different stages of prosecution as the "sieve effect":

> . . . initially its [the sieve effect] escape holes are somewhat broad and coarse. They begin to sift in an increasingly finite manner as we move structurally from the initial point of police handling to the court of preliminary hearing, then to the arena of the criminal court where felonies are tried. There the process almost freezes, and only infrequently from then on can the accused free himself from the procedural engine.

Sample statistics reflect the existence of the sieve effect. Having selected our sample by stage of final adjudication we are able to observe that different felony-charged offenses are likely to be adjudicated at different stages of adjudication (Table 1). For example, assaults comprise approximately 45 percent of Lower Court I adjudications (only 25 percent of the arraigned

TABLE 1
Offense Category by Stage of Adjudication, Sample Statistics, 1967, Metrocourt (percentages)

Offense Category	Lower Court I	Lower Court II (returned by Grand Jury)[a]	Grand Jury Dismissal	Superior Court
Assault	45%	38.3%	13.7%	12.4%
Burglary	15	12.2	6.9	8.3
Criminal possession	6	—	3.9	4.2
Drug abuse[b]	3	4.9	5.9	29.1
Fraud	5	1.2	5.9	2.1
Homicide	—	—	12.7	8.3
Larceny	20	7.4	11.8	8.3
Weapons possession	3	7.4	10.8	4.7
Robbery	2	16.0	12.7	19.2
Sexual abuse	1	12.3	15.7	3.1
Total	100	100.0	100.0	100.0
	(N = 100)	(N = 81)	(N = 102)	(N = 193)

[a] Cases sent to the Grand Jury and returned to the Lower Court for disposition.
[b] Drug statistics are inexact because an unknown percentage of these offenses are brought directly to the Grand Jury without Lower Court arraignment.

TABLE 2
Final Disposition of Felony Offenses by Stage of Adjudication and Type of Offense, Sample Statistics, 1967, Metrocourt (percentages)

Disposition by Stage of Adjudication	Total Cases	Assault	Burglary	Criminal Possession	Drug Abuse	Fraud	Homicide	Larceny	Weapons Possession	Robbery	Sexual Abuse
Dismissal†											
Lower Court*	48.1	60.5	37.5	33.3	28.6	—	—	—	22.2	60.0	45.4
Superior Court	6.1	7.7	6.3	—	3.6	—	18.7	—	—	10.5	16.7
Misdemeanor											
Lower Court	51.9	39.5	62.5	66.7	71.4	100.0	—	100.0	77.8	40.0	54.6
Superior Court	37.2	50.0	12.5	62.5	52.7	50.0	—	50.0	100.0	2.6	50.0
Felony											
Lower Court	—	—	—	—	—	—	—	—	—	—	—
Superior Court	56.7	42.3	81.3	37.5	43.7	50.0	81.3	50.0	—	86.9	33.3
Totals N											
Lower Court	N=156	76	24	6	7	6	0	2	9	15	11
Superior Court	N=194	26	16	8	55	4	16	16	9	38	6

* Includes cases adjudicated in the Lower Court as well as those sent to the Grand Jury and returned to the Lower Court for disposition.
† Includes dismissals and acquittals.

felonies are assaults) and 38 percent of Lower Court II adjudications. Homicides, which comprise almost 2 percent of felonies arraigned in the Lower Court, rarely reach final adjudication in this court, but they account for approximately 8 percent of the adjudications in the Superior Court. Robberies also usually find their way to the Superior Court, rather than being returned to the Lower Court as a misdemeanor; 19 percent of the Superior Court adjudications are for the robbery charge. In short, a sorting process takes place which results in some offenses being underrepresented or overrepresented at a specific stage of adjudication.

Dispositions of Felony Cases

The dispositions of cases involving various offenses initially arraigned as felonies in Metrocourt are presented in Table 2. This table indicates that only half the cases adjudicated in the Lower Court are adjudicated guilty of a misdemeanor (51.9 percent); the other half are dismissed or acquitted (48.1 percent).[6] Once a case is indicted by the Grand Jury and arraigned in Superior Court, few dismissals or acquittals occur (6.1 percent). More than half the cases (56.7 percent) adjudicated in the Superior Court are adjudicated guilty of a felony, while the remaining cases (37.2 percent) are adjudicated as misdemeanors (an adjudication which could have been made in the Lower Court as well). In other words, *few cases charged and arraigned as felonies in the Lower Court are adjudicated as felonies.*

Table 2 also documents the percent of each offense category which is adjudicated as dismissed, misdemeanor, or felony in both the Lower and Superior Courts. For example, approximately 60 percent of the assaults adjudicated in the Lower Court are dismissed or acquitted; the respective percentages for the offenses of robbery and sexual abuse are 60 percent and 45 percent. Superior Court statistics reveal that burglaries are likely to be given a felony disposition (81 percent), that assault and drug abuse cases are equally as likely to be disposed of as a misdemeanor or as a felony, and that a relatively high proportion of homicides and sexual abuse cases (18.7 percent and 16.7 percent, respectively) have their charges dismissed. In short, *discrepancies between original offense charge and final offense disposition exist which are offense specific.*

When this information is viewed in conjunction with the information in Table 1, a picture of felony adjudication in Metrocourt emerges which intimates that *different offenses have different probabilities: (1) of reaching a specific stage of adjudication* (i.e., Lower Court, Grand Jury, Superior Court and (2) *of receiving a specific disposition* (i.e., dismissal, misdemeanor conviction, felony conviction). To illustrate: few drug abuse offenses are adjudicated in the Lower Court (3 percent of all felony arraignments, Table

---

6. Acquittals account for 15 percent of this statistic.

1), but those that are adjudicated in this court are likely to be found guilty of (or plead guilty to) a misdemeanor (71 percent of all drug adjudications, Table 2). A relatively large proportion of drug offenses reach the Superior Court for adjudication, and dispositions are split almost equally between misdemeanor (52.7 percent) and felony (43.7 percent) dispositions. A similar analysis could be undertaken for each offense category.

Assessing Case Seriousness

Our observations, interviews and empirical data, supplemented by conclusions reached by other researchers, support the contention that extralegal factors play a major role in determining case outcome and that legal officials share a common orientation to this assessment. For instance, when legal officials were asked about those factors that influence adjudication, a typical first response focused on whether or not there was a potential for violence:

> Robberies are generally not reduced to misdemeanors. House burglaries, where there's a potential victim confrontation, aren't either. But car thefts, where kids are on a lark and there's no violence, are reduced all the time. (Private defense attorney)
>
> If a man has been convicted of a vicious crime [meaning violence was involved], he needs to be put away. (Legal aid, Lower Court)
>
> Reductions depend upon potential for personal injury for a victim—and on planning. (Private defense attorney)
>
> Most judges have antipathy to crimes of violence. (Private defense attorney)
>
> Crimes of violence are treated more severely in law and in plea bargaining. (Legal aid, Superior Court)

Wolfgang and Ferracuti (1967) have pointed out that the use of violence has differing meanings for differing subcultures. In some subcultures violence is expected in certain situations and is part of the shared normative system. The same behavior, transferred to a different subcultural setting, may be socially unacceptable.

In addition to the importance of potential violence, our data underline court officials' references to the meaning an act has for a particular community:

> They [the defendants and victims] live by different values. You have to go by the way they live. We must recognize their standards. (Judge, Superior Court)

The judge then illustrated his point with a case of a homicide resulting from a drinking situation:

> They'll spend money for liquor and then fight over who drank more. Take a homicide resulting from a simple stabbing of a friend—but the wound wasn't taken care of. . . . He's dead, his survivors know it's one of those things. He'll [the defendant] take a manslaughter plea and an assault sentence. (Judge, Superior Court)

The critical words in the above quotation are "they" when used in relation to a "simple stabbing" that is just "one of those things." The following statements made during interviews echo the point more clearly:

> People who get arrested are not up to middle-class standards. They're different. (Private defense attorney)

> A poor ghetto girl is sexually violated and has an illegitimate child. You can't expect her to adhere to our morals. (Judge, Lower Court)

The point being made is that court officials perceive certain criminal behavior (as defined in the criminal code) to be relatively acceptable forms of interacting in "certain" communities. *They share a common orientation to case assessment which focuses on the concept of "seriousness" and not upon the specifications of the criminal code.* The statistics discussed above, then, imply purpose, reason, and careful choice in case adjudication.

It is our conclusion that case assessment hinges, in large part, upon the concept of "seriousness." This concept has two prominent aspects: (1) the potential violence inherent in (or actually present in) an offense; and (2) the perceived threat of the offense to the community of reference. For heuristic purposes, "seriousness" can be visualized as the intersection of two coordinates (Figure 2). The "violence potential" ordinate ranges from minimum to

FIGURE 2
Between-Offense Comparison of Offense Seriousness

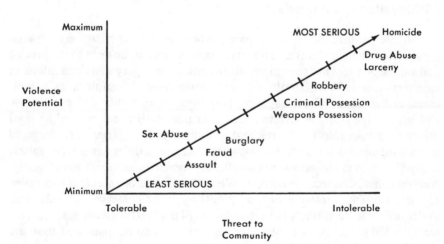

maximum and is defined as actual or potential physical harm to an individual. Under differing conditions in the referent's community, potential or actual violence may range from tolerable to intolerable along the "threat to community" ordinate. To determine case seriousness the court relies upon the perceptions and attitudinal values of legal officials: (1) to decide which community is the referent group, and (2) to assess the degree of behavior tolerance within that community.

Between-Offense Comparisons

The disposition statistics presented in Table 2 can be plotted (ranked) along a "seriousness" continuum, according to likelihood of adjudication in the Superior Court (Figure 2). Interpreted as a reflection of offense seriousness, the offenses of homicide, drug abuse, larceny, and robbery are likely to be perceived and evaluated as serious by legal officials and adjudicated primarily in the Superior Court. Similarly, the offenses of assault and sexual abuse are likely to be perceived and evaluated as less serious and adjudicated primarily in the Lower Court. Although the majority of assault cases involve violence, their form and nature are perceived by legal officials as tolerable to the referent community, and the assault case is adjudicated primarily in the Lower Court. In contrast, homicide is never viewed by legal officials as a tolerable offense, and all cases in the sample are sent directly to the Grand Jury and are typically adjudicated in the Superior Court.

Within-Offense Comparisons

While it is interesting to compare the perceived case seriousness between gross offense categories (i.e., robbery, assault), we can be even more precise and utilize our schema to explore within-offense category discriminations in case seriousness. For example, the large proportion of assault cases adjudicated in the Lower Court suggests that these cases either did not involve violence, or the violence involved (actual or potential) was perceived by legal officials as tolerable to the referent community. The large percentage of assault dismissals (60 percent) suggests that many defendants were falsely charged or that evidence was not available to reach an adjudication of guilty. Neither conclusion may be correct. When the offense of assault is controlled for victim-offender relationship an interesting pattern emerges: assaults on a police officer are less likely to be dismissed (14 percent) than are assaults on a stranger (50 percent), and the latter are less likely to be dismissed than are assaults on a friend or relative (73 percent).

These more detailed statistics suggest that an assault in which the victim and perpetrator are members of the same community is viewed as being less serious than a similar case in which the participants belong to different com-

FIGURE 3
Within-Offense Comparison of Offense Seriousness for Assault and Burglary

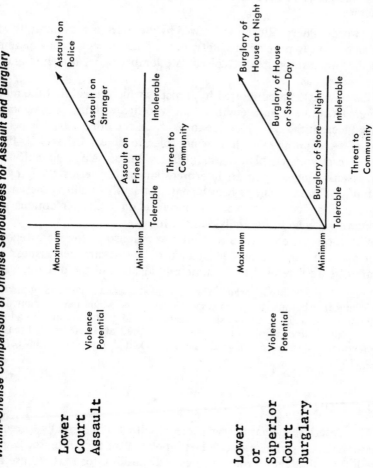

munities. Even this conclusion is inaccurate. The following statements reveal why:

> It's a [ghetto] type of crime. Puerto Ricans at a christening party and a fight over a wife. Someone picks up something and the district attorney prosecutes the winner. You never get the true story. (Judge, Lower Court)
> A stockbroker who shoots his wife for adultery will get a stiff sentence. A black man who shoots his girl friend for adultery may get three years. (Private defense attorney)

In other words, Puerto Ricans are viewed by the court as a community within which an assault is part of the lifestyle. As long as such behavior remains within the community, it is perceived as tolerable by legal agents and considered nonserious.

This conclusion is supported by statistics which reveal that the majority of dismissals result from a complainant who has withdrawn his complaint (Rovner-Pieczenik, 1973). The stockbroker, on the other hand, is perceived as part of a community which does not tolerate violent behavior. Although the legal terminology which distinguishes a misdemeanor assault from a felony assault hinges upon an interpretation of the terms "lengthy" and "substantial" impairment of health, pain, or loss of bodily function, legal officials interviewed place more importance on their perceptions of the meaning of violence to the individuals involved.

Within-offense comparisons of offense seriousness for the categories of assault and burglary are plotted in Figure 3. Assessing seriousness of the burglary offense is related to the time and location of the offense.

> Three kids break into a garage. There's a good chance a plea will be taken to a misdemeanor because the premises were empty and would have remained empty all night. The odds were small that someone would get hurt. But with a burglary in a house where people were asleep I'd set bail at $2,500 each because the defendant is a menace and could have attacked the residents. (Judge, Lower Court).

DISCUSSION

The descriptive characteristics legal officials informally agree upon indicate that case seriousness can be pinpointed for each offense. Once pinpointed, the adjudicatory route and case disposition for that offense can be surmised with relative assurance. Assessing case seriousness through such informal agreements quickens the pace of adjudication and limits case outcome uncertainties by narrowing the range of available dispositional alternatives. Sudnow's (1965) concept of "normal" crimes (cases in which typical features are attributed to offenders and offenses) can be readily extended into a concept of "normal case adjudication" (routine case adjudication based upon informal agreement among legal officials regarding case seriousness).

THE RESEARCH EXPERIENCE

Organizational Realities in Court

According to Selznick (1943), problems of organizational operation which are generated daily become the focus around which daily organizational behavior centers. These problems begin to consume an increasing proportion of time and thought and begin to be substituted for professed (formal) goals. Selznick has hypothesized, and we concur, that procedures of organizational activity tend to be molded by action toward those goals that provide operationally relevant solutions for the daily problems of organization.

In a context of limited resources, given the problem of adjudicating the overwhelming number of cases brought daily before the criminal court, our statistics on case screening and case dispositions reflect the organizational need to seek "operationally relevant solutions." Just as the police are neither equipped to nor desirous of making an arrest in all criminal cases (LaFave, 1965), the court and its legal officials are neither equipped to nor desirous of adjudicating each case as arraigned.

To keep case backlog to a minimum, the goals and objectives of the court become speed and ease, that is, efficiency, in case adjudication. Case screening becomes the rational[7] mode of daily operation which provides one solution to court administrative problems (Allison, 1971). Rationality, in an organizational context, can be equated with making "optimum choices," that is, selecting the most efficient alternative, the one that maximizes output for a given input or minimizes input for a given output. When applied to the court setting, differential case screening can be viewed as one technique for speeding adjudication and minimizing case backlog. Thus, screening is an alternative to full adjudication of all cases, and it is preferred because of the utility of its consequences.

Informal agreements on case seriousness simplify decision making and limit adjudicatory uncertainty. Although each legal subunit works within a varying set of constraints, functional interdependence in adjudication and agreement upon the goal of efficiency in administration promote the emergence of a consensus[8] on case evaluation—that is, shared norms of adjudication (Allison, 1971). In other words, the institutionalized common orientation among prosecutor, defense, and bench has the effect of arranging a negotiated environment which regularizes the reactions of each subunit and defines acceptable performance. Agreements on "case seriousness" are indispensable to routinization and standardization.

---

7. The "rational actor model" of organizational behavior is appropriate here. The model reduces organizational activity to the actions of a single actor, and it considers the goals which account for a choice of action and the alternative consequences of alternative choices.
8. The "organizational model" is a conceptual complement to the "rational actor model." It is concerned with the constraints an organization and its subunits place upon themselves and with the negotiations environment created in order to regularize the reactions of actors with whom they have to deal.

The Court as Labeler

Early in the history of the labeling movement, Erikson (1962) observed that social structure imposes patterns on human actors. Although he was referring to the person labeled, the structural problems and arrangements of the criminal court affect both the manner in which labels are applied in the court (i.e., stage of adjudication) and the labels themselves (i.e., dispositions). Both appear to be shaped more by legal officials responding to administrative pressures and priorities, and the resulting informal working codes, than to legalistic concerns. Thus questions pertaining to who is deviant and what is deviant are resolved by a triad of officials whose formal roles may conflict but whose informal working relationship must be one of consensus in judgment.

If a criminal act is defined as an infringement of a criminal statute, the labeled criminal should be an individual who has committed acts that the statutes have defined as criminal. Our data, however, reveal disparities between those acts for which an individual is charged and those for which an individual is convicted (labeled). Organizational constraints and informal codes impose patterns of behavior and decision making on court officials which result in *court-applied labels which may misrepresent the individual's criminal behavior.*

One defendant in the sample who was arrested, arraigned, and indicted for robbery (a mugging) pleaded guilty to petit larceny, misdemeanor, and was given one-year probation (a youthful age and lack of prior record were mitigating factors for both the disposition and sentence). Another defendant in the sample who was arrested, arraigned, and indicted for the same general robbery charge (wielding a knife at a bus driver) pleaded guilty to attempted robbery III (felony) and was given an indefinite sentence of up to five years (a prior record of three convictions and the appearance of a dangerous weapon were aggravating factors). The differences in case outcome—petit larceny vs. attempted robbery III—resulted less from the legal definitions available in the formal criminal code than from the willingness of legal officials to apply the informal code. The informal working code which was discussed earlier places significance on the potential for violence during the criminal act and the prior conviction record of the defendant. The consequences of its application are readily seen in the above example. In similar fashion, the sexual abuse charge may be adjudicated as assault, the burglary as larceny, the larceny as criminal possession.

Statistical and interview data reflect not only organizational and social concerns of labelers but also the *greater professional tolerance for deviance found among official labelers.* Emerson (1969:84) has encountered this situation in the juvenile courts: "Routinely encountering a wide range of youthful misconduct, the court develops a relatively narrow definition of delinquency. The definition generally requires quite frequent and serious manifestations of disturbing conduct before a youth will be categorized as 'really delin-quent.'" In the adult criminal court we find a similar phenomenon. When complainant and court disagree, the disparity of opinion regarding serious-ness of crime will find the informal working code of the court reflecting a judgment of less seriousness.

One legal aid attorney concretized the difference between the attitude of court and complainant in the following manner: In a fraud case, where an individual goes to a hotel and doesn't pay, or goes on a subway and doesn't pay, or uses a pass at an illegal hour, the complainant will see these acts as if they were the equivalent of a credit card theft, "and would give the guy a record for a 20 cents offense." Most judges, however, who "know it's baloney, give the guy a wink—and he goes away."

Much of the problem can be explained by the volume and the range of offenses to which legal officials must respond daily:

> If there was a special part for narcotics there would be a better perspective on narcotics by the judge. You can just see a husband and wife smacking each other and then see two marijuana cases: the smokers will get it. But in a special court part, when you could see smokers vs. heroin users and sellers, he'll [the judge] have a different perspective. (Prosecuting attorney)

Tolerance for deviance among legal officials is directly related to the context within which deviants are labeled.

SUMMARY AND CONCLUSIONS

This study has investigated the adjudication of felony cases in an urban criminal court, focusing on (1) the dropout of cases between initial arraign-ment and final adjudication, and (2) the discrepancy between initial charge and final disposition. The data clearly supported our conclusion that differ-ential patterns of adjudication exist for differing offense categories. We also found that few cases charged and initially arraigned as felonies were adjudicated as felonies. This finding was offense specific. We suggested that organizational theory and the labeling perspective converge to explain felony adjudications; the acquisition of the criminal label is mediated by an or-ganizational context within which labelers function.

We suggested that case screening is necessary for the continued opera-tional viability of the court. Screening is functional for speed of case adjudi-cation, ease of court operations, and limited case returns (i.e., few appeals). A shared normative consensus on case dispositions overrides the partisan group interests of judge, prosecution, and defense, limiting uncertainty of adjudication outcome and facilitating decision making. We feel that an investigation of decision making among court officials would be an impor-tant follow-up to this study; actual decisions made by authorized officials can be viewed as the result of bargaining among individuals with differing advan-tages (i.e., power differentials).

We suggested that the differential screening of cases results in criminal labels which misrepresent the original criminal act. In addition, we argued that the labelers, in daily contact with a large volume of crime, develop a greater tolerance for deviance than found in the community.

Deviant behavior is evaluated against other deviant behavior, and certain forms of deviance become viewed as acceptable. An extension of the reasoning behind the labeling perspective carries an inherent danger—the shifting of responsibility for behavior from both deviant and labeler. Both become victims of an overbearing and controlling "system," and individual responsibility becomes diffused to structural variables. Thus the philosophical consideration of "responsibility" is suggested as a necessary expansion and exploration of the labeling perspective.

REFERENCES

Allison, Graham T. *Essence of decision: Explaining the Cuban missile crisis.* Boston: Little, Brown & Co., 1971.

Becker, Howard S. *Outsiders.* New York: Free Press, 1963.

Blumberg, Abraham. *Criminal justice.* Chicago: Quadrangle Books, 1967.

Emerson, Robert M. *Judging delinquents.* Chicago: Aldine Press, 1969.

Erikson, Kai. Notes on the sociology of deviance. *Social Problems,* 1962, *9,* 307-314.

Kitsuse, John I. Societal reaction to deviant behavior. *Social Problems,* 1962, *9,* 247-256.

LaFave, Wayne. *Arrest: The decision to take a suspect into custody.* Boston: Little, Brown & Co., 1965.

Rovner-Pieczenik, Roberta. Urban justice: The adjudication of felony cases in an urban court. Unpublished doctoral dissertation, New York University, 1973.

Schur, Edwin M. *Labeling deviant behavior.* New York: Harper & Row, 1971.

Selltiz, Clarie; Jahoda, Marie; Deutsch, Morton; & Cook, Stuart W. *Research methods in social relations.* New York: Holt, Rinehart & Winston, 1959.

Selznick, Philip. An approach to a theory of bureaucracy. *American Sociological Review,* 1943, *8,* 47-54.

Sudnow, David. Normal crimes: Sociological features of the penal code in a public defender office. *Social Problems,* 1965, *12,* 255-276.

Wolfgang, Marvin E., & Ferracuti, Franco. *The subculture of violence: Towards an integrated theory in criminology.* London: Tavistock Publications, 1967.

B. ANOTHER KIND OF EDUCATION: RESEARCHING URBAN JUSTICE

THE BEGINNING

Which traitor to truth is responsible for the prevailing graduate student myth that social science research proceeds as a linear unfolding of information and insight, following a direct course from hypothesis formation through data gathering and analysis? Having spent nearly eight years attempting to complete a doctoral dissertation in sociology, I have staggered through a constant redefinition and clarification of terms, questions, interests, and problems. Although I tell myself that many of the depressing days and agonizing questions will eventually find meaning and resolution in the final product, I must periodically suppress the ever-present question: Is it worth it?

Sociology at the graduate school level had been a relatively diffuse and pallid experience for me until the magic combination of an exciting professor and fascinating material in a course in criminology. From that point on, I read, wrote, footnoted, and spouted crime and corrections. When it came to considering a dissertation topic, my specialization in criminology led me to consider, and disregard, a variety of subjects in which I had some interest. An intermingling of scholarly, practical, and personal reasons eventually resulted in my research on the informal aspects of the criminal court in daily operation.

Initially, I wanted to study some aspect of police operations, but I soon discovered the political realities (that is, difficulties) involved in "clearing" such a study and decided to choose another area. My second choice was to study the defense attorney and the quality of representation afforded the client. A review of the literature, however, revealed that this type of attorney—both public and private—had undergone extensive study by established scholars, with which I was somewhat reluctant to compare my novice efforts. A stray thought focused on the defendant (that is, the accused) as a possible research topic brought with it uncomfortable conjectures about the health and safety of this middle-class female, and such a thought was

Source: Prepared especially for this volume.
This piece was prepared during the period when my dissertation was being written. The dissertation has subsequently been completed, accepted by, and successfully defended before the graduate faculty of New York university.

peremptorily dismissed. Although I found criminology fascinating, at that time, at least, "criminals" scared me. Judges, while considered "safe," were fantasized as unapproachable, having more important things to do than speaking with a graduate student—who was not even studying law! It was thus by default that my path stopped at the door of the prosecuting attorney.

Sociologists had somehow neglected the prosecuting attorney. On first consideration I felt that a focus on either office organization or career patterns would be sociologically respectable and welcome in an area bereft of empirical investigation. Both topics seemed manageable on the operational level; similar studies had been undertaken with other professions and organizations. The decision to base my research on the adjudication of felony cases by the court (of which the prosecuting attorney was only one legal actor) was not made until midway through my observational period.

My knock at the prosecutor's office door was preceded by the appearance of every researcher's dream—a "contact." A cousin of a friend offered the assistance of still another friend who was a criminal court judge. Although I have never to this day met the judge nor understood why he used his influence in my behalf, I eagerly accepted a week of appointments with judges, prosecuting attorneys, and defense attorneys, with the hope that the interviews would lead to a more precise research topic. Four of the interviews were with chief prosecuting attorneys of large offices, and each attorney proved amenable to being "researched."

The interviews were exhilarating. Each increased my awareness of the hiatus between a sterile theoretical understanding of the legal system and its overwhelming affective reality. I saw my theoretical interests and the interviewees' anecdotes begin to mesh. For example, David Sudnow, a researcher whose work had impressed me, had defined "normal crime" as those crimes whose typical features—the ways they usually occurred and the characteristics of the persons who committed them—were known and responded to by the public defender. Although I had found the concept intriguing, it had remained coldly intellectual until interviewees, independently, began to give very similar miniprofiles of "garden variety" cases. The social history of the defendant (and sometimes the victim), the circumstances of the crime, and even the probable case procedure and outcome in court seemed predictable and well known to all.

For the criminal justice system, the "normal" rape case, for example, involved a willing, if underage, victim (female) who was assumed, for one of a few assumed reasons (e.g., pregnancy out of wedlock, an outraged mother), to have cried rape. Further, it was assumed that either the defendant and victim were friends, or the victim was known in her neighborhood as "easy." Both were apt to be poor or working class, either white or black, between 16 and 25 years of age, with a high school education or less. The victim was not likely to have had a prior arrest record, although the defendant might have been previously involved in a relatively minor incident and come to the attention of the court. The case would probably be dismissed in court. Either the victim would withdraw the complaint, with the passage of time and an informal resolution of the problems attendant to rape, or the Grand Jury would dismiss the case for lack of evidence (for conviction, the law prescribes independent corroboration of the act of rape).

I did not emerge from the interviews with a topic. I did find, however, confidence in my ability to do "research"—or at least to acquire information—and an appreciation of the practical necessity for a secure research base. I felt that the backing of an established, hopefully powerful, individual or group would add clout and legitimacy to my investigations. I told myself that a more refined topic would emerge at some time in the future.

My decision to seek an affiliation with the prosecutor attached to Metrocourt was made for reasons which were largely pragmatic. The office I selected was close to my residence. I could be there in ten minutes and travel against rush-hour traffic. Both the head prosecuting attorney and his chief assistant were friendly and encouraging. Perhaps most importantly, I felt comfortable with the office and the men. The majority of prosecutors were of a familiar type; they were of similar social class and religious background and of similar political persuasion. In retrospect, these similarities may also have influenced the prosecuting attorney's decision to allow me to conduct my research. The only constraint placed upon my affiliation with the office and on subsequent publications was the provision that my research remain apolitical.

ESTABLISHING CREDIBILITY

With a research base established, both the prosecutor and I felt that I needed an exploratory period in which to familiarize myself with office operations. During this period, which lasted three months, I shifted back and forth between the prosecutor's office, the court, and police precincts, as responsibility for me rotated from one assistant prosecuting attorney to another. I look back at these months of observation and informal interviews as the happiest of my research experience. Although I was little more than a walking sponge, my educational training had well qualified me for the role. I spent this time listening, questioning, and recording everything that crossed my sight or fell within earshot. In my attempts to include everything—from informal notes found on the outside flaps of case files, to questions I wanted to remind myself to ask attorneys in private, to my own freely associated thoughts—my daily process notes became unmanageable.

The chief assistant prosecuting attorney, who had the major responsibility for my supervision, introduced me to court personnel and to his office staff as a "special assistant" doing independent research in the office and having all the privileges of a regular assistant prosecuting attorney. The privileges gave me access to both public and private records and allowed me to attend confidential meetings between prosecutors and judges pertaining to office, staff, and case matters. All information, with the exception of the sealed Grand Jury minutes (which were unavailable to everyone except the Judge), was available to me. Resisting the daily urge to open the packets of Jury minutes contained in each case file became a minor ethical triumph.

Establishing credibility as a researcher was more difficult than I had anticipated. Initially, the assistant prosecutors (100 on the staff) decided I was a "spy" from "up front." After all, I was being given preferential treatment by "the boss" and I was seen lunching daily with the "big boys." It also unnerved some attorneys that during conversations I filled pages of legal pads with hurried notes. Over time, their discovery that I was naive in the law (and presented no threat to their legal acumen) diminished some of the problems. I helped the situation by lowering the visibility of my yellow pads and developing the ability to retain observations and remember conversations until they could be recorded in private. Lunching at the "assistants' tables" also helped my credibility.

The fact that I was a young female and therefore viewed as nonthreatening probably had as much to do with my eventual acceptance by the staff as any other factor. My presence was particularly noticeable in the male-dominated criminal court. The "me Tarzan, you Jane" approach was tried often. For a while I enjoyed the female status and the special attention and courtesies (like opened doors and clean language) it afforded. But I soon discovered the mutual exclusiveness of the statuses of female and serious researcher in the minds of court personnel. No doubt some of the difficulty lay with my own role confusion. Although the situation was never fully resolved, time taught me to assume the female status and its typical, ascribed sex-related role when it was useful for securing interviews and information. I have no doubt that the ethics of exploiting my sex when profitable in the research sense is one of those topics that should have been given some attention in graduate school, and something with which I might have forced myself to deal at the time.

LEARNING THE COURT

My investigation of the role of the prosecuting attorney took me through every phase of court operations (see Figure 1 in previous article). My initiation came through the Investigation Bureau, taking part in everything from "riding homicide"[1] to being present while potential witnesses were being interviewed. When attached to the Lower Court division, I sat beside the prosecutor at arraignment, hearings, and trials. I observed harried attorneys conduct hallway negotiations and questioned judges in their robing rooms during court recess. While attached to the Grand Jury division, I

---

1. "Riding homicide" is the term used by the prosecuting attorney for visits to the police precinct, the scene of the crime, and the streets to investigate a serious complaint and take statements from witnesses and the defendant.

attended staff case conferences and spoke with Jurors during recess. In the Superior Court, I again witnessed arraignments, conferences, and felony trials. I remained with each division until I felt competent in my understanding of the operation, its goals, and some of its problems. In addition, I interviewed attorneys staffing the complaint department and special assignments, among others.

Some of my most vivid and unforgettable memories are tied to this exploratory-observation phase of my research. The "feel" for case prosecution and the way in which the court adjudicates defendants provided by such research experiences is necessary for insightful interpretation of the empirical data (i.e., the case files). For instance, I remember nervously accompanying detectives from the homicide squad to the psychiatric ward of a large hospital to arrest a man suspected of having murdered his unfaithful girl friend (he attempted suicide thereafter, thus the hospitalization) and being amused when the detectives were asked to "check" their weapons. I recall with pride the day I discovered the wrong man was being arraigned in Superior Court for armed robbery. No one had compared the "mugshot" of the suspect with the man facing the bench; the defendant standing before the judge spoke no English and mistakenly nodded when another man's name was called in the lock-up area. There are other reasons for mistaken identity. The prosecuting attorney keeps card files on aliases. Hundreds of men and women are known to the criminal justice system only as "Cock-eye," "Lucky," "Kootch," "Lefty," "Killer." When these individuals are needed as witnesses, detectives attached to the prosecutor's office may be dispatched into the street to find "Cross-eye" who hangs around with "Spats" on 20th Street.

Uncovering the existence of the "nut file" was both tragic and comical. Individuals with a variety of psychiatric disorders appear routinely at the complaint desk of the prosecutor's office and ask the attorney in charge to investigate their "case" (usually someone is following them). Once the complainant is spotted as "a harmless nut" the complaint is recorded and the case is assigned to "Detective Maxwell," a fictitious detective who is forever out of the office investigating the case.

Although I thoroughly enjoyed this exploratory period, my observations and note taking remained largely unfocused and unstructured. I reached an important conclusion—I no longer wanted to focus my research solely on the work of the prosecuting attorney. As the everyday operation of the criminal court began to fascinate me, the prosecutor became just one of a number of legal actors who influence the flow of felony cases through the court. I discovered that the court had its independent needs (e.g., the need to save manpower and money wherever possible, the need to expedite the flow of cases) which resulted in "bargain justice."[2]

---

2. "Bargain justice" can be defined as a reduction of charge in exchange for a plea of guilty.

The phenomenon of "bargain justice," "trading out," "copping a plea" had already become a familiar topic in law journals, but description and discussion by sociologists had been limited. My interest was stimulated after observing the "conference and discussion" part of the Superior Court, which is devoted to discussion among judge, prosecutor, and defense attorney concerning the possibilities of a plea of guilty being offered and accepted, and the potential sentence involved. The social exchange relationship which existed among these legal actors was curious, for the dispersing of justice seemed to be the outcome of nothing more than bartering, with little relationship to the rule of law.

Although I could observe "bargain justice" on a case-by-case basis, quantitative data concerning the outcome of the bargaining sessions was not available in either the legal or the sociological literature. I concluded that the statistics on dispositions and sentences actually represent the outcome of bargaining, since the majority of cases was resolved by a plea of guilty. It was at this point in my observational experience that I decided to collect statistical information about the processing and outcome of a large number of individual cases. These statistics collectively would represent what was too difficult to observe directly: how, in fact, different case types were adjudicated by the courts.

GATHERING INFORMATION

An information file develops on every defendant arraigned in the criminal court. If the case is adjudicated in the Lower Court, the file is relatively slim; as a case continues to the Superior Court, the file thickens. For example, a short-form complaint is filed with the court clerk by an arresting police officer. This complaint describes the offense for which the defendant is accused and the circumstances of arrest. Bail information is noted on a separate form, containing the charge on arraignment and the terms of bail. A trial sheet contains the history of the defendant's appearances in each court part, including dates, names of legal officials involved, and actions taken in each court part. Grand Jury information, when present, reveals the indictment[3] charges or other decision reached by the Jury. The "yellow sheet," taking its name from the color of the paper it is printed on, lists (often incompletely) the defendant's prior arrest and conviction record. While the files of the court and the prosecution are similar (most of the above information is completed in duplicate), the prosecutor's files contain in addition private intradepartmental memoranda, assorted correspondence, and other notations which offer an interpretive dimension not available from the court records.

---

3. The accusation of the Grand Jury is called an "indictment," "bill of indictment," or "true bill."

I began with the assumption that the "raw scores" of charges and dispositions would reflect some of the reality of the court in operation. I decided that I could understand negotiated justice through the addition and subtraction of charges, indictments, and dispositions. This position was taken for two reasons: (1) to give the appearance of empiricism in research, a methodology expected by my advisors; and, (2) as an easy and quick way to amass a large quantity of data quickly, through what is usually viewed as an organized process.

To focus on court operations, rather than cases, I decided to stratify by critical adjudicatory stages, randomly choosing from among those cases adjudicated at each stage. Thus, I had four universes: (1) cases closed in the Lower Court, (2) cases presented to and dismissed by the Grand Jury, (3) cases presented to the Grand Jury and returned to the lower court for adjudication, and (4) cases closed in the Superior Court after Grand Jury indictment. My method of data collection on a self-crafted data form could euphemistically be termed "inclusive." To avoid omitting any information which might, at a later date, be important for statistical analysis, I collected and coded everything from time intervals between stages of prosecution, to names of legal officials present at each stage of adjudication, to initial charges and final dispositions. Such data-gathering "overkill," a technique which I now realize distinguishes the neophyte from the experienced researcher, was a cover for my still uncertain research focus.

My preparations for and activities in gathering the file information were tedious (as if an exacting process could compensate for a diffuse focus). I recall spending a two-hour train trip with my nose buried in the random number table of a statistics book, furiously scribbling down those 500 numbers which would soon represent "my" cases. After that came the task of sorting all cases closed during my specified information year into piles which would correspond to my four chosen universes. I spent the better part of one summer in a 100-year-old criminal court (without air conditioning!) collecting and recording data.

Following the collection of file information and a preliminary statistical analysis of charges and dispositions, I realized that my observational period and informal interviews were not only important for file date interpretation and speculation but also that they were a source of information significant enough to warrant expansion and formalization. For practical reasons related to travel and schedules, I decided to omit another observation period. Instead I focused on formal interviews with a small, selective sample of authorized court agents.

Choosing and obtaining acceptance of potential interviewees proved an easier task than anticipated. Each was selected on the basis of what insights he or she could offer with regard to the adjudication of "normal crimes." Approximately 40 formal interviews were eventually conducted with judges, defense attorneys, and prosecuting attorneys.

I compiled a list of private defense attorneys on the basis of their frequency of appearance in court, and a list of public defender attorneys in both the Lower and Superior Courts on the basis of varying length of service. Judges were listed on the basis of frequency of involvement (or strict non-involvement) in plea bargaining sessions. My preliminary list of prosecutors spanned the office divisions, reflecting those with whom I believed I had gained rapport over the preceding months. I discussed the issue of frankness of each potential interviewee with the chief assistant prosecuting attorney, and together we compiled a final list. A few well-placed telephone calls made by the chief assistant, with a follow-up letter sent by his office, asked prospective interviewees to extend me the courtesy of an interview and established me as an independent researcher doing vital and important research.

The interview schedule I constructed consisted of a series of open-ended questions intended to elicit extensive responses. Some questions were structured purely to gain the interviewees' opinions on an ongoing process, in a manner which was not apparently evaluative or personally threatening: "What do you think about the frequency with which the court uses plea bargaining to adjudicate cases?" Other questions were more focused on the individual's behavior: "Under what circumstances would you encourage your client to offer (accept) a plea of guilty?" I pretested the schedule and revised it until the questions covered the issues with which I was concerned and flowed in what seemed to me a logical sequence. It was only after conducting a number of formal interviews that I realized that each interview experience would be unique. Some interviewees had to be cajoled into talking; others, despite the questions being asked, insisted on discussing their pet interests; while others became defensive no matter what question was asked or how delicately it was put to them. Each interview had to be tailored to the differing expectations and attitudes of the interviewee. This meant reordering, deleting, and adding questions, in addition to changing my intonation and attitude as interviewer.

A TIME TO END

At what point does research conclude? External controls can help in this decision, such as time allotment and financial considerations. Mechanically-made decisions, such as the decision to limit a review to a stated number of files, which correspond to approved research techniques also help. Yet only a researcher's judgment is truly relevant in determining when formal data gathering should end and formal analysis begin. I had particular difficulties when I felt my research coming to an end because I so thoroughly enjoyed my liaison with the court. I did not relish returning to that innocuous and anonymous status of graduate student. Who knows, perhaps my decision to seek formal interviews had been a clever cover to prolong my time in court.

At some point, sense and sensibilities converged and led me to conclude that "it's time it's over." My court observations had ceased. My statistically reliable selection of case file data had been surveyed. Interview responses had become redundant. I was out of reasons to prolong data gathering.

BUT IT'S NOT OVER YET

Had I known that it would take six more years to complete a dissertation that was acceptable to a new advisory committee, I might have extended the data gathering stage interminably. In fairness to my academic advisors, I had been warned from the first day of entering the doctoral program that I should remain a full-time student at the university until my degree was "in hand." All sorts of horror stories were told, each with the explicit aim of revealing the virtues of singlemindedness of purpose. Had anyone told me that I would soon become a good subject for the next story, I would have laughed.

It would be too painful to reconstruct the six years of what I came to refer to as "my albatross." In outline form, it took the following turns: an attempt to analyze data and write a draft while settling into a new city and working full time; the acceptance of my dissertation by only two of my three advisors, leading to the postponement of my "defense"; the departure of my major advisor to another state; the departure of my second advisor to another country; an attempt to work with my third advisor on problems he found with the dissertation, resulting in an entirely new theoretical approach and the introduction of new substantive materials; the death of my third advisor (the one who objected) before he made any written comments on the dissertation; the return of my second advisor to this country, but to a position at another university; my attempt to recruit two new advisors; a defense taken and passed but with suggestions for revisions which involved the incorporation of materials originally suggested for deletion by the third advisor; receipt of the Ph. D. degree six months (and six years) later than planned because of difficulties with typists and university deadlines.

But there are compensations. My husband is terribly impressed with my perseverance. My parents can now honestly refer to me as "Dr.", a title they have been using jokingly for years. My siblings are now confirmed in their belief that I'm a bit strange. My friends can now enter my home without finding reprints, papers, and computer runs spread all over the dining room table. And my consolation? At this point in time, I am pleased to say that I've outlasted the system.

MEASUREMENT

A. RESEARCH BY
Anthony N. Doob &
Alan E. Gross
Zick Rubin

B. PERSONAL JOURNALS BY
Alan E. Gross &
Anthony N. Doob
Zick Rubin

CHAPTER 6 CHAPTER 6

MEASUREMENT

Problems of measurement have been discussed by a number of contributors in other chapters. The two contributions that constitute this chapter are included because the research was specifically conceived and designed with a measurement goal in mind. In the first case, Anthony Doob and Alan Gross sought to develop a study design which would use an "unobtrusive" measurement procedure. In the second case, Zick Rubin was interested in defining and measuring a particular concept, romantic love. Because of interest in questions of validity, both studies also consist of more than one phase. Doob and Gross compare the results obtained in their field study utilizing unobtrusive observations of subjects' responses (horn-honking behavior) to those obtained in a questionnaire experiment which relied on subjects' self-reports about how they would behave in a situation similar to the one in the field experiment. Rubin used a questionnaire study of dating couples to establish the construct validity of his love scale. To determine whether love-scale scores had predictive validity, he devised an experimental study to compare the behavior ("eye contact") of couples categorized as "strong-love" and "weak-love," based on their love scale scores.

There is much emphasis in the literature on doing studies which use unobtrusive methods, and which are, therefore, nonreactive. One way to be nonreactive is to do field experiments in which the subjects are not aware of their participation—this is suggested in E. J. Webb, D. T. Campbell, R. Schwartz, and L. Sechrest, *Unobtrusive Measures: Nonreactive Research in the Social Sciences* (Chicago: Rand McNally, 1966). In addition to minimizing reactivity, field experiments attempt to achieve naturalness without sacrificing control. As they acknowledge in their personal journal, Gross and Doob designed their study not to answer a particular question but to utilize a specific method. This "explicit, self-conscious attempt" was carried out in fulfillment of the requirements of a particular course. Content was of interest only as a vehicle for method.

To utilize their method of interest, Doob and Gross designed a study to examine the relationship between frustration and aggression in an everyday situation, one car blocking another at a traffic light. In particular, they were interested in the relationship between the status of the frustrator and the type of response elicited. To manipulate the independent variable, status of the car, they employed two automobiles, one a new luxury car, the other an older vehicle. Operationalization of the dependent variable, aggression, was accomplished by using an activity which was part of the ongoing action—horn honking. They recorded the number of times the subject had honked as well as the latency of the first honk. The authors considered the ethics of their experimental manipulation and concluded that, since it was such a common kind of minor frustration, and since it gave "the subject an easy way of 'opting out' of the experiment (by honking the horn)," the experiment was not a serious invasion of the subjects' lives.

When the authors presented their results to the other students in the course, few of their peers seemed interested. In fact, everyone they spoke to advised them that "nobody would be interested in publishing" their study. At that point, Doob and Gross became intrigued with the question of whether or not "psychology students sitting at a desk in a classroom" would produce similar data. Would such subjects think they would react in a way similar to the drivers in the field? The authors then decided to do the questionnaire study, which produced conflicting results: The behavior reported on the questionnaire was different from the behavior observed in the field. Because the two studies differed in *both* sample and method, it cannot be concluded that the different results are due to differences in the method of data collection. As Doob and Gross point out in their study, however, "it is clear that questionnaire data, obtained from this often used population of subjects [psychology majors and college students] do not always correspond to what goes on in the real world."

Probably the most intriguing and amusing aspect of Gross and Doob's personal journal is their report of their experiences in trying to get their research published. Having already received a lukewarm response from advisors and peers, the authors submitted their revised paper to the *Journal of Personality and Social Psychology,* only to be informed by the editor, nine days later, that their paper was unacceptable, a judgment apparently reached "without the customary comments from an independent reviewer." Though Doob and Gross were initially somewhat discouraged by this rapid rejection, they did not despair. Encouraged by the interest and support of people who had read mimeo copies of the paper, the authors submitted it to the *Journal of Social Psychology,* and within a month it had been accepted for publication. The experiences of Doob and Gross provide convincing evidence of the power of professional "gatekeepers." Decisions about what should or should not be published can be determined by a small group of individuals who control the editorial policy of a journal or journals. The shift in orientation which sometimes occurs when a journal changes editors provides further evidence of this.

Since publication, the paper by Doob and Gross has had an interesting history: "It has been reprinted at least eight times in various books of readings, has found its way into textbooks, has been reported in numerous newspapers from Cape Cod to San Francisco, and has been described in a national week-end magazine and in a photo feature in the April 1975 issue of *Playboy.*" The authors have also received innumerable requests for reprints, and their research has spawned a whole series of "horn-honk" studies and a growing literature on naturalistic studies of aggressive behavior. The authors conclude their personal journal with a review of those studies that have built on their "pioneering" effort. Their confidence in their work has been vindicated, and they are "glad we persevered in our attempts to make our technique and findings public."

Rubin chose to do his unconventional study of romantic love for conventional reasons. He needed a topic for his doctoral dissertation and love was *"there,"* a phenomenon important to human experience and yet "almost completely untouched by nonpoetic human hands." He also hoped, from a theoretical point of view, to extend the work of Theodore Newcomb on the bases of interpersonal attraction. That he is "by temperament and avocation" a songwriter may also have had, as he suggests, some effect on his choosing to measure love.

The first phase of Rubin's study, developing a paper-and-pencil love scale, involved several steps: (1) assembling a pool of questionnaire items; (2) initial sorting of the items into categories of "love" and "liking" by two successive panels of judges; (3) administering the revised set of items to a group of student subjects who were asked to complete the items with reference to their girl friend or boy friend (if they had one), and also with reference to a platonic friend of the opposite sex; and (4) performing separate factor analyses on the responses for "lovers" and on those for platonic friends. From this analysis two separate scales were constructed to measure "love" and "liking." These scales were used in the two subsequent phases of Rubin's research.

To establish the construct validity of his scales, Rubin recruited "dating couples" for the second phase of his research. The subjects completed both the love and the liking scales with respect to their dating partner and later with respect to a close, same-sex friend, as well as several personality scales. They also provided background information about the dating relationship. While this questionnaire study provided "evidence for the construct validity of the emerging conception of romantic love," Rubin wanted to test as well the predictive validity of his instrument. Using results from the questionnaire, and based on their scale scores, Rubin grouped his dating couples into "strong-love" and "weak-love" categories and hypothesized that "dating couples who loved each other a great deal would gaze into one another's eyes more than would partners who loved each other to a lesser degree." The main prediction was confirmed.

Rubin has chosen to devote the bulk of the discussion in his personal journal to his relationships with the dating couples he recruited on campus for participation in the later phases of the research. Recruiting the couples was easy, even given the minimal $1 payment Rubin could afford to make. In fact, he had to turn away about 200 couples.

Rubin notes that "People *are* interested in coming to a better understanding of their relationships with others," and their hope for such self-understanding may be responsible for their eagerness to participate in social-psychological experiments such as his. For Rubin, this presents a central question concerning his relations with his subjects: "Did the subjects in fact come away from their participation with increased insight into their relationship?" Rubin sought the subjects' reactions to their participation in a mail follow-up study six months after the initial sessions. In his personal journal, he considers some of the ethical issues raised by his research: the investigator's right to intervene in people's relationships; the subjects' awareness of the potential impact of participation; the asymmetrical nature and the impersonality of the researcher-subject relationship.

Rubin has misgivings about the "impersonal researcher-subject relationship." In his more recent research, he has made efforts to use more personal data gathering techniques (e.g., supplementing questionnaires with intensive interviews) and to explain to subjects the goals and initial results of his research (e.g., in postsession face-to-face interviews and in written research bulletins). These efforts "to personalize the researcher-subject relationship without sacrificing scientific rigor" are desirable and commendable. Rubin is right when he says that establishing mutual trust and respect in the research situation makes for both satisfied subjects and good research.

Anthony N. Doob and Alan E. Gross

A. STATUS OF FRUSTRATOR AS AN INHIBITOR OF HORN-HONKING RESPONSES

INTRODUCTION

Subjects may consciously attempt to present themselves in a favorable manner, they may cooperate with the experimenter or interviewer, and their reactions may be affected by the measurement process itself. In reviewing a number of such problems, Webb *et al.* (6, pp. 13-27) point out that some of these sources of contamination can be avoided when field data are collected from people who are unaware that they are subjects participating in an experiment. Although field procedures can reduce demand and reactivity effects, experimental manipulations outside of the laboratory may gain realism at the expense of control. The study reported here is an attempt to investigate unobtrusively some effects of frustration in a naturalistic setting without sacrificing experimental control.

Modern automobile traffic frequently creates situations which closely resemble classical formulations of how frustration is instigated. One such instance occurs when one car blocks another at a signal-controlled inter-section. Unlike many traffic frustrations, this situation provides a clearly identifiable frustrator and a fairly typical response for the blocked driver: sounding his horn. Horn honking may function instrumentally to remove the offending driver and emotionally to reduce tension. Both kinds of honks may be considered aggressive, especially if they are intended to make the frustrator uncomfortable by bombarding him with unpleasant stimuli.

One factor that is likely to affect aggressive responses is the status of the frustrator (2,3). The higher a person's status, the more likely it is he will have power to exercise sanctions, and although it is improbable that a high status driver would seek vengeance against a honker, fear of retaliation may

Source: Anthony N. Doob and Alan E. Gross, "Status of Frustrator as an Inhibitor of Horn-Honking Responses," *Journal of Social Psychology*, 1968, 76, 213-218.

We wish to thank Tina Fox and Mike Rosenberg, the observers in the field experiment, and Lorraine Soderstrum of Foothill College, Los Altos Hills, California, who made her class available for the questionnaire experiment. The first author was supported by a Public Health Service Predoctoral Fellowship.

generalize from other situations where aggression against superiors has been punished.

Aggression is not the only kind of social response that may be affected by status. High status may inhibit the initiation of any social response, even a simple informational signal. Although it is difficult in the present study to distinguish informational from aggressive motivation, it is hypothesized that a high status frustrator will generally inhibit horn honking.

METHOD

One of two automobiles, a new luxury model or an older car, was driven up to a signal controlled intersection and stopped. The driver was instructed to remain stopped after the signal had changed to green until 15 seconds had elapsed, or until the driver of the car immediately behind honked his horn twice. Subjects were the 82 drivers, 26 women and 56 men, whose progress was blocked by the experimental car. The experiment was run from 10:30 A.M. to 5:30 P.M. on a Sunday, in order to avoid heavy weekday traffic.

STATUS MANIPULATION

A black 1966 Chrysler Crown Imperial hardtop which had been washed and polished was selected as the high status car.[1] Two low status cars were used: a rusty 1954 Ford station wagon and an unobtrusive gray 1961 Rambler sedan. The Rambler was substituted at noon because it was felt that subjects might reasonably attribute the Ford's failure to move to mechanical breakdown. Responses to these two cars did not turn out to be different, and the data for the two low status cars were combined.

LOCATION

Six intersections in Palo Alto and Menlo Park, California, were selected according to these criteria: (a) a red light sufficiently long to insure that a high proportion of potential subjects would come to a complete stop behind the experimental car before the signal changed to green, (b) relatively light traffic so that only one car, the subject's, was likely to pull up behind the experimental car, and (c) a narrow street so that it would be difficult for the subject to drive around the car blocking him. Approximately equal numbers of high and low status trials were run at each intersection.

---

1. We have labeled this operation a "status manipulation" because a large expensive car is frequently associated with wealth, power, and other qualities which are commonly regarded as comprising high status. However, it could be argued that Chrysler is potentially inhibiting not because it is a status symbol, but because of some other less plausible attribute (e.g., physical size).

PROCEDURE

By timing the signal cycle, the driver of the experimental car usually managed to arrive at the intersection just as the light facing him was turning red. If at least one other car had come to a complete stop behind the experimental car before the signal had turned green, a trial was counted, and when the light changed, an observer started two stopwatches and a tape recorder. Observers were usually stationed in a car parked close to the intersection, but when this was not feasible, they were concealed from view in the back seat of the experimental car. High and low status trials were run simultaneously at different intersections, and the two driver-observer teams switched cars periodically during the day. Drivers wore a plaid sport jacket and white shirt while driving the Chrysler, and an old khaki jacket while driving the older car.

Dependent Measures

At the end of each trial, the observer noted whether the subject had honked once, twice, or not at all. Latency of each honk and estimated length of each honk were recorded and later double checked against tape recordings.

Subject Characteristics

Immediately after each trial, the observer took down the year, make, and model of the subject's car. Sex and estimated age of driver, number of passengers, and number of cars behind the experimental car when the signal changed were also recorded.

Results and Discussion

Eight subjects, all men, were eliminated from the analysis for the following reasons: four cars in the low status condition and one in the high status condition went around the experimental car; on one trial the driver of the experimental car left the intersection early; and two cars in the low status condition, instead of honking, hit the back bumper of the experimental car, and the driver did not wish to wait for a honk. This left 38 subjects in the low status condition and 36 in the high status condition.

Although the drivers of the experimental cars usually waited for 15 seconds, two of the lights used in the experiment were green for only 12 seconds; therefore 12 seconds was used as a cutoff for all data. There were no differences attributable to drivers or intersections.

The clearest way of looking at the results is in terms of the percentage in each condition that honked at least once in 12 seconds. In the low status condition 84 per cent of the subjects honked at least once, whereas in the high status condition, only 50 percent of the subjects honked ($\chi^2 = 8.37$, $df = 1$, $p < .01$). Another way of looking at this finding is in terms of the latency of the first honk. When no honks are counted as a latency of 12 seconds, it can be seen in Table 1 that the average latency for the new car was longer for both sexes ($F = 10.71$, $p \leq .01$).

Thus, it is quite clear that status had an inhibitory effect on honking even once. It could be argued that status would have even greater inhibitory effects on more aggressive honking. Although one honk can be considered a polite way of calling attention to the green light, it is possible that subjects felt that a second honk would be interpreted as aggression.[2]

Forty-seven percent of the subjects in the low status condition honked twice at the experimental car, as compared to 19 percent of the subjects in the high status condition ($\chi^2 = 5.26$, $df = 1$, $p < .05$). This difference should be interpreted cautiously because it is confounded with the main result that more people honk generally in the low status condition. Of those who overcame the inhibition to honk at all, 56 percent in the low status condition and 39 percent in the high status condition honked a second time, a difference which was not significant. First-honk latencies for honkers were about equal for the two conditions. The overall findings are presented in Table 2.

TABLE 1
Field Experiment: Mean Latency of First Honk (in seconds)

	Sex of Driver	
Frustrator	Male	Female
Low status	6.8 (23)	7.6 (15)
High status	8.5 (25)	10.9 (11)

Note: Numbers in parentheses indicate the number of subjects.

TABLE 2
Field Experiment: Number of Drivers Honking Zero, One, and Two Times

	Honking in 12 Seconds		
Frustrator	Never	Once	Twice
Low status	6	14	18
High status	18	11	7

Note: Overall $\chi^2 = 11.14$, $p < .01$.

TABLE 3
Questionnaire Experiment: Mean Latency of Honking (in seconds)

	Sex of Subject	
Frustrator	Male	Female
Low status	9.1 (18)	8.2 (10)
High status	5.5 (13)	9.2 (14)

Note: Numbers in parentheses indicate the number of subjects.

---

2. Series of honks separated by intervals of less than one second were counted as a single honk.

Sex of driver was the only other measure that was a good predictor of honking behavior. In both conditions men tended to honk faster than women ($F = 4.49$, $p < .05$). The interaction of status and sex did not approach significance ($F = 1.17$). These data are consistent with laboratory findings (1) that men tend to aggress more than women.

Most experiments designed to study the effects of frustration have been carried out in the laboratory or the classroom, and many of these have employed written materials (2,5).

It is undoubtedly much easier to use questionnaires, and if they produce the same results as field experiments, then in the interest of economy, they would have great advantage over naturalistic experiments. However, over 30 years ago, LaPiere warned that reactions to such instruments "may indicate what the responder would actually do when confronted with the situation symbolized in the question, but there is no assurance that it will" (4, p. 236).

In order to investigate this relationship between actual and predicted behavior, an attempt was made to replicate the present study as a questionnaire experiment. Obviously, the most appropriate sample to use would be one comprised of motorists sampled in the same way that the original drivers were sampled. Because this was not practicable, a questionnaire experiment was administered in a junior college classroom.

Subjects were 57 students in an introductory psychology class. Two forms of the critical item were included as the first of three traffic situations on a one-page questionnaire: "You are stopped at a traffic light behind a black 1966 Chrysler (gray 1961 Rambler). The light turns green and for no apparent reason the driver does not go on. Would you honk at him?" If subjects indicated that they would honk, they were then asked to indicate on a scale from one to 14 seconds how long they would wait before honking. Forms were alternated so that approximately equal numbers of subjects received the Chrysler and Rambler versions. Verbal instructions strongly emphasized that subjects were to answer according to what they actually thought they would do in such a situation. No personal information other than sex, age, and whether or not they were licensed to drive was required.

After the questionnaire had been collected, the class was informed that different kinds of cars had been used for the horn-honking item. The experimenter then asked subjects to raise their hands when they heard the name of the car that appeared in the first item of their questionnaire. All subjects were able to select the correct name from a list of four makes which was read.

One subject (a female in the high status condition) failed to mark the honk latency scale, and another subject in the same condition indicated that she would go around the blocking car. Both of these subjects were eliminated from the analysis, leaving 27 in the high status condition and 28 in the low status condition. The results were analyzed in the same manner as the latency data from the field experiment. Means for each condition broken down by sex are presented in Table 3. Males reported that they thought that they would honk considerably sooner at the Chrysler than at the Rambler, whereas this was slightly reversed for females (interaction of sex and status $F = 4.97$, $p < .05$). Eleven subjects, six males in the low status condition and five females in the high status condition, indicated that they would not honk within 12 seconds.

It is clear that the behavior reported on the questionnaire is different from the behavior actually observed in the field. The age difference in the samples may account for this disparity. Median estimated age of subjects in the field was 38, compared to a median age of 22 in the classroom. In order to check the possibility that younger males would indeed honk faster at the high status car, the field data were reanalyzed by age. The results for younger males, estimated ages 16 to 30, fit the general pattern of the field results and differed from the results of the classroom experiment. In the field, young males honked sooner at the Rambler than at the Chrysler ($t = 2.74$, $df = 11$, $p < .02$).

Unfortunately, because these two studies differed in both sample and method, it is impossible to conclude that the differences are due to differences in the method of collecting data. However, it is clear that questionnaire data obtained from this often used population of subjects do not always correspond to what goes on in the real world.

REFERENCES

1. Buss, A. H. Instrumentality of aggression, feedback, and frustration as determinants of physical aggression. *Journal of Personality and Social Psychology*, 1966, *3*, 153-162.
2. Cohen, A. R. Social norms, arbitrariness of frustration, and status of the agent in the frustration-aggression hypothesis. *Journal of Abnormal and Social Psychology*, 1955, *51*, 222-226.
3. Hokanson, J. E., & Burgess, M. The effects of status, type of frustration and aggression on vascular processes. *Journal of Abnormal and Social Psychology*, 1962, *65*, 232-237.
4. LaPiere, R. T. Attitudes vs. actions. *Social Forces*, 1934, *13*, 230-237.
5. Pastore, N. The role of arbitrariness in the frustration-aggression hypothesis. *Journal of Abnormal and Social Psychology*, 1952, *47*, 728-731.
6. Webb, E. J., Campbell, D. T., Schwartz, R. D., & Sechrest, L. *Unobtrusive measures: Nonreactive research in the social sciences.* Chicago: Rand McNally, 1966.

B. STATUS OF FRUSTRATOR AS AN INHIBITOR OF HORN-HONKING RESPONSES: HOW WE DID IT

Alan E. Gross and Anthony N. Doob

Most social science research looks as if it were planned in a straightforward, logical fashion. Reports are written as if the people involved had just finished reading the relevant literature and saw a need for a particular question to be answered. It generally looks as if these scientists thought a great deal about the best way to answer the question and then designed their research accordingly. The research described in the accompanying article does not conform to this pattern. Instead, it resulted from an explicit, self-conscious attempt to design a study utilizing a specific method which, at the time, was relatively underused in psychology. In fact, in this case, the content that was eventually studied was selected only because it was amenable to the method of interest.

Perhaps this focus on method can be better understood if we begin by describing how this study came into being. In the winter quarter of 1966 we were both graduate students at Stanford and enrolled in a seminar in social psychology taught by J. Merrill Carlsmith and Jonathan Freedman. The focus of this seminar was on methodology, or, more specifically, on using nonlaboratory methods to do social-psychological research. The core reading was a book (at that time still in mimeographed form) by E. J. Webb, D. T. Campbell, R. D. Schwartz, and Lee Sechrest entitled *Unobtrusive Methods: Nonreactive Research in the Social Sciences* (1966). One of its main points was that in most social-psychological investigations, especially door-to-door surveys or those set in laboratories or classrooms, the subjects are aware of the fact that they are being observed and measured. And further, when subjects become aware that they are being studied, they behave differently than they do under more normal circumstances. Webb and his colleagues call this the "guinea pig" effect (p. 13), and they point out that human guinea pigs may react to experimental scrutiny by attempting to present a good impression. In addition they warn that a measuring instrument such as a questionnaire may suggest ideas that the subject did not previously have in mind—that is, the research process itself can distort or create results. After reviewing a number of such "reactive measurement" problems inherent in

Source: Prepared especially for this volume.

traditional paper-and-pencil studies, Webb et al. suggest a wide range of ingenious means for unobtrusively observing behavior in natural settings.

We were lucky enough to have an advance copy of the book, which Merrill Carlsmith and Jon Freedman had managed to secure from Gene Webb, a visitor to Stanford that year. The major assignment in the course was to design and complete a nonlaboratory project modeled after the ideas and methods in the book. Since both of us had desks in research houses on the same block (the Stanford psychology department was at that time spread out across the campus in houses that the university had converted to offices and research rooms), and we met quite frequently, we decided to collaborate on the yet to be designed research project.

Most of the students, including ourselves, had had considerable experience in the laboratory. The research bias at the Stanford psychology department was decidedly experimental in that most studies involved the manipulation and control of one or more independent variables, as contrasted with correlational studies in which relationships between variables, none of which were manipulated by the experimenter, are measured. So even though we knew something about how to create experimental treatments in the lab, we had very little field experience. Furthermore if we were to follow the model of the Webb manuscript, we had to measure the effects of our treatments *unobtrusively*. We could not, as we were accustomed to do, hand questionnaires to our subjects or connect them to physiological measuring devices. We had to create experimental treatments (i.e., manipulate an independent variable) and measure the effects of these treatments, without letting the subjects know that they were being studied.

During the first few weeks of the course, we discussed various plans for the unobtrusive research. We discarded methods that required expensive instrumentation such as "electric eyes" and those that involved ethical problems such as invasion of privacy. One afternoon we were examining possibilities for unobtrusively testing some aspects of the classic frustration-aggression hypothesis. We thought about a number of different ways to frustrate people, eventually thinking about one of the day-to-day frustrations that most urban people experience, that of traffic jams. From there, it did not take long until one of us (each of us attributes this to the other, so it must be collaborative research in its most real sense) realized that it is easy to frustrate someone in traffic simply by not moving when a traffic light turns green. In a few minutes, then, we had developed our ideas for our dependent variable. We would drive up to a traffic light (being sure to be first in line). We would wait for the light to turn green, and then we would simply time how long it would take for the driver behind us in line to honk his or her horn.

We immediately began pretesting. Luckily, Doob had a 1949 Plymouth parked outside the door, so we headed for downtown Palo Alto. That afternoon, and for a few days thereafter, we collected beeps and honks at numerous local intersections. We did various things when the light was green and we weren't moving—we talked to each other, we studied maps, we looked around, but most of all we felt pretty stupid sitting at a green light and not moving. It was, in fact, a rather nerve-wracking experience.

So we had our dependent variable. All we had to do was to figure out a good independent variable and we were on our way to passing the course. We thought of lots of things that would affect how people would react in such a situation. Some of these were the subjects' cars (but since we couldn't bring this under "experimental control" we abandoned it as our major interest); sex and age of the driver (which we couldn't use because we only had two possible drivers—us—and none of our friends were willing to risk participating in our experiment); various bumper stickers; or the number of people in the car. Finally, Gross hit upon the idea of varying the status of the car that did the frustrating. In North America, it is fairly easy to translate operational definitions for high and low status into makes of automobiles. New luxury cars such as Rolls-Royces, Cadillacs, and expensive Chryslers are often sold via advertising in which the manufacturer attempts to associate the product with power, success, and status. Our prediction was that frustrated drivers would be less likely to honk their horns when they were stuck behind such a high-status vehicle than when they were stopped behind a cheap car.

We talked about, among other things, the ethics of such experimentation. Obviously, we were interfering with the subjects to some extent, possibly delaying them as much as 45 seconds or a minute. But we felt that since it was such a common kind of minor frustration, and since our design gave the subject an easy way of "opting out" of the experiment by honking the horn, it was not a serious invasion of the subjects' lives.

Now that we had our experiment designed, all we had to do was to get the equipment together to run it. We found it fairly easy to find clipboards (they are cheap), stopwatches (the department had some that we were able to borrow), and recording forms (as graduate students, we had access to the departmental ditto machine). Access to low-status cars was similarly no problem. Although Doob's old Plymouth could not be used (it had Connecticut license plates and the study was being run in California), Gross owned two low-status cars, registered in California, that were in running condition. However, procurement of a high-status automobile was more difficult. Most of the people we knew either had old cars, or if they had new ones, they were likely to be foreign sedans or sports cars. One of our fellow graduate students, John Masters, now a professor at the University of Minnesota, had a relatively new black Cadillac Fleetwood. It would have been perfect for our study, but he wasn't tempted by the offer of a trade for a day with a 1949 Plymouth, and more to the point, he was going to be out of town that weekend. We finally resorted to commercial car rental firms.

There were other expenses that we anticipated. Neither of us were any good at identifying the years or makes of other cars. Since some of the people we talked to in the course thought that there was a possibility of an inter-action between the status of the frustrating car and the status of the car behind (the subject's car), such that people in old cars would honk faster at new cars and people in new cars would honk faster at old cars, we thought it important to get a relatively good estimate of the types of cars that were behind us. This then meant that we needed to hire two high school students who could identify cars. In addition, we had to rent portable tape recorders to record the honks to check our on-the-spot timing. We estimated that the total cost would come to about $50 for these three items.

Being graduate students, we didn't relish the idea of paying for this our-selves. Luckily Sydney Burkhart, the departmental administrative assistant at Stanford, believed that we were not just planning a Sunday joy ride in a luxury car and assured us that she would arrange to have us reimbursed for our expenses.

On Sunday, February 20, 1966, we were ready to go. Six intersections with relatively light traffic had been preselected such that the red light was long enough so our car and the subject's car could pull up before the signal changed, and the street was narrow so that the subject's car could not easily drive around the frustrating car. Three of the intersections were located near the main shopping district of Palo Alto; the remainder were in residential areas. Gross arranged with Avis to rent a luxury car, and the evening before had gone to the Avis office to pick it up. Unfortunately, it was covered with road dust, the Avis maintenance crew was off for the weekend, the local car wash was closed, and neither of us was really thrilled with the prospect of polishing an Avis rent-a-car. Gross solved the problem: There was no need for the whole car to look great—only the back end. So he spent a few minutes polishing the back end of the car, and then we were, indeed, ready to begin experimenting. On Sunday morning we met with our two observers and proceeded to the first two intersections. The procedure as described in our report went smoothly, with only a few exceptions. Two subjects chose to hit the back of our low-status car rather than honk their horns (if their horns were in working order), and in the afternoon, one of our observers began feeling sick from riding around in the back seat of the cars, lying down so as not to be seen and popping up as soon as we started moving so as to be able to describe the subject and his or her car. As we mentioned in our report, during lunch we thought that it was possible that some people weren't honking at the Ford because they might have thought it was broken down. We then substituted the Rambler, but as it turned out, the data for the two cars were almost identical.

Otherwise, things went quite well. The driver of the car would pull up to an intersection in such a way that he would be the first in line, and generally would manage to have only one car behind him. He would then wait until the light turned green, and when it did, he would say "green" so that the time could be checked on the tape recorder, and then he would wait until the person behind us honked his or her horn. The observer, who often rode in the back seat of the car, lying down so as not to be seen, started two stopwatches when the light turned green and stopped one of them when the driver honked the horn in order to get the latency of the first honk. The second stopwatch was used to time second-honk latency. If the subject honked twice, the experimenter left. Often, by this time, the light had turned red, in which case we would turn right (right turns on red lights are legal in California), go around the block, and wait for another subject. The only real problem came in attempting to arrive back at the red light with a subject behind us. After a while, however, this became fairly easy as we learned the timing of the lights.

The two of us switched back and forth from intersection to intersection and from car to car a number of times during the day, and by six in the evening it seemed that we had enough data. Gross returned the car to Avis and the man there did not seem concerned about the fact that in the whole day we had only gone about 25 miles and had used somewhat over a half a tank of gas.

When we had finished collecting the data, neither of us thought that the experiment had worked out. As far as we were concerned, it seemed as if people sometimes honked at us and sometimes did not. It was not apparent that the data were as clear as they turned out to be. In any case, Gross had to leave soon after we started tabulating the data because he was, at that time, earning extra money by delivering the San Francisco *Chronicle* from 4 A.M. to 6 A.M. Doob then was left to tabulate the data. The first way he tried looking at them is essentially reported as Table 2 in the research report. Obviously, this was a welcome finding after a disturbing day's work. Doob telephoned Gross, who by this time was asleep; though groggy, he seemed pleased that things had worked out.

The next few days were devoted to more thorough analyses of the data. We recalculated all of the analyses and listened to the tape recordings we had made of each trial, with the driver saying "green" each time a trial began, and the sound of horns honking in the background. We looked at the data for both drivers separately and found, to our relief, that there were no differences; we looked for differences across the six intersections, but didn't find them; we looked for effects of different kinds of subjects and found only an effect of the driver's sex (as reported in Table 1 of the research paper). We also spent a good bit of time looking at the type of car driven by our subjects. We tried categorizing these cars by "status" but were not able to find any reliable effects. The major reason for this was that no matter how we divided up our subjects, their cars seemed remarkably alike. There were very few subject cars that even approached our Avis car on a perceived status dimension. Given the lack of range on this variable, then, it is not surprising that there was no effect.

We presented our results to the class, which didn't seem to be as interested in them as we had been. Everyone we spoke to at Stanford advised us that nobody would be interested in publishing the report, let alone reading it, and we ourselves began to question the value of it, other than as an example of how research could be done outside the laboratory. In particular, it had relatively little value if it could be shown that psychology students sitting at a desk in a classroom would produce data exactly like ours. It occurred to us, then, that we should try to find out whether the subjects we generally use think they would react similarly to our drivers in the field. This approach seemed more practical than other related questions such as whether subjects drawn from the same population as our subjects (i.e., drivers on a Sunday in Palo Alto, California) would predict that they would behave the way we had shown they would. We had thought about stopping cars and asking them to fill out a questionnaire, or taking their automobile license numbers and later interviewing them in person or on the telephone, but none of these schemes seemed practical. So we ended up doing the "questionnaire experiment" as described in the research report.

Gross had taught part-time at Foothill College and knew Lorraine Soderstrum, who gave us permission to administer our traffic questionnaire to her introductory psychology course during the summer of 1966. Among other things, being able to test a classroom full of people all at one time was important to us—Gross was in the midst of finishing his Ph.D. dissertation, and Doob was trying to prepare for a week's worth of doctoral exams which were to be held in September.

After running and analyzing the questionnaire study we felt that we had something worthwhile to report. We wrote up the study and in late August sent it off to the *Journal of Personality and Social Psychology* to be considered for publication. We hadn't shown the paper to anyone at Stanford, because no one there had been encouraging about publishing it in any form. As it was, it looked as if our advisors were correct. Nine days after submitting the paper we received a brief note from then *JPSP* editor, Daniel Katz. Katz not only informed us that he considered our paper unacceptable, but he had reached that judgment without the customary comments from an independent reviewer. The only substantive paragraph in Katz's letter read:

> ... We are under great space pressures and so can do very little with exploratory studies. The problem you are dealing with is not as novel as you imply. There have been studies over the years relating what people do to what they say they do. I don't understand why you have neglected this literature. For example, we have had a study in our Journal by Robbins comparing reports of child-rearing practices with the actual practices. What you have done has been to utilize a field experiment to give a measure of behavior in a natural setting. This should have given added precision but then this precision was lost when you had to use another sample for your questionnaire, and this sample is not really equated with the experimental sample.

This rapid rejection dampened our spirits, to put it mildly. Doob destroyed his copy of the letter, but not before reading the Robbins study cited by Katz. It was hard to see the relevance of Robbins's work, which demonstrates that parents' errors in their recall of child-rearing practices tended to go toward Dr. Spock's recommendations (from what they had earlier reported they did). Doob angrily suggested to Gross that the phrase "dictated but not read" appearing at the end of the *JPSP* letter indicated that the editor had dictated the letter but had not read the manuscript. As he prepared for the September exams, Doob wrote a brief note to Gross, who had taken a job at the University of California, Irvine, noting that "the whole thing makes me a little sick." Eventually, with exams successfully past and the new school year underway, our spirits revived and we decided to submit the paper to the *Journal of Personality,* which rejected it as inappropriate for the journal (which it probably was).

By this time, Doob was busy running subjects for his Ph.D. thesis and Gross was busy with courses at Irvine. As a result, neither of us had time to consider what to do about the paper. However, people who had received mimeo copies seemed interested and supportive, and we began to feel a bit better about the value of our study. Thus, in early July 1967, we submitted the paper to the *Journal of Social Psychology.* Within a month it had been accepted on the recommendation of one of their editors, John E. Horrocks. Horrocks had described the paper as using "an ingenious idea for research," a reaction which differed rather markedly from that we had received from Katz.

Since that time, the paper has had an interesting history. It has been reprinted at least eight times in various books of readings, has found its way into textbooks, has been reported in numerous newspapers from Cape Cod to San Francisco, and has been described in a national weekend feature magazine and in a photo feature in the April 1975 issue of *Playboy.* We have received innumerable requests for reprints.

In the past few years since publication a number of researchers have adopted variations of the horn-honk method. Kay Deaux, a social psychologist at Purdue University, found that both males and females honked more at female drivers in her study (1971). However, Steven Bochner (1971) found the opposite effect in Sydney, Australia; his subjects honked more quickly when a male drove the experimental car. Bochner also failed to find a status effect (in attempting to create a low-status frustrating car, he used a "P" license plate, which indicates an inexperienced driver), suggesting that there may be American-Australian cross-cultural differences, or that an inexperienced driver is not treated the same as a driver of a low-status car.

In the most extensive horn-honk study yet, Unger, Raymond, and Levine (1974) tested 408 subject-drivers and found that low-status individuals, operationally defined as women and hippies (whose cars were "festooned with stickers, peace signs, and pasted on flowers"), were honked at more rapidly. Unger et al. considered their results as an extension of our findings using low-status cars. Jeffrey Jerred, a student at the University of

Wisconsin, attempted to assess status and sex effects separately. His results, reported in an unpublished 1970 paper, indicated that drivers of both sexes waited twice as long before honking at a female when she was driving a brand new car as when she was driving an older model.

Other researchers have used variations of our technique to study the effects of race and modeling. Sally Hebert of Lake Charles, Louisiana, used both black and white drivers, and Mary Harris (1973), at the University of New Mexico, recorded aggressive responses of drivers after they had observed the behavior (horn-honking in one condition) of a model driver toward a bicyclist who was blocking both cars. Very recently a group of researchers at the University of Utah (Turner, Layton, & Simons, 1975) have developed ingenious means of studying the effects of aggressive stimuli and deindividuation on honking aggression. They used a pickup truck which in some conditions carried a rifle in a rear-window gunrack accompanied by aggressive ("Vengeance") or peaceful ("Friend") bumper stickers. In addition, a rear curtain obscured the pickup driver from view in some treatments. And Robert A. Baron (in press) at Purdue University found that drivers were less likely to honk in conditions designed to arouse feelings incompatible with anger. Three conditions were designed to reduce aggressive responses: a female confederate crossed the street, passing directly in front of the subject's car either using crutches (empathy), wearing a clown mask (humor), or wearing a revealing costume (sexual arousal).

Thus in early 1967, after two rejections, we had been seriously tempted to bury our data deep in a file drawer. Now, a few years later, as we exchange reprints and correspondence, we're glad we persevered in our attempts to make our technique and findings public.

REFERENCES

Baron, R. A. The reduction of human aggression: A field study of the influence of incompatible reactions. *Journal of Applied Social Psychology,* 1976 (in press).

Bochner, S. Inhibition of horn-honking as a function of frustrator's status and sex: An Australian replication and extension of Doob and Gross (1968). *Australian Psychologist,* 1971, *6,* 194-199.

Deaux, K. K. Honking at the intersection: A replication and extension. *Journal of Social Psychology,* 1971, *84,* 159-160.

Harris, M. B. Field studies of modeled aggression. *Journal of Social Psychology,* 1973, *89,* 131-139.

Turner, C. W., Layton, J. F. & Simons, L. S. Naturalistic studies of aggressive behavior: Aggressive stimuli, victim visibility, and horn-honking. *Journal of Personality and Social Psychology,* 1975, *31,* 1098-1107.

Unger, R. K., Raymond, B. J., & Levine, S. Are women a minority group sometimes? *International Journal of Group Tensions,* 1974, *4,* 71-81.

Webb, E. J., Campbell, D. T., Schwartz, R. D., & Sechrest, L. *Unobtrusive measures: Non-reactive research in the social sciences.* Chicago: Rand-McNally, 1966.

Zick Rubin ───────────────────────────────

A. MEASUREMENT OF ROMANTIC LOVE

Love is generally regarded to be the deepest and most meaningful of sentiments. It has occupied a preeminent position in the art and literature of every age, and it is presumably experienced, at least occasionally, by the vast majority of people. In Western culture, moreover, the association between love and marriage gives it a unique status as a link between the individual and the structure of society.

In view of these considerations, it is surprising to discover that social psychologists have devoted virtually no attention to love. Although interpersonal attraction has been a major focus of social-psychological theory and research, workers in this area have not attempted to conceptualize love as an independent entity. For Heider (1958), for example, "loving" is merely intense liking—there is no discussion of possible qualitative differences between the two. Newcomb (1960) does not include love on his list of the "varieties of interpersonal attraction." Even in experiments directed specifically at "romantic" attraction (e.g., Walster, 1965), the dependent measure is simply a verbal report of "liking."

The present research was predicated on the assumption that love may be independently conceptualized and measured. In keeping with a strategy of construct validation (cf. Cronbach & Meehl, 1955), the attempts to define love, to measure it, and to assess its relationships to other variables are all seen as parts of a single endeavor. An initial assumption in this enterprise is that love is an *attitude* held by a person toward a particular other person, involving predispositions to think, feel, and behave in certain ways toward that other person. This assumption places love in the mainstream of social-psychological approaches to interpersonal attraction, alongside such other

Source: Zick Rubin, "Measurement of Romantic Love," *Journal of Personality and Social Psychology,* 1970, *16,* 265-273.

This report is based on a doctoral dissertation submitted to the University of Michigan. The research was supported by a predoctoral fellowship from the National Institute of Mental Health and by a grant-in-aid from the Society for the Psychological Study of Social Issues. The author is grateful to Theodore M. Newcomb, chairman of the dissertation committee, for his invaluable guidance and support. Mitchell Baris, Cheryl Eisenman, Linda Muller, Judy Newman, Marlyn Rame, Stuart Katz, Edward Krupat, and Phillip Shaver served as observers in the experiment, and Mr. Shaver also helped design and assemble the equipment.

varieties of attraction as liking, admiration, and respect (cf. Newcomb, 1960).

The view of love as a multifaceted attitude implies a broader perspective than that held by those theorists who view love as an "emotion," a "need," or a set of behaviors. On the other hand, its linkage to a particular target implies a more restricted view than that held by those who regard love as an aspect of the individual's personality or experience which transcends particular persons and situations (e.g., Fromm, 1956). As Orlinsky (1970) has suggested, there may well be important common elements among different varieties of "love" (e.g., filial love, marital love, love of God). The focus of the present research, however, was restricted to *romantic love*, which may be defined simply as love between unmarried opposite-sex peers, of the sort which could possibly lead to marriage.

The research had three major phases. First, a paper-and-pencil love scale was developed. Second, the love scale was employed in a questionnaire study of student dating couples. Third, the predictive validity of the love scale was assessed in a laboratory experiment.

DEVELOPING A LOVE SCALE

The development of a love scale was guided by several considerations:

1. Inasmuch as the content of the scale would constitute the initial conceptual definition of romantic love, its items must be grounded in existing theoretical and popular conceptions of love.

2. Responses to these items, if they are tapping a single underlying attitude, must be highly intercorrelated.

3. In order to establish the discriminant validity (cf. Campbell, 1960) of the love scale, it was constructed in conjunction with a parallel scale of liking. The goal was to develop internally consistent scales of love and of liking which would be conceptually distinct from one another and which would, in practice, be only moderately intercorrelated.

The first step in this procedure was the assembling of a large pool of questionnaire items referring to a respondent's attitude toward a particular other person (the "target person"). Half of these items were suggested by a wide range of speculations about the nature of love (e.g., de Rougemont, 1940; Freud, 1955; Fromm, 1956; Goode, 1959; Slater, 1963). These items referred to physical attraction, idealization, a predisposition to help, the desire to share emotions and experiences, feelings of exclusiveness and absorption, felt affiliative and dependent needs, the holding of ambivalent feelings, and the relative unimportance of universalistic norms in the relationship. The other half of the items were suggested by the existing theoretical and empirical literature on interpersonal attraction (or liking; cf. Lindzey & Byrne, 1968). They included references to the desire to affiliate with the target in various settings, evaluation of the target on several dimensions, the

TABLE 1
Means, Standard Deviations, and Correlations with Total Scale Scores of Love-Scale and Liking-Scale Items

Love-Scale Items	Women				Men			
	$\bar{X}$	SD	r^a Love	r Like	$\bar{X}$	SD	r^a Love	r Like
1. If _____ were feeling badly, my first duty would be to cheer him (her) up.	7.56	1.79	.393	.335	7.28	1.67	.432	.304
2. I feel that I can confide in _____ about virtually everything.	7.77	1.73	.524	.274	7.80	1.65	.425	.408
3. I find it easy to ignore _____'s faults.	5.83	1.90	.184	.436	5.61	2.13	.248	.428
4. I would do almost anything for _____.	7.15	2.03	.630	.341	7.35	1.83	.724	.530
5. I feel very possessive toward _____.	6.26	2.36	.438	−.005	6.24	2.33	.481	.342
6. If I could never be with _____, I would feel miserable.	6.52	2.43	.633	.276	6.58	2.26	.699	.422
7. If I were lonely, my first thought would be to seek _____ out.	7.90	1.72	.555	.204	7.75	1.54	.546	.328
8. One of my primary concerns is _____'s welfare.	7.47	1.62	.606	.218	7.59	1.56	.683	.290
9. I would forgive _____ for practically anything.	6.77	2.03	.551	.185	6.54	2.05	.394	.237
10. I feel responsible for _____'s well-being.	6.35	2.25	.582	.178	6.67	1.88	.548	.307
11. When I am with _____, I spend a good deal of time just looking at him (her).	5.42	2.36	.271	.137	5.94	2.18	.491	.318
12. I would greatly enjoy being confided in by _____.	8.35	1.14	.498	.292	7.88	1.47	.513	.383
13. It would be hard for me to get along without _____.	6.27	2.54	.676	.254	6.19	2.16	.663	.464

Liking-Scale Items	Women				Men			
	$\bar{X}$	SD	r Love	r^b Like	$\bar{X}$	SD	r Love	r^b Like
1. When I am with _____, we are almost always in the same mood.	5.51	1.72	.163	.270	5.30	1.77	.235	.294
2. I think _____ is unusually well-adjusted.	6.36	2.07	.093	.452	6.04	1.98	.339	.610
3. I would highly recommend _____ for a responsible job.	7.87	1.77	.199	.370	7.90	1.55	.281	.422
4. In my opinion, _____ is an exceptionally mature person.	6.72	1.93	.190	.559	6.40	2.00	.372	.609
5. I have great confidence in _____'s good judgment.	7.37	1.59	.310	.538	6.68	1.80	.381	.562
6. Most people would react very favorably to _____ after a brief acquaintance.	7.08	2.00	.167	.366	7.32	1.73	.202	.287
7. I think that _____ and I are quite similar to each other.	6.12	2.24	.292	.410	5.94	2.14	.407	.417
8. I would vote for _____ in a class or group election.	7.29	2.00	.057	.381	6.28	2.36	.299	.297
9. I think that _____ is one of those people who quickly wins respect.	7.11	1.67	.182	.588	6.71	1.69	.370	.669
10. I feel that _____ is an extremely intelligent person.	8.04	1.42	.193	.155	7.48	1.50	.377	.415
11. _____ is one of the most likable people I know.	6.99	1.98	.346	.402	7.33	1.63	.438	.514
12. _____ is the sort of person whom I myself would like to be.	5.50	2.00	.253	.340	4.71	2.26	.417	.552
13. It seems to me that it is very easy for _____ to gain admiration.	6.71	1.87	.176	.528	6.53	1.64	.345	.519

Note: Based on responses of 158 couples. Scores on individual items can range from 1 to 9, with 9 always indicating the positive end of the continuum.
[a] Correlation between item and love scale total *minus that item.*
[b] Correlation between item and liking scale total *minus that item.*

salience of norms of responsibility and equity, feelings of respect and trust, and the perception that the target is similar to oneself.

To provide some degree of consensual validation for this initial categorization of items, two successive panels of student and faculty judges sorted the items into love and liking categories, relying simply on their personal understanding of the connotations of the two labels. Following this screening procedure, a revised set of 70 items was administered to 198 introductory psychology students during their regular class sessions. Each respondent completed the items with reference to his girlfriend or boyfriend (if he had one), and also with reference to a nonromantically viewed "platonic friend" of the opposite sex. The scales of love and of liking which were employed in the subsequent phases of the research were arrived at through factor analyses of these responses. Two separate factor analyses were performed—one for responses with reference to boyfriends and girlfriends (or "lovers") and one for responses with reference to platonic friends. In each case, there was a general factor accounting for a large proportion of the total variance. The items loading highest on this general factor, particularly for lovers, were almost exclusively those which had previously been categorized as love items. These high-loading items defined the more circumscribed conception of love adopted. The items forming the liking scale were based on those which loaded highly on the second factor with respect to platonic friends. Details of the scale development procedure are reported in Rubin (1969, Ch. 2).

The items forming the love and liking scales are listed in Table 1. Although it was constructed in such a way as to be factorially unitary, the content of the love scale points to three major components of romantic love:

1. *Affiliative and dependent need*—for example, "If I could never be with _____, I would feel miserable"; "It would be hard for me to get along without _____."

2. *Predisposition to help*—for example, "If _____ were feeling badly, my first duty would be to cheer him (her) up"; "I would do almost anything for _____."

3. *Exclusiveness and absorption*—for example, "I feel very possessive toward _____"; "I feel that I can confide in _____ about virtually everything."

The emerging conception of romantic love, as defined by the content of the scale, has an eclectic flavor. The affiliative and dependent need component evokes both Freud's (1955) view of love as sublimated sexuality and Harlow's (1958) equation of love with attachment behavior. The predisposition to help is congruent with Fromm's (1956) analysis of the components of love, which he identifies as care, responsibility, respect, and knowledge. Absorption in a single other person is the aspect of love which is pointed to most directly by Slater's (1963) analysis of the social-structural implications of dyadic intimacy. The conception of liking, as defined by the liking-scale items, includes components of favorable evaluation and respect for the target person, as well as the perception that the target is similar to oneself. It is in reasonably close accord with measures of "attraction" employed in previous research (cf. Lindzey & Byrne, 1968).

QUESTIONNAIRE STUDY

The 13-item love and liking scales, with their component items interspersed, were included in a questionnaire administered in October 1968 to 158 dating (but nonengaged) couples at the University of Michigan, recruited by means of posters and newspaper ads. In addition to the love and liking scales, completed first with respect to one's dating partner and later with respect to a close, same-sex friend, the questionnaire contained several personality scales and requests for background information about the dating relationship. Each partner completed the questionnaire individually and was paid $1 for taking part. The modal couple consisted of a junior man and a sophomore or junior woman who had been dating for about 1 year.

Each item on the love and liking scales was responded to on a continuum ranging from "Not at all true; disagree completely" (scored as 1) to "Definitely true; agree completely" (scored as 9), and total scale scores were computed by summing scores on individual items. Table 1 presents the mean scores and standard deviations for the items, together with the correlations between individual items and total scale scores. In several cases an inappropriate pattern of correlations was obtained, such as a love item correlating more highly with the total liking score than with the total love score (minus that item). These inappropriate patterns suggest specific revisions for future versions of the scales. On the whole, however, the pattern of correlations was appropriate. The love scale had high internal consistency (coefficient alpha was .84 for women and .86 for men)[1] and, as desired, was only moderately correlated with the liking scale ($r = .39$ for women and .60 for men). The finding that love and liking were more highly correlated among men than among women ($z = 2.48$, $p < .02$) was unexpected. It provides at least suggestive support for the notion that women discriminate more sharply between the two sentiments than men do (cf. Banta & Hetherington, 1963).

Table 2 reveals that the love scores of men (for their girlfriends) and women (for their boyfriends) were almost identical. Women *liked* their boyfriends somewhat more than they were liked in return, however ($t = 2.95$, $df = 157$, $p < .01$). Inspection of the item means in Table 1 indicates that this sex difference may be attributed to the higher ratings given by women to their boyfriends on such "task-related" dimensions as intelligence, good judgment, and leadership potential. To the extent that these items accurately represent the construct of liking, men may indeed tend to be more "likable"

---

1. Coefficient alpha of the liking scale was .81 for women and .83 for men.

(but not more "lovable") than women. Table 2 also reveals, however, that there was no such sex difference with respect to the respondents' liking for their same-sex friends. The mean liking-for-friend scores for the two sexes were virtually identical. Thus, the data do not support the conclusion that men are generally more likable than women, but only that they are liked more in the context of the dating relationship.

Table 2 also indicates that women tended to *love* their same-sex friends more than men did ($t = 5.33$, $df = 314$, $p < .01$). This result is in accord with cultural stereotypes concerning male and female friendships. It is more socially acceptable for female than for male friends to speak of themselves as "loving" one another, and it has been reported that women tend to confide in same-sex friends more than men do (Jourard & Lasakow, 1958). Finally, the means presented in Table 2 show that whereas both women and men *liked* their dating partners only slightly more than they liked their same-sex friends, they *loved* their dating partners much more than their friends.

TABLE 2
Love and Liking for Dating Partners and Same-Sex Friends

Index	Women		Men	
	$\bar{X}$	SD	$\bar{X}$	SD
Love for partner	89.46	15.54	89.37	15.16
Liking for partner	88.48	13.40	84.65	13.81
Love for friend	65.27	17.84	55.07	16.08
Liking for friend	80.47	16.47	79.10	18.07

Note: Based on responses of 158 couples.

TABLE 3
Intercorrelations among Indexes of Attraction

Index	1	2	3	4
Women				
1. Love for partner				
2. Liking for partner	.39			
3. "In love"[a]	.59	.28		
4. Marriage probability[b]	.59	.32	.65	
5. Dating length[c]	.16	.01	.27	.46
Men				
1. Love for partner				
2. Liking for partner	.60			
3. "In love"[a]	.52	.35		
4. Marriage probability[b]	.59	.35	.62	
5. Dating length[c]	.04	—.03	.22	.38

Note: Based on responses of 158 couples. With an N of 158, a correlation of .16 is significant at the .05 level and a correlation of .21 is significant at the .01 level (two-tailed values).
[a]Responses to question, "Would you say that you and _____ are in love?", scored on a 3-point scale ("No" = 0, "Uncertain" = 1, "Yes" = 2).
[b]Reponses to question, "What is your best estimate of the likelihood that you and _____ will marry one another?" Scale ranges from 0 (0%-10% probability) to 9 (91%-100% probability).
[c]The correlation across couples between the two partners' reports of the length of time they had been dating (in months) was .967. In this table, "dating length" was arbitrarily equated with the woman's estimates.

THE RESEARCH EXPERIENCE

Further insight into the conceptual distinction between love and liking may be derived from the correlational results presented in Table 3. As expected, love scores were highly correlated both with respondents' reports of whether or not they were "in love" and with their estimates of the likelihood that they would marry their current dating partners. Liking scores were only moderately correlated with these indexes.

Although love scores were highly related to perceived marriage probability, these variables may be distinguished from one another on empirical as well as conceptual grounds. As Table 3 indicates, the length of time that the couple had been dating was unrelated to love scores among men, and only slightly related among women. In contrast, the respondents' perceptions of their closeness to marriage were significantly correlated with length of dating among both men and women. These results are in keeping with the common observations that although love may develop rather quickly, progress toward marriage typically occurs only over a longer period of time.

The construct validity of the love scale was further attested to by the findings that love for one's dating partner was only slightly correlated with love for one's same-sex friend ($r = .18$ for women, and $r = .15$ for men) and was uncorrelated with scores on the Marlowe-Crowne Social Desirability Scale ($r = .01$ for both women and men). These findings are consistent with the assumption that the love scale was tapping an attitude toward a specific other person, rather than more general interpersonal orientations or response tendencies. Finally, the love scores of the two partners tended to be moderately symmetrical. The correlation across couples between the woman's and the man's love was .42. The corresponding intracouple correlation with respect to liking was somewhat lower ($r = .28$). With respect to the partners' estimates of the probability of marriage, on the other hand, the intracouple correlation was considerably higher ($r = .68$).

LABORATORY EXPERIMENT: LOVE AND GAZING

Although the questionnaire results provided evidence for the construct validity of the emerging conception of romantic love, it remained to be determined whether love-scale scores could be used to predict behavior outside the realm of questionnaire responses. The notion that romantic love includes a component of exclusiveness and absorption led to the prediction that in an unstructured laboratory situation, dating partners who loved each other a great deal would gaze into one another's eyes more than would partners who loved each other to a lesser degree.

The test of the prediction involved a comparison between "strong-love" and "weak-love" couples, as categorized by their scores on the love scale. To control for the possibility that "strong" and "weak" lovers differ from one another in their more general interpersonal orientations, additional groups were included in which subjects were paired with opposite-sex strangers. The love scores of subjects in these "apart" groups were equated with those of the subjects who were paired with their own dating partners (the "together" groups). In contrast to the prediction for the together groups, no difference in the amount of eye contact engaged in by the strong-apart and weak-apart groups was expected.

METHOD

Subjects

Two pools of subjects were established from among the couples who completed the questionnaire. Those couples in which both partners scored above the median on the love scale (92 or higher) were designated strong-love couples, and those in which both partners scored below the median were designated weak-love couples. Couples in which one partner scored above and the other below the median were not included in the experiment. Within each of the two pools, the couples were divided into two subgroups with approximately equal love scores. One subgroup in each pool was randomly designated as a together group, the other as an apart group. Subjects in the together group were invited to take part in the experiment together with their boyfriends or girlfriends. Subjects in the apart groups were requested to appear at the experimental session individually, where they would be paired with other people's boyfriends or girlfriends. Pairings in the apart conditions were made on the basis of scheduling convenience, with the additional guideline that women should not be paired with men who were younger than themselves. In this way, four experimental groups were created: strong together (19 pairs), weak together (19 pairs), strong apart (21 pairs), and weak apart (20 pairs). Only 5 of the couples contacted (not included in the above cell sizes) refused to participate—2 who had been preassigned to the strong together group, 2 to the weak together group, and 1 to the strong apart group. No changes in the preassignment of subjects to groups were requested or permitted. As desired, none of the pairs of subjects created in the apart groups were previously acquainted. Each subject was paid $1.25 for his participation.

Sessions

When both members of a scheduled pair had arrived at the laboratory, they were seated across a 52-inch table from one another in an observation room. The experimenter, a male graduate student, explained that the experiment was part of a study of communication among dating and unacquainted couples. The subjects were then asked to read a paragraph about "a couple contemplating marriage" (one of the "choice situations" developed by Wallach & Kogan, 1959). They were told that they would subsequently discuss the case, and that their discussion would be tape recorded. The experimenter told the pair that it would take a few minutes for him to set up the tape recorder, and that meanwhile they could talk about anything except the case to be discussed. He then left the room. After 1 minute had elapsed (to allow the subjects to adapt themselves to the situation), their visual behavior was observed for a 3-minute period.[2]

Measurement

The subjects' visual behavior was recorded by two observers stationed behind a one-way mirror, one facing each subject. Each observer pressed a button, which was connected to a cumulative clock, whenever the subject he was watching was looking across the table at his partner's face. The readings on these clocks provided measures of *individual gazing*. In addition, a third clock was activated whenever the two observers were pressing their buttons simultaneously. The reading on this clock provided a measure of *mutual gazing*. The mean percentage of agreement between pairs of observers in 12 reliability trials, interspersed among the experimental sessions, was 92.8. The observers never knew whether a pair of subjects was in a strong-love or weak-love group. They were sometimes able to infer whether the pair was in the together or the apart condition, however. Each observer's assignment alternated between watching the woman and watching the man in successive sessions.

TABLE 4
Mutual Gazing (in seconds)

Group	n	$\bar{X}$	SD
Strong together	19	56.2	17.1
Weak together	18[a]	44.7	25.0
Strong apart	21	46.7	29.6
Weak apart	20	40.0	17.5

[a]Because of an equipment failure, the mutual-gazing measure was not obtained for one couple in the weak-together group.

RESULTS

Table 4 reveals that, as predicted, there was a tendency for strong-together couples to engage in more mutual gazing (or "eye contact") than weak-together couples ($t = 1.52$, $p < .07$, one-tailed). Although there was also a tendency for strong-apart couples to make more eye contact than weak-apart couples, it was not a reliable one ($t = .92$).

---

2. Visual behavior was also observed during a subsequent 3-minute discussion period. The results for this period, which differed from those for the prediscussion waiting period, are reported in Rubin (1969, Ch. 5).

Another approach toward assessing the couples' visual behavior is to consider the percentage of "total gazing" time (i.e., the amount of time during which at least one of the partners was looking at the other) which was occupied by mutual gazing. This measure, to be referred to as *mutual focus,* differs from mutual gazing in that it specifically takes into account the individual gazing tendencies of the two partners. It is possible, for example, that neither member of a particular pair gazed very much at his partner, but that when they did gaze, they did so simultaneously. Such a pair would have a low mutual gazing score, but a high mutual focus score. Within certain limits, the converse of this situation is also possible. Using this measure (see Table 5), the difference between the strong-together and the weak-together groups was more striking than it was in the case of mutual gazing ($t = 2.31$, $p < .02$, one-tailed). The difference between the strong-apart and weak-apart groups was clearly not significant ($t = .72$).

Finally, the individual gazing scores of subjects in the four experimental groups are presented in Table 6. The only significant finding was that in all groups, the women spent much more time looking at the men than the men spent looking at the women ($F = 15.38$, $df = 1/150$, $p < .01$). Although there was a tendency for strong-together subjects of both sexes to look at their partners more than weak-together subjects, these comparisons did not approach significance.

DISCUSSION

The main prediction of the experiment was confirmed. Couples who were strongly in love, as categorized by their scores on the love scale, spent

TABLE 5
Mutual Focus

Group	n	X̄	SD
Strong together	19	44.0	9.8
Weak together	18	34.7	14.0
Strong apart	21	35.3	14.6
Weak apart	20	32.5	9.4

Note: Mutual focus = $100 \times \dfrac{\text{Mutual gazing}}{\text{woman's nonmutual gazing} + \text{man's nonmutual gazing} + \text{mutual gazing}}$

TABLE 6
Individual Gazing (in seconds)

Group	Women			Men		
	n	X̄	SD	n	X̄	SD
Strong together	19	98.7	23.2	19	83.7	20.2
Weak together	19	87.4	30.4	19	77.7	33.1
Strong apart	21	94.5	39.7	21	75.0	39.3
Weak apart	20	96.8	27.8	20	64.0	25.2

THE RESEARCH EXPERIENCE

more time gazing into one another's eyes than did couples who were only weakly in love. With respect to the measure of individual gazing, however, the tendency for strong-together subjects to devote more time than the weak-together subjects to looking at their partners was not substantial for either women or men. This finding suggests that the obtained difference in mutual gazing between these two groups must be attributed to differences in the *simultaneousness,* rather than in the sheer quantity, of gazing. This conclusion is bolstered by the fact that the clearest difference between the strong-together and weak-together groups emerged on the percentage measure of mutual focus.

This pattern of results is in accord with the assumption that gazing is a manifestation of the exclusive and absorptive component of romantic love. Freud (1955) maintained that "The more [two people] are in love, the more completely they suffice for each other [p. 140]." More recently, Slater (1963) has linked Freud's theory of love to the popular concept of "the oblivious lovers, who are all wrapped up in each other, and somewhat careless of their social obligations [p. 349]." One way in which this oblivious absorption may be manifested is through eye contact. As the popular song has it, "Millions of people go by, but they all disappear from view—'cause I only have eyes for you."

Another possible explanation for the findings is that people who are in love (or who complete attitude scales in such a way as to indicate that they are in love) are also the sort of people who are most predisposed to make eye contact with others, regardless of whether or not those others are the people they are in love with. The inclusion of the apart groups helped to rule out this possibility, however. Although there was a slight tendency for strong-apart couples to engage in more eye contact than weak-apart couples (see Table 5), it fell far short of significance. Moreover, when the percentage measure of mutual focus was employed (see Table 6), this difference virtually disappeared. It should be noted that no predictions were made concerning the comparisons between strong-together and strong-apart couples or between weak-together and weak-apart couples. It seemed plausible that unacquainted couples might make use of a relatively large amount of eye contact as a means of getting acquainted. The results indicate, in fact, that subjects in the apart groups typically engaged in as much eye contact as those in the weak-together group, with the strong-together subjects outgazing the other three groups. Future studies which systematically vary the extent to which partners are acquainted would be useful in specifying the acquaintance-seeking functions of eye contact.

The finding that in all experimental groups, women spent more time looking at men than vice versa may reflect the frequently reported tendency of women to specialize in the "social-emotional" aspects of interaction (e.g., Strodtbeck & Mann, 1956). Gazing may serve as a vehicle of emotional expression for women and, in addition, may allow women to obtain cues from their male partners concerning the appropriateness of their behavior. The present result is in accord with earlier findings that women tend to make more eye contact than men in same-sex groups (Exline, 1963) and in an interview situation, regardless of the sex of the interviewer (Exline, Gray, & Schuette, 1965).

CONCLUSION

"So far as love or affection is concerned," Harlow wrote in 1958, "psychologists have failed in their mission. The little we know about love does not transcend simple observation, and the little we write about it has been written better by poets and novelists [p. 673]." The research reported in this paper represents an attempt to improve this situation by introducing and validating a preliminary social-psychological conception of romantic love. A distinction was drawn between love and liking, and its reasonableness was attested to by the results of the questionnaire study. It was found, for example, that respondents' estimates of the likelihood that they would marry their partners were more highly related to their love than to their liking for their partners. In light of the culturally prescribed association between love and marriage (but not necessarily between liking and marriage), this pattern of correlations seems appropriate. Other findings of the questionnaire study, to be reported elsewhere, point to the value of a measurable construct of romantic love as a link between the individual and social-structural levels of analysis of social behavior.

Although the present investigation was aimed at developing a unitary conception of romantic love, a promising direction for future research is the attempt to distinguish among patterns of romantic love relationships. One theoretical basis for such distinctions is the nature of the interpersonal rewards exchanged between partners (cf. Wright, 1969). The attitudes and behaviors of romantic love may differ, for example, depending on whether the most salient rewards exchanged are those of security or those of stimulation (cf. Maslow's discussion of "Deficiency Love" and "Being Love," 1955). Some of the behavioral variables which might be focused on in the attempt to distinguish among such patterns are in the areas of sexual behavior, helping, and self-disclosure.

REFERENCES

Banta, T. J., & Hetherington, M. Relations between needs of friends and fiancees. *Journal of Abnormal and Social Psychology,* 1963, *66,* 401-404.

Campbell, D. T. Recommendations for APA test standards regarding construct, trait, and discriminant validity. *American Psychologist,* 1960, *15,* 546-553.

Cronbach, L. J., & Meehl, P. E. Construct validity in psychological tests. *Psychological Bulletin,* 1955, *52,* 281-302.

de Rougemont, D. *Love in the western world.* New York: Harcourt, Brace, 1940.

Exline, R. V. Explorations in the process of person perception: Visual interaction in relation to competition, sex, and need for affiliation. *Journal of Personality,* 1963, *31,* 1-20.

Exline, R., Gray, D., & Schuette, D. Visual behavior in a dyad as affected by interview content and sex of respondent. *Journal of Personality and Social Psychology,* 1965, *1,* 201-209.

Freud, S. Group psychology and the analysis of the ego. In *The standard edition of the complete psychological works of Sigmund Freud.* Vol. 18. London: Hogarth, 1955.

Fromm, E. *The art of loving.* New York: Harper, 1956.

Goode, W. J. The theoretical importance of love. *American Sociological Review,* 1959, *24,* 38-47.

Harlow, H. F. The nature of love. *American Psychologist,* 1958, *13,* 673-685.

Heider, F. *The psychology of interpersonal relations.* New York: Wiley, 1958.

Jourard, S. M., & Lasakow, P. Some factors in self-disclosure. *Journal of Abnormal and Social Psychology,* 1958, *56,* 91-98.

Lindzey, G., & Byrne, D. Measurement of social choice and interpersonal attractiveness. In G. Lindzey & E. Aronson (Eds.), *Handbook of social psychology.* Vol. 2. (2nd ed.) Reading, Mass.: Addison-Wesley, 1968.

Maslow, A. H. Deficiency motivation and growth motivation. *Nebraska Symposium on Motivation,* 1955, *2.*

Newcomb, T. M. The varieties of interpersonal attraction. In D. Cartwright & A. Zander (Eds.), *Group dynamics.* (2nd ed.) Evanston: Row, Peterson, 1960.

Orlinsky, D. E. Love relationships in the life cycle: A developmental interpersonal perspective. Unpublished manuscript, University of Chicago, 1970.

Rubin, Z. *The social psychology of romantic love.* Ann Arbor, Mich.: University Microfilms, 1969, No. 70-4179.

Slater, P. E. On social regression. *American Sociological Review,* 1963, *28,* 339-364.

Strodtbeck, F. L., & Mann, R. D. Sex role differentiation in jury deliberations. *Sociometry,* 1956, *19,* 3-11.

Wallach, M. A., & Kogan, N. Sex differences and judgment processes. *Journal of Personality,* 1959, *27,* 555-564.

Walster, E. The effect of self-esteem on romantic liking. *Journal of Experimental Social Psychology,* 1965, *1,* 184-197.

Wright, P. H. A model and a technique for studies of friendship. *Journal of Experimental Social Psychology,* 1969, *5,* 295-309.

B. ON STUDYING LOVE: NOTES ON THE RESEARCHER-SUBJECT RELATIONSHIP

When I first set out to study romantic love, it was still an unconventional object of study. But I chose this topic of investigation for largely conventional reasons. First, it was time for me to do my doctoral dissertation in social psychology, and so I had to find *something* to study. Second, love was *there*, like Mount Everest, shimmering in the distance, of obvious importance to the human experience, and yet almost completely untouched by nonpoetic human hands. Almost everyone embarking upon a doctoral dissertation searches for such an unspoiled, virgin subject. Third, romantic love seemed a particularly appropriate *social-psychological* topic. In my view, social psychology is not a subarea of psychology or of sociology, but rather the interface between the two—it deals with the links between the individual and his social environment. Love seemed to be one such link. It is simultaneously an element of individual experience and an ingredient and reflection of social structure. Especially in the context of the interdisciplinary doctoral program I was in (run jointly by the departments of psychology and sociology at the University of Michigan), I was eager to bridge these two levels of analysis.

Of course, there were some less conventional reasons as well. An important influence on the development of my interests in graduate school was Professor Theodore Newcomb. Newcomb had, some 15 years earlier, conducted an investigation which did much to pave the way for the scientific study of positive sentiments. Gordon Allport had observed, with special reference to the period between 1920 and 1950, that "Psychologists, in their research and in their theory, devote far more attention to aggressive, hostile, prejudiced behavior than to the softer acts of sympathy and love, which are equally important ingredients of social life" (Allport, 1968, p. 2). He suggested that social scientists, in their attempts to deal with pressing social problems, had indulged in a "flight from tenderness." Ted Newcomb helped to bring this flight back to earth. His pioneering study of the process of friendship formation was conducted in the mid-1950s, using a real boarding-house at the University of Michigan as his laboratory (Newcomb, 1961). This study helped to trigger a tremendous flood of research on the bases of interpersonal attraction.[1] Extending such research to romantic love was another

---

Source: Prepared especially for this volume.

1. For recent reviews of research in this area, see Berscheid and Walster (1969), Rubin (1973), and Huston (1974).

step in the direction Newcomb had taken. Throughout my research endeavor, from initial planning to final writeups, Newcomb, as my dissertation committee chairman, was an invaluable source of counsel, encouragement, and criticism.

All of the reasons I have listed so far represent what attribution theorists would call *situational* rather than *dispositional* explanations of my decision to study love. That is, they refer to aspects of the situation in which I found myself, rather than to personal dispositions or intentions residing uniquely in me. Edward Jones and Richard Nisbett (1972) suggest that it is hard for actors to recognize the internal causes of their own behavior, preferring instead to ascribe things to external factors. But if I try hard to take an outside observer's point of view, I can find a dispositional cause as well. I am, by temperament and avocation, a songwriter. Songwriters traditionally put love into measures. I set out to measure love. I think there may be a connection.

In further considering the process of studying love, I would like to focus on a single set of issues that may be of some wider interest both to researchers and to their subjects. The issues concern my relations with the subjects of my research.

ONLY DATING COUPLES CAN DO IT!
—GAIN INSIGHT INTO YOUR RELATIONSHiP
BY PARTICIPATING IN A UNIQUE
SOCIAL-PSYCHOLOGICAL STUDY
. . . AND GET PAID FOR IT TOO!!

- Who can participate? .

All Michigan student couples (heterosexual only) who are dating regularly, going together, or engaged. (Married couples are not eligible.)

- What do you have to do?

Simply show up with your boyfriend or girlfriend at one of the times and places listed. You will be asked to fill out a confidential questionnaire, and each of you will be paid $1 for the one-hour session.

- Then what?

All those who fill out the questionnaire will have a chance to be selected as subjects for a subsequent experiment, which (if you agree to participate) should be both exciting and lucrative.

BOTH MEMBERS OF A COUPLE MUST TAKE PART
TUESDAY, OCTOBER 29, 7:30 PM—AUDITORIUM C
WEDNESDAY, OCTOBER 30, 7:30 PM—AUDITORIUM C

Recruiting dating couples for a study of their relationship proved to be easier than I had anticipated. My limited budget permitted me to pay each participant only $1 for the initial questionnaire session. To induce couples to take part in spite of this low hourly wage, I launched a saturation campaign of posters and campus newspaper advertisements like the one in the accompanying illustration.

My advertising campaign was highly successful. On each of the two evenings, long lines of couples started forming outside Auditorium C by 7:00. By 7:30 they were snaking around the lobby of the auditorium complex, outdoing even the most popular features of the student cinema league. Approximately 400 couples showed up to take part. I had prepared questionnaires for about 180 couples, thinking this would be sufficient for the maximum conceivable turnout. As a result, each evening I had to make profuse apologies and send about 100 couples home. Although I do not have conclusive evidence on this, I do not think it was the $1 inducement that motivated most of the couples to participate. Nor do I think that the key factor was my flamboyant rhetoric, traceable in part to my college summer as a Madison Avenue copywriter. Except perhaps for one line: *Gain insight into your relationship.* People *are* interested in coming to a better understanding of their relationships with others, especially relationships that may still be in their relatively uncertain, formative stages. They may be willing—and, in my experience, often eager—to take part in research as one approach toward such understanding.

This hope for self-understanding leads to a central question concerning my relations with my subjects: Did the study live up to its billing? Did the subjects in fact come away from their participation with increased insight into their relationship? Not all of them did. As part of a mail follow-up study I conducted six months after the initial questionnaire sessions, I solicited the subjects' reactions to their participation. In at least one or two cases, subjects were disappointed that they did not learn more about their relationship as a result of their participation. One woman wrote, for example:

> Our participation had no effects on the relationship. I wanted to talk about it afterward but he refused to tell me anything he'd said or to listen to anything I had thought or felt about it. Not that I really had all that much to say. I was first interested in the questionnaire in the hope that it would give me some greater insight into our relationship, especially where my own, often ambiguous feelings were concerned. This did not occur. The questions seemed very matter of fact, external, etc. The objectives of the author of the test being different from my own as the taker of the test (or questionnaire), this is not too surprising.

I must agree with this subject's perception that my motives as investigator were different from hers, and probably from those of most other subjects as well. My primary motive was to develop a conceptual definition and measure of love, rather than to reveal anything to my subjects about their relationships. I was conducting basic research, whereas at least some of the subjects may have been interested in more immediate applications. Nevertheless, a sizable number of the subjects indicated that they *had* learned something about their relationships by virtue of their participation. For example:

> Mr. Rubin, when we got out of your experiment, we started comparing answers, or those which we could remember. We found out what we felt we knew before, but what you reinforced . . . that we *knew* each other.
>
> The only comment I have is that your study raised a lot of questions which Tim and I then discussed and we probably would not have talked about these otherwise. It also raised the question of whether we would marry and we are now talking about getting married at the end of next summer.
>
> Your questionnaire enabled my boyfriend and I to analyze our feelings about marriage. I have a very negative attitude toward marriage as a suburban, middle-class, split-level, station wagon, 2-3 kid institution and cannot envision myself in such a set-up. So I do not plan to marry unless I can work out a suitable arrangement. The subject of marriage had never come up between us before and it was definitely worth discussing, since we have rather disparate views to that subject on the original survey.
>
> We are living together in Berkeley, California. The experiment really made me think about the strength and motivation behind the relationship. Love & peace from sunny California.

The effect of such increased understanding, when it emerged, was not necessarily to strengthen the couples' relationships. In at least several cases participation in the study brought central conflicts to the surface and thus precipitated a weakening of the couple's tie. The general impression conveyed by several subjects' comments was that participation caused an acceleration of movement either toward or away from a permanent relationship that otherwise would have taken place over a longer period of time. "Your study was not the initial cause of the breakup," one respondent wrote, "just a little pusher. . . ."

If we acknowledge that completing a questionnaire about one's relationship can in some cases have a real impact upon the relationship, several new questions emerge. Can an investigator presume to intervene in people's relationships in this way, in the name of his research enterprise? Can we assume that subjects were fully aware of the possible impact of participation on their relationships? And if they were not, has the investigator violated the basic principle that he must obtain the *informed* consent of his subjects before commencing the research? These are ethical questions of considerable importance, and in the case of my initial study I am not certain of the answers to them. In my more recent research I have taken care to inform prospective subjects of possible effects and risks in advance of their actual participation. In practice, I have found that this information rarely if ever surprises or dissuades prospective subjects. Nevertheless, such a briefing seems a necessary ethical precaution.

As already suggested by these issues, the researcher-subject relationship is a fundamentally *asymmetrical* one.[2] Whereas the subjects provide to the researcher a great deal of personal information about themselves, the researcher gives them rather little in return, beyond a token monetary payment. In defiance of the generally held norm that self-disclosure should be reciprocal (Rubin, 1974), the researcher almost never reveals to the subject more than the most superficial sort of information about himself. And even though subjects may often desire specific feedback on their performance, the researcher rarely provides any. Many of my subjects, for example, may have entertained such questions as "Are we right for one another?" But they were never given any answers to such questions. Indeed, at the present stage of our knowledge about close relationships, the answers to such questions are far from certain. Thus, any attempt by the researcher to give his subjects a diagnosis of their relationship would run the risk of having an entirely unwarranted impact. The net result, however, was that my subjects gave me a great deal more information than I gave them.

My relationship to the subjects in this study was also quite *impersonal*. I had begun work on developing the love and liking scales in May 1968, administered the questionnaire to the sample of dating couples in October, and conducted the laboratory sessions in November and December. During this time I rarely interacted with subjects in ways that were not directly related to the tasks at hand, such as answering routine questions about the meaning of particular questionnaire items or scheduling laboratory sessions on the phone. During the first four months of 1969 I devoted myself to analyzing the large mass of data I had collected. In the process, I completely lost touch with the people who had provided the data in the first place. Symbolically they were close at hand in the form of identification numbers, love and liking scores, clock readings, and other such relics. But I almost never saw or spoke to any of them, nor have I since that time. (One exception was the student who appeared in my office early in 1969 and asked to see his girlfriend's questionnaire. He became rather upset when I told him that in accord with the guarantee of confidentiality I had given when the couples filled out the questionnaire, he could not see her responses.)

So we have a paradox. The researcher sets out to study relationships that are typically symmetrical and personal, and he does so in the context of a relationship that is asymmetrical and impersonal. The paradox is not, of course, peculiar to my study. It is characteristic of a great deal of social and psychological research. What I am describing is not an altogether undesirable state of affairs. Much important information about love may best be obtained in an impersonal atmosphere which stresses objectivity and anonymity. Just as people are sometimes able to disclose most about themselves to a passing stranger whom they know they will never see again

---

2. For a thoughtful discussion of the researcher-subject relationship, including consideration of ways to make it more symmetrical, see Kelman (1972).

THE RESEARCH EXPERIENCE

(Rubin, 1974), subjects may be able to reveal most about their relationships to an impersonal researcher who will never again cross their path.

I do confess to some misgivings about the impersonal researcher-subject relationship, however. In my more recent research I have supplemented questionnaires with intensive interviews and find that these more personal (though still asymmetrical) encounters provide invaluable information which could not be gained through questionnaires. I have also made efforts to explain to subjects the goals and initial results of our research, in postsession face-to-face discussions as well as in written research bulletins. I have tried to be approachable, and subjects have taken the opportunity to call me to ask questions about the research or even to seek help with personal problems. Further efforts to personalize the researcher-subject relationship without sacrificing scientific rigor seem desirable. The basic goal here is not researcher-subject equality, intimacy, or chumminess, but rather the establishment of mutual trust and respect.[3] The subject should know enough about the researcher's goals to be convinced of their legitimacy and should be assured of his candor, honesty, and willingness to entertain questions or complaints. It seems to me that such trust and respect, as facilitated by two-way communication between researcher and subject, makes for both satisfied subjects and good research. In the long run it may help all of us "gain insight into our relationships."

REFERENCES

Allport, G. W. The historical antecedents of modern social psychology. In G. Lindzey & E. Aronson (Eds.), *Handbook of Social Psychology,* 2nd ed., Vol. 1. Reading, Mass.: Addison-Wesley, 1968.

Berscheid, E., & Walster, E. H. *Interpersonal attraction.* Reading, Mass.: Addison-Wesley, 1969.

Huston, T. L. (Ed.), *Perspectives on interpersonal attraction.* New York: Academic Press, 1974.

Jones, E. E., & Nisbett, R. E. The actor and the observer: Divergent perceptions of the causes of behavior. In E. E. Jones, D. E. Kanouse, H. H. Kelley, R. E. Nisbett, S. Valins, & B. Weiber, *Attribution: Perceiving the causes of behavior.* Morristown, N.J.: General Learning Press, 1972.

Kelman, H. C. The rights of the subject in social research: An analysis in terms of the concepts of relative power and legitimacy. *American Psychologist,* 1972, *27,* 989-1016.

Newcomb, T. M. *The acquaintance process.* New York: Holt, Rinehart & Winston, 1961.

Rubin, Z. *Liking and loving: an invitation to social psychology.* New York: Holt, Rinehart & Winston, 1973.

Rubin, Z. Lovers and other strangers: The development of intimacy in encounters and relationships. *American Scientist.*

Rubin, Z. & Mitchell, C. Couples research as couples counseling. *American Psychologist,* 1976, *31,* 17-25.

---

3. For elaboration of these ideas, see Rubin, Z. & Mitchell, Cynthia (1976).

Contributors

Robert L. Arms. Assistant Professor of Psychology, University of Lethbridge, Canada.

James A. Banks. Professor of Education, University of Washington, Seattle, Washington 98195.

W. Curtis Banks. Assistant Professor of Psychology, Princeton University, Princeton, New Jersey 08540.

C. Daniel Batson. Assistant Professor of Psychology, University of Kansas, Lawrence, Kansas 66044.

Joy Browne. South Shore Counselling Associates, Hanover, Massachusetts 02339.

John Darley. Professor of Psychology, Princeton University, Princeton, New Jersey 08540.

Anthony N. Doob. Associate Professor of Psychology, University of Toronto, Toronto, 181, Canada.

Herbert Gans. Professor of Sociology, Columbia University, and Senior Research Associate, Center for Policy Research, 475 Riverside Drive, New York, New York 10027.

Philip A. Goldberg. Associate Professor of Psychology, Connecticut College, New London, Connecticut 06320.

Jeffrey H. Goldstein. Associate Professor of Psychology, Temple University, Philadelphia, Pennsylvania 19122.

Alan E. Gross. Associate Professor of Psychology, University of Missouri–St. Louis, St. Louis, Missouri 63121.

Craig Haney. Resident in Law and Social Science, Department of Psychology, Stanford University, Stanford, California 94305.

Laud Humphreys. Associate Professor of Sociology, Pitzer College, Claremont, California 91711.

Weldon T. Johnson. Assistant Professor of Sociology, University of Wisconsin, Madison, Wisconsin 53706.

Stella B. Jones. Assistant Professor

and Chair, Department of Sociology, Franklin College, Franklin, Indiana 46131.

John D. Kasarda. Associate Professor of Sociology, University of North Carolina, Chapel Hill, Chapel Hill, North Carolina.

Joseph J. Lengermann. Associate Professor of Sociology, University of Maryland, College Park, Maryland 20740.

Jack Levin. Associate Professor of Sociology, Northeastern University, Boston, Massachusetts 02115.

John H. McGrath, III. Professor and Chairman, Department of Sociology and Anthropology, Virginia Commonwealth University, Richmond, Virginia 23220.

Charles C. Moskos, Jr. Professor of Sociology, Northwestern University, Evanston, Illinois 60201.

H. Edward Ransford. Associate Professor of Sociology, University of Southern California, Los Angeles, California 90007.

Robert A. Rothman. Associate Professor of Sociology, University of Delaware, Newark, Delaware 19711.

Roberta Rovner-Pieczenik. Criminal Justice Research, Inc., 4701 Willard Avenue, Chevy Chase, Maryland 20015.

Zick Rubin. Professor of Social Psychology, Brandeis University, Waltham, Massachusetts.

Allan Schwartzbaum. Associate Professor of Sociology, Virginia Commonwealth University, Richmond, Virginia 23220.

Howard Schuman. Professor of Sociology and Faculty Associate, Institute for Social Research, University of Michigan, Ann Arbor, Michigan 48104.

James L. Spates. Assistant Professor of Sociology, Hobart and William Smith Colleges, Geneva, New York 14456.

Philip G. Zimbardo. Professor of Psychology, Stanford University, Stanford, California 94305.

Name Index

Abelson, R., 184, 189
Adams, Richard N., 58n
Adorno, T. W., 162, 165, 177
Ahlscwede, Ben F., 378n
Allen, A. A., 215
Allen, R. O., 195, 204
Allison, Graham T., 461, 464
Allport, Gordon W., 147, 153, 193, 194, 195, 201, 204, 207, 213, 219, 228, 508
Anderson, Astrid C., 377n
Anthony, Susan, 255, 257
Ardrey, Robert, 242, 246, 247, 250, 254
Argyle, M., 219, 232, 240
Arms, Robert, 27, 144, 145, 241, 249
Arnez, Nancy, 377n
Arnold, W. J., 247
Aronson, E., 181, 182, 187, 189, 211, 213, 247, 507, 513

Babbie, Earl R., 8, 24n, 31
Bachrach, Arthur J., 231, 240
Baldwin, Orrel T., 376n, 378n
Bales, R. F., 399, 446
Bandura, A., 241, 242, 247, 255, 257
Banks, James, 23, 369, 370, 375, 382n
Banks, W. Curtis, 6, 9, 11, 17, 141, 157
Banta, T. J., 499, 506
Barcus, Francis E., 405

Baris, Mitchell, 495n
Baritz, L., 182, 189
Baron, R. A., 494
Baston, C. Daniel, 8, 27, 28, 142, 143, 146, 191, 193, 194, 195, 201, 204, 205
de Beauvoir, Simone, 147, 153
Becker, Howard, 58n, 134, 138, 447, 464
Bell, Wendell, 115n, 125n, 129n, 137, 138
Berelson, Bernard, 376, 384, 385, 388
Berger, B. M., 390, 393n, 399
Berkowitz, L., 241, 242, 247
Berscheid, E., 508n, 513
Bettersworth, John K., 378n
Beverly, G., 219, 229
Bickman, L. B., 191, 204, 256, 257
Biller, Edward L., 376n
Birge, Kingsley H., 390n
Black, Hillel, 384, 389
Blalock, H. M., 412n, 414n, 424
Blau, Peter, 340, 341, 352, 354, 365
Bochner, Steven, 493, 494
Blum, R. H., 433, 439
Blumberg, Abraham, 448, 453, 464
Boisen, A., 215, 219, 228
Borg, Walter R., 376
Borgatta, Edgar, 424, 430n

Emerson, Robert M., 462, 464
Empey, L., 440
Engel, Gloria V., 340, 352
Erikson, Kai T., 111, 112, 462, 464
Exline, R. V., 506, 507

Feinberg, Helene, 253n
Ferracuti, Franco, 456, 464
Feshbach, S., 241, 242, 247
Festinger, Leon, 206, 213, 218, 219, 229, 438, 440
Fine, S., 180, 190
Fischer, Elizabeth, 267n, 289
Fisher, Beverly, 191n
Fleming, W. H., 219, 228
Follett, Dwight W., 378n
Fox, Tina, 481n
Francis, R. G., 340, 352
Freedman, Jonathan, 487, 488
Freedman, R. P., 215n, 229
Freidson, Eliot, 353, 364, 365
French, Elizabeth G., 147, 153
Frenkel-Brunswik, E., 162, 177
Freud, S., 193, 204, 205, 496, 498, 505, 507
Friedan, Betty, 147, 153
Fromm, E., 293, 304, 496, 498, 507
Froude, James Anthony, 115
Funk, R. W., 193, 204

Gabler, Robert E., 378n
Gabriel, Ralph H., 376n
Gans, Herbert, 6, 7, 9, 15, 35, 36, 37, 38, 40, 49n, 148n, 153, 315, 326
Garet, M., 178, 190
Gaskell, George D., 249n, 255
Geen, R. G., 241, 247
Geer, Blanche, 58
Geis, F. L., 162, 177
Gillespie, L. M., 219, 228
Gilmore, B., 219, 229
Ginglinger, G., 394, 399
Glass, D. C., 175, 177
Glasser, Karen, 191n
Glick, P., 215n, 229
Glock, C. Y., 195, 204, 215, 229
Gold, D., 300n, 304
Gold, Raymond L., 51n
Goldberg, Philip, 8, 141, 146, 147
Goldschmidt, W., 215, 219, 229
Goldstein, Jeffrey, 27, 144, 145, 241, 248, 249n, 255, 257

Goode, E., 215, 229
Goode, William J., 432, 440, 496, 507
Goodman, Leo A., 281n, 286
Gore, P. M., 304,
Gottlieb, David, 383, 389
Gouldner, Alvin, 341, 352, 354, 365
Graham, Billy, 143, 216, 217
Gray, D., 506, 507
Gray, L. N., 249n, 257
Greeley, A., 215n, 229
Greeley, A. M., 393, 399
Green, Robert L., 382n
Greenwald, Herbert J., 390n
Greenwood, Ernest, 341, 352
Gross, Alan, 6, 15, 21, 26, 28, 477, 478, 481
Gross, Herbert H., 378n
Gross, Llewellyn, 352, 365
Groves, D. P., 175, 177

Hagedorn, Robert, 292n
Hahn, Harlan, 271n, 286
Hall, Richard H., 341, 352, 354
Hammond, Phillip E., 30, 31
Haney, Craig, 6, 9, 11, 17, 141, 142, 143, 145, 146, 157, 177, 186, 190
Harlow, H. F., 506, 507
Harlow, James, 376n
Harris, Mary, 494
Hartshorne, H., 191, 204
Harvey, O. J., 219, 229
Hatt, Paul K., 424, 432, 440
Hawley, Amos, 412n, 417, 424, 427
Hebert, Sally, 494
Heider, F., 495, 507
Helgeson, Arlan C., 376n
Henchy, Thomas, 256, 257
Herberg, W., 219, 229
Hetherington, M., 499, 506
Hieronimus, R., 241, 247
Hokanson, J. E., 486
Holt, J., 215, 219, 229
Hooker, Evelyn, 89, 104, 105n
Hoopes, Townsend, 278n, 286
Horowitz, Irving L., 128, 136n, 137, 138
Horrocks, John E., 493
Horton, J. E., 293, 304, 305
Huber, Melissa, 432n
Hughes, E., 58n
Hughes, Everett C., 49
Humphrey, Norman D., 292n, 305

Humphreys, Laud, 25, 28, 35, 37, 38, 39, 85
Hunter, Floyd, 130n, 138
Hunter, S., 148n, 153
Huston, T. L., 508n, 513
Hyman, Herbert, 286, 424

Isard, Walter, 286

Jackson, George, 176, 177
Jacobson, Solomon, 271n, 286
Jaffe, David, 157n
Jahoda, Marie, 31, 389, 464
Janis, I., 218, 219, 229
Janowitz, Morris, 353
Johnson, B., 215n, 229
Johnson, David W., 375, 389
Johnson, Weldon, 15, 17, 23, 25, 143, 144, 145, 146, 215, 237n, 239, 240
Jones, E., 219, 229
Jones, Edward E., 185, 190, 509, 513
Jones, Jerrilyn, 432n
Jones, Stella, 12, 261, 263, 264, 265, 315
Jordan, W. D., 376n, 389
Josephson, E., 304
Josephson, M., 304
Jourard, S. M., 500, 507
Junker, Buford H., 51n

Kanouse, D. E., 513
Kasarda, John, 19, 23, 27, 371, 372, 412
Katz, D., 433, 440
Katz, Daniel, 492, 493
Katz, Stuart, 495n
Kelley, Harold, 341, 353, 354, 365
Kelley, H. H., 513
Kelman, H., 219, 229
Kelman, H. C., 512n, 513
Kerlinger, Fred N., 31, 376
Kerr, C., 292, 305
Kidder, Louise, 253n
Kiger, Joy, 432n
Killian, L. M., 241, 247, 316, 327
King, B., 219, 229
King, Fred M., 376n
Kitagawa, Evelyn, 316, 327
Kitay, P. M., 147, 153
Kitsuse, John I., 447, 464
Kittrie, 148n, 153
Klapper, J., 217, 219, 229
Kogan, N., 502, 507
Kornhauser, W., 292n, 293, 305, 340, 352

Korte, C., 191, 204
Krupat, Edward, 495n
Kunen, James S., 409, 411

LaFave, Wayne, 461, 464
Lana, Robert, 241n
Land, Kenneth, 414, 416n, 424, 430n
Landis, Judson, 316, 327
Lang, Gerhard, 383, 389
Lang, Kurt, 215, 216, 217, 218, 229, 231, 235, 236, 240, 341, 353
LePiere, R. T., 485, 486
Lasakow, P., 500, 507
Latané, B., 191, 204, 206, 207, 213, 214
Laumann, Edward O., 287n
Lawe, Elizabeth, 147n
Layton, J. F., 494
Lazerwitz, B., 215n, 229
Leik, Robert K., 24, 31
Lengermann, Joseph, 6, 12, 18, 261, 264, 265, 340, 345, 349n, 353, 365
Lenski, G., 215, 221, 229
Lesser, G. S., 147, 153
Lever, Janet, 241, 247
Levin, Jack, 19, 23, 370, 390, 400, 403, 404, 406, 407n, 410, 411
Levine, D., 247
Levine, L. W., 376n, 389
Levine, S., 493, 494
Levinson, D. J., 162, 177
Lewin, K., 167, 177, 182, 190, 218, 229, 256
Linder, D., 219, 229
Lindesmith, A. R., 134, 138
Lindzey, G., 189, 247, 496, 499, 507, 513
Lippitt, R., 167, 177
Lipset, S., 215, 230, 292n, 303, 304
Litcher, John H., 375, 389
Litwak, Eugene, 316, 327
Liverant, Shephard, 297n
Lobdell, George H., 376n
Lorenz, Konrad, 242, 246, 247, 250, 254

Macauley, William F., 390n
Maccoby, E., 229
MacConnell, Ann, 390n
Mack, Raymond, 129n
Madge, John, 445, 446
Manley, Norman W., 116, 122
Mann, 505, 507

Ross, J. M., 193, 194, 195, 201, 204, 207, 213
Ross, Sheila, 241, 247, 255, 257
Rossi, P., 215n, 229
Rossi, Peter H., 317, 327
Roszak, Theodore, 407, 411
Rothman, Robert, 26, 372, 432, 440, 441, 446
Rotter, Julian B., 297n, 304, 305
Rovner-Pieczenik, Roberta, 6, 15, 23, 373, 374, 447, 460, 464
Rubin, Zick, 26, 28, 477, 479, 480, 495, 503, 507, 508n, 512, 513
Runkel, Philip J., 9, 15, 31
Ryan, W., 190

Sabagh, George, 316, 327
Sanford, R. N., 162, 177
Schachter, S., 373, 433, 435, 437, 438, 439, 440, 444, 446
Scharyweller, Harry K., 316, 327
Schein, E., 172, 177
Schneider, L., 229
Schuette, D., 506, 507
Schuman, Howard, 11, 18, 261, 262, 267, 268n, 271n, 286, 287n, 288
Schur, Edwin M., 447, 464
Schwartz, Charlotte, 51n, 54n
Schwartz, Morris, 51n, 54n
Schwartz, S. H., 191, 205
Scott, Richard, 340, 352, 353
Schwartz, R. D., 31, 190, 256, 257, 477, 486, 487, 488, 494
Schwartzbaum, Allan, 26, 372, 373, 432, 440, 441, 446
Searles, R., 304, 305
Sears, R., 242, 247
Sechrest, Lee, 31, 190, 257, 477, 486, 487, 488, 494
Seeley, John R., 57n
Seeman, Melvin, 292n, 293n, 295n, 296, 305, 306
Seggar, John, 316, 327
Seidenberg, Robert, 315, 326
Seligman, M. E., 175, 177
Sellers, C. G., 376n, 389
Selltiz, Claire, 14n, 22, 31, 386, 389, 450, 464
Selznick, Philip, 461, 464
Sennett, Richard, 315, 327
Shafto, Mike, 191n
Shaver, Phillip, 495n

Sheras, Peter, 191n
Sherriffs, A. C., 147, 153
Shevky, Eshref, 137
Shils, E., 186, 190
Siegel, A., 292, 305
Siegel, S., 149, 153
Silverman, Irwin, 249n, 255
Simmel, Georg, 60
Simon, G., 390, 393n, 399
Simon, Herbert, 341, 353, 354, 365
Simon, William, 341, 353
Simons, L. S., 494
Singer, J. E., 175, 177
Slater, P. E., 496, 498, 505, 507
Sloan, Irving J., 377n
Slocum, W. L., 439, 440
Smith, Ramona, 316, 327
Smith, S., 147, 153
Smoke, G. L., 249n, 257
Soderstrum, Lorraine, 481n, 492
Sontag, S., 185, 188, 190
Sorensen, James E., 343, 353
Spates, James, 19, 23, 370, 390, 400, 401, 404, 406, 407n, 408, 409, 410, 411
Spilka, B., 195, 204
Stampp, Kenneth N., 376n, 381n, 384, 389
Stanton, F., 433, 440
Stare, F. G., 148n, 153
Stark, R., 195, 204, 215, 229
Steen, Ralph, W., 378n
Stein, M., 229, 240
Stocking, G. W., 376n, 389
Stoetzer, Louis, 316, 327
Stone, R. C., 340, 352
Storr, A., 242, 246, 247, 250, 254
Stouffer, S. A., 219, 230, 270, 286
Strauss, A., 58n
Streib, Gordon, 355
Strodtbeck, F. L., 505, 507
Suchman, E. A., 305, 433, 440
Sudnow, David, 447, 460, 464, 468
Suls, Jerry, 241n, 255, 257
Swanson, H., 440
Sweet, W., 215, 230
Sweezey, Kenneth, 390n

Tallent, M., 439, 440
Tamney, J., 228, 230
Tannenbaum, Mark, 267n
Taylor, M. Lee, 341, 353
Thelin, Ron, 394

Thibaut, John, 341, 353, 354, 365
Thomas, Marilyn, 390n
Thomas, William I., 315, 327, 445, 446
Thompson, Wayne, 356, 363
Thompson, W. E., 293, 304, 305
Thorp, Robert K., 376, 377, 384, 385, 389
Toch, H., 241, 247
Tolman, E. C., 203, 205
Trager, Helen G., 375, 384, 389
Trout, G., 390, 393n, 399
Turner, C. W., 494
Turner, R. H., 241, 247

Unger, R. K., 493, 494

Valins, S., 513
Van Arsdol, Maurice, 316, 327
Vernon, Raymond, 419, 424
Ver Steeg, Clarence L., 378n
Vollmer, Howard, 352, 353
Vossler, K., 148n, 153

Wager, L. Leslie, 340, 353
Wahler, R., 190
Wallace, D., 432, 440
Wallach, M. A., 502, 507
Walster, E. H., 174, 177, 495, 507, 508n, 513
Walters, R. H., 242, 247
Warner, W. Lloyd, 108n
Washburne, N. F., 304
Wax, Rosalie H., 22, 31
Webb, Eugene J., 21, 25, 31, 102, 104, 107n, 190, 256, 257, 477, 481, 486, 487, 488, 494
Weber, Max, 137
Weiber, B., 513
Wells, Robert, 191n
Westhoff, C., 215n, 228, 229

Wheeler, Stanton, 316, 326
Whelpton, P., 215n, 229
Whitam, F., 216, 228, 230
White, Greg, 157n
White, R., 167, 177
White, Ralph K., 394, 399, 405, 411
White, W., 391, 392, 399
Whyte, William F., 50, 52, 53
Wilensky, Harold, 341, 353
Williams, Eric, 123
Williams, J. A., Jr., 304, 305
Williams, R., Jr., 294n, 296, 305
Willmott, Peter, 43n
Wilson, B., 215n, 230
Wilson, F. D., 249n, 257
Wirth, Louis, 49
Wolfe, B. H., 396n, 399
Wolfgang, Marvin E., 456, 464
Wolin, S., 180, 190
Wolman, B. B., 204
Wright, P. H., 506, 507

Yablonsky, Lewis, 390, 391, 392, 393, 399, 405, 411
Yarrow, Marian R., 375, 384, 389
Yinger, J. M., 215n, 219, 230
Young, J., 219, 228
Young, Michael, 43n
Young, Pauline, 315, 327

Zald, Mayer, 353
Zander, Alvin, 440, 507
Zelditch, Morris Jr., 392, 393, 399, 445, 446
Zetterberg, H., 228, 230
Zillman, Dolf, 255, 257
Zimbardo, Philip G., 6, 9, 11, 17, 141, 157, 241, 247
Znaniecki, Florian, 315, 327, 445, 446

Subject Index

Adjudication of felonies, study of, 447–473

Affective observation, 54n

Aggression, 242, 246–247; field research, 248–257; measurement, 481–482, 488–494

Alienation, study of, 292–313

Allport-Ross scale of religiosity, 195, 201

American Journal of Sociology, 180

American Schoolbook, The, 384

American Social Science Association, 180

Analysis of data, *see* Data analysis

Analysis of variance, 212

Analytic induction, 134

Anonymity of data, 27

Anti-war protests, 267–291

Applied research, 5

Archival sources, 22–23, 107–108

Audio recordings, 170

Avatar, 402

Basic research, 5

Batson's Religious Life Inventory, 195

Before-after testing, 19–20

Behavior, 6–9; laws of, 186; violence, effects of observing, 241–257

Berkowitz and Daniels Social Responsibility Scale, 206

Bias, 78, 100

Budget costs, 265

Buss-Durkee Hostility Inventory, 144, 243, 245–246, 250

Bystander intervention, 191

Catharsis effect, 242, 246, 254

Causal research, 17, 19

Census data, 413, 424

Certified Public Accountants, study of, 340, 365

Christie's anomia scale, 206

Closed questions, 275, 289

Coding, 274, 275; accuracy, 311, 333, 387, 388, 396; jury method of ascertaining validity, 377–378; methodology, 291; open-ended responses, 289–291; thematic, 272–273, 275–278, 280–285, 290, 394

Cognitive dissonance, 218

Cohesiveness, measurement of, 435–437, 438

Collaborative research, 373, 445–446

Commitment, 138

Computers, 310, 332–334, 361, 371–372, 428–429; canned programs, 429;

Practical research, 5
Prejudice, 141; antisemitism, 154; misogyny, 147–156
Prisons, study of, 157–189
Professional autonomy, study of, 340–365
Professional community identification, 342, 344n, 345–350
Publication of research, 478
Public opinion polls, 268, 269; Vietnam war sentiment, 268, 269, 270, 273, 274
Pure research, 5

Qualitative and quantitative research, 20–22
Qualitative method of content analysis, 384–385
Quantitative method of content analysis, 384–385
Quest for universals, 134
Questioning, 22, 132, 133; closed, 275, 289; fixed-alternative, 37; open-ended, see Open-ended questions
Questionnaire, 22, 23, 477, 487, 492; construction, 336–338; cooperation from subjects, 444; CPA study, 343, 357–359; geographic mobility study, 316–317; mailed, 432; reactive, 487–488; respondent attitudes, study of, 432–446; response rates, 265, 358–359; results compared to field studies, 477, 485–486; romantic love, study of, 496, 499, 501; signed, 433; structured, 261; voluntary write-ins, study of, 432–446

Racial problems, 262; text book study, 375; Watts riot study, 292–313
Randomization of variables, 13–14
Random sampling, 13n, 14, 261, 309–310; stratified, 343
Reactivity, 20–21
Reader's Digest, 394, 396, 397
Real groups, 8
Reinforcement, 219
Relevance, measurement of, 435, 438
Religious behavior, 196, 215–239; Allport-Ross scale, 195, 201; Batson's Religious Life Inventory, 195; committment measurement, 221, 223–225; intrinsic vs extrinsic, 195; types measured, 195–196

Representative design, 183–185
Representativeness, 14–15, 17, 261, 262n, 263; field studies, 16; questionnaire, 434
Research-as-teaching, 178
Research constraints, 3–39; ethical, see Ethical considerations; financing, see Funding of research; personnel, 11–12; pragmatic, 6, 11–13; time, 11, 19–20
Research design, 21, 22, 129–130; 141–142; category formulation, 387; conceptualization of, 385; CPA study, 355–356; cross-sectional survey, 261; nonlaboratory, 488; utilizing specific method, 487
Research setting, see Setting
Research problem, 7; selection of, 328–329; see also, Research topic
Research purpose, 9–11
Research strategies, 9, 11–27, 29; comparing alternatives, 13–22; formulation of, 427
Research techniques, 71; observation, 367–470; setting, 9; write-up, 82–83
Research topic, 487, 508; selection, 5–6; see also Research problem
Research unit, 7–9
Researcher-subject relationship, 480, 512–513
Revivalism, 216–218
Role playing, 218–219, 222, 227
Romantic love, study of, 479, 495–513

Sample, 8–9, 334–336; Census data, 426; CPA study, 343; errors, 426; geographical mobility study, 317–318, 330; random, see Random sampling
Scales, 479; anomia, 206; Likert, 221; liking, 496–501; love, 496–501; Machiavellianism, 162, 165, 206; Need for Approval, 206; personality, 162, 165, 195, 206; religiosity, 195, 201; Social Desirability, 501; Social Responsibility, 206
Scientific American, 182, 288
Secondary analysis, 19, 369, 371, 435; census data, 424; importance to research, 444–445
Secondary Analysis of Sample Surveys, 424